JAVASCRIPT

SIXTH EDITION

Sasha Vodnik

Don Gosselin

CENGAGE
Learning®

Australia • Brazil • Mexico • Singapore • United Kingdom • United States

JavaScript, Sixth Edition
Sasha Vodnik and Don Gosselin

Product Director: Kathleen McMahon

Senior Product Manager: Jim Gish

Senior Content Developer: Alyssa Pratt

Marketing Manager: Eric LaScola

Senior Content Project Manager:
  Catherine DiMassa

Developmental Editor: Ann Shaffer

Quality Assurance Testers: Danielle Shaw
  and Serge Palladino

Art Director: Jack Pendleton

Manufacturing Planner: Julio Esperas

IP Analyst: Sara Crane

IP Project Manager: Kathryn Kucharek

Compositor: Integra Software Services Pvt. Ltd.

Cover Image: © Galyna Andrushko/
  Shutterstock.com

For product information and technology assistance, contact us at
Cengage Learning Customer & Sales Support, 1-800-354-9706

For permission to use material from this text or product, submit all requests online at **www.cengage.com/permissions.** Further permissions questions can be emailed to **permissionrequest@cengage.com.**

Library of Congress Control Number: 2014937483

ISBN-13: 978-1-305-07844-4

Cengage Learning
20 Channel Center Street
Boston, MA 02210
USA

Cengage Learning is a leading provider of customized learning solutions with office locations around the globe, including Singapore, the United Kingdom, Australia, Mexico, Brazil, and Japan. Locate your local office at **www.cengage.com/global**.

Cengage Learning products are represented in Canada by Nelson Education, Ltd.

To learn more about Cengage Learning, visit **www.cengage.com.**

Purchase any of our products at your local college store or at our preferred online store **www.cengagebrain.com**

Printed in China
2 3 4 5 6 7 18 17 16 15

BRIEF CONTENTS

CONTENTS

PREFACE

JavaScript is a client-side scripting language that allows web page authors to develop interactive web pages and sites. Although JavaScript is considered a programming language, it is also a critical part of web page design and authoring. This is because the JavaScript language enables web developers to add functionality directly to a web page's elements. The language is relatively easy to learn, allowing non-programmers to quickly incorporate JavaScript functionality into a web page. In fact, because it is used extensively in the countless web pages that are available on the World Wide Web, JavaScript is arguably the most widely used programming language in the world.

JavaScript, Sixth Edition teaches web page development with JavaScript for students with little programming experience. Although it starts with an overview of the components of web page development, students using this book should have basic knowledge of web page creation, including familiarity with commonly used HTML elements and CSS properties. This book covers the basics of ECMAScript Edition 3, which is compatible with older versions of Internet Explorer, as well as some features of ECMAScript 5.1, which is supported by all modern browsers. This book also covers advanced topics including object-oriented programming, the Document Object Model (DOM), touch and mobile interfaces, and Ajax. The HTML documents in this book are written to HTML5 standards, with some XHTML-compatible element syntax. After completing this course, you will able to use JavaScript to build professional quality web applications.

The Approach

This book introduces a variety of techniques, focusing on what you need to know to start writing JavaScript programs. In each chapter, you perform tasks that let you use a particular technique to build JavaScript programs. The step-by-step tasks are guided activities that reinforce the skills you learn in the chapter and build on your learning experience by providing additional ways to apply your knowledge in new situations. In addition to step-by-step tasks, each chapter includes objectives, short quizzes, a summary, key terms with definitions, review questions, and reinforcement exercises that highlight major concepts and let you practice the techniques you've learned.

Overview of This Book

The examples and exercises in this book will help you achieve the following objectives:

> Use JavaScript with HTML elements

> Work with JavaScript variables and data types and learn how to use the operations that can be performed on them

> Add functions and control flow within your JavaScript programs

> Trace and resolve errors in JavaScript programs

> Write JavaScript code that controls the web browser through the browser object model

> Use JavaScript to make sure data was entered properly into form fields and to perform other types of preprocessing before form data is sent to a server

> Create JavaScript applications that use object-oriented programming techniques

> Manipulate data in strings and arrays

> Save state information using hidden form fields, query strings, cookies, and Web Storage

> Incorporate touchscreen support and mobile capabilities in web applications

> Dynamically update web applications with Ajax

> Build a web application using the jQuery library

JavaScript, Sixth Edition presents twelve chapters that cover specific aspects of JavaScript programming. **Chapter 1** discusses basic concepts of the World Wide Web, reviews HTML documents, and covers the basics of how to add JavaScript to web pages. How to write basic JavaScript code, including how to use variables, data types, expressions, operators, and events, is also discussed in Chapter 1. This early introduction of key JavaScript concepts gives you a framework for better understanding more advanced concepts and techniques later in this book, and allows you to work on more comprehensive projects from the start. **Chapter 2** covers functions, data types, and how to build expressions. **Chapter 3** explains how to store data in arrays and how to use structured logic in control structures and statements. **Chapter 4** provides a thorough discussion of debugging techniques, including how to use the browser consoles integrated into all modern browsers. **Chapter 5** teaches how to use JavaScript to manipulate the web browser using the `Window`, `History`, `Location`, `Navigator`, and `Screen` objects. **Chapter 6** explains how to use JavaScript to make sure data was entered properly into form fields and how to perform other types of preprocessing before form data is sent to a server. **Chapter 7** presents object-oriented programming concepts, including how to use JavaScript's built-in `Date`, `Number`, and `Math` classes. **Chapter 8** covers advanced techniques for manipulating data in strings, arrays, and JSON. **Chapter 9** explains how to save state information using hidden form fields, query strings, cookies, and Web Storage, and also briefly discusses JavaScript security issues. **Chapter 10** covers supporting touch and pointer events in a web application, as well as using data provided by mobile device hardware and optimizing a web app for mobile users. **Chapter 11** introduces the basics of how to use Ajax to dynamically update portions of a web page with server-side data. **Chapter 12** introduces using the jQuery library to simplify common programming tasks in JavaScript. **Appendix A** provides detailed instructions on installing the XAMPP web server on a local machine. **Appendix B** gives a brief refresher on the basics of HTML, XHTML, and CSS. **Appendix C** serves as a one-stop reference for JavaScript syntax and usage covered throughout the book. **Appendix D**, which is online, lists answers for all Short Quizzes.

What's New in This Edition?

The sixth edition includes the following important new features:

> New, professionally-designed chapter projects, including mobile layouts in most chapters.

> All new Hands-On Projects in all chapters, along with new individual and group Case Projects.

> New boxed elements in each chapter: Best Practices box highlights a guideline for real world implementation of the topic at hand; Programming Concepts box explains a principle underlying the subject of the chapter; and Skills at Work box provides guidance for navigating the world of work.

> Multicolor code samples in each chapter identifying language components visually, with numbered lines for longer code blocks.

> Full-color figures showing the state of the project after each modification.

> Non-mobile projects coded for IE8 compatibility.

> Debugging coverage moved to Chapter 4, providing you with skills for finding and correcting errors in your apps before moving past the introductory chapters.

> Updated coverage of current industry best practices for creating arrays and objects, writing equality operators, and listening for events.

> Use of `document.write()`, `window.alert()`, and similar methods limited to earliest chapters, and replaced with modern techniques in remainder of book.

> New Chapter 10 on developing for touchscreen and mobile devices.

> New Chapter 12 on introductory programming with jQuery.

> Appendix A on installing a web server simplified to use the free, open-source XAMPP GUI installer rather than the command line.

> Appendix B on HTML and CSS updated to cover HTML5 instead of XHTML, and expanded to cover CSS selectors.

> New, streamlined layout that makes locating information easier.

Features

Each chapter in *JavaScript, Sixth Edition* includes the following features:

> **Chapter Objectives:** Each chapter begins with a list of the important concepts presented in the chapter. This list provides you with a quick reference to the contents of the chapter as well as a useful study aid.

> **Figures and Tables:** Plentiful full-color screenshots allow you to check your screen after each change. Tables consolidate important material for easy reference.

> **Code Examples:** Numerous code examples throughout each chapter are presented in any easy-to-read font, with key words shown in color. Longer code blocks include line numbers for easy reference.

> **New Terms:** New terms are printed in boldface to draw your attention to new material.

Note	*These elements provide additional helpful information on specific techniques and concepts.*

Caution	*These cautionary notes flag steps you need to perform with care to avoid potential pitfalls.*

> **Skills at Work:** These notes provide guidance for navigating the world of work.

> **Best Practices:** These notes highlight guidelines for real world implementation of various topics.

> **Programming Concepts:** These notes explain principles underlying the subject of each chapter or section.

> **Short Quiz:** Several short quizzes are included in each chapter. These quizzes, consisting of two to five questions, help ensure you understand the major points introduced in the chapter.

> **Summary:** These brief overviews revisit the ideas covered in each chapter, providing you with a helpful study guide.

> **Key Terms:** These lists compile all new terms introduced in the chapter along with their definitions, creating a convenient reference covering a chapter's important concepts.

> **Review Questions:** At the end of each chapter, a set of twenty review questions reinforces the main ideas introduced in the chapter. These questions help you determine whether you have mastered the concepts presented in the chapter.

> **Hands-On Projects:** Although it is important to understand the concepts behind every technology, no amount of theory can improve on real-world experience. To this end, each chapter includes detailed Hands-On Projects that provide you with practice implementing technology skills in real-world situations.

> **Case Projects:** These end-of-chapter projects are designed to help you apply what you have learned to open-ended situations, both individually and as a member of a team. They give you the opportunity to independently synthesize and evaluate information, examine potential solutions, and make decisions about the best way to solve a problem.

Instructor Resources

The following supplemental materials are available when this book is used in a classroom setting. All of the instructor resources available with this book are available on the Instructor Companion Site at *sso.cengage.com*. An instructor account is required.

Instructor's Manual. The Instructor's Manual that accompanies this textbook includes additional instructional material to assist in class preparation, including items such as Sample Syllabi, Chapter Outlines, Technical Notes, Lecture Notes, Quick Quizzes, Teaching Tips, Discussion Topics, and Additional Case Projects.

Cengage Learning Testing Powered by Cognero is a flexible, online system that allows you to:

> Author, edit, and manage test bank content from multiple Cengage Learning solutions.

> Create multiple test versions in an instant.

> Deliver tests from your LMS, your classroom, or wherever you want.

PowerPoint® Presentations. This book comes with Microsoft PowerPoint slides for each chapter. These are included as a teaching aid for classroom presentation, to make available to students on the network for chapter review, or to be printed for classroom distribution. Instructors can add their own slides for additional topics they introduce to the class.

Data Files. Files that contain all of the data necessary for the Hands-on Projects and Case Projects are also provided to students on *CengageBrain.com*.

Solution Files. Solutions to end-of-chapter questions and projects are available for this text.

Read This Before You Begin

The following information will help you prepare to use this textbook.

Data Files

To complete the steps, exercises, and projects in this book, you will need data files that have been created specifically for this book. The data files are available at *CengageBrain.com*. Note that you can use a computer in your school lab or your own computer to complete the steps, exercises, and projects in this book.

Using Your Own Computer

You can use a computer in your school lab or your own computer to complete the chapters. To use your own computer, you will need the following:

> **A modern web browser**, such as the current version of Chrome, Internet Explorer, Firefox, or Safari. If possible, you should have access to all of the most popular modern browsers (Chrome, Internet Explorer, and Firefox), as well as to Internet Explorer 8 for testing backward-compatible code.

> **A code-based HTML editor**, such as Aptana Studio 3, Komodo Edit, Notepad++, TextWrangler, Adobe Dreamweaver, or Sublime Text.

> **A web server** (for Chapter 11) such as Apache HTTP Server or Microsoft Internet Information Services and PHP. Appendix A contains detailed instructions on how to install a web server and PHP.

To The Instructor

To complete all the exercises and chapters in this book, your students must work with a set of user files called data files. The data files are available on the Instructor Companion Site and on *CengageBrain.com*.

Cengage Learning Data Files License

You are granted a license to copy the data files to any computer or computer network used by individuals who have purchased this book.

Feedback and Questions

We welcome feedback and questions about this book from instructors and students. You can contact author Sasha Vodnik on Twitter at *@sashavodnik*.

Acknowledgements

Creating the Sixth Edition of JavaScript has truly been a team effort. Thanks to the many people who helped shape and strengthen what I've written. Ann Shaffer provided great suggestions and great questions in equal numbers, and helped me keep an eye on the big picture while tending to the details. Alyssa Pratt kept us focused on getting this content out the door, while giving us the support and resources to make it all top-notch. Jim Gish connected me with both this project and an amazing group of people who helped make it all happen. Cathie DiMassa at Cengage, and Ramanan Sundararajan, along with the team at Integra, enhanced simple words on a page with an engaging visual layout, and labored over the tiniest details. Danielle Shaw and Serge Palladino read all the text, tested all the steps, and provided invaluable feedback. Kenji Oshima took the list of imaginary businesses and institutions for the chapter projects and created a unique, professional logo for each one.

Many, many thanks to the reviewers who provided feedback on early drafts of these chapters, and whose suggestions made the content clearer, made the examples more relevant, and helped me create better teaching tools for instructors and better learning materials for students: Jason Fleetwood-Boldt; Mark Murtha, Metropolitan Community College; Nicky Newell, Northeast Mississippi Community College; and Kevin Parker, Idaho State University.

Finally, thanks to my husband, Jason Bucy, for his love and support.

CHAPTER 1

INTRODUCTION TO JAVASCRIPT

When you complete this chapter, you will be able to:

> Explain the history of the World Wide Web
> Describe the differences between client-side and server-side scripting
> Understand the components of a JavaScript statement
> Add basic JavaScript code to your web pages
> Structure your JavaScript programs

The original purpose of the World Wide Web (WWW) was to locate and display information. However, once the web grew beyond a small academic and scientific community, people began to recognize that greater interactivity would make the web more useful. As commercial applications of the web grew, the demand for more interactive and visually appealing websites also grew.

To respond to the demand for greater interactivity, an entirely new web programming language was needed. Netscape filled this need in the mid-1990s by developing the JavaScript programming language. Originally designed for use in the Navigator web browser, JavaScript is now supported by all of the most popular web browsers, including Internet Explorer, Firefox, Chrome, Safari, and Opera.

Although JavaScript is considered a programming language, it is also a critical part of web page design and authoring. This is because the JavaScript language enables web developers to add functionality directly to a web page's elements. JavaScript can turn static documents into applications such as games or calculators. JavaScript code can change the contents of a web page after a browser has rendered it. It can also create visual effects such as animation, and it can control the web browser window itself. None of this was possible before the creation of JavaScript.

In this chapter, you will learn the skills required to create basic JavaScript programs. To be successful in your JavaScript studies, you should already possess a strong knowledge of techniques for authoring web pages. The first part of this chapter provides a quick refresher on the history of the World Wide Web and the basics of how to create web pages. Even if you are highly experienced with HTML, you might not be familiar with the formal terminology that is used in web page authoring. For this reason, be certain to read through these sections to ensure that you understand the terminology used in this book.

Introduction to the World Wide Web

The Internet is a vast network that connects computers all over the world. The original plans for the Internet grew out of a series of memos written by J. C. R. Licklider of the Massachusetts Institute of Technology (MIT), in August 1962, discussing his concept of a "Galactic Network." Licklider envisioned a global computer network through which users could access data and programs from any site on the network. The Internet was actually developed in the 1960s by the Advanced Research Projects Agency (or ARPA) of the U.S. Department of Defense, which later changed its name to Defense Advanced Research Projects Agency (or DARPA). The goal of the early Internet was to connect the main computer systems of various universities and research institutions that were funded by this agency. This first implementation of the Internet was referred to as the ARPANET. More computers were connected to the ARPANET in the years following its initial development in the 1960s, although access to the ARPANET was still restricted by the U.S. government primarily to academic researchers, scientists, and the military.

The 1980s saw the widespread development of local area networks (LANs) and the personal computer. Although at one time restricted to academia and the military, computers and networks soon became common in business and everyday life. By the end of the 1980s, businesses and individual computer users began to recognize the global communications capabilities and potential of the Internet, and they convinced the U.S. government to allow commercial access to the Internet.

In 1990 and 1991, Tim Berners-Lee created what would become the World Wide Web, or the web, at the European Laboratory for Particle Physics (CERN) in Geneva, Switzerland, as a way to easily access cross-referenced documents stored on the CERN computer network. When other academics and scientists saw the usefulness of Berners-Lee's system, the web as we know it today was born. In fact, this method of accessing cross-referenced documents, known as hypertext linking, was, in the early years, one of the most important aspects of the web because it allowed users to open other web pages quickly. A hypertext link, or hyperlink or link, contains a reference to a specific web page that you can click to open that web page.

A common misconception is that the words "web" and "Internet" are synonymous. The web is only one *part* of the Internet and is a means of communicating on the Internet. The Internet is also composed of other communication elements such as email systems that send and receive messages. However, because of its enormous influence on computing, communications, and the economy, the World Wide Web is arguably the most important part of the Internet today and is the primary focus of this book.

A document on the web is called a web page and is identified by a unique address called the Uniform Resource Locator, or URL. A URL is also commonly referred to as a web address. A URL is a type of Uniform Resource Identifier (URI), which is a generic term for many types of names and addresses on the World Wide Web. The term website refers to the location on the Internet of a set of web pages and related files (such as graphic and video files) that belong to a company, organization, or individual. You display a web page on the screen of a computer, tablet, or phone by using a program called a web browser. A person can retrieve and open a web page in a web browser either by entering a URL in the web browser's Address box or by clicking a link. No matter which method is used, the user's web browser asks a web server for the web page in what is referred to as a request. A web server is a computer that delivers web pages. What the web server returns to the user is called the response.

> **Note**   Many apps installed on smartphones and tablets are technically web documents that access web servers. They generally use the default web browsers on the devices where they're installed to connect with their servers, without requiring users to enter URLs.

Understanding Web Browsers
NCSA Mosaic was created in 1993 at the University of Illinois and was the first program to allow users to navigate the web by using a graphical user interface (GUI). In 1994, Netscape released Navigator, which soon controlled 75 percent of the market. Netscape maintained its control of the browser market until 1996, when Microsoft entered the market with the release of Internet Explorer, and the so-called browser wars began, in which Microsoft and Netscape fought for control of the browser market.

The browser wars began over dynamic HTML (DHTML), which is a combination of various technologies, including HTML and JavaScript, that allows a web page to change after it has been loaded by a browser. Examples of DHTML include the ability to reposition text and elements, change document background color, and create effects such as animation. Earlier versions of Internet Explorer and Navigator supported DHTML elements in ways that were exclusive to each browser, meaning that the DHTML code for Internet Explorer was incompatible with Navigator, and vice versa. Furthermore, Microsoft and Netscape each wanted its version of DHTML to become the industry standard.

To settle the argument, the World Wide Web Consortium set out to create a platform-independent and browser-neutral version of DHTML. The World Wide Web Consortium, or W3C, was established in 1994 at MIT to oversee the development of web technology standards. While the W3C was drafting a recommendation for DHTML, Internet Explorer version 4 and Navigator version 4 each added a number of proprietary DHTML elements that were completely incompatible with the other browser. As a result, when working with advanced DHTML techniques such as animation, a programmer had to write a different set of HTML code for each browser. Unfortunately for Netscape, the W3C adopted as the formal standard the version of DHTML found in version 4 of Internet Explorer, which prompted many loyal Netscape users to defect to Microsoft.

> **Note**
> The W3C does not actually release a version of a particular technology. Instead, it issues a formal recommendation for a technology, which essentially means that the technology is (or will be) a recognized industry standard.

One benefit of the browser wars was that they forced the web industry to rapidly develop and adopt advanced web page standards (including JavaScript, CSS, and DHTML) that are consistent across browsers. In 2004, Internet Explorer appeared to have essentially won the browser wars, as it controlled 95 percent of the browser market. However, Microsoft did not fully support web standards in subsequent versions of Internet Explorer, creating an opening for browsers that were more fully compliant with current standards. In the past decade, Internet Explorer has lost significant market share on desktop computers to Mozilla Firefox and Google Chrome. Other browsers—including Apple Safari and Opera—have also captured slices of the desktop browser market.

> **Note**
> Several companies collect and publish statistics on web browser usage. Each company uses a slightly different methodology, resulting in different conclusions. You can examine each company's findings by searching on web browser usage statistics with a search engine.

In the last few years, major technology companies have begun a new contest for browser market share on mobile devices. Apple Safari established a dominant position in this market as the default browser for both the iPhone and iPad. Google Chrome, the default browser on recent Android phones, also has significant market share, as does the mobile version of Opera. Unlike during the desktop browser wars of the 1990s, at the time of this writing Microsoft had yet to establish a significant market share in the mobile market.

Creating Web Pages

Originally, people created web pages using only Hypertext Markup Language. Hypertext Markup Language, or HTML, is a markup language used to create the web pages that appear on the World Wide Web. Web pages are also commonly referred to as HTML pages or documents. A markup language is a set of characters or symbols that defines a document's logical structure—that is, it indicates the meaning or function of each item in a document. HTML is based on an older language called Standard Generalized Markup Language, or SGML, which has a wider scope than HTML and can define the structure of documents in many different contexts.

Markup languages are designed to separate the data in a document from the way that data is formatted. Each element in an HTML document is marked according to its type, such as a paragraph or a heading. For a brief period in the early days of the web, the standards for HTML also incorporated specifications defining how elements should appear in a web browser—for example, the b element was used to format text in bold, and the i element to format text as italic. However, the people and organizations responsible for the growth of the web recognized the importance of keeping the appearance of documents independent from their structure, and restored HTML elements to their original purpose of identifying structure only. A separate, complementary language called Cascading Style Sheets (CSS) was developed for specifying the appearance of web page elements.

> **Note** | This textbook uses the terms web pages and HTML documents interchangeably.

Basic HTML Syntax

An HTML document is a text document that contains codes, called tags, which specify how the data in the document is treated by a web browser. HTML tags can indicate a wide range of elements, from different types of text content—like headings and paragraphs—to controls that allow user input—such as option buttons and check boxes. Other HTML tags allow you to display graphic images and other objects in a document. Tags are enclosed in brackets (< >), and most consist of an opening tag and a closing tag that surround the text or other items they format or control. The closing tag must include a forward slash (/) immediately after the opening bracket to define it as a closing tag. For example, to mark a line of text as a paragraph, you use the opening tag `<p>` and the closing tag `</p>`. When you open the HTML document in a web browser, the browser recognizes text enclosed in these tags as a paragraph.

A tag pair and any data it contains are referred to as an **element**. The information contained between an element's opening and closing tags is referred to as its **content**. Some elements do not require a closing tag. Elements that do not require a closing tag are called **empty elements** because they do not allow you to use a tag pair to enclose text or other elements. For instance, the `br` element, which inserts a line break on a web page, does not include a closing tag. You simply place the `<br />` tag anywhere in an HTML document where you want a line break to appear.

> **Note** | HTML documents must have a file extension of .htm or .html.

There are literally hundreds of HTML elements. Table 1-1 lists some commonly used elements.

HTML ELEMENT NAME	DESCRIPTION
article	Marks the main content of a web document
body	Marks the body of an HTML document
div	Marks a generic section of the web page body
head	Marks the page header and contains information about the entire page
h*n*	Marks heading level elements, where *n* represents a number from 1 to 6
html	Marks the content of an HTML document
img	Inserts an image file
nav	Marks navigation options, such as a navigation bar at the top or bottom of a page or along its side
p	Identifies the marked text as a paragraph

Table 1-1: Common HTML elements

All HTML documents must use the html element as the root element. A **root element** contains all the other elements in a document. This element tells a web browser to assemble any instructions between the tags into a web document. The opening <html> and closing </html> tags are required and contain all the text and other elements that make up the HTML document.

Two other important HTML elements are the head element and the body element. The head element contains information that is used by web browsers, and you place it at the beginning of an HTML document, after the opening <html> tag. You place several elements within the head element to help manage a document's content, including the title element, which contains text that appears in a browser's tab or title bar. A head element must contain a title element. With the exception of the title element, elements contained in the head element are not visible in the HTML document shown in the browser. The head element and the elements it contains are referred to as the **document head**.

Following the document head is the body element. The body element and the text and elements it contains are referred to as the **document body**.

HTML is not case sensitive, so you can use, for instance, <P> in place of <p>. However, an offshoot of HTML, a language called XHTML, is case sensitive, and requires the use of lowercase letters for tags. Because it can be useful to write code that works in both HTML and XHTML documents, this book uses lowercase letters for all tags. (You will learn more about XHTML shortly.)

You use various parameters, called **attributes**, to provide additional information about many HTML elements. You place an attribute before the closing bracket of the opening tag, and separate it from the tag name or other attributes with a space. You assign a value to an attribute using the syntax attribute="value". For example, to add an image to an HTML document, you use the img element with a number of attributes. One of these, the src attribute, specifies the filename of an image file. To add the file logo.jpg to a web document, you would use the src attribute within the img element, as follows:

```
<img src="logo.jpg" />
```

When you open an HTML document in a web browser, the document is assembled and formatted according to the instructions contained in its elements. The process by which a web browser assembles and formats an HTML document is called **parsing** or **rendering**. The final document that appears in the web browser includes only recognized HTML elements and text. When a web browser renders an HTML document, it ignores nonprinting characters such as tabs and line breaks. Although you can use the Enter or Return key on your keyboard to add line breaks to text within the body of an HTML document to make the code more legible, browsers ignore these line breaks when parsing the document. In addition, most web browsers ignore multiple contiguous spaces in a web document and replace them with a single space. The following code shows the document head and a portion of the document body for the web page shown in Figure 1-1.

```
1   <!DOCTYPE html>
2   <html>
3     <head>
4       <meta charset="utf-8" />
5       <title>Hotel Natoma - Reservations</title>
6       <link type="text/css" rel="stylesheet" media="screen"
7           href="natoma.css" />
8       <link type="text/css" rel="stylesheet" media="screen"
9           href="hnform.css" />
10      <link rel="shortcut icon" href="favicon.ico" />
11    </head>
12    <body>
13      <div id="box">
14        <h1>
15          <img src="images/natoma.gif" width="368"
16              height="65" alt="Hotel Natoma" title="" />
17        </h1>
18        <nav>
19          <ul id="mainnav">
20            <li><a href="index.html">Home</a></li>
21            <li><a href="nearby.html">
22                What&#39;s Nearby</a></li>
23            <li><a href="http://bit.ly/bb3Sic"
24                target="_blank">Location</a></li>
25            <li><a href="museums.html">SF Museums</a></li>
26            <li><a href="greensf.html">Green SF</a></li>
27            <li><a href="reserve.html">Reservations</a></li>
28          </ul>
29        </nav>
30        <article>
31          <h2 id="main">Reservations</h2>
32   ...
```

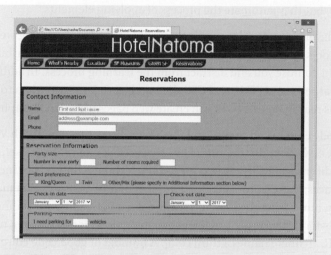

Figure 1-1: Web page in a browser
© 2015 Cengage Learning®

Creating an HTML Document

Because HTML documents are text files, you can create them in any text editor, such as Notepad or TextEdit, or any word-processing application capable of creating simple text files. If you use a text editor to create an HTML document, you cannot view the final result until you open the document in a web browser. Instead of a text editor or word processor, you could use a web development tool, which is an application designed specifically for creating web documents. Some popular web development tools, such as Adobe Dreamweaver and Microsoft Visual Studio, have graphical interfaces that allow you to create web pages and immediately view the results, similar to the WYSIWYG (what-you-see-is-what-you-get) interface in word-processing programs. Like text editors, web development tools create simple text files, but they automate the process of applying elements.

Graphical web development tools can greatly simplify the task of creating web pages. However, graphical tools automatically add many unfamiliar elements and attributes to documents that might confuse you and distract from the learning process. In addition, there's no better way to sharpen your HTML and CSS skills and learn JavaScript than to type the code yourself. For this reason, in this book you create web pages using a nongraphical text editor.

The choice of code editor is up to you, and the basic editors that come with Windows (Notepad) and OS X (TextEdit) are sufficient. However, you may find it useful to download and install an editor specifically created for coding. Although they do not incorporate graphical interfaces, these editors include a number of other features that make coding easier, including numbering the lines of code in a document and color coding text based on its meaning—for instance, giving element content one color, HTML tag names another color, and HTML attribute names a third color. A number of good code editors are available online to download for free, including the following:

> Aptana Studio 3 (Windows and Mac)—*http://www.aptana.com/products/studio3/*
> Komodo Edit (Windows and Mac)—*http://www.activestate.com/komodo-edit*
> Notepad++ (Windows)—*http://notepad-plus-plus.org*
> TextWrangler (Mac)—*http://www.barebones.com/products/textwrangler*

HTML and JavaScript code displayed in this book include colors to distinguish different parts of the code, as you might see in a code editor. Although many different color schemes are available, this book uses the following colors for HTML code:

> `black`: HTML syntax characters (<, >, =), DOCTYPE value, literal text
> `blue`: Element name, attribute name, character entity reference
> `green`: Attribute value
> `gray`: HTML comment

Later in the book, you'll learn about the colors used for JavaScript code as well.

Working with HTML5

HTML first became an Internet standard in 1993 with the release of version 1.0. The standard has been revised several times, and at the time of this writing, HTML5 is the most current version. HTML5 incorporated several significant changes from previous versions of HTML, including simplifying some coding practices and adding support for a number of semantic elements, such as `header` and `article`, that enable developers to indicate the role of specific content on the page.

Before HTML5 was developed, a different specification, known as **Extensible Hypertext Markup Language**, or **XHTML**, was seen as the future language for web development. XHTML modified HTML to conform to the rules of **Extensible Markup Language**, or **XML**, a language used to format data in many different applications. While initially seen as promising because of its ability to integrate web documents with other systems, several aspects of XHTML, including its inflexible syntax, have kept it from being widely embraced by developers. HTML5 has replaced XHTML as the standard for most web pages going forward. The web page examples and exercises in this book are written in HTML5.

Although you need to have a solid understanding of HTML to be successful with this book, you do not necessarily need to be an expert with HTML5. Because HTML5 is very similar to earlier versions of HTML, as well as to XHTML, you can easily adapt any of your existing HTML or XHTML skills to HTML5. If you are not familiar with HTML5, review the appendix titled "Working with HTML and CSS" before continuing with this chapter. Be sure you understand what semantic elements are and how they work. Also, you should thoroughly understand how to work with CSS.

In this chapter, you'll add JavaScript code to a web page for Tinley Xeriscapes, a landscaping company that specializes in plants that need minimal watering. A designer has created a new layout for the company's website, and they'd like you to incorporate JavaScript to enhance the functionality of one of the site's pages. Your Chapter folder for Chapter 1 contains the files you will need for the project. Figures 1-2 and 1-3 show desktop and mobile previews of the completed web page incorporating the functionality you'll create in this chapter.

> **Note**
>
> *Many of the projects and examples in this book use professionally designed websites because, in real-world situations, a JavaScript programmer is often asked to add code to a preexisting website. However, do not worry about trying to understand the design elements that you see in this book. Instead, simply focus on how JavaScript interacts with the web pages you work on.*

Figure 1-2: Desktop view of completed Tinley Xeriscapes Plants page using simple JavaScript code

U.S. Department of Agriculture

Before you begin the following steps, be certain to extract the data files for this book, which you can download from Cengage's website at *http://www.cengage.com*, as explained in the preface to this book. Save the files you create in the main body of each chapter within the Chapter folder.

To create the plants list page for Tinley Xeriscapes:

1. Start your text editor, and then open the **plants.htm** file from the Chapter folder for Chapter 1.

> **Note**
>
> *Some web servers do not correctly interpret spaces within the names of HTML files. For example, some web servers may not correctly interpret the filename* Mortgage Brokers.html, *because of the space between* Mortgage *and* Brokers, *making it impossible for some users to open this file in a browser. For this reason, filenames in this book do not include spaces.*

2. Examine the contents of the file in your editor. The file starts with the HTML5 DOCTYPE. The head section, marked with the opening <head> and closing </head> tags, specifies the character encoding, sets the viewport size for smaller screens, specifies a page title, links to two alternate style sheets based on screen width, and links to

picture changes to
show a plant when its
name is clicked in the
list above

Figure 1-3. Mobile view of completed Tinley Xeriscapes Plants
page using simple JavaScript code
U.S. Department of Agriculture

a web-hosted font. The body section, marked with the opening `<body>` and closing
`</body>` tags, includes a `header` element for the page header, a `nav` element for site
navigation, an `aside` element for sidebar content, an `article` element for main page
content, and a `footer` element for the page footer.

3. Open the **tinley.css** file in your text editor, and then examine its contents. The style
sheet starts with a number of rules to standardize the rendering of elements across
different browsers. These rules are followed by styles for the various sections of the
web page.

4. Open a web browser, press **Ctrl + O** (Windows) or **command + O** (Mac), navigate to the **Chapter** folder for Chapter 1, and then double-click **plants.htm** to open it in your web browser.

> **Note**
> *You can also open a local document in your system's default web browser by opening Windows Explorer (Windows 7), the File Explorer (Windows 8), or Finder (Mac), navigating to the location of the file, and double-clicking the filename. If you have multiple browsers installed and want to choose which browser to use to open the file, right-click (Windows) or control + click (Mac) the filename instead of double-clicking it, point to Open with, and then in the list that opens, click the name of the browser to use to open the file.*

Figure 1-4 displays the plants.html document as it appears in Firefox.

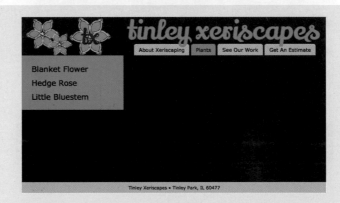

Figure 1-4: The plants.htm web page in a browser

> **Note**
> *Recent versions of Internet Explorer treat local documents differently than they treat documents opened from the Internet. To make both appear the same in Internet Explorer, press the Alt key to make the menu bar visible if necessary, click Tools on the menu bar, click Compatibility View settings, uncheck Display intranet sites in Compatibility View, close the Compatibility View Settings window, and then reload the document.*

5. Move the mouse pointer over the plant names **Blanket Flower**, **Hedge Rose**, and **Little Bluestem** on the left side of the page. Notice that a plant name's text and background colors change when the mouse pointer is over the name, and change back when the pointer is no longer over it. This effect is achieved with the CSS `:hover` pseudo-class.

6. Click the text **Blanket Flower**, click **Hedge Rose**, and then click **Little Bluestem**. Notice that nothing happens when you click the plant names. In the designer's plan for this page, clicking a plant name should trigger the browser to display a large photo of the selected plant to the right of the list of names. While this could be achieved by creating multiple versions of the same page and marking the plant names as links, JavaScript provides a method of creating the same effect that's faster for users and requires less code for developers to manage. In the rest of this chapter, you'll add this functionality to the web page using basic JavaScript code.

Short Quiz 1

1. What method of accessing documents did Tim Berners-Lee create? What was noteworthy about his system?

2. What does W3C stand for? What does the organization do?

3. What are the codes in an HTML document called? What function do they serve?

Introduction to Web Development

Web page design, or **web design**, refers to the visual design and creation of the documents that appear on the World Wide Web. Most businesses today—both prominent and small—have websites. High-quality web design plays an important role in attracting first-time and repeat visitors. However, the visual aspect of a website is only one part of the story. Equally important is the content of the website and how that content is structured.

Web design is an extremely important topic. However, this book is not about web design, even though you will certainly learn many web design concepts and techniques as you work through the chapters ahead. Instead, this book touches on both web page authoring and web development. **Web page authoring** (or **web authoring**) refers to the creation and assembly of the tags, attributes, and data that make up a web page. There is a subtle, but important, distinction between web design and web page authoring: web design refers to the visual and graphical design aspects of creating web pages, whereas web page authoring refers to the physical task of assembling the web page tags and attributes. **Web development**, or **web programming**, refers to the design of software applications for a website. Generally, a web developer works behind the scenes to develop software applications that access databases and file systems, communicate with other applications, and perform other advanced tasks. The programs created by a web developer will not necessarily be seen by a visitor to a website, although the visitor will certainly use a web developer's programs, particularly if the website writes and reads data to and from a database. Although JavaScript lives more in the realm of web page authoring, there is certainly some overlap between web authoring and web development, especially when it comes to sending and receiving data to and from a web server.

There are countless ways of combining the hundreds of HTML elements to create interesting web pages. One technique that professional web authors use to increase their HTML skill is examining the underlying HTML elements of a web page that they admire. All web browsers contain commands that allow you to view the underlying HTML code for a web page that appears in the browser. Using any major browser, you can right-click (Windows) or control-click (Mac) any part of a web page, and then on the context menu that opens, click Inspect element to view the code for that element.

Caution

Many JavaScript programmers make their code freely available for reuse by other developers, sometimes requesting only credit in the reused code. However, keep in mind that building your own JavaScript programming skills requires thinking through and solving programming tasks on your own. Relying on borrowed code can keep you from learning and understanding how to code. In addition, employers who hire programmers often focus in interviews on evaluating a candidate's ability to accomplish specific programming tasks, and want to review an applicant's existing portfolio of original code. Writing your own code now provides a crucial leg up in eventually getting a job based on your JavaScript skills.

Understanding Client/Server Architecture

To be successful in web development, you need to understand the basics of client/server architecture. There are many definitions of the terms "client" and "server". In traditional client/server architecture, the server is usually some sort of database from which a client requests information. A server fulfills a request for information by managing the request or serving the requested information to the client—hence the term, "client/server." A system consisting of a client and a server is known as a two-tier system.

One of the primary roles of the client, or front end, in a two-tier system is the presentation of an interface to the user. The user interface gathers information from the user, submits it to a server, or back end, then receives, formats, and presents the results returned from the server. The main responsibilities of a server are usually data storage, management, and communicating with external services. On client/server systems, heavy processing, such as calculations, usually takes place on the server. As devices that are used to access web pages—such as computers, tablets, and mobile phones—have become increasingly powerful, however, many client/server systems have placed increasing amounts of the processing responsibilities on the client. In a typical client/server system, a client computer might contain a front end that is used for requesting information from a database on a server. The server locates records that meet the client request, performs some sort of processing, such as calculations on the data, and then returns the information to the client. The client computer can also perform some processing, such as building the queries that are sent to the server or formatting and presenting the returned data. Figure 1-5 illustrates the design of a two-tier client/server system.

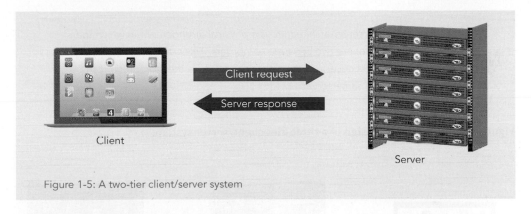

Figure 1-5: A two-tier client/server system

The web is built on a two-tier client/server system, in which a web browser (the client) requests documents from a web server. The web browser is the client user interface. You can think of the web server as a repository for web pages. After a web server returns the requested document, the web browser (as the client user interface) is responsible for formatting and presenting the document to the user. The requests and responses through which a web browser and web server communicate occur via Hypertext Transfer Protocol (HTTP), which is the main system used on the web for exchanging data. For example, if a web browser requests the URL *http://www.cengage.com*, the request is made with HTTP because the URL specifies the HTTP protocol. The web server then returns to the web browser an HTTP response containing the response header and the HTML for the Cengage Learning home page.

After you start adding databases and other types of applications to a web server, the client/server system evolves into what is known as a three-tier client architecture. A three-tier client/server system—also known as a multitier client/server system or *n*-tier client/server system—consists of three distinct pieces: the client tier, the processing tier, and the data storage tier. The client tier, or user interface tier, is still the web browser. However, the database portion of the two-tier client/server system is split into a processing tier and the data storage tier. The **processing tier**, or **middle tier**, handles the interaction between the web browser client and the data storage tier. (The processing tier is also sometimes called the processing bridge.) Essentially, the client tier makes a request of a database on a web server. The processing tier performs any necessary processing or calculations based on the request from the client tier, and then reads information from or writes information to the data storage tier. The processing tier also handles the return of any information to the client tier. Note that the processing tier is not the only place where processing can occur. The web browser (client tier) still renders web page documents (which requires processing), and the database or application in the data storage tier might also perform some processing.

> **Note** | Two-tier client/server architecture is a physical arrangement in which the client and server are two separate computers. Three-tier client/server architecture is more conceptual than physical, because the storage tier can be located on the same server.

Figure 1-6 illustrates the design of a three-tier client/server system.

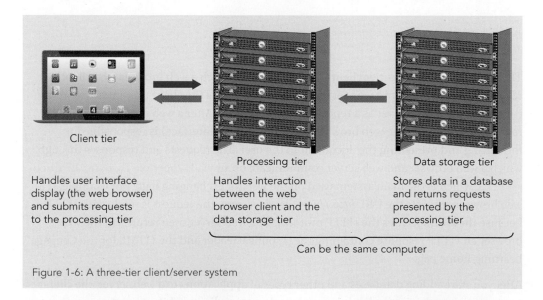

Client tier

Handles user interface
display (the web browser)
and submits requests
to the processing tier

Processing tier

Handles interaction
between the web
browser client and the
data storage tier

Data storage tier

Stores data in a database
and returns requests
presented by the
processing tier

Can be the same computer

Figure 1-6: A three-tier client/server system

JavaScript and Client-Side Scripting

As mentioned earlier, HTML was not originally intended to control the appearance of pages in a web browser. When HTML was first developed, web pages were static—that is, they couldn't change after the browser rendered them. However, after the web grew beyond a small academic and scientific community, people began to recognize that greater interactivity and better visual design would make the web more useful. As commercial applications of the web grew, the demand for more interactive and visually appealing websites also grew.

HTML could be used to produce only static documents. You can think of a static web page written in HTML as being approximately equivalent to a printed book; you can read it or move around in it, but the content is fixed. To respond to the demand for greater interactivity in web pages, an entirely new web programming language was needed. Netscape filled this need by developing JavaScript.

JavaScript is a client-side scripting language that allows web page authors to develop interactive web pages and sites. Client-side scripting refers to programming with a scripting language that runs on a local browser (on the client tier) instead of on a web server (on the processing tier). Originally designed for use in Navigator web browsers, JavaScript is now also used in all major web browsers, including Internet Explorer, Firefox, Chrome, Safari, and Opera.

> **Note**
>
> When you use HTML, CSS, and JavaScript in web development, each language plays a unique role. You use HTML to indicate the role and meaning of each part of web page content. You use CSS to describe how each web page element should be rendered in a browser or other user agent. You use JavaScript to add functionality to a web page. When attempting to enhance a web page, you should first identify which of these three main tasks you're trying to accomplish. The answer to this question will make it clear which language you'll use.

The term scripting language is a general term that originally referred to fairly simple programming languages that did not contain the advanced programming capabilities of languages such as Java or C++. When it comes to web development, the term scripting language refers to any type of language that is capable of programmatically controlling a web page or returning some sort of response to a web browser. It's important to note that, although the term "scripting language" originally referred to simple programming languages, today's web-based scripting languages are anything but simple. The part of a browser that executes scripting language code is called the browser's scripting engine. A scripting engine is just one kind of interpreter, with the term interpreter referring generally to any program that executes scripting language code. When a scripting engine loads a web page, it interprets any programs written in scripting languages, such as JavaScript. A web browser that contains a scripting engine is called a scripting host. Firefox and Internet Explorer are examples of scripting hosts that can run JavaScript programs.

> **Note**
>
> *Many people think that JavaScript is a simplified version of the Java programming language, or is related to Java in some other way. However, the languages are entirely different. Java is an advanced programming language that was created by Sun Microsystems and is considerably more difficult to master than JavaScript. Although Java can be used to create programs that can run from a web page, Java programs are usually external programs that execute independently of a browser. In contrast, JavaScript programs always run within a web page and control the browser.*

JavaScript was first introduced in Navigator and was originally called LiveScript. With the release of Navigator 2.0, the name was changed to JavaScript 1.0. Subsequently, Microsoft released its own version of JavaScript in Internet Explorer 4.0 and named it JScript.

When Microsoft released JScript, several major problems occurred. First, the Netscape and Microsoft versions of the JavaScript language differed so greatly that programmers were required to write almost completely different JavaScript programs for Navigator and Internet Explorer. To avoid similar problems in the future, an international, standardized version of JavaScript, called ECMAScript, was created. In this book you will learn to create JavaScript programs with ECMAScript edition 5.1, which is supported by all current web browsers including Internet Explorer version 9 and higher, Firefox version 4 and higher, Chrome version 7 and higher, and Safari version 5.1 and higher. You will also learn about aspects of the previous version of ECMAScript, ECMAScript 3, which are necessary for creating code that's compatible with older browsers such as Internet Explorer 8.

Although JavaScript is considered a programming language, it is also a critical part of web page authoring. This is because JavaScript programs are integrated with a web page's elements. JavaScript gives a developer the ability to:

> Turn static web pages into applications such as games or calculators.

> Change the contents of a web page after a browser has rendered it.

> Create visual effects such as animation.

> Control the web browser window itself.

> Work with information such as device orientation, speed, and geolocation reported by web-connected devices.

For security reasons, the JavaScript programming language cannot be used outside of specific environments. The most common environment where JavaScript is run is a web browser. For example, to prevent malicious scripts from stealing information, such as your email address or the credit card information you use for an online transaction, or from causing damage by changing or deleting files, JavaScript allows manipulation only of select files associated with the browser, and then with strict limitations. Another helpful limitation is the fact that JavaScript cannot run system commands or execute programs on a client. The ability to read and write cookies and a few other types of browser storage is the only type of access to a client that JavaScript has. Web browsers, however, strictly govern their storage and do not allow access to stored information from outside the domain that created it. This security also means that you cannot use JavaScript to interact directly with web servers that operate at the processing tier. Although programmers can employ a few tricks (such as forms and query strings) to allow JavaScript to interact indirectly with a web server, if you want true control over what's happening on the server, you need to use a server-side scripting language.

Understanding Server-Side Scripting

Server-side scripting refers to programming using a scripting language that is executed from a web server. Some of the more popular server-side scripting languages are PHP, ASP.NET, Python, and Ruby. One of the primary reasons for using a server-side scripting language is to develop an interactive website that communicates with a database. Server-side scripting languages work in the processing tier and have the ability to handle communication between the client tier and the data storage tier. At the processing tier, a server-side scripting language usually prepares and processes the data in some way before submitting it to the data storage tier. Some of the more common uses of server-side scripting language that you have probably already seen on the web include the following:

> Shopping carts
> Search engines
> Discussion and commenting systems

- Web-based email systems
- Authentication and security mechanisms
- Blogs and content management systems
- Multiplayer games

Without JavaScript, a server-side scripting language can't access or manipulate a web browser. In fact, a server-side scripting language cannot run on a client tier at all. Instead, a server-side scripting language exists and executes solely on a web server, where it performs various types of processing or accesses databases. When a client requests a server-side script, the script is interpreted and executed by the scripting engine within the web server software. After the script finishes executing, the web server software translates the results of the script (such as the result of a calculation or the records returned from a database) into HTML, which it then returns to the client. In other words, a client will never see the server-side script, only the HTML that the web server software returns from the script. Figure 1-7 illustrates how a web server processes a server-side script.

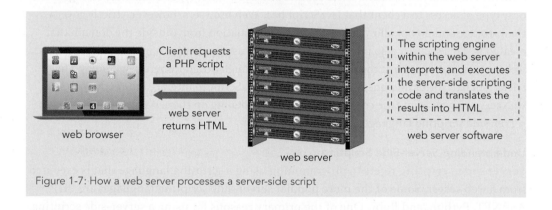

Figure 1-7: How a web server processes a server-side script

Should You Use Client-Side or Server-Side Scripting?

An important question in the design of any client/server system is deciding how much processing to place on the client and how much to place on the server. In the context of website development, you must decide whether to use client-side JavaScript or a server-side script. This is an important consideration because the choice you make can greatly affect the performance of your program. In some cases, the decision is simple. For example, if you want to control the web browser, you must use JavaScript. If you want to access a database on a web server, you must use a server-side script. However, there are tasks that both languages can accomplish, such as validating forms and manipulating cookies. Furthermore, both languages can perform the same types of calculations and data processing.

A general rule of thumb is to allow the client to handle the user interface processing and light processing, such as data validation, but have the web server perform intensive calculations and data storage. This division of labor is especially important when dealing with clients and servers over the web. Unlike with clients on a private network, it's not possible to know in advance the computing capabilities of each client on the web. You cannot assume that each client (browser) that accesses your client/server application (website) has the necessary power to perform the processing required by an application. For this reason, intensive processing should be performed on the server.

Because servers are usually much more powerful than client computers, your first instinct might be to let the server handle all processing and only use the client to display a user interface. Although you do not want to overwhelm clients with processing they cannot handle, it is important to perform as much processing as possible on the client for several reasons:

> Distributing processing among multiple clients creates applications that are more powerful, because the processing power is not limited to the capabilities of a single computer. Client devices—including computers, tablets, and smartphones—become more powerful every day. Thus, it makes sense to use a web application to harness some of this power and capability. A web application is a program that is executed on a server but is accessed through a web page loaded in a client browser.

> Local processing on client computers minimizes transfer times across the Internet and creates faster applications. If a client had to wait for all processing to be performed on the server, a web application could be painfully slow over a low-bandwidth Internet connection.

> Performing processing on client computers decreases the amount of server resources needed by application providers, decreasing costs for infrastructure and power use.

Short Quiz 2

1. In client/server architecture, what is a client? What is a server?

2. What does the middle tier do in a three-tier architecture?

3. What is ECMAScript? Why was it created?

Adding JavaScript to Your Web Pages

The following sections introduce basic procedures for adding JavaScript to your web pages.

Using the `script` Element

JavaScript programs run from within a web page (an HTML document). That is, you type the code directly into the web page code as a separate section. JavaScript programs contained within a web page are often referred to as scripts. When a web browser encounters a `script element` like the following one, it interprets the statements that the element contains in its scripting engine.

```
<script>
    statements
</script>
```

> **Note**
> The `type` attribute of the `script` element tells browsers which scripting language is being used. However, in HTML5, a value of `text/javascript` is assumed by default. This means you can omit the `type` attribute for any JavaScript code you create.

You'll start your work on the Tinley Xeriscapes Plants page by nesting a `script` element within the article section.

To add a script section to the Plants page for Tinley Xeriscapes:

1. Return to the **plants.htm** document in your text editor.

2. Scroll down to the **article** element, and then within the `figcaption` element, type **<script>**, add a blank line, and then type **</script>**. Your updated `article` element should match the following:

```
1    <article>
2        <figure>
3            <figcaption>
4                <script>
5
6                </script>
7            </figcaption>
8        </figure>
9    </article>
```

> **Note**
> Throughout this book, highlighting is used to draw your attention to code that you should type or edit. In the preceding example, the highlighting in lines 4 and 6 is used to draw your attention to the code you should have typed in Step 2.

3. Save the **plants.htm** document.

The individual lines of code, or statements, that make up a JavaScript program in a document are contained within a `script` element. The following script contains a single statement that writes the text "Plant choices" to a web browser window, using the `write()` method of the `Document` object, which you will study shortly:

```
document.write("<p>Plant choices</p>");
```

Notice that the preceding statement ends in a semicolon. Many programming languages, including C++ and Java, require you to end all statements with a semicolon. JavaScript statements are not required to end in semicolons. Semicolons are strictly necessary only when you want to separate statements that are placed on a single line. For example, the following script contains two statements on the same line, with each statement ending in a semicolon:

```
<script>
    document.write("<p>Plant ");document.write("choices</p>");
</script>
```

As long you place each statement on its own line, separated from other lines with line breaks, you are not required to end statements with semicolons. The following code shows another example of the preceding script, but this time, each statement is placed on its own line, without an ending semicolon.

```
1    <script>
2        document.write("<p>Plant ")
3        document.write("choices</p>")
4    </script>
```

Even though the statements do not end in semicolons, the preceding script is legal. However, that's not the end of the story. Programmers often adopt conventions in their code that make the code easier for themselves or other programmers to read in a text editor. In the case of semicolons, it is considered good JavaScript programming practice to end every statement with a semicolon. The semicolon serves to identify the end of each statement, making it easier for a programmer to read his or her own code (and for other programmers to read the code later on). In addition, a JavaScript parser must perform work on a script without semicolons to determine where each statement ends, which can slow down a web page and detract from the user experience. For these reasons, you should be sure to end all of your JavaScript statements with semicolons.

Understanding JavaScript Objects

Before you can use `script` elements to create a JavaScript program, you need to learn some basic terminology that is commonly used in JavaScript programming in particular, and in other programming languages in general. In addition to being an interpreted scripting language, JavaScript is considered an object-based programming language. An **object** is programming code and data that can be treated as an individual unit or component. For example, you might create a `carLoan` object that calculates the number of payments required to pay off a car loan. The `carLoan` object may also store information such as the principal loan amount and the interest rate. Individual statements used in a computer program are often grouped into logical units called **procedures**, which are used to perform specific tasks. For example, a procedure may contain a group of statements that calculate the sales tax based on the sales total. The procedures associated with an object are called **methods**. A **property** is a piece of data, such as a color or a name, which is associated with an object. In the `carLoan` object example, the programming code that calculates the number of payments required to pay off the loan is a method. The principal loan amount and the interest rate are properties of the `carLoan` object.

To incorporate an object and an associated method in JavaScript code, you type the object's name, followed by a period, followed by the method. For example, the following code references the `carLoan` object, followed by a period, followed by a method named `calcPayments()`, which calculates the number of payments required to pay off the loan:

```
carLoan.calcPayments();
```

For many methods, you also need to provide some more specific information, called an **argument**, between the parentheses. Some methods require numerous arguments, whereas others don't require any. Providing one or more arguments for a method is referred to as **passing arguments**. For example, the `calcPayments()` method may require an argument that specifies the number of months until the loan is paid off. In that case, the JavaScript statement would look like this:

```
carLoan.calcPayments(60);
```

You use an object's properties in much the same way you use a method, by appending the property name to the object with a period. However, a property name is not followed by parentheses. One of the biggest differences between methods and properties is that a property does not actually do anything; you only use properties to store data. You assign a value to a property using an equal sign, as in the following example:

```
carLoan.interest = .0349;
```

Programming Concepts | Objects, Properties, and Methods

Objects are one of the fundamental building blocks of JavaScript, as well as many other programming languages. You can think of an object as anything you want to be able to work with in your programs. Some objects, such as the Document object, are part of a document by definition. You can also create other objects that are necessary for the programs you want to create. Every object can have methods, which are actions that can be performed on it. Every object also has properties; each property is a different piece of information about the object. Understanding the relationship between objects, properties, and methods is an important part of building a strong foundation in JavaScript.

The next part of this chapter focuses on the write() method as a way of helping you understand how to program with JavaScript.

Using the write() Method

JavaScript treats many things as objects. One of the most commonly used objects in JavaScript programming is the Document object. The Document object represents the content of a browser's window. Any text, graphics, or other information displayed in a web page is part of the Document object. One of the most common uses of the Document object is to add new text to a web page. You create new text on a web page with the write() method of the Document object. For example, you could use the write() method to render a web page containing custom information such as a user's name or the result of a calculation.

You should understand that the only reason to use the write() method is to add new text to a web page while it is being rendered. For example, if your web page incorporates constantly changing data such as stock quotes from a web server, you might use the write() method to add the stock data to the HTML content of the web page as it loads. If you simply want to display text in a web browser when the document is first rendered, there is no need to use anything but standard HTML elements. The procedures for dynamically gathering information are a little too complicated for this introductory chapter. However, in this chapter you will use the write() method to display text in a web browser when the document is first rendered in order to learn the basics of creating JavaScript programs.

Different methods require different kinds of arguments. For example, the write() method of the Document object requires a text string as an argument. A text string, or literal string, is text that is contained within double or single quotation marks. The text string argument of the write() method specifies the text that the Document object uses to create new text on a web page. For example, document.write("Plant choices"); displays the text "Plant choices" in the web browser window (without the quotation marks). Note that you must place literal strings on a single line. If you include a line break within a literal string, you receive an error message.

<blockquote>
Caution

By convention, the first letter of the name of a built-in object is capitalized when writing about the language, but typed in all lowercase in actual JavaScript code. For this reason, we talk about the `Document` object, but specify the methods as `document.write()` and `document.writeln()` in JavaScript code. Be sure to enter object names in all lowercase in your programs.
</blockquote>

The `write()` method performs essentially the same function that you perform when you manually add text to the body of a standard web document. Whether you add text to a document by using standard elements, such as the p element, or by using the `write()` method, the text is added according to the order in which the statements appear in the document.

<blockquote>
Note

Programmers often talk about code that "writes to" or "prints to" a web browser window. For example, you might say that a piece of code writes a text string to the web browser window. This is just another way of saying that the code displays the text string in the web browser window.
</blockquote>

The following code contains a script that prints some text in a web browser by using the `write()` method of the `Document` object.

```
1   <script>
2       document.write("<p>Plant choices<br />");
3       document.write("for <a href=↵
4           'http://planthardiness.ars.usda.gov'>↵
5           hardiness zones</a> 5a-6b</p>");
6   </script>
```

Note the use of semicolons at the end of each statement. Remember that it is considered good JavaScript programming practice to end every statement with a semicolon.

Code throughout this book uses the following color scheme to signify the role of each character or string in JavaScript code:

- ⟩black: JavaScript syntax character (. and ;), method name
- ⟩blue: Object name, numeric value
- ⟩orange: Operator, keyword
- ⟩gray: JavaScript comment
- ⟩green: Literal string

Caution

The arrow symbol (↵) at the end of a line of code indicates the code is broken in this book because of space limitations. When you enter code in your editor from code samples in this book, you should not press the Enter or Return keys at the end of a line that finishes with ↵. You must continue typing the code that follows on the same line.

Figure 1-8 shows the output.

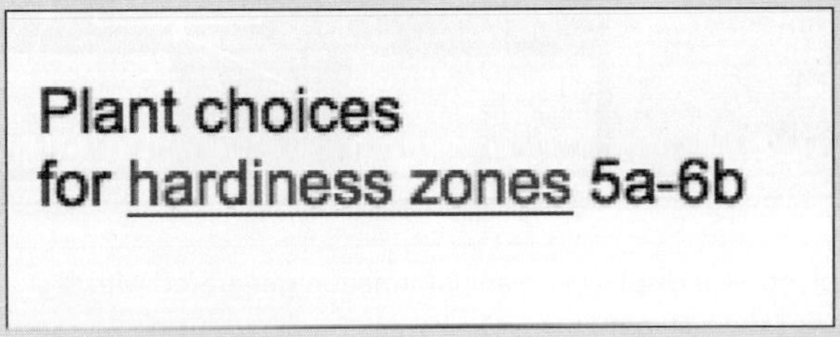

Plant choices
for hardiness zones 5a-6b

Figure 1-8: Output of a script that uses the write() method of the Document object

Next, you will add text and elements to the plants.htm file by using the write() method of the Document object.

To add text and elements to the plants.htm file by using the write() method of the Document object:

1. Return to the **plants.htm** document in your text editor.

2. Between the opening and closing <script> tags, add the following document.write() statement, which prints the text and elements that display information about the plants:

```
document.write("<p>Plant choices for <a href=↵
    'http://planthardiness.ars.usda.gov'>↵
    hardiness zones</a> 5a-6b</p>");
```

> **Caution** | *Because each line in this code ends with ↵ you should not press the Enter key, but rather type all of the above code on a single line.*

> **Note** | *Remember that the only reason you are using `write()` statements to add text to a web page when it is first rendered is to learn the basics of JavaScript.*

3. Save the **plants.htm** document, and refresh or reload it in your web browser. Your browser should appear similar to Figure 1-9.

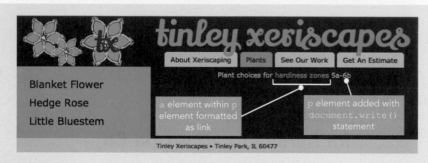

Figure 1-9: plants.htm displaying plant information generated with `document.write()` statements

Case Sensitivity in JavaScript

JavaScript is a case-sensitive language, meaning that it interprets differences in capitalization as differences in meaning. Within JavaScript code, object names must always be all lowercase. This can be a source of some confusion, because in written explanations about JavaScript, the names of objects are usually referred to with an initial capital letter. For example, throughout this book, the `Document` object is referred to with an uppercase *D*. However, you must use a lowercase *d* when referring to the `Document` object in a script, as in the code `document.write("Plant choices");`. Using a capital *D*, as in the statement `Document.write("Plant choices");`, causes an error message because the JavaScript interpreter cannot recognize an object named `Document` with an uppercase *D*.

Similarly, the following statements will also cause errors:

```
DOCUMENT.write("Plant choices");
```

```
Document.Write("Plant choices");
document.WRITE("Plant choices");
```

Note | Although HTML5 is not technically a case-sensitive language, it's considered good coding practice to write all HTML5 code in lowercase as well.

Adding Comments to a JavaScript Program

Just like in an HTML document, it's considered a good programming practice to add comments to any JavaScript code you write. Comments are lines of code that are not processed by browsers, which you use to add notes about your code. Comments are commonly used for specifying the name of the program, your name and the date you created the program, notes to yourself, or instructions to future programmers who may need to modify your work. When you are working with long scripts, comments make it easier to decipher how a program is structured.

JavaScript supports two kinds of comments: line comments and block comments. A line comment occupies only a single line or part of a line. To create a line comment, you add two slashes (//) before the text you want to use as a comment. The // characters instruct JavaScript interpreters to ignore all text following the slashes on the same line. You can place a line comment either at the end of a line of code or on its own line. Block comments hide multiple lines of code. You create a block comment by adding /* to the first line that you want included in the block, and you close a comment block by typing */ after the last character in the block. Any text or lines between the opening /* characters and the closing */ characters are ignored by JavaScript interpreters.

Note | A JavaScript block comment uses the same syntax as a comment in CSS, as well as in other programming languages including C++ and Java.

The following code shows a `script` element containing line and block comments (formatted in gray). If you opened a document containing the following script in a web browser, the browser would not render the text marked as comments.

```
1   <script>
2       /*
3           Information on available plants
4           including link to USDA website
5       */
6       document.write("<p>Plant choices for <a href=↵
```

```
7          'http://planthardiness.ars.usda.gov'>hardiness↵
8          zones</a> 5a-6b</p>"); // hardiness zones for Chicago↵
9          and surrounding area
10   </script>
```

Next, you will add comments to the plants.htm document.

To add comments to the plants.htm document:

1. Return to the **plants.htm** document in your text editor.

2. Add the following block comment immediately after the opening `<script>` tag:

```
/*
    Information on available plants
    including link to USDA website
*/
```

3. Position the insertion point after the ; at the end of the line containing the `document.write()` instruction, type a space, and then type the following line comment:

```
// hardiness zones for Chicago and surrounding area
```

The code for your `script` element should match the code sample shown above, just before these steps.

4. Save the **plants.htm** document, open it in your web browser, and then confirm that the comments are not displayed.

Skills at Work | Using Comments for Team Projects

JavaScript programmers generally work in teams with other programmers, especially on larger projects. This means that as a programmer, you'll be regularly reading and making changes to code that other programmers wrote; in addition, other team members will be changing and extending code that you created. When working as part of a team of programmers, it's important to use comments to document the code you write. Including a comment before each section of code to explain its purpose can help other team members understand the structure of your code. In addition, including comments makes it easier for everyone on the team to find and fix bugs, because they can compare the explanation of what a section should do, found in the comment, with the code that follows.

Short Quiz 3

1. JavaScript code in an HTML document goes within which HTML element?

2. Why should you end every JavaScript statement with a semicolon?

3. How do you create a single-line comment in JavaScript? How do you create a multiline comment in JavaScript?

Writing Basic JavaScript Code

So far, you've created a basic JavaScript program that stores comments and writes text to a web page. By incorporating a few additional JavaScript concepts into your program, you can make it flexible enough to apply to different situations, and responsive to user interaction.

Using Variables

The values a program stores in computer memory are commonly called variables. Technically speaking, though, a variable is actually a specific location in the computer's memory. Data stored in a specific variable often changes. You can think of a variable as similar to a storage locker—a program can put any value into it and then retrieve the value later for use in calculations. To use a variable in a program, you first have to write a statement that creates the variable and assigns it a name. For example, you may have a program that creates a variable named `curTime` and then stores the current time in that variable. Each time the program runs, the current time is different, so the value varies.

Programmers often talk about "assigning a value to a variable," which is the same as storing a value in a variable. For example, a shopping cart program might include variables that store customer names and purchase totals. Each variable will contain different values at different times, depending on the name of the customer and the items that customer is purchasing.

Assigning Variable Names

The name you assign to a variable is called an identifier. You must observe the following rules and conventions when naming a variable in JavaScript:

> Identifiers must begin with an uppercase or lowercase ASCII letter, dollar sign ($), or underscore (_).

> You can use numbers in an identifier but not as the first character.

> You cannot include spaces in an identifier.

> You cannot use reserved words for identifiers.

Reserved words (also called keywords) are special words that are part of the JavaScript language syntax. As just noted, reserved words cannot be used for identifiers. Figure 1-10 lists the JavaScript reserved words.

abstract	do	if	private	true
boolean	double	implements	protected	try
break	else	import	public	typeof
byte	enum	in	return	var
case	export	instanceof	short	void
catch	extends	int	static	volatile
char	false	interface	super	while
class	final	let	switch	with
const	finally	long	synchronized	yield
continue	float	native	this	
debugger	for	new	throw	
default	function	null	throws	
delete	goto	package	transient	

Figure 1-10: JavaScript reserved words

Variable names, like other JavaScript code, are case sensitive. Therefore, the variable name curTime is a completely different variable name than curtime, CurTime, or CURTIME. If a script doesn't perform as you expect, be sure you are using the correct case when referring to any variables in your code.

Note It's common practice to use an underscore (_) character to separate individual words within a variable name, as in my_variable_name. Another option is to use *camel case*, which is a method of capitalization that uses a lowercase letter for the first letter of the first word in a variable name, with subsequent words starting with an initial cap, as in myVariableName.

Declaring and Initializing Variables

Before you can use a variable in your code, you have to create it. In JavaScript, you usually use the reserved keyword var to create variables. For example, to create a variable named curTime, you use this statement:

```
var curTime;
```

Using the `var` keyword to create a variable is called **declaring** the variable. When you declare a variable, you can also assign a specific value to, or **initialize**, the variable by adding an equal sign (=) after the variable name, followed by the value you're assigning to the variable, as follows:

```
var variable_name = value;
```

The equal sign in the preceding statement is called an **assignment operator** because it assigns the value on the right side of the expression to the variable on the left side of the expression. The value you assign to a variable can be a literal string or a numeric value. For example, the following statement assigns the literal string *World News* to the variable `currentSection`:

```
var currentSection = "World News";
```

When you assign a literal string value to a variable, you must enclose the text in quotation marks, just as when you use a literal string with the `document.write()` method. However, when you assign a numeric value to a variable, do not enclose the value in quotation marks or JavaScript will treat the value as a string instead of a number. The following statement assigns the numeric value .05 to the `salesTax` variable:

```
var salesTax = .05;
```

You can declare multiple variables in a statement using a single `var` keyword followed by a series of variable names and assigned values separated by commas. For example, the following statement creates several variables using a single `var` keyword:

```
var orderNumber = "R0218", salesTotal = 47.58, salesTax = .05;
```

Notice in the preceding example that each variable is assigned a value. Although you can assign a value when a variable is declared, you are not required to do so. Your script may assign the value later, or you may use a variable to store user input. However, your script will not run correctly if it attempts to use a variable that has not been initialized. Therefore, it is good programming practice to always initialize your variables when you declare them.

In addition to assigning literal strings and numeric values to a variable, you can also assign the value of one variable to another. For instance, in the following code, the first statement creates a variable named `salesTotal` without assigning it an initial value. The second statement creates another variable, named `curOrder`, and assigns to it a numeric value of 47.58. The third statement then assigns the value of the `curOrder` variable to the `salesTotal` variable.

```
var salesTotal;
var curOrder = 47.58;
salesTotal = curOrder;
```

Displaying Variables

To print a variable (that is, display its value on the screen), you can pass the variable name to the `document.write()` method but without enclosing it in quotation marks. For instance, to display the value of the `salesTotal` variable in your document you could use the following code:

```
document.write(salesTotal);
```

This code would result in the value of the `salesTotal` variable, 47.58, being displayed in the browser window. Because the text `salesTotal` isn't enclosed in quotation marks in this line of code, a JavaScript parser treats it as the name of an object in the code, rather than as literal text.

You'll commonly want to combine literal text with variable values in your web documents. You can use a plus sign (+) with the `document.write()` method to combine a literal string with a variable containing a numeric value. You will learn more about performing similar operations as you progress through this chapter. However, for now you need to understand that using a plus sign to combine literal strings with variables containing numeric values does not add them together, as in an arithmetic operation. Rather, it combines the values to create a new string, which is then printed to the screen. For instance, to give some context to the `salesTotal` value, you could modify the `document.write()` statement to add text identifying the value, as follows:

```
document.write("<p>Your sales total is $" + salesTotal +↵
    ".</p>");
```

This code would produce the following result in a browser:

Your sales total is $47.58.

In addition to using a plus sign to combine a literal string with the numeric value of a variable, you can also use a plus sign to perform arithmetic operations involving variables that contain numeric values. For instance, the following code declares two variables and assigns numeric values to them. The third statement declares another variable and assigns to it the sum of the values stored in the other variables.

```
1   var salesTotal = 47.58;
2   var shipping = 10;
3   var grandTotal = salesTotal + shipping;
4   document.write("<p>Your sales total plus shipping is $" +↵
5       grandTotal + ".</p>");
```

This code would produce the following result in a browser:

Your sales total plus shipping is $57.58.

Modifying Variables

Regardless of whether or not you assign a value to a variable when it is declared, you can change the variable's value at any point in a script by using a statement that includes the variable's name, followed by an equal sign, followed by the value you want to assign to the variable. The following code declares a variable named salesTotal, assigns it an initial value of 47.58, and prints it using a document.write() method. The statement on line 5 changes the value of the salesTotal variable by adding its value to the value of another variable, named shipping. The final statement prints the new value of the salesTotal variable. Notice that it's only necessary to declare the salesTotal variable (using the var keyword) once.

```
1   var salesTotal = 47.58;
2   document.write("<p>Your sales total is $" +↵
3       salesTotal + ".</p>");
4   var shipping = 10;
5   salesTotal = salesTotal + shipping;
6   document.write("<p>Your sales total plus shipping is $" +↵
7       salesTotal + ".</p>");
```

This code would produce the following result in a browser:

Your sales total is $47.58.

Your sales total plus shipping is $57.58.

According to the design for the Tinley Xeriscapes Plants page, the main section should display an image that changes depending on which plant name a user clicks in the list on the left. To begin to create this effect, you'll first add an `img` element within the `article` element. Then you'll create a `script` section containing variables representing the path and filename for each of the three images.

To add the `img` element and variables to plants.htm:

1. Return to the **plants.htm** file in your text editor.

2. Within the `article` element, insert a new line just below the opening `<figure>` tag, and then enter the following code:

```
<img src="#" width="640" height="400" alt="" title="" />
```

This code creates a new `img` element, specifying `width` and `height` values, but setting the `src` attribute to #, which references the current page. Later you'll write JavaScript to replace the `src` attribute value with the relevant filename when a user clicks one of the plant names.

3. Within the existing script section, add the following comment and variables:

```
1   //define variables containing img src values
2   var blanket = "images/blanket.jpg";
3   var bluestem = "images/bluestem.jpg";
4   var rugosa = "images/rugosa.jpg";
```

Your code for the `figure` element should match the following:

```
1   <figure>
2       <img src="#" width="640" height="400" alt="" title=""↵
3       id="plantImg"/>
4   <figcaption>
5       <script>
6           /*
7               Information on available plants
8               including link to USDA website
9           */
10          document.write("<p>Plant choices for <a href=↵
11              'http://plainthardiness.ars.usda.gov'>hardiness↵
12              zones</a> 5a-6b</p>");↵
13              //hardiness zones for Chicago and surrounding area
14
15              //define variables containing img src values
```

```
16        var blanket = "images/blanket.jpg";
17        var bluestem = "images/bluestem.jpg";
18        var rugosa = "images/rugosa.jpg";
19      </script>
20     </figcaption>
21   </figure>
```

4. Save the **plants.htm** document. Later in this section, you will add code that changes the value of the img src attribute based on the variables you added in the last step.

Building Expressions

You can transform variables and data using expressions. An **expression** is a literal value or variable, or a combination of literal values, variables, operators, and other expressions, that can be evaluated by a JavaScript interpreter to produce a result. You use operands and operators to create expressions in JavaScript.

Operands are variables and literals contained in an expression. A **literal** is a value such as a literal string or a number. **Operators**, such as the addition operator (+) and multiplication operator (*), are symbols used in expressions to manipulate operands. You have already worked with several simple expressions that combine operators and operands. Consider the following statement:

```
votingAge = 18;
```

This statement is an expression that results in the value 18 being assigned to the variable votingAge. The operands in the expression are the votingAge variable name and the integer value 18. The operator is the equal sign (=). The equal sign operator is a special kind of operator, called an assignment operator, because it assigns the value 18 on the right side of the expression to the variable votingAge on the left side of the expression.

> **Caution**
>
> To assign a value to a variable, the value must be on the right side of the assignment operator, and the variable on the left, as in the expression `firstName = "Graham";`. Reversing the order could result in an error, as in the code `"Graham" = firstName;`, or it could produce unexpected results.

Understanding Events

One of the primary ways in which JavaScript is executed on a web page is through events. An **event** is a specific circumstance (such as an action performed by a user or an action performed by the browser) that is monitored by JavaScript and that your script can respond to in some way. You can use JavaScript events to allow users to interact with your web pages. The most common events are actions that users perform. For example, when a user clicks a form button, a `click` event is generated. You can think of an event as a trigger that can fire specific JavaScript code in response to a given situation. User-generated events, however, are not the only kinds of events monitored by JavaScript. Events that are not direct results of user actions, such as the `load` event, are also monitored. The `load` event, which is triggered automatically by a web browser, occurs when a document finishes loading in a web browser. Table 1-2 lists some JavaScript events and explains what triggers them.

EVENT	KEYBOARD TRIGGER	MOUSE TRIGGER	TOUCHSCREEN TRIGGER
blur	An element, such as a radio button, becomes inactive		
change	The value of an element, such as a text box, changes		
click	A user presses a key when an element is selected	A user clicks an element once	A user touches an element and then stops touching it
error	An error occurs when a document or image is being loaded		
focus	An element, such as a command button, becomes active		
keydown	A user presses a key		
keyup	A user releases a key		
load	A document or image loads		
mouseout		A user moves the mouse pointer off an element	A user stops touching an element
mouseover		A user moves the mouse pointer over an element	A user touches an element
reset	A form's fields are reset to its default values		
select	A user selects text		
submit	A user submits a form		
touchend			A user removes finger or stylus from the screen
touchmove			A finger or stylus already touching the screen moves on the screen
touchstart			A user touches a finger or stylus to the screen
unload	A document unloads		

Table 1-2: JavaScript events

Note that not all events happen with all devices. For instance, `keydown` and `keyup` are triggered only by a keyboard, and `touchend`, `touchmove`, and `touchstart` take place only on a touchscreen device. For this reason, it's important to choose trigger events that make your scripts available to users on all devices. You'll explore different methods of doing this as you build your JavaScript skills.

Working with Elements and Events

Events are associated with HTML elements. The events that are available to an element vary. The `click` event, for example, is available for a number of elements, including the `a` element and form controls created with the `input` element. In comparison, the `body` element does not have a `click` event, but it does have a `load` event, which occurs when a web page finishes loading, and an `unload` event, which occurs when a user goes to a different web page.

When an event occurs, your script executes any code that responds to that specific event on that specific element. This code is known as the **event handler**. There are a few different ways to specify an event handler for a particular event. One way is to include event handler code as an attribute of the element that initiates the event. For example, you can add an attribute that listens for a click to an `li` element in the navigation bar, and specify JavaScript code as the attribute value, such as code that changes the `display` attribute of the related submenu so it's visible. The syntax of an event handler within an opening tag is as follows:

```
<element onevent="JavaScript code">
```

The attribute name you use to specify an event handler combines the prefix `on` with the name of the event itself. For example, the attribute name for the `click` event is `onclick`, and the attribute name for the `load` event is `onload`. Table 1-3 lists various HTML elements and some of their associated event-related attributes.

The JavaScript code for an event handler in an attribute is contained within the quotation marks following the attribute name. The following code uses the `input` element to create a submit button.

```
<input type="submit" onclick="window.alert('Thanks for your↵
    order! We appreciate your business.')" />
```

This `input` element includes an `onclick` attribute that executes an event handler using the JavaScript `window.alert()` method, in response to a `click` event (which occurs when the mouse button is clicked or a user touches a touchscreen). The **`window.alert()` method** displays a dialog box with an OK button. You pass the `window.alert()` method a literal

ELEMENT	EVENT-RELATED ATTRIBUTES
a	onfocus, onblur, onclick, ondblclick, onmousedown, onmouseup, onmouseover, onmousemove, onmouseout, onkeypress, onkeydown, onkeyup, ontouchstart, ontouchend
img	onclick, ondblclick, onmousedown, onmouseup, onmouseover, onmousemove, onmouseout, onkeypress, onkeydown, onkeyup, ontouchstart, ontouchmove, ontouchend
body	onload, onunload, onclick, ondblclick, onmousedown, onmouseup, onmouseover, onmousemove, onmouseout, onkeypress, onkeydown, onkeyup
form	onsubmit, onreset, onclick, ondblclick, onmousedown, onmouseup, onmouseover, onmousemove, onmouseout, onkeypress, onkeydown, onkeyup
input	tabindex, accesskey, onfocus, onblur, onselect, onchange, onclick, ondblclick, onmousedown, onmouseup, onmouseover, onmousemove, onmouseout, onkeypress, onkeydown, onkeyup, ontouchstart, ontouchmove, ontouchend
textarea	onfocus, onblur, onselect, onchange, onclick, ondblclick, onmousedown, onmouseup, onmouseover, onmousemove, onmouseout, onkeypress, onkeydown, onkeyup, ontouchstart, ontouchmove, ontouchend
select	onfocus, onblur, onchange, ontouchstart, ontouchend

Table 1-3: HTML elements and some of their associated events

string containing the text you want to display. The syntax for the alert() method is window.alert(*message*);. The value of the literal string or variable is then displayed in the alert dialog box, as shown in Figure 1-11.

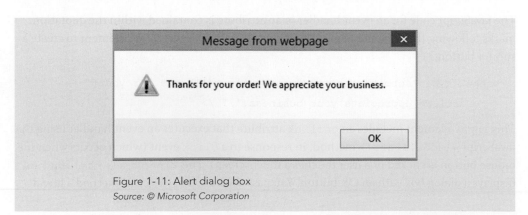

Figure 1-11: Alert dialog box
Source: © Microsoft Corporation

Notice that the event handler code specified as an attribute value—the `window.alert()` method—is contained within double quotation marks. Also notice that the literal string being passed is contained in single quotation marks. This is because the `window.alert()` method itself is already enclosed in double quotation marks. To ensure that browsers don't mistake the opening quote for the literal string as the closing quote for the value of the `onclick` event handler, JavaScript requires single quotes around the literal string.

The `window.alert()` method is the only statement being executed in the preceding event handler code. You can, however, include multiple JavaScript statements in event handler code, as long as semicolons separate the statements. For example, to include two statements in the event handler example—a statement that creates a variable and another statement that uses the `window.alert()` method to display the variable—you would type the following:

```
1    <input type="submit"
2            onclick="var message='Thanks for your order! We↵
3                appreciate your business.';↵
4                window.alert(message)" />
```

Referencing Web Page Elements

You can reference any element on a web page in your scripts using its `id` value. The `id` value is assigned using an element's HTML `id` attribute. For instance, the following HTML code creates an `input` element with the `id` value `firstName`:

```
<input type="text" id="firstName" />
```

To look up an element by its `id` value in your JavaScript code, you use the `getElementById()` method of the Document object. For instance, to create a variable named `total` that references the element with the `id` value `firstName`, you'd use the code

```
var fname = document.getElementById("firstName");
```

Specific properties of an element can then be appended to the element reference. This allows you to retrieve information about an element or change the values assigned to its attributes. For example, suppose you have a web page that contains an `input` element with the `id` value `firstName`. You could change the value of the `input` element using this statement:

```
document.getElementById("firstName").value = value;
```

As an alternative, using the `fname` variable created above to reference the element with the `id` value `firstName`, you could use this code:

```
fname.value = value;
```

Next, you will add event handlers to the three `li` elements containing plant names in the `aside` element of the plants.htm file. When a user's mouse pointer moves over one of these `li` elements, the `src` value of the `img` element with the `id` value `plantImg` will change to display the image of the plant.

To add event handlers to the plants.htm file:

1. Return to the **plants.htm** file in your text editor.

2. Within the `aside` element, in the opening tag for the first `li` element, add the following event handler:

```
onclick="document.getElementById('plantImg').src = blanket"
```

3. In the opening tag for the second `li` element, add the following event handler:

```
onclick="document.getElementById('plantImg').src = rugosa"
```

4. In the opening tag for the third `li` element, add the following event handler:

```
onclick="document.getElementById('plantImg').src = bluestem"
```

The code for your `aside` element should match the following:

```
1   <aside>
2       <ul>
3           <li onclick="document.getElementById('plantImg').src =↵
4               blanket">Blanket Flower</li>
5           <li onclick="document.getElementById('plantImg').src =↵
6               rugosa">Hedge Rose</li>
7           <li onclick="document.getElementById('plantImg').src =↵
8               bluestem">Little Bluestem</li>
9       </ul>
10  </aside>
```

5. Save the **plants.htm** document, refresh or reload it in your web browser, and then click each plant name on the left side of the page. The picture of each flower should be displayed in the main section of the web page when you click its name. If the page doesn't load, or if you receive error messages, make sure that you typed all the JavaScript code in the correct case. (Remember that JavaScript is case sensitive.) Figure 1-12 shows the web page after clicking Hedge Rose.

Figure 1-12: plants.htm web page after clicking Hedge Rose

U.S. Department of Agriculture

Short Quiz 4

1. What is an identifier? What limits does JavaScript place on an identifier?

2. What is the difference between declaring and initializing a variable?

3. How do you change the value of a variable?

4. What is an event handler for?

Structuring JavaScript Code

You can add JavaScript code just about anywhere in a document. However, there are a number of factors to consider in deciding the best location for particular code. In addition, there are rules to keep in mind regarding the organization of that code.

Including a `script` Element for Each Code Section

You can include as many script sections as you like within a document. However, when you include multiple script sections in a document, you must include a `script` element for each section. The following document fragment includes two separate script sections. The script sections create the information that is displayed beneath the h2 heading elements. Figure 1-13 shows the output.

```
1    <h2>Sales Total</h2>
2    <script>
3        var salesTotal = 47.58;
4        document.write("<p>Your sales total is $" + salesTotal +↵
5            ".</p>");
```

```
6    </script>
7    <h2>Sales Total with Shipping</h2>
8    <script>
9      var shipping = 10;
10     salesTotal = salesTotal + shipping;
11     document.write("<p>Your sales total plus shipping is $" +↵
12       salesTotal + ".</p>");
13   </script>
```

Figure 1-13: Output of a document with two script sections

Placing JavaScript in the Document Head or Document Body

You can place `script` elements in either the document head or the document body, or in both. However, in general, script elements are usually placed at the end of the body section, just before the closing `</body>` tag. The elements in an HTML document are rendered in the order in which they occur in the document, and each script is processed when the HTML element that contains it is parsed by a browser. When processing a script in the head section or in the middle of HTML content, most browsers do not continue rendering the web page until the script is loaded and executed. If a script is very large or complex, this could cause the page to be displayed with only some of its content and formatting until the script finishes loading. If you instead place your `script` elements just before the end of the body section, you allow browsers to render all the simple HTML content immediately on the user's screen, and then load and process any JavaScript that works with that content. This ensures that users can see and interact with the entire web page as quickly as possible.

Caution *You're unlikely to notice the effect of script position on the small scripts you're working with in this chapter. However, as you progress to working with larger, more complex scripts, correct placement can have significant effects on the usability of your web pages.*

You'll move the variable declarations in the Tinley Xeriscapes page to a script section at the end of the document body.

To move the variable declarations to a script section at the end of the document body:

1. Return to the **plants.htm** document in your text editor.

2. Create a new script section immediately above the closing `</body>` tag by entering the following tags:

```
<script>
</script>
```

3. Cut the variable declaration statements along with the comment that precedes them from the script section in the `article` element to the Clipboard, and then paste them into the script section at the end of the document body. The end of the document body section should appear as follows:

```
1     <script>
2         //define variables containing img src values
3         var blanket = "images/blanket.jpg";
4         var bluestem = "images/bluestem.jpg";
5         var rugosa = "images/rugosa.jpg";
6     </script>
7   </body>
```

The script section in the `article` element should contain only the `document.write` command.

4. Save the **plants.htm** document, reload or refresh it in your web browser, and test the functionality. The script should function the same as it did before you added the new script section.

Creating a JavaScript Source File

JavaScript is often incorporated directly into a web page. However, you can also save JavaScript code in an external file called a JavaScript source file. You can then write a statement in the HTML document that references the code saved in the source file. When a browser encounters a reference to a JavaScript source file, it loads the JavaScript source file and executes the code it contains.

A JavaScript source file is usually designated by the file extension .js, although it can technically have any extension that you like. The file contains only JavaScript statements, and it does not contain a `script` element. Instead, the `script` element is located within the document that calls the source file. To access JavaScript code that is saved in an external file, you use the `src` attribute of the `script` element. You assign to the `src` attribute the URL of a JavaScript source file. For example, to reference a JavaScript source file named *scripts.js*, you would include the following code in a document:

```
<script src="scripts.js"></script>
```

JavaScript source files cannot include HTML elements. If you include HTML elements in a JavaScript source file, the elements will be ignored or an error message will be generated, depending on which web browser you use. In addition, when you specify a source file in your document using the `src` attribute, the browser ignores any other JavaScript code located within the `script` element. For example, in the following code, the JavaScript source file specified by the `src` attribute of the `script` element is executed properly, but the `var` and `write()` statements within the `script` element are ignored.

```
1    <script src="scripts.js">
2        var salesTotal = 47.58;
3        document.write("<p>Your sales total is $" + salesTotal +↵
4            ".</p>");
5    </script>
```

If the JavaScript code you intend to use in a document is fairly short, then it is usually easier to include JavaScript code in a `script` element within the document itself. However, for longer JavaScript code, it is easier to include the code in a .js source file. There are several reasons you may want to use a .js source file instead of adding the code directly to a document.

> Your document will be neater. Lengthy JavaScript code in a document can be confusing. You may not be able to tell at a glance where the HTML code ends and the JavaScript code begins.

> The JavaScript code can be shared among multiple web pages. For example, your website may contain multiple pages that allow users to order an item. Each web page may display a different item but can use the same JavaScript code to gather order information. Instead of recreating the JavaScript order information code within each document, the web pages can share a central JavaScript source file. Sharing a single source file among multiple documents reduces the amount of bandwidth required to download any subsequent pages that use the same script, which is especially critical over slower connections, such as on mobile devices. In addition, when you share a source file among multiple documents, you make any additions or changes to the code in just one place, but they are immediately available to all the documents that use the script.

You can use a combination of embedded JavaScript code and JavaScript source files in your documents. The ability to combine embedded JavaScript code and JavaScript source files in a single web page is advantageous if you have multiple web pages. Each page can contain any code specific to that page, while all pages can share a single JavaScript source file containing code that they all use.

Suppose you have a website with multiple web pages. Each page displays a product that your company sells. You may have a JavaScript source file that collects order information, such as a person's name and address, which is shared by each of the product web pages. Each individual product page may also require other kinds of order information that you need to collect using JavaScript code. For example, one of your products might be a shirt, for which you need to collect size and color information. On another web page, you may sell jelly beans, for which you need to collect quantity and flavor information. Each of these products can share a central JavaScript source file to collect standard information, but each may also include embedded JavaScript code to collect product-specific information.

Next, you will move the variable declaration statements from the script section at the end of the document body of the plants.htm file to a JavaScript source file.

To move the variable declaration statements from the script section at the end of the document body of the plants.htm file to a JavaScript source file:

1. In your editor, create a new document, and then enter the following multiline comment, substituting your name and today's date where indicated:

```
1    /* JavaScript 6th Edition
2         Chapter 1
3         Chapter case
4
5         Tinley Xeriscapes
6         Author: Your Name
7         Date: Today's Date
8
9         Filename: plants.js
10   */
```

Note

If you're using a text editor that formats code with colors, use the editor's advanced options to specify that you want to create a JavaScript document. This ensures that the code will be colored appropriately for the JavaScript language. Consult the documentation for your editor if you're unsure how to specify the language for a document.

2. Switch to the **plants.htm** file in your editor, and then in the script section at the end of the document body, select the variable declaration statements and the comment that precedes them.

Caution | *Do not select the opening or closing `<script>` tags.*

3. Press **Ctrl** + **X** (Windows) or **command** + **X** (Mac) to cut the comment and statements to the Clipboard.

4. Switch back to the new file you created in your editor, click on a blank line below the comment section you created, and then press **Ctrl** + **V** (Windows) or **command** + **V** (Mac) to paste the variable declaration statements into the file.

5. Save the document as **plants.js** in the Chapter folder for Chapter 1 and then close the file.

6. Switch back to the **plants.htm** file in your editor, delete the spaces and the line break separating the opening and closing `<script>` tags, and then in the opening `<script>` tag at the end of the document body, add the attribute **src="plants.js"** as follows:

```
<script src="plants.js"></script>
```

7. Save the **plants.htm** document, refresh or reload it in your web browser, and test the functionality. The script should function the same as it did before you created the JavaScript source file.

Working with Libraries

In addition to storing scripts for multiple pages in the same website, sometimes JavaScript source files store especially useful generic scripts used on many different websites. These files, known as libraries, are often developed by a single programmer or a team of programmers and distributed online. Many libraries are developed to solve a problem on one website and turn out to be useful for other sites as well. Programmers often make libraries available for free reuse.

After downloading a .js file containing a library that you want to use on a web page, you incorporate it into your HTML code just as you would any other JavaScript source file: by creating a `script` element in the head section and using the `src` attribute to specify the filename of the library.

A handful of libraries are commonly used to perform a variety of functions on large, complex websites. For instance, Node.js and Backbone.js contain tools for creating and managing large web applications. Another library, Modernizr, is widely used to enable web authors to deliver a consistent design and functionality across different browsers, browser versions, and platforms.

Modernizr includes JavaScript code that enables older versions of Internet Explorer to work with HTML5 semantic elements, such as `nav` and `aside`. To ensure that the plants.htm web page is rendered correctly on the widest possible variety of browsers, you'll add a reference to a file containing the relevant parts of the Modernizr library.

To add a reference to a JavaScript source file containing parts of the Modernizr library:

1. Use Internet Explorer 8 (or an earlier version of Internet Explorer) to open **plants.htm**. As Figure 1-14 shows, several elements are not displayed as they are in modern browsers. This is because Internet Explorer 8 and earlier versions don't recognize HTML5 semantic elements.

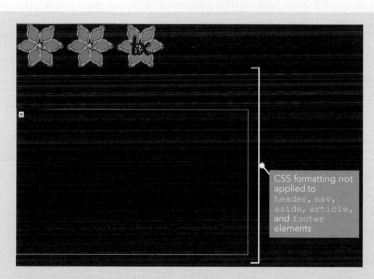

CSS formatting not applied to `header`, `nav`, `aside`, `article`, and `footer` elements

Figure 1-14: plants.htm in Internet Explorer 8

2. Return to the **plants.htm** file in your text editor.

3. Immediately above the closing `</head>` tag, add the following new script section:

```
<script src="modernizr.custom.05819.js"></script>
```

The modernizr.custom.05819.js file contains only the parts of the Modernizr library needed for the plants.htm web page. Note that unlike most script sections, you reference this file in the head section. For Modernizr to make semantic elements available in older browsers, it must be executed before the browser parses the page content.

4. Save the **plants.htm** file, and then refresh or reload the web page in Internet Explorer 8. The contents are now displayed as shown earlier in Figure 1-12.

5. Close Internet Explorer 8.

Validating Web Pages

When you use a web browser to open an HTML document that does not conform to the rules and requirements of the language, the browser simply ignores the errors and renders the web page as best it can. A document that conforms to these rules is said to be **well formed**. A web browser cannot tell whether an HTML document is well formed; instead, to ensure that a web page is well formed and that its elements are valid, you need to use a validating parser. A **validating parser** is a program that checks whether a web page is well formed and whether the document conforms to a specific language definition known as a DTD. The term **validation** refers to the process of verifying that your document is well formed and checking that the elements in your document are correctly written according to the element definitions in a specific DTD. If you do not validate a document and it contains errors, most web browsers will probably ignore the errors and render the page anyway. However, validation can help you spot errors in your code. Even the most experienced web page authors frequently introduce typos or some other types of errors into a document that prevent the document from being well formed.

Various web development tools, including Dreamweaver, offer validation capabilities. In addition, several validating services can be found online. One of the best available is W3C Markup Validation Service, a free service that validates HTML as well as other markup languages. The W3C Markup Validation Service is located at *http://validator.w3.org/*. The service allows you to validate a web page by entering its URL, by uploading a document from your computer, or by copying and pasting code.

Writing Valid XHTML Code with JavaScript

If you're working with XHTML instead of HTML, JavaScript can present a challenge to creating valid documents. This is because some JavaScript statements contain symbols such as the less-than symbol (<) symbol, the greater-than symbol (>), and the ampersand (&). This is not a problem with HTML documents, because the statements in a `script` element are interpreted as character data instead of as markup. A section of a document that is not interpreted as markup is referred to as **character data**, or **CDATA**. If you were to validate an HTML document containing a script section, the document would validate successfully because the validator would ignore the script section and not attempt to interpret the text and symbols in the JavaScript statements as HTML elements or attributes. By contrast, in XHTML documents, the statements in `script` elements are treated as **parsed character data**, or **PCDATA**, which identifies a section of a document that is interpreted as markup. Because JavaScript code in an XHTML document is treated as PCDATA, if you attempt to validate an XHTML document that contains a script section, it will fail the validation. To avoid this problem, you can do one of two things. One option is to move your code into a source file, which prevents the validator from attempting to parse the JavaScript statements. Alternatively, if you prefer to keep the JavaScript code within the document, you can enclose the code within a `script` element within a CDATA section, which marks sections of a document as CDATA. The syntax for including a CDATA section on a web page is as follows:

```
<![CDATA[
    statements to mark as CDATA
]]>
```

For instance, the following code snippet shows the body section of a web document containing JavaScript code that is enclosed within a CDATA section.

```
1    <body>
2        <script type="text/javascript">
3        <![CDATA[
4            document.write("<h1>Order Confirmation</h1>");
5            document.write("<p>Your order has been received.</p>");
6            document.write("<p>Thank you for your business!</p>");
7        ]]>
8        </script>
9    </body>
```

Validating HTML Code

Whenever you finish modifying an HTML document, you should validate it. Validating ensures that your code conforms to web standards, and it can help you eliminate coding errors, or **bugs**, which may not be obvious but which could at some point affect the functionality or appearance of your documents.

Before you return the modified plants.htm document to the Tinley Xeriscapes staff, you'll validate it using the W3C Markup Validation Service.

To validate your HTML document:

1. In your web browser, open the W3C Markup Validation Service page at **http://validator.w3.org/**. The service provides three methods for specifying code to validate.

2. Click the **Validate by File Upload** tab. Figure 1-15 shows the options on this tab.

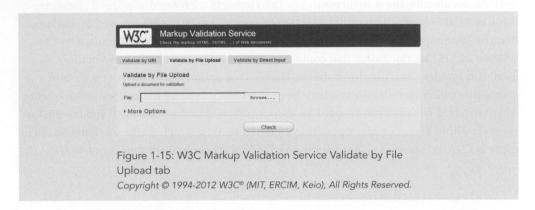

Figure 1-15: W3C Markup Validation Service Validate by File Upload tab
Copyright © 1994-2012 W3C® (MIT, ERCIM, Keio), All Rights Reserved.

3. Click the **Browse** or **Choose File** button, navigate to the **Chapter** folder for Chapter 1, and then double-click **plants.htm**. The filename is displayed in the File text box.

4. Click the **Check** button. The W3C Markup Validation Service validates the document. Figure 1-16 shows the results for a valid document. Note that the results include a warning. This is the W3C's method of reminding users that its HTML5 tools are still considered a work in progress. As long as the results page indicates that your document was found to be valid, you have completed the validation process.

Note *If your document is not found to be valid, review the list of errors, return to your document in your editor, fix one error, save your changes, and revalidate the document. Continue this process until the document passes validation.*

5. Close your web browser window, and then close the plants.htm document in your text editor.

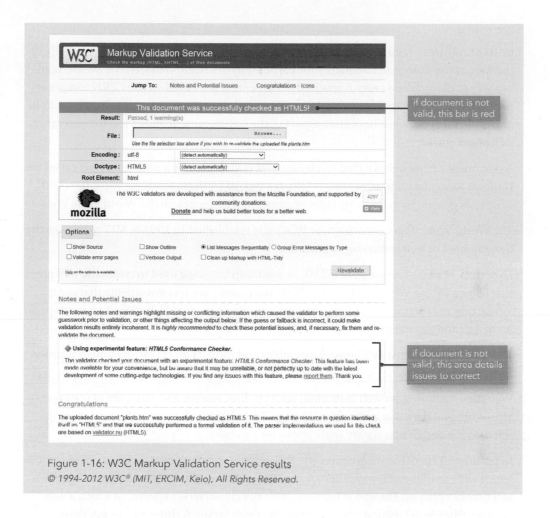

Figure 1-16: W3C Markup Validation Service results
© 1994-2012 W3C® (MIT, ERCIM, Keio), All Rights Reserved.

Short Quiz 5

1. Why should you place scripts at the end of an HTML document's body section?

2. How do you incorporate the contents of a JavaScript source file into an HTML document?

Summary

> In 1990 and 1991, Tim Berners-Lee created what would become the World Wide Web, or the web, at the European Laboratory for Particle Physics (CERN) in Geneva, Switzerland, as a way to easily access cross-referenced documents that existed on the CERN computer network. This method of accessing cross-referenced documents, known as hypertext linking, is probably the most important aspect of the web because it allows you to open other web pages quickly.

> A document on the web is called a web page and is identified by a unique address called the Uniform Resource Locator, or URL. A URL is a type of Uniform Resource Identifier (URI), which is a generic term for many types of names and addresses on the World Wide Web.

> The World Wide Web Consortium, or W3C, was established in 1994 at MIT to oversee the development of web technology standards.

> Hypertext Markup Language, or HTML, is a markup language used to create the web pages that appear on the World Wide Web. HTML documents are text documents that contain formatting instructions, called tags, which determine how data is displayed on a web page. A tag pair and any data it contains are referred to as an element.

> The process by which a web browser assembles and formats an HTML document is called parsing or rendering.

> Web page authoring (or web authoring) refers to the creation and assembly of the tags, attributes, and data that make up a web page. Web development, or web programming, refers to the design of software applications for a website.

> In traditional client/server architecture, the server is usually some sort of database from which a client requests information. A system consisting of a client and a server is known as a two-tier system. The web is built on a two-tier client/server system, in which a web browser (the client) requests documents from a web server. A three-tier, or multitier, client/server system consists of three distinct pieces: the client tier, the processing tier, and the data storage tier.

> JavaScript is a client-side scripting language that allows web page authors to develop interactive web pages and sites. Client-side scripting refers to a scripting language that runs on a local browser (on the client tier) instead of on a web server (on the processing tier).

> Server-side scripting refers to a scripting language that is executed from a web server.

- A general rule of thumb is to allow the client to handle the user interface processing and light processing, such as data validation, but have the web server perform intensive calculations and data storage.

- The `script` element tells a web browser that the scripting engine must interpret the commands it contains. The individual lines of code, or statements, that make up a JavaScript program in a document are contained within the `script` element.

- An object is programming code and data that can be treated as an individual unit or component. The procedures associated with an object are called methods. A property is a piece of data, such as a color or a name, which is associated with an object.

- You create new text on a web page with the `write()` method of the `Document` object.

- JavaScript is a case-sensitive language, meaning that it interprets differences in capitalization as differences in meaning.

- Comments are nonprinting lines that you place in your code to contain various types of remarks, including the name of the program, your name, and the date you created the program, notes to yourself, or instructions to future programmers who may need to modify your work.

- The values a program stores in computer memory are commonly called variables.

- Reserved words (also called keywords) are special words that are part of the JavaScript language syntax.

- An expression is a literal value or variable or a combination of literal values, variables, operators, and other expressions that can be evaluated by the JavaScript interpreter to produce a result.

- An event is a specific circumstance (such as an action performed by a user, or an action performed by the browser) that is monitored by JavaScript and that your script can respond to in some way. Code that executes in response to a specific event is called an event handler.

- You can place `script` elements in either the document head or the document body, or in both. However, in general, script elements are usually placed at the end of the body section, just before the closing `</body>` tag.

- You can save JavaScript code in an external file called a JavaScript source file.

Key Terms

argument—Specific information provided between the parentheses when using a method.

assignment operator—The operator (=) used to assign the value on the right side of an expression to the variable on the left side of the expression.

attribute—In HTML, a parameter used to provide additional information about an element.

back end—*See* server.

block comment—A comment that contains multiple lines of code; created by adding /* to the start of the first line that you want included in the block and */ after the last character in the block.

bug—A coding error.

camel case—A method of capitalization that uses a lowercase letter for the first letter of the first word in a variable name, with subsequent words starting with an initial cap.

Cascading Style Sheets (CSS)—A complementary language to HTML, developed for specifying the appearance of web page elements.

CDATA—*See* character data.

character data—A section of an HTML document that is not interpreted as markup.

client—In a two-tier system, the tier that presents an interface to the user.

client-side scripting—Programming written in a scripting language that runs on a local browser (on the client tier) instead of on a web server (on the processing tier).

comments—Lines of code that are not processed by browsers and which serve as notes about the rest of the code.

content—In HTML, the information contained between an element's opening and closing tags.

CSS—*See* Cascading Style Sheets (CSS)

declaring—Using the var keyword to create a variable.

document body—In HTML, the body element and the text and elements it contains.

document head—In HTML, the head element and the elements it contains.

element—In HTML, a tag pair (or a single tag) and any data it contains.

empty element—In HTML, an element that does not require a closing tag, and thus does not allow you to use a tag pair to enclose text or other elements.

ECMAScript—An international, standardized version of JavaScript.

event—A specific circumstance that is monitored by JavaScript and that your script can respond to in some way.

event handler—Code that tells a browser what to do in response to a specific event on a specific element.

expression—A literal value or variable or a combination of literal values, variables, operators, and other expressions that can be evaluated by a JavaScript interpreter to produce a result.

Extensible Hypertext Markup Language (XHTML)—A modified version of HTML that conforms to the rules of XML.

Extensible Markup Language (XML)—A markup language used to format data in many different applications.

front end—*See* client.

getElementById() method—A method of the `Document` object that you use in your JavaScript code to look up an element by its `id` value.

HTML—*See* Hypertext Markup Language (HTML).

HTML document—*See* web page.

HTML page—*See* web page.

HTTP—*See* Hypertext Transfer Protocol (HTTP).

hyperlink—*See* hypertext link.

hypertext link—A web page element that contains a reference to a specific web page that you can click to open that page.

hypertext linking—A method of accessing cross-referenced documents on the web by marking a reference with information necessary to access a related document.

Hypertext Markup Language (HTML)—A markup language used to create the web pages that appear on the web.

Hypertext Transfer Protocol (HTTP)—The main system used on the web for exchanging data.

identifier—The name assigned to a variable.

initialize—To assign a specific value to a variable when declaring it by adding an equal sign after the variable name, followed by the value you're assigning to the variable.

interpreter—Any program that executes scripting language code.

JavaScript—A client-side scripting language that allows web page authors to develop interactive web pages and sites.

JavaScript source file—An external file containing JavaScript code, which can be referenced in a web document.

keywords—*See* reserved words.

library—A JavaScript source file that contains especially useful generic scripts used on many different websites.

line comment—A comment that occupies only a single line or part of a line; created by adding two slashes (//) before the comment text.

link—*See* hypertext link.

literal—A value such as a literal string or a number.

literal string—*See* text string.

markup language—A set of characters or symbols that defines a document's logical structure, indicating the meaning or function of each item in the document.

method—A procedure associated with an object.

middle tier—*See* processing tier.

multitier client/server system—*See* three-tier client/server system.

n-tier client/server system—*See* three-tier client/server system.

object—Programming code and data that can be treated as an individual unit or component.

operand—A variable or a literal contained in an expression.

operator—A symbol such as + or * used in an expression to manipulate operands.

parsed character data—A section of an HTML document that is interpreted as markup.

parsing—The process by which a web browser assembles and formats an HTML document.

passing arguments—Providing one or more arguments for a method.

PCDATA—*See* parsed character data.

procedure—In a computer program, a logical unit composed of individual statements, which is used to perform a specific task.

processing tier—The part of a three-tier client/server system that handles the interaction between the web browser client and the data storage tier.

property—A piece of data, such as a color or a name, that is associated with an object.

rendering—*See* parsing.

request—The process by which a user's web browser asks a web server for a web page.

reserved words—Special words that are part of the JavaScript language syntax.

response—What a web server returns to a user in reply to a request.

root element—The element in an HTML document that contains all the other elements in the document.

script—A JavaScript program contained within a web page.

script element—The HTML element in which statements written in a scripting language are placed.

scripting engine—The part of a browser that executes scripting language code.

scripting host—A web browser that contains a scripting engine.

scripting language—Any type of language, including JavaScript, that is capable of programmatically controlling a web page or returning some sort of response to a web browser.

server—In traditional client/server architecture, a database from which a client requests information; a server fulfills a request for information by managing the request or serving the requested information to the client.

server-side scripting—Programming written in a scripting language that is executed from a web server.

SGML—*See* Standard Generalized Markup Language (SGML).

Standard Generalized Markup Language (SGML)—An older markup language on which HTML is based, which has a wider scope than HTML and can define the structure of documents in many different contexts.

statement—An individual line of code in a JavaScript program.

static—Description of a web page that can't change after a browser renders it.

tags—Codes in an HTML document that specify how the data in the document is treated by a web browser.

text string—Text passed as an argument, contained within double or single quotation marks.

three-tier client/server system—A system that consists of three distinct pieces: the client tier, the processing tier, and the data storage tier.

two-tier system—A system consisting of a client and a server.

Uniform Resource Identifier (URI)—A generic term for many types of names and addresses on the web, including URLs.

Uniform Resource Locator (URL)—The unique address of a document on the web.

URL—*See* Uniform Resource Locator (URL).

validating parser—A program that checks whether a web page is well formed and whether the document conforms to a specific DTD.

validation—The process of verifying that your document is well-formed and checking that the elements in your document are correctly written according to the element definitions in a specific DTD.

variables—The values a program stores in computer memory.

W3C—*See* World Wide Web Consortium (W3C)

web—*See* World Wide Web.

web address—*See* Uniform Resource Locator (URL).

web application—A program that is executed on a server but that clients access through a web page loaded in a browser.

web authoring—*See* web page authoring.

web browser—A program used to display a web page on the screen of a computer, tablet, or phone.

web design—*See* web page design.

web development—The design of software applications for a website.

web page—A document on the web.

web page authoring—The creation and assembly of the tags, attributes, and data that make up a web page.

web page design—The visual design and creation of the documents that appear on the web.

web programming—*See* web development.

web server—A computer that delivers web pages.

website—The location on the Internet of the web pages and related files (such as graphic and video files) that belong to a company, organization, or individual.

well formed—Term used to describe a document that conforms to the rules and requirements of a markup language such as HTML or XHTML.

`window.alert()` method—A method that displays a pop-up dialog box with an OK button; you pass the `window.alert()` method a literal string containing the text you want to display.

World Wide Web—A system for easily accessing cross-referenced documents using the Internet.

World Wide Web Consortium (W3C)—An organization established to oversee the development of web technology standards.

`write()` method—A method of the `Document` object used to create new text on a web page, without a line break at the end.

XHTML—*See* Extensible Hypertext Markup Language (XHTML).

XML—*See* Extensible Markup Language (XML).

Review Questions

1. A URL is a type of _____.
   a. web page
   b. URI
   c. link
   d. network

2. What organization oversees the development of web technology standards?
   a. U.S Department of Defense
   b. World Wide Web Consortium
   c. Stanford University
   d. United Nations

3. The markup language originally developed to create web pages and still in use today is called _____.
   a. HTML
   b. SGML
   c. XML
   d. CSS

4. _____ is a separate, complementary language to HTML that was developed for specifying the appearance of web page elements.
   a. XHTML
   b. SGML
   c. XML
   d. CSS

5. Elements that do not require a closing tag are called _____ elements.
   a. independent
   b. empty
   c. permanent
   d. constant

6. What is the root element of an HTML document?
   a. `head`
   b. `body`
   c. `html`
   d. `script`

7. A system consisting of a client and a server is known as a _____.
   a. mainframe topology
   b. double-system architecture
   c. two-tier system
   d. wide area network

8. What is usually the primary role of a client?
   a. locating records that match a request
   b. heavy processing, such as calculations
   c. data storage
   d. the presentation of an interface to the user

9. Which of the following functions does the processing tier *not* handle in a three-tier client/server system?
   a. Processing and calculations
   b. Reading and writing of information to the data storage tier
   c. The return of any information to the client tier
   d. Data storage

10. Which of the following uses the correct case?
    a. `Document.write()`
    b. `document.write()`
    c. `document.Write()`
    d. `Document.Write()`

11. Which of the following is *not* a valid identifier?
    a. $InterestRate
    b. 2QInterest Rate
    c. interestRate
    d. _interestRate

12. When you assign a specific value to a variable on its creation, you _____ it.
    a. declare
    b. call
    c. assign
    d. initialize

13. Code that tells a browser what to do in response to a specific event on a specific element is called a(n) _____.
    a. method
    b. event handler
    c. response
    d. procedure

14. Which method displays a dialog box with an OK button?
    a. `document.write()`
    b. `document.writeln()`
    c. `window.alert()`
    d. `window.popup()`

15. A section of a document that is not interpreted as markup is referred to as _____.
    a. PDATA
    b. CDATA
    c. PCDATA
    d. CPDATA

16. What is the difference between web page design, web page authoring, and web development?

17. What is the difference between character data and parsed character data? What does this have to do with JavaScript?

18. Write the JavaScript to add the text "Copyright 2017" as a line comment. Write the JavaScript to add the same text as a block comment.

19. Write a statement that creates a variable with the identifier `title` and the value "Dr."

20. What is a library?

Hands-On Projects

Before you begin working on the Hands-on Projects, be certain to extract the data files for this book, which you can download from Cengage's website at *http://www.cengage.com*, as explained in the preface to this book.

Hands-On Project 1-1

In this exercise you will use `document.write()` statements in a script section to add financial planning tips to a web page.

1. In your text editor, open **index.htm** from the HandsOnProject1-1 folder in the Chapter01 folder. Enter your name and today's date where indicated in the comment section in the document head.

2. Just above the closing `</head>` tag, add the following element to link the file containing the Modernizr library:

   ```
   <script src="modernizr.custom.05819.js"></script>
   ```

3. Within the article element, below the h2 element, enter `<script>`, insert a blank line, and then enter `</script>` to create a new script section.

4. Within the script section you created in the previous step, enter the following comment and `document.write()` statements. These statements create an ordered list element containing financial planning tips.

   ```
   1    // create ordered list
   2    document.write("<ol>");
   3    document.write("<li>Reduce spending on non ↵
   4        necessities.</li>");
   5    document.write("<li>Use extra money to pay off debt, starting↵
   6        with highest interest credit card.</li>");
   7    document.write("<li>Continue paying off debts until you are↵
   8        debt free.</li>");
   9    document.write("<li>Put a fixed percent of your pay aside in↵
   10       savings every payday.</li>");
   11   document.write("</ol>");
   ```

5. Save your work, and then open **index.htm** in a web browser. A numbered list containing four items should be displayed below the h2 heading "Financial Planning Tips," as shown in Figure 1-17.

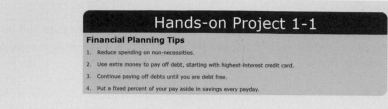

Financial Planning Tips

1. Reduce spending on non-necessities.
2. Use extra money to pay off debt, starting with highest-interest credit card.
3. Continue paying off debts until you are debt free.
4. Put a fixed percent of your pay aside in savings every payday.

Figure 1-17: Completed index.htm file

6. Use the W3C Markup Validation Service to validate the **index.htm** document, and then, if necessary, fix any errors that the document contains.

7. Close your web browser window.

Hands-On Project 1-2

In this exercise, you will create a web page that uses variables to display information about high-speed Internet plans offered by an Internet service provider.

1. In your text editor, open **index.htm** from the HandsOnProject1-2 folder in the Chapter01 folder. Enter your name and today's date where indicated in the comment section in the document head.

2. Just above the closing </head> tag, add the following element to link the file containing the Modernizr library:

```
<script src="modernizr.custom.05819.js"></script>
```

3. Within the article element, below the h2 element, enter **<script>**, insert a blank line, and then enter **</script>** to create a new script section.

4. Within the script section you created in the previous step, enter the following comment and var statements. These statements declare variables containing the names and speeds of the high-speed Internet plans.

```
1   //initialize variables for service names and speeds
2   var service1Name = "Basic";
3   var service2Name = "Express";
4   var service3Name = "Extreme";
5   var service4Name = "Ultimate";
6   var service1Speed = 5;
7   var service2Speed = 25;
8   var service3Speed = 50;
9   var service4Speed = 150;
```

5. In the `table` element, within the `thead` section, locate the first row. Within the first `td` element, enter the following code to create a `script` element containing a `document.write()` statement to write the name of the first type of service:

```
<script>
    document.write(service1Name);
</script>
```

6. Repeat Step 5 for each of the remaining table cells, using the following content:

```
<script>
    document.write(service1Speed);
</script>
<script>
    document.write(service2Name);
</script>
<script>
    document.write(service2Speed);
</script>
<script>
    document.write(service3Name);
</script>
<script>
    document.write(service3Speed);
</script>
<script>
    document.write(service4Name);
</script>
<script>
    document.write(service4Speed);
</script>
```

7. Save your work, and then open **index.htm** in a web browser. A table containing two columns and five rows should be displayed below the `h2` heading "High-Speed Internet Plans," as shown in Figure 1-18.

8. Use the W3C Markup Validation Service to validate the **index.htm** document, and then, if necessary, fix any errors that the document contains.

9. Close your web browser window.

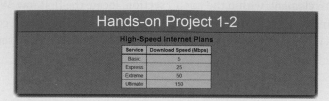

Figure 1-18: Table contents written by JavaScript statements

Hands-On Project 1-3

In this exercise, you will enhance a form to display an alert box when a user clicks the Submit button.

1. In your text editor, open **index.htm** from the HandsOnProject1-3 folder in the Chapter01 folder. Enter your name and today's date where indicated in the comment section in the document head.

2. Just above the closing `</head>` tag, add the following element to link the file containing the Modernizr library:

    ```
    <script src="modernizr.custom.05819.js"></script>
    ```

3. Locate the final `fieldset` element, with the id `submitbutton`, just before the closing `</form>` tag. Within the `input` element that creates the Submit button, add the following event handler:

    ```
    onclick="alert('Thanks for your order!');"
    ```

4. Save your work, open **index.htm** in a web browser, and then click the **Submit button**. As shown in Figure 1-19, an alert box should open, displaying the text "Thanks for your order!" Click the **OK** button to dismiss the alert box.

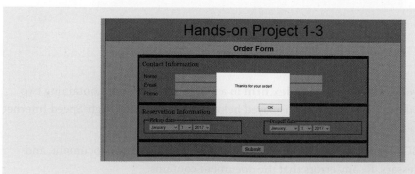

Figure 1-19: Alert box

5. Use the W3C Markup Validation Service to validate the **index.htm** document, and fix any errors that the document contains.

6. Close your web browser window.

Hands-On Project 1-4

In this chapter you learned how to dynamically change an image using the `getElementById()` method to set the value of the `src` attribute for an `img` element. You can apply this same process to many other web page elements. In this project, you'll use an event handler to automatically fill text boxes in a form with preassigned values based on the option button that a user clicks.

1. In your text editor, open **index.htm** from the HandsOnProject1-4 folder in the Chapter01 folder. Enter your name and today's date where indicated in the comment section in the document head.

2. Just above the closing `</head>` tag, add the following element to link the file containing the Modernizr library:

```
<script src="modernizr.custom.05819.js"></script>
```

3. Open **index.htm** in your browser, and familiarize yourself with the layout of the form.

4. Return to your text editor, locate the first `fieldset` element, with the id `addroptions`, and then find the first `input` element, with the id `homeoption`. Within the `input` element that creates the first option button, add the following event handler:

```
1   onclick="document.getElementById('streetinput').value =↵
2               '1 Main St.';
3           document.getElementById('cityinput').value =↵
4               'Sicilia';
5           document.getElementById('stateinput').value = 'MA';
6           document.getElementById('zipinput').value = '02103';"
```

5. Within the same `fieldset` element, locate the second `input` element, with the id `workoption`. Within the `input` element that creates the second option button, add the following event handler:

```
1   onclick="document.getElementById('streetinput').value = '15↵
2               Columbine Ln.';
3           document.getElementById('cityinput').value = 'Crab↵
4               City';
5           document.getElementById('stateinput').value = 'MA';
6           document.getElementById('zipinput').value = '02104';"
```

6. Save your work, open **index.htm** in a web browser, and then click the **Home** option button. The Street Address, City, State, and Zip fields should be filled with the information shown beneath the word "Home," as shown in Figure 1-20.

Figure 1-20: Fields populated with home address info

7. Click the **Work** option button. The contents of the Street Address, City, State, and Zip fields should be replaced with the information shown beneath the word "Work," as shown in Figure 1-21.

Figure 1-21: Fields populated with work address info

8. Use the W3C Markup Validation Service to validate the **index.htm** document, and fix any errors that the document contains.

9. Close your web browser window.

Hands-On Project 1-5

In this project, you'll fix errors in JavaScript code to make a broken program work.

1. In your text editor, open **index.htm** from the HandsOnProject1-5 folder in the Chapter01 folder. Enter your name and today's date where indicated in the comment section in the document head.

2. Just above the closing `</head>` tag, add the following code to link the file containing the Modernizr library:

   ```
   <script src="modernizr.custom.65897.js"></script>
   ```

3. In the `article` element, examine the contents of the `script` element, which contains several errors.

4. Delete the characters `*/` from the third line of the script section, and then at the end of the first line, after the text "Add content to web page," type the `*/` characters. Now only the first line of the script section is a comment.

5. In the second line of the script section, change the word `Document` to all lowercase.

6. After the opening parenthesis, replace the apostrophe character (`'`) with a double quote (`"`) to match the closing character at the end of the line.

7. After the closing parenthesis, add a semicolon (`;`). Your corrected script section should match the following:

   ```
   1  <script>
   2      /* Add content to web page */
   3      document.write("<p>We are closed for the holiday and will↵
   4          reopen at midnight tonight.</p>");
   5  </script>
   ```

8. Save your work, and then open **index.htm** in your browser. The `p` element is displayed on the web page, as shown in Figure 1-22.

Hands-on Project 1-5

We are closed for the holiday and will reopen at midnight tonight.

Figure 1-22: Text created by script section

9. Use the W3C Markup Validation Service to validate the **index.htm** document, and fix any errors that the document contains.

10. Close your web browser window.

Case Projects

Before you begin working on the Case Projects, be certain to extract the data files for this book, which you can download from Cengage's website at *http://www.cengage.com*, as explained in the preface to this book. Save any files you create for the Case Projects in the correct folder in your data files.

Individual Case Project

The Individual Case Project for each chapter in this book will build on a website that you create on a subject of your choice. To begin, choose a topic for your website. This can be a topic related to your major, or a personal interest or activity. Plan a website containing at least four pages with a common layout and navigation system. Note that you'll add pages to your site in later chapters, so ensure that your navigation system can support additional content. Add a `script` element that links to the modernizr.custom.05819.js file in each HTML document in your website. Ensure that all of your web pages pass validation.

Team Case Project

Throughout the Team Case Projects in this book you will continue to work on a website on a subject chosen by your team. Working in a team of 4–8 people, discuss and agree on a topic for your website. This may be a topic related to your major, another area of study, your college or university, or a shared interest. Work together to plan a website containing, at a minimum, a number of pages equal to the number of group members, and to create a common layout and navigation system. Note that you'll add pages to your site in later chapters, so ensure that your navigation system can support additional content. Decide as a group who will create which page, and create the pages individually. Add a `script` element that links to the modernizr.custom.05819.js file in each HTML document you create. When you've finished creating the individual pages, ensure they pass validation, and then work together to assemble the resulting website, identifying and fixing any issues as a group.

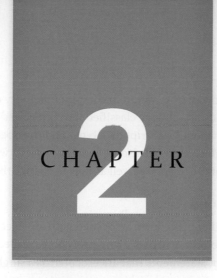

CHAPTER 2

WORKING WITH FUNCTIONS, DATA TYPES, AND OPERATORS

When you complete this chapter, you will be able to:

> Use functions to organize your JavaScript code
> Use expressions and operators
> Identify the order of operator precedence in an expression

So far, the code you have written has consisted of simple statements placed within script sections. However, like most programming languages, JavaScript allows you to group programming statements in logical units. In JavaScript, a group of statements that you can execute as a single unit is called a function. You'll learn how to create functions in this chapter, and you'll practice using them to organize your code.

In addition to functions, one of the most important aspects of programming is the ability to store values in computer memory and to manipulate those values. In the last chapter, you learned how to store values in computer memory using variables. The values, or data, contained in variables are classified into categories known as data types. In this chapter, you'll learn about JavaScript data types and the operations that can be performed on values of each type. You'll also explore the order in which different operations are performed by JavaScript processors, as well as how to change this order.

Working with Functions

In Chapter 1, you learned that procedures associated with an object are called methods. In JavaScript programming, you can write your own procedures, called functions. A function is a related group of JavaScript statements that are executed as a single unit. A function, like all JavaScript code, must be contained within a `script` element. In the following section, you'll learn more about incorporating functions in your scripts.

Defining Functions

JavaScript supports two different kinds of functions: named functions and anonymous functions. A **named function** is a set of related statements that is assigned a name. You can use this name to reference, or **call**, this set of statements in other parts of your code. An **anonymous function**, on the other hand, is a set of related statements with no name assigned to it. The statements in an anonymous function work only in a single context—the place in the code where they are located. You cannot reference an anonymous function anywhere else in your code.

Generally, you use a named function when you want to be able to reuse the function statements within your code, and you use an anonymous function for statements that you need to run only once.

Before you can use a function in a JavaScript program, you must first create, or define, it. The lines that make up a function are called the **function definition**.

The syntax for defining a named function is:

```
function name_of_function(parameters) {
    statements;
}
```

The syntax for defining an anonymous function is the same as that for a named function except that it does not specify a name:

```
function (parameters) {
    statements;
}
```

Parameters are placed within the parentheses that follow a function name. A parameter is a variable that is used within a function. Placing a parameter name within the parentheses of a function definition is the equivalent of declaring a new variable. However, you do not need to include the var keyword. For example, suppose that you want to write a function named calculateSquareRoot() that calculates the square root of a number contained in a parameter named number. The start of the function declaration would then be written as

```
calculateSquareRoot(number)
```

In this case, the function declaration is declaring a new parameter (which is a variable) named number. Functions can contain multiple parameters separated by commas. If you wanted to create a function that calculated the volume of a box, the function would need values for the length, width, and height of the box. You could write the start of the function declaration as

```
calculateVolume(length, width, height)
```

Note that parameters (such as length, width, and height) receive their values when you call the function from elsewhere in your program. (You will learn how to call functions in the next section.)

> **Note**
> Functions do not have to contain parameters. Many functions only perform a task and do not require external data. For example, you might create a function that displays the same message each time a user visits your website; this type of function only needs to be executed and does not require any other information.

Following the parentheses that contain the function parameters is a set of braces (called function braces) that contain the function statements. Function statements are the statements that do the actual work of the function, such as calculating the square root of the parameter, or displaying a message on the screen. Function statements must be contained within the function braces. The following is an example of a calculateVolume() function including function statements:

```
1    function calculateVolume(length, width, height) {
2        var volume = length * width * height;
3        document.write(volume);
4    }
```

Notice how the preceding function is structured. The opening brace is on the same line as the function name, and the closing brace is on its own line following the function statements. Each statement between the braces is indented. This structure is the preferred format among many JavaScript programmers. However, for simple functions it is sometimes easier to include the function name, braces, and statements on the same line. (Recall that JavaScript ignores line breaks, spaces, and tabs outside of string literals.) The only syntax requirement for spacing in JavaScript is that semicolons separate statements on the same line.

> **Note**
> *The code in this book is indented using three space characters. The number of spaces used for indenting isn't important, as long as you use the same number consistently throughout your code. Some programmers prefer to use tab characters instead of spaces for indents; this choice is also simply a question of personal preference, and has no effect on the quality of the code.*

It's common practice to place functions in an external .js file and include a script section that references the file at the bottom of an HTML document's body section.

In this chapter, you'll add JavaScript code to a web page for Fan Trick Fine Art Photography, a photography business that sells photographic prints and offers special event photography services. The owners want to expand their website to offer information about digital photography, and to provide a rate estimator for their services for prospective customers. Your Chapter folder for Chapter 2 contains the files you will need for the project. Figure 2-1 shows a preview of the completed web form in a desktop browser, and Figure 2-2 shows it in a mobile browser.

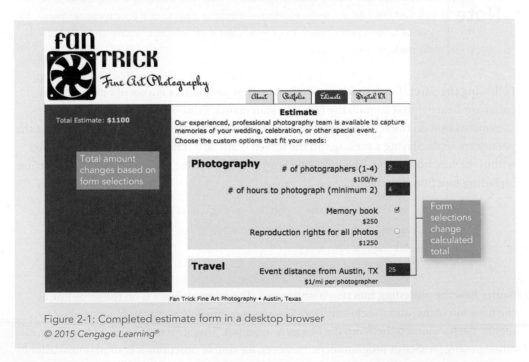

Figure 2-1: Completed estimate form in a desktop browser
© 2015 Cengage Learning®

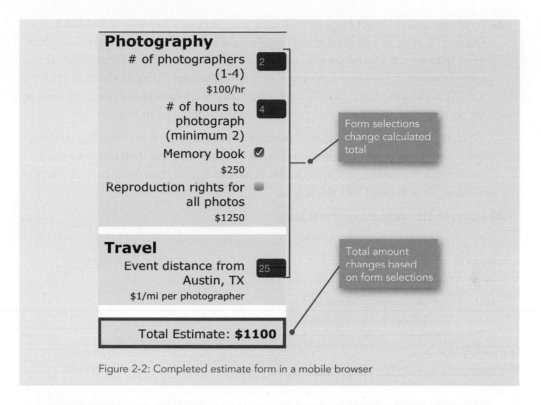

Figure 2-2: Completed estimate form in a mobile browser

The image contains the following labels and text:

Photography
# of photographers (1-4)   2
$100/hr
# of hours to photograph (minimum 2)   4
Memory book ☑
$250
Reproduction rights for all photos ⬤
$1250

Travel
Event distance from Austin, TX   25
$1/mi per photographer

Total Estimate: **$1100**

Form selections change calculated total

Total amount changes based on form selections

To start working on the estimate page:

1. In your text editor, open the **estimate.htm** file, located in your Chapter folder for Chapter 2.

2. In the comment section at the top of the document, type your name and today's date where indicated, and then save your work.

3. Scroll through the document to familiarize yourself with its contents. It includes a form as well as an `aside` element that contains the text "Total Estimate:". Later in the chapter, you'll write code that calculates the cost of the options selected in the form and displays them in the `aside` element.

4. Open **estimate.htm** in a browser, click the **# of photographers** text box, change the value to **2**, and then click the **Memory book** check box to insert a check. Nothing on the page changes when you make form selections because no JavaScript code is associated with the form fields. You'll add code later in this chapter.

5. Click your browser's **Refresh** or **Reload** button. Depending on which browser you're using, the form may still display the changes you made.

6. Press and hold the **Shift** key, and then click your browser's **Refresh** or **Reload** button. The form is reset to its default selections. Because your clients don't want to include a Reset button on the form, users could use Shift + Refresh or Shift + Reload to clear the form. However, many users don't know about this shortcut. To make the form as user-friendly as possible, your clients would instead like users to be able to clear the form by simply reloading the page. You'll create a function to accomplish this.

7. In your text editor, open the **ft.js** file located in your Chapter folder for Chapter 2, enter your name and today's date in the comment section, and then save your work. You'll create the code for your app in this external file, and then use a `script` element to reference it in the HTML document.

8. Enter the following code in the ft.js file:

```
1   // sets all form field values to defaults
2   function resetForm() {
3       document.getElementById("photognum").value = 1;
4       document.getElementById("photoghrs").value = 2;
5       document.getElementById("membook").checked = false;
6       document.getElementById("reprodrights").checked = false;
7       document.getElementById("distance").value = 0;
8   }
```

This code creates a function named `resetForm()`. Recall the `getElementById()` method of the `Document` object looks up an element by its HTML `id` attribute value. Each line in the `resetForm()` function references one of the `input` elements in the form and sets it to its default value. You use the `value` property to set the value for a text `input` element, and you use the `checked` property to specify whether a check box `input` element should be checked (`true`) or unchecked (`false`).

9. Save your work, return to the **estimate.htm** file in your text editor, and then near the bottom of the document, just before the closing `</body>` tag, enter the following `script` element:

```
<script src="ft.js"></script>
```

This element loads the code from the ft.js file.

10. Save your work, refresh or reload **estimate.htm** in your browser, click the **# of photographers** text box, change the value to **2**, click the **Memory book** check box to select it, and then click your browser's **Refresh** or **Reload** button. Unless your browser previously cleared input when you clicked Refresh or Reload, note that nothing happens. This is because browsers don't execute functions until they are triggered.

Calling Functions

A named function definition does not execute automatically. Creating a named function definition only names the function, specifies its parameters, and organizes the statements it will execute. To execute a named function, you must invoke, or call, it from elsewhere in your program. The code that calls a named function is referred to as a **function call** and consists of the function name followed by parentheses, which contain any variables or values to be assigned to the function parameters.

Passing Arguments to a Function

The variables or values that you place in the parentheses of the function call statement are called **arguments** or **actual parameters**. Sending arguments to the parameters of a called function is known as **passing arguments**. When you pass arguments to a function, the value of each argument is then assigned to the value of the corresponding parameter in the function definition. (Again, remember that parameters are simply variables that are declared within a function definition.)

For instance, the following code contains three functions. The `calculateSum()` and `calculateVolume()` functions each perform different mathematical manipulations on values passed to them when they are called. The last line of each function, however, is identical, passing the results of the calculation and the reference to an element as arguments to a third function, `updateResult()`. Based on the values passed to it, the `updateResult()` function updates the result value in the document.

```
1    function calculateSum(value1, value2, value3) {
2        var sum = value1 + value2 + value3;
3        var location = document.getElementById("sum");
4        updateResult(sum, location);
```

```
 5   }
 6   function calculateVolume(length, width, height) {
 7       var volume = length * width * height;
 8       var location = document.getElementById("volume");
 9       updateResult(volume, location)
10   }
11   function updateResult(result, element) {
12       element.innerHTML = result;
13   }
```

> **Note** Later in this chapter, you'll learn how the + and * operators work and what the `innerHTML` property does. For now, just notice that you can pass arguments to a function when you call it.

Handling Events with Functions

You can also call functions in response to browser events. Browsers support three different methods for doing this: HTML attributes, object properties, and event listeners.

The simplest way to specify a function as an event handler is to specify the function as the value for the associated HTML attribute. You saw in Chapter 1 how to use an event attribute to run a statement. For instance, the following code displays an alert box containing a message when a user clicks the `input` element in which it is located:

```
<input type="submit" onclick="window.alert('Thanks for your↵
    order! We appreciate your business.')" />
```

Instead of specifying a JavaScript statement as the value of the `onevent` attribute, you can instead specify a function name. Then, when the event fires, the function will be executed. For instance, if you had a named function called `showMessage()` that you instead wanted to specify as the event handler for the click event on the `input` element, you could replace the previous code with the following:

```
<input type="submit" onclick="showMessage()" />
```

Whenever a user clicks this `input` element, the browser runs the `showMessage()` function.

One drawback of specifying event handlers with HTML attributes is they require developers to place JavaScript code within HTML code. Just as developers generally avoid using inline CSS styles to keep HTML and CSS code separate, most developers prefer not to mix HTML and JavaScript code in the same file. Instead, they maintain separate HTML and JavaScript files. Fortunately, there are two other ways to specify functions as event handlers.

One alternative is to specify the function as a property value for the object representing the HTML element. Every element has an `onevent` property for each event it supports. For instance, a Submit button (an `input` element with a `type` value of `submit`) supports the `click` event, so you can specify a value for its `onclick` property. Within a .js file, you could specify the `showMessage()` function as the event handler for a submit button as follows:

```
document.getElementById("submitButton").onclick =
    showMessage;
```

This code references the Submit button using the value of its HTML `id` attribute. Note that the function name is not followed by parentheses.

Although this option enables you to separate HTML and JavaScript code, it has one major drawback: you can assign only one event handler per event. In more complex code, you might want to specify several event handlers to fire in response to a given event. To assign multiple event handlers to a single event, you need to use the third and final technique, which is the `addEventListener()` method. Every web page element has an `addEventListener()` method, which uses the following syntax:

```
element.addEventListener("event", function, false);
```

where `element` is a reference to the element, `event` names the event to handle, and `function` names a function that will handle the event. The third argument, `false`, is generally included for compatibility with some older browsers. Specifying an event handler with the `addEventListener()` method is known as **adding an event listener**. The following statement specifies the `showMessage()` function as an event handler for the `click` event on the element with the id `submitButton`:

```
var submit = document.getElementById("submitButton");
submit.addEventListener("click", showMessage, false);
```

Note that as in the object property above, the function name is not followed by parentheses in an event listener. Also notice that the event is specified by the event name only (`"click"`) rather than by prefixing the event name with `on` (`"onclick"`).

You can also specify an anonymous function as an event handler using the addEventListener() method. To do so, you simply substitute the entire function definition for the function name in the statement. For instance, the following statement replaces the showMessage function reference in the previous example with an anonymous function:

```
1   var el = document.getElementById("submitButton");
2   el.addEventListener("click", function() {
3       window.alert("Thanks for your order! We appreciate your↵
4           business.");
5   }, false);
```

The highlighted section of the above code represents the anonymous function. Notice that it comes after the name of the event, and is followed by the word false, a closing parenthesis, and a semicolon, just as in the previous statement that used a function name.

Next, you will add code to call the resetForm() function by using the addEventListener() method to specify the function as an event handler of the onload event handler of the Window object.

To specify the resetForm() function as an event handler:

1. Return to the **ft.js** file in your text editor.

2. On a new line below the function you added, type the following comment and statement:

```
// resets form when page is reloaded
document.addEventListener("load", resetForm, false);
```

This statement specifies the resetForm() function you just created as an event handler for the load event of the Window object. Because this statement is not part of the function, it is executed as soon as a browser parses it. This ensures whenever a user reloads or refreshes the page, your resetForm() function returns all form values to their defaults.

3. Save your work, refresh or reload **estimate.htm** in your browser, change the value in the **# of photographers** text box to **2**, click the **Memory book** check box, and then click your browser's **Refresh** or **Reload** button. Reloading the page should trigger the function you created, and the form values should return to their defaults.

Note	*If the form values don't reset as expected, check the contents of your function against Step 8 in the previous set of steps, check your* script *element against Step 9 in the previous set of steps, check your function call against Step 2 above, make any necessary changes, and then repeat Step 3. If your form values still don't reset, continue to the next section, where you'll use the browser console to identify errors in your code.*

Locating Errors with the Browser Console

Even the most careful developer introduces unintentional errors into code from time to time. Even a small mistake, such as incorrect capitalization or the omission of a closing quote, parenthesis, or brace, can prevent a browser from processing your code, and result in a document that doesn't function as you intended.

When a browser encounters an error that keeps it from understanding code, it generates an error message. However, this message is displayed in a pane known as a browser console, or simply console, which is hidden by default to avoid alarming users. As a developer, however, it can be useful to display the browser console pane to see any errors that your code may generate.

Next you'll introduce an intentional error in your code, and then open the browser console to view the error message generated by the error. You'll then fix the error, and verify that the error message does not reappear in the console.

To introduce an intentional error in your code and view an error message in the browser console:

1. Return to **ft.js** in your text editor.

2. At the end of the resetForm() function, delete the closing }. Function statements must always be enclosed in braces, so removing this brace causes an error when a browser processes the function.

3. Save your changes to **ft.js**, return to the **estimate.htm** document in your browser, and then click the **Reload** or **Refresh** button.

4. Click the **Memory book** check box to check it, click the **Reproduction rights** box to check it, and then click your browser's **Reload** or **Refresh** button. Depending on which browser you're using, the check boxes may remain checked, indicating your `resetForm()` function did not execute as expected. Next you'll open the browser console to view any error messages. Table 2-1 lists the keyboard shortcuts and menu commands to open the console in modern versions of the major browsers.

BROWSER	KEYBOARD SHORTCUT	MENU STEPS
Internet Explorer	**F12**, then **Ctrl + 2**	Click the **Tools** button, click **F12 Developer Tools** on the menu, and then in the window that opens, click the **Console** button.
Firefox	**Ctrl + Shift + K** (Win) **option + command + K** (Mac)	Click the **Firefox** button (Win) or **Tools** (Mac or Win), point to **Web Developer**, and then click **Web Console**.
Chrome	**Ctrl + Shift + J** (Win) **option + command + J** (Mac)	Click the **Customize and control Google Chrome** button, point to **Tools**, and then click **JavaScript console**.

Table 2-1: Steps to open the browser console in major browsers

5. Open the console in your browser using the appropriate command from Table 2-1, and then refresh or reload **estimate.htm**.

Note | *If your browser isn't listed, or if one of the listed methods doesn't work, check your browser's documentation for the correct steps, or try a different browser. Remember that different browsers may use different terms for the JavaScript console, including "web console" or "error console."*

The console indicates a syntax error resulting from a missing } after the function. Figure 2-3 shows the browser console in Internet Explorer, Figure 2-4 shows the console in Chrome, and Figure 2-5 shows the Firefox console.

Notice that each console specifies a line number where it identifies an error. IE and Firefox both indicate line 23, which is the start of the next statement after the function, as the place they ran into the error (your line number may differ depending on the number of blank lines in your code). Chrome identifies line 1, which is not particularly helpful in this case. Both IE and Firefox also recognize that the problem stems from a missing brace, while Chrome simply indicates "Unexpected end of input."

Figure 2-3: Internet Explorer browser console
Source: © Microsoft Corporation

Figure 2-4: Chrome browser console
Source: © Google Chrome

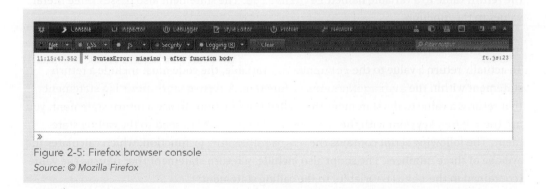

Figure 2-5: Firefox browser console
Source: © Mozilla Firefox

Note | *Because different browsers report errors differently, it can sometimes help to check the console in more than one browser to identify a hard-to-find error.*

6. Return to **ft.js** in your text editor, and then at the end of the `resetForm()` function, below the statement `document.getElementById("distance").value = 0;`, add a } character. This returns your function to its previous state. Your `resetForm()` function should match the one shown in the previous set of steps.

7. Save your changes to **ft.js**, and then in your browser reload or refresh the **estimate.htm** document. The browser console no longer displays an error message.

> **Note**
> *Don't worry if your console displays other informational messages. If it displays other error messages, though, examine your code for additional errors, and fix them until the console shows no further errors.*

Using Return Statements

In many instances, you may want your code to receive the results from a called function and then use those results in other code. For instance, consider a function that calculates the average of a series of numbers that are passed to it as arguments. Such a function would be useless if your code could not print or use the result elsewhere. As another example, suppose that you have created a function that simply prints the name of a student. Now suppose that you want to alter the code so it uses the student name in another section of code. You can return a value from a function to a calling statement by assigning the calling statement to a variable. The following statement calls a function named `averageNumbers()` and assigns the return value to a variable named `returnValue`. The statement also passes three literal values to the function.

```
var returnValue = averageNumbers(1, 2, 3);
```

To actually return a value to the `returnValue` variable, the code must include a return statement within the `averageNumbers()` function. A **return statement** is a statement that returns a value to the statement that called the function. To use a return statement, you use the `return` keyword with the variable or value you want to send to the calling statement. The following script contains the `averageNumbers()` function, which calculates the average of three numbers. The script also includes a return statement that returns the value (contained in the `result` variable) to the calling statement:

```
1    function averageNumbers(a, b, c) {
2        var sum_of_numbers = a + b + c;
3        var result = sum_of_numbers / 3;
4        return result;
5    }
```

Understanding Variable Scope

When you use a variable in a JavaScript program, particularly a complex JavaScript program, you need to be aware of the **variable scope**—that is, you need to think about where in your code a declared variable can be used. A variable's scope can be either global or local. A **global variable** is one that is declared outside a function and is available to all parts of your code. A **local variable** is declared inside a function and is available only within the function in which it is declared. Local variables cease to exist when a function ends. If you attempt to use a local variable outside the function in which it is declared, browsers log an error message to the console.

You must use the `var` keyword when you declare a local variable. However, when you declare a global variable, the `var` keyword is optional. For example, you can write the statement

```
var myVariable = "This is a variable.";
```

as

```
myVariable = "This is a variable.";
```

If you declare a variable within a function and do not include the `var` keyword, in most cases the variable automatically becomes a global variable. However, it is considered good programming technique to always use the `var` keyword when declaring variables because it indicates where in your code you intend to start using each variable. Also, it is considered poor programming technique to declare a global variable inside of a function by not using the `var` keyword because it makes it harder to identify the global variables in your scripts. Using the `var` keyword forces you to explicitly declare your global variables outside of any functions and local variables within functions.

The following code includes declarations for two global variables, `salesPrice` and `shippingPrice`, which are defined outside of the function. It also contains a declaration for a third variable, `totalPrice`, declared within the function using a `var` statement; this makes it a local variable. When the function is called, the global variables and the local variable print successfully from within the function. After the call to the function, the global variables again print successfully from the individual statements. However, the statement that tries to print the total price generates an error message because the local variable ceases to exist when the function ends.

```
1   var salesPrice = 100.00;
2   var shippingPrice = 8.95;
3   function applyShipping() {
4       var totalPrice = salesPrice + shippingPrice;
5       document.write(salesPrice); // prints successfully
6       document.write(shippingPrice); // prints successfully
7       document.write(totalPrice); // prints successfully
8   }
9   applyShipping();
10  document.write(salesPrice); // prints successfully
11  document.write(shippingPrice); // prints successfully
12  document.write(totalPrice); // error message
```

To correct this code, you could simply declare the totalPrice variable outside of the function without assigning it a value, making it a global variable, and then simply change its value within the function, as follows:

```
1   var salesPrice = 100.00;
2   var shippingPrice = 8.95;
3   var totalPrice;
4   function applyShipping() {
5       totalPrice = salesPrice + shippingPrice;
    . . .
```

> **Note** | An ellipsis (…) before or after code indicates that the code is a snippet from a larger document.

If code contains a global variable and a local variable with the same name, the local variable takes precedence when its function is called. However, the value assigned to a local variable within a function is not assigned to a global variable of the same name. For example, the following code contains a global variable named color, and a local variable named color.

The global variable `color` is assigned a value of "green". Next, the function that contains the local variable `color` is called. This function then assigns the local `color` variable a value of "purple". However, this has no effect on the value of the global variable `color`. After the function ends, "green" is still the value of the global `color` variable.

```
1    var color = "green";
2    function duplicateVariableNames() {
3        var color = "purple";
4        document.write(color);
5        // value printed is purple
6    }
7    duplicateVariableNames();
8    document.write(color);
9    // value printed is green
```

Figure 2-6 shows the output in a web browser.

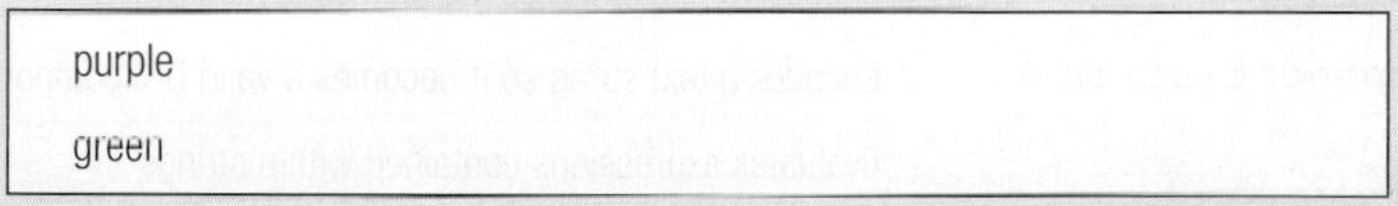

purple
green

Figure 2-6: Output of code that contains a global variable and a local variable with the same name

Note that, although the code that displays the output shown in Figure 2-6 is syntactically correct, it is poor programming practice to use the same name for local and global variables because it makes your scripts confusing, and it is difficult to track which version of the variable is currently being used by the code. Instead, you should ensure that all variable names within a related set of scripts are unique.

Next, you will add global variables to the ft.js file, for use with estimate.htm. The form fields on the estimate.htm page allow users to select options for special event photography, and the code you'll create will total these costs in response to user input. To start creating the program, you'll create global variables to store the total cost for photographers and the total estimate. You'll complete the estimate.htm page later in this chapter.

To add global variables to the ft.js file:

1. Return to the **ft.js** file in your text editor.

2. Below the comment section and above the `resetForm()` function, enter the following statements to define the two global variables:

```
// global variables
var photographerCost = 0;
var totalCost = 0;
```

3. Save your work.

Using Built-in JavaScript Functions

In addition to custom functions that you create yourself, JavaScript allows you to use the built-in functions listed in Table 2-2.

FUNCTION	DESCRIPTION
decodeURI(*string*)	Decodes text strings encoded with encodeURI()
decodeURIComponent(*string*)	Decodes text strings encoded with encodeURIComponent()
encodeURI(*string*)	Encodes a text string so it becomes a valid URI
encodeURIComponent(*string*)	Encodes a text string so it becomes a valid URI component
eval(*string*)	Evaluates expressions contained within strings
isFinite(*number*)	Determines whether a number is finite
isNaN(*number*)	Determines whether a value is the special value NaN (Not a Number)
parseFloat(*string*)	Converts string literals to floating-point numbers
parseInt(*string*)	Converts string literals to integers

Table 2-2: Built-in JavaScript functions

In this book, you will examine several of the built-in JavaScript functions as you need them. For now, you just need to understand that you call built-in JavaScript functions in the same way you call custom functions. For example, the following code calls the `isNaN()` function to determine whether the `socialSecurityNumber` variable is *not* a number.

```
var socialSecurityNumber = "123-45-6789";
var checkVar = isNaN(socialSecurityNumber);
document.write(checkVar);
```

Because the Social Security number assigned to the `socialSecurityNumber` variable contains dashes, it is not a true number. Therefore, the `isNaN()` function returns a value of `true` to the `checkVar` variable.

Short Quiz 1

1. What is the difference between a named function and an anonymous function?

2. Why does a named function not execute automatically? How do you execute it?

3. What alternatives exist to specifying an event handler using an HTML attribute?

4. How do you view any error messages that a browser might generate when processing your code?

5. Why is it poor programming practice to declare a global variable inside of a function by not using the `var` keyword?

Working with Data Types

Variables can contain many different kinds of values—for example, the time of day, a dollar amount, or a person's name. A **data type** is the specific category of information that a variable contains. The concept of data types is often difficult for beginning programmers to grasp because in real life you don't often distinguish among different types of information. If someone asks you for your name, your age, or the current time, you don't usually stop to consider that your name is a text string and that your age and the current time are numbers. However, a variable's specific data type is very important in programming because the data type helps determine how much memory the computer allocates for the data stored in the variable. The data type also governs the kinds of operations that can be performed on a variable.

Data types that can be assigned only a single value are called **primitive types**. JavaScript supports the five primitive data types described in Table 2-3.

DATA TYPE	DESCRIPTION
number	A positive or negative number with or without decimal places, or a number written using exponential notation
Boolean	A logical value of `true` or `false`
string	Text such as "Hello World"
undefined	An unassigned, undeclared, or nonexistent value
null	An empty value

Table 2-3: Primitive JavaScript data types

> **Note** | *The JavaScript language also supports a more advanced data type, object, which is used for creating a collection of properties. You will learn about the object type in Chapter 7.*

Null is a data type as well as a value that can be assigned to a variable. Assigning the value `null` to a variable indicates the variable does not contain a usable value. A variable with a value of `null` has a value assigned to it—`null` is really the value "no value." You assign the `null` value to a variable when you want to ensure the variable does not contain any data. In contrast, an undefined variable is a variable that has never had a value assigned to it, has not been declared, or does not exist.

The value `undefined` indicates that the variable has never been assigned a value—not even the `null` value. One use for an undefined variable is to determine whether a value is being used by another part of your script. As an example of an undefined variable, the following code declares a variable named `stateTax` without a value. When the second statement uses the `document.write()` method to print the `stateTax` variable, a value of `undefined` is printed because the variable has not yet been assigned a value. The variable is then assigned a value of 40, which is printed to the screen, and then a value of `null`, which is also printed to the screen.

```
1   var stateTax;
2   document.write(stateTax);
3   stateTax = 40;
4   document.write(stateTax);
5   stateTax = null;
6   document.write(stateTax);
```

Figure 2-7 shows the output in a web browser.

```
undefined
40
null
```

Figure 2-7: Variable assigned values of `undefined` and `null`

Many programming languages require that you declare the type of data that a variable contains. Programming languages that require you to declare the data types of variables are called strongly typed programming languages. A strongly typed language is also known as statically typed, because data types do not change after they have been declared. Programming languages that do not require you to declare the data types of variables are called loosely typed or duck typed programming languages. A loosely typed language is also known as dynamically typed, because data types can change after they have been declared. JavaScript is a loosely typed programming language. In JavaScript, you are not required to declare the data type of variables and, in fact, are not allowed to do so. Instead, a JavaScript interpreter automatically determines what type of data is stored in a variable and assigns the variable's data type accordingly. The following code demonstrates how a variable's data type changes automatically each time the variable is assigned a new literal value:

```
1   diffTypes = "Hello World"; // String
2   diffTypes = 8;             // Integer number
3   diffTypes = 5.367;         // Floating-point number
4   diffTypes = true;          // Boolean
5   diffTypes = null;          // Null
```

The next two sections focus on two especially important data types: number and Boolean data types.

Working with Numeric Values

Numeric values are an important part of any programming language and are particularly useful for arithmetic calculations. The number data type in JavaScript supports two types of numeric values: integers and floating-point numbers. An integer is a positive or negative number with no decimal places. Integer values in JavaScript can range from -9007199254740990 (-2^{53}) to 9007199254740990 (2^{53}). The numbers -250, -13, 0, 2, 6, 10, 100, and 10000 are examples of integers. The numbers -6.16, -4.4, 3.17, .52, 10.5, and 2.7541 are not integers; they are floating-point numbers because they contain decimal places. A floating-point number is a number that contains decimal places or that is written in exponential notation.

Programming Concepts | *Exponential Notation*

Exponential notation, or scientific notation, is a shortened format for writing very large numbers or numbers with many decimal places. Numbers written in exponential notation are represented by a value between 1 and 10 multiplied by 10 raised to some power. The value of 10 is written

Continued on next page...

with an uppercase *E* or lowercase *e*. For example, the number 200,000,000,000 can be written in exponential notation as 2.0e11, which means "two times ten to the eleventh power." Floating-point values in JavaScript range from approximately $\pm1.7976931348623157 \times 10^{308}$ to $\pm 5 \times 10^{-324}$. Floating-point values that exceed the largest positive value of $\pm1.7976931348623157 \times 10^{308}$ result in a special value of `Infinity`. Floating-point values that exceed the smallest negative value of $\pm5 \times 10^{-324}$ result in a value of `-Infinity`.

The owners of Fan Trick Fine Art Photography want to add a page to their website that explains the basics of digital photography for prospective clients. In addition to basic information about digital photography, they want to include a table comparing the many prefixes used in the metric system, to provide context for the term "megapixel." Next, you will create a script that uses variables containing integers, floating-point numbers, and exponential numbers to print the prefixes. A metric prefix, or SI prefix, is a name that precedes a metric unit of measure. For example, the metric prefix for centimeter is "centi," which denotes a value of 1/100th. In other words, a centimeter is the equivalent of 1/100th of a meter. Likewise, "mega" denotes a value of a million, meaning that a megapixel consists of roughly a million pixels.

To create a script that prints metric prefixes:

1. In your text editor, open the **digital.htm** document from the Chapter folder for Chapter 2.

2. Enter your name and today's date where indicated in the comment section, save the file, and then open **digital.htm** in a browser. The page displays explanatory text, followed by a table listing the prefixes. You'll add JavaScript statements to write values into the second column.

3. Return to your text editor and then, above the opening `<table>` tag, enter the following `script` element, which contains variable declarations for the 20 metric prefixes:

```
1   <script>
2       var yotta = 1e24;
3       var zetta = 1e21;
4       var exa = 1e18;
5       var peta = 1e15;
6       var tera = 1e12;
7       var giga = 1e9;
8       var mega = 1e6;
```

```
9        var kilo = 1000;
10       var hecto = 100;
11       var deca = 10;
12       var deci = .1;
13       var centi = .01;
14       var milli = .001;
15       var micro = 1e-6;
16       var nano = 1e-9;
17       var pico = 1c-12;
18       var femto = 1e-15;
19       var atto = 1e-18;
20       var zepto = 1e-21;
21       var yocto = 1e-24;
22   </script>
```

4. Within the `table` element, in the second row, within the empty `td` element, enter the following script section to print the value of the variable that corresponds to the prefix:

```
<script>
   document.write(yotta);
</script>
```

5. In the third row, within the empty `td` element, enter the following script section:

```
<script>
   document.write(zetta);
</script>
```

6. Repeat Step 5 for the remaining 18 rows of the table, replacing `zetta` with the relevant variable name for each row.

> **Note** Remember that capitalization counts when referencing variable names, so be sure to enter the variable names in all lowercase to match the variable definitions you created in Step 3.

7. Save your work, and then refresh or reload **digital.htm** in your browser. Figure 2-8 shows how the document looks in a web browser.

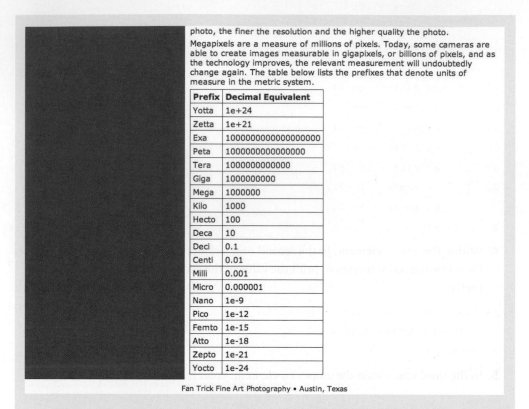

photo, the finer the resolution and the higher quality the photo.

Megapixels are a measure of millions of pixels. Today, some cameras are able to create images measurable in gigapixels, or billions of pixels, and as the technology improves, the relevant measurement will undoubtedly change again. The table below lists the prefixes that denote units of measure in the metric system.

Prefix	Decimal Equivalent
Yotta	1e+24
Zetta	1e+21
Exa	1000000000000000000000
Peta	1000000000000000
Tera	1000000000000
Giga	1000000000
Mega	1000000
Kilo	1000
Hecto	100
Deca	10
Deci	0.1
Centi	0.01
Milli	0.001
Micro	0.000001
Nano	1e-9
Pico	1e-12
Femto	1e-15
Atto	1e-18
Zepto	1e-21
Yocto	1e-24

Fan Trick Fine Art Photography • Austin, Texas

Figure 2-8: digital.htm document in a browser

Note that browsers automatically decide whether to display a large or small number in exponential notation. Also note that you never had to specify that the variables you declared contained numeric values. Instead, the JavaScript processor in your browser recognized that they contained numeric values and treated them accordingly. This is one of the benefits of JavaScript being a loosely typed language.

8. Close digital.htm in your browser, and then close digital.htm in your text editor.

JavaScript treats all numeric values as binary values, rather than as decimals—that is, the numbers are calculated using the two-digit binary system rather than the 10-digit decimal system. While the binary system can accurately represent any value that has a decimal equivalent, when it comes to floating point values, calculations performed on binary representations can result in slightly different results than the same calculations performed on decimal values. Because users enter decimal values in web interfaces and the interfaces display decimal results to users, this discrepancy can cause problems, especially when it comes to calculating exact monetary values such as dollars and cents. JavaScript programmers have developed a straightforward workaround, however: when manipulating a monetary value in a program, first multiply the value by 100, to eliminate the decimal portion of the number. In essence, this means calculating based on a value in cents (for instance, \$10.51 * 100 = 1051¢). Because calculations on integer values are the same in binary and decimal, any calculations you perform will be accurate. When your calculations are finished, simply divide the result by 100 to arrive at the correct, final value in dollars and cents.

Working with Boolean Values

A **Boolean value** is a logical value of `true` or `false`. You can also think of a Boolean value as being yes or no, or on or off. Boolean values are most often used for deciding which code should execute and for comparing data. In JavaScript programming, you can only use the words `true` and `false` to indicate Boolean values. In other programming languages, you can use the integer values of 1 and 0 to indicate Boolean values of `true` and `false`—1 indicates `true` and 0 indicates `false`. The following shows a simple example of two variables that are assigned Boolean values, one `true` and the other `false`.

```
1   var newCustomer = true;
2   var contractorRates = false;
3   document.write("<p>New customer: " + newCustomer + "</p>");
4   document.write("<p>Contractor rates: " + contractorRates +↵
5      "</p>");
```

Figure 2-9 shows the output in a web browser.

```
New customer: true

Contractor rates: false
```

Figure 2-9: Boolean values

Next, you will add Boolean global variables to the ft.js file for the Fan Trick Fine Art Photography site. These variables will determine whether the prospective client wants a memory book or reproduction rights for the photos.

To add two Boolean global variables to the ft.js file:

1. Return to the **ft.js** file in your text editor.

2. Below the statement `var totalCost = 0;`, add the following global variables for the memory book and reproduction rights selections:

```
var memoryBook = false;

var reproductionRights = false;
```

3. Within the `resetForm()` function, in the statements that set the values for the `checked` values of the `membook` and `reprodrights` elements, change the `false` values to the appropriate variable values as follows:

```
document.getElementById("membook").checked = memoryBook;

document.getElementById("reprodrights").checked = reproductionRights;
```

4. Save the **ft.js** file.

Working with Strings

As you learned in Chapter 1, a text string contains zero or more characters surrounded by double or single quotation marks. Examples of strings you may use in a script are company names, usernames, and comments. You can use a text string as a literal value or assign it to a variable.

A literal string can also be assigned a zero-length string value called an **empty string**. For example, the following statement declares a variable named `customerName` and assigns it an empty string:

```
var customerName = "";
```

This simply specifies that the variable is a string variable with no content.

When you want to include a quoted string within a literal string surrounded by double quotation marks, you surround the quoted string with single quotation marks. When you want to include a quoted string within a literal string surrounded by single quotation marks, you surround the quoted string with double quotation marks. Whichever method you use, a string must begin and end with the same type of quotation marks. For example, you can use either

```
document.write("Boston, MA is called 'Beantown.'")
```

or

```
document.write('Boston, MA is called "Beantown."')
```

Thus, the statement

```
document.write("This is a text string.");
```

is valid, because it starts and ends with double quotation marks, whereas the statement

```
document.write("This is a text string.');
```

is invalid, because it starts with a double quotation mark and ends with a single quotation mark. In the second case, you would receive an error message because a web browser cannot tell where the literal string begins and ends. The following code shows an example of a script that prints strings containing nested quotes.

```
1    document.write("<h1>Speech at the Berlin Wall↵
2        (excerpt)</h1>");
3    document.write("<p>Two thousand years ago, the proudest boast↵
4        was 'civis Romanus sum.'<br />");
5    document.write('Today, in the world of freedom, the proudest↵
6        boast is "Ich bin ein Berliner."</p>');
7    var speaker = "<p>John F. Kennedy</br>";
8    var date = 'June 26, 1963</p>';
9    document.write(speaker);
10   document.write(date);
```

Figure 2-10 shows the output.

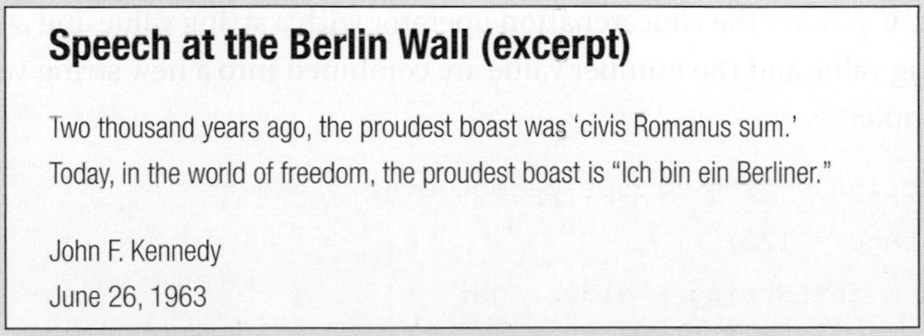

Speech at the Berlin Wall (excerpt)

Two thousand years ago, the proudest boast was 'civis Romanus sum.'
Today, in the world of freedom, the proudest boast is "Ich bin ein Berliner."

John F. Kennedy
June 26, 1963

Figure 2-10: String examples in a browser

> **Note** | Unlike other programming languages, JavaScript includes no special data type for a single character, such as the `char` data type in the C, C++, and Java programming languages.

String Operators

JavaScript has two operators that can be used with strings: + and +=. When used with strings, the plus sign is known as the concatenation operator. The **concatenation operator** (+) is used to combine two strings. You have already learned how to use the concatenation operator. For example, the following code combines a string variable and a literal string, and assigns the new value to another variable:

```
var destination = "Honolulu";
var location = "Hawaii";
destination = destination + " is in " + location;
```

The combined value of the location variable and the string literal that is assigned to the destination variable is "Honolulu is in Hawaii".

You can also use the compound assignment operator (+=) to combine two strings. You can think of += as meaning "Set the first operand equal to its current value plus the second operand." The following code combines the two text strings, but without using the location variable:

```
var destination = "Honolulu";
destination += " is in Hawaii";
```

The second line of this code tells the JavaScript interpreter to combine the current value of the destination variable—"Honolulu"—with the string "is in Hawaii". The result is the same as in the previous code.

Note that the same symbol—a plus sign—serves as both the concatenation operator and the addition operator. When used with numbers or variables containing numbers, expressions using the concatenation operator return the sum of the two numbers. As you learned earlier in this chapter, if you use the concatenation operator with a string value and a number value, the string value and the number value are combined into a new string value, as in the following example:

```
var textString = "The oldest person ever lived to ";
var oldestAge = 122;
newString = textString + oldestAge;
```

The value of `newString` is "The oldest person ever lived to 122".

Note that the value of the `textString` variable includes a space before the final quote. When values are concatenated, the last character of the first value is directly followed by the first character of the second value. If the space were not included at the end of the `textString` value, there would be no space between the two values, resulting in a `newString` value of "The oldest person ever lived to122". (Note the lack of space between "to" and "122".)

Escape Characters and Sequences

You need to use extra care when using single quotation marks with possessives and contractions in strings, because JavaScript interpreters always look for the first closing single or double quotation mark to match an opening single or double quotation mark. For example, consider the following statement:

```
document.write('<p>My mom's favorite color is blue.</p>');
```

This statement causes an error. A JavaScript interpreter assumes that the literal string ends with the apostrophe following "mom" and looks for the closing parentheses for the `document.write()` statement immediately following "mom'". To get around this problem, you include an escape character before the apostrophe in "mom's". An **escape character** tells compilers and interpreters that the character that follows it has a special purpose. In JavaScript, the escape character is the backslash (\ ). Placing a backslash before an apostrophe tells JavaScript interpreters that the apostrophe is to be treated as a regular keyboard character, such as *a*, *b*, *1*, or *2*, and not as part of a single quotation mark pair that encloses a text string. The backslash in the following statement tells the JavaScript interpreter to print the apostrophe following the word "mom" as an apostrophe.

```
document.write('<p>My mom\'s favorite color is blue.</p>');
```

You can also use the escape character in combination with other characters to insert a special character into a string. When you combine the escape character with a specific other character, the combination is called an **escape sequence**. The backslash followed by an apostrophe (\') and the backslash followed by a double quotation mark (\") are both examples of escape sequences. Most escape sequences carry out special functions. For example, the escape sequence \t inserts a tab into a string. Table 2-4 describes the escape sequences that can be added to a string in JavaScript.

ESCAPE SEQUENCE	CHARACTER
\\	Backslash
\b	Backspace
\r	Carriage return
\"	Double quotation mark
\f	Form feed
\t	Horizontal tab
\n	Newline
\0	Null character
\'	Single quotation mark (apostrophe)
\v	Vertical tab
\xXX	Latin-1 character specified by the XX characters, which represent two hexadecimal digits
\uXXXX	Unicode character specified by the XXXX characters, which represent four hexadecimal digits

Table 2-4: JavaScript escape sequences

Note *If you place a backslash before any character other than those listed in Table 2-4, the backslash is ignored.*

Notice that one of the characters generated by an escape sequence is the backslash. Because the escape character itself is a backslash, you must use the escape sequence \\ to include a backslash as a character in a string. For example, to include the path "C:\Users\me\Documents\Cengage\WebWarrior\JavaScript\" in a string, you must include two backslashes for every single backslash you want to appear in the string, as in the following statement:

```
document.write("<p>My JavaScript files are located in↵
    C:\\Users\\me\\Documents\\Cengage\\WebWarrior\\↵
    JavaScript\\</p>");
```

The following code shows an example of a script containing strings with several escape sequences.

```
1   <script>
2   document.write("<p>My personal files are in↵
3       C:\\Users\\me\\Documents\\.</p>"); // Backslash
4       document.write(("<p>Written letters are sometimes called↵
5       \"snail mail.\"</p>")); // Double quotation mark
6       document.write('<p>India\'s capital is New Delhi.</p>');
7       // Single quotation mark
8   </script>
```

Figure 2-11 shows the output.

My personal files are in C:\Users\me\Documents\.

Written letters are sometimes called "snail mail."

India's capital is New Delhi.

Figure 2-11: Output of script with strings containing escape sequences

Short Quiz 2

1. What is the difference between an integer and a floating-point number?

2. Which possible values can a Boolean variable have?

3. What is an empty string?

4. Why do you sometimes need to insert an extra space in a string when using the concatenation operator?

Using Operators to Build Expressions

In Chapter 1, you learned the basics of how to create expressions using basic operators, such as the addition operator (+) and multiplication operator (*). In this section, you will learn about additional types of operators you can use with JavaScript. Table 2-5 lists the operator types that you can use with JavaScript.

OPERATOR TYPE	OPERATORS	DESCRIPTION
Arithmetic	addition (+)	Perform mathematical calculations
	subtraction (−)	
	multiplication (*)	
	division (/)	
	modulus (%)	
	increment (++)	
	decrement (−−)	
	negation (−)	
Assignment	assignment (=)	Assign values to variables
	compound addition assignment (+=)	
	compound subtraction assignment (−=)	
	compound multiplication assignment (*=)	
	compound division assignment (/=)	
	compound modulus assignment (%=)	
Comparison	equal (==)	Compare operands and return a Boolean value
	strict equal (===)	
	not equal (!=)	
	strict not equal (!==)	
	greater than (>)	
	less than (<)	
	greater than or equal (>=)	
	less than or equal (<=)	
Logical	And (&&)	Perform Boolean operations on Boolean operands
	Or (||)	
	Not (!)	
String	concatenation (+)	Perform operations on strings
	compound concatenation assignment (+=)	

Continued on next page...

OPERATOR TYPE	OPERATORS	DESCRIPTION
Special	property access (`.`)	Various purposes; do not fit within other operator categories
	array index (`[]`)	
	function call (`()`)	
	comma (`,`)	
	conditional expression (`?:`)	
	delete (`delete`)	
	property exists (`in`)	
	object type (`instanceof`)	
	new object (`new`)	
	data type (`typeof`)	
	void (`void`)	

Table 2-5: JavaScript operator types

JavaScript operators are binary or unary. A **binary operator** requires an operand before and after the operator. The equal sign in the statement `myNumber = 100;` is an example of a binary operator. A **unary operator** requires just a single operand either before or after the operator. For example, the increment operator (`++`), an arithmetic operator, is used to increase an operand by a value of one. The statement `myNumber++;` changes the value of the `myNumber` variable to 101.

In the following sections, you will learn more about the different types of JavaScript operators.

> **Note** Another type of JavaScript operator, bitwise operators, operate on integer values; this is a fairly complex topic. Bitwise operators and other complex operators are beyond the scope of this book.

Arithmetic Operators

Arithmetic operators are used in JavaScript to perform mathematical calculations, such as addition, subtraction, multiplication, and division. You can also use an arithmetic operator to return the modulus of a calculation, which is the remainder left when you divide one number by another number.

Arithmetic Binary Operators

JavaScript binary arithmetic operators and their descriptions are listed in Table 2-6.

NAME	OPERATOR	DESCRIPTION
Addition	+	Adds two operands
Subtraction	–	Subtracts one operand from another operand
Multiplication	*	Multiplies one operand by another operand
Division	/	Divides one operand by another operand
Modulus	%	Divides one operand by another operand and returns the remainder

Table 2-6: Arithmetic binary operators

Note | *The operand to the left of an operator is known as the left operand, and the operand to the right of an operator is known as the right operand.*

The following code shows examples of expressions that include arithmetic binary operators.

```
1   var x = 0, y = 0, arithmeticValue = 0;
2   // ADDITION
3   x = 400;
4   y = 600;
5   arithmeticValue = x + y; // arithmeticValue changes to 1000
6   document.write("<p>arithmeticValue after addition↵
7     expression: " + arithmeticValue + "</p>");
8   // SUBTRACTION
9   x = 14;
10  y = 6;
11  arithmeticValue = x - y; // arithmeticValue changes to 8
12  document.write("<p>arithmeticValue after subtraction↵
13    expression: " + arithmeticValue + "</p>");
14  // MULTIPLICATION
15  x = 20;
16  y = 4;
17  arithmeticValue = x * y; // arithmeticValue changes to 80
```

```
18   document.write("<p>arithmeticValue after multiplication↵
19      expression: " + arithmeticValue + "</p>");
20   // DIVISION
21   x = 99;
22   y = 3;
23   arithmeticValue = x / y; // arithmeticValue changes to 33
24   document.write("<p>arithmeticValue after division↵
25      expression: " + arithmeticValue + "</p>");
26   // MODULUS
27   x = 5;
28   y = 3;
29   arithmeticValue = x % y; // arithmeticValue changes to 2
30   document.write("<p>arithmeticValue after modulus↵
31      expression: " + arithmeticValue + "</p>");
```

Figure 2-12 shows how the expressions appear in a web browser:

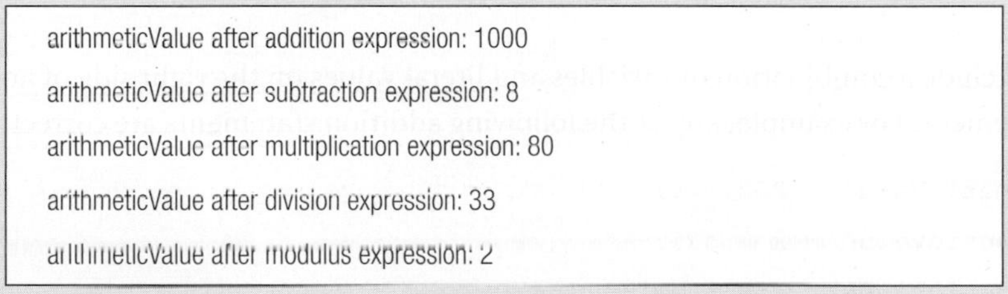

arithmeticValue after addition expression: 1000

arithmeticValue after subtraction expression: 8

arithmeticValue after multiplication expression: 80

arithmeticValue after division expression: 33

arithmeticValue after modulus expression: 2

Figure 2-12: Results of arithmetic expressions

Notice in the preceding code that when JavaScript performs an arithmetic calculation, it performs the operation on the right side of the assignment operator, and then assigns the value to the variable on the left side of the assignment operator. For example, in the statement arithmeticValue = x + y; on line 5, the operands x and y are added, then the result is assigned to the arithmeticValue variable on the left side of the assignment operator.

You may be confused by the difference between the division (/) operator and the modulus (%) operator. The division operator performs a standard mathematical division operation. For example, dividing 15 by 6 results in a value of 2.5. By contrast, the modulus operator returns the remainder that results from the division of two integers. The following code, for instance, uses the division and modulus operators to return the result of dividing 15 by 6. The division of 15 by 6 results in a value of 2.5, because 6 goes into 15 exactly 2.5 times. But if you allow only for whole numbers, 6 goes into 15 only 2 times, with a remainder of 3 left over. Thus the modulus of 15 divided by 6 is 3, because 3 is the remainder left over following the division.

```
1    var divisionResult = 15 / 6;
2    var modulusResult = 15 % 6;
3    document.write("<p>15 divided by 6 is "↵
4        + divisionResult + ".</p>"); // prints '2.5'
5    document.write("<p>The whole number 6 goes into 15 twice,↵
6        with a remainder of "+ modulusResult + ".</p>");↵
7        // prints '3'
```

Figure 2-13 shows the output.

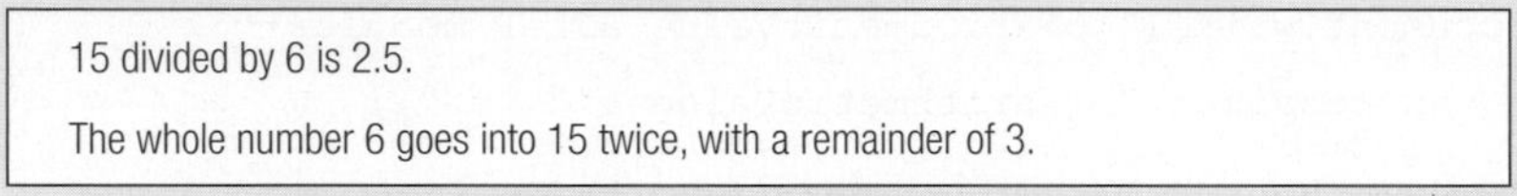

15 divided by 6 is 2.5.

The whole number 6 goes into 15 twice, with a remainder of 3.

Figure 2-13: Division and modulus expressions

You can include a combination of variables and literal values on the right side of an assignment statement. For example, any of the following addition statements are correct:

```
arithmeticValue = 250 + y;
arithmeticValue = x + 425;
arithmeticValue = 250 + 425;
```

However, you cannot include a literal value as the left operand because the JavaScript interpreter must have a variable to which to assign the returned value. Therefore, the statement `362 = x + y;` causes an error.

When performing arithmetic operations on string values, a JavaScript interpreter attempts to convert the string values to numbers. The variables in the following example are assigned as string values instead of numbers because they are contained within quotation marks. Nevertheless, JavaScript interpreters correctly perform the multiplication operation and return a value of 20.

```
x = "4";
y = "5";
arithmeticValue = x * y; // the value returned is 20
```

However, JavaScript interpreters do not convert strings to numbers when you use the addition operator. When you use the addition operator with strings, the strings are combined instead of being added together. In the following example, the operation returns a string value of "54" because the x and y variables contain strings instead of numbers:

```
x = "5";
y = "4";
arithmeticValue = x + y; // a string value of 54 is returned
```

Arithmetic Unary Operators

Arithmetic operations can also be performed on a single variable using unary operators. Table 2-7 lists the arithmetic unary operators available in JavaScript.

NAME	OPERATOR	DESCRIPTION
Increment	++	Increases an operand by a value of one
Decrement	--	Decreases an operand by a value of one
Negation	-	Returns the opposite value (negative or positive) of an operand

Table 2-7: Arithmetic unary operators

The increment (++) and decrement (--) unary operators can be used as prefix or postfix operators. A **prefix operator** is placed before a variable name. A **postfix operator** is placed after a variable name. The operands ++count and count++ both increase the count variable by one. However, the two statements return different values. When you use the increment operator as a prefix operator, the value of the operand is returned *after* it is increased by a value of one. When you use the increment operator as a postfix operator, the value of the operand is returned *before* it is increased by a value of one. Similarly, when you use the decrement operator as a prefix operator, the value of the operand is returned *after* it is decreased by a value of one, and when you use the decrement operator as a postfix operator, the value of the operand is returned *before* it is decreased by a value of one. If you intend to assign the incremented or decremented value to another variable, then whether you use the prefix or postfix operator makes a difference.

You use arithmetic unary operators in any situation in which you want to use a more simplified expression for increasing or decreasing a value by 1. For example, the statement count = count + 1; is identical to the statement ++count;. As you can see, if your goal is only to increase a variable by 1, then it is easier to use the unary increment operator.

While including comments in your code can make your code easier for you and other programmers to read and understand, using comments is not the only strategy for documenting code. Another strategy is to make your code self-documenting, meaning that the code is written as simply and directly as possible, so its statements and structures are easier to understand at a glance. For instance, it's a good idea to name variables with descriptive names so it's easier to remember what value is stored in each variable. Rather than naming variables `var1`, `var2`, and so on, you can use names like `firstName` or `lastName`. Creating statements that are easy to read is another instance of self-documenting code. For example, code that you create with the increment operator (++) is more concise than code that assigns a variable a value of itself plus 1. However, in this shortened form, the code can be more challenging to read and understand quickly. For this reason, some developers choose not to use the ++ operator at all, relying instead on the + and = operators to make their code easier for themselves and other developers to read. As you build your programming skills, you'll learn multiple ways to code many different tasks, but the best option is usually the one that results in code that is easy for you and other programmers to read and understand. This results in code that can be more easily maintained and modified by other developers when you move on to another job.

Remember that, with the prefix operator, the value of the operand is returned *after* it is increased or decreased by a value of 1. By contrast, with the postfix operator, the value of the operand is returned *before* it is increased or decreased by a value of 1.

For an example of when you would use the prefix operator or the postfix operator, consider an integer variable named `studentID` that is used for assigning student IDs in a class registration script. One way of creating a new student ID number is to store the last assigned student ID in the `studentID` variable. When it's time to assign a new student ID, the script could retrieve the last value stored in the `studentID` variable and then increase its value by 1. In other words, the last value stored in the `studentID` variable will be the next number used for a student ID number. In this case, you would use the postfix operator to return the value of the expression *before* it is incremented by using a statement similar to `currentID = studentID++;`. If you are storing the last assigned student ID in the `studentID` variable, you would want to increment the value by 1 and use the result as the next student ID. In this scenario, you would use the prefix operator, which returns the value of the expression after it is incremented using a statement similar to `currentID = ++studentID;`.

The following code uses the prefix increment operator to assign three student IDs to a variable named `curStudentID`. The initial student ID is stored in the `studentID` variable and initialized to a starting value of 100.

```
1    var studentID = 100;
2    var curStudentID;
3    curStudentID = ++studentID; // assigns '101'
4    document.write("<p>The first student ID is " +↵
5       curStudentID + "</p>");
6    curStudentID = ++studentID; // assigns '102'
7    document.write("<p>The second student ID is " +↵
8       curStudentID + "</p>");
9    curStudentID = ++studentID; // assigns '103'
10   document.write("<p>The third student ID is " +↵
11      curStudentID + "</p>");
```

Figure 2-14 shows the output.

The first student ID is 101

The second student ID is 102

The third student ID is 103

Figure 2-14: Output of the prefix version of the student ID script

The code below performs the same tasks, but using a postfix increment operator. Notice that the output in Figure 2-15 differs from the output in Figure 2-14. Because the first example of the script uses the prefix increment operator, which increments the `studentID` variable *before* it is assigned to `curStudentID`, the script does not use the starting value of 100. Rather, it first increments the `studentID` variable and uses 101 as the first student ID. By contrast, the second example of the script does use the initial value of 100 because the postfix increment operator increments the `studentID` variable *after* it is assigned to the `curStudentID` variable.

```
1    var studentID = 100;
2    var curStudentID;
3    curStudentID = studentID++; // assigns '100'
```

```
 4    document.write("<p>The first student ID is " +↵
 5        curStudentID + "</p>");
 6    curStudentID = studentID++; // assigns '101'
 7    document.write("<p>The second student ID is " +↵
 8        curStudentID + "</p>");
 9    curStudentID = studentID++; // assigns '102'
10    document.write("<p>The third student ID is " +↵
11        curStudentID + "</p>");
```

```
The first student ID is 100

The second student ID is 101

The third student ID is 102
```

Figure 2-15: Output of the postfix version of the student ID script

Assignment Operators

An **assignment operator** is used for assigning a value to a variable. You have already used the most common assignment operator, the equal sign (=), to assign values to variables you declared using the `var` statement. The equal sign assigns an initial value to a new variable or assigns a new value to an existing variable. For example, the following code creates a variable named `favoriteColor`, uses the equal sign to assign it an initial value, then uses the equal sign again to assign it a new value:

```
var favoriteColor = "blue";
favoriteColor = "yellow";
```

JavaScript includes other assignment operators in addition to the equal sign. Each of these additional assignment operators, called **compound assignment operators**, performs mathematical calculations on variables and literal values in an expression, and then assigns a new value to the left operand. Table 2-8 displays a list of the common JavaScript assignment operators.

NAME	OPERATOR	DESCRIPTION
Assignment	=	Assigns the value of the right operand to the left operand
Compound addition assignment	+=	Combines the value of the right operand with the value of the left operand (if the operands are strings), or adds the value of the right operand to the value of the left operand (if the operands are numbers), and assigns the new value to the left operand
Compound subtraction assignment	-=	Subtracts the value of the right operand from the value of the left operand, and assigns the new value to the left operand
Compound multiplication assignment	*=	Multiplies the value of the right operand by the value of the left operand, and assigns the new value to the left operand
Compound division assignment	/=	Divides the value of the left operand by the value of the right operand, and assigns the new value to the left operand
Compound modulus assignment	%=	Divides the value of the left operand by the value of the right operand, and assigns the remainder (the modulus) to the left operand

Table 2-8: Assignment operators

You can use the += compound addition assignment operator to combine two strings as well as to add numbers. In the case of strings, the string on the left side of the operator is combined with the string on the right side of the operator, and the new value is assigned to the left operator. Before combining operands, a JavaScript interpreter attempts to convert a nonnumeric operand, such as a string, to a number. This means that unlike the + operator, which concatenates any string values, using the += operator with two string operands containing numbers results in a numeric value. For instance, the following code defines two variables with string values: x with a value of "5" and y with a value of "4". In processing the third line of code, a JavaScript interpreter first converts the strings to the values 5 and 4, respectively, then adds them, and then assigns the result, the value 9, to the x variable.

```
x = "5";
y = "4";
x += y; // a numeric value of 9 is returned for x
```

If a nonnumeric operand cannot be converted to a number, you receive a value of NaN. The value NaN stands for "Not a Number" and is returned when a mathematical operation does not result in a numerical value. The sole exception to this rule is +=, which simply concatenates operands if one or both can't be converted to numbers.

The following code shows examples of the different assignment operators:

```
1   var x, y;
2   // += operator with string values
3   x = "Hello ";
4   x += "World"; // x changes to "Hello World"
5   // += operator with numeric values
6   x = 100;
7   y = 200;
8   x += y; // x changes to 300
9   // -= operator
10  x = 10;
11  y = 7;
12  x -= y; // x changes to 3
13  // *= operator
14  x = 2;
15  y = 6;
16  x *= y; // x changes to 12
17  // /= operator
18  x = 24;
19  y = 3;
20  x /= y; // x changes to 8
21  // %= operator
22  x = 3;
23  y = 2;
24  x %= y; // x changes to 1
25  // *= operator with a number and a convertible string
26  x = "100";
27  y = 5;
28  x *= y; // x changes to 500
29  // *= operator with a number and a nonconvertible string
30  x = "one hundred";
31  y = 5;
32  x *= y; // x changes to NaN
```

Next, you will add functions to the ft.js file to calculate the cost of hiring photography staff for an event. The calculation involves multiplying the number of staff by an hourly rate of $100 per photographer and by the total number of hours.

To modify the ft.js file to calculate the cost of hiring photography staff:

1. Return to the **ft.js** file in your text editor.

2. Above the `resetForm()` function you created earlier, add the following code to define the `calcStaff()` function:

```
// calculates all costs based on staff and adds to total cost
function calcStaff() {

}
```

3. Within the braces for the `calcStaff()` function, enter the following statements:

```
var num = document.getElementById("photognum");
var hrs = document.getElementById("photoghrs");
```

Each of these statements uses a variable to store a reference to an element in the web document. Using these variables will make the code for your calculations shorter and easier to understand at a glance.

4. Within the function, below the `var` statements you just entered, add the following statement:

```
totalCost -= photographerCost;
```

This statement uses the compound subtraction assignment operator to subtract the current value of the `photographerCost` variable from the value of the `totalCost` variable, and then assign the result as the new value of the `totalCost` variable. This results in a `totalCost` value that includes no `photographerCost` value. In the following steps, you'll add code to calculate the new `photographerCost` value and then add it back to the `totalCost` value.

5. Within the function, below the statement you just entered, add the following statement:

```
photographerCost = num.value * 100 * hrs.value;
```

This statement uses the variables you created in Step 3 that reference the input elements with the ids `photognum` and `photoghrs`. It multiplies the value entered for # of photographers (`num.value`) by 100 (the fixed hourly rate per photographer) and by the value entered for # of hours to photograph (`hrs.value`), and then assigns the result to the `photographerCost` variable.

6. Within the function, below the statement you just entered, add the following statement:

```
totalCost += photographerCost;
```

This statement uses the compound addition assignment operator to add the current value of the `photographerCost` variable to the value of the `totalCost` variable, and then assign the result as the new value of the `totalCost` variable. This reverses what the first statement in the function did, adding back the value of `photographerCost` into the calculation of `totalCost`.

7. Within the function, below the statement you just entered, add the following statement:

```
document.getElementById("estimate").innerHTML = "$" +↵
    totalCost;
```

This statement uses the `getElementById()` method of the `Document` object to locate the element with the `id` value of `estimate`, and then assigns a value to that element's `innerHTML` property. The value of an element's **innerHTML property** is the content between its opening and closing tags. By assigning a new value to an element's `innerHTML` property, you replace any existing content. The value assigned by this statement is the $ character followed by the value of the `totalCost` variable. Your `calcStaff()` function should match the following:

```
1   // calculates all costs based on staff and adds to total cost
2   function calcStaff() {
3       var num = document.getElementById("photognum");
4       var hrs = document.getElementById("photoghrs");
5       totalCost -= photographerCost;
6       photographerCost = num.value * 100 * hrs.value;
7       totalCost += photographerCost;
8       document.getElementById("estimate").innerHTML = "$" +↵
9           totalCost;
10  }
```

8. Scroll down to the `resetForm()` function you created earlier, and then, just above the closing brace (}), add the following statement:

```
calcStaff();
```

This statement calls the `calcStaff()` function whenever the `resetForm()` function runs. Because `resetForm()` is called each time the page loads, adding this statement will replace the empty value of the estimate element with the `totalCost` value calculated based on the default form values.

9. Below the closing } for the `resetForm()` function, enter the following code to create the `createEventListeners()` function:

```
// creates event listeners
function createEventListeners() {

}
```

To implement the `calcStaff()` function you just created, you have to add code to create event listeners.

10. Within the command block for the `createEventListeners()` function, enter the following two statements to add event listeners to the elements with the `id` values `photognum` and `photoghrs`:

```
1    document.getElementById("photognum").↵
2        addEventListener("change", calcStaff, false);
3    document.getElementById("photoghrs").↵
4        addEventListener("change", calcStaff, false);
```

The two event listeners will call the `calcStaff()` function each time a user changes the values for # of photographers or # of hours to photograph.

11. Scroll up to the `resetForm()` function, and then, just before the closing }, enter the following statement:

```
createEventListeners();
```

This calls the `createEventListeners()` function when the page loads. Your updated `resetForm()` function should match the following:

```
1    function resetForm() {
2        document.getElementById("photognum").value = 1;
3        document.getElementById("photoghrs").value = 2;
4        document.getElementById("membook").checked = memoryBook;
5        document.getElementById("reprodrights").checked =
6    reproductionRights;
7        document.getElementById("distance").value = 0;
8        calcStaff();
9        createEventListeners();
10   }
```

12. Save your changes to **ft.js**, and then in your browser, refresh or reload **estimate.htm**.

13. Change the value in the # of photographers box to **2**, press **Tab**, change the value in the # of hours to photograph box to **3**, and then press **Tab**. Pressing Tab fires the `change` event for an `input` element. Notice that the Total Estimate value in the side-bar is calculated automatically when the page reloads, and changes after each time you press Tab—first to $400 and then to $600.

> **Note**
>
> All modern browsers support the `textContent property` for web page elements. This property is similar to the `innerHTML` property, except that a `textContent` value excludes any HTML markup, while `innerHTML` includes it. Using `textContent` results in JavaScript code that's more secure. However, Internet Explorer 8 supports only `innerHTML`, not `textContent`. All the sites in this book are designed to work with IE8, so they use `innerHTML`. However, any site you create that doesn't need to support IE8 should use `textContent` instead of `innerHTML`.

Comparison and Conditional Operators

A **comparison operator**, or **relational operator**, is used to compare two operands and determine if one value is greater than another. A Boolean value of `true` or `false` is returned after two operands are compared. For example, the statement 5 < 3 would return a Boolean value of `false`, because 5 is not less than 3. Table 2-9 lists the JavaScript comparison operators.

NAME	OPERATOR	DESCRIPTION
Equal	==	Returns true if the operands are equal
Strict equal	===	Returns true if the operands are equal and of the same type
Not equal	!=	Returns true if the operands are not equal
Strict not equal	!==	Returns true if the operands are not equal or not of the same type
Greater than	>	Returns true if the left operand is greater than the right operand
Less than	<	Returns true if the left operand is less than the right operand
Greater than or equal	>=	Returns true if the left operand is greater than or equal to the right operand
Less than or equal	<=	Returns true if the left operand is less than or equal to the right operand

Table 2-9: Comparison operators

> **Note**
>
> *The comparison operators (`==` and `===`) consist of two and three equal signs, respectively, and perform a different function than the one performed by the assignment operator that consists of a single equal sign (`=`). The comparison operators compare values, whereas the assignment operator assigns values. Confusion between these two types of operators is a common source of bugs, and you should check for it if your code compares values and is not delivering expected results.*

You can use number or string values as operands with comparison operators. When two numeric values are used as operands, JavaScript interpreters compare them numerically. For example, the statement `arithmeticValue = 5 > 4;` results in `true` because the number 5 is numerically greater than the number 4. When two nonnumeric values are used as operands, the JavaScript interpreter compares them in lexicographical order—that is, the order in which they would appear in a dictionary. The statement `arithmeticValue = "b" > "a";` returns `true` because the letter *b* comes after than the letter *a* in the dictionary. When one operand is a number and the other is a string, JavaScript interpreters attempt to convert the string value to a number. If the string value cannot be converted to a number, a value of `false` is returned. For example, the statement `arithmeticValue = 10 === "ten";` returns a value of `false` because JavaScript interpreters cannot convert the string "ten" to a number.

> **Note**
>
> *The comparison operators `==` and `===` perform virtually the same function. However, for reasons that are beyond the scope of this book, using the `==` operator can occasionally produce unexpected results. The same is true of the `!=` and `!==` operators. For this reason, the code in this book uses `===` and `!==` unless otherwise noted.*

The comparison operator is often used with another kind of operator, the conditional operator. The **conditional operator** executes one of two expressions, based on the results of a conditional expression. The syntax for the conditional operator is

```
conditional expression ? expression1 : expression2;
```

If the conditional expression evaluates to `true`, then *expression1* executes. If the conditional expression evaluates to `false`, then *expression2* executes.

The following code shows an example of the conditional operator.

```
1   var intVariable = 150;
2   var result;
3   intVariable > 100 ?↵
4       result = "intVariable is greater than 100" :↵
5       result = "intVariable is less than or equal to 100";
6   document.write(result);
```

In line 3 of the example, the conditional expression checks to see if the `intVariable` variable is greater than 100. If `intVariable` is greater than 100, then the text "intVariable is greater than 100" is assigned to the `result` variable. If `intVariable` is not greater than 100, then the text "intVariable is less than or equal to 100" is assigned to the `result` variable. Because `intVariable` is equal to 150, the conditional statement returns a value of `true`, the first expression executes, and "intVariable is greater than 100" prints to the screen.

When a term in a conditional operator is particularly long or complex, you can add parentheses around it. This provides visual clarification of where the term starts and ends without changing its meaning.

Next, you will create functions for the estimate form that change the calculated estimate value based on whether a prospective client wants a memory book and photo reproduction rights. You'll use conditional operators in your functions to determine whether to add or subtract the cost of each item.

To create functions for the estimate form that add the cost of a memory book and reproduction rights:

1. Return to the **ft.js** file in your text editor.

2. Below the closing } for the `calcStaff()` function, add the following code to create the new `toggleMembook()` function:

```
// adds/subtracts cost of memory book from total cost
function toggleMembook() {

}
```

3. Within the braces for the `toggleMembook()` function, enter the following statement:

```
(document.getElementById("membook").checked === false) ?↵
   totalCost -= 250 : totalCost += 250;
```

This statement looks up the `checked` property of the element with the `id` of `membook`. For an `input` element with a `type` attribute set to `checkbox` or `radio`, the checked property is true if the element is selected, and false if it is not selected. If the checked value is false, the conditional expression subtracts the charge for a memory book, $250, from the totalCost value. If the checked value is true, the conditional expression adds $250 to the totalCost value.

4. Within the toggleMembook() function, below the statement you just entered, add the following statement:

```
document.getElementById("estimate").innerHTML =↵
    "$" + totalCost;
```

This statement changes the innerHTML value of the element with the id of estimate to a $ symbol followed by the current value of the totalCost variable.

5. Below the toggleMembook() function, add the following code to create the new toggleRights() function:

```
// adds/subtracts cost of reproduction rights from total cost
function toggleRights() {

}
```

6. Within the braces for the toggleRights() function, enter the following statement:

```
(document.getElementById("reprodrights").checked === false) ?↵
    totalCost -= 1250 : totalCost += 1250;
```

This statement is similar to the conditional statement for the toggleMembook() function. It subtracts $1250 from the totalCost variable if the input element with the id of reprodrights is unchecked, and adds that amount if the element is checked.

7. Within the toggleRights() function, below the statement you just entered, add the following statement:

```
document.getElementById("estimate").innerHTML =↵
    "$" + totalCost;
```

The following code shows the completed toggleMembook() and toggleRights() functions:

```
1    // adds/subtracts cost of memory book from total cost
2    function toggleMembook() {
3        (document.getElementById("membook").checked === false) ?↵
4            totalCost -= 250 : totalCost += 250;
```

```
5      document.getElementById("estimate").innerHTML =↵
6         "$" + totalCost;
7   }
8   // adds/subtracts cost of reproduction rights from total cost
9   function toggleRights() {
10     (document.getElementById("reprodrights").checked ===↵
11         false) ? totalCost -= 1250 : totalCost += 1250;
12     document.getElementById("estimate").innerHTML =↵
13        "$" + totalCost;
14  }
```

8. Scroll down to the `createEventListeners()` function, and then before the closing }, enter the following two statements to create event listeners for the elements with the id values `membook` and `reprodrights`:

```
1   document.getElementById("membook").↵
2       addEventListener("change", toggleMembook, false);
3   document.getElementById("reprodrights").↵
4       addEventListener("change", toggleRights, false);
```

9. Save your changes to the **ft.js** file, and then switch to **estimate.htm** in your text editor.

10. Save your work, switch to your browser, refresh or reload **estimate.htm**, click the **Memory book** check box to check it, and then click the **Reproduction rights box** to check it. Notice that the Total Estimate value in the sidebar changes each time you select a box, first to $450 and then to $1700.

11. Click the **Memory book** check box to uncheck it, and then click the **Reproduction rights box** to uncheck it. The Total Estimate value is reduced each time you uncheck a box, first to $1450, and then to $200.

Understanding Falsy and Truthy Values

JavaScript includes six values that are treated in comparison operations as the Boolean value `false`. These six values, known as *falsy values*, are

> ""
> -0
> 0
> NaN

```
> null
> undefined
```

All values other than these six falsy values are the equivalent of Boolean `true`, and are known as **truthy values**.

Developers commonly take advantage of falsy and truthy values to make comparison operations more compact. For instance, suppose you were writing a conditional statement that checks if a text field in a form contains a value. You could write the code for the conditional statement as

```
(document.getElementById("fname").value !== "") ?↵
    // code to run if condition is true :↵
    // code to run if condition is false;
```

However, another way to approach this is to simply check whether the value of the text field is falsy (an empty string) or truthy (anything else). You can do this by omitting the comparison operator and simplifying the code as follows:

```
(document.getElementById("fname").value) ?↵
    // code to run if condition is true :↵
    // code to run if condition is false;
```

Note that the revised code replaces the comparison in the first line with only a reference to the web page element. If this element is empty, then its value is "" (an empty string), which is a falsy value, in which case the conditional expression evaluates to `false`. However, if the element is not empty, then the value is truthy, and the conditional expression evaluates to `true`.

Logical Operators

Logical operators are used to modify Boolean values or specify the relationship between operands in an expression that results in a Boolean value. For example, a script for an automobile insurance company may need to determine whether a customer is male *and* under 21 in order to determine the correct insurance quote. As with comparison operators, a Boolean value of `true` or `false` is returned after two operands are evaluated. Table 2-10 lists the JavaScript logical operators.

The Or (`||`) and the And (`&&`) operators are binary operators (requiring two operands), whereas the Not (`!`) operator is a unary operator (requiring a single operand). Logical operators are often used with comparison operators to evaluate expressions, allowing you to combine the results of several expressions into a single statement. For example, the And (`&&`) operator is used for determining whether two operands return an equivalent value.

NAME	OPERATOR	DESCRIPTION
And	&&	Returns `true` if both the left operand and right operand return a value of `true`; otherwise, it returns a value of `false`
Or	||	Returns `true` if either the left operand or right operand returns a value of `true`; if neither operand returns a value of `true`, then the expression containing the Or || operator returns a value of `false`
Not	!	Returns `true` if an expression is false, and returns `false` if an expression is true

Table 2-10: Logical operators

The operands themselves are often expressions. The following code uses the And (`&&`) operator to compare two separate expressions:

```
1   var gender = "male";
2   var age = 17;
3   var riskFactor = gender === "male" && age <= 21;
4   // returns true
```

In the preceding example, the `gender` variable expression evaluates to `true` because it is equal to "male", and the `age` variable expression evaluates to `true` because its value is less than or equal to 21. Because both expressions are true, `riskFactor` is assigned a value of `true`. The statement containing the And (`&&`) operator essentially says, "if variable `gender` is equal to "male" *and* variable `age` is less than or equal to 21, then assign a value of `true` to `riskFactor`. Otherwise, assign a value of `false` to `riskFactor`."

In the following code, `riskFactor` is assigned a value of `false`, because the `age` variable expression does not evaluate to `true`:

```
1   var gender = "male";
2   var age = 25;
3   var riskFactor = gender === "male" && age <= 21;
4   // returns false
```

The logical Or (`||`) operator checks to see if either expression evaluates to `true`. For example, the statement in the following code says, "if the variable `speedingTicket` is greater than 0 *or* if the variable `age` is less than or equal to 21, then assign a value of `true` to `riskFactor`. Otherwise, assign a value of `false` to `riskFactor`."

```
1   var speedingTicket = 2;
2   var age = 25;
```

```
3    var riskFactor = speedingTicket > 0 || age <= 21;
4    // returns true
```

The `riskFactor` variable in the above example is assigned a value of `true`, because the `speedingTicket` variable expression evaluates to `true`, even though the `age` variable expression evaluates to `false`. This result occurs because the Or (`||`) statement returns `true` if *either* the left *or* right operand evaluates to `true`.

The following code is an example of the Not (`!`) operator, which returns `true` if an operand evaluates to `false` and returns `false` if an operand evaluates to `true`. Notice that since the Not operator is unary, it requires only a single operand.

```
var trafficViolations = true;
var safeDriverDiscount = !trafficViolations;
// returns false
```

Note | Logical operators are often used within conditional and looping statements such as the `if`, `for`, and `while` statements. You will learn about conditional and looping statements in Chapter 3.

Special Operators

JavaScript also includes the special operators that are listed in Table 2-11. These operators are used for various purposes and do not fit within any other category.

NAME	OPERATOR	DESCRIPTION
Property access	.	Appends an object, method, or property to another object
Array index	[]	Accesses an element of an array
Function call	()	Calls up functions or changes the order in which individual operations in an expression are evaluated
Comma	,	Allows you to include multiple expressions in the same statement
Conditional expression	?:	Executes one of two expressions based on the results of a conditional expression
Delete	delete	Deletes array elements, variables created without the `var` keyword, and properties of custom objects
Property exists	in	Returns a value of `true` if a specified property is contained within an object

Continued on next page...

NAME	OPERATOR	DESCRIPTION
Object type	`instanceof`	Returns `true` if an object is of a specified object type
New object	`new`	Creates a new instance of a user-defined object type or a predefined JavaScript object type
Data type	`typeof`	Determines the data type of a variable
Void	`void`	Evaluates an expression without returning a result

Table 2-11: Special operators

You will be introduced to the special JavaScript operators as necessary throughout this book. One special operator that you will use in this section is the `typeof` operator. This operator is useful because the data type of variables can change during the course of code execution. This can cause problems if you attempt to perform an arithmetic operation and one of the operands is a string or the `null` value. To avoid such problems, you can use the `typeof` operator to determine the data type of a variable. The syntax for the `typeof` operator is

```
typeof(variablename);
```

You should use the `typeof` operator whenever you need to be sure a variable is the correct data type. The values that can be returned by the `typeof` operator are listed in Table 2-12.

RETURN VALUE	RETURNED FOR
`number`	Integers and floating-point numbers
`string`	Text strings
`boolean`	True or false
`object`	Objects, arrays, and null variables
`function`	Functions
`undefined`	Undefined variables

Table 2-12: Values returned by `typeof` operator

Short Quiz 3

1. What is the difference between a binary operator and a unary operator?

2. How does JavaScript deal with code that performs arithmetic operations on string values?

3. What is a comparison operator? What kind of value does it return?

4. What is a falsy value? What are the six falsy values in JavaScript?

Understanding Operator Precedence

When using operators to create expressions in JavaScript, you need to be aware of the precedence of an operator. Operator precedence is the system that determines the order in which operations in an expression are evaluated. Table 2-13 shows the order of precedence for JavaScript operators. Operators in the same grouping in Table 2-13 have the same order of precedence. When performing operations with operators in the same precedence group, the order of precedence is determined by the operator's associativity—that is, the order in which operators of equal precedence execute. Associativity is evaluated from left-to-right or right-to-left, depending on the operators involved, as explained shortly.

OPERATORS	DESCRIPTION	ASSOCIATIVITY
.	Objects—highest precedence	Left to right
[]	Array elements—highest precedence	Left to right
()	Functions/evaluation—highest precedence	Left to right
new	New object—highest precedence	Right to left
++	Increment	Right to left
--	Decrement	Right to left
-	Unary negation	Right to left
+	Unary positive	Right to left
!	Not	Right to left
typeof	Data type	Right to left
void	Void	Right to left
delete	Delete object	Right to left

Continued on next page...

OPERATORS	DESCRIPTION	ASSOCIATIVITY
* / %	Multiplication/division/modulus	Left to right
	Addition/concatenation and subtraction	Left to right
< <= > >=	Comparison	Left to right
instanceof	Object type	Left to right
in	Object property	Left to right
== != === !==	Equality	Left to right
&&	Logical And	Left to right
||	Logical Or	Left to right
?:	Conditional	Right to left
=	Assignment	Right to left
+= -= *= /= %=	Compound assignment	Right to left
,	Comma—lowest precedence	Left to right

Table 2-13: Operator precedence

Note | *The preceding list does not include bitwise operators. As explained earlier, bitwise operators are beyond the scope of this book.*

In Table 2-13, operators in a higher grouping have precedence over operators in a lower grouping. For example, the multiplication operator (*) has a higher precedence than the addition operator (+). Therefore, the expression 5 + 2 * 8 evaluates as follows: the numbers 2 and 8 are multiplied first for a total of 16, then the number 5 is added, resulting in a total of 21. If the addition operator had a higher precedence than the multiplication operator, then the statement would evaluate to 56, because 5 would be added to 2 for a total of 7, which would then be multiplied by 8.

As an example of how associativity is evaluated, consider the multiplication and division operators. These operators have an associativity of left to right. Thus the expression 30 / 5 * 2 results in a value of 12. Although the multiplication and division operators have equal precedence, the division operation executes first due to the left-to-right associativity of both operators. Figure 2-16 conceptually illustrates the left to right associativity of the 30 / 5 * 2 expression.

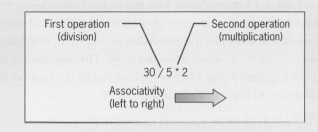

Figure 2-16: Conceptual illustration of left-to-right associativity

If the multiplication operator had higher precedence than the division operator, then the statement 30 / 5 * 2 would result in a value of 3 because the multiplication operation (5 * 2) would execute first. By contrast, the assignment operator and compound assignment operators—such as the compound multiplication assignment operator (*=)—have an associativity of right to left. Therefore, in the following code, the assignment operations take place from right to left.

```
var x = 3;
var y = 2;
x = y *= ++x;
```

The variable x is incremented by one *before* it is assigned to the y variable using the compound multiplication assignment operator (*=). Then, the value of variable y is assigned to variable x. The result assigned to both the x and y variables is 8. Figure 2-17 conceptually illustrates the right to left associativity of the x = y *= ++x statement.

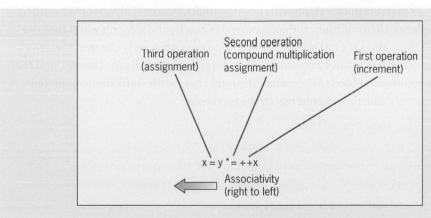

Figure 2-17: Conceptual illustration of right-to-left associativity

As you can see from Table 2-13, parentheses have the highest precedence. Parentheses are used with expressions to change the associativity with which individual operations in an expression are evaluated. For example, the expression `5 + 2 * 8`, which evaluates to 21, can be rewritten to `(5 + 2) * 8`, which evaluates to 56. The parentheses tell JavaScript interpreters to add the numbers 5 and 2 before multiplying by the number 8. Using parentheses forces the statement to evaluate to 56 instead of 21.

To finish the Fan Trick estimate form, you need to modify the `calcStaff()` function to calculate mileage costs. You'll edit the statement that calculates the value of the `photographerCost` variable, adding the product of the value entered in the # of photographers box and the value entered in the Event distance box. (The mileage charge is $1 per mile per photographer, but you will omit this from your calculation because multiplying by 1 will not change the result.)

To modify the `calcStaff()` function to include mileage charges:

1. Return to the **ft.js** file in your text editor.

2. In the `calcStaff()` function, below the statement that begins `var hrs`, insert the following statement:

   `var distance = document.getElementById("distance");`

   Similar to the `var` statements you created earlier for this function, this statement assigns a reference to the element with the `id` value `distance` to a variable.

3. Locate the statement `photographerCost = num.value * 100 * hrs.value;`, click before the closing `;`, type a **space**, and then type + **distance.value * num.value**

   This code multiplies the value entered in the box with the `id` value `distance` by the value entered in the box with the `id` value `photognum`, and adds the product to the earlier calculations in this statement. Because multiplication is higher in the order of precedence than addition, the code evaluates exactly the way you want: first the `num` and `hrs` values are multiplied to determine the staff hourly charges, then the `distance` and `num` values are multiplied to determine the mileage charges, and then the two results are added to determine the total charges for staff. Your completed `calcStaff()` function should match the following:

```
1   function calcStaff() {
2       var num = document.getElementById("photognum");
3       var hrs = document.getElementById("photoghrs");
4       var distance = document.getElementById("distance");
5       totalCost -= photographerCost;
```

```
6      photographerCost = num.value * 100 * hrs.value↵
7          + distance.value * num.value;
8      totalCost += photographerCost;
9      document.getElementById("estimate").innerHTML = "$" +↵
10         totalCost;
11 }
```

4. Scroll down to the createEventListeners() function, and then before the closing } add the following statement:

```
document.getElementById("distance").↵
    addEventListener("change", calcStaff, false);
```

Your completed createEventListeners() function should match the following:

```
1    function createEventListeners() {
2        document.getElementById("photognum").↵
3            addEventListener("change", calcStaff, false);
4        document.getElementById("photoghrs").↵
5            addEventListener("change", calcStaff, false);
6        document.getElementById("membook").↵
7            addEventListener("change", toggleMembook, false);
8        document.getElementById("reprodrights").↵
9            addEventListener("change", toggleRights, false);
10       document.getElementById("distance").↵
11           addEventListener("change", calcStaff, false);
12   }
```

5. Save the **ft.js** file, and then in your browser refresh or reload the **estimate.htm** file.

6. Change the # of hours value to **2**, change the # of photographers value to **3**, change the Event distance value to **50**, and then press **Tab**. Note that changing the event distance increases the estimate by $100, which is the product of the # of hours value (2) and the Event distance value (50).

Programming Concepts | *Creating Reusable Code*

In a small JavaScript program, each function you create generally serves a specific purpose. However, when writing more complex code for larger sites, you should try to build functions that you can apply to multiple situations. For instance, instead of specifying an element name within a function, you could use a variable whose value is specified elsewhere in your program, depending on the context in which the function is called. Because such functions are reusable in multiple contexts within a website, they allow you to perform the same amount of work with less code than would be required to create functions for each specific situation. You'll learn additional strategies for creating reusable code in later chapters of this book.

Short Quiz 4

1. When performing operations with operators in the same precedence group, how is the order of precedence determined?

2. How is the expression `5 + 2 * 8` evaluated? Explain your answer.

Summary

> A function is a related group of JavaScript statements that are executed as a single unit.

> To execute a function, you must invoke, or call, it from elsewhere in your program.

> The scope of a variable determines where in a program it can be used. A variable's scope can be global (for a variable declared outside a function, which is available to all parts of a program) or local (for a variable declared inside a function, which is available only within the function in which it is declared).

> A data type (such as number, Boolean, or string) is the specific category of information that a variable contains.

> JavaScript is a loosely typed programming language, meaning it does not require you to declare the data types of variables.

> The numeric data type in JavaScript supports both integers (positive or negative numbers with no decimal places) and floating-point numbers (numbers that contains decimal places or that are written in exponential notation).

> A Boolean value is a logical value of true or false.

> The JavaScript escape character (\) tells compilers and interpreters that the character that follows it has a special purpose.

> Operators are symbols used in expressions to manipulate operands, such as the addition operator (+) and multiplication operator (*).

> A binary operator (such as +) requires operands before and after the operator, while a unary operator (such as ++) requires a single operand either before or after the operator.

> Arithmetic operators (such as +, -, *, and /) are used in JavaScript to perform mathematical calculations, such as addition, subtraction, multiplication, and division.

> An assignment operator (such as = or +=) is used for assigning a value to a variable.

> A comparison operator (such as === or >) is used to compare two operands and determine if one numeric value is greater than another.

> The conditional operator (? :) executes one of two expressions, based on the results of a conditional expression.

> Logical operators (&&, ||, and !) are used for comparing two Boolean operands for equality.

> Operator precedence is the order in which operations in an expression are evaluated.

Key Terms

actual parameters—*See* arguments.

adding an event listener—Specifying an event handler with the `addEventListener()` method.

anonymous function—A set of related statements with no name assigned to it.

arguments—The variables or values that you place in the parentheses of a function call statement.

arithmetic operators—Operators used to perform mathematical calculations, such as addition, subtraction, multiplication, and division.

assignment operator—An operator used for assigning a value to a variable.

associativity—The order in which operators of equal precedence execute.

binary operator—An operator that requires an operand before and after it.

Boolean value—A logical value of `true` or `false`.

browser console—A browser pane that displays error messages.

call—To invoke a function from elsewhere in your code.

comparison operator—An operator used to compare two operands and determine if one value is greater than another.

compound assignment operators—Assignment operators other than the equal sign, which perform mathematical calculations on variables and literal values in an expression, and then assign a new value to the left operand.

concatenation operator—The plus sign (+) when used with strings; this operator combines, or concatenates, string operands.

conditional operator—The `?:` operator, which executes one of two expressions based on the results of a conditional expression.

console—*See* browser console.

data type—The specific category of information that a variable contains, such as numeric, Boolean, or string.

duck typed—*See* loosely typed.

dynamically typed—*See* loosely typed.

empty string—A zero-length string value.

escape character—The backslash character (\ ), which tells JavaScript compilers and interpreters that the character that follows it has a special purpose.

escape sequence—The combination of the escape character (\ ) with one of several other characters, which inserts a special character into a string; for example, the \b escape sequence inserts a backspace character.

exponential notation—A shortened format for writing very large numbers or numbers with many decimal places, in which numbers are represented by a value between 1 and 10 multiplied by 10 raised to some power.

falsy values—Six values that are treated in comparison operations as the Boolean value `false`.

floating-point number—A number that contains decimal places or that is written in exponential notation.

function—A related group of JavaScript statements that are executed as a single unit.

function braces—The set of curly braces that contain the function statements in a function definition.

function call—The code that calls a function, which consists of the function name followed by parentheses, which contain any arguments to be passed to the function.

function definition—The lines that make up a function.

function statements—The statements that do the actual work of a function, such as calculating the square root of the parameter, or displaying a message on the screen, and which must be contained within the function braces.

global variable—A variable that is declared outside a function and is available to all parts of your program, because it has global scope.

innerHTML property—The property of a web page object whose value is the content between the element's opening and closing tags.

integer—A positive or negative number with no decimal places.

local variable—A variable that is declared inside a function and is available only within the function in which it is declared, because it has local scope.

logical operators—The Or (`||`), And (`&&`), and Not (`!`) operators, which are used to modify Boolean values or specify the relationship between operands in an expression that results in a Boolean value.

loosely typed—Description of a programming language that does not require you to declare the data types of variables.

named function—A set of related statements that is assigned a name.

operator precedence—The system that determines the order in which operations in an expression are evaluated.

parameter—A variable that is used within a function.

passing arguments—Sending arguments to the parameters of a called function.

postfix operator—An operator that is placed after a variable name.

prefix operator—An operator that is placed before a variable name.

primitive types—Data types that can be assigned only a single value.

relational operator—*See* comparison operator.

return statement—A statement in a function that returns a value to the statement that called the function.

scientific notation—*See* exponential notation.

statically typed—*See* strongly typed.

strongly typed—Description of a programming language that requires you to declare the data types of variables.

`textContent` **property**—A property similar to the `innerHTML` property, except that its value excludes any HTML markup.

truthy values—All values other than the six falsy values; truthy values are treated in comparison operations as the Boolean value `true`.

unary operator—An operator that requires just a single operand either before or after it.

variable scope—The aspect of a declared variable that determines where in code it can be used, either globally (throughout the code) or locally (only within the function in which it is declared).

Review Questions

1. A(n) _____ allows you to execute a related group of statements as a single unit.
   a. variable
   b. statement
   c. event
   d. function

2. Parameters in a function definition are placed within _____ .
   a. braces
   b. parentheses
   c. double quotes
   d. single quotes

3. A variable that is declared outside a function is called a(n) _____ variable.
   a. class
   b. local
   c. global
   d. program

4. Which one of the following creates a local variable?
   a. Declaring it outside of a function with the `var` keyword
   b. Declaring it outside of a function without the `var` keyword
   c. Declaring it inside a function with the `var` keyword
   d. Declaring it inside a function without the `var` keyword

5. Which of the following is a primitive data type in JavaScript?
   a. Boolean
   b. Integer
   c. Floating-point
   d. Logical

6. Which of the following describes JavaScript?
    a. Strongly typed
    b. Statically typed
    c. Loosely typed
    d. Untyped

7. Which of the following is an integer?
    a. −2.5
    b. 6.02e23
    c. −11
    d. 0.03

8. Which of the following is a Boolean value?
    a. 3.04
    b. true
    c. "Greece"
    d. 6.02e23

9. Which of the following creates an empty string?
    a. `null`
    b. `undefined`
    c. `""`
    d. 0

10. Which of the following is a valid JavaScript statement?
    a. `document.write('Boston, MA is called 'Beantown.'')`
    b. `document.write("Boston, MA is called "Beantown."")`
    c. `document.write("Boston, MA is called 'Beantown."')`
    d. `document.write("Boston, MA is called 'Beantown.'")`

11. Which of the following is a concatenation operator?
    a. `>`
    b. `+`
    c. `||`
    d. `++`

12. Which of following is the JavaScript escape character?
    a. `"`
    b. `'`
    c. `\`
    d. `/`

13. Which of the following is an arithmetic binary operator?
    a. +
    b. ||
    c. =
    d. &&

14. Which of the following is an arithmetic unary operator?
    a. ++
    b. ||
    c. =
    d. &&

15. What is the result of the statement 5 < 4?
    a. 1
    b. yes
    c. true
    d. false

16. Write a simple function (or copy one used in this chapter), that includes the following parts, and then label the parts:
    > Name
    > Parameters
    > Function braces
    > Function statements

17. Explain the difference between prefix and postfix operators, and provide an example of each.

18. What is the result of the following expression?
    ```
    5 > 4 ? document.write("green") : document.write("blue");
    ```
    Name the operators, and explain the steps you took to arrive at your answer.

19. What is the result of the expression 5 % 4? Name the operator, and explain the steps you took to arrive at your answer.

20. Explain the difference between global and local variables, and describe how using or not using the var keyword can affect the scope of a variable.

Hands-On Projects

Hands-On Project 2-1

In this project, you'll create a script that calculates the Celsius equivalent of a Fahrenheit temperature. Note that your result should work on all modern browsers, but will not work on IE8 or previous versions of IE.

1. In your text editor, open **index.htm** from the HandsOnProject2-1 folder in the Chapter02 folder. Enter your name and today's date where indicated in the comment section in the document head.

2. At the bottom of the document, before the closing `</body>` tag, enter **<script>**, insert a blank line, and then enter **</script>** to create a new script section.

3. Within the script section you created in the previous step, enter the following function.

```
1    function convert() {
2        var degF = document.getElementById("fValue").value;
3        var degC = degF - 32 * 5 / 9;
4        document.getElementById("cValue").innerHTML = degC;
5    }
```

   This function, named `convert()`, starts by looking up the Fahrenheit value entered by users and assigning it to a variable named `degF`. It then performs calculations on `degF` to arrive at the Celsius equivalent, which is assigned to a variable named `degC`. Finally, it assigns the value of `degC` as the `innerHTML` value of the element with the `id` value `cValue`.

4. Below the closing `}` for the `convert()` function, but before the closing `</script>` tag, enter the following statement to add an event listener:

```
document.getElementById("button").↵
    addEventListener("click", convert, false);
```

5. Save your work, open **index.htm** in your browser, enter **–40** in the Enter temp in ° F box, and then click the **Convert to ° C** button. –40° Fahrenheit is actually equivalent to –40° Celsius. However, the formula incorrectly calculates that –40° F is equivalent to –57.7° C. This is because the calculations in the equation must take place in a different order than the order of precedence dictates.

6. Return to the **index.htm** file in your text editor, and then add two sets of parentheses to the first statement in the `convert()` function to modify the order in which the calculations are performed, as follows:

```
var degC = (degF - 32) * (5 / 9);
```

7. Save your work, refresh or reload **index.htm** in your browser, enter **–40** in the Enter temp in ° F box, and then click the **Convert to ° C** button. As Figure 2-18 shows, the temperature is now calculated correctly as –40° C.

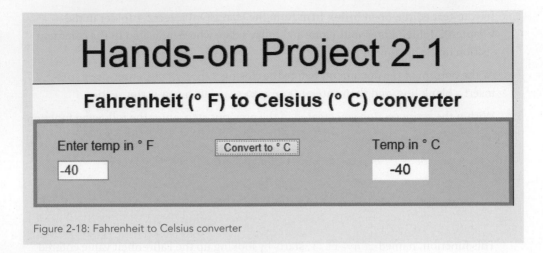

Hands-on Project 2-1

Fahrenheit (° F) to Celsius (° C) converter

Enter temp in ° F   Convert to ° C   Temp in ° C

-40   -40

Figure 2-18: Fahrenheit to Celsius converter

Hands-On Project 2-2

In this project, you'll create a script that uses logical operators and the conditional operator to give users feedback based on whether form fields are completed.

1. In your text editor, open **index.htm** from the HandsOnProject2-2 folder in the Chapter02 folder. Enter your name and today's date where indicated in the comment section in the document head.

2. At the bottom of the document, before the closing `</body>` tag, enter **`<script>`**, insert a blank line, and then enter **`</script>`** to create a new script section.

3. Within the script section you created in the previous step, enter the following function:

```
1   function submitInfo() {
2       var name = document.getElementById("nameinput");
3       var email = document.getElementById("emailinput");
4       var phone = document.getElementById("phoneinput");
5       (name.value && email.value && phone.value) ? ↵
6           alert("Thank you!") : alert("Please fill in all fields");
7   }
```

This function starts by declaring three variables, which point to three web page elements. The remaining code is a single conditional expression. The statement to be tested for a Boolean `true` or `false` value checks if the element with the `id` value of `nameinput` is truthy (in this case, is not ""), and (&&) if the element with the `id` of `emailinput` is truthy, and if the element with the `id` of `phoneinput` is truthy. If all of these statements are true, then the entire statement has the Boolean value `true`, and an alert box is displayed with the text "Thank you!". If any of these statements is false, then the entire statement has the Boolean value `false`, and an alert box is displayed with the text "Please fill in all fields".

4. Below the closing } for the `submitInfo()` function, but before the closing `</script>` tag, enter the following statement to add an event listener:

```
document.getElementById("submit").↵
    addEventListener("click", submitInfo, false);
```

5. Save your work, open **index.htm** in your browser, and then click the **Submit** button. The browser displays an alert box containing the text "Please fill in all fields" because the fields were all blank when you clicked the button. Click the **OK** button in the alert box, enter text in just the Name box, and then click **Submit**. The browser again displays an alert box containing the text "Please fill in all fields" because two of the fields were still blank when you clicked the button. Click the **OK** button in the alert box, enter text in all three fields, and then click **Submit**. As shown in Figure 2-19, the browser now displays an alert box containing the text "Thank you!" because none of the boxes were empty when you clicked the button. Click **OK**.

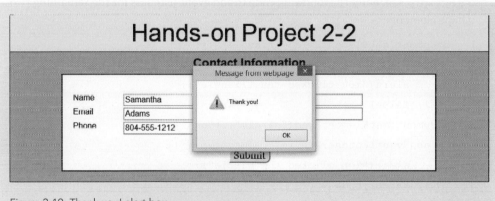

Figure 2-19: Thank you! alert box

Hands-On Project 2-3

In this project, you'll create a script that displays an alert box containing a custom message based on the element a user clicks. Note that your result should work on all modern browsers, but will not work on IE8 or previous versions of IE.

1. In your text editor, open **index.htm** from the HandsOnProject2-3 folder in the Chapter02 folder. Enter your name and today's date where indicated in the comment section in the document head.

2. Open **index.htm** in your browser. The web page displays three shapes: a square, a triangle, and a circle.

3. Return to your text editor. At the bottom of the document, before the closing `</body>` tag, enter **`<script>`**, insert a blank line, and then enter **`</script>`** to create a new script section.

4. Within the script section you created in the previous step, enter the following event listener:

```
1    document.getElementById("square").↵
2       addEventListener("click", function() {
3          alert("You clicked the square");
4       }, false);
```

This code adds an event listener to the element with the `id` of `square`. The code uses an anonymous function as the second argument for the `addEventListener()` method. When a user clicks the element, the anonymous function is executed, which generates an alert box containing the text "You clicked the square".

5. Below the event listener code you added in the previous step, but before the closing `</script>` tag, enter the following code to add event listeners for the remaining two shape elements:

```
1    document.getElementById("triangle").↵
2       addEventListener("click", function() {
3          alert("You clicked the triangle");
4       }, false);
5    document.getElementById("circle").↵
6       addEventListener("click", function() {
7          alert("You clicked the circle");
8       }, false);
```

6. Save your work, refresh or reload **index.htm** in your browser, and then click the **square**. As Figure 2-20 shows, the browser opens an alert box that displays the text "You clicked the square". Click **OK**, and then repeat for the triangle and the circle. Each alert box should name the shape you clicked.

Figure 2-20: Alert box displayed after clicking square element

Hands-On Project 2-4

In this project, you'll create a script that totals purchases and adds tax. Note that your result should work on all modern browsers, but will not work on IE8 or previous versions of IE.

1. In your text editor, open **index.htm** from the HandsOnProject2-4 folder in the Chapter02 folder. Enter your name and today's date where indicated in the comment section in the document head.

2. Open **index.htm** in your browser. The web page displays a form with five check boxes and a Submit button. Each check box allows users to select an item from a lunch menu. You'll create a script that totals the prices of all the elements a users selects, adds sales tax, and displays the order total in an alert box.

3. Return to your text editor. At the bottom of the document, before the closing </body> tag, enter <script>, insert a blank line, and then enter </script> to create a new script section.

4. Within the script section you created in the previous step, enter the following function.

```
1    function calcTotal() {
2       var itemTotal = 0;
3       var item1 = document.getElementById("item1");
4       var item2 = document.getElementById("item2");
5       var item3 = document.getElementById("item3");
```

```
6        var item4 = document.getElementById("item4");
7        var item5 = document.getElementById("item5");
8        (item1.checked) ? (itemTotal += 8) : (itemTotal += 0);
9        (item2.checked) ? (itemTotal += 9) : (itemTotal += 0);
10       (item3.checked) ? (itemTotal += 8) : (itemTotal += 0);
11       (item4.checked) ? (itemTotal += 13) : (itemTotal += 0);
12       (item5.checked) ? (itemTotal += 6) : (itemTotal += 0);
13       var salesTaxRate = 0.07;
14       var orderTotal = itemTotal + (itemTotal * salesTaxRate);
15       alert("Your order total is $" + orderTotal);
16   }
```

The `calcTotal()` function starts by creating six local variables—`itemTotal`, and one variable storing a reference to each check box element. Each statement in lines 8–12 contains a conditional statement that evaluates whether one of the check boxes on the page is checked. If so, the price corresponding to that check box is added to the `itemTotal` variable; if not, 0 is added to the `itemTotal` variable. After examining the values of all the check boxes, the function declares two additional variables. The `salesTaxRate` variable specifies the percentage of the purchase price that must be added to the total for tax. In line 14, the value of the `orderTotal` variable is calculated by first multiplying `itemTotal` and `salesTaxRate` to determine the sales tax amount and then adding that amount to the `itemTotal` value. The function ends by generating an alert box containing the text "Your order total is $" followed by the value of the `orderTotal` variable.

5. Below the closing } for the `calcTotal()` function, but before the closing `</script>` tag, enter the following code to add an event listener:

```
document.getElementById("submit").↵
    addEventListener("click", calcTotal, false);
```

6. Save your work, refresh or reload **index.htm** in your browser, click the **Fried chicken** check box, and then click the **Submit** button. As Figure 2-21 shows, the alert box displays a total of $8.56. Click **OK**.

Hands-on Project 2-4

Lunch selections

- ☑ Fried chicken ($8.00)
- ☐ Fried halibut ($9.00)
- ☐ Hamburger ($8.00)
- ☐ Grilled salmon ($13.00)
- ☐ Side salad ($6.00)

Submit

Message from webpage ×

⚠ Your order total is $8.56

OK

Figure 2-21: Alert box displaying order total

7. Select other items or combinations of items, and verify that the reported total realistically represents the total of the selected items plus 7% tax.

Hands-On Project 2-5

In this project, you'll enhance the document you worked on in Hands-On Project 2-4 to avoid potential differences between floating point and integer calculations. Note that your result should work on all modern browsers, but will not work on IE8 or previous versions of IE.

1. In the file manager for your operating system, copy the completed contents of the HandsOnProject2-4 folder to the HandsOnProject2-5 folder.

2. In your text editor, open the **index.htm** file from the HandsOnProject2-5 folder, change "Hands-on Project 2-4" to **Hands-On Project 2-5** in the comment section, in the `title` element, and in the `h1` element, and then save your changes.

3. In the `calcTotal()` function, after the statement `var SalesTaxRate = 0.07;`, add the following statement:

```
itemTotal *= 100;
```

This multiplies the total of selected items by 100 and assigns the result as the new value of `itemTotal`. This converts the item total from dollars (such as $7.99) to cents (such as 799¢), which is an integer, thus avoiding possible issues with floating point calculations.

4. In the next statement, which begins `var orderTotal`, before the first occurrence of `itemTotal`, add an opening parenthesis, before the closing `;` add a closing parenthesis, and then before the closing `;` add / **100**. Your updated statement should match the following:

```
var orderTotal =↵
    (itemTotal + (itemTotal * salesTaxRate)) / 100;
```

The existing content of the right operand is enclosed in parentheses, and the entire calculated value is divided by 100, converting it from cents back to dollars.

5. Save your changes, open **index.htm** in your browser, click the **Fried chicken** check box, and then click the **Submit** button. Verify that the alert box still displays a total of $8.56. Because the `orderTotal` calculation doesn't encounter any floating-point problems, you won't see different results based on the changes you made. However, if the page's requirements changed in the future to require a calculation that might introduce floating-point issues, your changes would prevent users from experiencing any problems.

Case Projects

Individual Case Project

Plan and add a feature to one of the web pages in your personal site that uses at least one function to perform a mathematical calculation based on user input. Test the page to ensure it works as planned.

Team Case Project

Choose one of the web pages from your team website to enhance with at least two functions. Common uses of functions include performing actions based on user input (validation, personalization of the web page) and performing calculations. Divide your team into subgroups equal to the number of functions your page will include. After each subgroup has created its function, come back together as a full group and incorporate the functions in the web page. Test the functions to verify the page works as planned, doing any troubleshooting and making any edits to the functions as a full team.

CHAPTER 3

BUILDING ARRAYS AND CONTROLLING FLOW

When you complete this chapter, you will be able to:

> Store data in arrays
> Use `while` statements, `do/while` statements, and `for` statements to repeatedly execute code
> Use `continue` statements to restart looping statements
> Use `if` statements, `if/else` statements, and `switch` statements to make decisions
> Nest one `if` statement in another

The code you have written so far has been linear in nature. In other words, your programs start at the beginning and end when the last statement in the program executes. However, sometimes it can be useful to change this default order of execution. Changing the order in which JavaScript code is executed is known as *controlling flow*. Controlling the flow of code is one of the most fundamental skills required in programming. In this chapter, you will learn about several statements that enable you to control flow. Before learning how to use these statements, you will first learn about the array data type, which is often used with these statements.

Storing Data in Arrays

An **array** contains a set of data represented by a single variable name. You can think of an array as a collection of variables contained within a single variable. You use an array when you want to store a group or a list of related information in a single, easily managed location. Lists of names, courses, test scores, and prices are typically stored in arrays. For example, Figure 3-1 shows a single array named `newsSections` that contains the names of the sections of a news website.

Figure 3-1: Conceptual illustration of an array
© 2015 Cengage Learning®

Note *The identifiers you use for an array name must follow the same rules as identifiers for variables. They must begin with an uppercase or lowercase ASCII letter, dollar sign ($), or underscore (_), can include numbers (but not as the first character), cannot include spaces, and cannot be reserved words.*

Declaring and Initializing Arrays

There are a couple ways to create arrays in JavaScript, but the most common by far is to use an **array literal**, which is a single statement that declares a variable and specifies array values as its content. To create an array using an array literal, you use the basic syntax for creating a variable, with one addition: the values in the array are separated by commas, and the entire set of array values is enclosed in square brackets ([ ]). The code to create an array using an array literal has the following syntax:

```
var name = [value1, value2, value3, ...];
```

where *name* is the variable name assigned to the array, and *value1*, *value2*, and *value3* are values in the array. To create the `newsSections` array illustrated in Figure 3-1, you'd use the statement shown in Figure 3-2.

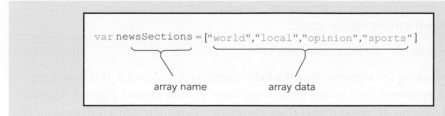

Figure 3-2: Code to create the newsSections array

When using an array literal to declare a large array, the var statement is sometimes quite long. Although in most cases you want to end every line of JavaScript code with a semicolon, it is safe to break an array literal over multiple lines. For instance, you might write an array literal for a long array as follows:

```
var name = [value1, value2, value3,
            value4, value5, value6,
            value7, value8];
```

Each value contained in an array is called an **element**. Each element has a number, known as an **index**, which represents the element's position within the array. While numbering in daily life generally starts with 1, in programming, numbering often starts with 0. This is the case for arrays.

> **Caution** Assuming that the first element in an array has an index number of 1 rather than 0 is a common source of programming errors. If you're working with an array and seeing results offset by 1 from what you expect, double check that your code accounts for 0 as the first index number.

You refer to a specific array element by enclosing its index number in brackets after the array name. For example, the first element in the newSections array is newSections[0], the second element is newSections[1], the third element is newSections[2], and so on. This also means that if you have an array consisting of 10 elements, you would refer to the 10th element in the array using an index of 9.

The var name = [value1, value2, value3, ...]; syntax allows you to create an array and specify the elements it contains. You can also add elements to an existing array. To do so, you use syntax similar to that for assigning a value to a standard variable, except that you also include the index for the new element in square brackets after the array name.

For instance, to add the value "entertainment" as a fifth element of the `newsSections` array, you'd use the following statement:

```
newsSections[4] = "entertainment";
```

Because the existing five elements have the index numbers 0, 1, 2, and 3, this statement uses the next number, 4, and assigns it the string value "entertainment". Figure 3-3 shows the updated contents of the array after using the above statement to add a fifth element.

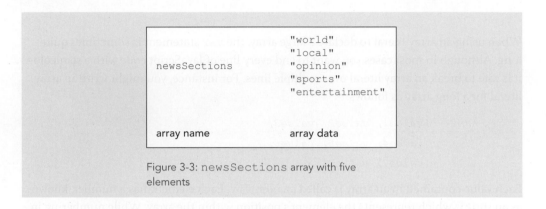

Figure 3-3: `newsSections` array with five elements

You can create an array that contains no elements, and then add elements to it later. You create a new, empty array using the following syntax:

```
var name = [];
```

The square brackets in this expression indicate that the new variable is an array. You can then add elements to the array just as you would for an array that already includes elements.

The size of an array can change dynamically. If you assign a value to an element that has not yet been created, the element is created automatically, along with any elements that might precede it. For example, the first statement in the following code creates the `colors` array without any elements. The second statement then assigns "yellow" to the third element, which also creates the first two elements (`colors[0]` and `colors[1]`) in the process.

```
var colors = [];
colors[2] = "yellow";
```

Note that until you assign values to `colors[0]` and `colors[1]`, their values will be `undefined`. Figure 3-4 illustrates the contents of the `colors` array after these statements are run.

array name	array index	array data
	[0]	undefined
colors	[1]	undefined
	[2]	"yellow"

Figure 3-4: `colors` array after adding an element with index 2

Most programming languages require that all of the elements in an array be of the exact same data type. However, in JavaScript the values assigned to array elements can be of different data types. For example, the following code creates an array and stores values with different data types in the array elements:

```
var hotelReservation = [];
// guest name (string)
hotelReservation[0] = "Minh Vuong";
// # of nights (integer)
hotelReservation[1] = 5;
// price per night (floating point)
hotelReservation[2] = 74.99;
// non-smoking room (Boolean)
hotelReservation[3] = true;
```

Note

A variable is sometimes referred to with `[]` at the end of its name to indicate that its value is an array. For instance, when diagramming a programming task, you might write `contactInfo[]` to refer to a `contactInfo` variable with an array data type. Note that this construction is not used in actual JavaScript code, though.

In this chapter, you'll be working on a web page to display the game schedule for the Tipton Turbines, a baseball team in Tipton, Iowa. The team wants to be able to post each month's schedule without needing to enter the information in each table cell. They'd like you to create the schedule for August 2016 as a first step. You'll start by creating arrays containing the different pieces of information that go in each table cell. Later in this chapter, you'll learn how to use control flow statements to insert information from arrays into table cells. Figure 3-5 shows a preview of the web page you'll create in this chapter in a desktop browser, and Figure 3-6 shows the page on a handheld device.

	Calendar August 2016					
Sunday	Monday	Tuesday	Wednesday	Thursday	Friday	Saturday
	1 @ Lightning	2 @ Combines	3 @ Combines	4 @ Combines	5 vs Lightning	6 vs Lightning
7 vs Lightning	8 vs Lightning	9 vs Barn Raisers	10 vs Barn Raisers	11 vs Barn Raisers	12 @ Sodbusters	13 @ Sodbusters
14 @ Sodbusters	15 @ Sodbusters	16 (off)	17 @ River Riders	18 @ River Riders	19 @ River Riders	20 @ Big Dippers
21 @ Big Dippers	22 @ Big Dippers	23 (off)	24 vs Sodbusters	25 vs Sodbusters	26 vs Sodbusters	27 vs Combines
28 vs Combines	29 vs Combines	30 (off)	31 (off)			

Tipton Turbines Baseball • Tipton, Iowa

Figure 3-5: Tipton Turbines schedule in a desktop browser

Figure 3-6: Tipton Turbines schedule on a handheld device

To create the arrays containing the schedule information:

1. In your text editor, open the **calendar.htm** file, located in your Chapter folder for Chapter 3.

2. In the comment section at the top of the document, type your name and today's date where indicated, and then save your work.

3. Scroll through the document to familiarize yourself with its content. The `article` element contains a table consisting of five rows and seven columns. The cells contain no data. Each of the 31 `td` elements that will eventually contain the schedule information has an `id` value. Later in this chapter, you'll use these `id` values to place each array element in the correct cell.

4. Open **calendar.htm** in a browser. As Figure 3-7 shows, the table is displayed as an empty grid.

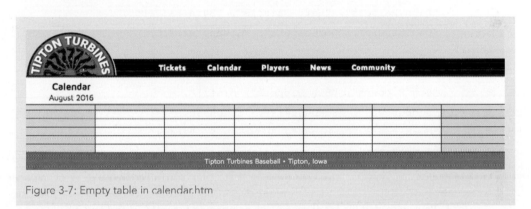

Figure 3-7: Empty table in calendar.htm

5. Return to your text editor, open a new document, and then enter the following comment, entering your name and today's date where indicated:

```
1    /*       JavaScript 6th Edition
2    *        Chapter 3
3    *        Chapter case
4    *        Tipton Turbines
5    *        Variables and functions
6    *        Author:
7    *        Date:
8    *        Filename: tt.js
9    */
```

6. Below the comment section, enter the following code to declare the `daysOfWeek` variable and set its value using an array literal:

```
// global variables
var daysOfWeek = ["Sunday", "Monday", "Tuesday",
  "Wednesday", "Thursday", "Friday", "Saturday"];
```

This code uses an array literal to declare a variable named `daysOfWeek` whose value is an array that contains the name of each day of the week.

7. Below the `daysOfWeek` variable declaration, enter the following code to declare the `opponents` variable and set its value:

```
1   var opponents =
2       ["Lightning", "Combines", "Combines", "Combines",
3        "Lightning", "Lightning", "Lightning", "Lightning",
4        "Barn Raisers", "Barn Raisers", "Barn Raisers",
5        "Sodbusters", "Sodbusters", "Sodbusters",
6        "Sodbusters", "(off)", "River Riders",
7        "River Riders", "River Riders", "Big Dippers",
8        "Big Dippers", "Big Dippers", "(off)",
9        "Sodbusters", "Sodbusters", "Sodbusters",
10       "Combines", "Combines", "Combines", "(off)",
11       "(off)"];
```

Note | *Be sure to start the list of values with an opening bracket ([ ) and end it with a closing bracket ( ]). Also make sure the entire statement ends with a semicolon (;).*

This array lists, in order, the Turbines' opponents for each of the 31 days in August 2016. For instance, the first day of the month, August 1, the team is playing the Lightning, on the second day they're playing the Combines, and on the last day, August 31, no game is scheduled.

8. Below the `opponents` variable declaration, enter the following code to declare the `gameLocation` variable and set its value:

```
1   var gameLocation =
2       ["away", "away", "away", "away", "home", "home",
```

```
3        "home", "home", "home", "home", "home", "away",
4        "away", "away", "away", "", "away", "away", "away",
5        "away", "away", "away", "", "home", "home", "home",
6        "home", "home", "home", "", ""];
```

This array lists whether the team is playing away or at home for each of the 31 days in August 2016. Note that this array combines the strings "away" and "home" with empty values, indicated by "", which denote days when no game is scheduled. For instance, the first four days of the month, August 1–4, the games are away, on the next 7 days, August 5–11, the games are at home, and on the last day, August 31, no game is scheduled.

9. Save the file as a text file with the name **tt.js** to your Chapter folder for Chapter 3, return to **calendar.htm** in your text editor, and then add the following line of code at the bottom of the document, just above the closing </body> tag:

```
<script src="tt.js"></script>
```

10. Save your changes to **calendar.htm**, and then refresh or reload **calendar.htm** in your browser. Although you've declared three array variables, you haven't yet referenced their values in any JavaScript code, so the web page still matches Figure 3-6. You'll create functions to insert the array values in the table later in this chapter.

Accessing Element Information

You access an element's value just as you access the value of any other variable, except that you include the element index in brackets. For example, the following code assigns the values contained in the first three elements of the newsSections array as the content of three web page elements:

```
1    var sec1Head = document.getElementById("section1");
2    var sec2Head = document.getElementById("section2");
3    var sec3Head = document.getElementById("section3");
4    sec1Head.innerHTML = newsSections[0]; // "world"
5    sec2Head.innerHTML = newsSections[1]; // "local"
6    sec3Head.innerHTML = newsSections[2]; // "opinion"
```

In Chapter 2, you used the browser console to check for errors generated by JavaScript code. The browser consoles included in the current versions of all major browsers also enable you to enter JavaScript statements and see the results of the statements displayed. Especially after entering large arrays like the opponents and gameLocation variables, it can be helpful to check the array values using the console to verify that you've declared the arrays accurately. You'll use your browser's console to check the arrays in the tt.js file now.

To check the array values using a browser console:

1. Return to **calendar.htm** in your browser. Table 3-1 lists the keyboard shortcuts and menu commands to open the console in the major browsers.

BROWSER	KEYBOARD SHORTCUT	MENU STEPS
Internet Explorer 9+	**F12**, then **Ctrl** + **2**	Click the **Tools** icon, click **F12 developer tools** on the menu, and then in the window that opens, click the **Console** button
Firefox	**Ctrl** + **Shift** + **K** (Win) **option** + **command** + **K** (Mac)	Click the **Open menu** button, click **Developer**, and then click **Web Console**
Chrome	**Ctrl** + **Shift** + **J** (Win) **option** + **command** + **J** (Mac)	Click the **Customize and control Google Chrome** button, point to **Tools**, and then click **JavaScript Console**

Table 3-1: Steps to open the browser console in major browsers

2. Open the console in your browser using the appropriate command from Table 3-1.

Note   *If your browser isn't listed, or if one of the listed methods doesn't work, check your browser's documentation for the correct steps, or try a different browser. Remember that different browsers may use different terms for the browser console, including "JavaScript console," "web console," or "error console."*

Figure 3-7 shows the browser console in Firefox. The browser console may be displayed differently in different browsers, but all share the same general components indicated in Figure 3-8.

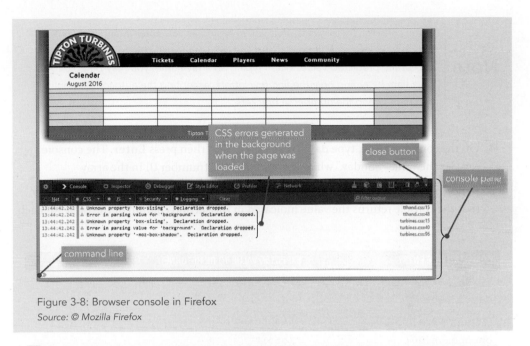

Figure 3-8: Browser console in Firefox
Source: © Mozilla Firefox

3. Click in the command line at the bottom of the console, type **daysOfWeek[1]**, and then press **Enter**. As Figure 3-9 shows, the console displays your entry on its own line and then displays the result on the following line. In this case, the result is "Monday".

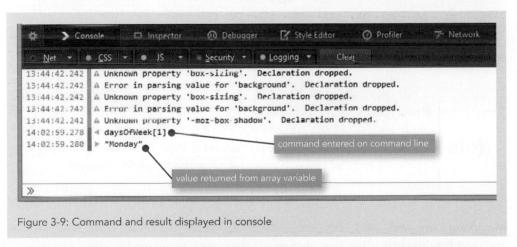

Figure 3-9: Command and result displayed in console

Notice that the console returned the value "Monday" for the command daysOfWeek[1], which requests the value of item 1 in the daysOfWeek array. The first value in the array is "Sunday." However, remember that array elements are numbered starting with 0, so daysOfWeek[1] refers to the *second* item in the daysOfWeek array, which is "Monday."

4. On the command line, type **daysOfWeek[0]**, and then press **Enter**. The console returns the value "Sunday," which is the first value (number 0) in the array.

5. Repeat Step 4 for each of the values in the first column in Table 3-2, and then verify that the console returns the value indicated in the second column of the table for each.

COMMAND LINE ENTRY	EXPECTED VALUE TO BE RETURNED
daysOfWeek[6]	"Saturday"
daysOfWeek[7]	Undefined
opponents[0]	"Lightning"
opponents[30]	"(off)"
opponents[31]	undefined
gameLocation[0]	"away"
gameLocation[30]	""
gameLocation[31]	undefined

Table 3-2: Command line entries to verify array contents

Modifying Elements

You modify values in existing array elements in the same way you modify values in a standard variable, except that you include the element index in brackets. The following code assigns a new value to the fifth element in the newSections array:

```
newSections[4] = "living";
```

Figure 3-10 illustrates the updated contents of the `newsSections` array after the above statement is executed.

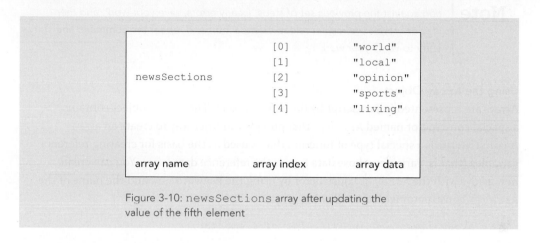

Figure 3-10: `newsSections` array after updating the value of the fifth element

Determining the Number of Elements in an Array

Every array has a `length` property, which returns the number of elements in the array. You append the `length` property to the name of the array whose length you want to retrieve using the syntax *name*`.length;`.

Note | *Remember that unlike method names, property names are not followed by parentheses.*

Although array indexes are numbered starting from 0, the `length` property counts from 1. This means that, for example, the `length` property for a 10-element array returns a value of 10, even though the final index value in the array is 9.

You'll use the `length` property in your browser's console to verify the number of elements in each of your three arrays.

To check the length of arrays using your browser's console:

1. Return to **calendar.htm** in your browser.

2. On the command line of the console, type **daysOfWeek.length**, and then press **Enter**. The console returns 7, which is the number of elements in the `daysOfWeek` array.

3. Repeat Step 2 to check the values of **opponents.length** and **gameLocation.length**. The console should return 31 for both.

Using the `Array` Object

Arrays are represented in JavaScript by the `Array` object. The `Array` object contains a special constructor named `Array()` that provides another way to create an array. A **constructor** is a special type of function that is used as the basis for creating reference variables (that is, variables whose data type is the reference data type). You can create new arrays with the `Array()` constructor by using the keyword `new` and the name of the `Array()` constructor with the following syntax:

```
var arrayName = new Array(number of elements);
```

Within the parentheses of the `Array()` construction, you include an integer that represents the number of elements to be contained in the array. The following code uses the `Array()` constructor to create an array named `newsSections` that has six elements:

```
var newsSections = new Array(6);
```

JavaScript programmers generally create arrays using literals rather than the constructor. Many programmers think using literals is easier than using the constructor, and the constructor offers no specific advantages over literals. For the remainder of this book, you'll create arrays using literals rather than using the `Array()` constructor.

Referencing Default Collections of Elements

You can reference web page elements by looking up the entire set of elements of a certain type in a web page, and then referencing one specific element in that collection. Although the set of elements isn't itself an array, you can reference specific items within the set using a system similar to the syntax for referencing an element in an array, by using an index number based on the order the element appears in the HTML code. For instance, assume you were working with a web page containing the following basic body section:

```
1    <h1>How to make salad</h1>
2    <ol>
3        <li>Wash lettuce</li>
4        <li>Rip into bite-sized pieces</li>
5        <li>Add dressing</li>
6    </ol>
```

If you wanted to manipulate the third `li` element with JavaScript, you could add an `id` attribute to its opening tag and then use the `getElementById()` method to access it. However, you could instead access the element using a different JavaScript method that would not require adding additional code to your HTML document. The `getElementsByTagName() method` returns a collection of references to all instances of a certain element in an HTML document. This method uses the following syntax:

```
getElementsByTagName("element")
```

For instance, the following code returns a set of references to all `li` elements in a document:

```
getElementsByTagName("li")
```

Note that the elements are ordered in the resulting collection by the order of their occurrence in the HTML code.

Caution	Unlike `getElementById()`, which uses the singular version of "element," the word "elements" in `getElementsByTagName()` has an s at the end. Be sure not to type `getElementByTagName()`, which is not a valid method name.

Although the collection returned is not technically an array, the syntax you use to access its contents is the same as the syntax to reference array elements—you simply specify an index value using a number in brackets. For instance, to reference the third `li` element in a document, you could use the `getElementsByTagName()` method to access the collection of all `li` elements in the document, and then add `[2]` to the end, indicating you want to access the third instance of the `li` element in the document, as follows:

```
document.getElementsByTagName("li")[2]
```

To access the contents of this element, you could add the `innerHTML` property, as follows:

```
document.getElementsByTagName("li")[2].innerHTML
```

If you loaded the document containing the above elements in a browser and then entered the preceding code in a browser console, the console would return the following:

```
"Add dressing"
```

You'll use the `getElementsByTagName()` method to view the values of the `li` elements in the navigation bar on the Tipton Turbines calendar page.

To use your browser's console to check the values of the `li` elements in the navigation bar:

1. Return to **calendar.htm** in your browser.

2. On the command line of the browser console, type `document.getElementsByTagName("li")[0].innerHTML`, and then press **Enter**. The browser console returns "<a href="#">Tickets</a>," which is the link code and text for the first item in the navigation bar.

3. On the command line of the browser console, type `document.getElementsByTagName("li")[1].innerHTML`, and then press **Enter**. The browser console returns "<a href="#">Calendar</a>," which is the linke code and text for the second item in the navigation bar.

4. Repeat Step 3 to check the third, fourth, and fifth `li` elements. The browser console should return the values "<a href="#">Players</a>," "<a href="#">News</a>," and "<a href="#">Community</a>," respectively.

5. Close the browser console by clicking the console's **Close button**, or by pressing the same key combination you used to open it. Figure 3-8 shows the location of the Close button on the Firefox console.

Programming Concepts | *Counting from 0*

The fact that programming languages often count items such as array elements starting with 0 rather than 1 is a common source of confusion for new programmers. While it can take some practice to get used to, counting from 0 rather than from 1 makes some advanced coding tasks much easier. In programming, it's often necessary to iterate through multiple sets of data and compare or combine the values. Using an agreed-on standard for the beginning of numbering makes it easier to perform these operations mathematically.

Short Quiz 1

1. How is an array different from a standard variable?

2. How do you create a new empty array?

3. How do you access an individual element in an array?

4. What property do you use to determine the number of elements in an array?

5. How do you use a browser to check the value of a specific array element?

Repeating Code

Often in programming, you need to repeat the same statement, function, or code section perhaps five times, 10 times, or 100 times. For example, you might want to perform the same calculation until a specific number is found. In that case, you would need to use a **loop statement**, a control flow statement that repeatedly executes a statement or a series of statements while the value of a specific condition is truthy or until the value of a specific condition becomes truthy. In this chapter, you'll learn about three types of loop statements: `while` statements, `do/while` statements, and `for` statements.

`while` Statements

One of the simplest types of loop statements is the **`while` statement**, which repeats a statement or series of statements as long as a given conditional expression evaluates to a truthy value. The syntax for the `while` statement is

```
while (expression) {
    statements
}
```

The conditional expression in the `while` statement is enclosed within parentheses following the keyword `while`. The conditional expression generally includes a variable whose value is changed by one or more statements in the `statements` code. Each time the statements finish executing, the expression is reevaluated. If the expression evaluates to a truthy value, the statements are executed again; if the expression evaluates to a falsy value, the `while` loop ends. Each repetition of a looping statement is called an **iteration**.

To ensure that a `while` statement ends after the desired tasks have been performed, you must include code that tracks the progress of the loop and changes the value produced by the conditional expression. You can track the progress of a `while` statement, or any other loop, with a **counter**. A **counter** is a variable that is incremented (increased) or decremented (decreased) with each iteration of a loop statement.

> **Note**
>
> Many programmers often name counter variables *count*, *counter*, or something similar. The letters *i*, *j*, *k*, *l*, *x*, *y*, and *z* are also commonly used as counter names. Using a name such as *count*, the letter *i* (for increment), or a higher letter helps you remember (and lets other programmers know) that the variable is being used as a counter.

The following code shows a simple script that includes a `while` statement. The script declares a variable named `count` and assigns it an initial value of 1. The `count` variable is then used in the `while` statement conditional expression (`count <= 5`). As long as the `count` variable is less than or equal to 5, the `while` statement loops. Within the body of the `while` statement, the `document.write()` statement prints the value of the `count` variable, then the `count` variable increments by a value of 1. The `while` statement loops until the `count` variable increments to a value of 6.

```
1    var count = 1;
2    while (count <= 5) {
3        document.write(count + "<br />");
4        count++;
5    }
6    document.write("<p>You have printed 5 numbers.</p>");
```

The preceding code prints the numbers 1 through 5, with each number representing one iteration of the loop. When the counter reaches 6, the message "You have printed 5 numbers." prints, thus demonstrating that the loop has ended. Figure 3-11 shows the output of this simple script.

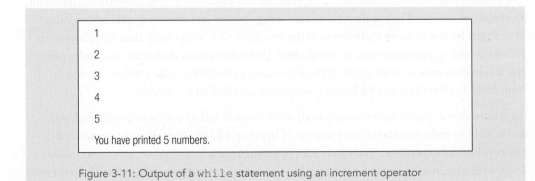

Figure 3-11: Output of a `while` statement using an increment operator

You can also control the repetitions in a `while` loop by decrementing (decreasing the value of) counter variables. Consider the following script:

```
1    var count = 10;
2    while (count > 0) {
3        document.write(count + "<br />");
4        count--;
5    }
6    document.write("<p>We have liftoff.</p>");
```

In this example, the initial value of the `count` variable is 10, and the decrement operator (--) is used to decrease the count by one. When the count variable is greater than 0, the statement within the `while` loop prints the value of the count variable. When the value of count is equal to 0, the `while` loop ends, and the statement immediately following it prints. Figure 3-12 shows the script output.

```
10

9

8

7

6

5

4

3

2

1

We have liftoff.
```

Figure 3-12: Output of a `while` statement using a decrement operator

There are many ways to change the value of a counter variable and to use a counter variable to control the repetitions of a `while` loop. The following example uses the `*=` assignment operator to multiply the value of the count variable by 2. When the `count` variable reaches a value of 128, which is greater than 100, the `while` statement ends, and 128 is not printed.

```
1    var count = 1;
2    while (count <= 100) {
3        document.write(count + "<br />");
4        count *= 2;
5    }
```

Figure 3-13 shows the script output.

```
1
2
4
8
16
32
64
```

Figure 3-13: Output of a `while` statement using the `*=` assignment operator

To ensure that a `while` statement will eventually end, you must include code within the command block that changes the value used by the conditional expression. If you do not include code that changes this value, your program will be caught in an infinite loop. In an **infinite loop**, a loop statement never ends because its conditional expression is never falsy. Consider the following `while` statement:

```
1    var count = 1;
2    while (count <= 10) {
3        window.alert("The number is " + count + ".");
4    }
```

Although the `while` statement in the preceding example includes a conditional expression that checks the value of a `count` variable, there is no code within the command block that changes the `count` variable value. The `count` variable will continue to have a value of 1 through each iteration of the loop. That means an alert dialog box containing the text string "The number is 1." will appear over and over again, no matter how many times the user clicks the OK button.

Note

In most cases, to end an infinite loop you must close the browser tab or window. If the loop is generating dialog boxes, as in the preceding example, you may need to force the browser to close. The method for forcing an application to close varies from one operating system to another. For most versions of Windows, press Ctrl + Alt + Delete, click Task Manager, click the Applications tab (Windows 7 and earlier only), right-click the browser name, and then click End Task. In Mac OS X, press command + option + esc, and then in the window that opens, click the browser name in the list and click Force Quit.

Next, you will create a function to add strings containing the days of the week to the column headers for the Tipton Turbines calendar table. To do this, you'll use a `while` statement to increment a counter variable, and you'll use the value of the counter variable to identify the array index of the string to work with as well as the index of the `th` element in which to place it.

To create a function using a `while` statement to place the days of the week in the table:

1. Return to the **tt.js** document in your text editor.

2. Below the variable declarations, enter the following code to add a comment and create the structure of a function named **addColumnHeaders()**:

```
1    // function to place daysOfWeek values in header row
2       cells
3    function addColumnHeaders() {

4

5    }
```

3. Within the command block, enter the following statement:

```
var i = 0;
```

This statement creates a counter variable called `i` and sets its value to 0.

4. Below the variable declaration, enter the following code:

```
while (i < 7) {


}
```

This code creates a `while` statement that sets the condition `i < 7`. This means that every time the loop restarts and the value of the counter variable is less than 7, the loop will go through another iteration.

5. Within the command block for the `while` statement, enter the following statement:

```
document.getElementsByTagName("th")[i].innerHTML =
   daysOfWeek[i];
```

Starting at the end, the second part of this statement, `daysOfWeek[i]`, fetches the value from the `daysOfWeek` array that has the index value equal to the counter variable, `i`. The first part of the statement uses the `getElementsByTagName()` method to identify the `th` element that has the index value equal to the counter variable, `i`, and sets the value of its `innerHTML` property to the corresponding value fetched from the `daysOfWeek` array. For instance, in the first iteration of this loop, the value of `i` will be 0. The `getElementsByTagName()` method will identify the first `th` element, representing the column heading for the first column, and set its value to the first value of the `daysOfWeek` array, which is "Sunday".

6. Below the statement you created in the previous step, enter the following statement:

```
i++;
```

This statement increments the counter variable. Following is the completed code for the addColumnHeaders() function.

```
1   // function to place daysOfWeek values in header row↵
2       cells
3       function addColumnHeaders() {
4       var i = 0;
5       while (i < 7) {
6           document.getElementsByTagName("th")[i].innerHTML↵
7               = daysOfWeek[i];
8           i++;
9       }
10  }
```

7. Below the function you just created, enter the following comment and statement:

```
// runs addColumnHeaders() function when page loads
window.addEventListener("load", addColumnHeaders, false);
```

This statement calls the addColumnHeaders() function when the page finishes loading in a browser.

8. Save your changes to **tt.js**, and then reload **calendar.htm** in your browser. As Figure 3-14 shows, the table header rows are now populated with the days of the week in the same order you entered them in the daysOfWeek array.

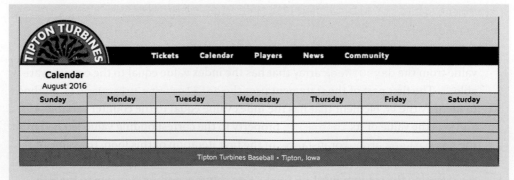

Figure 3-14: The calendar.htm document displaying the column header values

do/while Statements

Another JavaScript looping statement, similar to the while statement, is the do/while statement. The **do/while statement** executes a statement or statements once, then repeats the execution as long as a given conditional expression evaluates to a truthy value. The syntax for the do/while statement is as follows:

```
do {
    statements;
} while (expression);
```

As you can see in the syntax description, the statements execute before the conditional expression is evaluated. Unlike the simpler while statement, the statements in a do/while statement always execute at least once, before the conditional expression is evaluated the first time.

The following do/while statement executes once before the conditional expression evaluates the count variable. Therefore, a single line that reads "The count is equal to 2." prints. When the conditional expression (count < 2) is evaluated, the count variable is equal to 2. This causes the conditional expression to return a value of false, and the do/while statement ends.

```
1    var count = 2;
2    do {
3       document.write("<p>The count is equal to " + count +↵
4          ".</p>");
5       count++;
6    } while (count < 2);
```

Note that this do/while example includes code that operates on a counter variable within the command block. As with the while statement, you need to include code that changes the value of the counter variable in order to prevent an infinite loop.

The following example uses the same basic code as the previous example, but it uses a while statement instead of a do/while statement. Unlike in the do/while statement above, where the code block was executed once before the loop ended, the code block in the while statement below is never executed because the count variable does not fall within the range of the conditional expression:

```
1    var count = 2;
2    while (count < 2) {
3       document.write("<p>The count is equal to " + count +↵
4          ".</p>");
5       count++;
6    }
```

In the previous set of steps, you used a `while` statement to add the values from the `daysOfWeek` array to the Tipton Turbines calendar table. The following statement performs the same action using a `do/while` statement instead:

```
1   var i = 0;
2   do {
3       document.getElementsByTagName("th")[i].innerHTML =↵
4           daysOfWeek[i];
5       i++;
6   } while (i < 7);
```

Notice that the code `while (i < 7)` is moved from before the command block to after it, and the word `do` takes its place. Otherwise, the code using `do/while` is the same as the earlier code using just `while`.

Next, you'll add a function to the tt.js document that will add the days of the month to the calendar table using a `do/while` statement.

To add the days of the month to the calendar using a `do/while` statement:

1. Return to the **tt.js** document in your text editor.

2. Below the `addColumnHeaders()` function, enter the following code to add a comment and create the structure of a new function named `addCalendarDates()`:

```
1   // function to place day of month value in first p↵
2       element
3   // within each table data cell that has an id
4   function addCalendarDates() {
5
6   }
```

3. Within the command block, enter the following statements:

```
var i = 1;
var paragraphs = "";
```

The first statement creates a counter variable called `i` and sets its value to 1. The second statement creates a variable named `paragraphs` and sets its value to an empty string.

4. Below the variable declarations, enter the following code:

```
do {


}
```

This code starts a `do/while` statement with the `do` keyword.

5. Within the code block for the `do` statement, enter the following statement:

```
var tableCell = document.getElementById("08-" + i);
```

This statement creates a variable called `tableCell` and uses the `getElementById()` method to set its value to the element with an `id` value that starts with 08- followed by the value of `i`. This means that in the first iteration of the loop, the table cell variable references the element with the `id` of 08-1, which is the second `td` element in the second row of the table.

6. Below the statement you created in the previous step, enter the following statement:

```
paragraphs = tableCell.getElementsByTagName("p");
```

This statement uses the `getElementsByTagName()` method to look up all `p` elements within the current cell (designated by the `tableCell` variable), and stores the values as an array in the `paragraphs` variable.

7. Below the statement you created in the previous step, enter the following statement:

```
paragraphs[0].innerHTML = i;
```

This statement assigns the value of the counter variable, `i`, as the content of the first paragraph (numbered 0) in the current cell. The first time through the loop, this places the value 1 in the cell for the first day of the month.

8. Below the statement you created in the previous step, enter the following statement:

```
i++;
```

This statement increments the counter variable.

9. After the closing } for the `do` command block, but before the closing } for the function, add the following statement:

```
while (i <= 31);
```

This conditional statement determines whether the `do` command block is repeated for another iteration. Because the month of August has 31 days, the block should be executed 31 times. After the 31st time, the counter variable will be 32, which is not less than or equal to 31, so the do/while statement will end without iterating again. The following shows the completed code for the addCalendarDates() function.

```
1   // function to place day of month value in first p↵
2      element
3   // within each table data cell that has an id
4   function addCalendarDates() {
5      var i = 1;
6      var paragraphs = "";
7      do {
8         var tableCell = document.getElementById("08-" + i);
9         paragraphs = tableCell.getElementsByTagName("p");
10        paragraphs[0].innerHTML = i;
11        i++;
12     } while (i <= 31);
13  }
```

Because you now have multiple functions to run when the page loads, you'll create a master function to call when the page loads. This function will in turn call each of the functions that needs to run on page load.

10. Below the function you just created, enter the following comment and statement:

```
1   // function to populate calendar
2   function setUpPage() {
3      addColumnHeaders();
4      addCalendarDates();
5  }
```

This code creates a new function named setUpPage() that calls the addColumnHeaders() and addCalendarDates() functions. You need to change the event listener to call this function when the page finishes loading.

11. In the last two lines of the tt.js file, replace both occurrences of addColumnHeaders with **setUpPage** so your code matches the following:

```
// runs setUpPage() function when page loads
window.addEventListener("load", setUpPage, false);
```

12. Save your changes to **tt.js**, and then reload **calendar.htm** in your browser. As Figure 3-15 shows, the table cells containing the days of the month have been populated with consecutive numbers from 1-31.

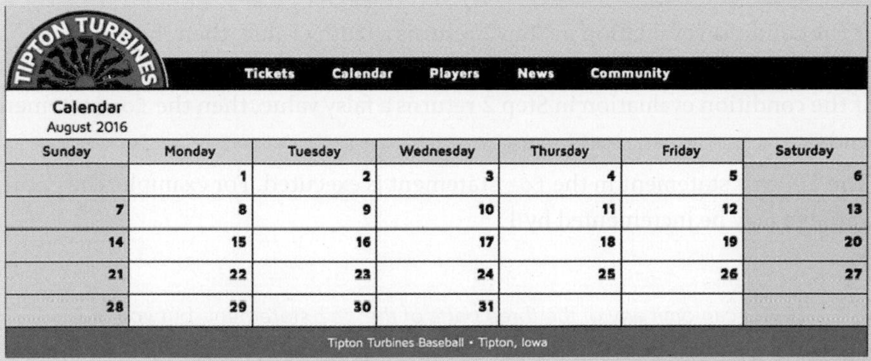

Figure 3-15: The calendar.htm document displaying the days of the month

for Statements

So far you have learned how to use the `while` and the `do/while` statements to repeat, or loop through, code. You can also use the `for` statement to loop through code. The `for statement` is used to repeat a statement or series of statements as long as a given conditional expression evaluates to a truthy value. The `for` statement performs essentially the same function as the `while` statement: if a conditional expression within the `for` statement evaluates to a truthy value, then the code block in the `for` statement is executed, and then the conditional expression is reevaluated. The loop continues to execute repeatedly until the conditional expression evaluates to a falsy value.

One of the primary differences between the `while` statement and the `for` statement is that, in addition to a conditional expression, the parentheses after the `for` keyword at the start of the expression can also include code that initializes a counter and changes its value with each iteration. This is useful because it provides a specific place for you to declare and initialize a counter, and to update its value, which helps prevent infinite loops. The syntax of the `for` statement is as follows:

```
for (counter_declaration; condition; counter_operation) {
    statements
}
```

When a JavaScript interpreter encounters a `for` loop, the following steps occur:

1. The counter variable is declared and initialized. For example, if the initialization expression in a `for` loop is `var count = 1;`, then a variable named `count` is declared and assigned an initial value of 1. The initialization expression is only executed once, when the `for` loop is first encountered.

2. The `for` loop condition is evaluated.

3. If the condition evaluation in Step 2 returns a truthy value, then the `for` loop statements are executed, Step 4 occurs, and the process starts over again with Step 2. If the condition evaluation in Step 2 returns a falsy value, then the `for` statement ends.

4. The `update` statement in the `for` statement is executed. For example, the `count` variable may be incremented by 1.

> **Note**
>
> You can omit any of the three parts of the `for` statement, but you must include the semicolons that separate the sections. If you omit a section, be sure that you include code within the command block that will end the `for` statement or your program may get caught in an infinite loop.

The following script demonstrates a `for` statement that prints the contents of an array:

```
1    var brightestStars =
2        ["Sirius", "Canopus", "Arcturus", "Rigel", "Vega"];
3    for (var count = 0; count < brightestStars.length;↵
4        count++) {
5        document.write(brightestStars[count] + "<br />");
6    }
```

As you can see in this example, the counter is initialized, evaluated, and incremented within the parentheses. You do not need to include a declaration for the `count` variable before the `for` statement, nor do you need to increment the `count` variable within the command block of the `for` statement. Figure 3-16 shows the output.

Figure 3-16: Output of brightest stars script

Using a `for` statement is more efficient than a `while` statement because you do not need as many lines of code. Consider the following `while` statement:

```
1    var count = 1;
2    while (count < brightestStars.length) {
3        document.write(count + "<br />");
4        count++;
5    }
```

You could achieve the same flow control more efficiently by using a `for` statement as follows:

```
1    for (var count = 1; count < brightestStars.length;↵
2            count++) {
3        document.write(count + "<br />");
4    }
```

The following code shows a revised version of the `addColumnHeaders()` function you created earlier in the chapter. You originally created this function using a `while` statement, but the rewritten version below performs the same actions using a `for` statement instead.

```
1    function addColumnHeaders() {
2        for (var i = 0; i < 7; i++) {
3            document.getElementsByTagName("th")[i].innerHTML↵
4                = daysOfWeek[i];
5        }
6    }
```

Notice that the declaration of the `count` variable, the conditional expression, and the statement that increments the `count` variable are now all contained in the parentheses after the `for` keyword. Using a `for` statement instead of a `do/while` statement simplifies the script somewhat, because you do not need as many lines of code.

Next, you add another function to the tt.js file. This function will use a `for` statement to add the names of the opposing teams from the `opponents` array to the second paragraph in each table cell that represents a date in August.

To add a function to populate the calendar dates with the opposing team names using a `for` statement:

1. Return to the **tt.js** document in your text editor.

2. Below the `addCalendarDates()` function, enter the following code to add a comment and create the structure of a new function named `addGameInfo()`:

```
1   // function to place opponents values in
2   // second p element within each table data cell that has an id
3   function addGameInfo() {

4

5   }
```

3. Within the command block, enter the following code:

```
var paragraphs = "";
```

This code creates a variable named `paragraphs` and sets its value to an empty string.

4. Below the variable declaration, enter the following code:

```
for (var i = 0; i < 31; i++) {

}
```

This code starts a `for` statement. It creates a counter variable named `i` and sets its value to 0. It specifies the condition `i < 31`; as long as this condition is satisfied, the `for` command block will repeat. Finally, the code `i++` increments the `i` counter variable with each iteration.

5. Within the code block for the `for` statement, enter the following statement:

```
var date = i + 1;
```

This statement creates a variable called `date` and assigns a value to it equal to the value of the counter variable, `i`, plus 1.

6. Below the statement you created in the previous step, enter the following statement:

```
var tableCell = document.getElementById("08-" + date);
```

This statement creates a variable called `tableCell` and uses the `getElementById()` method to set its value to the element with an `id` value that starts with 08- followed by the value of `i`.

7. Below the statement you created in the previous step, enter the following statement:

```
paragraphs = tableCell.getElementsByTagName("p");
```

This statement uses the `getElementsByTagName()` method to look up all p elements within the current cell (designated by the `tableCell` variable) and stores the values as an array in the `paragraphs` variable.

8. Below the statement you created in the previous step, enter the following statement:

```
paragraphs[1].innerHTML = opponents[i];
```

This statement fetches the value in the `opponents` array whose index matches the current value of the counter variable, `i`, and assigns its value as the content of the second paragraph (numbered 1) in the current cell. The following shows the completed code for the `addGameInfo()` function.

```
1    // function to place opponents in second
2    // p element within each table data cell that has an id
3    function addGameInfo() {
4        var paragraphs = "";
5        for (var i = 0; i < 31; i++) {
6            var date = i + 1;
7            var tableCell = document.getElementById("08-" +↵
8                date);
9            paragraphs = tableCell.getElementsByTagName("p");
10           paragraphs[1].innerHTML += opponents[i];
11       }
12   }
```

9. Within the `setUpPage()` function, before the closing `}`, add the statement **addGameInfo();** so your `setUpPage()` function matches the following:

```
1    function setUpPage() {
2        addColumnHeaders();
3        addCalendarDates();
4        addGameInfo();
5    }
```

> **Note** | This book uses a yellow highlight to call attention to changes in existing code.

Calling the `addGameInfo()` function you just created within the `setUpPage()` function ensures that the calendar is populated with opponent information when the page is loaded.

10. Save your changes to **tt.js**, and then reload **calendar.htm** in your browser. As Figure 3-17 shows, the table cells containing the days of the month now also display the name of each day's opponent, or "(off)" if no opponent is scheduled.

Figure 3-17: The calendar.htm document displaying the opposing team names

Using `continue` Statements to Restart Execution

In some situations, you want a loop to continue even when its condition evaluates to a falsy value. You can do this using the **continue statement**, which restarts a loop with a new iteration. For example, suppose that you have a script that uses a `for` statement to loop through the elements of an array containing a list of stocks. For stocks worth more than $10, the script prints information such as purchase price and number of shares on the screen. However, for stocks worth less than $10, you use the `continue` statement to skip that stock and move on to a new iteration. In this situation, the `continue` statement allows you to check all the contents of an array while performing operations only on those array elements that satisfy the condition.

In the following code, when the `count` variable equals 3, the `continue` statement also stops the current iteration of the `for` loop, and the script skips printing the number 3. However, the loop continues to iterate until the conditional expression `count <= 5` is `false`.

```
1    for (var count = 1; count <= 5; count++) {
2        if (count === 3) {
3            continue;
4        }
5        document.write("<p>" + count + "</p>");
6    }
```

Figure 3-18 shows the output in a web browser.

```
1
2
4
5
```

Figure 3-18: Output of a `for` loop with a `continue` statement

Skills at Work | *Communicating the Structure of a Program with a Flow Chart*

When designing a program that involves loops, especially a large and complex program, it can be challenging to explain the structure of the program and the relationships between its parts to other team members who might be working with you to create it. It's common for programmers to create a visual representation to illustrate the parts of a program and how they fit together, both before and during development. For loops, such diagrams often take the form of a flow chart, which shows program components as boxes of different shapes, with lines connecting those components that communicate with each other. A flow chart often includes arrows to indicate the direction that information flows between components. While software is available to create professional-looking flow charts, most programmers create flowcharts on white boards.

Short Quiz 2

1. What is the role of a counter in a repetition statement?
2. What are the differences between a `while` and `do/while` statement?
3. Which repetition statement allows you to initialize a counter variable as part of its syntax?
4. How do you force a new iteration of a loop even when its condition evaluates to a falsy value?

Making Decisions

When you write a computer program, regardless of the programming language, you often need to execute different sets of statements depending on some predetermined criteria. For example, you might create a program that needs to execute one set of code in the morning and another set of code at night. Or you might create a program that must execute one set of code when it's running on a larger screen, like a desktop or notebook computer, and another when it runs on a smaller screen, like a tablet or mobile phone. Additionally, you might create a program that depends on user input to determine exactly what code to run. For instance, suppose you create a web page through which users place online orders. If a user clicks the Add to Shopping Cart button, a set of statements that builds a list of items to be purchased must execute. However, if the user clicks the Checkout button, an entirely different set of statements, which completes the transaction, must execute.

The process of choosing which code to execute at a given point in an application is known as **decision making**. The special types of JavaScript statements used for making decisions are called **decision-making statements**, **decision-making structures**, or **conditional statements**. The most common type of decision-making statement is the `if` statement.

`if` Statements

The `if statement` is used to execute specific programming code if the evaluation of a conditional expression returns a truthy value.

> **Note** | *Recall that a falsy value is one of six values that are treated in comparison operations as the Boolean value `false`, and that a truthy value is any value other than the six falsy values.*

The syntax for a simple `if` statement is as follows:

```
if (condition) {
    statements
}
```

The term `condition` is a conditional expression and `statements` represents one or more executable statements. The `if` statement always starts with the keyword `if`, and the conditional expression must be enclosed within parentheses. While the braces are optional around a single statement, always including them is considered a best practice for creating self-documenting code, as well as for avoiding unexpected results when a browser processes your code. In JavaScript, a set of statements contained within a set of braces is known as a **command block**. If the condition being evaluated by an `if` statement returns a truthy value, then the statements within the command block are executed. After the command block executes, the program continues on to execute any code after the command block. If the condition instead evaluates to a falsy value, the `if` statement command block is skipped, and the program continues on to execute any statements after the command block.

So far, you've created functions to add column headers, dates, and opponent names to the calendar page for the Tipton Turbines. To complete the calendar, you need to add one additional piece of information: whether each game is being played at home or away. You've stored this information in the `gameLocation` array. You'll add `if` statements to the `addGameInfo()` function to insert the appropriate content in the calendar based on whether the game is home or away, or the team is off for the day. If the team is playing at home, you'll insert the value "vs" followed by a space. If the team is playing away, you'll insert the character "@" followed by a space. If the team is off for the day, you won't insert any text.

To add the home/away information to the calendar using `if` statements:

1. Return to the **tt.js** document in your text editor.

2. Within the `addGameInfo()` function, within the data block for the `for` loop, insert a new line before the final statement, enter the code `if (gameLocation[i] === "away") {`, press **Enter** twice, and then enter a closing `}` as shown below:

```
1          paragraphs = tableCell.getElementsByTagName("p");
2          if (gameLocation[i] === "away") {
3
4          }
5      }
6  }
```

This code starts with the `if` keyword to create an `if` statement, followed by parentheses containing the `if` condition. The statement tests whether the element of the `gameLocation` array with the index value equal to the counter variable, `i`, equals the string "away".

> **Note**
>
> *Some developers add comments to their closing braces to indicate what statement each brace ends. For instance, after the first closing brace in Step 2, you might add the comment `// end if` to indicate that the brace closes the preceding `if` statement. Especially when your code includes structures nested several levels deep, such comments can make it easier to add or remove levels of nesting.*

3. Within the command block for the `if` statement, enter the statement `paragraphs[1].innerHTML = "@ ";` as shown below:

```
1    var paragraphs = "";
2            if (gameLocation[i] === "away") {
3                paragraphs[1].innerHTML = "@ ";
4            }
```

This statement sets the content of the first paragraph in the current cell equal to "@ ".

4. Below the command block you just created, in the final line of code for the `for` loop, change = to **+=** so the statement matches the following:

```
paragraphs[1].innerHTML += opponents[i];
```

Because you've just added content to the second paragraph using your `if` statement, you want to ensure that the name of the opposing team is concatenated to the existing content (+=) rather than replacing it (=).

5. Save your changes to **tt.js**, and then reload **calendar.htm** in your browser. As Figure 3-19 shows, "@" followed by a space is now displayed before the opponent names in some of the table cells. These dates correspond to the elements in the `gameLocation` array with a value of "away."

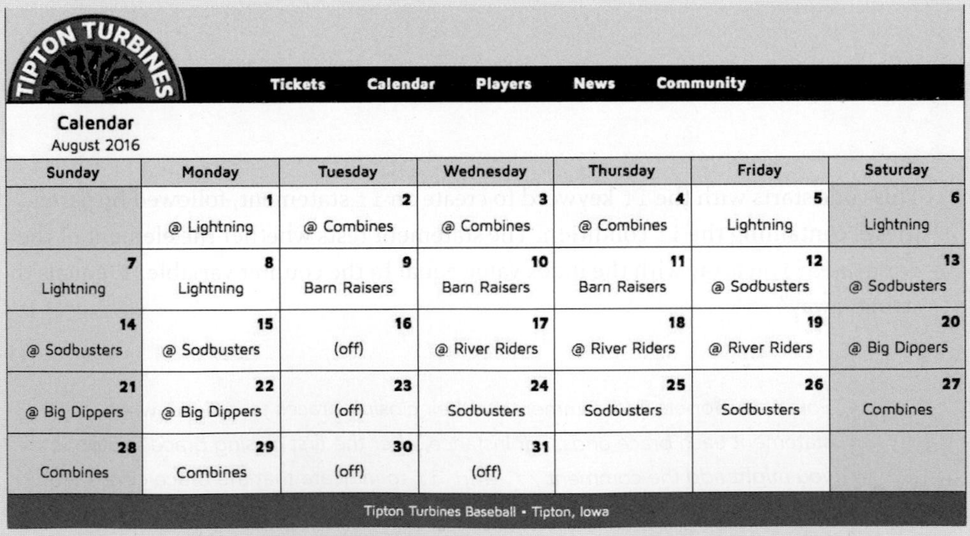

Figure 3-19: The calendar.htm document displaying @ before the names of away opponents

To add the text "vs" followed by a space before the names of opponents for home games, you need to create another if statement.

6. Return to **tt.js** in your text editor, and then, immediately after the closing } for the if statement you created in the previous steps, enter the following code to create a second if statement:

```
if (gameLocation[i] === "home") {
   paragraphs[1].innerHTML = "vs ";
}
```

This statement creates a second if statement. It checks if the element in the gameLocation array with the index equal to the counter variable is equal to "home" and if so, sets the content of the second paragraph of the current cell to "vs ".

7. In the first comment line before the start of the addGameInfo() function, after the word "opponents," insert **and gameLocation values**. The following code shows the completed addGameInfo() function:

```
1    // function to place opponents and gameLocation values in
2    // second p element within each table data cell that has an id
3    function addGameInfo() {
4       var paragraphs = "";
5       for (var i = 0; i < 31; i++) {
6          var date = i + 1;
7          var tableCell = document.getElementById("08-" +↵
8             date);
9          paragraphs = tableCell.getElementsByTagName("p");
10         if (gameLocation[i] === "away") {
11            paragraphs[1].innerHTML = "@ ";
12         }
13         if (gameLocation[i] === "home") {
14            paragraphs[1].innerHTML = "vs ";
15         }
16         paragraphs[1].innerHTML += opponents[i];
17      }
18   }
```

8. Save your changes to **tt.js**, and then reload **calendar.htm** in your browser. As Figure 3-20 shows, "vs" followed by a space is now displayed before the opponent names in some of the table cells. These dates correspond to the elements in the `gameLocation` array with a value of "home."

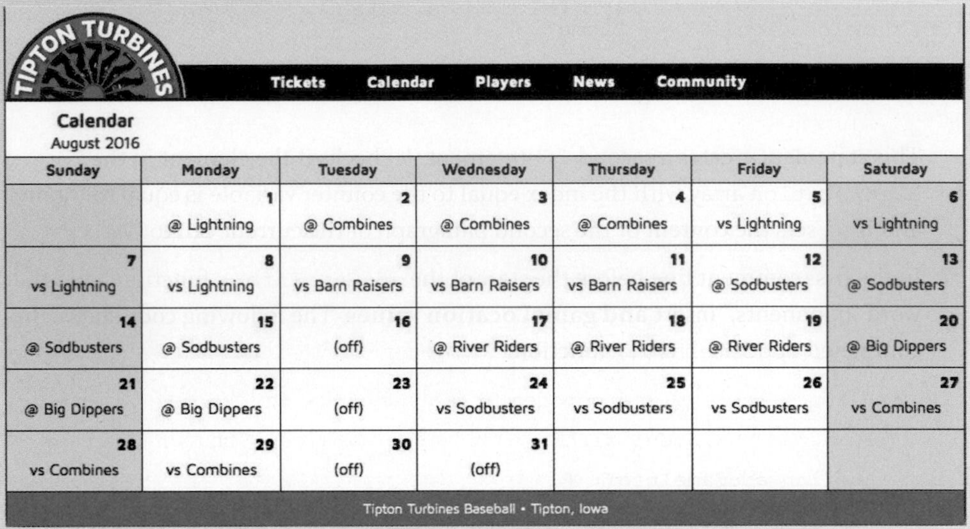

Sunday	Monday	Tuesday	Wednesday	Thursday	Friday	Saturday
	1 @ Lightning	2 @ Combines	3 @ Combines	4 @ Combines	5 vs Lightning	6 vs Lightning
7 vs Lightning	8 vs Lightning	9 vs Barn Raisers	10 vs Barn Raisers	11 vs Barn Raisers	12 @ Sodbusters	13 @ Sodbusters
14 @ Sodbusters	15 @ Sodbusters	16 (off)	17 @ River Riders	18 @ River Riders	19 @ River Riders	20 @ Big Dippers
21 @ Big Dippers	22 @ Big Dippers	23 (off)	24 vs Sodbusters	25 vs Sodbusters	26 vs Sodbusters	27 vs Combines
28 vs Combines	29 vs Combines	30 (off)	31 (off)			

Tipton Turbines Baseball • Tipton, Iowa

Figure 3-20: The calendar.htm document displaying "vs" before the names of home opponents

Note

You could add a third `if` statement to the `addGameInfo()` function to cover the case when an element of the `gameLocation` array has a value of "". However, because no text needs to be inserted in such a case, there's no need to add this extra code to your function.

if/else Statements

So far you've learned how to use an `if` statement to execute one or more statements if a condition evaluates to a truthy value. In some situations, however, you may want to execute one set of statements when a condition evaluates to a truthy value and another set of statements when the condition evaluates to a falsy value. You can accomplish this by adding an `else` clause to your `if` statement. For instance, suppose you create a web page form that asks users to indicate by clicking an option button whether they invest in the stock market. An `if` statement in the script might contain a conditional expression that evaluates the user's input. If the condition evaluates to `true` (that is, if the user clicked the "yes" option), then the `if` statement would display a web page on recommended stocks. If the condition evaluates to `false` (that is, if the user clicked the "no" option), then the statements in an `else` clause would display a web page on other types of investment opportunities.

An `if` statement that includes an `else` clause is called an **if/else statement**. You can think of an `else` clause as a backup plan that is implemented when the condition returns a falsy value. The syntax for an `if/else` statement is as follows:

```
1    if (expression) {
2        statements
3    }
4    else {
5        statements
6    }
```

> **Note** The `if/else` statement is equivalent to the conditional operator (`?:`), which you learned about in Chapter 1. Although the conditional operator is more compact, it's easier to recognize at a glance what an `if/else` statement is doing.

The following code shows an example of an `if/else` statement:

```
1    var today = "Tuesday"
2    if (today === "Monday") {
3        document.write("<p>Today is Monday</p>");
4    }
5    else {
6        document.write("<p>Today is not Monday</p>");
7    }
```

In the preceding code, the `today` variable is assigned a value of "Tuesday". If the condition (`today === "Monday"`) evaluates to `false`, control of the program passes to the `else` clause, and the statement `document.write("<p>Today is not Monday</p>");` is executed, causing the string "Today is not Monday" to print. If the `today` variable had instead been assigned a value of "Monday," the condition (`today === "Monday"`) would have evaluated to `true`, and the statement `document.write("<p>Today is Monday</p>");` would have been executed. Only one set of statements executes in an `if/else` statement: either the statements following the `if` statement or the statements following the `else` clause.

The JavaScript code for the calendar.htm document you created earlier uses multiple *if* statements to evaluate the contents of the gameLocation array and decide what value to insert into the current table cell. Although the multiple *if* statements function properly, they can be combined into an if/else statement. Next, you will replace the multiple if statements in the addGameInfo() function with a single if/else statement.

To add an *if/else* statement to the *addGameInfo()* function:

1. Return to the **tt.js** document in your text editor.

2. Within the addGameInfo() function, within the data block for the for loop, insert **/*** before the start of the first *if* statement, and add ***/** after the closing } for the second *if* statement, as shown below:

```
1    for (var i = 0; i < 31; i++) {
2        var date = i + 1;
3        var tableCell = document.getElementById("08-" + date);
4        paragraphs = tableCell.getElementsByTagName("p");
5    /*   if (gameLocation[i] === "away") {
6            paragraphs[1].innerHTML = "@ ";
7        }
8        if (gameLocation[i] === "home") {
9            paragraphs[1].innerHTML = "vs ";
10       }*/
11       paragraphs[1].innerHTML += opponents[i];
12   }
```

The if statements are now treated as comments, and will not be processed by JavaScript interpreters. This allows you to keep the code available for reference without it being part of your program.

3. Within the command block for the `for` statement, add a new line below the closing `*/` you entered in the previous step, and then enter the following code:

```
if (gameLocation[i] === "away") {
    paragraphs[1].innerHTML = "@ ";
}
```

This is the same `if` statement you entered in the previous set of steps. Instead of standing alone, however, this time it will serve as the start of an `if/else` construction.

4. Below the command block you just created, enter the following code:

```
else {
    paragraphs[1].innerHTML = "vs ";
}
```

In place of the `if` statement from the previous set of steps, which had its own condition, this `else` statement simply provides a single line of code to be executed if the original condition evaluates to `false`. The revised `for` statement in the `addGameInfo()` function should match the following code:

```
1    for (var i = 0; i < 31; i++) {
2        var date = i + 1;
3        var tableCell = document.getElementById("08-" + date);
4        paragraphs = tableCell.getElementsByTagName("p");
5    /*    if (gameLocation[i] === "away") {
6            paragraphs[1].innerHTML = "@ ";
7        }
8        if (gameLocation[i] === "home") {
9            paragraphs[1].innerHTML = "vs ";
10       }*/
11       if (gameLocation[i] === "away") {
12           paragraphs[1].innerHTML = "@ ";
13       }
14       else {
15           paragraphs[1].innerHTML = "vs ";
16       }
17       paragraphs[1].innerHTML += opponents[i];
18   }
```

5. Save your changes to **tt.js**, and then reload **calendar.htm** in your browser. As Figure 3-21 shows, the text "@" and "vs" is still inserted into the cells containing August dates. However, note that "vs" is also inserted before the text "(off)" for the four dates when no game will be played. Because you removed the condition specified by the second `if` statement and replaced it with a default value for all instances where the first condition didn't evaluate to `true`, the text "vs" is displayed in cells whose corresponding `gameLocation` values are "home" as well as in those whose value is "". To fix this issue, you need to use a nested `if` statement.

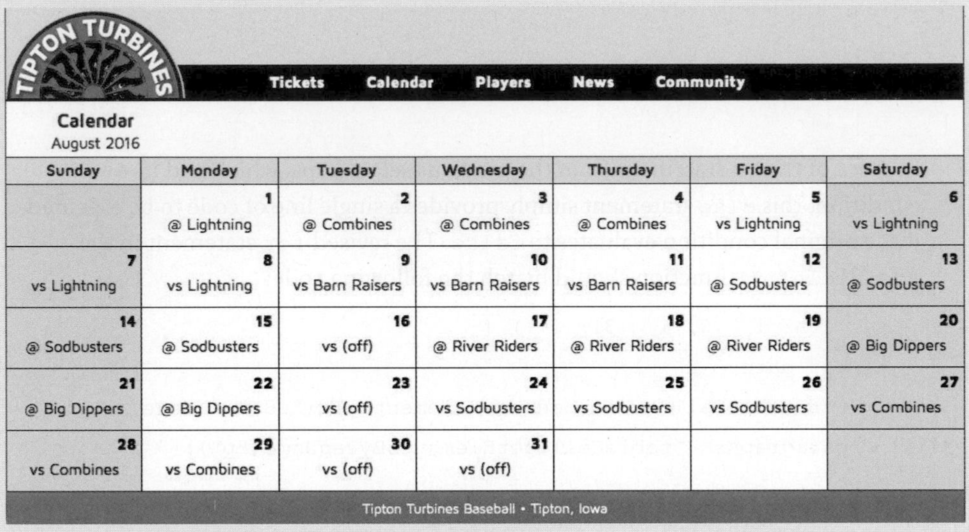

Sunday	Monday	Tuesday	Wednesday	Thursday	Friday	Saturday
	1 @ Lightning	2 @ Combines	3 @ Combines	4 @ Combines	5 vs Lightning	6 vs Lightning
7 vs Lightning	8 vs Lightning	9 vs Barn Raisers	10 vs Barn Raisers	11 vs Barn Raisers	12 @ Sodbusters	13 @ Sodbusters
14 @ Sodbusters	15 @ Sodbusters	16 vs (off)	17 @ River Riders	18 @ River Riders	19 @ River Riders	20 @ Big Dippers
21 @ Big Dippers	22 @ Big Dippers	23 vs (off)	24 vs Sodbusters	25 vs Sodbusters	26 vs Sodbusters	27 vs Combines
28 vs Combines	29 vs Combines	30 vs (off)	31 vs (off)			

Figure 3-21: The calendar.htm document populated using an `if/else` statement

Nested `if` and `if/else` Statements

As you have seen, you can use a decision-making statement such as an `if` or `if/else` statement to allow a program to make decisions about which statements to execute. In some cases, however, you may want the statements executed by the decision-making statement to make other decisions. For instance, you may have a program that uses an `if` statement to ask users if they like sports. If users answer yes, you may want to run another `if` statement that asks users whether they prefer team sports or individual sports. You can include any code you like within the code block for an `if` statement or an `if/else` statement, and that includes other `if` or `if/else` statements.

Nesting one decision-making statement within another decision-making statement creates a **nested decision-making structure**. An `if` statement contained within an `if` statement or within an `if/else` statement is called a nested `if` statement. Similarly, an `if/else` statement contained within an `if` or `if/else` statement is called a nested `if/else` statement. You use nested `if` and `if/else` statements to perform conditional evaluations that must be executed after the original conditional evaluation. For example, the following code evaluates two conditional expressions before the `write()` statement is executed:

```
1    var salesTotal = 75;
2    if (salesTotal > 50) {
3        if (salesTotal < 100) {
4            document.write("<p>The sales total is between 50↵
5                and 100.</p>");
6        }
7    }
```

The `document.write()` statement in the preceding example is executed only if the conditional expressions in both `if` statements evaluate to `true`.

The `if/else` statement you added to the `addGameInfo()` function doesn't work correctly because it can't differentiate between `gameLocation` values of `"home"` and `""`. To add back the ability to make this distinction, you'll make the second clause a nested `if` statement that tests for the second condition.

To add a nested `if` statement to the `addGameInfo()` function:

1. Return to the **tt.js** document in your text editor.

2. Within the `addGameInfo()` function, add a new line below the code `else {`, and then enter the code `if (gameLocation[i] === "home") {`.

3. Add a new line below the statement `paragraphs[1].innerHTML = "vs ";`, and then type a closing `}`. Your completed `if/else` statement containing a nested `if` statement should match the code shown below:

```
1    if (gameLocation[i] === "away") {
2        paragraphs[1].innerHTML = "@ ";
3    }
4    else {
5        if (gameLocation[i] === "home") {
6            paragraphs[1].innerHTML = "vs ";
7        }
8    }
```

The nested `if` statement you just created specifies that the text "vs " should be inserted only if the current element in the `gameLocation` array has a value of "home". This means that any `gameLocation` elements with values of `""` will not meet the condition and the text "vs " will not be added to those cells.

4. Save your changes to **tt.js**, and then reload **calendar.htm** in your browser. As Figure 3-22 shows, the text "vs" is still inserted into the cells for home games, but it is no longer added to cells that contain the text "(off)".

		Tipton Turbines				
Tickets		Calendar	Players	News	Community	

Calendar
August 2016

Sunday	Monday	Tuesday	Wednesday	Thursday	Friday	Saturday
	1 @ Lightning	2 @ Combines	3 @ Combines	4 @ Combines	5 vs Lightning	6 vs Lightning
7 vs Lightning	8 vs Lightning	9 vs Barn Raisers	10 vs Barn Raisers	11 vs Barn Raisers	12 @ Sodbusters	13 @ Sodbusters
14 @ Sodbusters	15 @ Sodbusters	16 (off)	17 @ River Riders	18 @ River Riders	19 @ River Riders	20 @ Big Dippers
21 @ Big Dippers	22 @ Big Dippers	23 (off)	24 vs Sodbusters	25 vs Sodbusters	26 vs Sodbusters	27 vs Combines
28 vs Combines	29 vs Combines	30 (off)	31 (off)			

Tipton Turbines Baseball • Tipton, Iowa

Figure 3-22: The calendar.htm document populated using a nested `if` statement

else if Statements

JavaScript supports a compact version of nested `if`/`else` statements known as an **else if construction**. In an `else if` construction, you combine an `else` statement with its nested `if` statement. The resulting statement requires fewer characters to create and is easier to read. For example, you could replace the `else` statement and its nested `if` statement from the previous steps with the following `else if` statement:

```
else if (gameLocation[i] === "home") {
   paragraphs[1].innerHTML = "vs ";
}
```

These three lines of code replace five lines in the previous version. In addition, these lines consist of only a single command block, rather than one nested inside another.

The `else if` construction is commonly used to enhance event listeners so they're backward-compatible with older browsers. Although modern browsers have all standardized on the `addEventListener` method for creating event listeners, Internet Explorer version 8 and earlier used the `attachEvent` method instead. You can use an `else if` statement to create code that checks if either method is supported in the current browser, and if so, adds an event listener using the correct syntax. For instance, if your web page included a submit button with the id of button, and you wanted to submit its contents with a function named submitForm(), you could use the following cross-browser code to create an event listener:

```
1    // add backward compatible event listener to Submit↵
2      button
3    var submitButton = document.getElementById("button");
4    if (submitButton.addEventListener) {
5        submitButton.addEventListener("click", submitForm, ↵
6            false);
7    }
8    else if (submitButton.attachEvent) {
9        submitButton.attachEvent("onclick", submitForm);
10   }
```

This code checks if the addEventListener method exists for the button. If it does, the standard code using the addEventListener method is executed. If not, the program checks if the attachEvent method exists for the button. If it does, the older IE-specific attachEvent syntax is used to add an event listener. If neither of these conditions evaluates to a truthy value, then neither method is executed. Note that the attachEvent method always includes "on" at the start of the event name—in this example, onclick instead of simply click.

> **Note**
>
> Just as in the previous set of steps, you could use a nested if statement instead of an else if statement to create a backward-compatible event listener. The advantage to using an else if statement is that it makes your code more compact without making it more difficult to understand.

You'll enhance the event listener for the load event on the window object to incorporate an else if construction for compatibility with IE8.

To add an else if construction to the event listener:

1. If you have access to Internet Explorer 8, open **calendar.htm** in that browser. The calendar cells are empty, as in Figure 3-7. Because IE8 doesn't recognize the addEventListener() method, the browser doesn't run the page setup functions after loading the page.

> **Note**
>
> Even if you don't have access to Internet Explorer 8, you should still complete the remaining steps.

2. Return to the **tt.js** document in your text editor, and then scroll down to the event listener code at the end of the document.

3. Enclose the existing `addEventListener()` statement within an `if` statement, as follows:

```
if (window.addEventListener) {
    window.addEventListener("load", setUpPage, false);
}
```

4. After the closing } you just entered, on the same line, type a **space** followed by **else if (window.attachEvent) {**.

5. Below the `else if` statement, enter the following code:

```
    window.attachEvent("onload", setUpPage);
}
```

Your completed `else if` construction should match the following:

```
if (window.addEventListener) {
    window.addEventListener("load", setUpPage, false);
} else if (window.attachEvent) {
    window.attachEvent("onload", setUpPage);
}
```

6. Save your changes to **tt.js** and then, if available, reload **calendar.htm** in Internet Explorer 8. All of the calendar content is now displayed as shown in Figure 3-22. This is because IE8 returns a truthy value for the `window.attachEvent` condition of the `else if` clause, and then it executes the `attachEvent()` method to call the `setUpPage` when the document finishes loading.

switch Statements

Another JavaScript statement used for controlling flow is the `switch` statement. The `switch statement` executes a specific set of statements, depending on the value of an expression. The `switch` statement compares the value of an expression to a value contained within a special statement called a `case` label. A **case label** in a `switch` statement represents a specific value. Each `case` label is followed by one or more statements that are executed if the value of the `case` label matches the value of the `switch` statement's expression. The syntax for the `switch` statement is as follows:

```
1    switch (expression) {
2        case label:
3            statements;
4            break;
```

```
 5      case label:
 6          statements;
 7          break;
 8          ...
 9      default:
10          statements;
11          break;
12   }
```

A `case` label consists of the keyword `case`, followed by a literal value or variable name, followed by a colon. JavaScript compares the value returned from the `switch` statement expression to the literal value or variable name following the `case` keyword. If a match is found, the statements following that `case` label are executed.

For example, imagine you were creating a web page for a community pool that offers swimming lessons for children. Your script might store the child's age entered by a user in a variable named `swimmerAge`. You could then use a `switch` statement to evaluate the variable and compare it to `case` labels within the `switch` construct for different ages. One case label might be 6, with statements following it that are executed if the age a user provides is 6. Although you could accomplish the same task by using `if` or `if/else` statements, a `switch` statement makes it easier to organize the different branches of code that can be executed.

> **Note**
>
> A single statement or multiple statements can follow a `case` label. However, unlike `if` statements, multiple statements for a `case` label do not need to be enclosed within a command block.

Another type of label used within `switch` statements is the `default` label. The **default label** is followed by statements that are executed when the value returned by the `switch` statement expression does not match a `case` label. A `default` label consists of the keyword `default` followed by a colon.

Best Practices | Ending `case` Statements with `break;`

When a `switch` statement is executed, the value returned by the expression is compared to each `case` label in the order in which it is encountered. When a matching label is found, its statements are executed. Unlike with the `if/else` statement, though, execution of a `switch` statement

Continued on next page...

does not automatically stop after the statements for a particular case label are executed. Instead, by default the switch statement continues evaluating the rest of the case labels in the list, an event known as **fallthrough**. Generally, though, once a matching case label is found, evaluation of additional case labels is unnecessary. In addition, the fact that statements for multiple case labels can be executed is a common source of bugs in JavaScript. To ensure that your switch statements perform as expected and that fallthrough does not occur, the last statement for each case label should be break;. A **break statement** is a special kind of statement that is used to end the execution of a switch statement. To end a switch statement once it performs its required task, include a break statement at the end of the statements associated with each case label. A break statement can also be used to end a loop statement prematurely. However, it's usually possible to achieve this in a more straightforward manner by changing the loop conditions themselves, so programmers generally avoid using break statements in loops.

The following code shows a switch statement contained within a function. When the function is called, it is passed an argument named americanCity. The switch statement compares the value of the americanCity argument to the case labels. If a match is found, the city's state is returned and a break statement ends the switch statement. If a match is not found, the value "United States" is returned from the default label. Remember that JavaScript is a case-sensitive language, so a value must use the same capitalization as a case label to be considered a match.

```
1    function city_location(americanCity) {
2        switch (americanCity) {
3            case "Boston":
4                return "Massachusetts";
5                break;
6            case "Chicago":
7                return "Illinois";
8                break;
9            case "Los Angeles":
10               return "California";
11               break;
12           case "Miami":
13               return "Florida";
14               break;
15           case "New York":
```

```
16              return "New York";
17              break;
18          default:
19              return "United States";
20              break;
21      }
22  }
23  document.write("<p>" + city_location("Boston") + "</p>");
```

Note that case labels must be discrete values and cannot use operators. This means that for numeric values, you cannot use greater than, less than, or ranges for case labels—only individual values. If you need your code to make decisions based on comparison operators, such as > 25, then if/else and else if statements are a better choice.

Next, you will modify the addGameInfo() function program to use a switch statement instead of the if/else if statements. Each case statement in the modified function will check the value that is passed from the gameLocation array. The switch statement makes better programming sense than the if/else if statements, because it eliminates the need to check the gameLocation value multiple times.

To add a switch statement to the addGameInfo() function:

1. Return to the **tt.js** document in your text editor.

2. Within the addGameInfo() function, within the data block for the for loop, insert /* before the start of the if/then statement, and add */ after the closing } for the second if/then statement, as shown below.

```
1   for (var i = 0; i < 31; i++) {
2       var date = i + 1;
3       var tableCell = document.getElementById("08-" + date);
4       paragraphs = tableCell.getElementsByTagName("p");
5   /*  if (gameLocation[i] === "away") {
6           paragraphs[1].innerHTML = "@ ";
7       }
8       if (gameLocation[i] === "home") {
9           paragraphs[1].innerHTML = "vs ";
10      }*/
11  /*  if (gameLocation[i] === "away") {
12          paragraphs[1].innerHTML = "@ ";
13      }
```

```
14        else {
15            if (gameLocation[i] === "home") {
16                paragraphs[1].innerHTML = "vs ";
17            }
18        } */
19        paragraphs[1].innerHTML += opponents[i];
20    }
```

3. Within the command block for the `for` statement, add a new line below the closing `*/` you entered in the previous step, and then enter the following code:

```
switch (gameLocation[i]) {

}
```

This code uses the `switch` keyword to create a `switch` statement, and specifies in parentheses the expression to evaluate. In this code, the expression is the element from the `gameLocation` array that corresponds to the current value of the counter variable.

4. Within the command block you just created, enter the following code:

```
case "away":
    paragraphs[1].innerHTML = "@ ";
    break;
```

This code uses the `case` keyword to create a `case` statement. The `case` label "away" specifies that if the value of the switch expression—`gamelocation[i]`—equals "away," the JavaScript processor should execute the code that follows. The first statement adds "@ " as the content for the second paragraph in the current cell, and the second statement, `break;`, specifies that the JavaScript processor should end execution of the `switch` statement.

5. Below the last line of code you entered in the previous step, enter the following code:

```
case "home":
    paragraphs[1].innerHTML = "vs ";
    break;
```

This code creates a second `case` statement. The `case` label "home" specifies that if the value of the `switch` expression equals "home," the JavaScript processor should execute the code that follows. The first statement adds "vs " as the content for the second paragraph in the current cell, and the second statement specifies that the JavaScript processor should end execution of the `switch` statement.

6. Save your changes to **tt.js**, and then reload **calendar.htm** in your browser. The calendar content still matches that shown earlier in Figure 3-21, meaning that the switch statement has exactly replicated the results created by the if/else and if statements.

The following code shows the final version of the tt.js file.

```
1    // global variables
2    var daysOfWeek = ["Sunday", "Monday", "Tuesday", "Wednesday",
3       "Thursday", "Friday", "Saturday"];
4    var opponents = ["Lightning", "Combines", "Combines",
5        "Combines", "Lightning", "Lightning", "Lightning",
6        "Lightning", "Barn Raisers", "Barn Raisers",
7        "Barn Raisers", "Sodbusters", "Sodbusters", "Sodbusters",
8        "Sodbusters", "(off)", "River Riders", "River Riders",
9        "River Riders", "Big Dippers", "Big Dippers",
10       "Big Dippers", "(off)", "Sodbusters", "Sodbusters",
11       "Sodbusters", "Combines", "Combines", "Combines",
12       "(off)", "(off)"];
13   var gameLocation =
14      ["away", "away", "away", "away", "home", "home", "home",
15       "home", "home", "home", "home", "away", "away", "away",
16       "away", "", "away", "away", "away", "away", "away",
17       "away", "", "home", "home", "home", "home", "home",
18       "home", "", ""];
19   // function to place daysOfWeek values in header row cells
20   function addColumnHeaders() {
21      var i = 0;
22      while (i < 7) {
23         document.getElementsByTagName("th")[i].innerHTML =↵
24            daysOfWeek[i];
25         i++;
26      }
27   }
28   // function to place day of month value in first p element
29   // within each table data cell that has an id
30   function addCalendarDates() {
31      var i = 1;
```

```
32       var paragraphs = "";
33       do {
34          var tableCell = document.getElementById("08-" + i);
35          paragraphs = tableCell.getElementsByTagName("p");
36          paragraphs[0].innerHTML = i;
37          i++;
38       } while (i <= 31);
39    }
40    // function to place opponents and gameLocation values in
41    // second p element within each table data cell that has an id
42    function addGameInfo() {
43       var paragraphs = "";
44       for (var i = 0; i < 31; i++) {
45          var date = i + 1;
46          var tableCell = document.getElementById("08-" + date);
47          paragraphs = tableCell.getElementsByTagName("p");
48    /*      if (gameLocation[i] === "away") {
49             paragraphs[1].innerHTML = "@ ";
50          }
51          if (gameLocation[i] === "home") {
52             paragraphs[1].innerHTML = "vs ";
53          }*/
54    /*      if (gameLocation[i] === "away") {
55             paragraphs[1].innerHTML = "@ ";
56          }
57          else {
58             if (gameLocation[i] === "home") {
59                paragraphs[1].innerHTML = "vs ";
60             }
61          } */
62          switch (gameLocation[i]) {
63             case "away":
64                paragraphs[1].innerHTML = "@ ";
65                break;
66             case "home":
```

```
67                    paragraphs[1].innerHTML = "vs ";
68                    break;
69                }
70            paragraphs[1].innerHTML += opponents[i];
71        }
72    }
73    // function to populate calendar
74    function setUpPage() {
75        addColumnHeaders();
76        addCalendarDates();
77        addGameInfo();
78    }
79    // runs setUpPage() function when page loads
80    if (window.addEventListener) {
81        window.addEventListener("load", setUpPage, false);
82    } else if (window.attachEvent) {
83        window.attachEvent("onload", setUpPage);
84    }
```

> **Note**
>
> Normally when you finish writing JavaScript code, you remove any comments
> that aren't relevant to the final product. On an actual JavaScript project, you
> would remove the `if` and `if/else` versions of the code you replaced with
> a `switch` statement. However, while you are learning, it can be useful to
> be able to compare different versions of code you've created, so you'll leave
> these comments in your file.

Short Quiz 3

1. What does an `if` statement do when its condition evaluates to a falsy value?

2. What can you do with an `if/else` statement that you can't do with an `if` statement?

3. Why would you nest decision-making statements?

4. How do you specify possible values for the expression in a `switch` statement?

5. What statement should you include at the end of the code for each `case` label in a `switch` statement? Why is it important to include this statement?

Summary

> An array contains a set of data represented by a single variable name. You can think of an array as a collection of variables contained within a single variable. Each piece of data contained in an array is called an element. An index is an element's numeric position within the array.

> A loop statement is a control flow statement that repeatedly executes a statement or a series of statements while a specific condition is true or until a specific condition becomes true. Loop statements in JavaScript include the `while`, `do/while`, and `for` statements.

> The `while` statement is used for repeating a statement or series of statements as long as a given conditional expression evaluates to `true`.

> Each repetition of a looping statement is called an iteration.

> An infinite loop is a situation in which a loop statement never ends because its conditional expression is never false.

> The `do/while` statement executes a statement or statements once, and then repeats the execution as long as a given conditional expression evaluates to `true`.

> The `for` statement is used to repeat a statement or series of statements as long as a given conditional expression evaluates to `true`.

> The `continue` statement halts a looping statement and restarts the loop with a new iteration.

> The process of choosing which code to execute at a given point in an application is known as decision making. In JavaScript, you use the `if`, `if/else`, `else if`, and `switch` statements to create decision-making structures.

> The `if` statement is used to execute specific programming code if the evaluation of a conditional expression returns a value of `true`.

> A command block is a set of statements contained within a set of braces.

> An `if` statement that includes an `else` clause is called an `if/else` statement.

> When one decision-making statement is contained within another decision-making statement, they are referred to as nested decision-making structures.

> The `switch` statement controls program flow by executing a specific set of statements, depending on the value of an expression.

> A `break` statement is used to exit control statements, such as the `switch` statement or the `while`, `do/while`, and `for` looping statements.

Key Terms

array—A set of data represented by a single variable name.

array literal—A single statement that declares a variable and specifies array values as its content.

break statement—A special kind of statement that is used to end the execution of a control statement.

case label—A term in a switch statement that represents a specific possible expression value.

command block—A set of statements contained within a set of braces.

conditional statements—*See* decision-making statement.

constructor—A special type of function that is used as the basis for creating reference variables.

continue statement—A statement that restarts a loop with a new iteration even when its condition evaluates to a falsy value.

controlling flow—Changing the order in which JavaScript code is executed.

counter—A variable that is incremented or decremented with each iteration of a loop statement, which you use to track the progress of the loop.

decision making—The process of choosing which code to execute at a given point in an application.

decision-making statement—A special type of JavaScript statement used for making decisions.

decision-making structure—*See* decision-making statement.

default label—A case label in a switch statement that contains statements that are executed when the value returned by the switch statement expression does not match a case label.

do/while statement—A loop statement that executes a statement or statements once, then repeats the execution as long as a given conditional expression evaluates to a truthy value.

element—An individual value contained in an array.

else if construction—A compact version of nested if/else statements that combines an else statement with its nested if statement.

fallthrough—A situation in which execution of a switch statement does not stop after the statements for a particular case label are executed, but continues evaluating the rest of the case labels in the list.

for statement—A loop statement that repeats a statement or series of statements as long as a given conditional expression evaluates to a truthy value.

getElementsByTagName() method—A method that returns a collection of references to all instances of a certain element in an HTML document.

if statement—A conditional statement used to execute specific programming code if the evaluation of a conditional expression returns a truthy value.

if/else statement—An `if` statement that includes an `else` clause.

index—A number associated with an element in an array, which represents the element's position within the array.

infinite loop—A loop statement that never ends because its conditional expression is never falsy.

iteration—Each repetition of a looping statement.

loop statement—A control flow statement that repeatedly executes a statement or a series of statements while a specific condition is truthy or until a specific condition becomes truthy.

nested decision-making structure—The type of structure created by nesting one decision-making statement within another decision-making statement.

switch statement—A conditional statement that executes a specific set of statements depending on the value of an expression.

while statement—One of the simplest types of loop statements, which repeats a statement or series of statements as long as a given conditional expression evaluates to a truthy value.

Review Questions

1. What is the correct syntax for creating an empty array named `taxRules`?
   a. `var taxRules = {};`
   b. `var taxRules;`
   c. `var taxRules = [];`
   d. `var taxRules[5];`

2. Which of the following statements adds the value "oak" as the third element of the `trees` array?
   a. `trees += "oak";`
   b. `trees += "","","oak";`
   c. `trees[2] = "oak";`
   d. `trees[3] = "oak";`

3. Which of the following properties returns the number of elements in an array?
   a. `length`
   b. `size`
   c. `elements`
   d. `indexes`

4. Which characters are used to create a command block?
   a. ( )
   b. [ ]
   c. { }
   d. <>

5. You track the progress of a loop with a(n) _____.
   a. counter
   b. iteration
   c. increment
   d. decrement

6. The statements in a(n) _____ statement always execute at least once.
   a. for
   b. do/while
   c. switch
   d. if

7. If you do not include code that changes the counter value in a loop statement, your program will be caught in a(n) _____.
   a. iteration
   b. condition
   c. fallthrough
   d. infinite loop

8. When is a for statement initialization expression executed?
   a. When the for statement begins executing
   b. With each repetition of the for statement
   c. When the counter variable is incremented
   d. When the for statement ends

9. The parentheses at the start of a(n) _____ statement can include code that initializes a counter and changes its value with each iteration.
   a. while
   b. do
   c. do/while
   d. for

10. The _____ statement halts a looping statement and restarts the loop with a new iteration.
    a. restart
    b. continue
    c. break
    d. halt

11. An `if` statement can include multiple statements provided that they _____.
    a. execute after the `if` statement's closing semicolon
    b. are not contained within a command block
    c. do not include other `if` statements
    d. are contained within a command block

12. A simple `if/else` statement enables you to specify code for _____ alternatives.
    a. 2
    b. 3
    c. 4
    d. unlimited

13. The _____ statement is equivalent to the conditional operator (`?:`).
    a. `if`
    b. `if/else`
    c. `nested if`
    d. `switch`

14. A `switch` statement compares the value of an expression to a value contained in a(n) _____.
    a. `default` label
    b. `case` label
    c. fallthrough
    d. `break` statement

15. When the value returned by a `switch` statement expression does not match a `case` label, then the statements within the _____ label execute.
    a. `error`
    b. `else`
    c. `exception`
    d. `default`

16. What is the difference between an array and a standard variable?

17. Provide the code to access the value of the fourth element in the `projectTeam` array, and explain how you determined the index value.

18. Explain what causes an infinite loop, and what you can to do ensure that your programs do not contain infinite loops.

19. What does an `else if` statement replace? What are the advantages of using an `else if` statement?

20. Explain what "fallthrough" means and how to prevent it.

Hands-On Projects

Hands-On Project 3-1

In this exercise, you will total the prices for items selected on an order form, using both a `for` statement and an `if` statement. You'll also add an event listener to the Submit button that supports both modern browsers and older versions of Internet Explorer.

1. In your text editor, open **index.htm** from the HandsOnProject3-1 folder in the Chapter03 folder. Enter your name and today's date where indicated in the comment section in the document head.

2. At the bottom of the document, before the closing `</body>` tag, enter **<script>**, insert a blank line, and then enter **</script>** to create a new script section.

3. Within the script section you created in the previous step, enter the following function:

```
1   // function to add values of selected check boxes and↵
2       display total
3   function calcTotal() {
4
5   }
```

4. Within the function braces, define the following global variables:

```
var itemTotal = 0;
var items = document.getElementsByTagName("input");
```

5. Below the global variables, enter the following `for` statement:

```
1   for (var i = 0; i < 5; i++) {
2       if (items[i].checked) {
3           itemTotal += (items[i].value * 1);
4       }
5   }
```

> **Note**   `items[i].value` is multiplied by 1 to ensure that it is treated as a number rather than a string.

6. Below the closing `}` for the `for` statement, enter the following statement to write the result to the web document:

```
document.getElementById("total").innerHTML =↵
    "Your order total is $" + itemTotal + ".00";
```

7. Below the closing } for the function, enter the following code to create an event listener that's compatible with older versions of Internet Explorer:

```
// add backward compatible event listener to Submit button
var submitButton = document.getElementById("sButton");
if (submitButton.addEventListener) {
    submitButton.addEventListener("click", calcTotal,↵
        false);
} else if (submitButton.attachEvent) {
    submitButton.attachEvent("onclick", calcTotal);
}
```

8. Save your work, open **index.htm** in a browser, check the **Fried chicken** and **Side salad** check boxes, and then click **Submit**. The text "Your order total is $14.00" should be displayed on the right side of the page as shown in Figure 3-23.

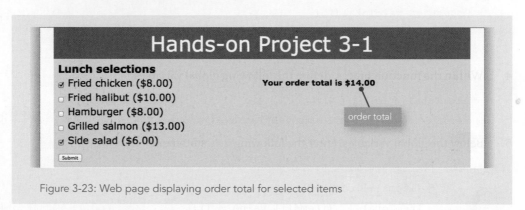

Figure 3-23: Web page displaying order total for selected items

Hands-On Project 3-2

In this project, you'll use a conditional statement to check for browser support of the HTML5 placeholder feature, and execute code to replicate this feature if the condition returns a falsy value.

1. In your text editor, open **index.htm** from the HandsOnProject3-2 folder in the Chapter03 folder. Enter your name and today's date where indicated in the comment section in the document head.

2. Open **index.htm** in a modern browser. As Figure 3-24 shows, the placeholder text created by the `placeholder` attribute is displayed in the form fields.

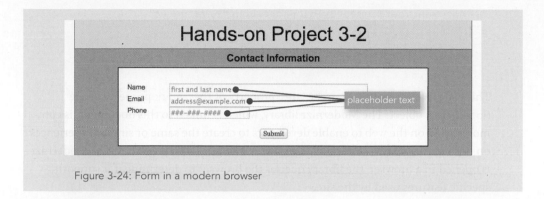

Figure 3-24: Form in a modern browser

3. If you have access to Internet Explorer version 9 or earlier, use it to open **index.htm**. The placeholder text is not displayed in older versions of Internet Explorer because the attribute that creates them, `placeholder`, is not recognized by those browsers. Figure 3-25 shows the form in IE8.

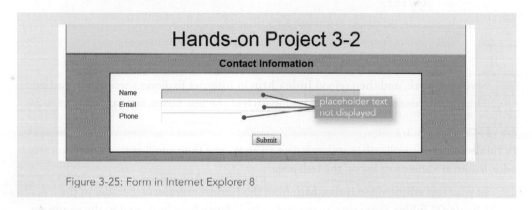

Figure 3-25: Form in Internet Explorer 8

4. At the bottom of the document, before the closing `</body>` tag, enter **<script>**, insert a blank line, and then enter **</script>** to create a new script section.

5. Within the script section you created in the previous step, enter the following function:

```
function insertPlaceholders() {
    if (!Modernizr.input.placeholder) {
        document.getElementById("nameinput").value =↵
            "first and last name";
        document.getElementById("emailinput").value =↵
            "address@example.com";
```

```
document.getElementById("phoneinput").value =↵
    "###-###-####";
    }

}
```

This code references the `placeholder` property of the `input` property of the `Modernizr` object. The Modernizr library, which is linked to this document, is commonly used on the web to enable developers to create the same or similar experiences on both modern browsers and older browsers. When a web page that uses Modernizr is opened in a browser, the library queries the browser to determine if it supports specific features used by the site.

6. Below the code for the function, add the following backward-compatible event listener to call the function when the window finishes loading:

```
1   if (window.addEventListener) {
2       window.addEventListener("load", insertPlaceholders,↵
3           false);
4   } else if (window.attachEvent) {
5       window.attachEvent("onload", insertPlaceholders);
6   }
```

7. Save your work, and then reload **index.htm** in Internet Explorer version 9 or earlier. The placeholder text is now displayed in each of the text boxes, similar to Figure 3-24.

Hands-On Project 3-3

In this exercise, you will create and populate an array, and then you'll create a function that adds the array values to a list on the web page.

1. In your text editor, open **index.htm** from the HandsOnProject3-3 folder in the Chapter03 folder. Enter your name and today's date where indicated in the comment section in the document head.

2. At the bottom of the document, before the closing `</body>` tag, create a new script section.

3. Within the script section create a global variable named **places**. The value of `places` should be an array, which you should populate with the names of five places of your choice.

4. Below your array definition, create a function with the name **processPlaces()**. Within the function, create a **for** statement. It should create a counter variable named **i** with a starting value of **0**. As long as the counter variable is less than 5, it should increment by 1 on each iteration. Each loop of the `for` statement should perform the following actions:
    a. Set the value of the `listItem` variable to the string "item" concatenated with (i + 1).

b. Change the content of the element with the `id` equal to the value of the `listItem` variable to the value of the element in the `places` array with an index equal to the value of `i`.

5. Below the code for the `processPlaces()` function, add the following statement to run the function when the window finishes loading:

```
1    if (window.addEventListener) {
2        window.addEventListener("load", processPlaces, false);
3    } else if (window.attachEvent) {
4        window.attachEvent("onload", processPlaces);
5    }
```

6. Add comments to document your work, and then save your work. Open **index.htm**, and verify that the page displays the five places you specified in your array as a bulleted list, as shown in Figure 3-26. If your web page is not displayed as expected, examine your JavaScript code for errors. After fixing each error, save and reload your page.

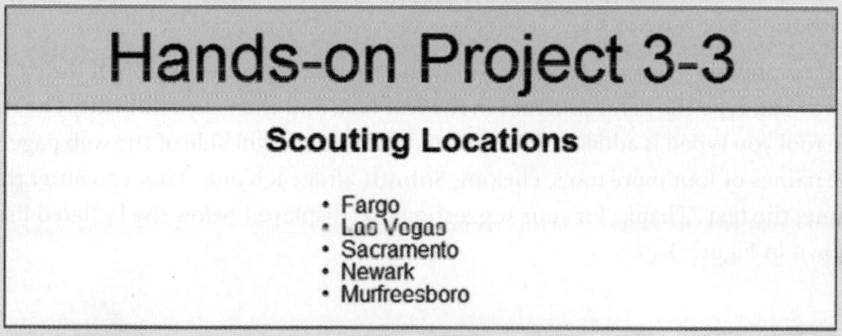

Hands-on Project 3-3

Scouting Locations

- Fargo
- Las Vegas
- Sacramento
- Newark
- Murfreesboro

Figure 3-26: Places displayed in bulleted list

Hands-On Project 3-4

In this exercise, you will create a program that writes user input from a text box to a list on the web page. Your program will also write a thank-you message to the page after the user has entered five items. Finally, you'll also create a backward-compatible event listener for the Submit button.

1. In your text editor, open **index.htm** from the HandsOnProject3-4 folder in the Chapter03 folder. Enter your name and today's date where indicated in the comment section in the document head.

2. At the bottom of the document, before the closing `</body>` tag, create a new script section.

3. Within the script section create two global variables: one named **i** with a value of **1**, and the other named **listItem** with its value set to an empty string.

4. Below the variables, create a function called **processInput()**. Within the function, create an **if** statement that runs if the value of i is less than or equal to 5. The if statement should perform the following actions:
   a. Set the value of the listItem variable to the string "item" concatenated with the value of i.
   b. Set the content of the element with an id equal to listItem to the value of the element with the id of toolbox.
   c. Set the value of the element with the id of toolbox to an empty string.

5. Before the closing } of the if statement, create a nested **if** statement. If the value of i is equal to 5, the statement should change the content of the element with the id of resultsExpl to the string "Thanks for your suggestions."

6. Before the closing } of the main if statement, after the nested if statement, add a statement to increment the value of i by 1.

7. Add a backward-compatible event listener for the click event to the Submit button (with the id of button).

8. Add comments to document your work, and then save your work. Open **index.htm** in a browser, type the name of a tool in the text box, and then click **Submit**. The name of the tool you typed is added to the bulleted list on the right side of the web page. Enter the names of four more tools, clicking **Submit** after each one. After you enter the fifth name, the text "Thanks for your suggestions." is displayed below the bulleted list, as shown in Figure 3-27.

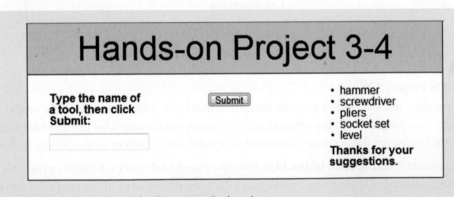

Figure 3-27: Tools and thank-you text displayed

9. Fix any errors in your code until it works as you expect.

Hands-On Project 3-5

In this exercise, you will rewrite the code you created in Hands-On Project 3-4 to use a `switch` statement.

1. In the file manager for your operating system, copy the completed contents of the HandsOnProject3-4 folder to the HandsOnProject3-5 folder.

2. In your text editor, open the **index.htm** file from the HandsOnProject3-5 folder, change "Hands-on Project 3-4" to **Hands on Project 3-5** in the comment section, in the `title` element, and in the `h1` element, and then save your changes.

3. Convert the `if` statement to a comment, and then enter code to perform the same task using a `switch` statement. The `switch` statement should check the value of the variable `i`, and should contain two cases: one for the value 5, and a default case. Be sure to include code that prevents fallthrough. Edit or add comments as necessary to document your work.

4. Save your work, and then test the web page as described in Step 8 of Hands-On Project 3-4. Adjust your code as necessary until it works just as it did at the end of the steps for Hands-On Project 3-4.

5. Fix any errors in your code until it works as you expect.

Case Projects

Individual Case Project

Plan and add a feature to one of the web pages in your personal site that incorporates content or functionality created by a series of `if`, `if/else`, and/or `else if` statements, or by a `switch` statement. If your page requires an event listener, create one that's backward-compatible with older versions of Internet Explorer. View and test your page in one or more browsers as appropriate to ensure it works as you expect.

Team Case Project

Choose one of the web pages from your team web site to enhance with code that uses an array and a loop. Arrays are often used to store a set of related data, either provided by the developer or added by a user. Loops are often used in combination with arrays to perform a common action on each element in an array. Plan the structure of the code as a team, then divide into two groups. One group should create the code for the array, and the other the code for the loop. After each group has completed its work, come back together as a full group and incorporate the code in the group web page. Test the code to verify the page works as planned, doing any troubleshooting and making any edits to the functions as a full team.

CHAPTER 4

DEBUGGING AND ERROR HANDLING

When you complete this chapter, you will be able to:

> Recognize error types
> Trace errors with dialog boxes and the console
> Use comments to locate bugs
> Trace errors with debugging tools
> Write code to respond to exceptions and errors

The more JavaScript programs you write, the more likely you are to write programs that generate error messages. At times it may seem like your programs never function quite the way you want. Regardless of experience, knowledge, and ability, all programmers incorporate errors in their programs at one time or another. Thus, all programmers must devote part of their programming education to mastering the art of debugging, which is the process of tracing and resolving errors in a program. Debugging is an essential skill for any programmer, regardless of the programming language.

In this chapter, you will learn techniques and tools that you can use to trace and resolve errors in JavaScript programs. However, you will not create any new programs. Instead, you will learn how to use JavaScript debugging techniques to locate errors in an existing program.

Introduction to Debugging

All programming languages, including JavaScript, have their own syntax, or rules. To write a program, you must understand the syntax of the programming language you are using. You must also understand computer-programming logic. The term logic refers to the order in which various parts of a program run, or execute. The statements in a program must execute in the correct order to produce the desired results. In an analogous situation, although you may know how to drive a car well, you're unlikely to reach your destination if you do not follow the correct route. Similarly, you might be able to write statements using the correct syntax but be unable to construct an entire, logically executed program that works the way you want. A typical logical error might be multiplying two values when you meant to divide them. Another might be producing output before obtaining the appropriate input (for example, adding order confirmation text to a document before asking the user to enter the necessary order information).

Any error in a program that causes it to function incorrectly, whether because of incorrect syntax or flaws in logic, is called a bug. The term "debugging" refers to the act of tracing and resolving errors in a program. Grace Murray Hopper, a mathematician who was instrumental in developing Common Business-Oriented Language (COBOL), a programming language, is said to have first coined the term "debugging." As the story from the 1940s goes, a moth short-circuited a primitive computer that Hopper was using. Removing the moth from the computer "debugged" the system and resolved the problem. Today, the term "bug" refers to any sort of problem in the design and operation of a program.

> **Note**
>
> *Do not confuse bugs with computer viruses or worms. Bugs are problems within a program that occur because of syntax errors, design flaws, or run-time errors. Viruses and worms are self-contained programs designed to infect a computer system and cause damage, compromise security, and/or steal information.*

Three types of errors can occur in a program: syntax errors, run-time errors, and logic errors.

Recognizing Syntax Errors

A syntax error occurs when the interpreter fails to recognize code. In JavaScript, statements that are not recognized by a browser's scripting engine generate syntax errors. (Recall from Chapter 1 that a scripting engine is just one kind of interpreter, with the term "interpreter" referring generally to any program that executes scripting language code.) Syntax errors can be caused by incorrect use of JavaScript code or references to objects, methods, or variables that do not exist. For example, if a programmer attempts to use a method that does not exist or omits a method's closing parenthesis, the scripting engine generates a syntax error. Many syntax errors are generated by incorrectly spelled or mistyped words. For example, the statement `document.writ("Hello World");` causes a syntax error because the `write()` method is misspelled as *writ()*. Similarly, the statement `Document.write("Hello World");` causes a syntax error because the `Document` object is incorrectly typed with an uppercase *D*. (Remember that most JavaScript objects, such as the `Document` object, should be all lowercase letters when used within statements.)

> **Note**
> Syntax errors in compiled languages, such as C++, are also called compile-time errors, because they are usually discovered when a program is compiled. Because JavaScript is an interpreted language, syntax errors are not discovered until a program executes.

A code editor designed for coding in JavaScript—such as Notepad++, Aptana Studio, or KomodoEdit—can highlight syntax errors while you type, saving you the trouble of locating and fixing them later.

Recognizing Run-Time Errors

The second type of error, a **run-time error**, occurs when the JavaScript interpreter encounters a problem while a program is executing. Run-time errors differ from syntax errors in that they do not necessarily represent JavaScript language errors. Instead, run-time errors occur when the interpreter encounters code that it cannot execute. For example, consider the statement `createRecommendation();`, which calls a custom JavaScript function. This statement does not generate a syntax error, because it is legal (and usually necessary) to create and then call custom functions in a JavaScript program. However, if your program includes the call statement but does not include code that creates the function in the first place, your program generates a run-time error. The error occurs when the interpreter attempts to call the function and is unable to find it.

The following shows another example of a run-time error. In this example, a `write()` method attempts to print the contents of a variable named `messageVar`. Because the `messageVar` variable is not declared (you can assume it has not been declared in another script section elsewhere in the document), a run-time error occurs.

```
document.write(messageVar);
```

Another point to remember is that a run-time error can be caused by a syntax error, because a syntax error does not occur until the interpreter attempts to execute the code. For example, you may have a function that contains a statement with a syntax error. However, the syntax error will not be caught until the function executes at run time. When the function does execute, it generates a run-time error because of the syntax error within the function.

Recognizing Logic Errors

The third type of error, a logic error, is a flaw in a program's design that prevents the program from running as you anticipate. In this context, the term "logic" refers to the execution of program statements and procedures in the correct order to produce the desired results. You're already accustomed to performing ordinary, nonprogramming tasks according to a certain logic. For example, when you do the laundry, you normally sort, then wash, then dry, and finally fold your clothes. If you decided to dry, sort, fold, and then wash the clothes, you would end up with a pile of wet laundry rather than the clean and pressed garments you desired. The problem, in that case, would be a type of logic error—you performed the steps in the wrong order.

One example of a logic error in a computer program is multiplying two values when you mean to divide them, as in the following code:

```
var divisionResult = 10 * 2;
document.write("Ten divided by two is equal to "
    + divisionResult);
```

Another example of a logic error is the creation of an infinite loop, in which a loop statement never ends because its conditional expression is never updated or is never false. The following code creates a for statement that results in the logic error of an infinite loop. The cause of the infinite loop is that the third argument in the for statement's parentheses never changes the value of the count variable.

```
for (var count = 10; count >= 0; count) {
    document.write("We have liftoff in " + count);
}
```

Because the count variable is never updated in the preceding example, it continues to have a value of 10 through each iteration of the loop, resulting in the repeated display of an alert dialog box containing the text "We have liftoff in 10." To correct this logic error, you would add a decrement operator to the third argument in the for statement's constructor, as follows:

```
for (var count = 10; count >= 0; count--) {
    document.write("We have liftoff in " + count);
}
```

Note

As you work through this book, keep in mind that debugging is not an exact science. Every program you write is different and requires different methods of debugging. While there are some tools available to help you debug your JavaScript code, your own logical and analytical skills are the best debugging resources you have.

You've been hired by Tuba Farm Equipment, located in Fargo, North Dakota, to finalize a web application that recommends tractor models based on four user selections. The web application has been coded, but it doesn't work as expected. You'll use debugging techniques to identify and fix the bugs in the program so it functions as designed. Figure 4-1 shows the completed form in action.

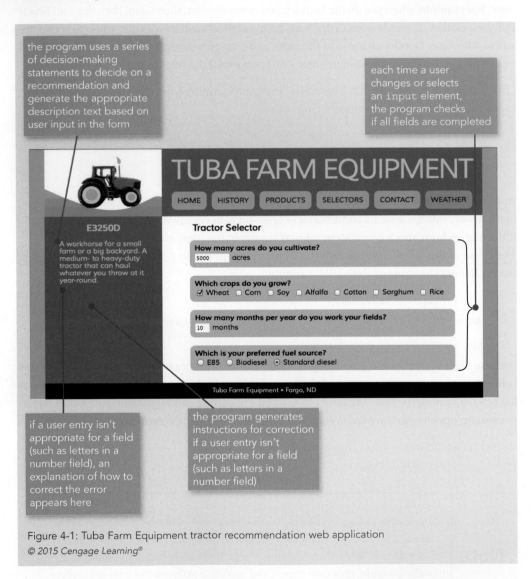

Figure 4-1: Tuba Farm Equipment tractor recommendation web application

© 2015 Cengage Learning®

The tractor selector application accepts user answers to four questions. Each time a user types a character or clicks a box, the program uses a series of decision-making statements to identify the tractor model that best fits the user's answers, and then adds the name and description of that model to the page's sidebar. If the user enters inappropriate data (such as text where a number is expected) the program displays an explanation of how to correct the erroneous input.

The version of the application that you'll start with does not work as described above, however. It contains several bugs that prevent it from working as designed. You'll start by opening and testing the application.

To open and test the tractor selector application:

1. In your text editor, open the **tractor.htm** file, located in your Chapter folder for Chapter 4.

2. In the comment section at the top of the document, type your name and today's date where indicated, and then save your work.

3. Scroll through the document to familiarize yourself with its content. The `article` element contains the form, and the `aside` element contains empty `h2` and `p` elements where the program writes either a warning or a recommendation.

4. Repeat Steps 1 and 2 to open **tuba.js** and save a personalized copy, and then scroll through the document to familiarize yourself with its content. The file contains definitions for 12 global variables, followed by four functions that call the `createRecommendation()` function. Even though these four functions currently all perform the same task, the program design includes adding code to each of them to verify whether a particular `fieldset` element is complete. (Your work will include adding this code to two of these functions, with the remainder to be completed in a later stage of the project.) The file also contains the following: a function that tests whether the user has completed all parts of the form, a function that generates a recommendation and writes it within the `aside` element, and a function that creates event listeners for the `input` elements in each `fieldset` element. At the bottom of the file, a single command sets the `createEventListeners()` function to run when the page finishes loading.

5. Open **tractor.htm** in a browser, and then in the first text box (with the label "acres"), type your first name. Because the program expects a number in this box, your entry of text should generate an error. However, nothing happens when you type text in the box.

> **Note** | The tractor selector app uses the input event to execute a function every time a user enters or removes characters in an input box. However, IE8 does not support this event, so IE8 users must move to a different element after entering or removing characters before the function is executed.

6. Delete the text you entered, enter a number in each of the two input boxes, click at least one check box, and then click one option button. As Figure 4-2 shows, even though you've completed the form, no recommendation is displayed.

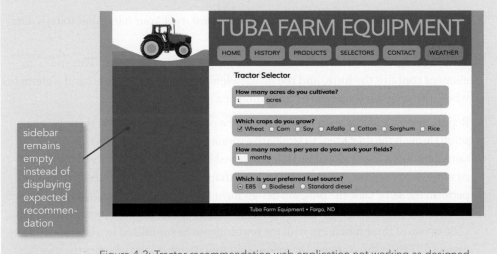

sidebar remains empty instead of displaying expected recommendation

Figure 4-2: Tractor recommendation web application not working as designed

Interpreting Error Messages

The first line of defense in locating bugs in JavaScript programs consists of the error messages displayed in a browser's console when the JavaScript interpreter encounters a syntax or run-time error. Two important pieces of information displayed in error messages in the console are the line number in the document where the error occurred and a description of the error. Note that the line number in an error message is counted from the start of the document, not just from the start of a script section. Also, different browsers may report different line numbers for error messages. For example, in a program missing a closing brace, Firefox reports the line number of the final statement before where the brace should occur, while Chrome reports the line number of the following line, assuming the brace would be placed on a new line. All error messages generated by a browser are run-time errors. However, keep in mind that run-time errors can be caused by syntax errors. Logic errors do not generate error messages because they do not prevent a script from running (as syntax errors do) or from executing properly (as run-time errors do). Instead, they prevent the program from running the way you anticipated. Computers are not smart enough (yet) to identify a flaw in a program's logic. For example, if you create an infinite loop with a `for` statement, the interpreter has no way of telling whether you really wanted to continually execute the `for` statement's code. Later in this chapter, you will learn how to trace the flow of your program's execution in order to locate logic errors.

Consider the following function, which causes a syntax error because it is missing the closing brace (}).

```
function missingClosingBrace() {
    var message = "This function is missing a closing brace.";
    window.alert(message);
```

Figure 4-3 shows the resulting error messages in the Firefox browser console.

Figure 4-3: Firefox error messages

Source: © Mozilla Firefox

> **Note**
> *All console figures in this section show the Firefox console. Although the appearance of the console may be slightly different in each of the major browsers, they all display the same information in roughly the same layout.*

You can rely on error messages in the console only to find the general location of an error in a program and not as the exact indicator of an error. You cannot always assume that the line specified by an error message is the actual problem in your program. For example, consider the following code:

```
1    function variableDeclarations() {
2        var percentage = .25;
3        var amount = 1600;
4    }
5    function calculatePercentage() {
6        var result = amount * percentage;
7        document.write("<p>Twenty-five percent of "↵
8            + amount + " is ");
9        document.write(result + "</p>");
10   }
```

The `var result = amount * percentage;` statement in line 6 causes a run-time error because the interpreter cannot locate the `amount` and `percentage` variables included in the statement. The `amount` and `percentage` variables are declared within the `variableDeclarations()` function, on lines 2 and 3, making them local variables, which are available only inside that function. Because the `amount` and `percentage` variables are not global variables, they are not visible to the `calculatePercentage()` function, which causes a run-time error. The `var result = amount * percentage;` statement on line 6 generates the run-time error because it attempts to access variables that are local to another function. However, the real problem is that the `percentage` and `amount` variables are not declared at a global level.

When debugging JavaScript, it is important that you understand how a browser interprets a web page and JavaScript code. A common complaint among professional programmers is that web browsers do not strictly enforce JavaScript syntax. For example, browsers can interpret JavaScript statements that do not end in a semicolon. In contrast, in high-level languages such as C++ and Java, you *must* end a statement with a semicolon or you receive an error.

You can compare the way browsers render HTML and interpret JavaScript to the way human beings comprehend language. Someone can speak to you using grammatical variations that you're not familiar with, or with a strong regional or foreign accent. Yet, provided the other person is speaking to you in the same root language, you can usually understand what the person is saying. The same applies to a browser and JavaScript: even if you write sloppy JavaScript code, a browser can often (but not always) figure out what the code is supposed to do. This means that a browser can run JavaScript code and render HTML, even though your program contains bugs.

This lack of common bug enforcement makes writing and debugging programs more difficult.

Next, you will use console messages to help locate bugs in the tractor selector application.

To use console messages to help locate bugs in the tractor selector program:

1. Return to **tractor.htm** in your browser, and then open your browser's console.

   Figure 4-4 shows the log message.

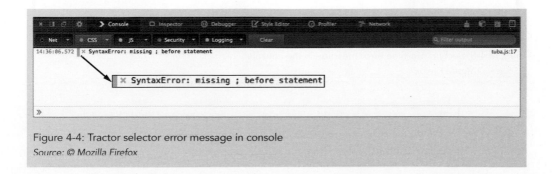

Figure 4-4: Tractor selector error message in console
Source: © Mozilla Firefox

If the console instead opens in a separate window, for Internet Explorer press Ctrl + P, for Firefox click the "Dock to bottom of browser window" button in the top-left corner, or for Chrome click the "Dock to main window" button in the bottom-left corner.

2. Leave the **tractor.htm** document open in your browser, and return to **tuba.js** in your text editor. The error message in the browser console indicates an error on line 17. The statement on this line declares the `fuelComplete` variable; this statement is missing the letter *v* in the `var` keyword.

3. In the section of the tuba.js file where the global variables are defined, locate the statement `ar fuelComplete = true;`, and then insert a **v** at the start of the line so the statement reads as follows:

```
var fuelComplete = true;
```

4. Save the **tuba.js** document in your text editor, return to your browser, and then press and hold **Shift** while clicking the **Refresh** or **Reload** button to reset the form and reload the page. The console now displays the error message shown in Figure 4-5.

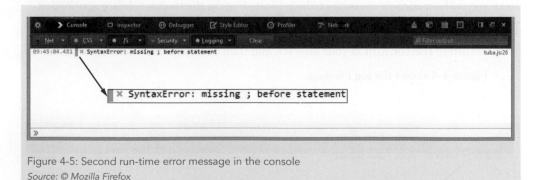

Figure 4-5: Second run-time error message in the console
Source: © Mozilla Firefox

Note that this is a different error than the one you saw above in Figure 4-4. Generally when a browser encounters a syntax error, the browser is unable to process any JavaScript code that follows the error. Because there are a number of possible reasons for — and ways of fixing — any given error, the processor can no longer reliably parse the code that comes after the error. Because you fixed the error on line 17, however, when you reloaded the page, your browser was able to continue processing code after that line. However, this time it encountered a different syntax error on line 26, so it reported this error and then again stopped processing the tuba.js file.

5. Return to the **tuba.js** document in your text editor, and locate line 26, which contains the statement `var monthsFieldset document.getElementsByTagName("fieldset")[2];`. As written, the processor sees the `var` keyword followed by a variable name, which is then followed by code that has no specified relation to the variable that has been created. In this instance, the line is simply missing an operator—an assignment operator (=) setting the remainder of the statement as the value of the `monthsFieldset` variable.

6. After the code `var monthsFieldset`, insert a space and an equal sign, so the line reads as follows:

```
var monthsFieldset = document.↵
   getElementsByTagName("fieldset")[2];
```

7. Save the **tuba.js** document in your text editor, return to your browser, and then refresh or reload the web page. The console now displays the error message shown in Figure 4-6.

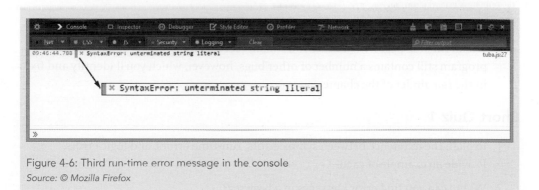

Figure 4-6: Third run-time error message in the console
Source: © Mozilla Firefox

8. Return to the **tuba.js** document in your text editor, and locate line 27. The error, which Firefox describes as "unterminated string literal," is a missing closing quote around a string. Examining line 27, you can see that the line ends with `("fieldset)[3];`, missing the closing quote (") after the word `fieldset`.

9. In line 27, after the word `fieldset` and before the closing), insert a quotation mark.

10. Save the **tuba.js** document in your text editor, return to your browser, and then refresh or reload the web page. The console now displays the error message shown in Figure 4-7.

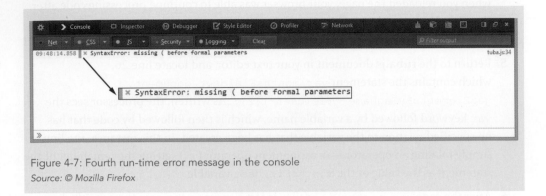

Figure 4-7: Fourth run-time error message in the console
Source: © Mozilla Firefox

11. Return to the **tuba.js** document in your text editor, and locate line 34, which is the first line of the declaration for the `verifyAcres()` function. Notice that the opening parenthesis is missing after the name of the function.

12. After the name `verifyAcres` and before the closing parenthesis, insert an opening parenthesis so line 34 matches the following:

```
function verifyAcres() {
```

13. Save the **tuba.js** document in your text editor, then return to your web browser and reload the web page a final time. You should receive no more error messages. The program still contains a number of other bugs, however, which you'll identify and fix in the remainder of the chapter.

Short Quiz 1

1. Explain the difference between syntax errors, run-time errors, and logic errors. Provide an example of each.

2. Where can you find error messages in a browser?

3. Suppose your browser console lists a single error, which you find and fix. Why is it important to save your work and reload the page in the browser?

Using Basic Debugging Techniques

Although error and warning messages will help you catch basic syntax errors, some syntax errors are still difficult to pinpoint. For example, if you have a deeply nested set of control structures and one of the control structures is missing a closing brace, the syntax error may not be able to tell you exactly which control structure is malformed. This section covers a few basic techniques for debugging JavaScript.

Tracing Errors with the `window.alert()` Method

If you are unable to locate a bug in your program by using error messages, or if you suspect a logic error (which does not generate error messages), then you must trace your code. Tracing is the examination of individual statements in an executing program. The `window.alert()` method provides one of the most useful ways to trace JavaScript code. You place a `window.alert()` method at different points in your program and use it to display the contents of a variable, an array, or the value returned from a function. Using this technique, you can monitor values as they change during program execution.

For example, examine the following function, which calculates weekly net pay, rounded to the nearest integer. The program is syntactically correct and does not generate an error message. However, the function as written does not return the correct result, which should be 485. Instead, the function returns a value of 5169107.

```
1   function calculatePay() {
2       var payRate = 15; numHours = 40;
3       var grossPay = payRate * numHours;
4       var federalTaxes = grossPay * .06794;
5       var stateTaxes = grossPay * .0476;
6       var socialSecurity = grossPay * .062;
7       var medicare = grossPay * .0145;
8       var netPay = grossPay - federalTaxes;
9       netPay *= stateTaxes;
10      netPay *= socialSecurity;
11      netPay *= medicare;
12      return netPay;
13  }
```

To trace the problem, one technique is to place a `window.alert()` method at the point in the program where you think the error may be located. For example, the first thing you may want to check in the `calculatePay()` function is whether the `grossPay` variable is being calculated correctly. To check whether the program calculates `grossPay` correctly, you can place a `window.alert()` method in the function following the calculation of the `grossPay` variable as follows:

```
1   function calculatePay() {
2       var payRate = 15; numHours = 40;
3       var grossPay = payRate * numHours;
4   window.alert(grossPay);
5       var federalTaxes = grossPay * .06794;
6       var stateTaxes = grossPay * .0476;
7       var socialSecurity = grossPay * .062;
8       var medicare = grossPay * .0145;
9       var netPay = grossPay - federalTaxes;
10      netPay *= stateTaxes;
11      netPay *= socialSecurity;
12      netPay *= medicare;
13      return Math.round(netPay);
14  }
```

Best Practices | *Use a Distinguishing Indent for Debugging Code*

When adding statements such as `window.alert()` to your code to trace program execution, it's helpful to place them at a different level of indentation to clearly distinguish them from the actual program. This makes it easier to identify and delete all such statements after debugging is completed.

Because the `grossPay` variable contains the correct value (600), you might next move the `window.alert()` method to check the value of the `netPay` variable. You would then continue with this technique until you discovered the error. In this case, you would discover that the `calculatePay()` function does not perform properly because the lines that should subtract the `stateTaxes`, `socialSecurity`, and `medicare` variables from the `netPay` variable are incorrect; they use the multiplication assignment operator (`*=`) instead of the subtraction assignment operator (`-=`).

An alternative to using a single `window.alert()` method is to place multiple `window.alert()` methods throughout your code to check values as the code executes. For example, you could trace the `calculatePay()` function by using multiple `window.alert()` methods as follows:

```
1    function calculatePay() {
2        var payRate = 15; numHours = 40;
3        var grossPay = payRate * numHours;
4    window.alert(grossPay);
5        var federalTaxes = grossPay * .06794;
6        var stateTaxes = grossPay * .0476;
7        var socialSecurity = grossPay * .062;
8        var medicare = grossPay * .0145;
9        var netPay = grossPay - federalTaxes;
10   window.alert(netPay);
11       netPay *= stateTaxes;
12   window.alert(netPay);
13       netPay *= socialSecurity;
14   window.alert(netPay);
15       netPay *= medicare;
16   window.alert(netPay);
17       return Math.round(netPay);
18   }
```

When using multiple `window.alert()` methods to trace values, you must close each dialog box for your code to continue executing. While this can be a drawback if you're simply trying to view values, it has the advantage of freezing the program at the current point each time an alert box is displayed, and not continuing until you click OK. This can allow you to carefully observe what's displayed in the browser at each of these moments. Additionally, using multiple `window.alert()` methods is sometimes more efficient than moving a single `window.alert()` method. The key to using multiple `window.alert()` methods to trace program values is using them selectively at key points throughout a program. For example, suppose that you were debugging a large accounting program with multiple functions. You could place a `window.alert()` method at key positions within the program, such as wherever a function returns a value or a variable is assigned new data. In this way, you could get the general sense of what portion of the program contains the bug. Once you discover the approximate location of the bug, for instance, in a particular function, you can then concentrate your debugging efforts on that one function.

Your contacts at Tuba Farm Equipment have tested the updated version of the tractor selector page. They're happy that the syntax errors are gone and that the recommendations are now displayed, but they've detected some logical errors in the recommendations that the application is making. You'll use alert dialog boxes to narrow down the location of the first error and fix it.

To use alert dialog boxes to locate a bug in the tractor selector program:

1. Return to the **tuba.js** document in your web browser.

2. Enter **5** in the acres box, check the **Wheat** check box, enter **8** in the months box, and then click the **E85** option button. As Figure 4-8 shows, the application recommends the W1205E, which is described as a tractor for a large farm. However, 5 acres is considered a small farm, so a different model should be recommended.

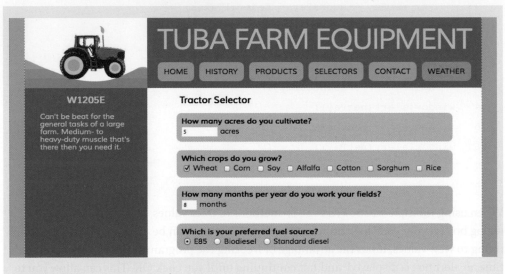

Figure 4-8: Erroneous recommendation

3. Return to the **tuba.js** document in your text editor, and locate the `createRecommendation()` function.

4. On a new line below the second line in the function—the `if` statement that checks the value entered in the acres box—enter the following statement:

```
window.alert("After first if clause: " + acresBox.value);
```

5. On a new line below the 10th line of the function, which reads

```
} else { // more than 5000 acres
```

enter the following statement:

```
window.alert("After second else clause: " + acresBox.value);
```

This `if/else` statement makes the distinction between people farming small and large farms, with any farm less than or equal to 5000 acres considered a small farm. The tractors for small farms are in the first section of the `if/else` statement, so the first dialog box should be displayed after entering a value less than or equal to 5000, and the second dialog box should be displayed after entering a value over 5000. The start of your `createRecommendation()` function should match the following:

```
1    function createRecommendation() {
2        if (acresBox.value >= 5000) { // 5000 acres or less, ↵
3            no crop test needed
4    window.alert("After first if clause: " + acresBox.value);
5            if (monthsBox.value <= 10) { // 10+ months of farming↵
6                per year
7                messageHeadElement.innerHTML = "E3250";
8                messageElement.innerHTML = "A workhorse for a small↵
9                farm or a big backyard. A medium- to heavy-duty↵
10               tractor that can haul whatever you throw at it↵
11               year-round.";
12           } else { // 9 or fewer months per year
13               messageHeadElement.innerHTML = "E2600";
14               messageElement.innerHTML = "Perfect for a small↵
15               farm, or just a big backyard. A light- to medium-↵
16               duty tractor that can make short work of most any↵
17               chore.";
18           }
19       } else { // more than 5000 acres
20    window.alert("After second else clause: " + acresBox.value);
```

6. Save your work, return to your browser, refresh or reload **tractor.htm**, click the **acres** box, and then type **5**. As Figure 4-9 shows, an alert dialog box appears with the text "After second else clause: 5". This is the value you expected. However, because this is the message you specified in the `else` clause rather than in the `if` clause, its appearance indicates that the `else` clause is executing rather than the `if` clause for values under 5000, which is the reverse of the programmer's intent.

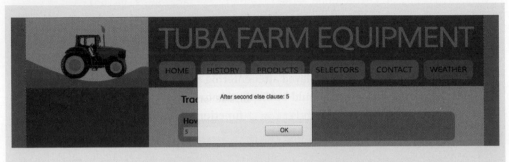

Figure 4-9: First alert dialog box displayed

7. Click the **OK** button, return to your text editor, and then examine the statement above the first `window.alert()` statement. Note that the `if` clause is true if the `acresBox.value` is greater than or equal to (>=) 5000. Because the number you entered, 5, is less than this value, the statement evaluated to `false` and the function moved on to the `else` statement that decides among tractors for large farms. Your contacts at Tuba Farm Equipment specified that the first `if` clause should be true if the acres value is less than or equal to 5000, so you need to change the >= operator to <=.

8. In the `if` statement above the first `window.alert()` statement, replace >= with **<=**, so the line reads as follows:

```
if (acresBox.value <= 5000) {
```

9. Delete the two `window.alert()` statements from the `createRecommendation()` function.

10. Save your work, return to your browser, refresh or reload **tractor.htm**, and then in the acres box, type **5**. As Figure 4-10 shows, the application now generates a recommendation for a tractor geared toward small farms.

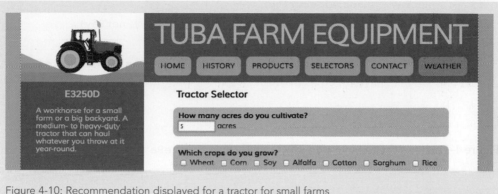

Figure 4-10: Recommendation displayed for a tractor for small farms

Tracing Errors with the `console.log()` Method

There may be situations in which you want to trace a bug in your program by analyzing a list of values rather than by trying to interpret the values displayed in alert dialog boxes on a case-by-case basis. You can create such a list by writing, or **logging**, values directly to the console using the `console.log()` method. This method has the syntax

```
console.log(value);
```

where `value` can be a string literal, the value of a variable, or a combination of the two. For instance, the following code shows an example of the `calculatePay()` function logging values. Multiple `console.log()` methods that log values to the console are included throughout the function.

```
1    function calculatePay() {
2        var payRate = 15; numHours = 40;
3        var grossPay = payRate * numHours;
4    console.log("grossPay is " + grossPay);
5        var federalTaxes = grossPay * .06794;
6        var stateTaxes = grossPay * .0476;
7        var socialSecurity = grossPay * .062;
8        var medicare = grossPay * .0145;
9        var netPay = grossPay - federalTaxes;
10   console.log("grossPay minus federalTaxes is " + netPay);
11       netPay *= stateTaxes;
12   console.log("netPay minus stateTaxes is " + netPay);
```

```
13      netPay *= socialSecurity;
14    console.log("netPay minus socialSecurity is " + netPay);
15      netPay *= medicare;
16    console.log("netPay minus medicare is " + netPay);
17      return netPay;
18    }
19    calculatePay();
```

Figure 4-11 shows the console after executing the `calculatePay()` function.

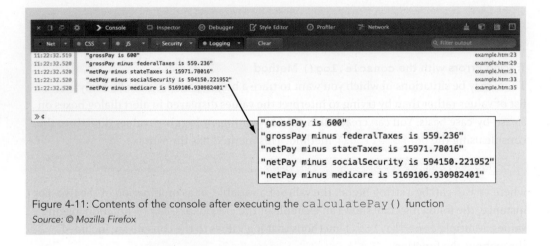

Figure 4-11: Contents of the console after executing the `calculatePay()` function
Source: © Mozilla Firefox

Using the contents of the console log in Figure 4-11, you can evaluate each variable in the `calculatePay()` function as values change throughout the function execution. Quickly viewing a list of variable values in the console is a simple, yet effective technique for testing many types of code.

Note

When using the `console.log()` method to trace bugs, it can be helpful to use a *driver program*, which is a simplified, temporary program that is used for testing functions and other code. A driver program is simply a JavaScript program that contains only the code you are testing. Driver programs do not have to be elaborate; they can be as simple as a single function you are testing. This technique allows you to isolate and test an individual function without having to worry about web page elements, event handlers, global variables, and other code that form your program's functionality as a whole.

After reviewing your most recent change to the tractor selector application, your contacts at Tuba Farm Equipment have reported another logic error. Entering an acreage less than or equal to 5000 correctly produces recommendations for small farms. However, the all-season tractor is being recommended for usage of 10 months or fewer, while the partial-year tractor is being recommended for 11 or 12 months of use. You'll use `console.log()` statements to help you verify that the program is receiving the correct value from the form and identify which branch of the `if/else` statement is being executed.

To use `console.log()` statements to help locate a bug in the `createRecommendation()` function:

1. Return to the **tuba.js** document in your web browser.

2. Enter **5** in the acres box, check the **Wheat** check box, enter **8** in the months box, and then click the **E85** option button. As Figure 4-12 shows, the application recommends the E3250E, which is described as a year-round tractor. However, because you entered 8 months, a non-year-round model should be recommended.

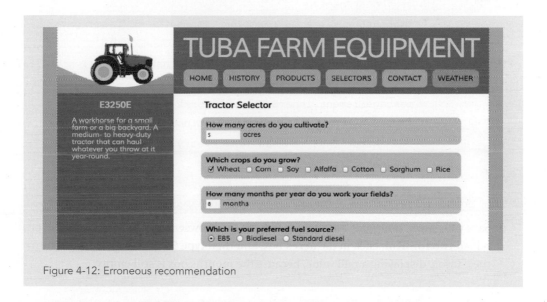

Figure 4-12: Erroneous recommendation

3. Return to the **tuba.js** document in your text editor, and locate the `createRecommendation()` function.

4. Below the third line of the function—the `if` statement that checks the value entered in the months box—enter the following statement:

```
console.log("After second if clause: " + monthsBox.value);
```

5. On a new line below the sixth line of the function, which reads

```
} else { // 9 or fewer months per year
```

enter the following statement:

```
console.log("After else clause: " + monthsBox.value);
```

This `if/else` statement makes the distinction between people who farm year round and people who farm only part of the year, with any farm working 10 or more months out of the year considered a year-round operation. The small farm, year-round tractor is in the first section of the `if/else` statement, so the first message should be logged after a value of 10, 11, or 12 is entered in the months box, and the second message should be logged after entering a value of 1–9. The start of your `createRecommendation()` function should match the following:

```
1    function createRecommendation() {
2        if (acresBox.value <= 5000) { // 5000 acres or less,↵
3          no crop test needed
4          if (monthsBox.value <= 10) { // 10+ months of farming↵
5            per year
6      console.log("After second if clause: " + monthsBox.value);
7            messageHeadElement.innerHTML = "E3250";
8            messageElement.innerHTML = "A workhorse for a small↵
9              farm or a big backyard. A medium- to heavy-duty↵
10             tractor that can haul whatever you throw at it↵
11             year-round.";
12         } else { // 9 or fewer months per year
13     console.log("After else clause: " + monthsBox.value);
```

6. Save your work, return to your browser, ensure the browser console is open, refresh or reload **tractor.htm**, click in the **acres** box, and then type **5**. A message is logged to the console displaying a null value, because the months box is still empty.

Caution

If you open or reload a document containing a `console.log()` statement in Internet Explorer without first opening the console, the browser itself may crash. For this reason, always ensure the IE console is open before opening or reloading a document that uses `console.log()`. In addition, be sure to remove all `console.log()` statements from your code before publishing an app, or IE users may to be unable to use it.

7. Click the **months** box, and then type **12**. Because the event listener fires after any input to the box, a message is logged in the console displaying a value of 1, followed by another message displaying a value of 12, as shown in Figure 4-13.

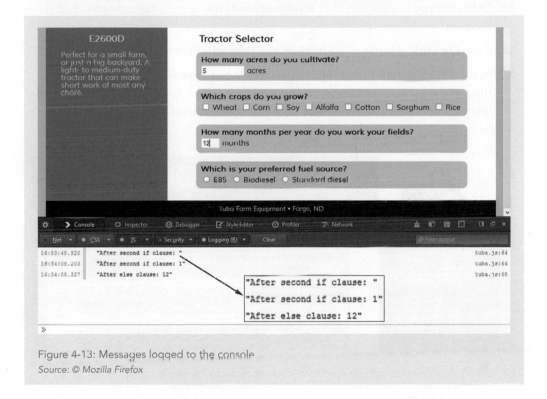

Figure 4-13: Messages logged to the console
Source: © Mozilla Firefox

Note that according to the log messages in the console, the contents of the `if` clause were executed for the value of 1, while the `else` clause contents were executed for the value of 12. This is the reverse of what the people at Tuba Farm Equipment want.

8. Return to your text editor, and examine the statement above the first `console.log()` statement. Note that the `if` clause is true if `monthsBox.value` is less than or equal to (`<=`) 10. Because your final entry 12, is greater than this value, the statement evaluated to `false` and the function moved on to the `else` statement that recommends the small farm year-round tractor. Your contacts at Tuba Farm Equipment specified that this `if` clause should be true if the months value is greater than or equal to 10, so you need to change the `<=` operator to `>=`.

9. In the `if` statement directly above the first `console.log()` statement, replace `<=` with `>=`, so the line reads as follows:

```
if (monthsBox.value >= 10) { // 10+ months of farming per year
```

10. Delete the two `console.log()` statements from the `createRecommendation()` function.

11. Save your work, return to your browser, and then refresh or reload **tractor.htm**.

12. In the acres box, type **5**, and then in the months box, type **8**. As Figure 4-14 shows, the application now generates a recommendation for the E2600D, the tractor geared toward small farms that is not billed as a year-round tractor.

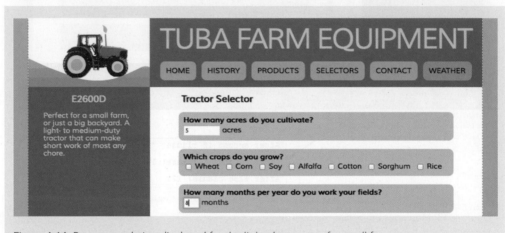

Figure 4-14: Recommendation displayed for the light-duty tractor for small farms

Using Comments to Locate Bugs

Another method of locating bugs in a JavaScript program is to identify lines that you think may be causing problems and transform them into comments. To do so, you simply add `//` to the start of a single line, or `/*` to the start of a block and `*/` to the end of the block, just as you would to create any other comment. This process is known as commenting out code. This technique can help you isolate a particular statement that may be causing an error. In some cases, you may choose to comment out individual lines that may be causing an error, or you may choose to comment out all lines except the lines that you know work. When you first receive an error message, you can start by commenting out only the statement specified by the line number in the error message. You can then save the document, and then open it again in your browser to see if you receive another error. If you receive additional error messages, you comment out those statements as well. Once you eliminate the error messages, you can examine the commented out statements for the cause of the bug.

The last five statements in the following code are commented out because they generate error messages stating that `yearlyIntrest` is not defined. The problem with the code is that the `yearlyInterest` variable is incorrectly spelled as *yearlyIntrest* in several of the statements. Commenting out the lines isolates the problem statements.

```
1    var amount = 100000;
2    var percentage = .08;
3    document.write("<p>The interest rate for a loan in the amount↵
4       of " + amount + " is " + percentage + "<br />");
5    var yearlyInterest = amount * percentage;
6    // document.write("The amount of interest for one year is "
7    // + yearlyIntrest + "<br />");
8    // var monthlyInterest = yearlyIntrest / 12;
9    // document.write("The amount of interest for one month is "
10   // + monthlyInterest + "<br />");
11   // var dailyInterest = yearlyIntrest / 365;
12   // document.write("The amount of interest for one day is " +
13   // dailyInterest + "</p>");
```

Although the error in the preceding code may seem somewhat simple, it is typical of the types of errors you will encounter. Often you will see the error right away and, therefore, have no need to comment out code or use any other tracing technique. However, when you have been staring at the same code for long periods of time, simple spelling errors, like `yearlyIntrest`, are not always easy to spot. Commenting out the lines you know are giving you trouble is a good technique for isolating and correcting even the simplest types of bugs.

Combining Debugging Techniques

You can combine debugging techniques to aid in your search for errors. For example, the following code uses comments combined with an alert dialog box to trace errors

in the `calculatePay()` function. Suppose that the `var grossPay = payRate *`
`numHours;` statement is the last statement in the function that operates correctly.
Therefore, all of the lines following that statement are commented out. You could then
use an alert dialog box or log message to check the value of each statement, removing
comments from each statement in a sequential order, and checking and correcting
syntax as you go.

```
1    function calculatePay() {
2        var payRate = 15;
3        var numHours = 40;
4        var grossPay = payRate * numHours;
5        window.alert(grossPay);
6    //    var federalTaxes = grossPay * .06794;
7    //    var stateTaxes = grossPay * .0476;
8    //    var socialSecurity = grossPay * .062;
9    //    var medicare = grossPay * .0145;
10   //    var netPay = grossPay - federalTaxes;
11   //    netPay *= stateTaxes;
12   //    netPay *= socialSecurity;
13   //    netPay *= medicare;
14   //    return Math.round(netPay);
15   }
```

Your contacts at Tuba Farm Equipment have reported another bug, which you'll work
on tracking down next. When a user indicates that they run a large farm (> 5000 acres)
year-round (>= 10 months), two tractor recommendations are possible based on the
crops they grow. If a user indicates that they grow wheat or corn or soy, the program
should recommend the W2500. However, the program currently only recommends this
tractor for wheat farmers. You'll use comments to identify the line of code that's causing
the issue.

To use comments to locate a bug in the `createRecommendation()` function:

1. Return to the **tractor.htm** document in your browser, reload or refresh the web page,
   enter **10000** in the acres box, enter **12** in the months box, and then click the **Wheat**
   check box to check it. As Figure 4-15 shows, the application recommends a tractor
   especially for wheat, corn, and soy farmers.

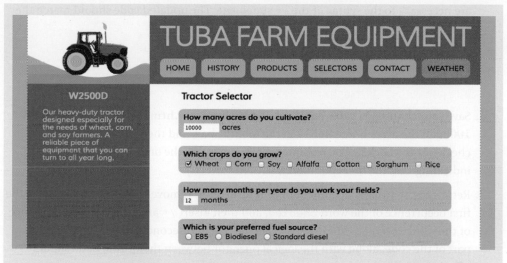

Figure 4-15: Recommendation displayed for the heavy-duty tractor for large wheat, corn, and soy farms

2. Uncheck the **Wheat** check box, and then check the **Corn** check box. Notice that the tractor recommendation changes to a general-purpose tractor.

3. Check the **Wheat** check box. Notice that when the Wheat check box is checked, the recommendation reverts to the tractor specialized for wheat, corn, and soy farmers.

4. Return to the **tuba.js** document in your text editor, and then locate the following line of code, which is roughly in the middle of the `createRecommendation()` function:

```
if (document.getElementById("wheat").checked ||
    document.getElementById("corn").checked &&
    document.getElementById("soy").checked) {
```

To debug this condition statement, you'll comment out two of its three parts and then add back the commented out sections one at a time.

5. Click after the first occurrence of the word `checked`, type **/***, and then after the third occurrence of the word `checked`, type ***/**. These insertions comment out the second and third parts of the condition, while leaving the final) and opening { that

are necessary to the syntax of the `if` statement. The updated code should match the following:

```
if (document.getElementById("wheat").checked /*||↵
    document.getElementById("corn").checked &&↵
    document.getElementById("soy").checked*/) {
```

6. Save your changes to **tuba.js**, reload or refresh **tractor.htm** in your browser, enter **10000** in the acres box, enter **12** in the months box, and then click the **Wheat** check box to check it. The recommendation matches the one shown in Figure 4-15, indicating that the first condition is written correctly.

7. Return to the **tuba.js** document in your text editor, remove the `/*` characters after the first occurrence of the word `checked`, and then insert `/*` after the second occurrence of the word `checked`. These edits make the first and second parts of the condition part of the code, along with the logical operator between them. Your code should match the following:

```
if (document.getElementById("wheat").checked ||↵
    document.getElementById("corn").checked /*&&↵
    document.getElementById("soy").checked*/) {
```

8. Save your changes to **tuba.js**, reload or refresh **tractor.htm** in your browser, enter **10000** in the acres box, enter **12** in the months box, and then click the **Corn** check box to check it. Unlike when you checked Corn in your initial test, this time the recommendation continues to match the correct one shown in Figure 4-15. This indicates that the first two conditions, along with the logical operator that joins them, are written correctly, and that the bug must be in either the condition or operator that is still commented out.

9. Return to the **tuba.js** document in your text editor. Notice that although any of the three options—wheat, corn, or soy—are supposed to trigger the recommendation for the specialized tractor, the operator after the second part of the condition is `&&`, meaning "and." For the program to work as designed, both of the logical operators must be `||` ("or"). This allows a `true` value for any of the three conditions to trigger the code block that follows.

10. After the second occurrence of the word `checked`, delete `/*`, replace `&&` with `||`, and then near the end of the line, remove the `*/` characters. Your revised code should match the following:

```
if (document.getElementById("wheat").checked ||↵
    document.getElementById("corn").checked ||↵
    document.getElementById("soy").checked) {
```

11. Save your changes to **tuba.js**, reload or refresh **tractor.htm** in your browser, enter **10000** in the acres box, enter **12** in the months box, and then click the **Soy** check box to check it. This time the recommendation matches the correct one shown in Figure 4-15.

12. Uncheck the **Soy** box, and then check the **Corn** box. The recommendation for Corn is accurate as well.

13. Uncheck the **Corn** box, and then check the **Wheat** box. The recommendation for Wheat is accurate as well.

Programming Concepts | *Dependencies*

Any program longer than a handful of lines includes statements that depend on the successful execution of other statements or functions. These relationships, known as **dependencies**, can add an extra layer of complexity to debugging. An error that seems to be caused by code in one function, for example, can actually be the result of an error in another part of your program. In addition, an error in one part of your code can stop dependent code from executing, preventing you from receiving error messages for the dependent code. After finding and fixing a bug, it's important to test related functionality that worked correctly before the bug fix. In some cases, fixing one bug exposes another, or itself creates another problem, so it's important not to assume that everything that worked before fixing a bug will continue to work after fixing it.

Short Quiz 2

1. What are the two different statements you can add to your code to provide you with additional information while you're debugging?

2. What statement would you use to log the text "itemTotal: " plus the value of the `itemTotal` variable to the console?

3. When is commenting out code useful in debugging?

Tracing Errors with Debugging Tools

Many high-level programming languages, such as Visual C++, have debugging capabilities built directly into their development environments. These built-in debugging capabilities provide sophisticated commands for tracking errors. While various JavaScript editors include different debugging features, these tools are also widely available as part of the current versions of the three major web browsers: Internet Explorer, Firefox, and Chrome.

> **Note** | *Another popular debugging tool, Firebug, is available as a free extension for Firefox. The term "extension" refers to additional functionality that can be added to a program.*

In all the major browsers, debugging tools are accessible through the same panel that opens when you use the console. The tools provided with all three browsers allow you to debug HTML, CSS, and web page scripts, and they also include tools that you can use to gauge your web site's performance.

Up to this point, you have learned how to interpret error messages and correct the statements that cause the errors. As helpful as they are, error messages are useful only in resolving syntax and run-time errors. You have also learned some techniques that assist you in locating logic errors. Examining your code manually is usually the first step in resolving a logic error, or you may use alert boxes or console log messages to track values. These techniques work fine with smaller programs. However, when you are creating a large program that includes many lines of code, logic errors can be very difficult to spot. For instance, you may have several functions that perform calculations and pass the results to other functions for further processing. Attempting to trace the logic and flow of such a program using simple tools such as the alert boxes and log messages can be difficult. Browser debuggers provide several tools that can help you trace each line of code, creating a much more efficient method of finding and resolving logic errors.

Understanding the IE, Firefox, and Chrome Debugger Windows

To debug JavaScript with any of the three major browsers, you open the document you want to debug in the browser and then open the debugger. Table 4-1 describes how to access the debugging tools in all three of the major browsers.

BROWSER	KEYBOARD SHORTCUT	MENU STEPS
Internet Explorer 9+	**F12**, then **Ctrl + 3**	Click the **Tools** icon, click **F12 developer tools** on the menu, then in the window that opens, click the **Debugger** button
Firefox	**Ctrl + Shift + S** (Win) or **option + command + S** (Mac)	Click the **Open menu** button, click **Developer**, and then click **Debugger**
Chrome	**Ctrl + Shift + J** (Win) or **option + command + J** (Mac), then in the window that opens, click the **Sources** button	Click the **Customize and control Google Chrome** button, click **Tools**, click **JavaScript Console**, then in the window that opens, click the **Sources** button

Table 4-1: Steps to open debuggers in IE, Firefox, and Chrome

The debugger window is usually displayed as a separate pane attached to the bottom of the browser window, as shown in Figure 4-16. However, you can also detach the pane into a separate window.

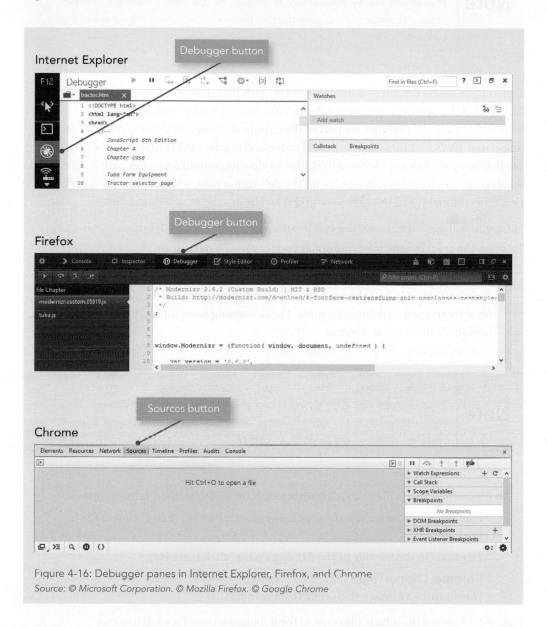

Figure 4-16: Debugger panes in Internet Explorer, Firefox, and Chrome

Source: © Microsoft Corporation. © Mozilla Firefox. © Google Chrome

Different browsers default to different views of open files. Internet Explorer shows the code for the HTML document; you can click the View sources button to select a different file to view from a list of files that are part of the current document. Firefox displays a list of associated JavaScript files in alphabetical order, and displays the contents of the first file in the list; you can click any filename in the list to view its content and work with it. Chrome displays no files by default; instead, with the debugging pane selected, you press Ctrl + O (Win) or command + O (Mac) to view and select from a list of associated files.

Next, you will open the tractor selector program in your browser's debugger.

To open the tractor selector program in your browser's debugger:

1. Return to the **tractor.htm** document in your browser.

2. Refer to Table 4-1, and then use the keyboard shortcut or the menu steps for your browser to open its debugging tools. The debugging pane should be displayed at the bottom of the browser window.

3. Open the **tuba.js** file in the debugging tools using the method for your browser:
   › **Internet Explorer**: Click the **Open document** button, then click **tuba.js** in the list.
   › **Firefox**: On the left side of the debugger pane, click **tuba.js**.
   › **Chrome**: Click an empty area of the debugger pane, press **Ctrl + O** (Win) or **command + O** (Mac), then click **tuba.js** in the list.

Figure 4-17 shows the tuba.js file open in the debugging tools for each browser.

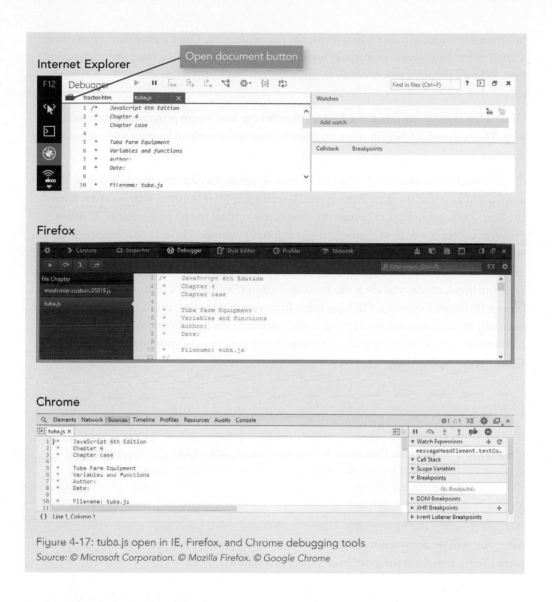

Figure 4-17: tuba.js open in IE, Firefox, and Chrome debugging tools

Source: © Microsoft Corporation. © Mozilla Firefox. © Google Chrome

Setting Breakpoints

The browser debugging tools in all three major browsers include commands that you can use to control program execution after your scripts enter break mode. The term **break mode** refers to the temporary suspension of program execution so you can monitor values and trace program execution. Entering break mode requires inserting breakpoints into your code. A **breakpoint** is a designation added to a specific statement in a program that causes program execution to pause when it reaches that statement. Once a program is paused at a breakpoint, you can use command buttons within each window to trace program execution. When a program enters break mode, program execution is not stopped—it is only suspended.

To set a breakpoint, you click the line number for the line where program execution should stop. The browser debugging tools mark each breakpoint with an icon on or next to the line number.

Once you add a breakpoint, Firefox and Chrome automatically stop the program at the breakpoint anytime the statement is run. Internet Explorer requires that you first click the Start Debugging button before the program is subject to any breakpoints. When a program enters break mode, program execution is not stopped—it is only suspended. When a program is paused at a breakpoint, browser debugging tools display different types of information about the current state of the program. To resume program execution after entering break mode, you click the Resume button (Firefox and Chrome) or the Continue button (Internet Explorer). Clicking these buttons executes the rest of the program normally or until another breakpoint is encountered. Multiple breakpoints provide a convenient way to pause program execution at key positions in your code at which you think there may be a bug.

> **Note** *You can end a debugging session without executing the rest of the program in Internet Explorer by clicking the Stop Debugging button, or in Chrome by clicking the Deactivate breakpoints button, followed by the Resume script execution button. At the time of this writing, Firefox debugging tools don't include this option.*

Next, you will set breakpoints in the `createRecommendation()` function and use them to track the results of entering different values in the form.

To set breakpoints in the `createRecommendations()` function:

1. In your browser, enter **100** in the acres box, click the **Wheat** check box to check it, enter **12** in the months box, and then click the **E85** option button to select it. Your form should match Figure 4-18.

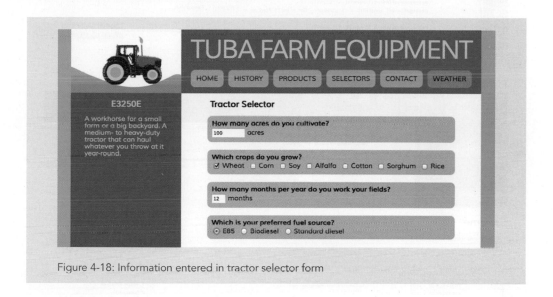

Figure 4-18: Information entered in tractor selector form

2. In your browser debugger tools, scroll down to line 63, which reads `if (monthsBox .value >= 10) { // 10+ months of farming per year`, and then click **63** (the line number) to set a breakpoint.

   Figure 4-19 shows the breakpoint set in the debugging tools for all three browsers.

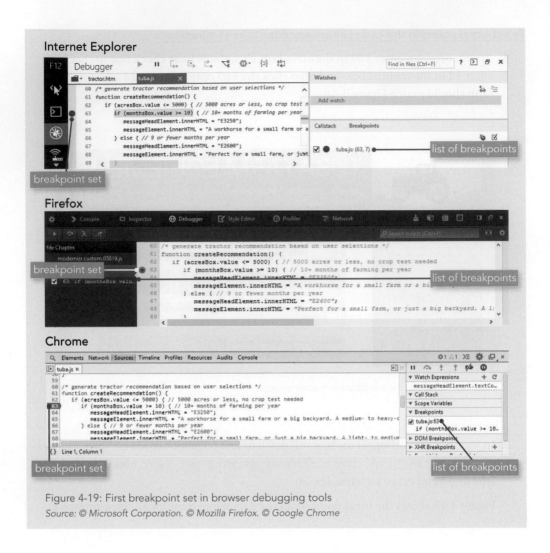

Figure 4-19: First breakpoint set in browser debugging tools
Source: © Microsoft Corporation. © Mozilla Firefox. © Google Chrome

3. Repeat Step 2 to set additional breakpoints on lines **64**, **67**, **71**, **72** and **75**. You should now have six breakpoints marked in the code for tuba.js in your browser debugging tools.

4. In the tractor selector form, click at the end of the value in the acres box, and then type **0** to change the value to 1000. Your input triggers an event listener, which executes the `createRecommendation()` function. The focus switches to the debugging tools, where line 63 is highlighted, as shown in Figure 4-20. The highlighting indicates that the program has stopped at this breakpoint.

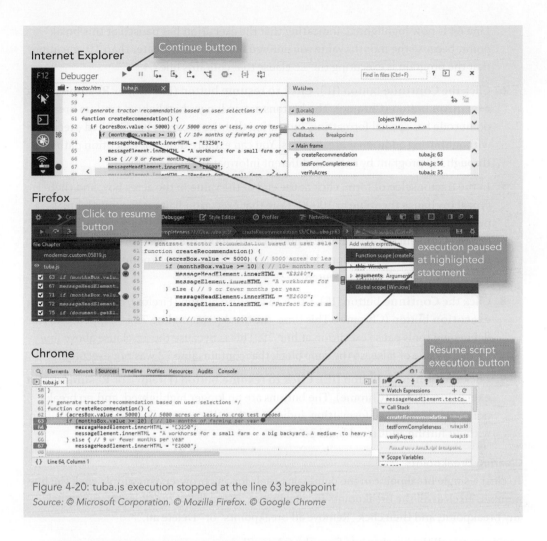

Figure 4-20: tuba.js execution stopped at the line 63 breakpoint

Source: © Microsoft Corporation. © Mozilla Firefox. © Google Chrome

Execution halted at line 63, the first breakpoint you created, because the value you entered in the acres box is less than 5000.

5. Click the **Continue** button (IE), **Click to resume** button (Firefox), or **Resume script execution** button (Chrome).

Note | *See Figure 4-20 for the location of the appropriate button in each browser.*

Line 64 is now highlighted, indicating that the execution has paused at this breakpoint, because the months value you entered in the form is greater than 10, meaning that the program is executing the `if` clause that contains line 64.

6. Click the **Continue** button (IE), **Click to resume** button (Firefox), or **Resume script execution** button (Chrome). The buttons are no longer highlighted, and no breakpoint code has special formatting, indicating that the program has finished execution without hitting additional breakpoints. You can explore different execution paths through the program by entering different information in the form.

7. In the tractor selector form, click at the end of the value in the acres box, and then type **0** to change the value to 10000. Note that execution halts at the fourth breakpoint you set, on line 71, rather than at the first breakpoint on line 63. Because the changed value in the acres box was greater than 5000, the `if` clause that contains lines 63, 64, and 67 was skipped. Execution is halted at a breakpoint only when the breakpoint is about to be executed.

8. Click the **Continue** button (IE), **Click to resume** button (Firefox), or **Resume script execution** button (Chrome). This time, the breakpoint on line 72 is skipped, and the debugging tools pause execution at line 75. This is because the `if` clause above line 72 had a value of false, so the code block that contains line 72 was not executed.

9. Click the **Continue** button (IE), **Click to resume** button (Firefox), or **Resume script execution** button (Chrome). The buttons are no longer highlighted, and no breakpoint code has special formatting, indicating that the program has finished execution without hitting additional breakpoints.

Clearing Breakpoints

To clear a single breakpoint in the debugging tools for any browser, you simply click the line number. To clear all the breakpoints in a document, in the list of breakpoints, right-click any breakpoint, and then click "Remove all breakpoints" or "Delete all."

You'll remove all the breakpoints from the tuba.js file.

To remove breakpoints from the tuba.js file:

1. If necessary, scroll to line 63, then click **63** (the line number) to remove the breakpoint.

2. In the list of breakpoints, right-click the description of any breakpoint, and then click **Remove all breakpoints** (Firefox and Chrome) or **Delete all** (IE). All remaining breakpoints are removed.

Stepping Through Your Scripts

The debugging tools in all three browsers include a set of alternative options known as stepping options, which allow you to continue program execution after you enter break mode. The first, known as stepping in or stepping into, executes an individual line of code and then pauses until you instruct the debugger to continue. This feature gives you an opportunity to evaluate program flow and structure as code is being executed.

As you use the Step Into button to move through code, the debuggers stop at each line within every function of the JavaScript program. However, when stepping through a program to trace a logical error, it is convenient to be able to skip functions that you know are functioning correctly. The second option, known as stepping over, allows you to skip function calls. The program still executes each function that you step over, but it appears in each debugger as if a single statement executes.

The final option, stepping out, executes all remaining code in the current function. If the current function was called from another function, all remaining code in the current function executes and the debugger stops at the next statement in the calling function.

Next, you will trace the execution of the program using the stepping options.

To trace program execution using the stepping options:

1. In your browser's debugging tools, scroll up to line 50, and then click **50** (the line number) to set a breakpoint.

2. On the tractor selector form, click the **E85** option button. Because this is an option button that's already selected, clicking it doesn't change its value; however, it triggers the event listener for the button, which executes the functions associated with the form. The focus switches to the debugging tools, which show that the program is paused at line 50, which calls the `testFormCompleteness()` function.

3. Click the **Step into** (IE and Chrome) or **Step In** (Firefox) button, as shown in Figure 4-21. The debugging tools move the highlight to line 55, the first statement in the `testFormCompleteness()` function.

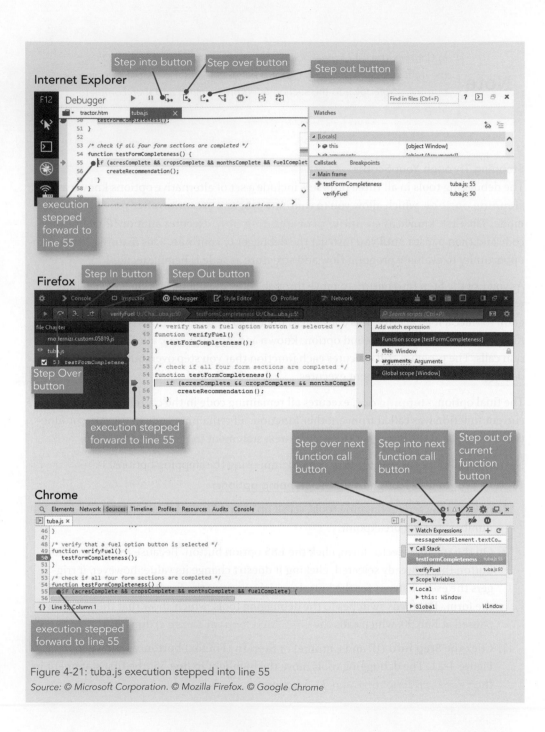

Figure 4-21: tuba.js execution stepped into line 55

Source: © Microsoft Corporation. © Mozilla Firefox. © Google Chrome

4. Click the **Step into** or **Step In** button again to move to the next statement, `createRecommendation();`, on line 56. You've already explored the `createRecommendation()` function, so you'll step over it.

5. Click the **Step over** button to execute the `createRecommendation()` function. Script execution either stays on line 56, indicating that the function call has been skipped, or moves to line 58, the end of the `testFormCompleteness()` function, which called the `createRecommendation()` function.

6. Click the **Step into** or **Step In** button. Script execution returns to line 50 or 51, within the `verifyFuel()` function.

7. Click the **Step out** button to complete debugging and program execution.

8. On line 50, click **50** (the line number) to remove the breakpoint.

Note	*The tractor selector program is structured to eventually support validation that finds additional types of errors, which you'll study in Chapter 6. Even though the program could be simplified by removing functions such as `verifyFuel()`, such functions are included in the program's architecture to support this future functionality.*

Tracing Variables and Expressions

As you trace program execution by using step commands and breakpoints, you may also need to trace how variables and expressions change during the course of program execution. For example, suppose that you have a statement that reads `resultNum = firstNum / secondNum;`. If you attempt to divide by zero, a value of `infinity` is returned. You know this line is causing a divide-by-zero error, but you do not know exactly when `secondNum` is being changed to a zero value. To pinpoint the cause of the logic problem, you need a way to trace program execution and locate the exact location at which `secondNum` is being changed to a zero value.

The debugging tools in all browsers display lists of local variables within the currently executing function, regardless of whether they have been initialized. The **variables lists** help you see how different values in the currently executing function affect program execution. In addition, each browser lets you create a **watch list**, which is a list of expressions whose values are displayed and updated throughout the execution of the program.

In all three browsers, the watch list and the variables list are displayed in the right section of the debugging tools pane:

> **Internet Explorer**: The Watches list is displayed by default on the right side of the debugging tools pane. In break mode, local and global variables are displayed automatically in the Watches list.

> **Firefox**: Click the Expand Panes button to open a pane on the right side of the debugging tools; this pane contains both the watch and variables lists.

> **Chrome**: Both the Watch Expressions and Scope Variables lists are displayed by default on the right side of the debugging tools pane, beneath the stepping buttons.

To add an expression to the watch list in any browser, you first locate an instance of the expression in the program, select it, and copy it to the Clipboard. You next click "Click to add" (IE) or "Add watch expression" (Firefox or Chrome), paste the expression from the Clipboard, and then press Enter. The expression is then displayed in the list, along with its current value.

Your contacts at Tuba Farm Equipment have tested out your most recent changes to the tractor selector application, and they have found one additional bug. A single letter should be added to the end of the model name to denote the selected fuel source—*E* for E85, *B* for biodiesel, or *D* for standard diesel. The letters are correctly appended for E85 and standard diesel. However, when a user selects biodiesel, the model number is changed to simply *B*. You'll create a watched expression to monitor changes to the model name during program execution to identify the source of this bug.

To add an expression to the watch list to monitor the value of the model name:

1. Scroll down to line 84, and then click **84** (the line number) to add a breakpoint. Line 84 is the start of the `if/else` statement that determines the letter to be appended to the model name.

2. In line 85, select the text `messageHeadElement.innerHTML`, and then press **Ctrl + C** (Win) or **command + C** (Mac) to copy it to the clipboard.

3. Follow the instructions for your browser to add the expression to your watch list:

   > **Internet Explorer:** On the right side of the debugging tools pane, click **Add watch**, press **Ctrl + V** to paste the clipboard contents, and then press **Enter**.

   > **Firefox:** On the right side of the debugging tools pane, click the **Expand panes** button if necessary to display the watch and variables lists, click **Add watch expression**, press **Ctrl + V** (Win) or **command + V** (Mac) to paste the clipboard contents, and then press **Enter**.

   > **Chrome:** On the right side of the debugging tools pane, scroll up if necessary to the Watch Expressions section, click the **Add watch expression** button, press **Ctrl + V** (Win) or **command + V** (Mac) to paste the clipboard contents, and then press **Enter**.

   Figure 4-22 shows the debugging tools pane for each browser after adding the expression to the watch list.

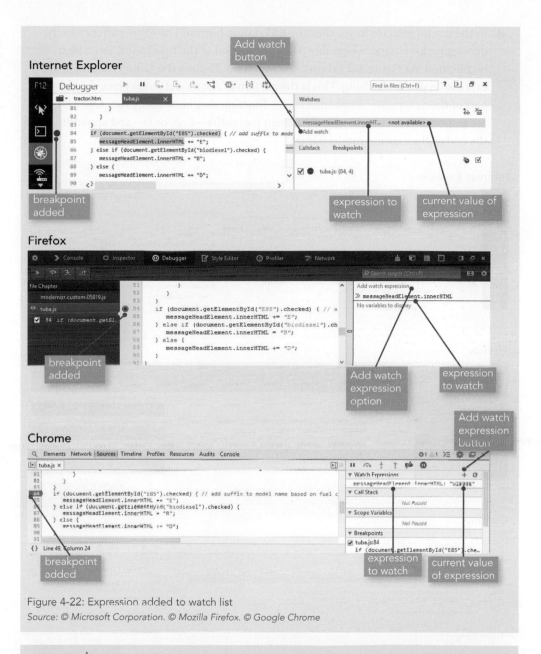

Figure 4-22: Expression added to watch list

Source: © Microsoft Corporation. © Mozilla Firefox. © Google Chrome

> **Note**
>
> If the watch list in your browser is not as wide as the one shown in Figure 4-22, move the pointer over the border between the tuba.js code and the watch list until the pointer becomes a double-headed arrow, and then click and drag to the left until the width of your watch list matches the one in the figure.

4. In the tractor selector form, click the **E85** option button. The focus switches to the debugging tools pane, where line 84—the location of the breakpoint you added—is highlighted. As Figure 4-23 shows, the watch list displays the value W2500 for the expression you're watching. This is the portion of the model name generated by the part of the `createRecommendation()` function that has already run. Lines 84–90 are responsible for identifying the correct fuel suffix—*E*, *B*, or *D*—and appending it to the end of the existing model name.

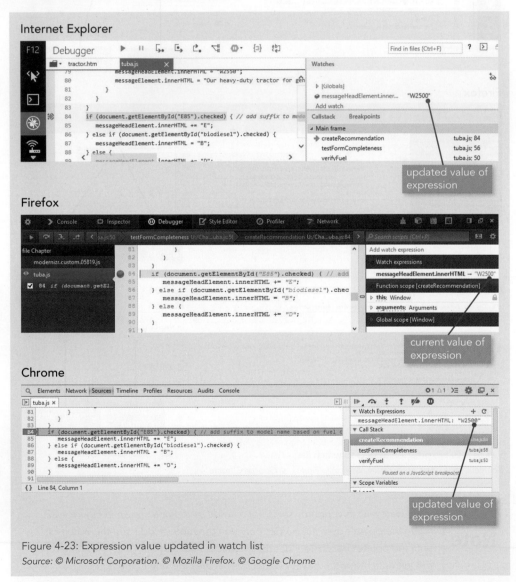

Figure 4-23: Expression value updated in watch list

Source: © Microsoft Corporation. © Mozilla Firefox. © Google Chrome

5. Click the **Step into** or **Step In** button. Because the `if` clause in line 84 evaluates to `true`, script execution moves to line 85.

6. Click the **Step into** or **Step In** button again. The expression on line 85 is executed, and the value of the expression in the watch list is correctly updated to W2500E.

7. Click the **Resume** or **Continue** button. The script execution finishes, with the expression value remaining W2500E. Next you'll watch how the expression value changes after clicking the Biodiesel option button.

8. Click the **Biodiesel** option button, click the **Step into** or **Step In** button, and then click the **Step into** or **Step In** button again. The expression value starts at W2500, as it did when you first clicked E85. This time the program execution moves to line 86 because the expression in the first `if` statement evaluates to `false`, and then moves to line 87 because the expression in the second `if` statement evaluates to `true`.

9. Click the **Step into** or **Step In** button again. As Figure 4-24 shows, the watch list now shows the expression value as simply *B*. This indicates a problem with the code in line 87.

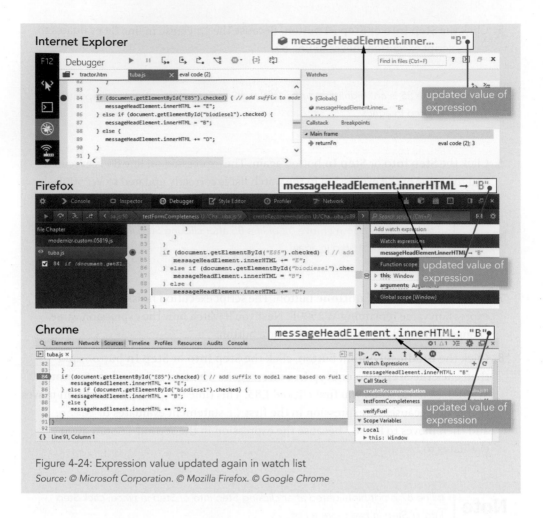

Figure 4-24: Expression value updated again in watch list

Source: © Microsoft Corporation. © Mozilla Firefox. © Google Chrome

10. Click the **Resume** or **Continue** button, remove the breakpoint on line 84, and then return to **tuba.js** in your text editor.

11. In line 87, which reads `messageHeadElement.innerHTML = "B";`, change = to +=, so your code matches the following:

```
messageHeadElement.innerHTML += "B";
```

12. Save your changes to **tuba.js**, refresh or reload **tractor.htm** in your browser, enter **10000** in the acres box, check the **Wheat** box, enter **12** in the months box, and then click the **Biodiesel** option button. As Figure 4-25 shows, the model number is now correctly listed as W2500B instead of just *B*, indicating that you fixed the bug.

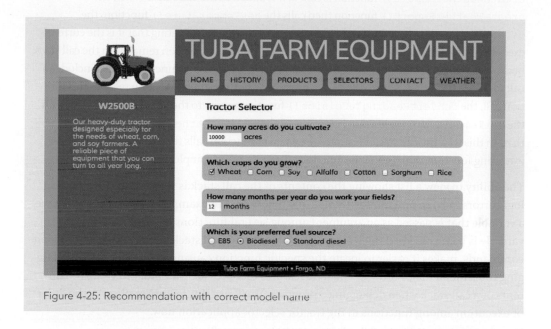

Figure 4-25: Recommendation with correct model name

Examining the Call Stack

When you are working with a JavaScript program that contains multiple functions, the processor must remember the order in which functions are executed. For example, if you have an `accountsPayable()` function that calls an `accountsReceivable()` function, the computer must remember to return to the `accountsPayable()` function after the `accountsReceivable()` function finishes executing. Similarly, if the `accountsReceivable()` function calls a `depositFunds()` function after it has been called by the `accountsPayable()` function, then the computer must remember to return to the `accountsReceivable()` function after the `depositFunds()` function finishes executing, and then return to the `accountsPayable()` function after the `accountsReceivable()` function finishes executing. The **call stack** is the ordered list maintained by a JavaScript processor containing all the procedures, such as functions, methods, or event handlers, that have been called but have not yet finished processing. Each time a program calls a procedure, the procedure is added to the top of the call stack, and then removed after it finishes executing.

For instance, suppose you are working with a program that includes a `createWeatherReport()` function, which in turn contains a call to a `getTemperature()` function. When the `createWeatherReport()` function is called, it is added to the call stack. When the `createWeatherReport()` function then calls the `getTemperature()` function, the `getTemperature()` function is added to the top of call stack, indicating that it is the currently executing function. However, the `createWeatherReport()` function remains on the call stack because it has not yet finished executing. The `getTemperature()` function in turn includes a call to a `convertReadingToCelsius()` function; when program execution reaches this function call, the `convertReadingToCelsius()` function moves to the top of the call stack, with the `getTemperature()` function below it, and the `createWeatherReport()` function below that. In this way, the call stack illustrates the chain of function calls that leads to the currently executing function, and lists all the functions that have yet to complete execution.

The ability to view a list showing the contents of the call stack is very useful when tracing logic errors in large programs with multiple functions. For example, suppose that you have a variable that is passed as an argument among several functions. Suppose also that the variable is being assigned the wrong value. Viewing the call stack, along with using tracing commands, makes it easier to locate the specific function causing the problem. The debugging tools for all major browsers include features that provide the ability to view the contents of a call stack when debugging a program. You'll use this feature to observe the order of execution among functions in the tractor selector application now.

To monitor the call stack while the tractor selector application executes:

1. Scroll up to line 50, and then click **50** (the line number) to add a breakpoint.

> **Note**
> If you're using Chrome, you might need to scroll to the top of the right section of the debugging tools pane so the heading "Call Stack" is visible. In Internet Explorer, you might need to scroll down the right section of the debugging tools pane. If you're using Firefox, the call stack is displayed by default.

2. On the tractor selector form, click the **E85** option button to trigger execution of the `verifyFuel()` function. The focus returns to the debugging tools, and line 50 is highlighted. The function name `verifyFuel` is added to the call stack, as shown in Figure 4-26.

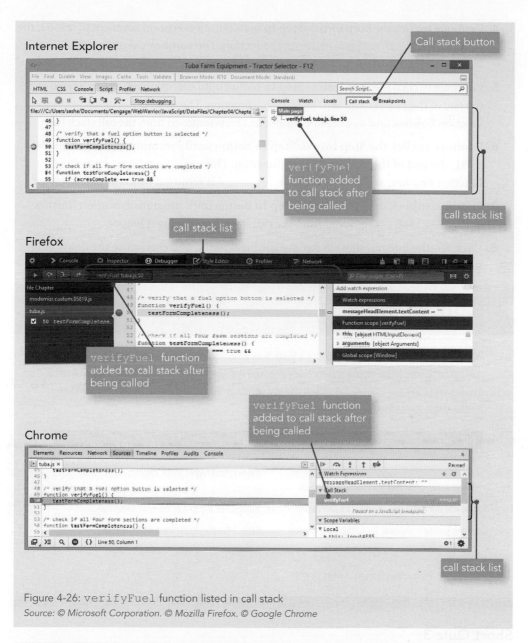

Figure 4-26: `verifyFuel` function listed in call stack

Source: © Microsoft Corporation. © Mozilla Firefox. © Google Chrome

3. Click the **Step into** or **Step In** button. The `testFormCompleteness` function is added to the top of the call stack, while `verifyFuel` remains on the call stack as well. This indicates that `testFormCompleteness` is the currently executing function, and that when it's finished executing, the program flow will return to the `verifyFuel` function.

4. Continue to click the **Step into** or **Step In** button until execution advances to line 62, the start of the createRecommendation() function. The name createRecommendation is added to the top of the call stack, above testFormCompleteness and verifyFuel.

5. Continue to click the **Step into** or **Step In** button until execution returns to line 56 or 58, the end of the testFormCompleteness() function. The createRecommendation() function finishes, and createRecommendation is removed from the call stack list.

6. Continue to click the **Step into** or **Step In** button until execution returns to line 50 or 51, the end of the verifyFuel() function. The testFormCompleteness() function finishes, and testFormCompleteness is removed from the call stack list.

7. Continue to click the **Step into** or **Step In** button until program execution finishes and verifyFuel is removed from the call stack list, leaving it empty.

8. Click **50** (the line number) to remove the breakpoint, and then close the debugging tools pane.

Skills at Work | *Reporting Bugs*

Whether you are working as a member of a team or as an individual technical support person, you need to be able describe clearly and concisely any bugs that you encounter in an application. Follow the do's and don't's in Table 4-2 to ensure that you generate reports that will be useful to whomever is responsible for tracking down and resolving the issue.

DO	DON'T
Describe in detail the steps required to reproduce the error, what you expected would result from these steps, and what you observed instead	Jump to conclusions about what may be causing the bug and report those instead
Provide the exact text of any error messages	Summarize the gist of an error message
Make yourself available for further questions or demonstration	Expect the bug to be fixed immediately

Table 4-2: Bug reporting do's and don't's

Short Quiz 3

1. What is a breakpoint? How do you set a breakpoint?

2. Explain the differences between stepping in (or into), stepping over, and stepping out.

3. What is the call stack? How do you use it in debugging?

Handling Exceptions and Errors

Any good programmer wants to create bug-free programs. However, in practice, even the best-written and most thoroughly debugged code may be released to users with some undetected bugs. In addition, programs that require user input can sometimes fail if that input doesn't fit with the guidelines provided to users, such as a user entering a word in a number field. Thus, a good programmer should also strive to write code that anticipates any problems that may occur and includes graceful methods of dealing with those problems. Writing code that anticipates and handles potential problems is often called bulletproofing. One common bulletproofing technique is to validate submitted form data. For example, you might run a script when the Submit button is clicked that verifies that the value of any required text box isn't an empty string.

> **Note** | You'll learn additional validation techniques for form data in Chapter 6.

Another method of bulletproofing your code is to use exception handling, which allows a program to handle errors, or exceptions as they are often called, as they occur in the execution of the program. Many advanced programming languages, including ECMAScript Edition 5.1, include exception-handling capabilities. You use exception handling to test any type of input or functionality that is external to a program. For most programming languages, exception handling is most useful when connecting to a database or when trying to access some other type of external program. Because JavaScript does not currently support robust methods for connecting to databases, the main reason for using exception handling is to evaluate user input. Although you could technically use exception handling for all of your JavaScript programs, your code should be tested thoroughly enough that it anticipates any potential problems that may occur. However, one area that you cannot control is whether users enter the correct type of data.

JavaScript includes four statements specifically for exception handling: try, throw, catch, and finally.

Using the try and throw Statements

You enclose code that may contain an exception in a try statement. The syntax for a try statement is as follows:

```
try {
    statements;
}
```

If the result of evaluating statements is an error—for instance, the result of trying to divide a number by 0—then an error is triggered, or thrown.

Alternately, you can test a condition within the `try` statement, and then add a `throw` statement to specify an error message if the result is `false`.

For instance, if you wanted to throw an error if a user leaves the element with the `id` value `1Name` blank when submitting a form, you could use the following structure:

```
1    try {
2        var lastName = document.getElementById("1Name").value;
3        if (lastName === "") {
4            throw "Please enter your last name.";
5        }
6    }
```

Creating a `try` statement by itself only generates a text string that's identified as a message. To specify how that message is to be used, you use a `catch` statement.

Catching Exceptions

After you throw an error, you use a **`catch()` statement** to handle, or "catch" the error. The syntax for a catch statement is as follows:

```
catch(error) {
    statements;
}
```

The `catch` statement accepts a single argument that assigns a name to the error message specified by the exception thrown by a `try` statement. Whatever argument name you specify when creating the `catch` statement is the variable name you use within *statements* to refer to the text of the thrown exception. The following `catch` statement demonstrates how to catch the exception that is thrown by the `try` statement that evaluates the `1Name` field value. Notice that the `window.alert()` statement displays the passed `1NameError` variable as its value. The `catch` statement also returns a value of `false` to the calling statement, which indicates that the form's `submit` event listener should not execute.

```
1    catch(1NameError) {
2        window.alert(1NameError);
3        return false;
4    }
```

In combination with the preceding `try` statement, this code would result in an alert dialog box containing the text "Please enter your last name." if a user tried to submit the form with a blank `1Name` field.

Whenever a `try` statement throws an exception, the JavaScript interpreter executes the nearest `catch` statement. If a `catch` statement is not located within the construct that throws an exception, the JavaScript interpreter looks at the next higher level of code for a `catch` statement. For example, if an `if` statement contains a `throw` statement, but it does not contain a `catch` statement, the JavaScript interpreter looks in a function that contains the `if` statement. Then, if the function does not contain a `catch` statement, the JavaScript interpreter looks for a `catch` statement at the global level. If a construct contains `try` and `finally` statements, but no `catch` statement, the `finally` statement executes before the JavaScript constructor begins searching at a higher level for a `catch` statement.

Executing Final Exception Handling Tasks

JavaScript's exception handling functionality also includes a **finally statement** that executes regardless of whether its associated `try` block throws an exception. You normally use a `finally` statement to perform some type of cleanup or any necessary tasks after code is evaluated with a `try` statement. The syntax for a `finally` statement is as follows:

```
finally {
    statements;
}
```

The following example contains the entire `validateLName()` function, with `try`, `throw`, `catch`, and `finally` statements that evaluate the first name value:

```
1    function validateLName() {
2        try {
3            var lastName = document.getElementById("lName");
4            if (lastName.value === "") {
5                throw "Please enter your last name.";
6            }
7        }
8        catch(lNameError) {
9            window.alert(lNameError)
10           return false;
11       }
12       finally {
13           lNameValid = true;
14       }
```

```
15      return true;
16   }
```

Your contacts at Tuba Farm Equipment are happy with the state of the application. They'd now like you to add code to handle cases where users enter text in the acres or months boxes, or where they enter 0 in the acres box or a number outside the range 1–12 in the months box. Any of these situations would prevent the createRecommendation() function from working as designed. You'll add exception handlers to deal with these situations.

To add exception handling to the tractor selector application:

1. Return to the **tuba.js** document in your text editor.

2. Locate the verifyAcres() function, and then delete its contents—the statement testFormCompleteness();—so the function is empty.

3. Within the code block for the verifyAcres() function, enter the following statements to create variables:

```
var validity = true;
var messageText = "";
```

You'll use these variables to track whether the user's entry is valid, and the text of the message to be written to the sidebar.

4. Below the variable declarations, enter the following try statement:

```
1   try {
2       if (!(acresBox.value > 0)) {
3           throw "Please enter a number of acres greater than↵
4               0.";
5       }
6   }
```

This statement checks if the value of the acresBox variable (which references the input box with the id value acres) is greater than 0. If not, it throws an error with the message "Please enter a number of acres greater than 0."

5. Below the try statement, enter the following catch statement:

```
1   catch(message) {
2       validity = false;
3       messageText = message;
4       acresBox.value = ""; // remove erroneous entry from↵
5           input box
6   }
```

This statement sets the value of the `validity` variable to `false`, sets the value of the `messageText` variable to the text of the error message thrown by the `try` statement, and then sets the value of the input box to an empty string, removing the erroneous entry.

6. Below the `catch` statement, enter the following `finally` statement:

```
1    finally {
2        acresComplete = validity;
3        messageElement.innerHTML = messageText;
4        messageHeadElement.innerHTML = ""; // remove any↵
5            former recommendation heading
6        testFormCompleteness();
7    }
```

This statement sets the value of the global variable `acresComplete` to the value of the `validity` variable. This allows other functions to identify whether the user input in the acres box is ready for a recommendation to be generated. Next, the text content of the sidebar element displaying any error message (referenced with the variable `messageElement`) is set to the value of the `messageText` variable. If an error was thrown, this places the text of the error in the sidebar; otherwise, it sets the value of the sidebar text to an empty string. Next, the text content of the sidebar element displaying the model name for any previous recommendation is set to an empty string, in case the error message is replacing a previous recommendation. Finally, the `testFormCompleteness()` function is called.

Your `verifyAcres()` function should match the following:

```
1    function verifyAcres() {
2        var validity = true;
3        var messageText = "";
4        try {
5            if (!(acresBox.value > 0)) {
6                throw "Please enter a number of acres greater than↵
7                    0.";
8            }
9        }
10       catch (message) {
11           validity = false;
12           messageText = message;
13           acresBox.value = ""; // remove erroneous entry from↵
14               input box
```

```
15    }
16    finally {
17        acresComplete = validity;
18        messageElement.innerHTML = messageText;
19        messageHeadElement.innerHTML = ""; // remove any↵
20            former recommendation heading
21        testFormCompleteness();
22    }
23  }
```

7. Scroll down to the verifyMonths() function, remove its contents, and then add the variables and error handling statements shown below so your verifyMonths() function matches the following:

```
1   function verifyMonths() {
2       var validity = true;
3       var messageText = "";
4       try {
5           if (!(monthsBox.value >= 1 && monthsBox.value <= 12)) {
6               throw "Please enter a number of months between 1↵
7                   and 12.";
8           }
9       }
10      catch(message) {
11          validity = false;
12          messageText = message;
13          monthsBox.value = ""; // remove erroneous entry from↵
14              input box
15      }
16      finally {
17          monthsComplete = validity;
18          messageElement.innerHTML = messageText;
19          messageHeadElement.innerHTML = ""; // remove any former↵
20              recommendation heading
21          testFormCompleteness();
22      }
23  }
```

The structure of this error handling code matches the code you added to the `verifyAcres()` function above.

8. Save your changes to **tuba.js**, reload or refresh **tractor.htm** in your browser, and then in the acres box, type **0**. As Figure 4-27 shows, the error message "Please enter a number of acres greater than 0." is displayed in the sidebar, and the invalid entry is removed from the acres box.

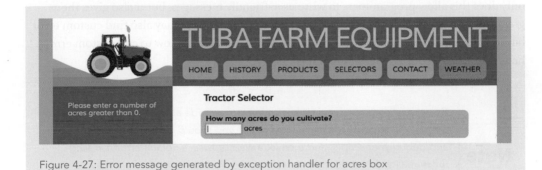

Figure 4-27: Error message generated by exception handler for acres box

9. Type **10** in the acres box. The error message is removed from the sidebar.

10. In the months box, type **13**. As Figure 4-28 shows, the error message "Please enter a number of months between 1 and 12." is displayed in the sidebar, and the invalid entry is removed from the months box.

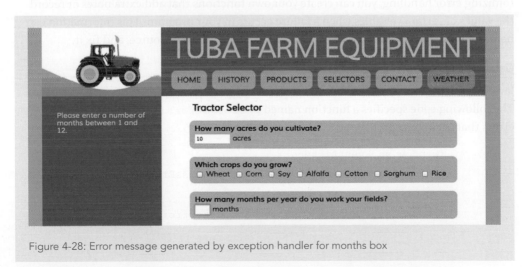

Figure 4-28: Error message generated by exception handler for months box

11. Type **8** in the months box. The error message is removed from the sidebar.

Implementing Custom Error Handling

The primary purpose of exception handling is to provide a graceful way to handle errors that may occur in your programs. As you learned earlier in this chapter, the main reason for using exception handling with JavaScript is to evaluate user input. Instead of just using exception handling with specific types of code, you can also write your own custom code for handling any types of errors that occur on a web page. Regardless of the programming language, many programmers often prefer to write their own error-handling code. Not only does this allow programmers to write user-friendly messages, but it also gives them greater control over any errors that occur in their programs. You may also find custom error handling useful in debugging your scripts. This section explains how to add custom error-handling code to your JavaScript programs.

> **Note**
>
> *Be warned that this section explains how to override a web browser's default error-handling functionality. In most cases, you should just thoroughly test and debug your scripts, and then let a web browser's default error-handling functionality deal with whatever errors you missed. However, there may be cases when you will find it necessary to write your own error-handling functionality, particularly with interactive web pages that require user input.*

As you saw earlier in this chapter, modern browsers generally send error messages to the console, where developers can view them but where users aren't bothered by them. By customizing error handling, you can create your own functions that add extra notes or record the values of certain variables when a failure occurs in your program. This information can help you more quickly understand the nature of a bug, locate its source, and fix it.

Catching Errors with the `error` Event

JavaScript includes an `error` event that executes whenever an error occurs on a web page. The following code specifies a function named `processErrors()` to handle any JavaScript errors that occur on a page.

```
1   if (window.addEventListener) {
2      window.addEventListener("error", processErrors, false);
3   } else if (window.attachEvent) {
4      window.attachEvent("onerror", processErrors);
5   }
```

To prevent a web browser from executing its own error-handling functionality, you return a value of `true` from the `error` event function, as demonstrated in the following example of the `processErrors()` function:

```
1    function processErrors() {
2        custom error handling code
3        return true;
4    }
```

> **Note**
>
> Creating an `error` event function does not fix errors in your JavaScript programs; its only purpose is to give you an opportunity to handle them with custom code.

Writing Custom Error-Handling Functions

When you specify a custom error-handling function by assigning it to the `error` event, the JavaScript interpreter automatically passes three arguments in the following order to the function for any JavaScript errors that occur: error message, URL, and line number. You can use the values in your custom error-handling function by adding parameters to the function definition. You can then use the parameters in your function to send information to the console about the location of any JavaScript errors that may occur. For example, the following code shows a modified version of the `processErrors()` function containing parameters that are assigned the three arguments that are passed by the JavaScript interpreter.

```
1    function processErrors(errMessage, errURL, errLineNum) {
2        console.log("The file " + errURL
3            + " generated the following error: "
4            + errMessage + " on line " + errLineNum);
5        return true;
6    }
7    if (window.addEventListener) {
8        window.addEventListener("error", processErrors, false);
9    } else if (window.attachEvent) {
10       window.attachEvent("onerror", processErrors);
11   }
```

If you include the preceding code on your web page, messages will be written to the console log noting any JavaScript errors the page contains.

Short Quiz 4

1. When is it necessary to include exception handling in your code? Give an example.

2. What statement in the code to handle an exception do you use to specify an error message?

3. How do you reference a previously generated error message in a `catch()` statement?

Additional Debugging Techniques

The rest of this chapter discusses additional methods and techniques for locating and correcting errors in your JavaScript programs, including checking HTML elements, analyzing logic, testing statements with the console command line, using the `debugger` statement, executing code in strict mode, linting, and reloading a web page.

Checking HTML Elements

There will be occasions when you cannot locate the source of a bug, no matter how long you search. In such cases, the flaw may not lie in your JavaScript code at all, but in your HTML elements. If you cannot locate a bug using any of the methods described in this chapter, then perform a line-by-line analysis of your HTML code, making sure that all tags have opening and closing brackets. Also, be sure that all necessary opening and closing tags, such as the `<script></script>` tag pair, are included.

You can also take advantage of free tools to perform some of this analysis for you. One of these is writing code in an editor specialized for web development, such as Notepad++, Aptana Studio, or KomodoEdit. These editors, and others like them, automatically highlight syntax errors in HTML, CSS, and JavaScript code as you type. This means that rather than needing to scrutinize each line of code, you can count on the editor to draw your attention visually to any errors it identifies—often even before you test your code.

Another tool for automatically examining your code is the W3C Markup Validation Service (*http://validator.w3.org*), which you used in Chapter 1. Many validation errors also cause problems in the browser, so validating your HTML and fixing any issues the validator identifies can help you remove bugs in your HTML code, while at the same time helping you ensure that your HTML works across browsers.

The following code contains flawed HTML elements that can cause problems with JavaScript. Examine the code, and look for the errors, which can be difficult to spot.

```
1   <!DOCTYPE html>
2   <html lang="en">
3   <head>
4       <title>Error Example</title>
```

```
5      <meta charset="utf-8" />
6      <script
7          document.write("<h2>Tractor Selector</h2>");
8      </script>
9    </head>
10   <body>
11      <h1>Tuba Farm Equipment</h1>
12   </body>
13   </html>
```

The problem with the preceding code is that the opening `<script>` element is missing a closing bracket. Without the closing bracket, the browser sees only the script section that you want to include in the head section of the document. Because the contents of the head section are not rendered, you never receive an error message, nor do you see the output from the `document.write()` method. In your debugging efforts, you may think the JavaScript code is not functioning properly when actually it does not function at all. It's worth mentioning again that the W3C Markup Validation Service would have caught this immediately, so validate your web pages frequently.

Analyzing Logic

At times, errors in JavaScript code stem from logic problems that are difficult to spot using tracing techniques. When you suspect that your code contains logic errors, you must analyze each statement on a case-by-case basis. For example, the following code contains a logic flaw that prevents it from functioning correctly:

```
1    var displayAlert = false;
2    var conditionTrue;
3    if (displayAlert === true)
4        conditionTrue = "condition is true";
5        window.alert(conditionTrue);
```

If you were to execute the preceding code, you would always see the alert dialog box, although it should not appear, because the `displayAlert` variable is set to `false`. However, if you examine the `if` statement more closely, you would see that the `if` statement ends after the declaration of the `conditionTrue` variable. The `window.alert()` method following the variable declaration is not part of the `if` structure, because the `if` statement does not include a set of braces to enclose the lines it executes when the conditional evaluation returns `true`. The `window.alert()` method also displays the value `undefined`. This is because the `conditionTrue` variable was not assigned a value when it was declared in the second statement, and because the statement that assigns a value to the `conditionTrue` variable is bypassed when the `if` statement conditional expression evaluates to `false`. For the code to execute properly, the `if` statement must include braces as follows:

```
1    var displayAlert = false;
2    var conditionTrue;
3    if (displayAlert === true) {
4        conditionTrue = "condition is true";
5        window.alert(conditionTrue);
6    }
```

The following `for` statement shows another example of an easily overlooked logic error:

```
1    var count = 0;
2    for (count = 1; count < 6; count++); {
3        document.write(count + "<br />");
4    }
```

The preceding code should print the numbers 1 through 5 to the screen. However, the line `for (var count = 1; count < 6; count++);` contains an ending semicolon, which marks the end of the `for` loop. The loop executes five times and changes the value of count to 6, but does nothing else, because there are no statements before its ending semicolon. The line `document.write(count + "<br />");` is a separate statement that executes only once, printing the number 6 to the screen. The code is syntactically correct but does not function as you anticipated. As you can see from these examples, it is easy to overlook very minor logic errors in your code.

Testing Statements with the Console Command Line

If you find that the error in your code is the result of a single statement, you can test the statement using the console command line without rerunning the entire program. You saw in Chapter 3 that a browser evaluates a variable name that you enter in the browser tools command line and returns its value. You can also enter a statement at the command line, which the browser evaluates and executes. For example, to display the results of a calculation, you could enter `15000 * .08` at the command line.

As long as you remain on the same page without refreshing it, the browser stores any values you assign to variable names. This enables you to enter multiple statements that build on each other on the command line. For instance, to declare a variable and then use its value in a calculation, you could enter the following statements:

```
var price = 15000
price * .08
```

Notice that you do not need to include a semicolon at the end of a statement entered at the command line. This is because each entry is considered a single line of code by default.

The command line is particularly useful if you are trying to construct the correct syntax for a mathematical expression. The following code calculates the total amount due on a mortgage of $100,000. The calculation adds eight percent interest and a $35 late fee. However, the calculation does not function correctly because of an order of precedence problem.

```
1    var mortgageBalance = 100000;
2    var interest = .08;
3    var lateFees = 35;
4    document.write(mortgageBalance + lateFees * 1 + interest);
```

Although you can modify the structure of the formula directly within a JavaScript program, you can also use the command line to test the calculation. The following statements declare the variables and then display the result of the formula in the console. Parentheses that correct the order of precedence problem have been added to the formula.

```
1    var mortgageBalance = 100000
2    var interest = .08
3    var lateFees = 35
4    (mortgageBalance + lateFees) * (1 + interest)
```

Figure 4-29 shows the results in the Chrome console.

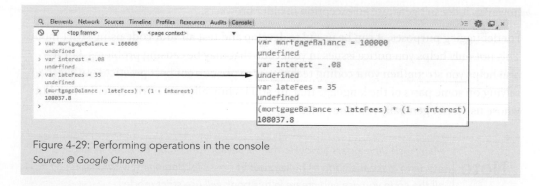

Figure 4-29: Performing operations in the console
Source: © Google Chrome

Using the debugger Statement

JavaScript includes a statement, debugger, that can make debugging easier in some situations. When you add the statement debugger to your code and then run it in a browser with debugging tools open, the browser stops executing the program when it reaches the debugger statement and switches the focus to the debugging tools.

The `debugger` statement works like a breakpoint that's part of your JavaScript code.

Using Strict Mode

Starting with version 5.1, ECMAScript included a new feature: the ability to request processors to treat code using strict mode. In strict mode, some features are removed from the language, while other features require more stringent syntax. For instance, you can create a variable with or without the `var` keyword, although for a number of reasons, most developers recommend always using this keyword. In strict mode, declaring a variable without the `var` keyword triggers an exception.

While coding in strict mode may in fact generate more errors, it can be a helpful debugging tool. Many of the features that strict mode prohibits or requires to be used in a certain way are well known for causing hard-to-find bugs in code that implements them using nonstrict syntax.

To request that JavaScript processors parse your code in strict mode, you add the following statement to your code:

```
"use strict";
```

If you add this statement at the start of a script section, then all the code in that script section will be processed in strict mode. If you instead add the statement at the start of a function, then just the code within the function will be processed in strict mode.

Note that not all browsers support strict mode; in particular, many older browsers don't support it. Because the statement `"use strict"` is a string rather than a set of keywords, however, it doesn't generate an exception in older browsers.

For debugging purposes, it can be useful to develop and test all your code using strict mode. This not only helps you notice issues in your code that may be causing problems, but it also helps you strengthen your coding techniques to use current best practices, rather than relying on some parts of the language that are still technically part of the specification but whose use is not generally recommended.

> **Note** Many web developers advocate that all JavaScript coding be done in strict mode to make the code as bulletproof as possible. Beginning with Chapter 5, all the code you use and create in this book will use strict mode.

Linting

Linting involves running your code through a program that flags some common issues that may affect the quality of your code. Such programs are available for many programming languages. One of the most commonly used for JavaScript code is called jslint. Linting your code with jslint catches many of the same errors as executing it in strict mode. However, while strict mode helps you strengthen your code by generating error messages in a browser console, jslint generates a report that identifies the line number in the code for each issue it flags. This makes it easier to find and fix most errors with jslint.

There are two main ways to lint your code with jslint. You can visit *jslint.com*, paste your code into the interface, and then lint it and view the report. However, if you are writing JavaScript on a regular basis, this method quickly becomes time consuming and impractical. Instead, you can turn on the jslint capabilities built into many common code editors, which mark potential issues as you type. Check the documentation or online support for your editor to learn how to enable and configure jslint support.

Note that some jslint recommendations are the subject of debate. For instance, by default, jslint recommends grouping all variable declarations into a single `var` statement rather than using multiple `var` statements. However, many JavaScript developers believe their code is stronger with multiple `var` statements, and thus do not implement this jslint suggestion. Both the web interface and many editor features enable you to turn on selected jslint options only. When in doubt, check with your instructor or search the web for other programmers' advice on a particular issue.

Reloading a Web Page

When you edit the JavaScript code in a document, it is usually sufficient to save the document and click the Reload or Refresh button in your browser to test your changes. However, it is important to understand that with complex scripts, a web browser cannot always completely clear its memory of the remnants of an old bug, even though you have fixed the code. Therefore, it is sometimes necessary to close and then reopen the document in your browser. You can also force the reload of a web page by holding down your Shift key and clicking the browser's Reload or Refresh button. At times, however, even reopening the file does not completely clear the browser memory of the old JavaScript code. Instead, you must close the browser window completely and start a new session. You may also find it necessary to delete the frequently visited web pages that your browser temporarily stores either in your computer's memory or on the hard drive.

Short Quiz 5

1. How can code editors designed for web development help you in identifying errors in your HTML?

2. What code would you enter on the command line to declare a variable named `cost` with a value of 75, and then log to the console the result of multiplying the `cost` variable by 1.2?

3. Explain how coding in strict mode can help you write better code.

Summary

> Three types of errors can occur in a program: syntax errors, run-time errors, and logic errors. Syntax errors occur when the interpreter fails to recognize code. Run-time errors occur when the JavaScript interpreter encounters a problem while a program is executing. Logic errors are flaws in a program's design that prevent the program from running as you anticipate.

> The first line of defense in locating bugs in JavaScript programs consists of the error messages you receive when the JavaScript interpreter encounters a syntax or run-time error.

> Tracing is the examination of individual statements in an executing program. You can use the `window.alert()` and `console.log()` methods to trace JavaScript code.

> When using the `console.log()` method to trace bugs, it is helpful to use a driver program, which is a simplified, temporary program that is used for testing functions and other code.

> Another method of locating bugs in a JavaScript program is to identify lines that you think may be causing problems and transform them into comments.

> The current versions of all three major browsers—Internet Explorer, Firefox, and Chrome—contain built-in debugging tools.

> The term "break mode" refers to the temporary suspension of program execution so that you can monitor values and trace program execution.

> A breakpoint is a statement in the code at which program execution enters break mode.

> The step in (or into), step over, and step out options in browser debugging tools allow you to continue program execution after you enter break mode.

> You can add an expression to the watch list in browser debugging tools to monitor its value as you step through the program.

> The term "call stack" refers to the order in which procedures, such as functions, methods, or event handlers, execute in a program.

> Writing code that anticipates and handles potential problems is often called bulletproofing.

> Exception handling allows programs to handle errors as they occur in the execution of a program. The term "exception" refers to some type of error that occurs in a program.

> You execute code that may contain an exception in a `try` statement. You use a `throw` statement to indicate that an error occurred within a `try` block. After a program throws an error, you can use a `catch()` statement to handle, or "catch" the error. A `finally` statement that is included with a `try` statement executes regardless of whether its associated `try` block throws an exception.

> You can assign a custom function to JavaScript's `error` event for handling any types of errors that occur on a web page.

> Additional methods and techniques for locating and correcting errors in your JavaScript programs include checking your HTML elements, analyzing your logic, testing statements with the console command line, using the `debugger` statement, executing code in strict mode, linting, and reloading a web page.

Key Terms

break mode—The temporary suspension of program execution in a browser so you can monitor values and trace program execution.

breakpoint—A designation added to a specific statement in a program that causes program execution to pause when it reaches that statement.

bug—Any error in a program that causes it to function incorrectly, whether because of incorrect syntax or flaws in logic.

bulletproofing—Writing code that anticipates and handles potential problems.

call stack—The ordered list maintained by a JavaScript processor containing all the procedures, such as functions, methods, or event handlers, that have been called but have not yet finished processing.

catch() statement—The statement used to handle an error that has been thrown.

commenting out—Identifying lines of code that you think may be causing problems and transforming them into comments.

debugging—The act of tracing and resolving errors, or bugs, in a program.

dependencies—The relationships that exist when statements depend on the successful execution of other statements or functions.

driver program—A simplified, temporary program that is used for testing functions and other code.

exception—An error that occurs in the execution of a program.

exception handling—A method of bulletproofing code that allows a program to handle errors as they occur in the execution of the program.

finally statement—The final statement in exception-handling code, which executes regardless of whether its associated `try` block throws an exception.

linting—Running your code through a program that flags some common issues that may affect the quality of your code.

logging—Writing values directly to the browser console.

logic—The order in which various parts of a program run, or execute.

logic error—A flaw in a program's design that prevents the program from running as you anticipate.

run-time error—An error that occurs when a JavaScript interpreter encounters a problem while a program is executing.

stepping in—The stepping option that executes an individual line of code and then pauses until you instruct the debugger to continue; also known as *stepping into*.

stepping into—*See* stepping in.

stepping options—Options in browser debugging tools that allow you to continue program execution after you enter break mode.

stepping out—The stepping option that executes all remaining code in the current function.

stepping over—The stepping option that allows you to skip function calls; the program still executes each function that you step over, but it appears in the debugger as if a single statement executes.

strict mode—A JavaScript processing mode in which some features are removed from the language and other features require more stringent syntax.

syntax—The rules for a programming language.

syntax error—An error that occurs when an interpreter fails to recognize code, such as a statement that is not recognized by a browser's scripting engine.

throw—To trigger an error.

tracing—A debugging technique that involves examining individual statements in an executing program.

try statement—The statement used to enclose code that may contain an exception.

variables list—In browser debugging tools, a list of all local variables within the currently executing function, regardless of whether they have been initialized; the value of each variable is displayed and updated throughout the execution of the program.

watch list—In browser debugging tools, a list of user-specified expressions whose values are displayed and updated throughout the execution of the program.

Review Questions

1. What type of error occurs when the interpreter fails to recognize code?
   a. Debugging
   b. Syntax
   c. Run-time
   d. Logic

2. _____ errors are problems in the design of a program that prevent it from running as you anticipate.
   a. Application
   b. Syntax
   c. Logic
   d. Run-time

3. When a JavaScript interpreter encounters a problem while a program is executing, that problem is called a(n) _____ error.
   a. application
   b. syntax
   c. logic
   d. run-time

4. Which of the following statements causes a syntax error?
   a. `var firstName = "";`
   b. `document.write(Available points: " + availPoints);`
   c. `readyState = true;`
   d. `"use strict";`

5. Which of the following statements writes the value of the `selection` variable to the console?
   a. `console.log("selection");`
   b. `document.console("selection");`
   c. `console.alert(selection);`
   d. `console.log(selection);`

6. Which of the following `for` statements is logically incorrect?
   a.
   ```
   for (var count = 10; count <= 0; count++) {

       document.write(count);

   }
   ```
   b.
   ```
   for (var count = 0; count <= 10; count++) {

       document.write (count);

   }
   ```
   c.
   ```
   for (var count = 10; count >= 0; count--) {

       document.write (count);

   }
   ```
   d.
   ```
   for (var count = 5; count >= 0; count--) {

       document.write (count);

   }
   ```

7. Which of the following modes temporarily suspends, or pauses, program execution so that you can monitor values and trace program execution?
   a. Suspend
   b. Step
   c. Break
   d. Continue

8. Which command executes all the statements in the next function in browser debugging tools?
   a. Step out
   b. Step over
   c. Step
   d. Step in/into

9. After you throw an error, you use a(n) _____ statement to handle the error.
   a. `try`
   b. `throw`
   c. `catch`
   d. `finally`

10. In _____, some features are removed from the JavaScript language, while other features require more stringent syntax.
    a. exception handling
    b. strict mode
    c. debugging tools
    d. debugger mode

11. Which of the following pieces of information is passed as an argument from a `throw` statement to a `catch` statement?
    a. Error number
    b. Error message
    c. Line number
    d. URL

12. What statement can you add to your code to effectively serve the same role as a breakpoint?
    a. `break;`
    b. `breakpoint;`
    c. `debug;`
    d. `debugger;`

13. The watch list in browser debugging tools lets you monitor the value of a(n) _____ during program execution.
    a. function
    b. exception handler
    c. expression
    d. statement

14. The _____ is the ordered list maintained by a JavaScript processor containing all the procedures, such as functions, methods, or event handlers, that have been called but have not yet finished processing.
    a. variables list
    b. watch list
    c. strict mode
    d. call stack

15. Which of the following exception handling code executes regardless of whether its associated `try` block throws an exception?
    a. `throw "Please enter your last name.";`
    b.
    ```
    catch(lNameError) {

        return false;

    }
    ```
    c.
    ```
    catch(lNameError) {

        window.alert(lNameError)

        return false;

    }
    ```
    d.
    ```
    finally {

        lNameValid = true;

    }
    ```

16. What is the advantage of tracing errors using the `window.alert()` method? What is the advantage of using the `console.log()` method instead?

17. Explain how to debug code by commenting it out.

18. Explain two different ways that a text editor specialized for web development can help you in preventing errors and debugging code.

19. When and why should you use exception handling with your JavaScript programs?

20. Explain what strict mode is, how to implement it, and how it's useful in reducing coding errors.

Hands-On Projects

Hands-On Project 4-1

In this project, you'll continue working with the tuba.js and tractor.htm files from the chapter. You'll add error handling to the `verifyCrops()` function so users receive an error message if they remove checkmarks from all the crop boxes.

1. Use the file manager for your operating system to copy all the files and subfolders from the Chapter04/Chapter directory in your Data Files, and paste them in the Chapter04/HandsOnProject4-1 folder. Verify that you still have a copy in the Chapter04/Chapter directory.

2. In your text editor, open **tuba.js** from the Chapter04/HandsOnProject4-1 folder, and then in the comment section, replace the text "Chapter case" with **Hands-on Project 4-1**.

3. Scroll down to the `verifyCrops()` function, and then delete the line `testFormCompleteness();` so the command block is empty.

4. Enter the following `try` statement within the command block of the `verifyCrops()` function:

```
1   try {
2       for (var i = 0; i < 7; i++) {
3           if (cropsFieldset.getElementsByTagName("input")[i].↵
4               checked) {
5               cropscomplete = true;
6               messageElement.innerHTML = ""; // clear previous↵
7                   message or recommendation
8               testFormCompleteness();
9               i = 8;
10          }
11      }
12      if (i === 7) {
13          throw "Please select at least one crop.";
14      }
15  }
```

Note that the code shown in Steps 4 and 5 is not free of bugs. You will debug the code later in the next project.

5. Below the `try` statement but before the closing } of the `verifyCrops()` function, add the following `catch()` statement:

```
1  catch(message) {
2      cropsComplete = false;
3      messageHeadElement.innerHTML = ""; // remove any former↵
4          recommendation heading
5      messageElement.innerHTML = message; // display error↵
6          message
7  }
```

6. Scroll to the top of the document, and then change the values for the variables `acresComplete`, `cropsComplete`, and `monthsComplete` to `false`. Note that the value for the `fuelComplete` variable should remain `true`.

7. Save your changes to **tuba.js**, and open **tractor.htm** in a browser, and then test the crops boxes by selecting some and then unselecting all of them. Notice that an error message is displayed when no crops boxes are checked, as shown in Figure 4-30, and the message is removed when any crops box is checked.

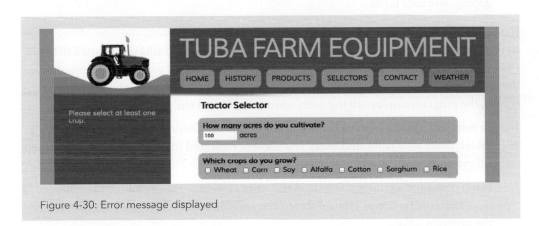

Figure 4-30: Error message displayed

8. Close the **tractor.htm** file in your browser.

Hands-On Project 4-2

In this project, you'll continue working with the **tuba.js** and **tractor.htm** files from Hands-On Project 4-1. You'll debug the exception handling code in the `verifyCrops()` function.

1. Use the file manager for your operating system to copy all the files and subfolders from the Chapter04/HandsOnProject4-1 directory in your Data Files, and paste them in the Chapter04/HandsOnProject4-2 folder. Verify that you still have a copy in the Chapter04/HandsOnProject4-1 directory.

2. In your text editor, open **tuba.js** from the Chapter04/HandsOnProject4-2 folder, and then in the comment section, replace the text "Hands-on Project 4-1" with **Hands-on Project 4-2**.

3. Open the **tractor.htm** file in your browser. Test the entire form by entering appropriate content in each of the four sections. Notice that no recommendation is displayed no matter what data you enter. This indicates that the code you entered in the previous project contains a bug.

4. Use the techniques you learned in this chapter to debug the `verifyCrops()` function. Applicable techniques may include looking for highlighted syntax errors in your text editor, setting breakpoints, stepping through the program, and commenting out code. When you finish debugging, the appropriate error messages should continue to appear based on user entries in the first three form sections. In addition, a recommendation should be displayed in the sidebar when the first three sections contain appropriate user input.

Hands-On Project 4-3

In this project, you will examine an existing program and use the skills you learned in this chapter to debug it until it works as designed. When a user enters a string in the input box, the program is designed to add the string to an array. When the array reaches a certain length, the program displays all the users' entries in a list on the page.

1. In your text editor, open the **index.htm** file from the Chapter04/HandsOnProject4-3 folder. Enter your name and today's date where indicated in the head section, and then save your changes.

2. Scroll down and examine the code in the script section at the bottom of the body section. Examine the loops, control structures, and comments until you understand how the program works.

3. Open **index.htm** in a browser. To test the program, enter the name of a place in the input box, click **Submit**, and then repeat four more times. The string in the input box should be cleared after each submission, and the list of places should be displayed after the fifth string is submitted. The fact that these things don't happen indicates that the program contains one or more bugs.

4. Use the techniques you learned in this chapter to debug the program. Applicable techniques may include looking for highlighted syntax errors in your text editor, setting

breakpoints, stepping through the program, and commenting out code. When you finish debugging, the user's entry in the input box should be cleared each time the Submit button is clicked. Additionally, after five strings are submitted, the entire list of submitted strings should be displayed on the page.

Hands-On Project 4-4

In this project, you will use strict mode to strengthen the code used in one of the functions from Project 4-3. Strict mode enforces a number of rules that are considered good coding practices but are not enforced by default in JavaScript. One of the most basic of these rules is that all variables must be declared with the `var` keyword. In strict mode, declaring a new variable without the `var` keyword throws an error. The `processInput()` function in the file you debugged in Project 4-3 includes a number of variables declared without the `var` keyword. You'll specify that the function is to be executed in strict mode, and then use the resulting errors to identify and add the missing keywords.

1. Use the file manager for your operating system to copy all the files and subfolders from the Chapter04/HandsOnProject4-3 directory in your Data Files, and paste them in the Chapter04/HandsOnProject4-4 folder. Verify that you still have a copy in the Chapter04/HandsOnProject4-3 directory.

2. In your text editor, open **index.htm** from the Chapter04/HandsOnProject4-4 folder, and then in the comment section, `title` element, and `h1` element, replace the text "Hands-on Project 4-3" with **Hands-on Project 4-4**.

3. Scroll down to the script section at the bottom of the body section.

4. Add a new line at the top of the code block for the `processInput()` function, and then add a statement requesting that browsers interpret the function using strict mode.

5. Save your changes, open **index.htm** in a browser, and then test the operation of the page. The features that worked at the end of Project 4-3 no longer work.

6. Open the browser console, and examine any error messages that are logged. Use the browser tools to identify the lines missing `var` keywords, add the keywords in your text editor, save your changes, and then retest the page. Continue debugging until the page works as it did at the end of Project 4-3.

Hands-On Project 4-5

In this project, you'll debug a program that converts a distance in miles to a distance in kilometers.

1. In your text editor, open the **index.htm** file from the Chapter04/HandsOnProject4-5 folder. Enter your name and today's date where indicated in the head section, and then save your changes.

2. Scroll down and examine the code in the script section at the bottom of the body section. Examine the program and comments until you understand how the program works.

3. Open **index.htm** in a browser. To test the program, enter a number in the input box, and then click **Convert to Km**. The answer should be displayed in the box below the "Distance in Km" label on the right side of the page. The fact that this doesn't happen indicates that the program contains one or more bugs.

4. Use the techniques you learned in this chapter to debug the program. When you finish debugging, you should be able to enter a number in the Distance in Mi box, click the Convert to Km button, and see the result in the Distance in Km box. (*Hint*: Keep in mind that a kilometer is shorter than a mile, so a distance in kilometers should be a larger number than the same distance in miles. To convert miles to kilometers, you multiply the miles value by 1.6.)

Case Projects

Individual Case Project

Add exception handling to the code for one of the forms on your personal web site. If your site does not include a form, add one first. Your code should display one or more relevant error messages in an appropriate location. After you finalize your code, write a summary of the debugging methods from this chapter that you used in this project, describing how you used each one in your code.

Team Case Project

Divide your team into two subgroups and assign each group a page from your team project website that includes JavaScript code. Within each subgroup, introduce at least three bugs into the code for the page you've been assigned. Exchange documents with the other subgroup, and then work as a team to debug the code provided by the other team. As you debug, record which debugging methods you use, including whether each was helpful in resolving a given issue. When the document works as expected, create a report. For each bug, describe the behavior you expected as well as the erroneous behavior that the bug caused and describe the methods you used to debug it, including whether each method was helpful or not. Also specify the line number or numbers of the code that contained the error, and show the incorrect as well as the corrected code in your report.

CHAPTER **5**

WORKING WITH THE DOCUMENT OBJECT MODEL (DOM) AND DHTML

When you complete this chapter, you will be able to:

> Access elements by id, tag name, class, name, or selector
> Access element content, CSS properties, and attributes
> Add and remove document nodes
> Create and close new browser tabs and windows with an app
> Use the `setTimeout()` and `setInterval()` methods to specify a delay or a duration
> Use the `History`, `Location`, `Navigation`, and `Screen` objects to manipulate the browser window

One of the most powerful uses of JavaScript on the web is to modify page content based on external events, such as clicks or other user interactions. Doing so requires a way of referring to different components of the web browser and of the current document. JavaScript specifies the objects, properties, and methods of the browser and the relationship between them through a convention called the browser object model (BOM). One part of the BOM, the `Document` object, represents the contents of a document within the browser. Because the `Document` object is where many of the changes happen in a dynamic web page, this object has its own object model, known as the document object model (DOM). In this chapter, you'll explore the structure of the BOM and the DOM, and you'll learn how to reference some of the basic properties and methods of objects in the browser and in a document to increase the amount of interactivity in your apps. You'll apply these skills to build an app that displays a photo gallery of images and allows users to navigate through the images, as well as to view a larger version of each image. Figure 5-1 shows a preview of the photo gallery application you'll create, and Figure 5-2 shows a preview of an enlarged image from the gallery.

Figure 5-1: Photo gallery application
© Jason Bucy. © Sasha Vodnik. © 2015 Cengage Learning®

Figure 5-2: Enlarged image view
© Jason Bucy. Source: © Mozilla Firefox.

Understanding the Browser Object Model and the Document Object Model

JavaScript treats the content of an HTML document as a set of related components, which are referred to as objects. JavaScript treats every element on a web page as an object. In addition, you can create objects within a JavaScript app itself. For instance, every function that you create is also an object.

The Browser Object Model

The **browser object model (BOM)** (or **client-side object model**) describes the relationship between objects within the web browser, including within the current document. The existence of this model is important because, as you'll see shortly, it enables you to refer to specific browser objects without confusion about what you mean.

The objects in the BOM are arranged in a hierarchy. As Figure 5-3 shows, the Window object is at the top, with the `History`, `Location`, `Navigator`, `Screen`, and `Document` objects below it. Although this is the model used by all major browsers, note that the

BOM is not a standard agreed on by any organization. Instead, it is a general model that all browser manufacturers follow by convention.

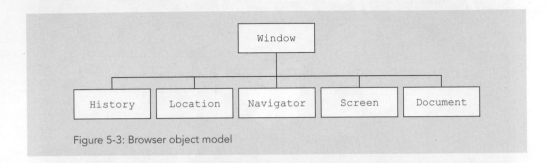

Figure 5-3: Browser object model

You do not have to create any of the objects explicitly in the browser object model; they are created automatically when a web browser opens a web page. The top-level object in the browser object model is the **Window object**, which represents a web browser window. The web browser automatically creates the `Window` object for you. The `Window` object is called the **global object** because all other objects in the browser object model are contained within it. For example, the `Window` object contains the `Document` object, just as a web browser window contains a web page document. You use the methods and properties of the `Window` object to control the web browser window, while you use the methods and properties of the `Document` object to control the web page.

Relationships between the objects in the BOM are usually described with the same terms used for members of a family. In Figure 5-3, the `Window` object is the parent object of all the other objects, such as `History` and `Location`. `History` is a sibling object to the `Location`, `Navigator`, `Screen`, and `Document` objects, which are all child objects of the `Window` object.

The Document Object Model

The `Document` object is the most important object in the browser object model because it represents the web page displayed in a browser. You are already familiar with the `document.write()` method. The "`document.`" at the start indicates that it is a method of the `Document` object. All elements on a web page are contained within the `Document` object, and each element is represented in JavaScript by its own object. This means that the `Document` object contains all of the elements you create on a web page.

In this book, objects in the browser object model are referred to with an initial uppercase letter (`Document` object). However, when you use the object name in code, you must always use a lowercase letter. For example, the following statement refers to the `Document` object:

```
document.write("Go Patriots!");
```

Note the use of the lowercase *d* in `document`.

The `Document` object branch of the browser object model is represented by its own object model called the **Document Object Model**, or **DOM**. Unlike the BOM, which is a loose convention, the DOM is a formal specification of the World Wide Web Consortium (W3C), like HTML and CSS.

The DOM and DHTML

While the web started out as a collection of static documents, today most web content is dynamic—user interaction can change the content displayed without the need to load a new document, as well as changing the way that content is presented, such as its size, arrangement, and color. The combination of HTML and CSS with JavaScript, which enables this interactivity on the modern web, is sometimes referred to as **dynamic HTML (DHTML)**.

The DOM is what allows you to write JavaScript that changes the HTML and CSS of a web document. The DOM is an example of an **application programming interface (API)**, which is a specification of how different software components can interact with each other. By codifying a structure for the objects in a web document, along with a standard set of properties and methods, the DOM creates tools for making web documents dynamic. This makes it possible for you to write JavaScript apps that have predictable results in browsers that conform to the DOM specification.

The DOM represents the HTML of a web page that is displayed in a browser. Each element on a web page is represented in the DOM by its own object. The fact that each element is an object makes it possible for a JavaScript app to access individual elements on a web page and change them individually, without having to reload the page from the server.

The DOM tree

As in the BOM, objects in the DOM are represented hierarchically, based on the nesting of elements in an HTML document. However, while all the objects in the standard BOM are present in a browser at all times, the DOM hierarchy—known as the **DOM tree**—for any given web page depends on its contents. For instance, Figure 5-4 shows the DOM tree for the following HTML document:

```
1    <html lang="en">
2        <head>
3            <meta charset="utf-8" />
4            <title>Photo Gallery</title>
5        </head>
6        <body>
```

```
7        <header>
8            <h1>Garden Photo</h1>
9        </header>
10       <article>
11          <figure>
12             <figcaption>Butterfly bush</figcaption>
13             <img src="image016.jpg" alt="Butterfly bush" />
14          </figure>
15       </article>
16    </body>
17 </html>
```

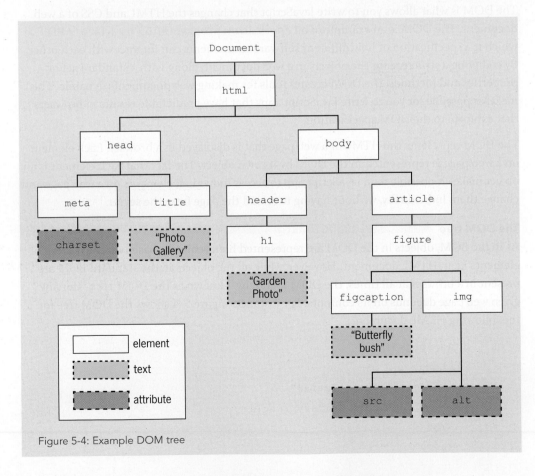

Figure 5-4: Example DOM tree

Chapter 5 **Working with the Document Object Model (DOM) and DHTML**

In Figure 5-4, the HTML elements are arranged hierarchically according to their nesting in the document. For instance, the `figcaption` and `img` elements, which are nested within the `figure` element in lines 11–14 of the code, are shown in the DOM tree as children of the `figure` element.

Notice that in addition to the objects corresponding to the HTML elements, the DOM tree also shows the text of elements that contain text content, as well as the attributes of elements that include them. Each item in the DOM tree is known as a **node**. Other types of nodes exist, but those corresponding to elements, attributes, and text content are the most commonly used.

DOM Document Object Methods

The DOM `Document` object includes several methods used for dynamically generating web pages and manipulating elements. Table 5-1 lists some of the most useful methods of the `Document` object that are specified in the W3C DOM. You'll learn more about several of these methods in this chapter.

METHOD	DESCRIPTION
`getElementById(ID)`	Returns the element with the `id` value `ID`
`getElementsByClassName(class1 [class2 ...])`	If one class name, `class1`, is specified, returns the collection of elements that belong to `class1`; if two or more space-separated class names are specified, the returned collection consists of those elements that belong to all specified class names
`getElementsByName(name)`	Returns the collection of elements with the name `name`
`getElementsByTagName(tag)`	Returns the collection of elements with the tag (element) name `tag`
`querySelectorAll(selector)`	Returns the collection of elements that match the CSS selector specified by `selector`
`write(text)`	Writes `text` to the document

Table 5-1: HTML DOM `Document` object methods

DOM Document Object Properties

The DOM `Document` object has various properties used for manipulating web page objects. Table 5-2 lists some of the most important properties of the `Document` object that are specified in the W3C DOM.

PROPERTY	DESCRIPTION
body	Document's body element
cookie	Current document's cookie string, which contains small pieces of information about a user that are stored by a web server in text files on the user's computer
domain	Domain name of the server where the current document is located
lastModified	Date the document was last modified
location	Location of the current document, including its URL
referrer	URL of the document that provided a link to the current document
title	Title of the document as specified by the title element in the document head section
URL	URL of the current document

Table 5-2: Selected DOM Document object properties

Short Quiz 1

1. What is the `Window` object?

2. What is the DOM?

3. What is the difference between the `Window` object and the `Document` object? What is the relationship between the two?

Accessing Document Elements, Content, Properties, and Attributes

In previous chapters, you've learned several methods for referring to elements in a web document, including `document.getElementById()` and `document.getElementsByTagName()`. Both of these are methods of the `Document` object in the DOM. Next, you'll review these two methods, and then explore a few other useful methods of the `Document` object for referencing elements in a web document as well as their content, CSS properties, and attributes.

Accessing Elements by id Value

If you need to directly access a specific element that has an `id` value, nothing is easier than the `getElementById()` method. Recall that you set the `id` value in HTML using an element's `id` attribute. You then pass the `id` value with quotes around it as an argument to the `getElementById()` method. For example, suppose your HTML document includes this element:

```
<input type="number" id="zip" />
```

You could reference this element in JavaScript code as follows:

```
var zipField = document.getElementById("zip");
```

Caution | *Be sure to use the capitalization "Id" and not "ID" when using this method. Entering the method as* getElementByID() *returns an error.*

Next, you will create event listeners for the photo gallery application using the getElementById() method.

To add event listeners to the photo gallery application using the getElementById() method:

1. In your text editor, open the **photos.htm** file located in your Chapter folder for Chapter05.

2. In the comment section at the top of the document, type your name and today's date where indicated, and then save your work.

3. Scroll through the document to familiarize yourself with its content. Below the header element, the article element contains a div element, three figure elements, and two more div elements. The first two div elements will serve as the back and forward buttons for navigating through the gallery, and the final div element will serve as the button that enables users to switch between viewing three and five images at a time. Each figure element contains an img element, which will display one of five images. Notice that no src attribute is specified for the img elements. You'll use JavaScript to specify the src values based on user actions.

4. Repeat Steps 1 and 2 to open **photos.js**, save a personalized copy, and then scroll through the document to familiarize yourself with its content. The file defines a photoOrder variable, which you'll use to track the order of photos as users move through the gallery. It also contains rightArrow() and leftArrow() functions, which work with the photoOrder variable to shift the images to the left or to the right. The file contains an empty function, zoomFig(), where you'll add code to view an image at a larger size. Finally, it includes a setUpPage() function and code for an event listener to run the setUpPage() function when the page loads. The existing functions include references to the populateFigures() and createEventListeners() functions, which you'll create.

5. Open **photos.htm** in a browser. The navigation buttons are displayed, but the area where the images would appear is empty. No images will be displayed until you add src values to the img elements, which you'll do later in the chapter.

6. Return to the **photos.js** file in your text editor, and then below the `leftArrow()` function, before the `setUpPage()` function, enter the following statements to create the `createEventListeners()` function:

```
1   /* create event listeners for left arrow, right arrow, and
2   center figure element */
3   function createEventListeners() {
4   }
```

7. Within the code block for the function, add the following statement:

```
var leftarrow = document.getElementById("leftarrow");
```

This statement creates a local variable named `leftarrow`, and then uses the `getElementById()` method to specify the variable value as the document element with the `id` value `leftarrow`.

8. Below the variable declaration and within the code block for the function, enter the following `if/else` statement to create the event listener for the left navigation arrow:

```
1   if (leftarrow.addEventListener) {
2     leftarrow.addEventListener("click", leftArrow, false);
3   } else if (leftarrow.attachEvent)  {
4     leftarrow.attachEvent("onclick", leftArrow);
5   }
```

9. Below the code from Step 8, and within the code block for the function, enter the following code to create a variable and assign an event listener for the right navigation arrow:

```
1   var rightarrow = document.getElementById("rightarrow");
2   if (rightarrow.addEventListener) {
3     rightarrow.addEventListener("click", rightArrow, false);
4   } else if (rightarrow.attachEvent)  {
5     rightarrow.attachEvent("onclick", rightArrow);
6   }
```

The code for your `createEventListeners()` function should match the following:

```
1   /* create event listeners for left arrow, right arrow, and
2   center figure element */
3   function createEventListeners() {
4     var leftarrow = document.getElementById("leftarrow");
5     if (leftarrow.addEventListener) {
```

```
 6         leftarrow.addEventListener("click", leftArrow, false);
 7      } else if (leftarrow.attachEvent) {
 8         leftarrow.attachEvent("onclick", leftArrow);
 9      }
10   var rightarrow = document.getElementById("rightarrow");
11      if (rightarrow.addEventListener) {
12         rightarrow.addEventListener("click", rightArrow, false);
13      } else if (rightarrow.attachEvent) {
14         rightarrow.attachEvent("onclick", rightArrow);
15      }
16   }
```

10. Save your work.

Accessing Elements by Tag Name

Another method of the `Document` element that you've already used is
`getElementsByTagName()`. You pass this method the name of an element—also known
as a tag name—as an argument, and the method returns a collection of all the elements of
that name in the document. For instance, the following statement returns a collection of all
the p elements in a document:

```
var docParagraphs = document.getElementsByTagName("p");
```

> **Note** | Be sure not to include brackets (such as "`<p>`") in the argument you pass to the `getElementsByTagName()` method.

This method returns a collection of objects in order by their appearance in the document.
Depending on the browser, this collection may be either a node list or an HTML collection.
A **node list** is simply an indexed collection of nodes. Similarly, an **HTML collection** is an
indexed collection of HTML elements. The technical differences between these two types of
objects are not important. However, they share two important features. First, they are not
actual arrays, which means that array properties and methods are not available for these
objects. However, because their organization is similar to that of an array, you can reference their contents just as you would reference the contents of an array. This means that
you can reference a specific element on the page by using its index number in the collection returned by `getElementsByTagName()`. For instance, if you wanted to work with the
second h1 element on the page, you could use the code

```
var secondH1 = document.getElementsByTagName("h1")[1];
```

Just as in an array, the index numbers start at 0, so to reference the second element in collection you use the index number 1, as in the preceding statement.

You want users of your photo gallery to be able to click the center image to see a larger version. To enable this feature, you'll use the getElementsByTagName() method to add an event listener for the third img element in the document, which has the index value 2.

To add an event listener using the getElementsByTagName() method:

1. Return to the **photos.js** file in your text editor.

2. Within the code block for the createEventListeners() function, just before the closing }, add the following statement:

```
var mainFig = document.getElementsByTagName("img")[1];
```

This statement creates a local variable named mainFig, and then it uses the getElementsByTagName() method to specify the variable value as the second img element in the document (with the index value of 1).

3. Below the variable declaration and before the closing } for the function, enter the following if/else statement to create the event listener for the center image:

```
1    if (mainFig.addEventListener) {
2       mainFig.addEventListener("click", zoomFig, false);
3    } else if (mainFig.attachEvent) {
4       mainFig.attachEvent("onclick", zoomFig);
5    }
```

This code calls a function when a user clicks the middle image in the gallery. Your completed createEventListeners() function should match the following:

```
1    /* create event listeners for left arrow, right arrow, and
2    center figure element */
3    function createEventListeners() {
4       var leftarrow = document.getElementById("leftarrow");
5       if (leftarrow.addEventListener) {
6          leftarrow.addEventListener("click", leftArrow, false);
7       } else if (leftarrow.attachEvent) {
8          leftarrow.attachEvent("onclick", leftArrow);
9       }
10      var rightarrow = document.getElementById("rightarrow");
11      if (rightarrow.addEventListener) {
12         rightarrow.addEventListener("click", rightArrow, false);
```

```
13        } else if (rightarrow.attachEvent)    {
14          rightarrow.attachEvent("onclick",  rightArrow);
15        }
16        var mainFig = document.getElementsByTagName("img")[1];
17        if (mainFig.addEventListener) {
18          mainFig.addEventListener("click", zoomFig, false);
19        } else if (mainFig.attachEvent)    {
20          mainFig.attachEvent("onclick", zoomFig);
21        }
22    }
```

4. Save your work.

Accessing Elements by Class Name

Another method that's similar to the previous two is the `getElementsByClassName()` **method.** Like `getElementById()`, `getElementsByClassName()` references elements based on the value of an HTML attribute—in this case, the `class` attribute. Like `getElementsByTagName()`, `getElementsByClassName()` returns a node list or HTML collection of all the elements in the document with the class name or names specified by the attribute. For instance, if you wanted to access all the elements in a document with the `class` value `side`, you could use the following statement:

```
var sideElements = document.getElementsByClassName("side");
```

Because the HTML `class` attribute can take multiple values, the `getElementsByClassName()` method accepts multiple arguments. For instance, the following code returns all the elements in a document with the `class` values `side` and `green`:

```
var sideGreenElements = document.↵
    getElementsByClassName("side green");
```

Note that all class names provided as arguments are enclosed in a single set of quotes, with class names separated by spaces.

All modern browsers support the `getElementsByClassName()` method, but IE8 does not. If your app needs to support IE8 users, you should instead use other methods for selecting web page elements.

Accessing Elements by Name

A fourth method, the `getElementsByName()` **method,** returns a node list or HTML collection of elements with a `name` attribute that matches a specified value. The preceding three methods are generally more useful. However, `getElementsByName()` can enable you to create more concise code when you need to access a set of option buttons or check boxes in a form. Because each input element in a set shares the same `name` value, you can use the `getElementsByName()` method to access the entire set at once. For example, suppose your form includes the following set of option buttons:

```
1    <legend><span>Choose a color:</span></legend>
2    <input type="radio" name="color" id="redOption" value="red" />
3    <label for="redOption">Red</label>
4    <input type="radio" name="color" id="greenOption"↵
5       value="green" />
6    <label for="greenOption">Green</label>
7    <input type="radio" name="color" id="blueOption"↵
8       value="blue" />
9    <label for="blueOption">Blue</label>
```

You could use the following statement to return a collection of all three `input` elements in the above code:

```
var colorButtons = document.getElementsByName("color");
```

The results returned by this method in IE9 and earlier versions of Internet Explorer are inconsistent with web standards. Therefore, if you use this method and need to support either IE9 or older versions of Internet Explorer, you should test your app on these browsers to ensure that the method performs as you expect.

Accessing Elements with CSS Selectors

The preceding methods all let you reference elements based on specific aspects of their HTML markup. The `Document` object also includes two methods that let you reference elements or collections of elements using the syntax of CSS. The **querySelector()** **method** returns the first occurrence of an element matching a specified CSS selector. The method uses the following syntax:

```
querySelector("selector")
```

When using this method, *selector* is any valid CSS selector. For instance, assume you're working on a project containing the following HTML structure:

```
1    <header>
2       <h1><img class="logo" src="images/logo.png"↵
3          alt="Blue Jay Photography" /></h1>
4    </header>
```

You could reference the img element using the querySelector() method as follows:

```
querySelector("header h1 img")
```

IE8 supports only simple selectors with the querySelector() method, so it would not recognize a descendent selector as in the previous code. Fortunately, there are usually multiple ways to write a CSS selector to reference the same elements, so you could rewrite the preceding selector to be compatible with IE8 as follows:

```
querySelector("img.logo")
```

In addition to the querySelector() method, the Document object also includes the **querySelectorAll() method**, which returns a collection of elements matching a specified selector, rather than just the first element. For instance, assume you're working with the following HTML code:

```
1    <nav>
2        <ul>
3            <li>About Us</li>
4            <li>Order</li>
5            <li>Support</li>
6        </ul>
7    </nav>
```

Assuming this is the only nav element in the document, you could return a collection of the three li elements with the following code:

```
querySelectorAll("nav ul li")
```

As with querySelector(), IE8 supports only simple selectors for querySelectorAll(). Therefore, to write IE8-compatible code, you would need to use a simpler selector. In this case, writing IE8-compatible code would require adding attributes to your HTML code. For instance, if all li elements in the above code had the attribute class="topNav" then you could use the following code to select these li elements in all modern browsers as well as IE8:

```
querySelectorAll("li.topNav")
```

Accessing an Element's Content

Once you create a reference to a document element, the DOM provides tools for accessing and modifying its content, properties, and attributes. You've already used the innerHTML property to access and change an element's content. The DOM specification also includes another property, the **textContent property**, which you use to access and change just the text that an element contains. In practice, the main difference between innerHTML and textContent is that `innerHTML` allows you to access and write HTML tags along with text, while `textContent` strips these out. For example, assume you are working with the following HTML code:

```
1   <ul>
2       <li class="topnav"><a href="aboutus.htm">About Us</a></li>
3       <li class="topnav"><a href="order.htm">Order</a></li>
4       <li class="topnav"><a href="support.htm">Support</a></li>
5   </ul>
```

You could use the following statements to reference the first `li` element and then access the `innerHTML` and `textContent` values of this element:

```
1   var button1 = querySelectorAll("li.topNav")[0];
2   var allContent = button1.innerHTML;
3       // <a href="aboutus.htm">About Us</a>
4   var justText = button1.textContent;
5       // About Us
```

The `innerHTML` statement on line 2 returns the value shown in the comment on line 3, which includes the element text as well as the `a` element that formats it as a link. By contrast, the `textContent` statement on line 4 returns the value shown in the comment on line 5, which consists only of the element text.

In general, for security reasons you should use the `textContent` property when possible instead of the `innerHTML` property. This is because use of `innerHTML` leaves you theoretically vulnerable to a code injection attack, in which someone replaces an `innerHTML` value in your code with HTML code that includes malicious JavaScript statements. However, IE8 does not support the `textContent` property, so if your code needs to support IE8, you must continue to use the `innerHTML` property. Because all the code in this book is designed to be IE8-compatible, this book uses `innerHTML` rather than `textContent`.

Some developers balance the security and compatibility issues around these properties by using `if/else` constructions to check whether a browser supports `textContent`, and then provide statements that use `textContent` for compatible browsers, with `innerHTML` only as a fallback for noncompliant browsers. However, the drawback of this approach is increased code size and complexity.

> **Note**
> *If you need to add an element within an existing element in the DOM tree, the standard method is to directly create and append a DOM node rather than using an element's `innerHTML` property to create a new child element. You'll learn to work with nodes later in this chapter.*

Accessing an Element's CSS Properties

You can also access and change an element's CSS properties through the DOM. To do so, you use dot notation to reference the element's `style` property followed by the name of the CSS property, as follows:

```
element.style.property
```

The term `element` is a reference to a document element, and `property` is a CSS property name. For instance, the following statement changes the value of the CSS `display` property to `none` for the element with the `id` value `logo`:

```
document.getElementById("logo").style.display = "none";
```

When a CSS property name includes a hyphen, you need to remove the hyphen and capitalize the letter following the hyphen when you reference it using dot notation. For instance, to reference the CSS property `font-family` in JavaScript, you would specify it in your code as `fontFamily`, as in the following statement:

```
var font = document.getElementById("logo").style.fontFamily;
```

When you specify a CSS value using a DOM reference, it is added as an inline style to the relevant element. This means that the setting generally has higher priority than styles set in embedded or external style sheets. To remove a style that you previously added using a DOM reference, you simply set its value to an empty string, as in the following statement:

```
document.getElementById("navbar").style.color = "";
```

Setting the style value to an empty string removes the inline style, reverting the style for the element to whatever settings are specified in the style sheet(s) for the document.

Accessing Element Attributes

You can also access an element's attributes, such as the `href` attribute of an `a` element, or the `src` attribute of an `img` element. To do so, you use dot syntax by adding a period and the name of the attribute after the element reference. For instance, to reference an `a` element with the `id` value `homeLink`, you could use the following `getElementById()` method:

```
document.getElementById("homeLink")
```

To reference the `href` attribute of this element, you add `.href` to the end of the element reference, as follows:

```
document.getElementById("homeLink").href
```

You can use this code to look up the value of the `href` attribute and assign that value to a variable, as follows:

```
var homeURL = document.getElementById("homeLink").href;
```

You can also use the attribute reference to assign a new value to the attribute, as follows:

```
document.getElementById("homeLink").href = "http://w3.org";
```

This code changes the value of the `href` attribute for this element to "http://w3.org". After this script executed, clicking the `homeLink` element would open the website at *w3.org*.

You can use dot notation to access the value of almost any existing element attribute. You can also use it to assign a value to almost any valid attribute of a given element, even if the original HTML code doesn't include that variable.

The exception to the use of dot notation for accessing or assigning attribute values is the `class` attribute. Because many programming languages treat the word "class" as a reserved word, the DOM does not recognize it for working with the HTML `class` attribute. Instead, you use the `className` property. If an element has a single `class` value, the `className` property returns that `class` name. If the element has more than one `class` value, the `className` property returns a string of all the `class` values, separated by spaces.

Programming Concepts   *Getting Values and Setting Values*

You can reference properties of DOM objects in two different ways: to get a value, or to set a value. Most properties, including those you use to access document element attributes, allow you to do either: you can both look up an existing attribute value, and set the attribute value. When working with properties of DOM objects, it's important to be aware of whether you're trying to get or set a property value, and to write your code accordingly. For instance, there's a big difference between the following two examples:

```
captionText = document.getElementById("logoImage").alt;
document.getElementById("logoImage").alt = captionText;
```

The first statement *gets* the `alt` value of the element with the `id` value `logoImage` and stores the result in the variable `captionText`. The second statement does the reverse: it retrieves the value of the variable `captionText` and *sets* it as the value of the `alt` attribute value of the element with the `id` value `logoImage`.

Next, you'll create the `populateFigures()` function for the photo gallery. The navigation works by changing the `src` attribute values of the three `img` elements. You'll create a `for` loop that changes the value of each `img` `src` attribute.

To create the `populateFigures()` function to change the `src` attribute values of the `img` elements:

1. Return to the **photos.js** file in your text editor.

2. Below the global variable declaration, enter code to declare the `populateFigures()` function as follows:

```
1    /* add src values to img elements based on order specified in↵
2    photoOrder array */
3    function populateFigures() {
4        var filename;
5        var currentFig;
6    }
```

In addition to declaring the function, this code also declares two local variables for use within the function.

3. Within the function code block and below the local variable declarations, enter the following `for` loop:

```
1    for (var i = 1; i < 4; i++) {
2        filename = "images/IMG_0" + photoOrder[i] + "sm.jpg";
3        currentFig = document.getElementsByTagName("img")[i - 1];
4        currentFig.src = filename;
5    }
```

This loop runs three times, setting the value of the `filename` variable using the corresponding value in the `photoOrder` array, then looking up the element corresponding to one less than the counter variable value, and then assigning the value of `filename` to the `src` attribute of the `img` element.

4. Save your work, and then open **photos.htm** in your browser. Your screen should match Figure 5-1.

5. Click the > button on the right side of the screen. As Figure 5-5 shows, all the figures shift to the left, and the photo of the flower growing through the fence is now in the center.

all images shifted to the left, with new image displayed on the right

right arrow

Figure 5-5: Photo gallery after clicking right arrow
© Jason Bucy. © Sasha Vodnik.

Short Quiz 2

1. What statement would you use to create a variable named `logo` and assign as its value a reference to the element with the `id` value `logoImage`?

2. What statement would you use to create a variable named `firstPriority` and assign as its value a reference to the first `li` element in the document?

3. What statement would you use to create a variable named `language` and assign as its value the value of the `lang` attribute of the `html` element?

4. What statement would you use to change the value of the `lang` attribute of the `html` element to the value of the `language` variable?

Adding and Removing Document Nodes

You've seen that you can change an element's attribute values to alter web page content without reloading the page. The DOM also includes methods that let you create brand new elements and add or remove elements from the DOM tree. These methods enable you to add additional dynamic aspects to your apps without any interaction with the server.

Your plan for the photo gallery app includes giving users the option to add two additional images to the screen so users can (1) see parts of all the images in the slideshow at once, and (2) use the buttons to navigate to any image they want to view. In this section, you'll learn about DOM methods for creating new nodes and adding them to the DOM tree, as well as a method for removing a node from the tree. You'll use these methods to enable users to switch between seeing three and five image previews at once.

Creating Nodes

You create a new element node using the `createElement()` method of the Document object, which has the following syntax:

```
document.createElement("element")
```

The term *element* is an HTML element name. For example, to create a new `div` element, you'd use the following statement:

```
document.createElement("div");
```

To add additional preview images to the photo gallery app, you need to create new `figure` elements and new `img` elements. Figure 5-6 shows the changes to the DOM tree you will make in this section.

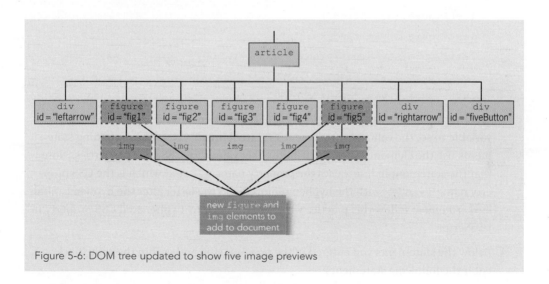

Figure 5-6: DOM tree updated to show five image previews

Note that for simplicity, Figure 5-6 merges element nodes with their attribute nodes, rather than breaking them out as in Figure 5-4.

You'll continue your work on the photo gallery by creating the first `figure` and `img` elements and setting their attributes and styles using the methods you learned earlier in this chapter.

To create the figure and img nodes for the first new preview image:

1. Return to the **photos.js** file in your text editor, and then below the `leftArrow()` function, add the following code to create a `previewFive()` function:

```
/* switch to 5-image layout */
function previewFive() {

}
```

2. Within the `previewFive()` function, enter the following comment and statement:

```
// create figure and img elements for fifth image
var lastFigure = document.createElement("figure");
```

The statement uses the `createElement()` method to create a new `figure` element and assign it to the variable name `lastFigure`.

3. Below the statement you entered in the previous step and within the code block, enter the following statements:

```
1    lastFigure.id = "fig5";
2    lastFigure.style.zIndex = "5";
3    lastFigure.style.position = "absolute";
4    lastFigure.style.right = "45px";
5    lastFigure.style.top = "67px";
```

The first statement uses the `id` property of the element stored in the `lastFigure` variable to set the value of the element's `id` attribute to `fig5`. The remaining statements use the element's `style` attribute to set values for CSS style properties. Note that the statement in line 2 uses the property name `zIndex`, which is the CSS property name `z-index` with the hyphen removed and the letter after the hyphen capitalized. You must follow this practice when referring to any hyphenated CSS property in JavaScript.

4. Below the statements you entered in the previous step and within the code block, enter the following statements:

```
var lastImage = document.createElement("img");
lastImage.width = "240";
lastImage.height = "135";
```

The first statement uses the `createElement()` method to create a new `img` element and assign it to the `lastImage` variable name. The second and third lines assign values to the element's `width` and `height` attributes. Your `previewFive()` function should match the following:

```
1    function previewFive() {
2        // create figure and img elements for fifth image
3        var lastFigure = document.createElement("figure");
4        lastFigure.id = "fig5";
5        lastFigure.style.zIndex = "5";
6        lastFigure.style.position = "absolute";
7        lastFigure.style.right = "45px";
8        lastFigure.style.top = "67px";
9        var lastImage = document.createElement("img");
10       lastImage.width = "240";
11       lastImage.height = "135";
12   }
```

5. Scroll down to the `createEventListeners()` function and then, just before the closing `}`, enter the following code:

```
1    var showAllButton = document.querySelector("#fiveButton p");
2    if (showAllButton.addEventListener) {
3        showAllButton.addEventListener("click", previewFive, ↵
4            false);
5    } else if (showAllButton.attachEvent) {
6        showAllButton.attachEvent("onclick", previewFive);
7    }
```

This code adds an event listener that calls the `previewFive()` function when a user clicks the Show more images button.

6. Save your changes to **photos.js**, return to your browser, and then open the browser tool that lets you inspect the DOM of the current web page using the method for your browser:

   › Internet Explorer DOM Inspector: Press **F12**, then **Ctrl + 1**.

   › Firefox Inspector: Press **Ctrl + Shift + C** (Windows) or **command + option + C** (Mac).

   › Chrome Elements: Press **Ctrl + Shift + I** (Windows) or **command + option + I** (Mac), then click **Elements**.

The pane that displays the console for each browser also contains an option to view the DOM tree of the current web page.

7. Refresh or reload **photos.htm** in your browser, and then click the **Show more images** button.

8. In the console pane, click the **right-pointing triangle (▶)** for each element that displays one to view its child elements. Notice that the new `figure` element you created, with the `id` value `fig5`, does not appear anywhere in the DOM tree.

Attaching Nodes

A node you create with the `createElement()` method is not automatically attached to the DOM tree or to any other nodes. Instead, it exists independently of the DOM tree. The `Document` object includes several methods for attaching nodes to the DOM tree. The most basic method is `appendChild()`, which has the following syntax:

```
parentNode.appendChild(childNode)
```

To use this method, you specify the node to be attached, which is the child node, and the node to attach it to, which is the parent node. For instance, the following code creates a new `li` element and then attaches it to the element with the `id` value `navList`:

```
var list = document.getElementById("navList");
var contact = document.createElement("li");
list.appendChild(contact);
```

The first statement sets the value of the `list` variable to the element with the `id` value `navList`. The second statement creates a new `li` element and assigns it to the variable name `contact`. The final statement appends the new element stored in the `contact` variable as a child of the `navList` element referenced by the `list` variable.

In the previous steps, you created a new `img` element and stored it with the variable name `newImage`. You also created a new `figure` element that you stored with the variable name `last`. Next you'll use the `appendChild()` method to add the `img` element as a child of the `figure` element to match the nesting of the existing `figure` and `img` elements in the photo gallery app. This creates a **document fragment**, which is a set of connected nodes that are not part of a document. You'll then use the `appendChild()` method to add the document fragment to the DOM tree for the document, as a child of the `article` element. Figure 5-7 illustrates the process you'll follow.

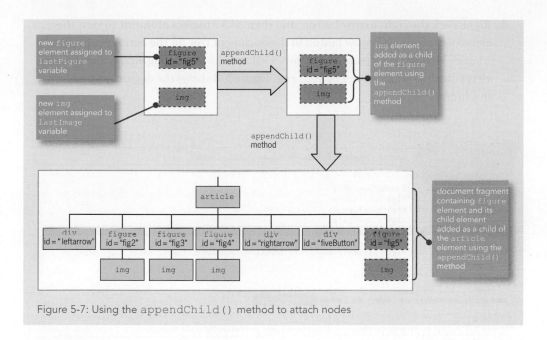

Figure 5-7: Using the appendChild() method to attach nodes

To append the img node to the figure node and the resulting document fragment to the DOM tree:

1. Return to the **photos.js** file in your text editor.

2. Within the previewFive() function, at the top of the function block, add the following statement:

```
var articleEl = document.getElementsByTagName("article")[0];
```

3. Just before the closing }, add the following statement:

```
lastFigure.appendChild(lastImage);
```

This statement uses the appendChild() method to add the lastImage node as a child node of the lastFigure node, creating a document fragment.

4. Below the statement you entered in the previous step and before the closing }, enter the following statement:

```
articleEl.appendChild(lastFigure);
```

This statement uses the appendChild() method to attach the lastFigure document fragment as a child of the article element in the document (referenced by the articleEl variable).

5. Save your changes to **photos.js**, return to your browser, refresh or reload **photos.htm**, and then click the **Show more images** button.

6. Right-click the **right arrow** button, and then click **Inspect element** to view the div element for the right arrow button in the document tree for the current page. The figure element you created with the id value fig5 is a sibling element of the div element with the id value rightarrow. Figure 5-8 shows the document tree in Chrome.

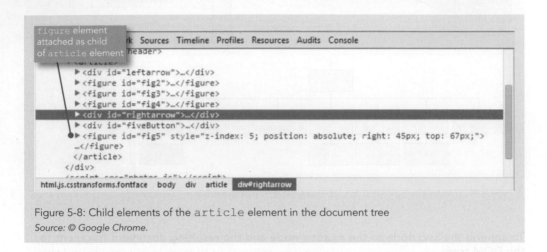

Figure 5-8: Child elements of the article element in the document tree
Source: © Google Chrome.

Note | If you don't see the figure element with the id value fig5 in the document tree, you may have forgotten to click the Show more images button. Click the Show more images button, and then examine the child elements of the article element in the document tree.

7. Click the **triangle** (▶) for the figure element with the id value rightarrow, as indicated in Figure 5-8, to view the child element of the figure element you added. As Figure 5-9 shows, the img element you added as a child of the figure element is displayed in the document hierarchy.

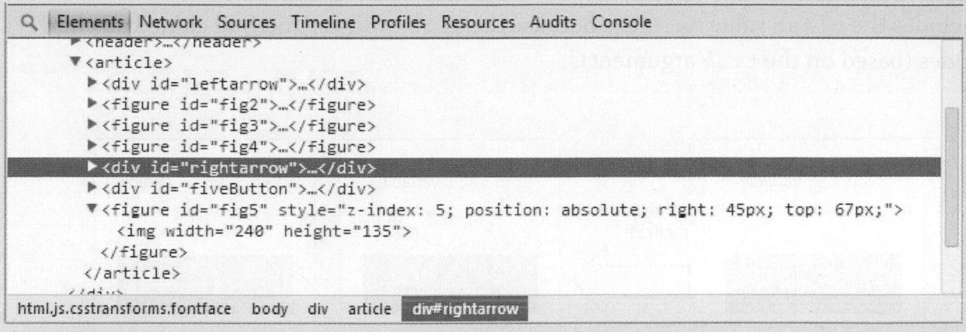

Figure 5-9: Child element of the `figure` element displayed

Source: © Google Chrome.

Note that the document fragment containing the `figure` element and its child `img` element is the last child of the `article` element. A node attached with the `appendChild()` method is always added as the last child element of the parent element.

Next you need to create the `figure` and `img` elements to display the first image in the gallery. Rather than create and configure new elements from scratch, you can create a copy of the document fragment you already created.

Cloning Nodes

Sometimes you want to create a new node that is the same as or similar to an existing node in your document. Rather than duplicate all the statements necessary to create and configure a new node, you can use the `cloneNode()` method of the `Document` object to duplicate an existing node. The `cloneNode()` method has the following syntax:

```
existingNode.cloneNode(true | false)
```

In this method, `existingNode` is a reference to the node that you want to clone. The method takes a Boolean value as an argument to indicate whether the cloned node should include any child nodes of the existing node (`true`) or only the specified parent node (`false`). For instance, the following code creates a new `li` element and assigns it to the contact variable, and then specifies a class name of `mainNav` for this element. The final statement clones the `contact` node and stores the copy in the `directions` variable.

```
var contact = document.createElement("li");
contact.className = "mainNav";
var directions = contact.cloneNode(true);
```

Figure 5-10 illustrates this process. The cloned node stored in the `directions` variable includes the `class` value `mainNav` because the `cloneNode()` method cloned all child nodes (based on the `true` argument).

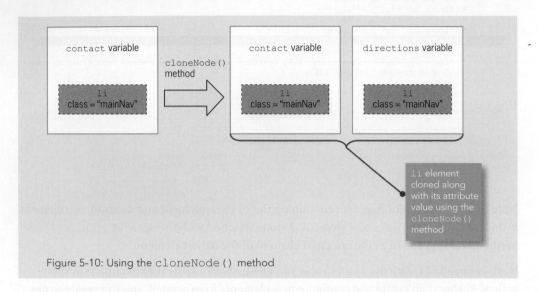

Figure 5-10: Using the `cloneNode()` method

For the photo gallery app, you need to add another `img` element nested in a `figure` element to display the first image. Instead of creating, attaching, and configuring two new nodes, you'll use the `cloneNode()` method to clone the node you created in the previous steps. You'll then add statements to change only the attribute values and style properties that are different for the new `figure` and `img` elements.

To clone the `lastFigure` node to create the `firstFigure` node:

1. Return to the **photos.js** file in your text editor.

2. Within the `previewFive()` function, just before the final `}`, enter the following comment and statement:

```
//clone figure element for fifth image and edit to be first↵
   image
var firstFigure = lastFigure.cloneNode(true);
```

This statement uses the `cloneNode()` method to duplicate the `lastFigure` node and assign the result to the variable name `firstFigure`. Because the `cloneNode()` method includes the `true` argument, the copy includes the child `img` node of the `lastFigure` node.

3. Below the code you added in the previous step, and before the final `}`, enter the following statements:

```
firstFigure.id = "fig1";
firstFigure.style.right = "";
firstFigure.style.left = "45px";
```

This code changes the `id` value for the `firstFigure` node from `fig5`, the value cloned from the `lastFigure` node, to `fig1`. It also removes the cloned value for the `right` CSS style and specifies a new value for the `left` CSS style.

4. Below the code you added in the previous step, and before the final `}`, enter the following statement:

```
articleEl.appendChild(firstFigure);
```

This statement uses the `appendChild()` method to add the `firstFigure` node to the document tree.

5. Save your changes to **photos.js**, and then refresh or reload **photos.htm** in your browser.

6. Click the **Show more images** button, right-click the **right arrow** button, and then click **Inspect element**. As Figure 5-11 shows, the `figure` element with the `id` value `fig1` is now the last child of the `article` element, right after the `figure` element with the `id` value `fig5`.

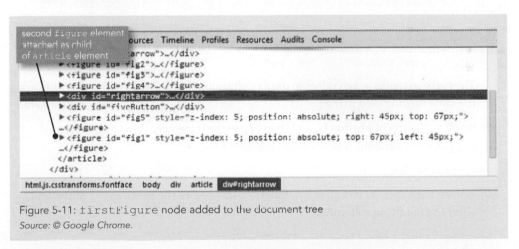

Figure 5-11: `firstFigure` node added to the document tree
Source: © Google Chrome.

7. Click the **triangle** (▶) next to the `figure` element with the `id` value `fig5` and the **triangle** next to the `figure` element with the `id` value `fig1` to view the child elements of the `figure` elements you added. As Figure 5-12 shows, the child `img` element of the node you cloned was copied as part of the cloning process.

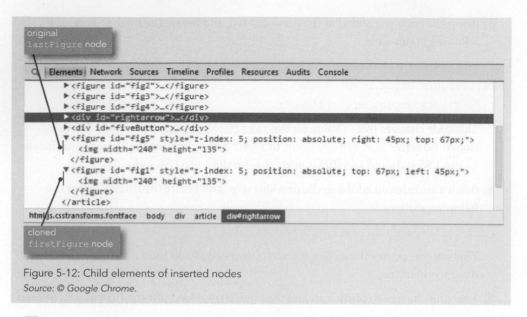

Figure 5-12: Child elements of inserted nodes
Source: © Google Chrome.

8. Return to **photos.js** in your editor, and then in the `previewFive()` function, just before the closing `}`, enter the following code:

```
1   // add appropriate src values to two new img elements
2   document.getElementsByTagName("img")[3].src = "images/IMG_0"↵
3       + photoOrder[4] + "sm.jpg";
4   document.getElementsByTagName("img")[4].src = "images/IMG_0"↵
5       + photoOrder[0] + "sm.jpg";
```

The two statements assign values to the `src` attributes for the two new `img` elements using the same method used in the `populateFigures()` function for the other `img` elements.

9. Scroll to the top of **photos.js**, and then below the statement declaring the global `photoOrder` variable, add the following statement:

```
var figureCount = 3;
```

10. Within the `populateFigures()` function, just before the existing `for` statement, enter the following statement:

```
if (figureCount === 3) {
```

11. After the `for` loop but before the closing `}` for the function, enter the following code:

```
1   } else {
2       for (var i = 0; i < 5; i++) {
3           filename = "images/IMG_0" + photoOrder[i] + "sm.jpg";
```

```
4          currentFig = document.getElementsByTagName("img")[i];
5          currentFig.src = filename;
6      }
7  }
```

This code ensures that when five images are displayed in the app, the
populateFigures() function assigns an image to each of the img elements
in the gallery each time a user clicks one of the arrow buttons. Your revised
populateFigures() function should match the following:

```
1  function populateFigures() {
2      var filename;
3      var currentFig;
4      if (figureCount === 3) {
5          for (var i = 1; i < 4; i++) {
6              filename = "images/IMG_0" + photoOrder[i] + "sm.jpg";
7              currentFig = document.↵
8                  getElementsByTagName("img")[i - 1];
9              currentFig.src = filename;
10         }
11     } else {
12         for (var i = 0; i < 5; i++) {
13             filename = "images/IMG_0" + photoOrder[i] + "sm.jpg";
14             currentFig = document.getElementsByTagName("img")[i];
15             currentFig.src = filename;
16         }
17     }
18 }
```

12. Scroll down to the previewFive() function, and then just before the closing },
enter the following statement:

```
figureCount = 5;
```

By default, the figureCount variable is set to 3 when the page opens. This statement
changes it to 5 when a user switches to viewing five images, ensuring that the
populateFigures() function assigns a photo to each img element.

13. Save your changes to **photos.js**, refresh or reload **photos.htm** in your browser, and
then click the **Show more images** button. The two additional images are displayed,
one at each end of the gallery, as shown in Figure 5-13.

two additional images displayed in gallery

Photo gallery

Show more images

Figure 5-13: Gallery showing five images
© Jason Bucy. © Sasha Vodnik.

14. Click the **right arrow** button, and then click the **right arrow** button again. Notice that the images don't change the first time you click the button, but then advance the second time you click the button.

Because the first image is the final image in the `article` element, the first time you click the right arrow button the images do not change position. You can avoid this glitch by adding the first and last `figure` elements at specific positions within the `article` element.

Inserting Nodes at Specific Positions in the Document Tree

The `createElement()` method creates a node that is not attached to the DOM tree. The final step in creating new nodes is to add them to the DOM tree in the appropriate place. You can use the `appendChild()` method to add a node as a child of a parent node that you specify. However, the new child node is always appended after any existing child nodes. If you need to add a node in a specific place among existing children of the same parent element, you instead use the `insertBefore()` method, which has the following syntax:

```
parentNode.insertBefore(newChildNode, existingChildNode)
```

For instance, assume you're working with the following HTML code:

```
1    <ul id="topnav">
2        <li><a href="aboutus.htm">About Us</a></li>
3        <li><a href="order.htm">Order</a></li>
4        <li><a href="support.htm">Support</a></li>
5    </ul>
```

The following JavaScript statements create a new `li` element and then attach it as a child of the `ul` element before the first `li` element in the existing HTML:

```
1    var list = document.getElementById("topnav");
2    var directions = document.createElement("li");
3    directions.innerHTML = "Directions";
4    var aboutus = document.querySelectorAll("#topnav li")[0];
5    list.insertBefore(directions, aboutus);
```

The statement in line 1 creates the variable `list` with a value pointing to the `ul` element with the `id` value topnav. Line 2 creates a new `li` element and assigns it to the variable `directions`. Line 4 assigns the `aboutus` variable to the existing first `li` element in the topnav list. The `insertBefore()` method in line 5 specifies `list` as the parent element, `directions` as the child element to add, and `aboutus` as the existing child element that `directions` is inserted before. Figure 5-14 illustrates the changes to the DOM tree in this example.

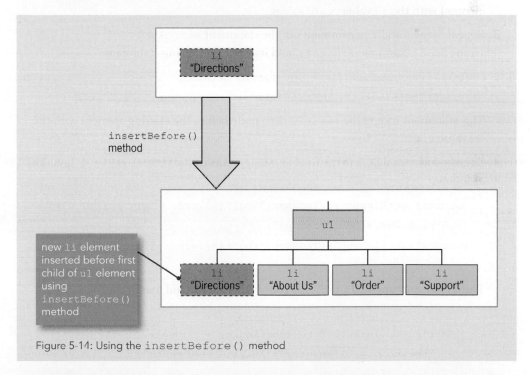

Figure 5-14: Using the `insertBefore()` method

Because the existing code for the photo gallery app uses the order of the `img` elements to determine where each image is displayed, you'll need to insert the `first` node before the existing first `figure` element in the document. To ensure that your additions to the document tree correspond to what users see on the screen, you'll also place the `last` node before the button displaying the right arrow. Next, you'll use the `insertBefore()` method to add the nodes for the first and fifth figure elements to the appropriate places in the DOM tree for the photo gallery app.

To insert the `firstFigure` and `lastFigure` nodes in the appropriate places in the DOM tree:

1. Return to the **photos.js** file in your text editor, then within the `previewFive()` function locate the statement `articleEl.appendChild(lastFigure);`, and then insert `//` at the start of the line.

2. On the next line, enter the following statement:

```
articleEl.insertBefore(lastFigure, ↵
    document.getElementById("rightarrow"));
```

This statement uses the `insertBefore()` method to add the `lastFigure` node as a child of the element specified by the `articleEl` variable, and before the child element with the `id` value `rightarrow`.

3. Repeat Steps 1 and 2 to comment out the statement `articleEl.appendChild(firstFigure);`, and insert the following statement:

```
articleEl.insertBefore(firstFigure, ↵
    document.getElementById("fig2"));
```

This statement inserts the `firstFigure` node before the existing element with the `id` value `fig2`.

4. Edit the index numbers in the final two statements of the `previewFive()` function as follows:

```
1    document.getElementsByTagName("img")[0].src = "images/IMG_0"↵
2        + photoOrder[0] + "sm.jpg";
3    document.getElementsByTagName("img")[4].src = "images/IMG_0"↵
4        + photoOrder[4] + "sm.jpg";
```

The end of your updated `previewFive()` function should match the following:

```
1    //    articleEl.appendChild(lastFigure);
2        articleEl.insertBefore(lastFigure, ↵
3          document.getElementById("rightarrow"));
4        //clone figure element for fifth image and edit to be first
5        image
6        var firstFigure = lastFigure.cloneNode(true);
7        firstFigure.id = "fig1";
```

```
 8        firstFigure.style.right = "";
 9        firstFigure.style.left = "45px";
10   //   articleEl.appendChild(firstFigure);
11        articleEl.insertBefore(firstFigure,↵
12          document.getElementById("fig2"));
13        figureCount = 5;
14   // add appropriate src values to two new img elements
15        document.getElementsByTagName("img")[0].src =↵
16          "images/IMG_0" + photoOrder[0] + "sm.jpg";
17        document.getElementsByTagName("img")[4].src =↵
18          "images/IMG_0" + photoOrder[4] + "sm.jpg";
19   }
```

5. Save your changes to **photos.js**, refresh or reload **photos.htm** in your browser, click the **Show more images** button, and then click the **right arrow** button. The photos now advance the first time you click the right arrow button.

6. Right-click the first image on the left, click **Inspect Element**, and then in the console pane examine the placement of the figure elements in the document tree. As Figure 5-15 shows, the figure element with the id value fig1 precedes the figure element with the id value fig2, and the figure element with the id value fig5 precedes the div element with the id value rightarrow.

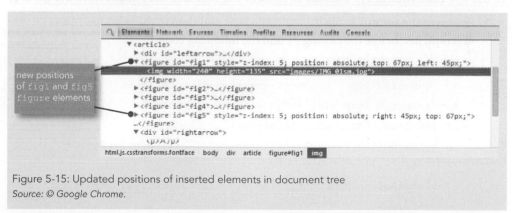

Figure 5-15: Updated positions of inserted elements in document tree
Source: © Google Chrome.

Removing Nodes

In addition to creating and attaching nodes, creating interactive apps can also involve removing nodes from the DOM tree. You can do this with the removeChild() method, which has the following syntax:

```
parentNode.removeChild(childNode)
```

You can assign the removed node to a variable to keep it available for future use, as in the following code:

```
var list = document.getElementById("topnav");
var aboutus = document.querySelectorAll("#topnav li")[0];
var aboutNode = list.removeChild(aboutus);
```

The final line of this code uses the removeChild() method to remove the aboutus node from the list parent node. The statement assigns the removed node to the aboutNode variable. You can then reference the aboutNode variable elsewhere in your code to reattach or clone the removed node.

> **Note**
> If you remove a node from the DOM tree without assigning it to a variable, JavaScript processors delete the node from memory when performing regular garbage collection. If you store a node using a variable and later want to delete the node from memory, you can do so by setting the value of the variable to null.

You want to give users the option of returning to the original layout of the photo gallery app by removing the first and fifth image previews. Next, you'll add code to achieve this using the removeChild() method.

To use the removeChild() method to remove the first and last images from the gallery:

1. Return to the **photos.js** file in your text editor, and then in the previewFive() function, just before the closing }, add the following code:

```
1   //change button to hide extra images
2   var numberButton = document.querySelector("#fiveButton p");
3   numberButton.innerHTML = "Show fewer images";
4   if (numberButton.addEventListener) {
5      numberButton.removeEventListener("click", previewFive, ↵
6         false);
7      numberButton.addEventListener("click", previewThree, ↵
8         false);
9   } else if (numberButton.attachEvent) {
10     numberButton.detachEvent("onclick", previewFive);
11     numberButton.attachEvent("onclick", previewThree);
12  }
```

After five images are displayed on the screen, this code changes the text of the button at the bottom of the gallery to "Show fewer images." It also removes the event listener that calls the previewFive() function when a user clicks the button and replaces it with an event listener that calls the previewThree() function, which you'll create in the following steps.

2. Below the previewFive() function, add the following code to create a new previewThree() function and declare the variables it will use:

```
1    /* switch to 3-image layout */
2    function previewThree() {
3        var articleEl =↵
4            document.getElementsByTagName("article")[0];
5        var numberButton = document.querySelector("#fiveButton p");
6    }
```

3. Before the closing }, enter the following statements to remove the first and fifth figure elements:

```
articleEl.removeChild(document.getElementById("fig1"));
articleEl.removeChild(document.getElementById("fig5"));
```

The first statement uses the removeChild() method to remove the element with the id value fig1, and the second uses removeChild() to remove the element with the id value fig5. Because neither of these statements assign the result to a variable, the removed nodes are deleted and do not remain in computer memory.

4. Before the closing }, enter the following statements to complete the feature:

```
1    figureCount = 3;
2    numberButton.innerHTML = "Show more images";
3    if (numberButton.addEventListener) {
4        numberButton.removeEventListener("click", previewThree,↵
5            false);
6        numberButton.addEventListener("click", previewFive, false);
7    } else if (numberButton.attachEvent) {
8        numberButton.detachEvent("onclick", previewThree);
9        numberButton.attachEvent("onclick", previewFive);
10   }
```

5. Save your changes to **photos.js**, refresh or reload **photos.htm** in your browser, and then click the **Show more images** button. The two additional images are displayed, and the button text changes to "Show fewer images."

6. Right-click the first image in the gallery, click **Inspect element**, and then in the document tree, verify that all five `figure` elements are displayed in order.

7. Click the **Show fewer images** button, and then examine the document tree. As Figure 5-16 shows, the first and fifth `figure` elements are removed from the document tree, and the button text changes back to "Show more images."

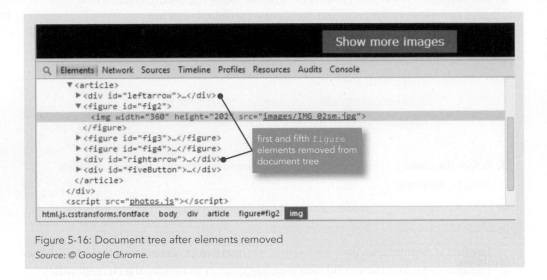

Figure 5-16: Document tree after elements removed
Source: © Google Chrome.

Short Quiz 3

1. What statement creates a new `footer` element?

2. Name two methods you can use to add a node to the DOM tree, and explain the difference between them.

3. How would the results of the following two statements differ?

Manipulating the Browser with the `Window` Object

The `Window` object includes several properties that contain information about the web browser window or tab. For instance, the `name` property contains the name of the current window or tab. Also contained in the `Window` object are various methods that allow you to manipulate the web browser window or tab itself. You have already used some methods of the `Window` object, including the `window.alert()` method, which displays a dialog box. Table 5-3 lists some commonly used `Window` object properties, and Table 5-4 lists some commonly used `Window` object methods.

PROPERTY	DESCRIPTION
closed	Boolean value that indicates whether a window or tab has been closed
document	Reference to the Document object
history	Reference to the History object
innerHeight	Height of the window area that displays content, including the scrollbar if present
innerWidth	Width of the window area that displays content, including the scrollbar if present
location	Reference to the Location object
name	Name of the window or tab
navigator	Reference to the Navigator object
opener	Reference to the window that opened the current window or tab
outerHeight	Height of the entire browser window
outerWidth	Width of the entire browser window
screen	Reference to the Screen object
self	Self-reference to the Window object; identical to the window property
status	Temporary text that is written to the status bar
window	Self-reference to the Window object; identical to the self property

Table 5-3: Window object properties

METHOD	DESCRIPTION
alert()	Displays a simple message dialog box with an OK button
blur()	Removes focus from a window or tab
clearInterval()	Cancels an interval that was set with setInterval()
clearTimeout()	Cancels a timeout that was set with setTimeout()
close()	Closes a web browser window or tab
confirm()	Displays a confirmation dialog box with OK and Cancel buttons
focus()	Makes a Window object the active window or tab
moveBy()	Moves the window relative to the current position
moveTo()	Moves the window to an absolute position
open()	Opens a new web browser window or tab
print()	Prints the document displayed in the current window or tab
prompt()	Displays a dialog box prompting a user to enter information

Continued on next page...

METHOD	DESCRIPTION
resizeBy()	Resizes a window by a specified amount
resizeTo()	Resizes a window to a specified size
scrollBy()	Scrolls the window or tab by a specified amount
scrollTo()	Scrolls the window or tab to a specified position
setInterval()	Repeatedly executes a function after a specified number of milliseconds have elapsed
setTimeout()	Executes a function once after a specified number of milliseconds have elapsed

Table 5-4: Window object methods

Another way of referring to the Window object is by using the **self property**, which refers to the current Window object. Using the self property is identical to using the window property to refer to the Window object. For example, the following lines are identical:

```
window.close();
self.close();
```

Some JavaScript programmers prefer to use the window property, while other JavaScript programmers prefer to use the self property. The choice is yours. However, when attempting to decipher JavaScript code created by other programmers, be aware that both of these properties refer to the current Window object.

Because a web browser assumes that you are referring to the global object, you generally do not need to refer explicitly to the Window object when using one of its properties or methods. For example, the alert() method is a method of the Window object. Throughout this text, you have used the full syntax of window.alert(*text*);, although the syntax alert(*text*); (without the Window object) works equally well. However, it's good practice to use the window or self references when referring to a property or method of the Window object in order to clearly identify them as belonging to the Window object. If you do not use the window or self reference, then you or another programmer might confuse a property or method of the Window object with JavaScript variables or functions.

Opening and Closing Windows and Tabs

Most web browsers allow you to open new web browser windows or tabs in addition to the web browser window(s) and tab(s) that may already be open. There are several reasons why you may need to open a new web browser window or tab. You may want to launch a new web page in a separate window or tab, allowing users to continue viewing the current page in the current window or tab. Or, you may want to use an additional window or tab to display information such as a picture or an order form.

Whenever a new web browser window or tab is opened, a new `Window` object is created to represent the new window or tab. You can have as many web browser windows or tabs open as your system will support, each displaying a different web page.

You can use simple HTML, without any JavaScript, to open a link in a new window or tab by using the `target` attribute of the `a` element. For example, the following link opens the Wikipedia home page in a new window or tab, named `wikiWindow`:

```
<a href="http://www.wikipedia.org/"↵
    target="wikiWindow">Wikipedia home page</a>
```

Whenever a user clicks the preceding link, the browser first checks for a browser window or tab named `wikiWindow`. If the window or tab exists, then the link is opened in it. If the window or tab does not exist, then a new window or tab, named `wikiWindow`, is created where the link opens.

Opening a Window or Tab

There are many scenarios in which you may want to open a window or tab but it doesn't make sense to use the HTML-only method. For instance, you may want a window or tab to open when a user clicks an element other than an `a` element. You may also want to name the new window or tab based on a variable, rather than hard-coding it into your HTML. For situations like these, you can instead create a new window or tab with JavaScript using the **open() method** of the `Window` object. The syntax for the `open()` method is

```
window.open(url, name, options, replace);
```

Table 5-5 describes the arguments of the `window.open()` method.

ARGUMENT	DESCRIPTION
`url`	Represents the web address or filename to be opened
`name`	Assigns a value to the `name` property of the new `Window` object
`options`	Represents a string that allows you to customize the new web browser window's appearance
`replace`	A Boolean value that determines whether the URL should create a new entry in the web browser's history list (`true`) or replace the existing entry (`false`); if not specified, `false` is the default value

Table 5-5: Arguments of the `Window` object's `open()` method

You can include all or none of the arguments for the `window.open()` method. For instance, the statement `window.open("http://www.wikipedia.org");` opens the Wikipedia home page in a new web browser window or tab. If you exclude the *url* argument, then a blank web page opens. For example, the statement `window.open();` opens a blank web browser window or tab.

> ### Note
> If you are writing code that requires a user to click a link or a button, then you can use an event listener to call the `window.open()` method, and the window or tab will open successfully. However, if you include JavaScript code that opens a new window or tab without a request from the user, then the pop-up blocker feature built into the current versions of all major browsers will prevent the window or tab from opening. The pop-up blocker functionality built into browsers examines the event that triggers code to open a window, and executes the code only if the event is a click, touch, or other user-generated event.

When you open a new web browser window or tab, you can customize its appearance by using the *options* argument of the `window.open()` method. Table 5-6 lists some common options that you can use with the `window.open()` method.

NAME	DESCRIPTION
height	Sets the window's height
left	Sets the horizontal coordinate of the left of the window, in pixels
location	Includes the URL Location text box
menubar	Includes the menu bar
personalbar	Includes the bookmarks bar (or other user-customizable bar)
resizable	Determines if the new window can be resized
scrollbars	Includes scroll bars
status	Includes the status bar
toolbar	Includes the Standard toolbar
top	Sets the vertical coordinate of the top of the window, in pixels
width	Sets the window's width

Table 5-6: Common options of the `Window` object's `open()` method

All the options listed in Table 5-6, with the exception of the `width` and `height` options, are set using values of "yes" or "no", or 1 for yes and 0 for no. For instance, to include the status bar, the options string should read `"status=yes"`. You set the `width` and `height` options using integers representing pixels. For example, to create a new window that is 200 pixels high by 300 pixels wide, the string should read `"height=200,width=300"`. When including multiple items in the options string, you must separate the items by commas. If you exclude the options string of the `window.open()` method, then all the standard options are included in the new web browser window. However, if you include the options string, you must include all the components you want to create for the new window; that is, the new window is created with only the components you explicitly specify.

For instance, suppose you're working on a web site for a company that sells printers. A user can view a page showing icons and summarized information about all the printers and can click any printer for details. To display the information about a specific printer in a new window, you might use the following code:

```
window.open("htx23specs.htm","SpecsWindow","toolbar=no, ↵
    menubar=no,location=no,scrollbars=no,resizable=no, ↵
    width=380,height=405");
```

Browsers have many security features built in to ensure that users are in control of their experiences while browsing. Part of this security system specifies that a browser window or tab cannot be changed by any other window or tab except the one that created it. For reasons that are beyond the scope of this chapter, in order to be able to make changes to a new window or tab, you need to create it using a variable, as in the following code:

```
var openWin = window.open("htx23specs.htm","SpecsWindow", ↵
    "toolbar=no,menubar=no,location=no,scrollbars=no, ↵
    resizable=no,width=380,height=405");
```

This code declares a variable named `openWin` and assigns as its value the window created by the specified `window.open()` method. This window displays the htx23specs.htm document; has the name `SpecsWindow`; displays no toolbar, menu bar, location box, or scroll bars; is not resizable; and has a width of 380px and a height of 405px.

The `name` argument of the `window.open()` method is essentially the same as the value assigned to the `target` attribute in that it specifies the name of the window where the URL should open. If the `name` argument is already in use by another window or tab, then JavaScript changes focus to the existing window or tab instead of creating a new one.

For instance, the code above opens the htx23specs.htm web page and assigns it a name of `SpecsWindow`. If the `SpecsWindow` window already exists when you select another menu item from the main web page, then the `SpecsWindow` window is reused; another window does not open. This is especially important with a web page such as the page displaying information on printers, which might allow you to view dozens of different web pages for each of the printers shown. Imagine how crowded a user's screen would be if the app kept opening a new window for each selected printer.

> ## Skills at Work | *Using New Windows Judiciously*
>
> As a programmer, it can be tempting to create new windows—whether with methods like `alert()` or with `window.open()`—whenever your app generates information that you think users should pay attention to. However, in most cases, creating new windows gets in the way of users, so you should minimize your use of this technique. It's appropriate to create new windows in two general situations. First, if a user has initiated an action that could have significant repercussions, triggering a dialog box with a method like `alert()` can be a good idea—for instance, to confirm that a user wants to delete information stored by a web service when the deletion is irrevocable. The other situation is when a user is taking a meta action—an action about the current document—such as linking to the document via social media. In this case, it can be helpful to launch a new window in which the user finishes and confirms the action—like adding text to provide context for a link, and then clicking a Post button—after which the window closes and the user is returned to the original page.

The design for your photo gallery specifies that when a user clicks the photo in the center, it should open in a separate window at full size. You've already created an event listener to trigger the `zoomFig()` function when a user clicks the center photo. Next, you'll create the `zoomFig()` function, which will incorporate the `window.open()` method to open the image in a separate window.

To create the `zoomFig()` function:

1. In your text editor, open the **zoom.htm** file, located in your Chapter folder for Chapter05.

2. In the comment section at the top of the document, type your name and today's date where indicated, and then save your work.

3. Scroll through the document to familiarize yourself with its content. The body section contains only two elements: `figure` and `footer`. The `figure` element contains a single `img` element.

4. Repeat Steps 1 and 2 to open **zoom.js** and save a personalized copy, and then scroll through the document to familiarize yourself with its content. The file contains global variable declarations and a `pageSetup()` function.

5. Return to the **photos.js** document in your text editor.

6. Within the function block for the `zoomFig()` function, add the following statement:

```
var zoomWindow = window.open("zoom.htm", "zoomwin",↵
    "width=960,height=600");
```

This statement creates a variable named `zoomWindow` and assigns to it the window created by the `window.open()` method. This window, which displays the contents of the zoom.htm document, has the name `zoomwin` and is 960px wide and 600px high. Assigning this window to a variable will enable to you to modify it in other parts of your app.

7. Save your work, refresh or reload **photos.htm** in your browser, and then click the photo in the center of the page. As Figure 5-17 shows, a larger version of the photo opens in a separate window.

Figure 5-17: Window opened with the `open()` method
© Jason Bucy. Source: © Mozilla Firefox.

> **Note**
>
> *For security reasons, some browsers do not display files referenced by documents launched by local files. If the new window opens but does not display the image, repeat Step 8 using a different browser. Note that this issue may affect you as a developer testing an app locally, but does not affect end users accessing the content over the web.*

8. Close the window showing the larger version of the photo. Note that clicking the "Close Window" text at the bottom of the window has no effect. You'll add this functionality in the next section.

A `Window` object's `name` property can be used to specify a target window only with a link and cannot be used in JavaScript code. If you want to control the new window by using JavaScript code located within the web browser in which it was *created*, then you must assign the new `Window` object created with the `window.open()` method to a variable. The statement that opens the photo gallery slideshow web page assigns an object representing the new web browser window to a variable named `zoomWindow`. You can use any of the properties and methods of the `Window` object with a variable that represents a `Window` object.

One problem with web pages such as your photo gallery is that windows that open in response to the user clicking a link can get hidden or "lost" behind other windows on the user's screen. For example, suppose that the user clicks the main image, as you did, thereby opening a new window. If the user then returned to the main page without closing the new window, navigated through the slideshow until a different photo was in the center, and then clicked that image, the new image would open in the same window created previously, with the name `zoomwin`. However, if that window is hidden behind the main browser window, it would appear to the user that the application was broken, because clicking an image would no longer have a noticeable effect. The user may continuously click images, thinking that nothing is happening in response to his or her clicks, when in fact the code is actually working fine. The problem might be that the windows are open but not visible. To make a window the active window, you use the **focus()** **method** of the `Window` object. You append the `focus()` method to the variable that represents the window, not to the name argument of the `window.open()` method. For example, to make the external photo gallery window the active window, you would use the statement

```
zoomWindow.focus();
```

This statement appends the `focus()` method to the name of the variable that represents the window, `zoomWindow`. Note that you would not use the name of the second window, as in the statement `zoomwin.focus()`, because for browser security reasons, JavaScript code cannot directly affect a different window.

Next, you will add a `focus()` method to the `zoomFig()` function in the photo gallery application.

To add a `focus()` method to the `zoomFig()` function:

1. Return to the **photos.js** document in your text editor.

2. Just before the closing brace for the `zoomFig()` function, add the following statement:

`zoomWindow.focus();`

   Your completed `zoomFig()` function should match the following:

```
1    /* open center figure in separate window */
2    function zoomFig() {
3        var zoomWindow = window.open("zoom.htm", "zoomwin",↵
4            "width=960,height=600");
5        zoomWindow.focus();
6    }
```

3. Save your work, refresh or reload **photos.htm** in your browser, and then click the **photo** in the center of the page. A larger version of the photo opens in a separate window.

4. Without closing the new window, return to the window containing the main photo gallery page, click the **right arrow**, and then click the **photo** in the center of the page. The window that displays the larger versions of photos should become the active window and should display the larger version of the image you clicked.

5. Close the window showing the larger version of the photo.

Closing a Window

The `close()` method, which closes a web browser window, is the method you will probably use the most with variables representing other `Window` objects. To close the web browser window represented by the `zoomWindow` variable, you use the statement `zoomWindow.close();`. To close the current window, you use the statement `window.close()` or `self.close()`.

> **Note**
>
> It is not necessary to include the `Window` object or `self` property when using the `open()` and `close()` methods of the `Window` object. However, the `Document` object also contains methods named `open()` and `close()`, which are used for opening and closing web pages for writing. Therefore, the `Window` object is usually included with the `open()` and `close()` methods to distinguish between the `Window` object and the `Document` object.

Next, you'll create a function and an event listener to close the `zoomwin` window when a user clicks the text "Close Window".

To create a function and an event listener to close the window using the `close()` method:

1. Return to the **zoom.js** document in your text editor.

2. Below the `pageSetup()` function, enter the following code to declare the `closeWin()` function:

```
/* close window */
function closeWin() {

}
```

3. Within the code block for the `closeWin()` function, enter the following statement:

```
window.close();
```

   Your completed function should match the following:

```
1   /* close window */
2   function closeWin() {
3       window.close();
4   }
```

4. Below the `closeWin()` function, add the following `createEventListener()` function:

```
1   /* create event listener for close button */
2   function createEventListener() {
3       var closeWindowDiv =↵
4           document.getElementsByTagName("p")[0];
5       if (closeWindowDiv.addEventListener) {
6         closeWindowDiv.addEventListener("click", closeWin,↵
7             false);
8       } else if (closeWindowDiv.attachEvent) {
9         closeWindowDiv.attachEvent("onclick", closeWin);
10      }
11  }
```

   Because the p element containing the text "Close Window" is the first p element in the document, you use the `getElementsByTagName()` method with an index of 0 to reference it.

5. Scroll up to the `pageSetup()` function, and then, just before the closing brace, add the following statement:

```
createEventListener();
```

Your completed `pageSetup()` function should match the following:

```
1   /* populate img element and create event listener */
2   function pageSetup() {
3       document.getElementsByTagName("img")[0].src = figFilename;
4   // assign filename to img element
5       createEventListener();
6   }
```

6. Save your work, refresh or reload **photos.htm** in your browser, and then click the **center image**. The large version of the image is displayed in a new window, as shown in Figure 5-18.

Figure 5-18: New window
© Jason Bucy. Source: © Mozilla Firefox.

> **Note**
>
> *If the image is not displayed in your browser, the link will not work either, due to the browser's security policy. Repeat Step 7 using a different browser. As before, this issue may affect you as a developer testing an app locally, but does not affect end users accessing the content over the web.*

7. At the bottom of the new window, click **Close Window**. The window closes.

Working with Timeouts and Intervals

As you develop web pages, you may need to have some JavaScript code execute repeatedly, without user intervention. Alternately, you may want to allow for some kind of repetitive task that executes automatically. For example, you may want to create a slideshow in which the image displayed changes automatically every few seconds.

You use the `Window` object's timeout and interval methods to create code that executes automatically. The **`setTimeout()` method** is used in JavaScript to execute code after a specific amount of time has elapsed. Code executed with the `setTimeout()` method executes only once. The syntax for the `setTimeout()` method is

```
var variable = setTimeout("code", milliseconds);
```

This statement declares that the variable will refer to the `setTimeout()` method. The code argument must be enclosed in double or single quotation marks and can be a single JavaScript statement, a series of JavaScript statements, or a function call. The amount of time the web browser should wait before executing the code argument of the `setTimeout()` method is expressed in milliseconds.

> **Note** A millisecond is one thousandth of a second; there are 1,000 milliseconds in a second. This means that, for example, 5 seconds is equal to 5,000 milliseconds.

The **`clearTimeout()` method** is used to cancel a `setTimeout()` method before its code executes. The `clearTimeout()` method receives a single argument, which is the variable that represents a `setTimeout()` method call. The variable that represents a `setTimeout()` method call must be declared as a global variable. (Recall that a global variable is a variable declared outside of a function and is available to all parts of a JavaScript app.)

The script section in the following code contains a `setTimeout()` method and a `clearTimeout()` method call. The `setTimeout()` method is set to execute after 10,000 milliseconds (10 seconds) have elapsed. If a user clicks the OK button, the `buttonPressed()` function calls the `clearTimeout()` method.

```
1    var buttonNotPressed = setTimeout("window.alert('Your↵
2       changes have been saved')",10000);
3    function buttonPressed() {
4       clearTimeout(buttonNotPressed);
5       window.open(index.htm);
6    }
```

Two other JavaScript methods that create code that executes automatically are the `setInterval()` method and the `clearInterval()` method. The **`setInterval()` method** is similar to the `setTimeout()` method, except that it repeatedly executes the same code after being called only once. The **`clearInterval()` method** is used to clear a `setInterval()` method call in the same way that the `clearTimeout()` method clears a `setTimeout()` method call. The syntax for the `setInterval()` method is the same as the syntax for the `setTimeout()` method:

```
var variable = setInterval("code", milliseconds);
```

As with the `clearTimeout()` method, the `clearInterval()` method receives a single argument, which is the global variable that represents a `setInterval()` method call.

Next, you will modify the photo gallery page so it automatically advances one image every 5 seconds.

To use the `setInterval()` method to make the photo gallery images advance automatically:

1. Return to the **photos.js** document in your text editor.

2. Near the top of the document, below the comment section, add the following statement to the global variables section:

```
var autoAdvance = setInterval(rightArrow, 5000);
```

3. Save your work, refresh or reload **photos.htm** in your browser, and then wait 5 seconds. The images should all shift to the left, with the center image replaced by the image of the flower growing through the fence. The images should continue to change every 5 seconds.

The automated slide show can be helpful for users, but undoubtedly some users will want to navigate through the images at their own pace. You'll incorporate the `clearInterval()` method so when a user clicks the left or right arrow, the `setInterval()` method is canceled, and the images will move only in response to the user's navigation.

To use the `clearInterval()` method to enable users to cancel the photo gallery slide show:

1. Return to the **photos.js** document in your text editor.

2. Within the `leftArrow()` function, before the other statements in the command block, add the following statement:

```
clearInterval(autoAdvance);
```

Your updated `leftArrow()` function should match the following:

```
1    function leftArrow() {
2        clearInterval(autoAdvance);
3        for (var i = 0; i < 5; i++) {
```

```
4        if ((photoOrder[i] - 1) === 0) {
5            photoOrder[i] = 5;
6        } else {
7            photoOrder[i] -= 1;
8        }
9        populateFigures();
10   }
11 }
```

3. Save your work, and then refresh or reload **photos.htm** in your browser. The photos should still switch every 5 seconds.

4. On the left side of the window, click the **left arrow**. The slideshow should return to displaying the previous image. In addition, because you added a `clearInterval()` method to the function called by the left arrow, the images should no longer change automatically every 5 seconds.

   You can add the same functionality to the right arrow. However, coding this feature is more involved. Because the `rightArrow()` function is used by the `setInterval()` method, adding a `clearInterval()` method to this function would result in only one change in images before the slide show was halted. To enable users to stop the animation with the right arrow, you'll separate the current functionality of the `rightArrow()` function into a separate function, and you'll create a new `rightArrow()` function that clears the interval and then calls the new function.

5. Return to the **photos.js** document in your text editor, and then in the `rightArrow()` function, change the function name to **rightAdvance()**. Your updated function should match the following:

```
1    /* shift all images one figure to the left, and
2    change values in photoOrder array to match */
3    function rightAdvance() {
4        for (var i = 0; i < 5; i++) {
5            if ((photoOrder[i] + 1) === 6) {
6                photoOrder[i] = 1;
7            } else {
8                photoOrder[i] += 1;
9            }
10           populateFigures();
11       }
12   }
```

6. Above the `rightAdvance()` function, add the following new `rightArrow()` function:

```
1    /* stop automatic image switching and call rightAdvance()
2    function */
3    function rightArrow() {
4        clearInterval(autoAdvance);
5        rightAdvance();
6    }
```

This function clears the interval set with the `autoAdvance` variable, and then calls the `rightAdvance()` function to shift the images as it previously did.

> **7.** Scroll up to the declaration of the `autoAdvance` variable, and then in the `setInterval()` method, replace `rightArrow` with **rightAdvance**. Your revised variable declaration should match the following:

```
var autoAdvance = setInterval(rightAdvance, 5000);
```

> **8.** Save your work, and then refresh or reload **photos.htm** in your browser. The photos should still switch every 5 seconds.

> **9.** On the right side of the window, click the **right arrow**. The slideshow should display the next image. In addition, because you added a `clearInterval()` method to the function called by the right arrow, the images should no longer change automatically every 5 seconds.

Short Quiz 4

1. What statement do you use to create a new, blank window?

2. What happens if your apps include JavaScript code that opens a new window or tab without a request from the user?

3. What extra step do you need to take in code to create a new window if you want to be able to control the new window from the window that created it?

Working with the `History`, `Location`, `Navigator`, and `Screen` objects

While the `Document` object is arguably the most important child of the `Window` object, it's important to understand the roles of the other child objects as well. In this section, you'll work with the `History`, `Location`, `Navigator`, and `Screen` objects.

The `History` Object

The `History` object maintains an internal list (known as a **history list**) of all the documents that have been opened during the current web browser session. Each web browser window contains its own internal `History` object. You cannot view the URLs contained in the history list, but you can write a script that uses the history list to navigate to web pages that have been opened during a web browser session.

The `History` object will not actually display the URLs contained in the history list. This is important because individual user information in a web browser, such as the types of web sites a user likes to visit, is private information. Preventing others from viewing the URLs in a `History` list is an essential security feature because it keeps people's browsing history confidential.

The `History` object includes three methods, listed in Table 5-7.

METHOD	DESCRIPTION
back()	Produces the same result as clicking a browser's Back button
forward()	Produces the same result as clicking a browser's Forward button
go()	Opens a specific document in the history list

Table 5-7: Methods of the `History` object

When you use a method or property of the `History` object, you must include a reference to the `History` object itself. For example, the `back()` and `forward()` methods allow a script to move backward or forward in a browser's history. To use the `back()` method, you must use the following: `history.back()`.

The `go()` method is used for navigating to a specific web page that has been previously visited. The argument of the `go()` method is an integer that indicates how many pages in the history list, forward or backward, you want to navigate. For example, `history.go(-2);` opens the web page that is two pages back in the history list; the statement `history.go(3);` opens the web page that is three pages forward in the history list. The statement `history .go(-1);` is equivalent to using the `back()` method, and the statement `history.go(1);` is equivalent to using the `forward()` method.

The `History` object contains a single property, the `length` property, which contains the specific number of documents that have been opened during the current browser session. To use the `length` property, you use the syntax `history.length;`. The `length` property does not contain the URLs of the documents themselves, only an integer representing how many documents have been opened. The following code uses the `length` property with the `go()` method to return to the first document opened in the current browser session:

```
history.go(-(history.length - 1));
```

The Location Object

When you want to allow users to open one web page from within another web page, you usually create a link with the a element. You can also use JavaScript code and the Location object to open web pages. The **Location object** allows you to change to a new web page from within JavaScript code. One reason you may want to change web pages with JavaScript code is to briefly display a message letting a user know that the action they took—such as submitting a request or changing account information—was successful, and then automatically redirect the visitor back to the content they were viewing before making their request. The Location object contains several properties and methods for working with the URL of the document currently open in a web browser window. When you use a method or property of the Location object, you must include a reference to the Location object itself. For example, to use the href property, you must write location.href = URL;. Table 5-8 lists the Location object's properties, and Table 5-9 lists the Location object's methods.

PROPERTIES	DESCRIPTION
hash	URL's anchor
host	Host and domain name (or IP address) of a network host
hostname	Combination of the URL's host name and port sections
href	Full URL address
pathname	URL's path
port	URL's port
protocol	URL's protocol
search	URL's search or query portion

Table 5-8: Properties of the Location object

METHOD	DESCRIPTION
assign()	Loads a new web page
reload()	Causes the page that currently appears in the web browser to open again
replace()	Replaces the currently loaded URL with a different one

Table 5-9: Methods of the Location object

The properties of the Location object allow you to modify individual portions of a URL. When you modify any properties of the Location object, you generate a new URL, and the web browser automatically attempts to open that new URL. Instead of modifying individual portions of a URL, it is usually easier to change the `href` property, which represents the entire URL. For example, the following statement opens the Google home page:

```
location.href = "http://www.google.com";
```

The `assign()` method of the `Location` object performs the same action as changing the `href` property: it loads a new web page. The following two statements are equivalent:

```
location.assign("http://www.google.com");
location.href = "http://www.google.com";
```

The `reload()` method of the `Location` object is equivalent to clicking a browser's Reload or Refresh button. It causes the page that currently appears in the browser to open again. You can use the `reload()` method without any arguments, as in `location.reload();`, or you can include a Boolean argument of `true` or `false`. Including an argument of `true` forces the current web page to reload from the server where it is located, even if no changes have been made to it. For example, the statement `location.reload(true);` forces the current page to reload. If you include an argument of `false`, or do not include any argument at all, then the web page reloads only if it has changed.

The `replace()` method of the `Location` object is used to replace the currently loaded URL with a different one. This method works somewhat differently from loading a new document by changing the `href` property. The `replace()` method actually overwrites one document with another and replaces the old URL entry in the web browser's history list. In contrast, the `href` property opens a different document and adds it to the history list.

The Navigator Object

The **Navigator object** is used to obtain information about the current browser. It gets its name from Netscape Navigator, but it is supported by all major browsers. Some browsers support unique methods and properties of the `Navigator` object that cannot be used with other browsers. Table 5-10 lists properties of the `Navigator` object that are supported by current versions of all major browsers.

PROPERTIES	DESCRIPTION
appName	Name of the web browser displaying the page
appVersion	Version of the web browser displaying the page
geolocation	API for accessing the user's current location and user permission settings denying or allowing access to that information

Continued on next page...

PROPERTIES	DESCRIPTION
onLine	Whether the browser currently has a network connection
platform	Operating system in use on the client computer
userAgent	String stored in the HTTP user-agent request header, which contains information about the browser, the platform name, and compatibility

Table 5-10: Properties of the Navigator object

For instance, the following code labels and logs several properties of the Navigator object:

```
1   console.log("Web browser name: " + navigator.appName);
2   console.log("Web browser version: " + navigator.appVersion);
3   console.log("Operating platform: " + navigator.platform);
4   console.log("User agent: " + navigator.userAgent);
```

Figure 5-19 shows the results of these commands in the Firefox console.

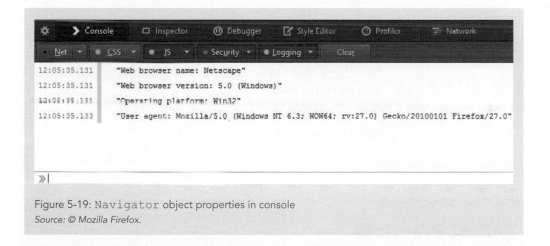

Figure 5-19: Navigator object properties in console
Source: © Mozilla Firefox.

In the past, the Navigator object was commonly used to determine which type of browser was running, in order to execute the correct code for different implementations of JavaScript. Today, JavaScript implementations are standardized across the current versions of all major browsers, so this technique, known as browser sniffing, is rarely used. One application remains for browser sniffing, however: some browser implementations of JavaScript themselves contain bugs, making it useful to identify the browser and version in order to work around the bugs. However, browser sniffing is a challenge, and it can be difficult to get conclusive information about what browser a user is running. For this reason, many developers use browser detection capabilities built into libraries such as Modernizr rather than coding this complicated task themselves.

The `Screen` Object

Computer displays can vary widely, depending on the type and size of the monitor, the type of installed graphics card, and the screen resolution and color depth selected by the user. For example, some notebook computers have small screens with limited resolution, while some desktop systems can have large monitors with very high resolution. The wide range of possible display settings makes it challenging to determine the size and positioning of windows generated by JavaScript. The `Screen object` is used to obtain information about the display screen's size, resolution, and color depth. Table 5-11 lists the properties of the `Screen` object that are supported by current versions of all major web browsers.

PROPERTIES	DESCRIPTION
`availHeight`	Height of the display screen, not including operating system features such as the Windows taskbar
`availWidth`	Width of the display screen, not including operating system features such as the Windows taskbar
`colorDepth`	Display screen's bit depth if a color palette is in use; if a color palette is not in use, returns the value of the `pixelDepth` property
`height`	Height of the display screen
`pixelDepth`	Display screen's color resolution in bits per pixel
`width`	Width of the display screen

Table 5-11: Properties of the `Screen` object

Best Practices *Use `meta` Viewport Instead of `Screen` Properties for Responsive Design*

You could use the properties of the `Screen` object to implement responsive design principles, optimizing the appearance of your documents at different screen sizes. However, wide support for the viewport property of the HTML `meta` element has made that an easier option for creating responsive designs, so this is not a common use of the `Screen` object properties.

One of the more common uses of the `Screen` object properties is to center a web browser window in the middle of the display area. For windows generated with the `window.open()` method, you can center a window when it is first displayed by assigning values to the `left` and `top` options of the options argument. To center a window horizontally, subtract the width of the window from the screen width, divide the remainder by two, and assign the result to the `left` option. Similarly, to center a window vertically, subtract the height of the window from the screen height, divide the remainder by two, and assign the result to the top option. The following code demonstrates how to create a new window and center it in the middle of the display area:

```
1   var winWidth = 300;
2   var winHeight = 200;
3   var leftPosition = (screen.width - winWidth) / 2;
4   var topPosition = (screen.height - winHeight) / 2;
5   var optionString = "width=" + winWidth + ",height="↵
6      + winHeight + ",left=" + leftPosition + ",top="↵
7      + topPosition;
8   var openWin = window.open("", "CtrlWindow", optionString);
```

> **Note**
>
> *Remember that the statements for opening a new window must be called from an event handler, or a web browser's pop-up blocker will prevent the window from opening.*

Next, you will modify the slide show application so when the new window opens, it's centered on the user's screen.

To modify the slide show application so the window showing larger images is centered on the user's screen:

1. Return to the **photo.js** document in your text editor.

2. Within the `zoomFig()` command block, above the existing statements, enter the following code:

```
1   var propertyWidth = 960;
2   var propertyHeight = 600;
3   var winLeft = ((screen.width - propertyWidth) / 2);
4   var winTop = ((screen.height - propertyHeight) / 2);
5   var winOptions = "width=960,height=600";
6   winOptions += ",left=" + winLeft;
7   winOptions += ",top=" + winTop;
```

The calculation of the `winLeft` variable starts with the width of the existing browser window minus the width of the new browser window, divided by two. This determines the amount the new window should be offset from the left edge of the existing window. The calculation for the `winTop` variable is similar to `winLeft`, using vertical properties instead of horizontal ones. The `winOptions` variable creates an options string for the `window.open()` method that incorporates the calculated values.

3. In the next line of the `zoomFig()` function, which declares the `zoomWindow` variable, replace the argument `"width=960,height=600"` with **winOptions**. Your revised `zoomFig()` function should match the following:

```
1    /* open center figure in separate window */
2    function zoomFig() {
3        var propertyWidth = 960;
4        var propertyHeight = 600;
5        var winLeft = ((screen.width - propertyWidth) / 2);
6        var winTop = ((screen.height - propertyHeight) / 2);
7        var winOptions = "width=960,height=600,";
8        winOptions += ",left=" + winLeft;
9        winOptions += ",top=" + winTop;
10       var zoomWindow = window.open("zoom.htm", "zoomwin",↵
11           winOptions);
12       zoomWindow.focus();
13   }
```

4. Save your work, refresh or reload **photos.htm** in your browser, and then click the **center image**. The new window that opens should be centered on your screen.

Short Quiz 5

1. Provide two statements that display the previous page in the browser history.

2. What is the effect of the statement `location.reload(true);`?

3. What types of information can you access using the `Screen` object?

Summary

> The browser object model (BOM) or client-side object model is a hierarchy of objects, each of which provides programmatic access to a different aspect of the web browser window or the web page.

> The top-level object in the browser object model is the `Window` object, which represents a web browser window.

> The `Document` object is the most important object in the browser object model because it represents the web page displayed in a browser.

> The Document Object Model, or DOM, represents the web page displayed in a window.

> Through the `Document` object, you can access other objects that represent elements on a web page.

> The `getElementById()` method returns the first element in a document with a matching `id` attribute.

> The `getElementsByTagName()` method returns an array of elements that matches a specified element (tag) name.

> The `getElementsByClassName()` method returns an array of elements with a `class` attribute that matches a specified value.

> The `getElementsByName()` method returns an array of elements with a `name` attribute that matches a specified value.

> Whenever a new web browser window is opened, a new `Window` object is created to represent the new window.

> When you open a new web browser window, you can customize its appearance by using the options argument of the `window.open()` method.

> A `Window` object's `name` property can be used only to specify a target window with a link and cannot be used in JavaScript code.

> To control a new window by using JavaScript code located within the web browser in which it was created, you must assign the new `Window` object created with the `window.open()` method to a variable.

> The `setTimeout()` method is used in JavaScript to execute code after a specific amount of time has elapsed, and the `clearTimeout()` method is used to cancel a `setTimeout()` method before its code executes.

> The `setInterval()` method repeatedly executes the same code after being called only once, and the `clearInterval()` method is used to clear a `setInterval()` method call.

> The `History` object maintains an internal list of all the documents that have been opened during the current web browser session.

> The `Location` object allows you to change to a new web page from within JavaScript code.

> The `Navigator` object is used to obtain information about the current web browser.

> The `Screen` object is used to obtain information about the display screen's size, resolution, and color depth.

Key Terms

API—*See* application programming interface.

application programming interface (API)—A specification of how different software components can interact with each other.

browser object model (BOM)—The model that describes the relationship between objects within the web browser, including within the current document.

`clearInterval()` method—The method of the `Window` object that's used to clear a `setInterval()` method call.

`clearTimeout()` method—The method of the `Window` object that's used to cancel a `setTimeout()` method before its code executes.

client-side object model—*See* browser object model.

`close()` method—The method of the `Window` object that's used to close a web browser window.

DHTML—*See* dynamic HTML.

document fragment—A set of connected nodes that are not part of a document.

Document Object Model (DOM)—The object model that represents the `Document` object branch of the browser object model.

DOM—*See* document object model.

DOM tree—The DOM hierarchy for a web page.

dynamic HTML (DHTML)—The combination of HTML and CSS with JavaScript, which enables interactivity on the modern web.

`focus()` method—The method of the `Window` object that's used to make a window the active window.

`getElementsByName()` method—The method of the `Document` object that returns a collection of elements with a `name` attribute that matches a specified value.

getElementsByClassName() method—The method of the Document object that returns a collection of elements with a class attribute that matches a specified value.

global object—A term for the Window object, based on the fact that all other objects in the browser object model are contained within it.

history list—The internal list maintained by the History object of all the documents that have been opened during the current web browser session.

History object—The child object of the Window object that maintains an internal list of all the documents that have been opened during the current web browser session.

HTML collection—An indexed collection of HTML elements.

Location object—The child object of the Window object that allows you to change to a new web page from within JavaScript code.

Navigator object—The child object of the Window object that is used to obtain information about the current browser.

node—Each item in the DOM tree.

node list—An indexed collection of nodes.

open() method—The method of the Window object that you can use to create a new window or tab with JavaScript.

querySelector() method—The method of the Document object that returns the first occurrence of an element matching a specified CSS selector.

querySelectorAll() method—The method of the Document object that returns a collection of elements matching a specified CSS selector.

Screen object—The child object of the Window object that is used to obtain information about the display screen's size, resolution, and color depth.

self property—Another way of referring to the Window object; using the self property is identical to using the window property to refer to the Window object.

setInterval() method—A method of the Window object that repeatedly executes the same code after being called only once.

setTimeout() method—A method of the Window object that is used to execute code once after a specific amount of time has elapsed.

tag name—The name of an element.

textContent property—The property of a web page element that you use to access and change just the text that an element contains; unlike the innerHTML property, textContent strips out any HTML tags.

Window object—The top-level object in the browser object model, which represents a web browser window.

Review Questions

1. Which of the following objects is also referred to as the global object?
   a. `Browser` object
   b. `Screen` object
   c. `Document` object
   d. `Window` object

2. In the browser object model, the `History` object is a _____ object to the `Location` object.
   a. parent
   b. grandparent
   c. sibling
   d. child

3. Each item in the DOM tree is known as a _____.
   a. node
   b. document
   c. object
   d. element

4. Which of the following is the correct syntax for accessing an element with the `id` value `headline`?
   a. `document.getElementsByID("headline")`
   b. `document.getElementById("headline")`
   c. `document.getElementByID("headline")`
   d. `document.getElementById(headline)`

5. Which of the following is the correct syntax for using the `getElementsByTagName()` method to return all of a document's p elements?
   a. `document.getElementsByTagName("<p>")`
   b. `document.getElementsByTagName("p")`
   c. `document.getElementsByTagName(<p>)`
   d. `document.getElementsByTagName() = "<p>"`

6. Which of the following is the correct syntax for accessing the value of the `href` attribute for the third `a` element in a document?
   a. `document.getElementsByTagName("a")[2].href`
   b. `document.getElementsByTagName("a")[3].href`
   c. `document.getElementById("a").href`
   d. `document.getElementsByTagName("href")[3]`

7. A set of connected nodes that are not part of a document is known as a(n) _____.
   a. history list
   b. node list
   c. HTML collection
   d. document fragment

8. Which method allows you to insert a node at a position among its sibling nodes that you specify?
   a. `createElement()`
   b. `appendChild()`
   c. `cloneNode()`
   d. `insertBefore()`

9. How do you increase the likelihood that a new window you create with the `window.open()` method will open as a new window rather than a new tab?
   a. Specify the `window=true` option.
   b. Specify a `height` and/or a `width` value.
   c. Ensure the method is initiated by a user action.
   d. Close all open tabs in the user's browser.

10. How do you control a new window that you have created with JavaScript code?
    a. You cannot control a new window with JavaScript code.
    b. Assign the new `Window` object created with the `window.open()` method to a variable.
    c. Use the `name` argument of the `window.open()` method.
    d. Use the `name` argument of the `document.open()` method.

11. To make a window the active window, you use the _____ method of the Window object.
    a. `focus()`
    b. `open()`
    c. `close()`
    d. `active()`

12. Which method do you use to execute code only once after a specific amount of time has elapsed?
    a. `setTimeout()`
    b. `setInterval()`
    c. `clearTimeout()`
    d. `clearInterval()`

13. Which method do you use to execute code repeatedly, with a specific amount of time between each execution?
    a. `setTimeout()`
    b. `setInterval()`
    c. `clearTimeout()`
    d. `clearInterval()`

14. The properties of which object describe a user's browser?
    a. `History`
    b. `Location`
    c. `Navigator`
    d. `Screen`

15. Which object allows you to change to a new, unvisited web page from within JavaScript code?
    a. `History`
    b. `Location`
    c. `Navigator`
    d. `Screen`

16. List the six main objects that make up the browser object model. Describe the relationships between these objects using the terms parent, child, and sibling.

17. Suppose you're working with a document that includes one `img` element, which has the `id` value `logoImage`. Provide the code for two ways of referencing this element.

18. Write code that displays a document named modelHDescription.htm in a new browser window that is 400px wide and 300px high, and then brings that window to the front of any other browser windows.

19. Explain the difference between the `setTimeout()` and `setInterval()` methods. Provide an example of when you'd use each one.

20. Explain how to center a window on the screen when it is created with the `window.open()` method.

Hands-On Projects

Hands-On Project 5-1

In this project, you'll create an app that prints information from a browser's `Navigator` object to the screen. You'll then compare the information reported by different browsers.

1. In your text editor, open the **index.htm** file from the HandsOnProject5-1 folder in the Chapter05 folder, add your name and today's date where indicated in the comment section, and then save the file.

2. Within the body section, just before the closing `</body>` tag, add a `script` element, and then add the following statements within the `script` element:

```
1        "use strict";
2        document.getElementsByTagName("p")[0].innerHTML =↵
3            "Web browser name: " + navigator.appName;
4        document.getElementsByTagName("p")[1].innerHTML =↵
5            "Web browser version: " + navigator.appVersion;
6        document.getElementsByTagName("p")[2].innerHTML =↵
7            "Operating platform: " + navigator.platform;
8        document.getElementsByTagName("p")[3].innerHTML =↵
9            "User agent: " + navigator.userAgent;
```

3. Save your changes.

4. Open **index.htm** in a browser, print the page or save it as a PDF, and then examine the results shown for each property. Figure 5-20 shows sample output from Firefox for Windows.

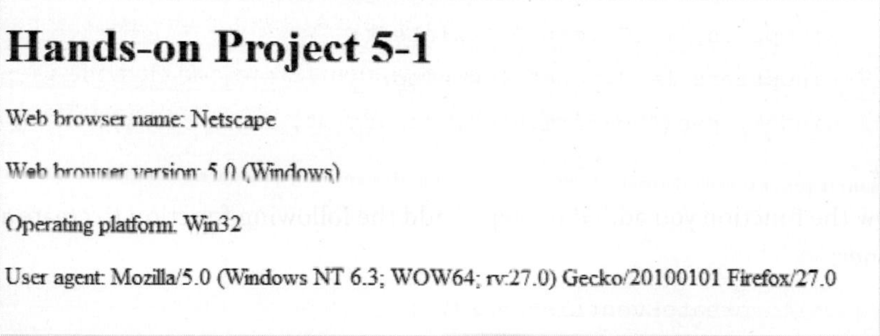

Hands-on Project 5-1

Web browser name: Netscape

Web browser version: 5.0 (Windows)

Operating platform: Win32

User agent: Mozilla/5.0 (Windows NT 6.3; WOW64; rv:27.0) Gecko/20100101 Firefox/27.0

Figure 5-20: `Navigator` object properties in Firefox

5. Repeat Step 4 using at least two additional browsers on multiple operating systems (Windows, OS X, Linux) if possible.

6. Compare the results for each browser you tested, and then answer the following questions:
   a. For each of the four properties, specify whether the information returned seems accurate.
   b. Which of the properties are consistently different in each browser? Which of the properties, if any, are the same for each browser?

c. Based on your results, explain any challenges you see in using the properties of the `Navigator` object to tell which browser an app is open in. Also explain which property or properties would deliver useful information.

Hands-On Project 5-2

In this project you'll create a function that opens a confirmation window when a user clicks a button. The window you create will be centered on the user's screen.

1. In your text editor, open the **index.htm** file from the HandsOnProject5-2 folder in the Chapter05 folder, add your name and today's date where indicated in the comment section, and then save the file.

2. Within the body section, just before the closing `</body>` tag, add a `script` element, and then add the following function within the `script` element:

```
1    function processInput() {
2        var propertyWidth = 300;
3        var propertyHeight = 100;
4        var winLeft = ((screen.width - propertyWidth) / 2);
5        var winTop = ((screen.height - propertyHeight) / 2);
6        var winOptions = "width=300,height=100";
7        winOptions += ",left=" + winLeft;
8        winOptions += ",top=" + winTop;
9        window.open("confirm.htm", "confirm", winOptions);
10   }
```

3. Below the function you added in Step 3, add the following function to create an event listener:

```
1    function createEventListener() {
2        var submitButton = document.getElementById("submit");
3        if (submitButton.addEventListener) {
4            submitButton.addEventListener("click", processInput, ↵
5                false);
6        } else if (submitButton.attachEvent) {
7            submitButton.attachEvent("onclick", processInput);
8        }
9    }
```

4. Below the function you created in Step 3, add the following code to create the event listener when the page finishes loading:

```
1   if (window.addEventListener) {
2     window.addEventListener("load", createEventListener, false);
3   } else if (window.attachEvent) {
4     window.attachEvent("onload", createEventListener);
5   }
```

5. Save your work, open **index.htm** in a browser, and then click the **Submit** button. A window opens displaying the message "Your address has been updated", as shown in Figure 5-21.

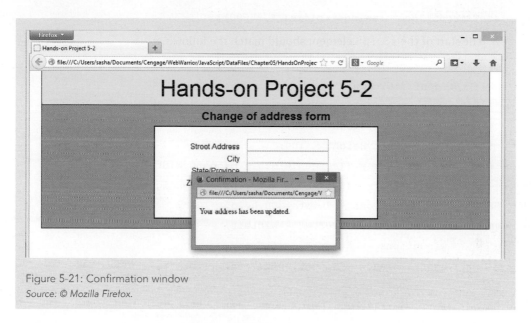

Figure 5-21: Confirmation window
Source: © Mozilla Firefox.

6. Close the window containing the message.

Hands-On Project 5-3

In this project you'll enhance the work you did in Hands-On Project 5-2, setting the confirmation window to close 5 seconds after it opens.

1. In the file manager for your operating system, copy the completed contents of the HandsOnProject5-2 folder to the HandsOnProject5-3 folder.

2. In your text editor, open the **index.htm** file from the HandsOnProject5-3 folder, and then change "Hands-on Project 5-2" to **Hands-on Project 5-3** in the comment section, in the `title` element, and in the `h1` element.

3. Within the `script` element, before the `processInput()` function, enter the following statement:

```
var confirmWindow;
```

4. Within the `processInput()` function, in the last statement, remove the `var` keyword at the start of the line.

5. Before the closing brace for the `processInput()` function, add the following statement:

```
setTimeout("confirmWindow.close()", 5000);
```

The start of the `script` element should match the following:

```
1    "use strict";
2    var confirmWindow;
3    function processInput() {
4        var propertyWidth = 300;
5        var propertyHeight = 100;
6        var winLeft = ((screen.width - propertyWidth) / 2);
7        var winTop = ((screen.height - propertyHeight) / 2);
8        var winOptions = "width=300,height=100";
9        winOptions += ",left=" + winLeft;
10       winOptions += ",top=" + winTop;
11       confirmWindow = window.open("confirm.htm", "confirm",↵
12           winOptions);
13       setTimeout("confirmWindow.close()", 5000);
14   }
```

6. Save your work, open **index.htm** in a browser, and then click the **Submit** button. After 5 seconds, the confirmation window should close.

Hands-On Project 5-4

In this project you'll enhance Hands-On Project 5-2 in a different way, replacing the timeout with a close button.

1. In the file manager for your operating system, copy the completed contents of the HandsOnProject5-2 folder to the HandsOnProject5-4 folder.

2. In your text editor, open the **confirm.htm** file from the HandsOnProject5-4 folder, change "Hands-on Project 5-2" to **Hands-on Project 5-4** in the comment section, and then add your name and today's date to the comment section.

3. Just below the existing p element, add the following new p element:

```
<p id="closeB">Close</p>
```

4. Just above the closing `</body>` tag, create a `script` element.

5. Within the `script` element, enter the following function:

```
function closeWindow() {
   window.close();
}
```

6. Below the `closeWindow()` function, enter the following function:

```
1    // add event listener to Close button
2    function createEventListener() {
3       var closeButton = document.getElementById("closeB");
4       if (closeButton.addEventListener) {
5          closeButton.addEventListener("click", closeWindow, ↵
6             false);
7       } else if (closeButton.attachEvent) {
8          closeButton.attachEvent("onclick", closeWindow);
9       }
10   }
```

7. Below the `createEventListener()` function, add the following statement:

```
if (window.addEventListener) {
   window.addEventListener("load", createEventListener, false);
} else if (window.attachEvent) {
   window.attachEvent("onload", createEventListener);
}
```

8. Save your work, open **index.htm** in a browser, and then click the **Submit** button. The confirm window opens, as shown in Figure 5-22.

Figure 5-22: Confirm window with Close button
Source: © Mozilla Firefox.

9.   Click the **Close** button. The confirm window closes.

Hands-On Project 5-5

In this project, you'll create and reference document elements as a means of generating a table of contents for a document containing the United States Bill of Rights.

1.   In your text editor, open the **index.htm** file from the HandsOnProject5-5 folder in the Chapter05 folder, add your name and today's date where indicated in the comment section, and then save the file.

2.   Within the body section, just before the closing `</body>` tag, add a `script` element.

3.   Within the `script` element, declare a variable named `list` that contains a reference to the only `ul` element in the document. Also declare empty variables named `headingText` and `TOCEntry`.

4.   Below the variable declarations, create a `for` statement that sets a counter variable equal to 1, repeats the loop as long as the value of the counter variable is less than or equal to 10, and increments the counter variable by 1 each time through the loop.

5.   Within the `for` loop, add statements that perform the following tasks:
     a.   Set the value of the `headingText` variable to the content of the element with an `id` value equal to the current value of the counter variable.

b. Create a new `li` element, and assign it as the value of the `TOCEntry` variable.

c. Set the content of the `TOCEntry` node to the following:

```
"<a href=#" + i + ">" + headingText + "</a>"
```

d. Add the `TOCEntry` node as the last child of the `list` node.

6. Add a backward-compatible event listener that calls the `createTOC()` function when the page finishes loading.

7. Save your work, and then open **index.htm** in a browser. Beneath the "Table of Contents" heading, a list of the 10 sections should be displayed, with each section name formatted as a link, as shown in Figure 5-23.

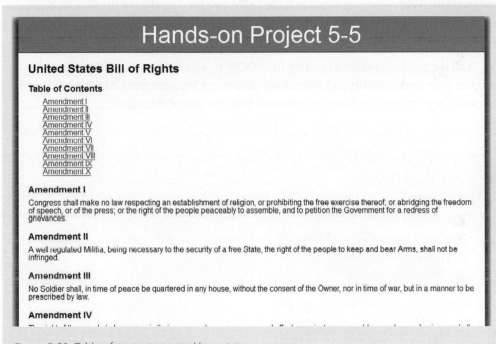

Figure 5-23: Table of contents created by script

8. In the Table of Contents, click the **Amendment III** link. If the entire page was not visible in your browser window, the window should scroll up until the Amendment III heading is at the top of the window.

Case Projects

Individual Case Project

Add a page to your individual website that educates visitors about web security. Report the values of at least six properties from Tables 5-10 and 5-11 to illustrate the breadth of information about a user's computer that a web app can access. Perform a web search on practices for using the web safely, and include links to at least three sources, along with a one-sentence summary of each.

Team Case Project

In this project, your team will draw the DOM tree for an HTML document.

To start, break into pairs, with each pair responsible for a different HTML document in your team website. With your partner, sketch the DOM tree for the selected document. Your tree should show the hierarchy of the site, including elements, attributes, and text content, similar to Figure 5-4.

When all the pairs are finished creating their DOM trees, assemble as a full group and compare your trees. Identify and discuss any differences between trees. Make any changes necessary to your own tree based on feedback from the rest of the team.

CHAPTER 6

ENHANCING AND VALIDATING FORMS

When you complete this chapter, you will be able to:

> Enhance form usability with JavaScript
> Customize browser-based HTML validation
> Implement custom validation to check for errors
   and display error messages

Forms are one of the most common web page elements used with JavaScript. You use JavaScript to make sure that data was entered properly into the form fields and to perform other types of processing before the data is sent to the server. Without JavaScript, the only actions that a web page can take on form data are to perform limited validation and to send it to a server for processing. In this chapter, you will learn how to use JavaScript to make forms easier for users to complete, and to implement custom data validation before submission.

Using JavaScript with Forms

JavaScript is commonly used with forms for two reasons: to add functionality that makes forms easier for users to fill out, and to validate or process the data that a user enters before that data is submitted to a server-side script. **Validation** is the process of checking that information provided by users conforms to rules to ensure that it appropriately answers the form's questions and is provided in a format that the site's back-end programs can work with. For example, customers may use an online form to order merchandise from your web site. When customers click the form's Submit button, you need to make sure that their information, such as the shipping address and credit card number, is entered correctly.

> ## Programming Concepts | *Validation*
>
> Validation involves checking user input against a set of rules or standards. While JavaScript lets you perform validation in a user's browser, the server-side programs that receive form data generally perform validation as well. Although some validation can be performed only by the server, you can implement many types of validation on the client using JavaScript. There are many ways to present feedback to users based on client-side validation. As a programmer, your choices include whether to present all validation results at once, or highlight one erroneous field at a time; and whether to validate while a user is typing, after a user leaves a field, or only when a user clicks a submit button.

A `form` object represents a `form` element in an HTML document. You use the properties, events, and methods of a `form` object to access the form and its data with JavaScript. Tables 6-1, 6-2, and 6-3 list some properties, an event, and some methods, respectively, of `form` objects.

PROPERTY	DESCRIPTION
`autocomplete`	Enables autocompletion of previously saved form data by a browser when set to `true`
`elements`	Returns a collection of a form's elements
`length`	Returns an integer representing the number of elements in the form
`novalidate`	Disables browser-based validation by a browser when set to `false`

Table 6-1: Properties of `form` objects

EVENT	DESCRIPTION
submit	Fires when a form's submit button is clicked

Table 6-2: Event of `form` objects

METHOD	DESCRIPTION
checkValidity()	Initiates browser-based validation of form controls, returning `true` if all controls are valid
submit()	Submits a form without the use of a submit button

Table 6-3: Methods of `form` objects

The elements used for collecting data within a form include `input`, `select`, `option`, `textarea`, and `button`. Tables 6-4, 6-5, and 6-6 list properties, methods, and events that are common to most or all of these elements. Note that properties, methods, and events related to validity do not apply to `button` elements or `input` elements of type `button`. Later in this chapter you'll learn about additional properties, methods, and events that are element specific.

PROPERTY	DESCRIPTION
autofocus	Returns the value `true` if the HTML autofocus attribute is set, indicating that the element should receive the focus when the form is loaded
placeholder	Returns the value of the `placeholder` attribute, which contains text to be displayed when a field has no value
required	Returns the value `true` if the HTML `required` attribute is set, indicating that the control must contain a value before the form can be submitted
validationMessage	Sets or returns the text of the message to be displayed to the user after a failed `submit` event if the field's `validity` value is `false`
validity	Returns the value `true` if the control value passes browser-based validation rules
value	Sets or returns the value of the control
willValidate	Returns the value `true` if constraint validation is enabled for the control

Table 6-4: Properties of elements within forms

METHOD	DESCRIPTION
checkValidity()	Runs constraint validation against a form element; returns a value of true if the value is valid, and false if the value is invalid
setCustomValidity ("message")	Sets the string message as the text to be displayed to users if the control value is found to be invalid; passing a nonempty string sets the control's validity to false, and passing an empty string as the parameter sets the control's validity to true

Table 6-5: Methods of elements within forms

EVENT	TRIGGERED WHEN
blur	The focus leaves the element, meaning that the element is initially selected or contains the insertion point, and then another element is selected or contains the insertion point (usually by clicking another element or pressing Tab to move to another element)
change	The focus leaves the element, and the value or selected state of the current element has changed
focus	The element receives the focus, meaning the element is selected or the insertion point moves into the current element (usually by clicking the current element or pressing Tab to move to the current element)
formchange	Another control in the form fires a change event
forminput	Another control in the form fires an input event
input	The value or selected state of the current element changes
invalid	A control's value is found to be invalid during constraint validation

Table 6-6: Events of elements within forms

Referencing Forms and Form Elements

While most developers use methods such as getElementById() and getElementsByTagName() to access and work with web page objects, you should be aware that there's another way to address form objects. By default, browsers create collections of a few types of objects in an HTML document, including anchors, images, links, and forms. This book uses the code

```
document.getElementsByTagName("form")[0]
```

to refer to the form object in a document that contains only one form. However, you may also encounter the reference

```
document.forms[0]
```

that refers to the first `form` object within the default array of `form` objects created by browsers. In addition, the `forms` array contains an array of objects within a `form` element, known as the `elements` array. You could reference the third object within the first form in a web document using

```
document.forms[0].elements[2]
```

Especially in a larger form, using the `elements` array can be tedious. However, when referencing a form using the `forms` array, you can instead reference any element within the form by the element's `name` value. This means that to reference an element with the name `DeliveryZip` in the first form in a web document, you could use the syntax

```
document.forms[0].DeliveryZip
```

One advantage of referencing `form` objects using methods such as `getElementById()` rather than the `forms` array is that you don't need to switch between using one syntax for referencing `form` objects and another syntax for non-`form` objects. In addition, using `Document` object methods makes your code more flexible when you need the same code to be able to refer to both `form` and non-form elements. Finally, use of the `name` attribute is not allowed in the strict DTD for XHTML, so if you're writing JavaScript to work with XHTML documents, you cannot use the forms array or other browser arrays. However, you should understand how it works in case you encounter it when working with code written by other developers.

In this chapter, you'll work with a form for Snoot Flowers, a flower shop in Davenport, Iowa. The shop has commissioned an order form for their website, which has been completed. Your task will be to create JavaScript code to enhance the form and validate user entries before the form data is submitted to the back-end software on the company's server.

You'll start your work by opening the order form page and familiarizing yourself with it.

To open and view the order form:

1. In your text editor, open the **snoot.htm** file, located in your Chapter folder for Chapter 6.

2. In the comment section at the top of the document, type your name and today's date where indicated, and then save your work.

3. Scroll through the document to familiarize yourself with its content. The article contains a form, which is composed of six fieldsets, which are created with the HTML `fieldset` element.

4. Open **snoot.htm** in a web browser. Figure 6-1 shows the current content of the document.

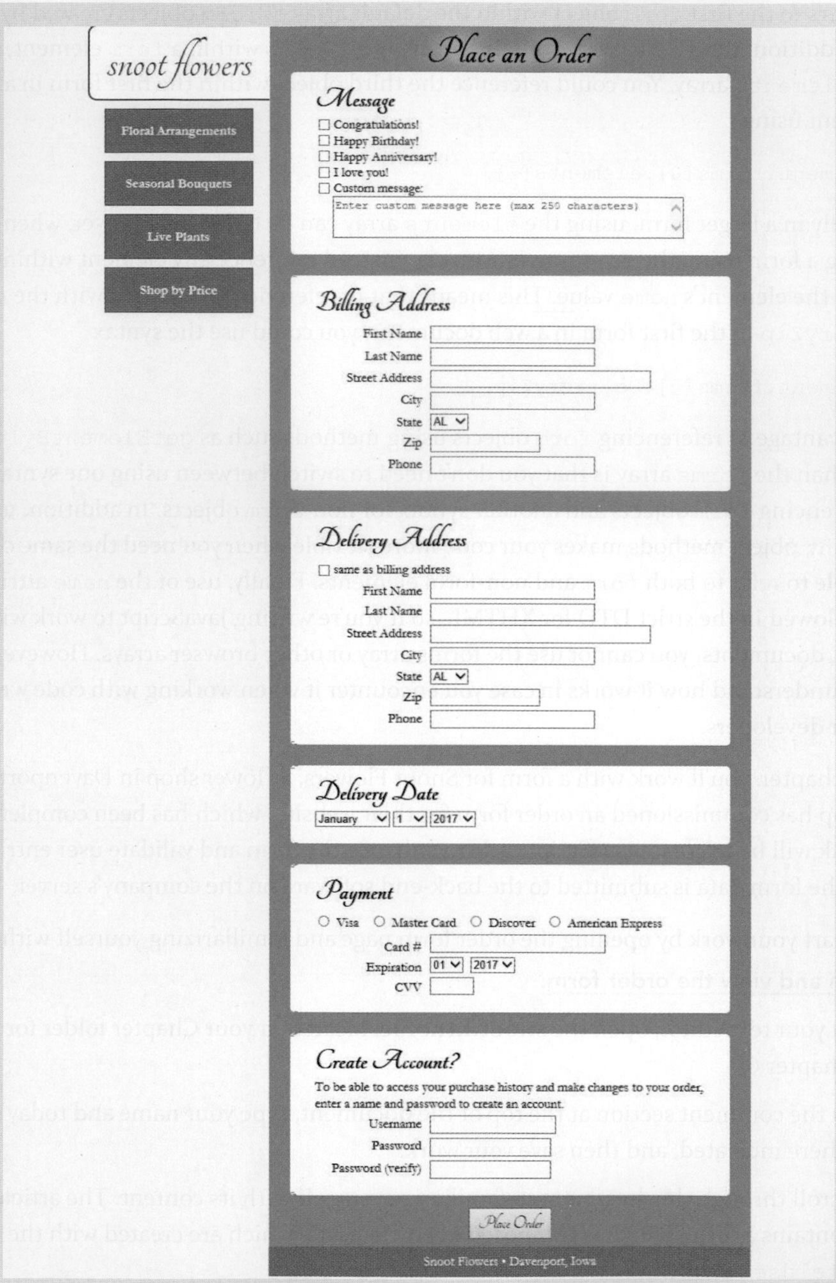

Figure 6-1: snoot.htm in a browser

© 2015 Cengage Learning®

Short Quiz 1

1. Describe two common uses of JavaScript with forms.

2. Name two advantages of identifying `form` elements using the `getElementById()` method rather than by specifying their index numbers within the form.

Improving Form Usability

One of the most important form-related roles for JavaScript programs is validating user input. Before you actually write code to validate user input, however, there are a few steps you can take to reduce the amount of validation necessary.

Designing Forms to Collect More Accurate Content

Most form validation involves checking data that users have typed into `input` and `textarea` boxes to ensure its accuracy. For instance, in the form in Figure 6-2, you'd want to ensure that a user's entry in the Card Type box was the name or abbreviation for a type of credit card that your company accepts. Likewise, you'd want to check that the entry in the Expiration box specified a month and a year.

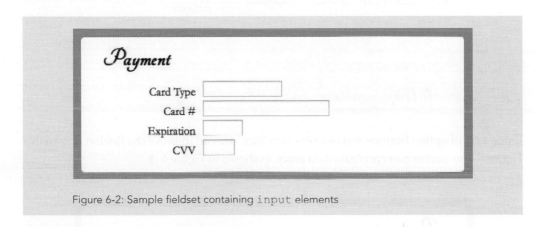

Figure 6-2: Sample fieldset containing `input` elements

However, the information requested for the Card Type and Expiration fields is restricted to a small, discrete list—the names of a few credit cards, for instance, in the case of the Card Type field. Asking users to type this information opens your form to the possibility that they'll misspell a word, use an abbreviation that your back-end system doesn't recognize, or simply enter data that's not within the acceptable parameters (such as "65" for the month, or "Check" for the card type). Instead, you can use other types of form fields to present users with acceptable choices, and limit their options to those choices. Table 6-7 lists some alternative form elements and the types of information they're best for.

NAME	CODE TO CREATE	USE TO DISPLAY
Option buttons	`<input type="radio" />`	A small set of options at once, from which a user can select one
Check boxes	`<input type="checkbox" />`	One or more yes/no choices

Selection lists	`<select>`
	
	   `<option>value1</option>`
	
	   `<option>value2</option>`
	
	   `...`
	
	`</select>`
		A truncated list of options that's fully displayed when a user interacts with it

Sliders	`<input type="range" />`	A bar with an indicator that users can drag to increase or decrease a value; used with `min` and `max` attributes to specify bottom and top of range (supported in IE10+ and all other modern browsers)

Data lists	`<input type="text" list="listname" />`
	
	`<datalist id="listname">`
	
	   `<option value="value1" />`
	
	   `...`
	
	`</datalist>`
		A text box that suggests values from the `datalist` element as a user types, but enables a user to enter a value not in the list

Table 6-7: Selected form elements for providing limited choices

Using a set of option buttons and two selection lists, you can improve the fieldset shown in Figure 6-2 to ensure more accurate data entry, as shown in Figure 6-3.

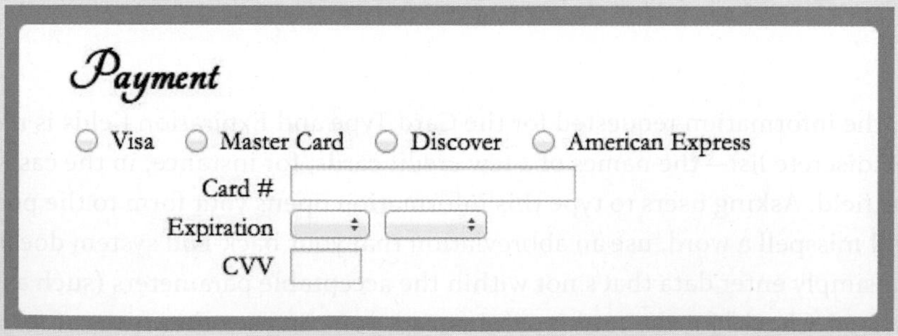

Figure 6-3: Sample fieldset updated with option buttons and selection lists

The fieldset in Figure 6-3 uses option buttons to display credit card choices, and provides selection lists from which users can select the month and year of credit card expiration. Although user input is still required for the Card # and CVV fields, this redesign reduces the amount of necessary validation on the data provided by users.

> **Note**
>
> *You can restrict user entries in text fields by specifying* `type` *values specific to the data being collected, such as* `number` *or* `email`*, as well as by specifying the* `maxlength` *and* `required` *attributes. You'll learn more about validating data based on these* `input` *types and attributes later in this chapter.*

Programming Forms to Increase Content Accuracy

In addition to providing users with limited sets of possibilities for different form fields, you can create JavaScript functions that reduce the likelihood of user errors when completing a form. Such functions, known as **assistive functions**, do not perform validation themselves—that is, they don't check user content for errors. Instead, these functions prevent users from entering erroneous data in the first place. Many types of assistive functions are possible; which ones you implement depends on the design of your form and the type of data you're trying to collect.

Removing Default Values from Selection Lists

Two aspects of the Snoot Flowers order form would benefit from assistive functions. First, the form includes a number of selection lists. By default, browsers select the first item in each list. However, Snoot Flowers wants to be sure that users have made a deliberate choice for these fields, rather than simply overlooking the default and submitting the form with that information. For instance, erroneously submitting a form with the default delivery date of January 1, 2017 might result in orders being delivered on the wrong date.

You can use HTML to set the default value for a selection list, but only to one of the menu options. However, you can use JavaScript to set the `selectedIndex` property of a `select` object to –1, which corresponds to no selection. This ensures that any selection is made by a user, rather than being a default value. Table 6-8 describes this and other properties of `select` elements that you can manipulate with JavaScript.

PROPERTY	DESCRIPTION
length	Returns the number of `option` elements nested within the `select` element
multiple	Sets or returns a Boolean value that determines whether multiple options can be selected in the selection list
options	Returns a collection of the elements nested within the `select` element
selectedIndex	Returns a number representing the element number in the `options` collection of the first option selected in a selection list; returns −1 if no option is selected
size	Sets or returns the number of options to be displayed at once
type	Returns the type of selection list, which is either `select-one` if the `select` element does not include the `multiple` attribute, or `select-multiple` if the `select` element does include the `multiple` attribute

Table 6-8: `select` element properties

You'll start your work by creating a function that sets the `selectedIndex` property to -1 for the form's `select` elements.

> **Note** Another usability approach for the delivery date might be to change the default date to the current date whenever the form is opened. You'll learn how to access and use the current date with JavaScript in Chapter 7.

To change the `selectedIndex` property for `select` elements:

1. In your text editor, create a new JavaScript document, and then enter the following comment section, typing your name and today's date where indicated:

```
1   /*      JavaScript 6th Edition
2    *      Chapter 6
3    *      Chapter case
4
5    *      Snoot Flowers
6    *      Functions
7    *      Author: your name
8    *      Date:   today's date
9
10   *      Filename: snoot.js
11   */
```

2. Save the document as **snoot.js**.

3. Below the comment section, enter the following statement to tell processors to interpret the document comments in strict mode:

```
"use strict"; // interpret document contents in JavaScript strict↵
   mode
```

4. Below the code you entered in the previous step, enter the following code to create a function with the name removeSelectDefaults():

```
1    /* remove default values and formatting from state and delivery
2    date selection lists */
3    function removeSelectDefaults() {
4    }
```

5. Within the command block for the function you created in the previous step, enter the following statement to declare the variable emptyBoxes:

```
var emptyBoxes = document.getElementsByTagName("select");
```

This variable references a collection that includes all the select elements in the document.

6. Below the variable declaration and within the command block, enter the following code to create a for loop:

```
for (var i = 0; i < emptyBoxes.length; i++) {

}
```

This for loop iterates as long as the value of i is less than the length of the emptyBoxes collection, and it increments the value of i each time through the loop. You'll use the loop to run commands on the select element at position i each time through the loop.

7. Within the command block for the for statement, enter the following code to set the selectedIndex value:

```
emptyBoxes[i].selectedIndex = -1;
```

The code for your removeSelectDefaults() function should match the following:

```
1    /* remove default values and formatting from state and delivery
2    date selection lists */
3    function removeSelectDefaults() {
4       var emptyBoxes = document.getElementsByTagName("select");
5       for (var i = 0; i < emptyBoxes.length; i++) {
6          emptyBoxes[i].selectedIndex = -1;
7       }
8    }
```

8. Below the function you just created, enter the following comment and event listener code to call the function after the page finishes loading:

```
1    /* run setup function when page finishes loading */
2    if (window.addEventListener) {
3        window.addEventListener("load", removeSelectDefaults, false);
4    } else if (window.attachEvent) {
5        window.attachEvent("onload", removeSelectDefaults);
6    }
```

9. Save your work, return to **snoot.htm** in your editor, and then just before the closing `</body>` tag, add the following `script` element to reference the snoot.js file you just created:

```
<script src="snoot.js"></script>
```

10. Save your changes to snoot.htm, and then refresh or reload **snoot.htm** in your browser. As Figure 6-4 shows, the `select` elements now display no default values.

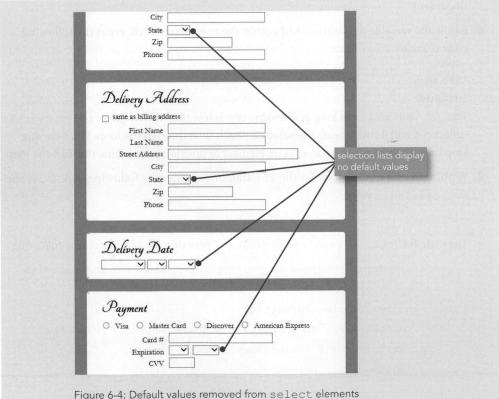

Figure 6-4: Default values removed from `select` elements

Dynamically Updating Selection List Values

Using the properties in Table 6-8 in combination with the methods you learned about in Chapter 5 for creating and attaching nodes in the node tree, you can add and remove `option` elements in a `select` element. In addition to using the properties of the `select` element, you can also look up and set properties of `option` elements, which are described in Table 6-9.

PROPERTY	DESCRIPTION
`defaultSelected`	Returns a Boolean value that determines whether the `option` element representing the currently selected item includes the `selected` attribute
`index`	Returns a number representing the element number within the `options` collection
`label`	Sets or returns alternate text to be displayed for the option in the selection list
`selected`	Sets or returns a Boolean value that determines whether an option is selected
`text`	Sets or returns the text displayed for the option in the selection list
`value`	Sets or returns the text that is assigned to the `option` element's `value` attribute; this value is submitted to the server

Table 6-9: Properties of `option` elements

One common use of adding and removing options from a `select` element is to change the options shown in a list based on another selection a user has made in the same form. For instance, the three selection lists in the Delivery Date fieldset of the Snoot Flowers order form contain lists of months, days, and years. However, the number of days shown to users should depend on the selected month. For instance, if a user selects March, the selection list for days should display the numbers 1–31. However, if a user selects April, the days list should display only 1–30.

To add this functionality to the Snoot Flowers order form, you'll start by creating three nodes. The first will contain a single child node, consisting of an `option` element with the value 29. The second node will contain two child nodes consisting of `option` elements with the values 29 and 30. The final node you'll create will contain three child nodes, which will be `option` elements with the values 29, 30, and 31. With these three building blocks in place, you'll then truncate the existing selection list (showing the numbers 1–31) so it contains only options for the values 1–28. Then, based on the user's month selection, you'll either make no additional changes to the list (for February in a nonleap year) or you'll add one of the three nodes you created to increase the date values to the length that corresponds with the selected month. In addition, when February is the selected month, your program will check if the selected year is 2018, which is a leap year; if so, you'll add the node containing only the option value 29 to the days selection list. Figure 6-5 illustrates the code you'll create.

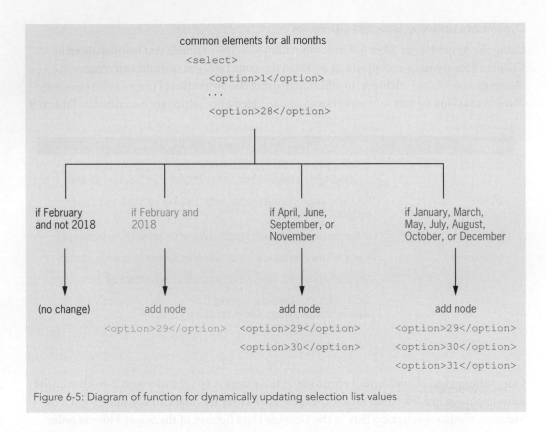

Figure 6-5: Diagram of function for dynamically updating selection list values

To program the days list to change dynamically based on the selected month and year:

1. In your browser, scroll down the order form to the Delivery Date field, click the **arrow** for the first selection list, click **April**, click the **arrow** for the second selection list, and then if necessary, scroll to the bottom of the second selection list. Although April contains only 30 days, the days list includes 31 as an option. This makes it possible for a user to select a delivery date of April 31, which would be invalid.

2. Return to **snoot.js** in your text editor, and then, below the `"use strict";` statement, enter the following code to create three global variables:

```
1  /* global variables */
2  var twentyNine = document.createDocumentFragment();
3  var thirty = document.createDocumentFragment();
4  var thirtyOne = document.createDocumentFragment();
```

You use the `createDocumentFragment()` **method** to create an empty document fragment. Because you'll use one function to populate the three nodes when the page loads, and another function to append the correct node to the day selection list each time the month or year changes, the nodes must be represented by global variables.

3. Below the global variables, enter the following function to populate the three nodes:

```
1    /* set up node building blocks for selection list of days */
2    function setupDays() {
3        var dates = document.getElementById("delivDy").↵
4            getElementsByTagName("option");
5        twentyNine.appendChild(dates[28].cloneNode(true));
6        // add 29th
7        thirty.appendChild(dates[28].cloneNode(true));
8        thirty.appendChild(dates[29].cloneNode(true));
9        // add 29th & 30th
10       thirtyOne.appendChild(dates[28].cloneNode(true));
11       thirtyOne.appendChild(dates[29].cloneNode(true));
12       thirtyOne.appendChild(dates[30].cloneNode(true));
13       // add 29th, 30th, & 31st
14   }
```

The code first creates a local variable containing references to all the option elements within the day selection list. It then copies the 29th option element (with index number 28) to the twentyNine node. The remaining code copies the 29th and 30th option elements to the thirty node and the 29th, 30th, and 31st option elements to the thirtyOne node. This creates the building blocks for any changes required to the content of the day selection list.

4. Below the code for the function you just created, but before the removeSelectDefaults() function, enter the following code to create the updateDays() function and declare its local variables:

```
1    function updateDays() {
2        var deliveryDay = document.getElementById("delivDy");
3        var dates = deliveryDay.getElementsByTagName("option");
4        var deliveryMonth = document.getElementById("delivMo");
5        var deliveryYear = document.getElementById("delivYr");
6        var selectedMonth = deliveryMonth.options↵
7            [deliveryMonth.selectedIndex].value;
8    }
```

5. Below the code for the local variables, but within the code block for the function, enter the following `while` statement:

```
1   while (dates[28]) {
2       // remove child with index of 28 until this index is empty
3       deliveryDay.removeChild(dates[28]);
4   }
```

This code removes the child with an index of 28, and repeats this until no child exists at index 28. This has the effect of removing the options for the 29th, 30th, and 31st from the selection list.

6. Below the `while` loop, but within the code block for the function, enter the following `if` statement:

```
1   if (deliveryYear.selectedIndex === -1) {
2   // if no year is selected, choose the default year so length of↵
3       Feb can be determined
4       deliveryYear.selectedIndex = 0;
5   }
```

This statement checks the `selectedIndex` value of the year selection list. If the value is –1, meaning no value is selected, the value is changed to 0, which is the first item in the list. Because the function must determine whether the current year is a leap year, a date value must be selected before the subsequent conditional statements run.

7. Below the `if` statement from the previous step, enter the following `if` statement:

```
1   if (selectedMonth === "2" &&↵
2       deliveryYear.options[deliveryYear.selectedIndex].value ===↵
3       "2018") {
4       // if leap year, Feb has 29 days
5       deliveryDay.appendChild(twentyNine.cloneNode(true));
6   }
```

This `if` statement adds the `twentyNine` node to the end of the day selection list if February is selected and the year is 2018—a leap year.

8. Add the following `else if` statement to the end of the `if` statement from the previous step:

```
1   else if (selectedMonth === "4" || selectedMonth === "6" ||↵
2       selectedMonth === "9" || selectedMonth === "11") {
3       // these months have 30 days
4       deliveryDay.appendChild(thirty.cloneNode(true));
5   }
```

This `if` statement checks if the selected month contains 30 days (April, June, September, or November), and if so, it adds the `thirty` node to the end of the day selection list.

9. Add the following `else if` statement to the end of the `if/else` statement from the previous steps:

```
1   else if (selectedMonth === "1" || selectedMonth === "3" ||↵
2       selectedMonth === "5" || selectedMonth === "7" ||↵
3       selectedMonth === "8" || selectedMonth === "10" ||↵
4       selectedMonth === "12") {
5       // these months have 31 days
6       deliveryDay.appendChild(thirtyOne.cloneNode(true));
7   }
```

This `if` statement checks if the selected month contains 31 days (January, March, May, July, August, October, or December), and if so, it adds the `thirtyOne` node to the end of the day selection list.

10. At the bottom of snoot.js, before the `window.addEventListener` statement, enter the following function:

```
1   /* create event listeners */
2   function createEventListeners() {
3       var deliveryMonth = document.getElementById("delivMo");
4       if (deliveryMonth.addEventListener) {
5         deliveryMonth.addEventListener("change", updateDays,↵
6           false);
7       } else if (deliveryMonth.attachEvent)  {
8         deliveryMonth.attachEvent("onchange", updateDays);
9       }
```

```
10        var deliveryYear = document.getElementById("delivYr");
11        if (deliveryYear.addEventListener) {
12          deliveryYear.addEventListener("change", updateDays, false);
13        } else if (deliveryYear.attachEvent)   {
14          deliveryYear.attachEvent("onchange", updateDays);
15        }
16    }
```

This code adds two event listeners: the first to call the updateDays() function when the value in the month selection list changes, and the second to call the same function when the value in the year selection list changes. This second event listener ensures that the list of days remains accurate if a user chooses February and then changes the year from a leap year to a nonleap year, or vice versa.

11. Below the createEventListeners() function and before the event listener code, enter the following function:

```
1    /* run initial form configuration functions */
2    function setUpPage() {
3        removeSelectDefaults();
4        setupDays();
5        createEventListeners();
6    }
```

Because multiple functions must run when the page is first loaded, you add references to them to the setUpPage() function, which you'll then call when the page finishes loading.

12. Change the event listener code at the bottom of snoot.js to call setUpPage:

```
1    if (window.addEventListener) {
2        window.addEventListener("load", setUpPage, false);
3    } else if (window.attachEvent) {
4        window.attachEvent("onload", setUpPage);
5    }
```

13. Save your changes to **snoot.js**, and refresh or reload **snoot.htm** in your browser. Then, in the Delivery Date fieldset, click the **arrow** for the first selection list, click **April**, click the **arrow** for the second selection list, and if necessary scroll to the bottom of the list. As Figure 6-6 shows, the final number in the list is now 30, which is appropriate for April.

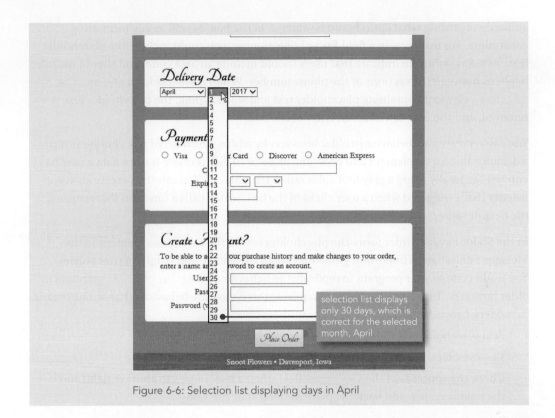

Figure 6-6: Selection list displaying days in April

14. Check the days displayed for each month in both 2017 and 2018 to verify that the code you just created works as intended.

Adding Placeholder Text for Older Browsers

Recent additions to HTML include features that enhance usability with minimal work on the part of developers. However, older browsers don't support all of these features, so some of these enhancements are available only to users of current versions of popular browsers. You can, however, use JavaScript to simulate the behavior of these features in older browsers. One popular recent feature in form creation is the `placeholder` attribute of the `input` and `textarea` elements. You can specify a word or phrase as the value of the `placeholder` attribute; this word or phrase is then displayed in the `input` or `textarea` box, generally in gray rather than black characters. For instance, in the Custom message box in Figure 6-1, the text "Enter custom message here (max 250 characters)" is specified using the `placeholder` attribute. The value of the `placeholder` attribute generally provides guidance regarding what data should be entered in the box, as well as any formatting constraints. For instance, in a field for a phone number, you could include the placeholder text "###-###-####" to indicate that users should include an area code, and should include hyphens between the sections of the phone number. When a user clicks in an `input` or `textarea` element containing placeholder text and starts typing, the placeholder text is removed, and the user can make an entry in the box.

You can recreate this behavior in older browsers by adding the desired placeholder text as a default value for an element and changing its color to differentiate it from data a user has entered (generally using a gray font color rather than black). You can then create an event listener that's triggered when a user clicks in the box, which calls a function that removes the default value.

In the Snoot Flowers order form, the placeholder text in the `textarea` element in the Message fieldset gives important guidelines about the nature and length of user entries. You'll add code to your program to replicate the behavior of the `placeholder` attribute in older browsers. To do this, you need to replicate three separate behaviors that are automatic in modern browsers:

> Add placeholder text when the page finishes loading.

> Remove placeholder text when a user selects the `textarea` field.

> Check the contents of the `textarea` field when a user moves to another field, and if the field is empty, add back the placeholder text as the value.

You'll start by creating a function to add the placeholder text in older browsers. The order form page already includes the Modernizr library for making semantic HTML elements available in older browsers. You'll check the value of the `Modernizr.input.placeholder` value to see if the browser opening the page supports the `placeholder` attribute. If so, your function isn't necessary and will do nothing. But if the attribute isn't recognized, your function will add the text of the `placeholder` attribute as the value for the `textarea` control.

To add placeholder text to the Custom message box in older browsers:

1. If you have access to Internet Explorer 8, use it to open **snoot.htm**. Notice that no placeholder text is displayed in the `textarea` box below the Custom message check box. See Figure 6-7.

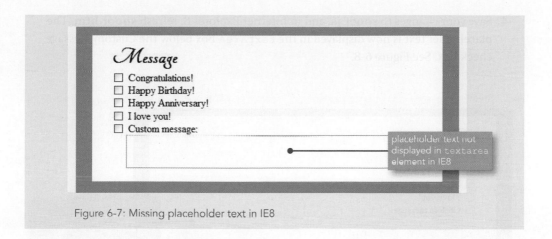

Figure 6-7: Missing placeholder text in IE8

2. Return to the **snoot.js** file in your editor and then, above the `createEventListeners()` function, enter the following code to create the `generatePlaceholder()` function:

```
1   function generatePlaceholder() {
2       if (!Modernizr.input.placeholder) {
3           var messageBox = document.getElementById("customText");
4           messageBox.value = messageBox.placeholder;
5           messageBox.style.color = "rgb(178,184,183)";
6       }
7   }
```

The function contains a single `if` statement. If the browser doesn't support the `placeholder` attribute, this `if` statement sets the value of the `placeholder` attribute as the value of the `textarea` element, and then changes the text color of the `textarea` element to a shade of gray.

3. Scroll down to the `setUpPage()` function, and then add a call to the `generatePlaceholder()` function, as shown below:

```
1   function setUpPage() {
2       removeSelectDefaults();
3       setupDays();
4       createEventListeners();
5       generatePlaceholder();
6   }
```

4. Save your changes to **snoot.js**, and in Internet Explorer 8, refresh **snoot.htm**. The placeholder text is now displayed in the `textarea` box below the Custom message check box. See Figure 6-8.

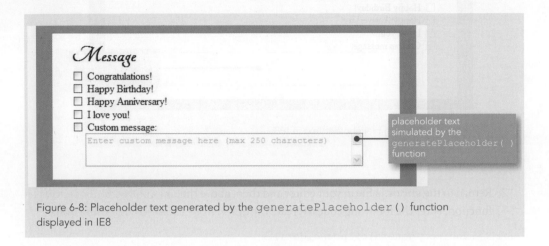

Figure 6-8: Placeholder text generated by the `generatePlaceholder()` function displayed in IE8

Next you'll add code to clear the value in the `textarea` box when a user clicks in the box.

To add code to clear the value in the `textarea` box:

1. In Internet Explorer 8, click in the **textarea** box below the Custom message check box, and then type **Thanks a million**. Instead of replacing the placeholder text, as it would in a modern browser, the text you typed is added to the placeholder text, creating a garbled mixture of instructions and custom message text. See Figure 6-9.

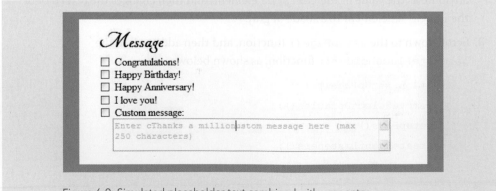

Figure 6-9: Simulated placeholder text combined with user entry

2. Return to the **snoot.js** file in your editor and then, above the `generatePlaceholder()` function, enter the following code to create the `zeroPlaceholder()` function and declare a variable:

```
1   /* remove fallback placeholder text */
2   function zeroPlaceholder() {
3       var messageBox = document.getElementById("customText");
4   }
```

3. Below the variable declaration, add the following statements:

```
1   messageBox.style.color = "black";
2   if (messageBox.value === messageBox.placeholder) {
3       messageBox.value = "";
4   }
```

When this function is called to remove the placeholder text, it starts by setting the font color back to black, in preparation for a user entry. In addition, if the only content of the control is the value of the `placeholder` attribute, the content is reset to an empty string. This `if` statement ensures that if a user has entered text in this control, then left the control, and then returned to it, the user's earlier entry is not deleted when they click in the control for a second time. Your completed `zeroPlaceholder()` function should match the following:

```
1   function zeroPlaceholder() {
2       var messageBox = document.getElementById("customText");
3       messageBox.style.color = "black";
4       if (messageBox.value === messageBox.placeholder) {
5           messageBox.value = "";
6       }
7   }
```

4. Within the `generatePlaceholder()` function you created in the previous set of steps, just before the closing `}` for the `if` statement, add the following code to create an event listener to call the `zeroPlaceholder()` function:

```
1   if (messageBox.addEventListener) {
2       messageBox.addEventListener("focus", zeroPlaceholder, false);
3   } else if (messageBox.attachEvent) {
4       messageBox.attachEvent("onfocus", zeroPlaceholder);
5   }
```

Your updated `generatePlaceholder()` function should match the following:

```
1    function generatePlaceholder() {
2        if (!Modernizr.input.placeholder) {
3            var messageBox = document.getElementById("customText");
4            messageBox.value = messageBox.placeholder;
5            messageBox.style.color = "rgb(178,184,183)";
6            if (messageBox.addEventListener) {
7                messageBox.addEventListener("focus", zeroPlaceholder, ↵
8                    false);
9            } else if (messageBox.attachEvent)   {
10                messageBox.attachEvent("onfocus", zeroPlaceholder);
11            }
12        }
13    }
```

5. Save your changes to **snoot.js**, refresh **snoot.htm** in IE8, click in the **textarea** control, and then type **Thanks a million**. When you click in the `textarea` control, the simulated placeholder text is removed, and the text you type is the only text in the box.

To finish simulating placeholder text for older browsers, you'll add code to restore the placeholder text when a user leaves the `textarea` field without typing anything.

To restore placeholder text when the textarea is left empty:

1. In Internet Explorer 8, refresh **snoot.htm**, and then click in the **textarea** control. The placeholder text is removed.

2. Click in the **First Name** box. Notice that the `textarea` control remains blank. This means that users who click in the `textarea` but don't type anything and decide to come back to it later won't see the placeholder text. You'll create a function to restore the placeholder text if a user removes the focus from the `textarea` control without making an entry.

3. Return to **snoot.js** in your editor, and then above the `generatePlaceholder()` function, enter the following code to create the `checkPlaceholder()` function and declare a variable:

```
1    /* restore placeholder text if box contains no user entry */
2    function checkPlaceholder() {
3        var messageBox = document.getElementById("customText");
4    }
```

4. Below the variable declaration, add the following `if` statement:

```
1    if (messageBox.value === "") {
2        messageBox.style.color = "rgb(178,184,183)";
3        messageBox.value = messageBox.placeholder;
4    }
```

This `if` statement checks if the `textarea` value is an empty string, and if so, changes the text color back to gray and assigns the value of the `placeholder` attribute as the value of the field. Your completed `checkPlaceholder()` function should match the following:

```
1    function checkPlaceholder() {
2        var messageBox = document.getElementById("customText");
3        if (messageBox.value === "") {
4            messageBox.style.color = "rgb(178,184,183)";
5            messageBox.value = messageBox.placeholder;
6        }
7    }
```

5. In the `generatePlaceholder()` function you created earlier, add the code highlighted below to create an event listener (or attach an event in older browsers):

```
1    function generatePlaceholder() {
2        if (!Modernizr.input.placeholder) {
3            var messageBox = document.getElementById("customText");
4            messageBox.value = messageBox.placeholder;
5            messageBox.style.color = "rgb(178,184,183)";
6            if (messageBox.addEventListener) {
7                messageBox.addEventListener("focus", zeroPlaceholder,↵
8                    false);
9                messageBox.addEventListener("blur", checkPlaceholder,↵
10                    false);
11            } else if (messageBox.attachEvent)  {
12                messageBox.attachEvent("onfocus", zeroPlaceholder);
13                messageBox.attachEvent("onblur", checkPlaceholder);
14            }
15        }
16    }
```

6. Save your changes to **snoot.js**, refresh **snoot.htm** in IE8, click in the `textarea` box, and then click the **First Name** field. When you click in the `textarea` box, the simulated placeholder text is removed, as you saw earlier. This time, when you click in the First Name field without making an entry in the `textarea` box, the simulated placeholder text is displayed once again in the `textarea` box.

Automatically Updating an Associated Field Based on a User Entry

The order form includes a Custom message check box that a user can check to send a message with an order. Below this option is a `textarea` element where the user can enter the text of the custom message. However, suppose a form is submitted in which the `textarea` field contains text, but the Custom message text box is not checked. Depending on the back-end program processing form data, this ambiguity might cause problems with the order, because the back-end program would have to decide whether the user meant to send the message. You can keep this mismatch from happening and reduce the amount of time it takes for a user to complete the form by adding a function that checks a user's entry in the `textarea` field and checks the Custom message box for them if they've entered custom text. Table 6-10 lists some commonly used properties associated with `textarea` elements, and Table 6-11 describes a `textarea` method.

PROPERTY	REFERENCES
`placeholder`	Value of the `placeholder` attribute
`defaultValue`	Default value displayed in the `textarea` element when the page loads

Table 6-10: Properties of `textarea` elements

METHOD	DESCRIPTION
`select()`	Selects the element contents

Table 6-11: Method of `textarea` elements

The logic of any program designed to increase form usability involves interpreting users' intentions. For instance, the order form validation code you've written assumes that users might overlook default values for selection lists, and that any default values might not reflect users' actual choices. At the same time, the function for the message box will assume that users intend to use whatever text they type into the Custom message `textarea` box, even if they haven't checked the associated check box. Depending on the importance of the form you're creating and the image the owner wants to project, you may choose to be stricter or looser in your interpretations. In general, the more important it is for a form to collect precise data, the less you should assume intent in validating it. For instance, in a form collecting confidential health care information, you would likely want to make few, if any, assumptions. On the other hand, for a form collecting general feedback about an event, you might be safer making more assumptions about user intent.

To create a function to automatically check the Custom message check box when a custom message has been entered:

1. Return to the **snoot.js** file in your editor and then, above the `createEventListeners()` function, enter the following code to create the `autocheckCustom()` function and declare a local variable:

```
1    /* automatically check Custom message check box if user makes
2    entry in customText box */
3    function autocheckCustom() {
4        var messageBox = document.getElementById("customText");
5    }
```

2. Below the variable declaration, add the following `if` statement:

```
1    if (messageBox.value !== "" && messageBox.value !==↵
2        messageBox.placeholder) {
3        // if user entry in textarea, check Custom check box
4        document.getElementById("custom").checked = "checked";
5    }
```

This `if` statement checks if the value of the `textarea` element is something other than an empty string or the value of the `placeholder` attribute. If so, the `checked` attribute for the custom check box is set to `checked`, which adds a check to the box. Your completed `autocheckCustom()` function should match the following:

```
1   function autocheckCustom() {
2      var messageBox = document.getElementById("customText");
3      if (messageBox.value !== "" && messageBox.value !==↵
4         messageBox.placeholder) {
5         // if user entry in textarea, check Custom check box
6         document.getElementById("custom").checked = "checked";
7      }
8   }
```

3. Within the `createEventListeners()` function, add the following code to create an event listener that calls the `autoCheckCustom()` function when a user leaves the `textarea` control:

```
1   var messageBox = document.getElementById("customText");
2   if (messageBox.addEventListener) {
3     messageBox.addEventListener("blur", autocheckCustom, false);
4   } else if (messageBox.attachEvent) {
5     messageBox.attachEvent("onblur", autocheckCustom);
6   }
```

4. Save your changes to **snoot.js**, in your browser reload or refresh **snoot.htm**, click in the **textarea** control, type **Thanks a million**, and then click in the **First Name** box. The Custom message check box is automatically checked when you click outside of the `textarea` control.

Transferring Duplicate Field Values

Another way that JavaScript is commonly used to improve form usability is to copy data entered in one field to another field that a user indicates should contain the same data. In fact, if you've ever placed an order online, you've likely used such a function to indicate that items should be shipped to the address you already provided as the billing address. This feature is often linked to a check box labeled "shipping address same as billing address" or something similar. When a user checks the box, the contents of all billing address fields are copied to the corresponding shipping address fields.

As Figure 6-1 shows, the Snoot Flowers form contains fields for both billing and shipping address, and already incorporates a "same as billing address" check box. Next you'll create a function that copies the contents of each field in the billing address fieldset to the corresponding field in the shipping address fieldset. You'll also add an event listener to call this function when a user checks this box, and another event listener to clear the values in the shipping address fieldset when a user unchecks the box.

To enable users to use billing address information for the shipping address:

1. Return to the **snoot.js** file in your editor and then, above the `createEventListeners()` function, enter the following code to create the `copyBillingAddresses()` function and declare local variables:

```
1   /* copy values for Billing Address fields to Delivery Address
2   fields */
3   function copyBillingAddress() {
4       var billingInputElements =↵
5           document.querySelectorAll("#billingAddress input");
6       var deliveryInputElements =↵
7           document.querySelectorAll("#deliveryAddress input");
8   }
```

2. After the `var` statement, enter the following `if` statement:

```
1       if (document.getElementById("sameAddr").checked) {
2           for (var i = 0; i < billingInputElements.length; i++) {
3               deliveryInputElements[i + 1].value =↵
4                   billingInputElements[i].value;
5           }
6           document.querySelector("#deliveryAddress select").value =↵
7               document.querySelector("#billingAddress select").value;
8       }
```

This `if` statement runs if the "same as billing address" text box is checked. It first loops through the `input` elements in the Billing Address section, assigning the value of each to its corresponding element in the Delivery Address section. Note that the index `i + 1` is used for the Delivery Address elements because the first input element in this section is the "same as billing address" check box, which has no matching field in the Billing Address section. After all `input` values are copied, the final line of code copies the value of the single `select` element in the Billing Address section to the corresponding element in the Delivery Address section.

3. Add the following `else` statement to the `if` statement you created in the previous step:

```
1   else {
2       for (var i = 0; i < billingInputElements.length; i++) {
3           deliveryInputElements[i + 1].value = "";
4       }
5       document.querySelector("#deliveryAddress select").↵
6           selectedIndex = -1;
7   }
```

This `if` statement runs if the "same as billing address" text box is unchecked. It first loops through the `input` elements in the Delivery Address section, setting the value of each to an empty string. It finishes by setting the `selectedIndex` for the single `select` element in the Delivery Address section to -1, meaning that no value is selected.

4. Within the command block for the `createEventListeners()` function, before the closing `}`, enter the following code to create an event listener for the `copyBilling-Address()` function:

```
1   var same = document.getElementById("sameAddr");
2   if (same.addEventListener) {
3       same.addEventListener("click", copyBillingAddress, false);
4   } else if (same.attachEvent) {
5       same.attachEvent("onclick", copyBillingAddress);
6   }
```

5. Save your changes to **snoot.js**, then refresh or reload **snoot.htm** in your browser.

6. In the Billing Address section of the form, make an entry or selection in each field (don't worry about entering accurate information), and then in the Delivery Address section, click the **same as billing address** check box to check it. As Figure 6-10 shows, the values you specified in the Billing Address section are copied to their corresponding controls in the Delivery Address section.

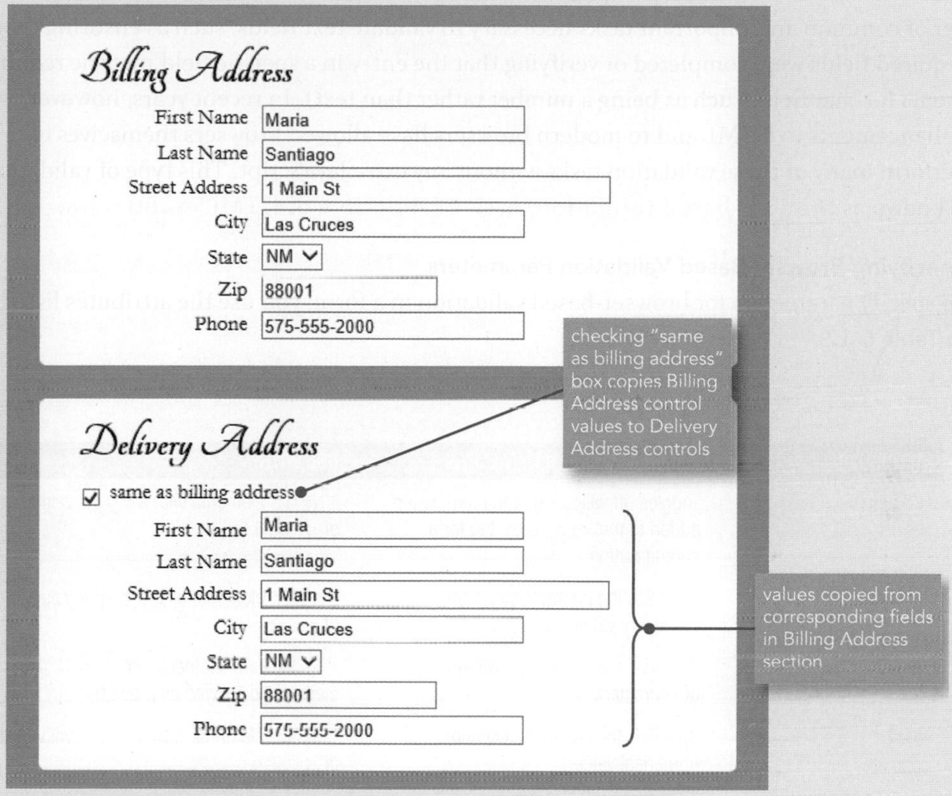

Figure 6-10: Billing Address entries copied to Delivery Address section

7. Click the **same as billing address** check box again to uncheck it. The values are removed from the controls in the Delivery Address section.

Short Quiz 2

1. If you were designing a form with a question that asked users if they owned a bicycle, would you expect more accurate input using a text input box or a check box? Why?

2. What property do you use to change the selected option element in a selection list? What value do you use to specify that no option element is selected?

Customizing Browser-Based Validation

Almost without exception, even the best-designed form needs validation. One of the main reasons is that most forms contain text boxes, and any text box can have incorrect data entered in it.

Historically, much of the JavaScript code written to validate web forms performed a number of common and important tasks necessary to validate text fields, such as ensuring that required fields were completed or verifying that the entry in a specific field met the requirements for that field (such as being a number rather than text). In recent years, however, enhancements to HTML and to modern browsers have allowed browsers themselves to perform many of these validation tasks without any extra JavaScript. This type of validation is known as browser-based validation, native validation, or HTML5 validation.

Specifying Browser-Based Validation Parameters

To specify parameters for browser-based validation in a form, you use the attributes listed in Table 6-12.

ATTRIBUTE	DESCRIPTION	USE WITH
formnovalidate	Toggles off validation of the form when added to the `<input>` tag for a submit button	`input` elements with a `type` value of `submit`
max	Specifies the control's maximum numerical value	`input` elements with a `type` value of `number`
maxlength	Specifies the control's maximum number of characters	`textarea` elements, or `input` elements displayed as a text box
min	Specifies the control's minimum numerical value	`input` elements with a `type` value of `number`
novalidate	Toggles off validation of the form when added to the opening `<form>` tag	the `form` element
pattern	Specifies a pattern that a control's value must match, expressed as a regular expression	`textarea` elements, or `input` elements displayed as a text box
required	Indicates that the control must have a value	`input`, `select`, or `textarea` elements
step	Specifies the increment that a numerical value must adhere to	`input` elements with a `type` value of `number`

Table 6-12: HTML attributes to set browser-based validation parameters

Additional browser-based validation is linked to several values for the `type` attribute of the `input` element, which are described in Table 6-13. For instance, if a field is created with the tag `<input type="number" />`, modern browsers automatically reject nonnumeric content.

VALUE	CONTENT DESCRIPTION	SAMPLE CONTENT
color	# followed by a 6-digit hexadecimal color value, with any letters in lower case	#ffcc00
date, datetime, week, month, time, datetime-local	Relevant components of coordinated universal time (UTC), a standardized date/time format	2019-10-14T12:00:00.001-04:00
email	An email address	president@whitehouse.gov
number	A numerical value	73.54

Table 6-13: Values for `type` attribute that trigger browser-based validation

When you include any of the attributes from Table 6-12 (aside from `novalidate` or `formnovalidate`) or the input `type` values from Table 6-13 in the HTML code for a form, modern browsers automatically perform validation when the `submit` event is triggered on the form—usually when a user clicks the form's submit button.

Note | HTML also includes the values `tel` (telephone number) and `url` as values for the `input type` attribute. However, browsers do not enforce any rules for content validity on elements that use these types.

To see how browser-based validation works, you'll try submitting the form with missing or invalid data.

To see how browser-based validation deals with missing or invalid data in the order form:

1. Return to **snoot.htm** in your editor.

2. Within the code for the order form, examine the `type` values for the `input` elements. Notice that the `input` elements for the zip codes, the phone numbers, the credit card number, and the CVV all use a `type` value of `number`.

3. Note which `input` and `select` elements include the `required="required"` attribute. All the `input` and `select` elements in the form are marked as required except for those in the Message and Create Account? fieldsets.

Note | You can flag an element in a form as required in HTML with the attribute `required`, which doesn't need a value. However, to make your code valid XHTML as well, you add the attribute name as the value, using the code `required="required"`.

4. Open **snoot.htm** in a modern browser, such as the current version of Internet Explorer, Firefox, Chrome, or Safari. Without completing any of the form fields, scroll to the bottom of the form, and click the **Place Order** button. A modern browser scrolls up to the first required field, adds a red background or box shadow, and displays a rounded rectangle, known as a bubble, next to the control. The bubble contains text describing the validation error found in the highlighted field and instructions for fixing it. Figure 6-11 shows the bubbles and error formatting in current versions of Internet Explorer, Firefox, and Chrome at the time this book was written.

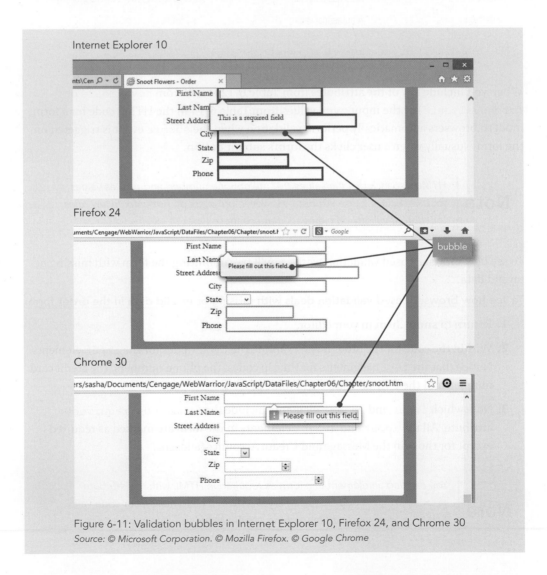

Figure 6-11: Validation bubbles in Internet Explorer 10, Firefox 24, and Chrome 30
Source: © Microsoft Corporation. © Mozilla Firefox. © Google Chrome

5. Type your first name (or a fictional one) in the highlighted First Name field, and then press **Enter**. The highlight moves to the Last Name field, with a bubble displaying the same error information.

6. Continue completing the form fields, pressing **Enter** after completing each one, until you get to the Zip field.

7. In the Zip field, type **none**, and then press **Enter**. New bubble text may be displayed after you type the first character, indicating that the field value must be a number.

8. Enter your zip code (or a fictional one) in the Zip field, and press **Enter**, and then complete each remaining form field that displays an error message. After you enter a numerical value in the CVV box and press Enter, all the browser-based validation requirements are satisfied, and the form is submitted. Figure 6-12 shows the submission results page.

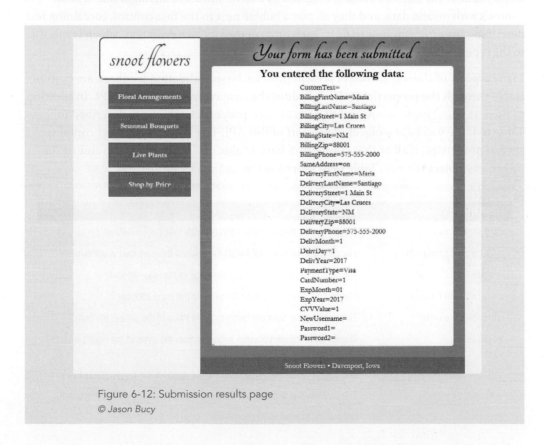

Figure 6-12: Submission results page
© Jason Bucy

> **Note**
>
> *Because the focus of this book is client-side JavaScript, the form action value is set to submit the data to another HTML document named results. htm rather than to a web server. The document results.htm, which is located in your Chapter folder for Chapter 6, uses JavaScript code to display the values submitted from a form. The only purpose of the results.htm document is to display the form data that would be submitted to a server. A finished form would be integrated with a program on a server, which would return a confirmation message.*

Customizing Browser-Based Validation Feedback

As you saw in the preceding steps, modern browsers display browser-based validation feedback in similar ways, with some variation between browsers. In general, feedback is displayed after the `submit` event is triggered by a form. Browsers highlight one or more controls with invalid data, and they display a bubble next to the first control, containing text describing the error and how to fix it. Each browser uses its own error text, which is specific to the type of error found.

Many aspects of the way browsers present browser-based validation feedback are customizable through the properties and methods of the **constraint validation API**. In addition to the `validationMessage` and `willValidate` properties, which are described in Table 6-4, the `validity` object is also part of this API. The `validity` object contains several properties; if all of these properties have a value of `false`, then the value of the `validity` object is `true`. Table 6-14 describes the `validity` properties.

PROPERTY	RETURNS `true` IF
customError	A custom error message has been set with `setCustomValidity()`
patternMismatch	The control value does not match the value of the `pattern` attribute
rangeOverflow	The control value is greater than the value of the `max` attribute
rangeUnderflow	The control value is less than the value of the `min` attribute
stepMismatch	The control value does not conform to the value of the `step` attribute
tooLong	The length of the control value is greater than the value of the `maxlength` attribute
typeMismatch	The control value does not conform to the rules for the `type` attribute value
valueMissing	The control value is empty but the control has a `required` attribute set
valid	None of the preceding properties are `true`

Table 6-14: `validity` properties

Note that setting a custom error message for a control changes the validity of that control to `false`. This means that additional code is required for validating fields when you use custom error messages.

Table 6-15 describes the methods of the constraint validation API.

METHOD	DESCRIPTION
checkValidity()	Returns `true` for a control if the control value is valid
setCustomValidity()	Sets custom validation message and rules

Table 6-15: Constraint validation API methods

In conjunction with these properties and methods, you can use the CSS `:invalid` and `:valid` pseudo-classes to change the properties of form elements based on their validity status. Using all of these tools, you can customize the behavior of browser-based validation so users get similar feedback in all modern browsers.

For instance, the following JavaScript code checks the `valueMissing` property of the `fname` element, and if the value is `true`, it sets the bubble text to "Please fill out this field". This bubble text would then be displayed consistently in all modern browsers.

```
1    var fname = document.getElementbyId("firstName");
2    if (fname.valueMissing) {
3        setCustomValidity("Please fill out this field.");
4    }
```

The addition of the following CSS sets the background of the field to a pink color as long as the validity state of the field is invalid:

```
#firstName:invalid {
    background: rgb(255,233,233);
}
```

Figure 6-13 shows the result of this code when the form is submitted without a value for the `firstName` field.

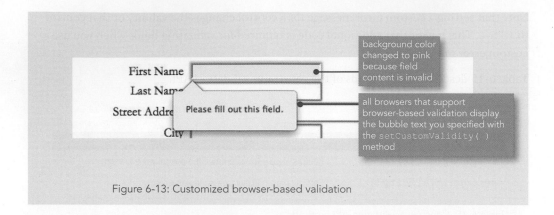

Figure 6-13: Customized browser-based validation

At the time this book was written, no aspect of bubble appearance aside from text is customizable, meaning that the color, shape, and size vary among browsers. If creating a uniform appearance in every browser is a goal, you can instead use the `preventDefault()` method and the `invalid` event to keep the bubbles from being displayed in any browser. If you choose to do this, you instead need to program your own mechanism for displaying feedback to users.

Also note that, at the time this book was written, browser-based validation was missing a couple features, and their absence made it more challenging to use browser-based validation in more complex situations. One of these missing features was the inability to set multiple validation messages for the same field at the same time. This meant that if a field had two validation issues—for instance, if it had to be a value less then 100 (`max="100"`) and an even number (`step="2"`)—it wouldn't be possible to provide two separate custom validation messages for an entry such as 105, which violates both rules.

It's important to Snoot Flowers that their form behaves similarly not only in modern browsers, but also in Internet Explorer 8, which does not perform browser-based validation. It's possible to write a program to perform validation in older browsers, and then incorporate code that incorporates browser-based validation properties and methods to perform the same task. This method makes a lot of sense for smaller forms—for instance, a form requesting just a username and password. However, for a form as large as the Snoot Flowers order form, simply writing one set of custom validation functions that will run on all browsers, including modern ones, saves programming time and reduces the amount of validation code required.

A person filling out a web form wants the process to be as easy and fast as possible. For that reason, design principles for user interaction aim to minimize **friction**, which is a loose measure of the persistence required for a user to accomplish a goal, such as placing an order. In general, the more steps a process requires of a user, the more friction it exposes a user to, and the less likely the user is to complete the process. One important practice in minimizing friction in forms is to provide feedback in a way that doesn't interfere with the task at hand. For instance, if you used an alert box to display an error message on form submission, a user would have to click OK before correcting the form, which would add a step to the user's process of submitting the form—and increase the friction of the transaction. Providing accurate and complete form instructions is another way of reducing friction; incomplete instructions might cause user input to fail validation and require reentry. You can also add attributes such as `placeholder` and `autofocus` to elements in your form to guide users through it.

In preparation for writing custom validation functions for all browsers, you'll add the `novalidate` attribute to the `form` element to disable browser-based validation in modern browsers.

To disable browser-based validation for the order form:

1. Return to **snoot.htm** in your editor.

2. Within the opening `<form>` tag, add the attribute **novalidate="novalidate"**. Your opening `<form>` tag should match the following code:

```
<form action="results.htm" novalidate="novalidate">
```

3. Save your changes to **snoot.htm**, return to your browser, press and hold the **Shift** key, and then click the **Refresh** or **Reload** button. Refreshing or reloading while holding the Shift key clears any previous entries in the form in most browsers, leaving all fields blank.

Note | *If holding the Shift key while refreshing or reloading doesn't clear the field values, close the page and then reopen it to display a blank form.*

4. Without entering data in any field, scroll to the bottom of the form, and then click the **Place Order** button. The browser skips browser-based validation and submits the form data to the results page. Note that the results page lists each field name followed by an equal sign, but with no value.

Short Quiz 3

1. List two attributes that specify parameters for browser-based validation in child elements of a form, and describe what each does.

2. List a value for the `type` attribute of the `input` element that triggers browser-based validation, and describe what content browsers check for.

3. What is the constraint validation API?

4. What is one drawback of using browser-based validation?

Programming Custom Validation

The requirements of the form you're validating determine the kind of logic you need to incorporate into a custom validation program. However, a few types of validation functions are particularly common:

> Checking that required fields contain entries

> Checking values that are dependent on the values of other controls

> Checking for an appropriate content type in one or more fields

The plan for the Snoot Flowers order form envisions using red backgrounds and borders, along with custom error messages displayed at the top of the page and within each fieldset containing an error, as shown in Figure 6-14.

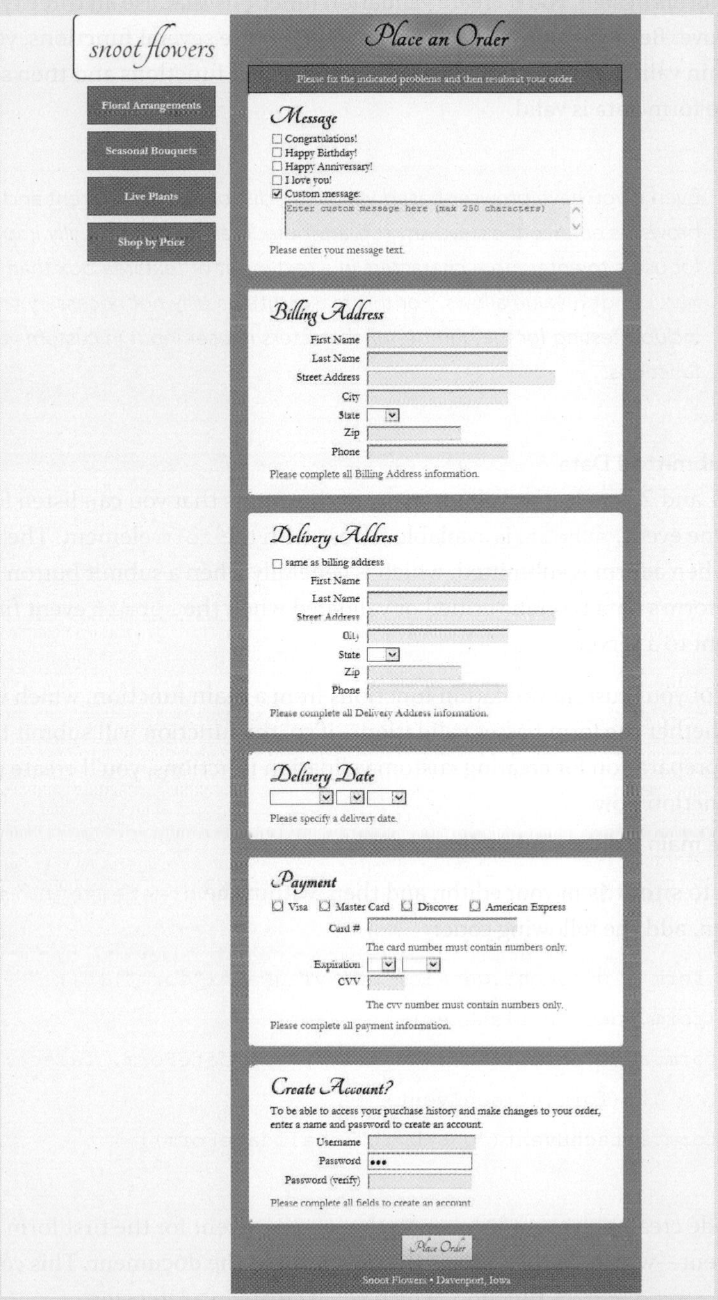

Figure 6-14: Preview of order form with error messages and styles

To implement this design, you'll create validation functions that use all three types of logic described above. Because your validation plans will require several functions, you'll start by creating a main validation function that will call the other functions and then submit the form if all the form data is valid.

<table>
<tr><td>**Note**</td><td>*Even if you have browser-based validation disabled, both current and older browsers enforce the* maxlength *attribute, making it essentially impossible for users to enter more characters in a text input or textarea box than the* maxlength *value allows. For this reason, it's usually not necessary to include testing for the number of characters in user input in custom validation functions.*</td></tr>
</table>

Validating Submitted Data

In Chapters 1 and 2, you learned about many of the events that you can listen for in JavaScript. One event, submit, is available for use with the form element. The **submit event** fires when a form is submitted, which is generally when a submit button is selected on a form. A form's data is often verified or validated when the submit event fires, before the data is sent to a server.

You'll call all of your custom validation functions from a main function, which will determine whether the form passes validation—if so, the function will submit the form contents. In preparation for creating custom validation functions, you'll create the main validation function now.

To create the main validation function:

1. Return to **snoot.js** in your editor, and then, within the createEventListeners() function, add the following code:

```
1   var form = document.getElementsByTagName("form")[0];
2   if (form.addEventListener) {
3      form.addEventListener("submit", validateForm, false);
4   } else if (form.attachEvent) {
5      form.attachEvent("onsubmit", validateForm);
6   }
```

This code creates an event listener on the submit event for the first form in the document—which, in this case, is the only form in the document. This code triggers the validateForm() function, which you'll create in a later step.

2. In the global variables section at the top of the snoot.js document, add the following statement:

```
var formValidity = true;
```

This code declares the `formValidity` variable, which you'll use to track if the form is valid or if the user needs to add or change entries.

3. Before the `createEventListeners()` function, add the following code to create the `validateForm()` function:

```
1    /* validate form */
2    function validateForm(evt) {
3        if (evt.preventDefault) {
4            evt.preventDefault(); // prevent form from submitting
5        } else {
6            evt.returnValue = false; // prevent form from submitting↵
7                in IE8
8        }
9        formValidity = true; // reset value for revalidation
10   }
```

The form receives a single parameter, `evt`, when it's called. This parameter references the event that called the function—the `submit` event for the form. The statement `evt.preventDefault()` disables the default behavior for the referenced event. You use the `preventDefault()` method on an object to block the action normally associated with an event. However, the `preventDefault()` method is not supported in Internet Explorer 8, so you use a conditional statement to instead set the `returnValue` property of the event to `false` in browsers that don't support `preventDefault()`; setting `returnValue` to `false` accomplishes the same task in older browsers that `preventDefault()` does in modern browsers.

You generally follow the `preventDefault()` method with code that performs a different task for the specified event. In this case, the `preventDefault()` method stops the form from being submitted. You'll complete the function by specifying custom validation functions to run, and then you'll manually call the `submit()` method to submit the form if the contents pass validation.

4. Save your changes to **snoot.js**, return to **snoot.htm** in your browser, refresh or reload the page, and then click the **Place Order** button. Notice that the results page is not displayed. This is because the `preventDefault()` method stopped the page from being submitted.

5. Return to **snoot.js** in your editor, and then, within the `validateForm()` function, after the `formValidity = true` statement, enter the following `if/then` statement:

```
1    // replace with calls to validation functions
2    if (formValidity === true) {
3        document.getElementById("errorText").innerHTML = "";
4        document.getElementById("errorText").style.display = "none";
5        document.getElementsByTagName("form")[0].submit();
6    } else {
7        document.getElementById("errorText").innerHTML = "Please fix↵
8            the indicated problems and then resubmit your order.";
9        document.getElementById("errorText").style.display = "block";
10       scroll(0,0);
11   }
```

As you write your validation functions, you'll add calls to each of these functions before the `if` statement. Any function that finds invalid content will change the value of the global `formValidity` variable to false, making the execution of the `if` statement contingent on the form data passing all validation checks. The statement `document.getElementsByTagName("form")[0].submit()` uses the `submit()` method to submit the form contents manually if your custom validation functions find that the data is valid. If any of the data is invalid—that is, if the `formValidity` variable has been assigned a value of `false`—the `else` clause runs three statements. The first two set the display for the element with the `id` value `errorText` to `block`, making it visible on the page, and add an appropriate message to the user as the element's content. This element is above the top of the form and informs users that the form entries require correction before the form can be submitted. The third statement, `scroll(0,0)`, moves the browser back to the top of the page so users can see the `errorText` section and then examine the form from the top down for issues they need to fix.

6. Save your changes to **snoot.js**, return to **snoot.htm** in your browser, refresh or reload the page, and then click the **Place Order** button. This time the results.htm page is displayed. Because no validation functions yet exist that might change the value of `formValidity` to `false`, the `if` statements executed, and the form was submitted manually by the `submit()` method.

7. Return to **snoot.js** in your editor, and then, within the `validateForm()` function, change the value of `formValidity` to `false`, as follows:

```
1    function validateForm(evt) {
2        if (evt.preventDefault) {
```

```
3           evt.preventDefault(); // prevent form from submitting
4        } else {
5           evt.returnValue = false; // prevent form from submitting↵
6              in IE8
7        }
8        formValidity = false; // reset value for revalidation
```

8. Save your changes to **snoot.js**, return to **snoot.htm** in your browser, refresh or reload the page, and then click the **Place Order** button. This time the form is not submitted, the browser scrolls to the top of the page, and the `errorText` block is displayed, as shown in Figure 6-15.

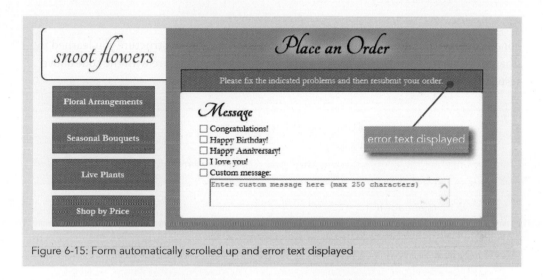

Figure 6-15: Form automatically scrolled up and error text displayed

9. Return to **snoot.js** in your editor, and then, within the `validateForm()` function, change the value of `formValidity` back to `true`, as follows:

```
1    function validateForm(evt) {
2       if (evt.preventDefault) {
3          evt.preventDefault(); // prevent form from submitting
4       } else {
5          evt.returnValue = false; // prevent form from submitting↵
6             in IE8
7       }
8       formValidity = true; // reset value for revalidation
```

10. Save your changes to **snoot.js**.

Next you'll create custom validation functions to validate different types of content and display custom error messages.

Validating Required Fields with Custom Functions

Creating a function to validate required fields generally involves retrieving the values of the required fields and checking if the value of any of them is an empty string. These functions have the general form

```
1   if (element.value === "") {
2       // code to display message and highlight error
3       formValidity = false;
4   }
```

For all custom validation, it can be helpful to use the `try/catch` structure you learned in Chapter 4 to handle and display error messages. Using this structure with the code above results in the following general form:

```
1   try {
2       if (element.value === "") {
3           throw "message";
4       }
5   }
6   catch(message) {
7       // code to display message and highlight error
8       formValidity = false;
9   }
```

In the order form, the design calls for a single error message to be displayed in a fieldset if any of the fields contain an error.

Checking for Empty Text Input Fields

You use different properties to validate each form element and `input` type. For text boxes—including any object created with an `input` element that displays a box allowing character input—you can use the `value` property to check for a value. Table 6-16 lists the most commonly used properties of `input` elements, and Table 6-17 lists commonly used `input` element methods.

PROPERTY	DESCRIPTION	FORM CONTROLS
accept	Sets or returns a comma-separated list of MIME types that can be uploaded	File boxes
alt	Sets or returns alternate text for an image	Image submit buttons
autocomplete	Sets or returns whether a browser is permitted to automatically fill in the control value based on data from other websites that a user has stored	Text boxes, password boxes
checked	Sets or returns the checked status of a check box or radio button	Check boxes, option buttons
defaultChecked	Determines the control that is checked by default in a check box group or radio button group	Check boxes, option buttons
defaultValue	Sets or returns the default text that appears in a form control	Text boxes, password boxes, file boxes
files	Collection of files selected by a user	File boxes
list	A collection of option elements that can be used to provide options or suggest values for the control	Text boxes
max	Sets or returns the largest allowed value for the control	Text boxes
maxLength	Sets or returns the maximum number of characters that can be entered into a field	Text boxes, password boxes
min	Sets or returns the smallest allowed value for the control	Text boxes
multiple	Sets or returns whether the control accepts more than one value	Text boxes, file boxes
name	Sets or returns the value assigned to the element's name attribute	Check boxes, option buttons, submit buttons, image submit buttons, text boxes, password boxes, file boxes, hidden text boxes
pattern	Sets or returns a regular expression describing a pattern that a valid control value must match	Text boxes, password boxes
placeholder	Sets or returns text displayed in an empty control to provide user guidance	Text boxes, password boxes

Continued on next page...

PROPERTY	DESCRIPTION	FORM CONTROLS
size	Sets or returns a field's width (in characters)	Text boxes, password boxes
step	Sets or returns the increment between allowable values	Text boxes
src	Sets or returns the URL of an image	Image submit buttons
type	Returns the type of input element	Check boxes, option buttons, submit buttons, image submit buttons, text boxes, password boxes, file boxes, hidden text boxes

Table 6-16: Commonly used input element properties and their associated form controls

METHOD	DESCRIPTION	FORM CONTROLS
blur()	Removes focus from a form control	Check boxes, option buttons, submit buttons, text boxes, text areas, password boxes, file boxes
click()	Activates a form control's click event	Check boxes, option buttons, submit buttons
focus()	Changes focus to a form control	Check boxes, option buttons, submit buttons, text boxes, password boxes, file boxes
select()	Selects the text in a form control	Text boxes, password boxes, file boxes

Table 6-17: Commonly used input element methods and their associated form controls

For instance, to check if the input element with the id value firstName is blank, you could use the following statement:

```
if (document.getElementById("firstName").value === "") {
    // code to run if the field is blank
}
```

You can use a loop statement to check a group of fields and trigger an error message if any of them is empty. Next you'll create a custom validation function that uses a loop statement to check if each input field in the Billing Address fieldset is empty, and if so, to change the background color of that field, and display an error message within the fieldset. Because your plan for the order form includes displaying a single message for any errors in a fieldset, you'll separate the code for highlighting each error from the code that displays a message.

To create a custom validation function for input fields in the Billing Address fieldset:

1. Return to **snoot.js** in your editor, and then, above the `validateForm()` function, enter the following code to create the `validateAddress()` function and declare variables:

```
1   /* validate address fieldsets */
2   function validateAddress(fieldsetId) {
3      var inputElements = document.querySelectorAll("#" +↵
4         fieldsetId + " input");
5      var errorDiv = document.querySelectorAll("#" + fieldsetId +↵
6         " .errorMessage")[0];
7      var fieldsetValidity = true;
8      var elementCount = inputElements.length;
9      var currentElement;
10  }
```

The function accepts a single parameter, `fieldsetId`. Because you need to validate the same fields in the Billing Address and Delivery Address sections, you can use the same code to validate both sections, specifying the `id` value for the fieldset to validate when you call the function. The `fieldsetValidity` variable has an initial value of `true`. Because the final function will run multiple tests on each address section, you'll use the `fieldsetValidity` variable to track whether any part of the section is invalid.

2. After the variable declarations, add the following `try` statement:

```
1      try {
2         for (var i = 0; i < elementCount; i++) {
3            // validate all input elements in fieldset
4            currentElement = inputElements[i];
5            if (currentElement.value === "") {
6               currentElement.style.background =↵
7                  "rgb(255,233,233)";
8               fieldsetValidity = false;
9            } else {
10               currentElement.style.background = "white";
11            }
12         }
13         if (fieldsetValidity === false) {
14            // throw appropriate message based on current fieldset
15            if (fieldsetId === "billingAddress") {
```

```
16          throw "Please complete all Billing Address↵
17              information.";
18      } else {
19          throw "Please complete all Delivery Address↵
20              information.";
21      }
22  } else {
23      errorDiv.style.display = "none";
24      errorDiv.innerHTML = "";
25  }
26  }
```

Note that you can simply loop through all the fields in this fieldset because all of them are required. For a fieldset in which only some fields are required, you could expand the conditional statement each time through the loop to check if the element's `required` property is `true`, and alert users about blank fields for required fields only.

3. After the `try` statement, add the following `catch` statement:

```
catch (msg) {
    errorDiv.style.display = "block";
    errorDiv.innerHTML = msg;
    formValidity = false;
}
```

4. In the `validateForm()` function, replace the comment `// replace with calls to validation functions` with the two statements shown below:

```
1  function validateForm(evt) {
2    if (evt.preventDefault) {
3      evt.preventDefault(); // prevent form from submitting
4    } else {
5      evt.returnValue = false; // prevent form from submitting in↵
6        IE8
7    }
8    formValidity = true; // reset value for revalidation
9    validateAddress("billingAddress");
10   validateAddress("deliveryAddress");
```

The first statement calls the function with the string "billingAddress" as the argument, and the second does the same with the string "deliveryAddress". Recall that the function treats the supplied parameter value as the `id` value of the fieldset to validate. As a result, the first statement calls the function to validate the `billingAddress` fieldset, and the second statement calls it to validate the `deliveryAddress` fieldset.

5. Save your changes to **snoot.js**, refresh or reload **snoot.htm** in your browser, clear the form if necessary, and then click the **Place Order** button without completing any of the fields. The browser scrolls to the top of the document, and the error message is displayed at the top of the page.

6. Scroll down to the Billing Address and Shipping Address sections. The backgrounds of the text input fields are pink, and each fieldset displays custom error text at the bottom. Figure 6-16 shows the error formatting and messages in Firefox.

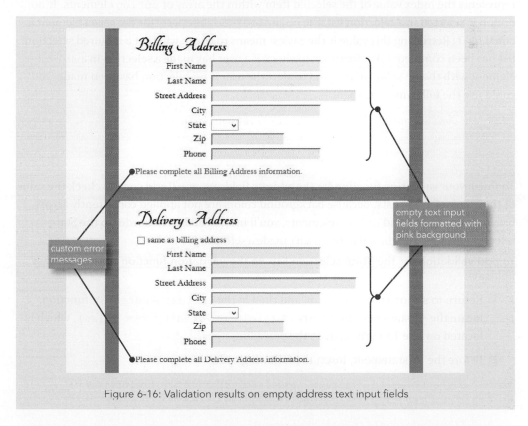

Figure 6-16: Validation results on empty address text input fields

7. Enter fictitious values in all the text input fields in both address sections, and then click the **Place Order** button. All validation checks are successful, and the results page is displayed.

Checking for Selection Lists with No Values

The function you created to validate the address fieldsets is almost complete. However, in addition to the text boxes, each fieldset also contains a single selection list—the State field. Instead of checking the `value` property as you do for a text `input` element, to validate whether a selection has been made in a selection list, you check the value of the `selectedIndex` property. Recall from earlier in the chapter that the `selectedIndex` property represents the index value of the selected item within the array of `option` elements. If no option is selected in a selection list, the `selectedIndex` property for the select element is equal to -1. Retrieving this value is the easiest means to check whether a required selection list has been completed. For instance, to check if a user has made a selection in a `select` element with the `id` value `state`, and to alert the user if no selection has been made, you could use the following statement:

```
if (document.getElementById("state").selectedIndex === -1 {
    // code to run if the field is blank
}
```

To finish your validation function for the address fieldsets, you'll add code to check the value of the State selection lists. Because background colors are not applied consistently across browsers to `select` and `option` elements, you'll instead add a red border to the State selection list to highlight it if a user hasn't made a selection.

To add validation for the State selection lists to the validation function for the address fieldsets:

1. Return to **snoot.js** in your editor, and then in the `validateAddress()` function, locate the `if` statement that starts `if (fieldsetValidity === false)`, which is located on line 13 in the code in the preceding steps.

2. Before the `if` statement, insert the following code:

```
1    currentElement = document.querySelector("#" + fieldsetId +↵
2       " select");
3    // validate state select element
4    if (currentElement.selectedIndex === -1) {
5        currentElement.style.border = "1px solid red";
```

```
6        fieldsetValidity = false;
7    } else {
8        currentElement.style.border = "";
9    }
```

3. Save your changes to **snoot.js**, refresh or reload **snoot.htm** in your browser, clear the form if necessary, and then click the **Place Order** button without entering information in any fields. The text input fields have pink backgrounds, and in addition, the state selection lists now have red borders. Figure 6-17 shows the Billing Address fieldset in Firefox.

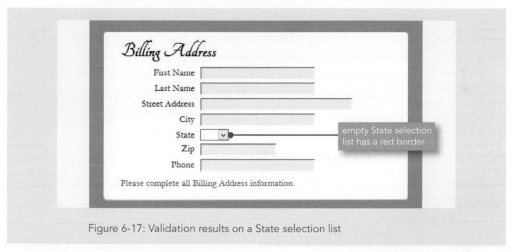

Figure 6-17: Validation results on a State selection list

4. Enter fictitious values in all the text input fields in both address sections, select a state from each State selection list, and then click the **Place Order** button. All validation checks are successful, and the results page is displayed.

Next, you'll create a function to validate the required fields in the Delivery Date fieldset. All three of the controls in this fieldset are selection lists. You'll use a loop to check each one for a value, and apply a red border to any empty select element, as you did previously for the State selection lists.

To create a function to validate the required fields in the Delivery Date fieldset:

1. Return to **snoot.js** in your editor, and then, above the validateForm() function, enter the following code to create the validateDeliveryDate() function and declare variables:

```
1    /* validate delivery date fieldset */
2    function validateDeliveryDate() {
```

```
3      var selectElements = document.querySelectorAll(↵
4        "#deliveryDate select");
5      var errorDiv = document.querySelector(↵
6        "#deliveryDate .errorMessage");
7      var fieldsetValidity = true;
8      var elementCount = selectElements.length;
9      var currentElement;
10  }
```

2. After the variable declarations, enter the following `try` statement:

```
1   try {
2       for (var i = 0; i < elementCount; i++) {
3           currentElement = selectElements[i];
4           if (currentElement.selectedIndex === -1) {
5               currentElement.style.border = "1px solid red";
6               fieldsetValidity = false;
7           } else {
8               currentElement.style.border = "";
9           }
10      }
11      if (fieldsetValidity === false) {
12          throw "Please specify a delivery date.";
13      } else {
14          errorDiv.style.display = "none";
15          errorDiv.innerHTML = "";
16      }
17  }
```

3. After the `try` statement, enter the following `catch` statement:

```
1   catch(msg) {
2       errorDiv.style.display = "block";
3       errorDiv.innerHTML = msg;
4       formValidity = false;
5   }
```

4. In the `validateForm()` function, before the `if` statement, add a call to the `validateDeliveryDate()` function as follows:

```
1    function validateForm(evt) {
2        if (evt.preventDefault) {
3            evt.preventDefault(); // prevent form from submitting
4        } else {
5            evt.returnValue = false; // prevent form from submitting in↵
6                IE8
7        }
8        formValidity = true; // reset value for revalidation
9        validateAddress("billingAddress");
10       validateAddress("deliveryAddress");
11       validateDeliveryDate();
```

5. Save your changes to **snoot.js**, refresh or reload **snoot.htm** in your browser, clear the form, and then without entering any data in the fields, click the **Place Order** button. The empty selection lists in the Delivery Date section are displayed with red borders, and error text is displayed at the bottom of the fieldset. Figure 6-18 shows the validation results in Firefox.

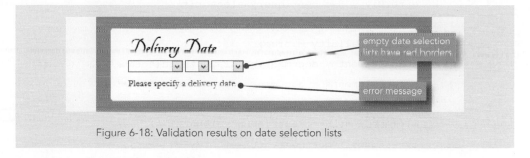

Figure 6-18: Validation results on date selection lists

6. Enter fictitious values in all the text input fields in both address sections, select a state from each State selection list, select a month, day, and year in the Delivery Date section, and then click the **Place Order** button. All validation checks are successful, and the results page is displayed.

Checking for Option Button Sets with No Selection

Next, you'll create a function to validate the required fields in the Payment fieldset. In addition to both text boxes and selection lists, the Payment fieldset contains a set of option buttons.

To check if an option button is selected, you access the value of its `checked` property. To check if none of the option buttons in a set are selected, you can create a conditional statement using And (`&&`) operators. For instance, to check if none of the three option buttons with the name `Color` are selected you could use the following code:

```
1   var buttons = document.getElementsByName("Color");
2   if (!buttons[0].checked && !buttons[1].checked && ↵
3       !buttons[2].checked) {
4     // code to run if no button is selected
5   }
```

This code checks if the first button is not selected (using the ! operator), And (`&&`) if the second button is not selected, and if the third button is not selected. If all of those conditions are true, the `if` statement is true, meaning that no button is checked. You'll use a statement like this to verify that an order form user has selected a credit card in the Payment fieldset.

To create a validation function for the Payment fieldset:

1. Return to **snoot.js** in your editor, and then, above the `validateForm()` function, enter the following code to create the `validatePayment()` function and declare variables:

```
1   /* validate payment fieldset */
2   function validatePayment() {
3     var errorDiv = document.querySelector(↵
4       "#paymentInfo .errorMessage");
5     var fieldsetValidity = true;
6     var ccNumElement = document.getElementById("ccNum");
7     var selectElements = document.querySelectorAll(↵
8       "#paymentInfo select");
9     var elementCount = selectElements.length;
10    var cvvElement = document.getElementById("cvv");
11    var cards = document.getElementsByName("PaymentType");
12    var currentElement;
13  }
```

2. Below the variable declarations, add the following `try` statement:

```
1   try {
2     if (!cards[0].checked && !cards[1].checked &&↵
3         !cards[2].checked && !cards[3].checked) {
4       // verify that a card is selected
5       for (i = 0; i < 4; i++) {
```

```
6            cards[i].style.outline = "1px solid red";
7        }
8        fieldsetValidity = false;
9    } else {
10       for (i = 0; i < 4; i++) {
11           cards[i].style.outline = "";
12       }
13   }
14 }
```

This `try` statement checks if all of the option buttons are unselected, and if so, it adds a red border to each of them and sets `fieldsetValidity` to `false`. Because the fieldset contains text input fields and selection lists as well, you'll create additional code to check if any of those fields are blank. Then at the end, you'll check the value of the `fieldsetValidity` variable to determine whether to throw an error.

3. Within the `try` statement, below the `if/else` statement you entered in the previous step, enter the following `if` statement to check the value of the card number field:

```
1    if (ccNumElement.value === "") {
2        // verify that a card number has been entered
3        ccNumElement.style.background = "rgb(255,233,233)";
4        fieldsetValidity = false;
5    } else {
6        ccNumElement.style.background = "white";
7    }
```

4. Within the `try` statement, below the `if/else` statement you entered in the previous step, enter the following `for` statement to check the values of the month and year selection lists:

```
1    for (var i = 0; i < elementCount; i++) {
2        // verify that a month and year have been selected
3        currentElement = selectElements[i];
4        if (currentElement.selectedIndex === -1) {
5            currentElement.style.border = "1px solid red";
6            fieldsetValidity = false;
7        } else {
8            currentElement.style.border = "";
9        }
10   }
```

5. Within the `try` statement, below the `for` statement you entered in the previous step, enter the following `if` statement to check the value of the card number field:

```
1   if (cvvElement.value === "") {
2       // verify that a cvv value has been entered
3       cvvElement.style.background = "rgb(255,233,233)";
4       fieldsetValidity = false;
5   } else {
6       cvvElement.style.background = "white";
7   }
```

6. Within the `try` statement, below the `if/else` statement you entered in the previous step, enter the following `if/else` statement to check the value of the `fieldsetValidity` variable and, if necessary, throw an exception:

```
1   if (!fieldsetValidity) { // check if any field is blank
2       throw "Please complete all payment information.";
3   } else {
4       errorDiv.style.display = "none";
5   }
```

7. Below the `try` statement, enter the following `catch` statement:

```
1   catch (msg) {
2       errorDiv.style.display = "block";
3       errorDiv.innerHTML = msg;
4       formValidity = false;
5   }
```

8. In the `validateForm()` function, add a call to the `validatePayment()` function after the call to the `validateDeliveryDate()` function, as follows:

```
1    function validateForm(evt) {
2        if (evt.preventDefault) {
3            evt.preventDefault(); // prevent form from submitting
4        } else {
5            evt.returnValue = false; // prevent form from submitting↵
6                in IE8
7        }
8        formValidity = true; // reset value for revalidation
9        validateAddress("billingAddress");
10       validateAddress("deliveryAddress");
```

```
11        validateDeliveryDate();
12        validatePayment();
```

9. Save your changes to **snoot.js**, refresh or reload **snoot.htm** in your browser, clear the form, and then without entering any data in the fields, click the **Place Order** button. The empty set of option buttons in the Payment section are displayed with a red border, and the empty text input boxes and selection lists are displayed as in previous fieldsets, along with the error text at the bottom of the fieldset. Figure 6-19 shows the validation results in Firefox.

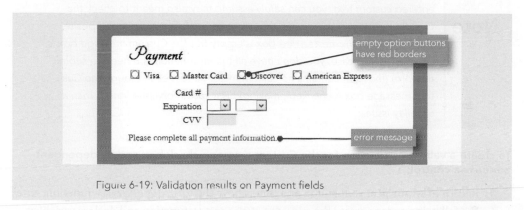

Figure 6-19: Validation results on Payment fields

10. Complete all fields in the Billing Address, Delivery Address, Delivery Date, and Payment sections with fictitious information, and then click the **Place Order** button. All validation checks are successful, and the results page is displayed.

Validating Dependent Fields with Custom Functions

The custom functions you've created so far follow general patterns for common web form data. However, in some cases you need to create functions to test logic that's specific to the form you're creating. For instance, if a set of option buttons provides several choices along with "other" and is followed by a text box, you could add validation logic that verifies that the text box contains an entry, but only if the "other" option button is selected. You'll create two additional functions for the Snoot Flowers order form to perform validation that's specific to the information you're collecting.

Validating Based on the State of a Check Box

In the order form, the Message fieldset includes a set of check boxes that allow users to select common messages, such as "Happy Birthday!" None of these check boxes are required. However, if the final check box, "Custom message," is checked, a user must enter custom text in the `textarea` element at the bottom of the fieldset. A message is not required for an order, so if a user submits the form without any boxes checked in the Message fieldset, the form is still valid. However, you need to create a function that checks if the Custom message box is checked, and if it is, verifies that the user has entered custom text in the `textarea` control. To identify whether a check box is selected, you use the same `checked` property that you use to access the status of an option button.

To create a validation function for the Custom message check box and its dependent textarea control:

1. Return to **snoot.js** in your editor, and then, above the `validateForm()` function, enter the following code to create the `validateMessage()` function and declare variables:

```
1    /* validate message fieldset */
2    function validateMessage() {
3        var errorDiv = document.querySelector("#message .errorMessage");
4        var msgBox = document.getElementById("customText");
5    }
```

2. Below the variables, add the following `try` statement:

```
1    try {
2        if (document.getElementById("custom").checked && ((msgBox.value↵
3            === "") || (msgBox.value === msgBox.placeholder))) {
4            // custom checked but message box empty
5            throw "Please enter your message text.";
6        } else {
7            errorDiv.style.display = "none";
8            msgBox.style.background = "white";
9        }
10   }
```

3. Below the `try` statement, add the following `catch` statement:

```
1    catch (msg) {
2        errorDiv.style.display = "block";
3        errorDiv.innerHTML = msg;
4        msgBox.style.background = "rgb(255,233,233)";
5        formValidity = false;
6    }
```

4. In the `validateForm()` function, add a call to the `validateMessage()` function after the call to the `validatePayment()` function, as follows:

```
1    function validateForm(evt) {
2        if (evt.preventDefault) {
3            evt.preventDefault(); // prevent form from submitting
4        } else {
5            evt.returnValue = false; // prevent form from submitting↵
6                in IE8
7        }
8        formValidity = true; // reset value for revalidation
9        validateAddress("billingAddress");
10       validateAddress("deliveryAddress");
11       validateDeliveryDate();
12       validatePayment();
13       validateMessage();
```

5. Save your changes to **snoot.js**, refresh or reload **snoot.htm** in your browser, and then clear the form.

6. In the Message fieldset, click the **Custom message** check box to check it, and then without entering any data in any other fields, click the **Place Order** button. The textarea is displayed with a pink background, and the error text is shown at the bottom of the fieldset. Figure 6-20 shows the validation results in Firefox.

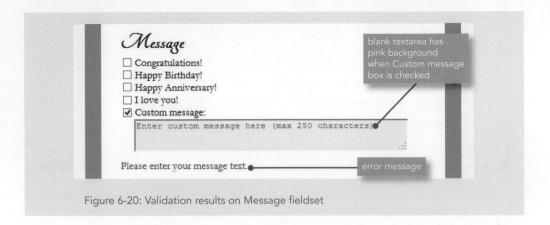

Figure 6-20: Validation results on Message fieldset

7. Enter a word or phrase in the custom message textarea, complete all fields in the Billing Address, Delivery Address, Delivery Date, and Payment sections with fictitious information, and then click the **Place Order** button. All validation checks are successful, and the results page is displayed.

Validating Based on Text Input Box Contents

One additional fieldset in the order form contains fields whose valid values depend on other fields: the Create Account fieldset. Like many online retailers, Snoot Flowers customers aren't required to create accounts, so the Username, Password, and Password (verify) fields can all be left blank. However, if a user enters data in one or more of these fields, two checks need to happen:

1. If at least one field contains a user entry, all three fields must be completed. This means that if a user makes an entry in one field, all three fields become required.

2. The values in the Password and Password (verify) fields must match. Because password entries aren't visible to users—browsers represent each character with a bullet, by default—requiring a user to enter the password twice helps ensure that the user has entered what they intended.

You'll create a function using nested `if` statements to account for all possibilities when validating this fieldset. Your code will throw two possible error messages depending on which of the two validity checks fails. Figure 6-21 shows a flowchart of the logic you'll incorporate into this function.

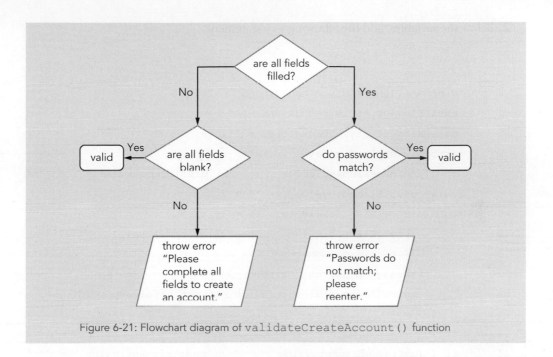

Figure 6-21: Flowchart diagram of `validateCreateAccount()` function

To create a validation function for the Create Account fieldset:

1. Return to **snoot.js** in your editor, and then, above the `validateForm()` function, enter the following code to create the `validateCreateAccount()` function and declare variables:

```
1   /* validate create account fieldset */
2   function validateCreateAccount() {
3      var errorDiv = document.querySelector(↵
4         "#createAccount .errorMessage");
5      var usernameElement = document.getElementById("username");
6      var pass1Element = document.getElementById("pass1");
7      var pass2Element = document.getElementById("pass2");
8      var passwordMismatch = false;
9      var invColor = "rgb(255,233,233)";
10  }
```

2. Below the variables, add the following `try` statement:

```
1   try {
2      // reset styles to valid state
3      usernameElement.style.background = "";
4      pass1Element.style.background = "";
5      pass2Element.style.background = "";
6      errorDiv.style.display = "none";
7      if ((usernameElement.value !== "" && pass1Element.value !== ""↵
8         && pass2Element.value !== "")) {
9         // all fields are filled
10        if (pass1Element.value !== pass2Element.value) {
11           // passwords don't match
12           passwordMismatch = true;
13           throw "Passwords entered do not match; please reenter.";
14        }
15     }
16     if (!(usernameElement.value === "" && pass1Element.value === ""↵
17        && pass2Element.value === "")) {
18        // not all fields are blank
19        throw "Please complete all fields to create an account.";
20     }
21  }
```

3. Below the `try` statement, add the following `catch` statement:

```
1   catch(msg) {
2      errorDiv.innerHTML = msg;
3      errorDiv.style.display = "block";
4      if (passwordMismatch) {
5         usernameElement.style.background = "";
6         pass1Element.style.background = invColor;
7         pass2Element.style.background = invColor;
8      } else {
9         if (usernameElement.value === "") {
10           usernameElement.style.background = invColor;
11        }
```

```
12          if (pass1Element.value === "") {
13              pass1Element.style.background = invColor;
14          }
15          if (pass2Element.value === "") {
16              pass2Element.style.background = invColor;
17          }
18      }
19      formValidity = false;
20  }
```

4. In the `validateForm()` function, add a call to the `validateCreateAccount()` function after the call to the `validateMessage()` function, as follows:

```
1   function validateForm(evt) {
2       if (evt.preventDefault) {
3           evt.preventDefault(); // prevent form from submitting
4       } else {
5           evt.returnValue = false; // prevent form from submitting↵
6               in IE8
7       }
8       formValidity = true; // reset value for revalidation
9       validateAddress("billingAddress");
10      validateAddress("deliveryAddress");
11      validateDeliveryDate();
12      validatePayment();
13      validateMessage();
14      validateCreateAccount();
```

5. Save your changes to **snoot.js**, refresh or reload **snoot.htm** in your browser, and then clear the form.

6. In the Create Account fieldset, enter a fictitious name in the **Username** box, and then without entering any data in any other fields, click the **Place Order** button.

7. Scroll down to the Create Account section. Both password fields are displayed with pink backgrounds, and the relevant error text is shown at the bottom of the fieldset. Figure 6-22 shows the validation results in Firefox.

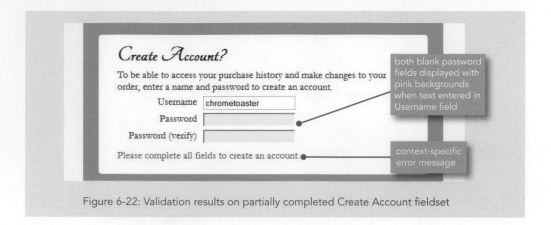

Figure 6-22: Validation results on partially completed Create Account fieldset

8. Enter one or more characters in the Password field, in the Password (verify) field enter different characters, and then click the **Place Order** button. Both password fields are again displayed with pink backgrounds, and new error text is shown at the bottom of the fieldset. Figure 6-23 shows the validation results in Firefox.

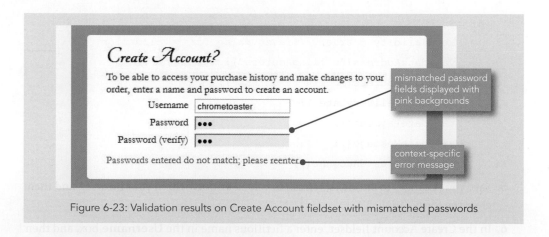

Figure 6-23: Validation results on Create Account fieldset with mismatched passwords

9. Enter the same character or characters in both password fields, complete all fields in the Billing Address, Delivery Address, Delivery Date, and Payment sections with fictitious information, and then click the **Place Order** button. All validation checks are successful, and the results page is displayed.

Validating Content Type with Custom Functions

The final type of validation function you need to create for the Snoot Flowers order form is one that checks user input to verify that it conforms to the content rules for each field. You'll add this type of validation to two fields in the form: the card number field and the CVV field, both of whose values must be numbers.

Note that many other field values in the order form should ideally conform to stricter rules. For instance, to be a valid U.S. zip code, a value must be either five digits (#####) or five digits followed by a hyphen and then four more digits (#####-####). For this form, you'll leave this more complex validation to the back-end program that processes the data submitted by the form. In Chapter 8, you'll learn how to specify and check for character patterns like a zip code, phone number, or email address.

For any fields that require numeric values, you can use JavaScript's built-in `isNaN()` function to determine whether the user actually entered a number. Recall from Chapter 2 that the `isNaN()` function determines whether a value is the special value NaN (not a number). The `isNaN()` function returns a value of `true` if it is passed a value that is not a number; if passed a value that is a number, the function returns a value of `false`. The following function shows a statement that passes the value of a text box with the `id` value `subtotal` to the `isNaN()` function:

```
isNaN(document.getElementById("subtotal").value)
```

You'll use the `isNaN()` function to check that the values of the Card # and CVV fields are numbers.

To validate the Card # and CVV numeric fields:

1. Return to **snoot.js** in your editor, and then, above the `validateForm()` function, enter the following code to create the `validateNumbers()` function and declare variables:

```
1    /* validate number fields for older browsers */
2    function validateNumbers() {
3        var ccNotNum;
4        var cvvNotNum;
5        var ccNumElement = document.getElementById("ccNum");
6        var cvvElement = document.getElementById("cvv");
7        var ccNumErrMsg = document.getElementById("ccNumErrorMessage");
8        var cvvErrMsg = document.getElementById("cvvErrorMessage");
9    }
```

2. Below the variables, enter the following `try` statement:

```
1   try {
2       if (isNaN(ccNumElement.value) || ccNumElement.value === "") {
3           ccNotNum = true;
4       } else { // ccNum value is a number
5           ccNumElement.style.background = "";
6           ccNumErrMsg.style.display = "none";
7       }
8       if (isNaN(cvvElement.value) || cvvElement.value === "") {
9           cvvNotNum = true;
10      } else { // cvv value is a number
11          cvvElement.style.background = "";
12          cvvErrMsg.style.display = "none";
13      }
14      if (ccNotNum || cvvNotNum) {
15          throw "must contain numbers only.";
16      }
17  }
```

3. Below the `try` statement, enter the following `catch` statement:

```
1   catch(msg) {
2       if (ccNotNum) {
3           ccNumElement.style.background = "rgb(255,233,233)";
4           ccNumErrMsg.style.display = "block";
5           ccNumErrMsg.innerHTML = "The card number " + msg;
6       }
7       if (cvvNotNum) {
8           cvvElement.style.background = "rgb(255,233,233)";
9           cvvErrMsg.style.display = "block";
10          cvvErrMsg.innerHTML = "The cvv number " + msg;
11      }
12      formValidity = false;
13  }
```

4. In the `validateForm()` function, add a call to the `validateNumbers()` function after the call to the `validateCreateAccount()` function, as follows:

```
1    function validateForm(evt) {
2        if (evt.preventDefault) {
3            evt.preventDefault(); // prevent form from submitting
4        } else {
5            evt.returnValue = false; // prevent form from submitting↵
6                in IE8
7        }
8        formValidity = true; // reset value for revalidation
9        validateAddress("billingAddress");
10       validateAddress("deliveryAddress");
11       validateDeliveryDate();
12       validatePayment();
13       validateMessage();
14       validateCreateAccount();
15       validateNumbers();
```

5. Save your changes to **snoot.js**, refresh or reload **snoot.htm** in your browser, and then clear the form.

6. In the Payment fieldset, enter text (not numbers) in the Card # box, enter text (not numbers) in the CVV box, and then without entering any data in any other fields, click the **Place Order** button.

7. Scroll down to the Payment section. Note that some browsers clear non-numeric entries from number fields automatically. In other browsers, both the Card # and CVV fields are displayed with pink backgrounds, and the relevant error text is shown beneath each field. Figure 6-24 shows the validation results in Firefox.

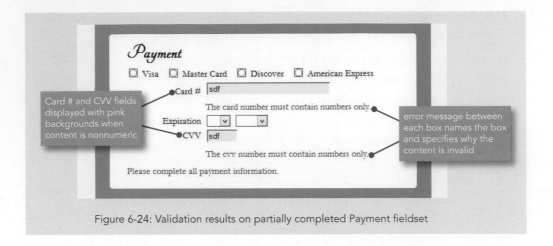

Figure 6-24: Validation results on partially completed Payment fieldset

8. Change your entries in the Card # and CVV fields to numbers, complete all fields in the Billing Address, Delivery Address, Delivery Date, and Payment sections with fictitious information, and then click the **Place Order** button. All validation checks are successful, and the results page is displayed.

Short Quiz 4

1. Which event fires when a form is submitted?

2. What method do you use to disable the default behavior associated with an event?

3. What property do you check to determine if a text input box contains user input?

4. What built-in JavaScript function do you use to test whether a value is not a number?

Summary

> Validation is the process of checking that information provided by users conforms to rules to ensure that it appropriately answers the form's questions and is provided in a format that the site's back-end programs can work with.

> You can create JavaScript functions that reduce the likelihood of user errors when completing a form. Such functions aren't themselves validation, but are instead aimed at preventing users from entering erroneous data in the first place. Many types of assistive functions are possible; which ones you implement depends on the design of your form and the type of data you're trying to collect.

> You can use JavaScript to set the `selectedIndex` property of a `select` element to -1, which corresponds to no selection. This ensures that any selection is made by a user, rather than being a default value.

> You can add or remove options from a select element in response to another selection a user has made in the same form. One way to accomplish this is to create child nodes containing one or more option elements, and then writing a function that adds the appropriate node in response to a user's selection.

> In older browsers, you can replicate the behavior of the `placeholder` attribute available in modern browsers by adding the desired placeholder text as a default value for an element and changing its color to differentiate it from data a user has entered (generally using a gray font color rather than black). You can then create an event listener that's triggered when a user clicks in the box, which calls a function that removes the default value.

> You can use a script to check or uncheck a check box by changing the value of the element's `checked` attribute.

> Recent enhancements to HTML and to modern browsers allow browsers themselves to perform many common validation tasks without any extra JavaScript. This type of validation is known as browser-based validation or native validation.

> Many aspects of the way browsers present browser-based validation feedback are customizable through the properties and methods of the constraint validation API.

> You use the `preventDefault()` method on an object to block the action normally associated with an event. You generally follow the `preventDefault()` method with code that performs a different task for the specified event.

> Creating a function to validate required text input fields generally involves retrieving the values of the required fields and checking if the value of any of them is an empty string.

> To validate required selection lists, you retrieve the `selectedIndex` value and check whether it's equal to -1.

> To check if an option button is selected, you access the value of its `checked` property. To check if none of the option buttons in a set are selected, you can create a conditional statement using And (`&&`) operators.

> In some cases, you need to create validation functions to test logic that's specific to the form you're creating.

Key Terms

assistive functions—JavaScript functions that reduce the likelihood of user errors when completing a form by preventing users from entering erroneous data in the first place.

browser-based validation—Validation tasks performed by browsers themselves without any extra JavaScript, enabled by recent enhancements to HTML and to modern browsers; also known as native validation.

constraint validation API—The set of properties and methods that enables developers to customize aspects of the way browsers present browser-based validation feedback.

createDocumentFragment() method—The method of the `Document` object that creates an empty document fragment.

friction—A loose measure of the persistence required for a website user to accomplish a goal, such as placing an order.

HTML5 validation—*See* browser-based validation.

native validation—*See* browser-based validation.

submit event—The event that fires when a form is submitted, which is generally when a submit button is selected on a form.

validation—The process of checking that information provided by users conforms to rules to ensure that it appropriately answers the form's questions and is provided in a format that the site's back-end programs can work with.

Review Questions

1. Objects representing each of the controls in a form are stored in the _____ collection.
    a. `forms`
    b. `controls`
    c. `inputs`
    d. `elements`

2. Which of the following type values for the input element does *not* enable you to provide users with a limited set of choices?

   a. `radio`

   b. `email`

   c. `checkbox`

   d. `range`

3. What value of the `selectedIndex` property of a `select` object corresponds to no selection?

   a. `-1`

   b. `0`

   c. `1`

   d. `false`

4. To simulate the behavior of placeholder text in older browsers, you can instead set the value of the _____ property.

   a. `src`

   b. `all`

   c. `title`

   d. `value`

5. Which event do you use to call a function when a user selects a field or moves the insertion point into a field?

   a. `blur`

   b. `focus`

   c. `input`

   d. `forminput`

6. Which event do you use to call a function when a field is no longer selected, or a user moves the insertion point to a different field?

   a. `blur`

   b. `focus`

   c. `click`

   d. `forminput`

7. Which of the following attributes determines whether a check box or option button is selected?

   a. `checked`

   b. `defaultChecked`

   c. `selected`

   d. `focus`

8. What do you assign to the `value` property of a text input box to remove its content?

    a. `false`

    b. `true`

    c. `""`

    d. `null`

9. Which of the following attributes triggers browser-based validation in modern browsers?

    a. `max`

    b. `title`

    c. `alt`

    d. `src`

10. Which of the following input `type` values triggers browser-based validation in modern browsers?

    a. `password`

    b. `text`

    c. `radio`

    d. `number`

11. Which of the following properties has a value of `true` when a user has left a required field blank?

    a. `required`

    b. `valueMissing`

    c. `patternMismatch`

    d. `typeMismatch`

12. Which of the following attributes for form child elements would you use for a field that must have a value before the form can be submitted?

    a. `novalidate`

    b. `min`

    c. `required`

    d. `max`

13. What method do you use to disable the default behavior for an event?

    a. `preventDefault()`

    b. `checkValidity()`

    c. `select()`

    d. `getElementById()`

14. Which statement moves the browser to the top of the page?
    a. `scroll(top)`
    b. `scroll(0,0)`
    c. `move(top)`
    d. `move(0,0)`

15. For any fields that require numeric values, you can use JavaScript's built-in _____ function to determine whether the user actually entered a number.
    a. `value()`
    b. `integer()`
    c. `isNumber()`
    d. `isNaN()`

16. Explain how to transfer the contents of one field to another field.

17. What is the purpose of the `novalidate` attribute?

18. Explain how the `validity` object of the constraint validation API is used for checking the validity of form data.

19. Explain how to check if any option button in a set is selected.

20. Explain how to check if a user's entry is a number.

Hands-On Projects

Hands-On Project 6-1

In this exercise, you will create validation functions for a form that work in all browsers.

1. In your text editor, open the **index.htm** file from the HandsOnProject6-1 folder in the Chapter06 folder, add your name and today's date where indicated in the comment section, and then save the file.

2. Create a new document in your editor, add JavaScript comments containing the text **Hands-on Project 6-1**, your name, and today's date, and then save the file to the HandsOnProject6-1 folder with the name **script.js**.

3. Return to the **index.htm** file in your browser, within the body section, just before the closing `</body>` tag, add a **script** element, and then specify the file **script.js** as the source.

4. In the opening `<form>` tag, add code to disable browser-based validation, and then save your changes.

5. In the **script.js** file, add code instructing processors to interpret the contents in strict mode, and then create a global variable named `formValidity` and set its value to `true`.

6. Add the following function to validate the required form elements:

```
1   /* validate required fields */
2   function validateRequired() {
3       var inputElements = document.querySelectorAll(↵
4           "#contactinfo input");
5       var errorDiv = document.getElementById("errorText");
6       var elementCount = inputElements.length;
7       var requiredValidity = true;
8       var currentElement;
9       try {
10          for (var i = 0; i < elementCount; i++) {
11              // validate all input elements in fieldset
12              currentElement = inputElements[i];
13              if (currentElement.value === "") {
14                  currentElement.style.background = "rgb(255,233,233)";
15                  requiredValidity = false;
16              } else {
17                  currentElement.style.background = "white";
18              }
19          }
20          if (requiredValidity === false) {
21              throw "Please complete all fields.";
22          }
23          errorDiv.style.display = "none";
24          errorDiv.innerHTML = "";
25      }
26      catch (msg) {
27          errorDiv.style.display = "block";
28          errorDiv.innerHTML = msg;
29          formValidity = false;
30      }
31  }
```

7. Add the following function to create an event listener for the `submit` event:

```
1   /* create event listeners */
2   function createEventListeners() {
3       var form = document.getElementsByTagName("form")[0];
4       if (form.addEventListener) {
5           form.addEventListener("submit", validateForm, false);
6       } else if (form.attachEvent) {
7           form.attachEvent("onsubmit", validateForm);
8       }
9   }
```

8. Add the following function to trigger validation of required fields when the Submit button is clicked:

```
1   /* validate form */
2   function validateForm(evt) {
3       if (evt.preventDefault) {
4           evt.preventDefault(); // prevent form from submitting
5       } else {
6           evt.returnValue = false; // prevent form from submitting↵
7               in IE8
8       }
9       formValidity = true; // reset value for revalidation
10      validateRequired();
11      if (formValidity === true) {
12          document.getElementsByTagName("form")[0].submit();
13      }
14  }
```

9. Add the following code to call the `createEventListeners()` function when the page finishes loading:

```
1   /* run setup functions when page finishes loading */
2   if (window.addEventListener) {
3       window.addEventListener("load", createEventListeners, false);
4   } else if (window.attachEvent) {
5       window.attachEvent("onload", createEventListeners);
6   }
```

10. Save your changes to **script.js**, open **index.htm** in a browser, and then test various combinations of invalid and valid data to ensure that the scripts you wrote behave as you expect. Debug your code as necessary until it functions correctly.

11. Return to **script.js** in your editor, and then add the following function to validate `input` **elements with the** `number` **type:**

```
1   /* validate number fields for older browsers */
2   function validateNumbers() {
3       var numberInputs = document.querySelectorAll(↵
4          "#contactinfo input[type=number]");
5       var elementCount = numberInputs.length;
6       var numErrorDiv = document.getElementById("numErrorText");
7       var numbersValidity = true;
8       var currentElement;
9       try {
10          for (var i = 0; i < elementCount; i++) {
11              // validate all input elements of type "number" in fieldset
12              currentElement = numberInputs[i];
13              if (isNaN(currentElement.value) || (currentElement.value↵
14                  === "")) {
15                  currentElement.style.background = "rgb(255,233,233)";
16                  numbersValidity = false;
17              } else {
18                  currentElement.style.background = "white";
19              }
20          }
21          if (numbersValidity === false) {
22              throw "Zip and Social Security values must be numbers.";
23          }
24          numErrorDiv.style.display = "none";
25          numErrorDiv.innerHTML = "";
26      }
27      catch(msg) {
28          numErrorDiv.style.display = "block";
```

```
29        numErrorDiv.innerHTML = msg;
30        formValidity = false;
31    }
32 }
```

12. In the `validateForm()` function, add a call to the `validateNumbers()` function as follows:

```
1  function validateForm(evt) {
2      if (evt.preventDefault) {
3          evt.preventDefault(); // prevent form from submitting
4      } else {
5          evt.returnValue = false; // prevent form from submitting↵
6              in IE8
7      formValidity = true; // reset value for revalidation
8      validateRequired();
9      validateNumbers();
10     if (formValidity === true) {
11         document.getElementsByTagName("form")[0].submit();
12     }
13 }
```

13. Save your changes to **script.js**, open **index.htm** in a browser, and then test various combinations of invalid and valid data, including nonnumeric entries in number fields, to ensure that the scripts you wrote behave as you expect. Debug your code as necessary until it functions correctly.

Hands-On Project 6-2

In this exercise, you'll enhance the form you worked with in Hands-on Project 6-1 to simulate the behavior of the `placeholder` attribute in IE8.

1. In the file manager for your operating system, copy the completed contents of the HandsOnProject6-1 folder to the HandsOnProject6-2 folder.

2. In your text editor, open the **index.htm** file from the HandsOnProject6-2 folder, change "Hands-on Project 6-1" to **Hands-on Project 6-2** in the comment section, in the `title` element, and in the `h1` element, and then save your changes.

3. Open **script.js**, and then in the comment section, change "Hands-on Project 6-1" to **Hands-on Project 6-2**.

4. Add the following three functions to replicate the behavior in modern browsers of the placeholder attribute:

```
1   /* remove fallback placeholder text */
2   function zeroPlaceholder() {
3       var addressBox = document.getElementById("addrinput");
4       addressBox.style.color = "black";
5       if (addressBox.value === addressBox.placeholder) {
6           addressBox.value = "";
7       }
8   }
9   /* restore placeholder text if box contains no user entry */
10  function checkPlaceholder() {
11      var addressBox = document.getElementById("addrinput");
12      if (addressBox.value === "") {
13          addressBox.style.color = "rgb(178,184,183)";
14          addressBox.value = addressBox.placeholder;
15      }
16  }
17  /* add placeholder text for browsers that don't support placeholder
18  attribute */
19  function generatePlaceholder() {
20      if (!Modernizr.input.placeholder) {
21          var addressBox = document.getElementById("addrinput");
22          addressBox.value = addressBox.placeholder;
23          addressBox.style.color = "rgb(178,184,183)";
24          if (addressBox.addEventListener) {
25              addressBox.addEventListener("focus", zeroPlaceholder,↵
26                  false);
27              addressBox.addEventListener("blur", checkPlaceholder,↵
28                  false);
29          } else if (addressBox.attachEvent) {
30              addressBox.attachEvent("onfocus", zeroPlaceholder);
```

```
31              addressBox.attachEvent("onblur", checkPlaceholder);
32          }
33      }
34  }
```

5.   Create the following function to call other functions to set up the page:

```
1   /* run initial form configuration functions */
2   function setUpPage() {
3       createEventListeners();
4       generatePlaceholder();
5   }
```

6.   Change the event listener code at the end of the file to the following:

```
1   if (window.addEventListener) {
2       window.addEventListener("load", setUpPage, false);
3   } else if (window.attachEvent) {
4       window.attachEvent("onload", setUpPage);
5   }
```

7.   Save your changes to **script.js**, open **index.htm** in IE8, and verify that the placeholder
     text is displayed. Click in the Street Address field, and verify that the placeholder text
     is removed. Without typing in the Street Address field, click elsewhere on the page
     and verify that the placeholder text is displayed once again. Click in the Street Address
     field, type a fictional address, and verify that the text is displayed in black rather than
     gray. If necessary, debug your code until it functions correctly.

Hands-On Project 6-3

In this exercise, you'll enhance the form you worked with in Hands-on Project 6-2 to automatically move the focus to the next box when a user has typed the maximum number of
characters for each component of the Social Security number.

1.   In the file manager for your operating system, copy the completed contents of the
     HandsOnProject6-2 folder to the HandsOnProject6-3 folder.

2.   In your text editor, open the **index.htm** file from the HandsOnProject6-3 folder,
     change "Hands-on Project 6-2" to **Hands-on Project 6-3** in the comment section, in
     the title element, and in the h1 element, and then save your changes.

3.   Open **script.js**, and then in the comment section, change "Hands-on Project 6-2" to
     Hands-on Project 6-3.

4. Add the following function to check after each character a user types whether the focus should move to the next SSN box:

```
1    function advanceSsn() {
2        var ssnFields = document.getElementsByClassName("ssn");
3        var currentField = document.activeElement;
4        if (currentField.value.length === currentField.maxLength) {
5            if (currentField === ssnFields[0]) {
6                ssnFields[1].focus();
7            }
8            if (currentField === ssnFields[1]) {
9                ssnFields[2].focus();
10           }
11           if (currentField === ssnFields[2]) {
12               document.getElementById("submitBtn").focus();
13           }
14       }
15   }
```

5. In the `createEventListeners()` function, add the following code:

```
1        var ssnFields = document.getElementsByClassName("ssn");
2        for (var i = 0; i < ssnFields.length; i++) {
3            if (ssnFields[i].addEventListener) {
4                ssnFields[i].addEventListener("input", advanceSsn, false);
5            } else if (ssnFields[i].attachEvent) {
6                ssnFields[i].attachEvent("oninput", advanceSsn);
7            }
8        }
```

6. Save your changes to **script.js**, and then open **index.htm** in a browser. Click in the first **Social Security Number** field, type four characters, and then verify that the focus moves automatically to the second Social Security Number field. Type two characters, and then verify that the focus moves to the third Social Security Number field. Type four characters, and verify that the focus moves to the Submit button.

Hands-On Project 6-4

In this exercise, you will enhance a form to replicate the behavior of the `placeholder` attribute in IE8 and to remove the default selection from the `select` element.

1. In your text editor, open the **index.htm** file from the HandsOnProject6-4 folder in the Chapter06 folder, add your name and today's date where indicated in the comment section, and then save the file.

2. Create a new document in your editor, add JavaScript comments containing the text **Hands-on Project 6-4**, your name, and today's date, and then save the file to the HandsOnProject6-4 folder with the name **script.js**.

3. Return to the **index.htm** file in your browser, within the body section, just before the closing `</body>` tag, add a `script` element, and then specify the file **script.js** as the source.

4. In the **script.js** file, add code instructing processors to interpret the contents in strict mode.

5. Add the following function to remove the default selection from the `select` element:

```
1    /* remove default value and formatting from selection list */
2    function removeSelectDefault() {
3        var selectBox = document.getElementById("size");
4        selectBox.selectedIndex = -1;
5        selectBox.style.boxShadow = "none";
6    }
```

6. Add the following function to set up the page:

```
/* run initial form configuration functions */
function setUpPage() {
    removeSelectDefault();
}
```

7. Add the following code to call the `setUpPage()` function when the page finishes loading:

```
1    /* run setup functions when page finishes loading */
2    if (window.addEventListener) {
3        window.addEventListener("load", setUpPage, false);
4    } else if (window.attachEvent) {
5        window.attachEvent("onload", setUpPage);
6    }
```

8. Save your changes to **script.js**, open **index.htm** in a browser, and then verify that the select element is displayed with no default value. If necessary, debug your code until the function works as expected.

9. Return to **script.js** in your editor, and then add the following three functions to replicate the behavior of the `placeholder` attribute in IE8:

```
1   /* remove fallback placeholder text */
2   function zeroPlaceholder() {
3       var instrBox = document.getElementById("instructions");
4       instrBox.style.color = "black";
5       if (instrBox.value === instrBox.placeholder) {
6           instrBox.value = "";
7       }
8   }
9   /* restore placeholder text if box contains no user entry */
10  function checkPlaceholder() {
11      var instrBox = document.getElementById("instructions");
12      if (instrBox.value === "") {
13          instrBox.style.color = "rgb(178,184,183)";
14          instrBox.value = instrBox.placeholder;
15      }
16  }
17  /* add placeholder text for browsers that don't support
18  placeholder attribute */
19  function generatePlaceholder() {
20      if (!Modernizr.input.placeholder) {
21          var instrBox = document.getElementById("instructions");
22          instrBox.value = instrBox.placeholder;
23          instrBox.style.color = "rgb(178,184,183)";
24          if (instrBox.addEventListener) {
25              instrBox.addEventListener("focus", zeroPlaceholder, false);
26              instrBox.addEventListener("blur", checkPlaceholder, false);
27          } else if (instrBox.attachEvent) {
28              instrBox.attachEvent("onfocus", zeroPlaceholder);
29              instrBox.attachEvent("onblur", checkPlaceholder);
30          }
31      }
32  }
```

10. In the `setUpPage()` function, add a call to the `generatePlaceholder()` function as follows:

```
function setUpPage() {
  removeSelectDefault();
  generatePlaceholder();
}
```

11. Save your changes to **script.js**, open **index.htm** in IE8, and then verify that the placeholder text is displayed. Click in the textarea box, and verify that the placeholder text is removed. Without typing in the textarea box, click elsewhere on the page and verify that the placeholder text is displayed once again. Click in the textarea box, type a word, and verify that the text is displayed in black rather than gray. If necessary, debug your code until it functions correctly.

Hands-On Project 6-5

In this exercise, you'll enhance the form you worked with in Hands-on Project 6-4 with validation functions that work in all browsers.

1. In the file manager for your operating system, copy the completed contents of the HandsOnProject6-4 folder to the HandsOnProject6-5 folder.

2. In your text editor, open the **index.htm** file from the HandsOnProject6-5 folder, change "Hands-on Project 6-4" to **Hands-on Project 6-5** in the comment section, in the `title` element, and in the `h1` element, and then save your changes.

3. Open **script.js**, and then in the comment section, change "Hands-on Project 6-4" to **Hands-on Project 6-5**.

4. In the **index.htm** file, in the opening `<form>` tag, add code to disable browser-based validation, and then save your changes.

5. In the **script.js** file, create a global variable named **formValidity**, and set its value to `true`.

6. Add the following function to validate required fields:

```
1  /* validate required fields */
2  function validateRequired() {
3    var inputElements = document.querySelectorAll("input[required]");
4    var errorDiv = document.getElementById("errorMessage");
5    var crustBoxes = document.getElementsByName("crust");
6    var fieldsetValidity = true;
```

```
7    var elementCount = inputElements.length;
8    var currentElement;
9    try {
10       for (var i = 0; i < elementCount; i++) {
11          // validate all required input elements in fieldset
12          currentElement = inputElements[i];
13          if (currentElement.value === "") {
14             currentElement.style.background = "rgb(255,233,233)";
15             fieldsetValidity = false;
16          } else {
17             currentElement.style.background = "white";
18          }
19       }
20       currentElement = document.querySelectorAll("select")[0];
21       // validate state select element
22       if (currentElement.selectedIndex === -1) {
23          currentElement.style.border = "1px solid red";
24          fieldsetValidity = false;
25       } else {
26          currentElement.style.border = "";
27       }
28       if (!crustBoxes[0].checked && !crustBoxes[1].checked) {
29          // verify that a crust is selected
30          crustBoxes[0].style.outline = "1px solid red";
31          crustBoxes[1].style.outline = "1px solid red";
32          fieldsetValidity = false;
33       } else {
34          crustBoxes[0].style.outline = "";
35          crustBoxes[1].style.outline = "";
36       }
37       if (fieldsetValidity === false) {
38          throw "Please complete all required fields.";
39       } else {
40          errorDiv.style.display = "none";
```

```
41            errorDiv.innerHTML = "";
42        }
43     }
44     catch(msg) {
45         errorDiv.style.display = "block";
46         errorDiv.innerHTML = msg;
47         formValidity = false;
48     }
49  }
```

7. Add the following function to run form validation:

```
1   /* validate form */
2   function validateForm(evt) {
3      if (evt.preventDefault) {
4          evt.preventDefault(); // prevent form from submitting
5      } else {
6          evt.returnValue = false; // prevent form from submitting↵
7              in IE8
8      }
9      formValidity = true; // reset value for revalidation
10     validateRequired();
11     if (formValidity === true) {
12         document.getElementById("errorMessage").innerHTML = "";
13         document.getElementById("errorMessage").style.display =↵
14             "none";
15         document.getElementsByTagName("form")[0].submit();
16     } else {
17         document.getElementById("errorMessage").innerHTML =↵
18             "Please complete the highlighted fields.";
19         document.getElementById("errorMessage").style.display =↵
20             "block";
21         scroll(0,0);
22     }
23  }
```

8. Add the following function to create an event listener for the `submit` event:

```
1   /* create event listeners */
2   function createEventListeners() {
3      var orderForm = document.getElementsByTagName("form")[0];
4      if (orderForm.addEventListener) {
5         orderForm.addEventListener("submit", validateForm, false);
6      } else if (orderForm.attachEvent) {
7         orderForm.attachEvent("onsubmit", validateForm);
8      }
9   }
```

9. In the `setUpPage()` function, add a call to the `createEventListeners()` function as follows:

```
/* run initial form configuration functions */
function setUpPage() {
   removeSelectDefault();
   createEventListeners();
   generatePlaceholder();
}
```

10. Save your changes to **script.js**, open **index.htm** in a browser, and then test various combinations of invalid data as well as valid data to ensure that the scripts you wrote behave as you expect. Debug your code as necessary until it functions correctly.

Case Projects

For the following projects, save the documents you create in your Projects folder for Chapter 6. Be sure to validate each web page with the W3C Markup Validation Service.

Individual Case Project

Add validation the code for one of the forms on your individual website. First, ensure that your form uses at least three of the following field types: check boxes, text boxes, option buttons, selection lists, and text areas. Then, program validation for your form ensuring that users enter values or make selections in all fields, and verifying at least one other aspect of at least one of the fields. Provide appropriate feedback to users when the form fails validation. Test your completed program until all validation works reliably with different combinations of valid and erroneous data.

Team Case Project

Add validation code to one of the forms on your team website. First, ensure that your form uses at least three of the following field types: check boxes, text boxes, option buttons, selection lists, and text areas. Next, as a team, plan validation for each field in the form. Your validation should require a value in each field, and should verify at least one other aspect of at least one field. Divide your team into two groups—one that will write code to verify that all fields have values, and the other to write code to verify another aspect of the entered data. Each group's code should also incorporate appropriate feedback to users when it encounters validation errors. When both groups are done, work as a team to integrate the code into the document. Strategize as a team about how to test for all possible validation scenarios. Test and debug the code until your completed program until all validation works reliably with different combinations of valid and erroneous data.

CHAPTER

7

USING OBJECT-ORIENTED JAVASCRIPT

When you complete this chapter, you will be able to:

> Explain basic concepts related to object-oriented programming
> Use the `Date`, `Number`, and `Math` objects
> Define your own custom JavaScript objects

In this chapter, you will learn how to use object-oriented programming techniques in your JavaScript programs. Essentially, object-oriented programming allows you to use and create self-contained pieces of code and data, called objects, which can be reused in your programs. You already have some experience with object-oriented programming, after working with browser objects (including the `Window` and `Document` objects) in Chapter 5. The browser objects, however, are part of the web browser itself. The objects you will study in this chapter are part of the JavaScript programming language. Additionally, you will learn how to create your own custom JavaScript objects.

Introduction to Object-Oriented Programming

The JavaScript programs you have written so far have primarily been tailored for specific situations. That is, most of your variables, statements, and functions have referenced elements and values specific to one document. The problem with that approach is that it limits the usefulness of your code. For example, you might create a web page for an online retailer that uses JavaScript to calculate the total for a sales order that includes state sales tax and shipping. However, the retailer might sell different types of products on different web pages, with one page selling books, another page selling sporting goods, and so on. If you wanted to reuse the JavaScript sales total code on multiple web pages, you would have to rewrite all of the statements for each web page. Object-oriented programming takes a different approach. It allows you to reuse code without having to rewrite it for a specific situation.

Reusing Software Objects

Object-oriented programming (OOP) refers to the creation of reusable software objects that can be easily incorporated into multiple programs. The term object specifically refers to programming code and data that can be treated as an individual unit. Objects are also called components. The term data refers to information contained within variables or other types of storage structures. In Chapter 1, you learned that the procedures associated with an object are called "methods," and the variables that are associated with an object are called "properties" or "attributes."

Objects can range from simple controls, such as a button, to entire programs, such as a database application. In fact, some programs consist entirely of other objects. You'll often encounter objects that have been designed to perform a specific task. For example, in a retail sales program, you could refer to all of the code that calculates the sales total as a single object. You could then reuse that object over and over again in the same program just by typing the object name.

> **Note** | Popular object-oriented programming languages include C++, Java, and Visual Basic.

Using an object-oriented language, programmers can create objects themselves or use objects created by other programmers. For example, if you are creating an accounting program, you might use an existing object named `Payroll` that contains several methods— one to calculate the amount of federal and state tax to deduct, another that calculates the FICA amount to deduct, and so on. Properties of the `Payroll` object may include an employee's number of tax withholding allowances, federal and state tax percentages, and the cost of insurance premiums. You do not need to know how the `Payroll` object was created. You only need to know how to access the methods and properties of the `Payroll` object from your program.

At its core, object-oriented programming involves creating components that can be used by themselves or in combination with other components. OOP shares some similarities with putting together an entertainment center, which might contain a television, DVD or Blu-Ray player, DVR, and streaming media device (such as a Roku or Apple TV). Many companies manufacture devices that can be connected to a TV—there are many different brands of DVD players, DVRs, and streaming media devices. Even though different manufacturers build each of these hardware components, if they are designed to work with a TV, then they all share common ways of attaching to it or to each other. Most of today's hardware components connect using HDMI, which is a standard interface for connecting audio and video devices. As a result, you can create an entertainment center by buying different components, connecting them using a standard interface, and then using them in combination. Likewise, you can create a program by using existing objects (or creating your own) and connecting them together to accomplish a purpose. Figure 7-1 illustrates the difference between creating self-contained programs you've written up to this point and programming with modular objects.

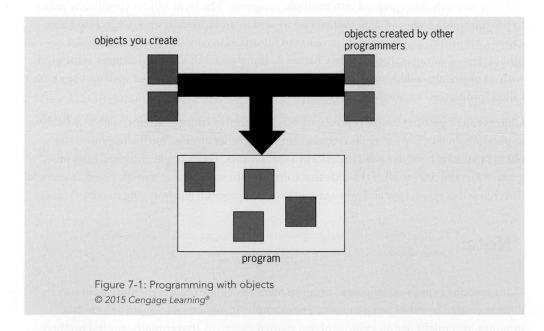

Figure 7-1: Programming with objects
© 2015 Cengage Learning®

Understanding Encapsulation

Objects are **encapsulated**, which means that all code and required data are contained within the object itself. In most cases, an encapsulated object consists of a single computer file that contains all code and required data. Encapsulation places code inside what programmers like to call a black box; when an object is encapsulated, other parts of the program cannot read or modify the code itself—all internal workings are hidden. The code (methods and statements) and data (variables and constants) contained in an encapsulated object are instead accessed through an interface. The term **interface** refers to the programmatic elements required for a source program to communicate with an object. For example, interface elements required to access a `Payroll` object might be a method named `calcNetPay()`, which calculates an employee's net pay, and properties containing the employee's name and pay rate.

When you include encapsulated objects in your programs, users can see only the methods and properties of the object that you allow them to see. Essentially, the principle of **information hiding** states that any methods and properties that other programmers do not need to access or know about should be hidden. By removing the ability to see inside the black box, encapsulation reduces the complexity of the code, allowing programmers who use the code to concentrate on the task of integrating the code into their programs. Encapsulation also prevents other programmers from accidentally introducing a bug into a program, or from possibly even stealing the code and claiming it as their own.

You can compare a programming object and its interface to a handheld calculator. The calculator represents an object, and you represent a program that wants to use the object. You establish an interface with the calculator object by entering numbers (the data required by the object) and then pressing calculation keys (which represent the methods of the object). You do not need to know about, nor can you see, the inner workings of the calculator object. As a programmer, you are concerned only with an object's methods and properties. To continue the analogy, you are only concerned with the result you expect the calculator object to return. Figure 7-2 illustrates the idea of the calculator interface.

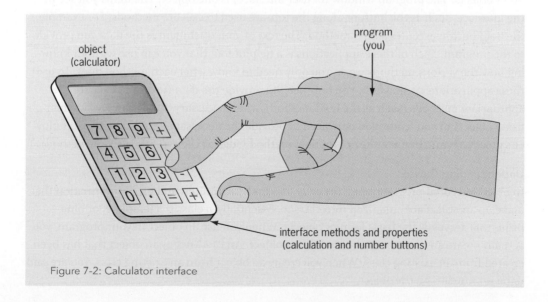

Figure 7-2: Calculator interface

In JavaScript, the `Document` object is encapsulated, making it a black box. You can access the `Document` object using its interface, which consists of its properties and its methods. For instance, you can incorporate the `getElementById()` method of the `Document` object in your programs. However, doing so does not require you to work with the code that makes up the `Document` object itself. Figure 7-3 illustrates the concept of a black box using JavaScript and the `Document` object.

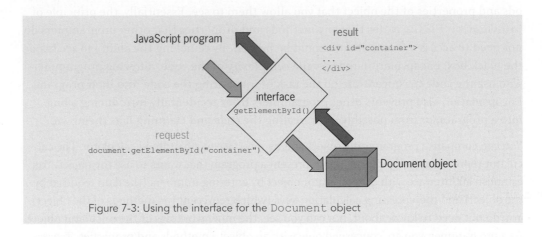

Figure 7-3: Using the interface for the `Document` object

Another example of an object and its interface is a word-processing application such as Microsoft Word or Google Docs. Each application is itself an object made up of numerous other objects. The program window (or user interface) is one object. The items you see in the interface, such as the buttons along the top, are used to execute methods. For example, the Bold button executes a bold method. The text of your document is the data you provide to the program. Each of these applications is a helpful tool that you can use without knowing how the various methods work. You only need to know what each method does. To use these applications successfully, you only need to provide the data (text) and execute the appropriate methods (such as the bold method), when necessary. In the same way, when using objects in your code, you only need to provide the necessary data (such as an employee's gross pay) and execute the appropriate method (such as the `calcNetPay()` method).

Understanding Classes

In object-oriented programming, the code, methods, attributes, and other information that make up an object are organized into **classes**. Essentially, a class is a template, or blueprint, that serves as the basis for new objects. When you use an object in your program, you actually create an instance of the class of the object. An **instance** is an object that has been created from an existing class. When you create an object from an existing class, you are said to be **instantiating** the object.

> **Note** | Class names in traditional object-oriented programming usually begin with an uppercase letter. This convention is also followed in JavaScript.

Later in this chapter, you will learn how to create, or instantiate, an object from built-in JavaScript classes and from custom classes that you write yourself. However, as a conceptual example, consider an object named `BankAccount` that contains methods and properties that you might use to record transactions associated with a checking or savings account. The `BankAccount` object is created from a `BankAccount` class. To use the `BankAccount` class, you create an instance of the class. A particular instance of an object *inherits* its methods and properties from a class—that is, it takes on the characteristics of the class on which it is based. The `BankAccount` object, for instance, would inherit all of the methods and properties of the `BankAccount` class.

To give another example, when you create a new word-processing document, which is a type of object, it usually inherits the properties of a template on which it is based. The template is a type of class. The document inherits characteristics of the template such as font size, line spacing, and boilerplate text. In the same manner, a program that include instances of an object inherits the object's functionality.

Because objects in the browser object model are actually part of the web browser, you do not need to instantiate them in order to use them in your programs. For example, you do not need to instantiate a `Document` object from the `Document` class in your JavaScript programs because the web browser automatically instantiates one for you. However, you do need to instantiate some objects from the built-in JavaScript classes that you will study next.

Using Built-In JavaScript Classes

The JavaScript language includes the 13 built-in classes listed in Table 7-1. Each object contains various methods and properties for performing a particular type of task.

CLASS	DESCRIPTION
Arguments	Retrieves and manipulates arguments within a function
Array	Creates new array objects
Boolean	Creates new Boolean objects
Date	Retrieves and manipulates dates and times
Error	Returns run-time error information
Function	Creates new function objects

Continued on next page...

CLASS	DESCRIPTION
Global	Stores global variables and contains various built-in JavaScript functions
JSON	Manipulates objects formatted in JavaScript Object Notation (JSON); available in ECMAScript 5 and later
Math	Contains methods and properties for performing mathematical calculations
Number	Contains methods and properties for manipulating numbers
Object	Represents the base class for all built-in JavaScript classes; contains several of the built-in JavaScript functions
RegExp	Contains methods and properties for finding and replacing characters in text strings
String	Contains methods and properties for manipulating text strings

Table 7-1: Built-in JavaScript classes

> **Note** You will study the `Date`, `Number`, `Math`, and `Object` classes in this chapter. You will study the `Array`, `String`, `RegExp`, and `JSON` classes in Chapter 8.

Instantiating an Object

You can use some of the built-in JavaScript objects directly in your code, while other objects require you to instantiate a new object. The `Math` object is one that you can use directly in your programs without instantiating a new object. The following example shows how to use the `Math` object's PI (π) property and `pow()` method in a statement:

```
1   // calculate the area of a circle based on its radius
2   function calcCircleArea() {
3       var r = document.getElementById("radius").value;
4       var area = Math.PI * Math.pow(r, 2); // area is pi times ↵
5       radius squared
6       return area;
7   }
```

Unlike the `Math` object, other objects require you to instantiate a new object before you can use them. There are two different ways to create a new object—using the object's constructor or using a literal. For instance, as you learned in Chapter 3, arrays are represented in JavaScript by the `Array` object. The following statement shows an example of how to instantiate an empty array named `deptHeads` using an array literal:

```
var deptHeads = [];
```

Likewise, you can create an empty generic object using an object literal. The following code creates an object with the name `accountsPayable` using an object literal:

```
var accountsPayable = {};
```

Notice that unlike an array literal, which uses square brackets, an object literal uses curly braces around its values.

Instantiating objects with literals is generally the preferred method among programmers because it's easier than using a constructor. However, one built-in object, `Date`, does not support the literal format. Therefore, to create a `Date` object, you must use the `Date()` constructor. For instance, the following statement creates a `Date` object:

```
var today = new Date();
```

You may be wondering why the preceding statements instantiate new objects using the `var` keyword. As you know, the `var` keyword is used for declaring variables. The name you use for an instantiated object is really a variable, just like an integer or string variable. In fact, programmers use the terms "variable" and "object" interchangeably. The difference is that, in this case, the data the variable represents happens to be an object instead of a number or string. Recall from Chapter 1 that variables are the values a program stores in computer memory. Recall, too, that the JavaScript language also supports reference data types, which can contain multiple values or complex types of information, as opposed to the single values stored in primitive data types. In other words, in the same manner that you use a variable name to represent a primitive data type, such as an integer, in computer memory you also use a variable name to represent an object. Because the objects you declare in your JavaScript program are actually a certain type of variable, you use the `var` keyword to identify them as variables.

Note

If you have worked with other object-oriented programming languages, then you may be familiar with the term garbage collection, *which refers to cleaning up, or reclaiming, memory that is reserved by a program. When you declare a variable or instantiate a new object, you are actually reserving computer memory for the variable or object. With some programming languages, you must write code that deletes a variable or object after you are through with it in order to free the memory for use by other parts of your program or by other programs running on your computer. With JavaScript, you do not need to worry about reclaiming memory that is reserved for your variables or objects; JavaScript knows when your program no longer needs a variable or object and automatically cleans up the memory for you.*

In this chapter, you'll use object-oriented programming to add functionality to a web page for Outer Orbits, a space tourism company based in Virginia Beach, Virginia. The company has created a page that enables potential customers to enter the names of one or more passengers, select a prospective launch date, and see payment options. You'll add a calendar widget that uses Date objects to specify a date in the correct format and a countdown widget that simulates a countdown clock to show the time remaining before the selected flight. You'll also use methods of the Math and Number objects to perform mathematical functions and control the display of the results. Finally, you'll create a custom object with its own properties and methods to store all the ticket information entered in the form. Figure 7-4 shows a preview of the page you'll create in a desktop browser, and Figure 7-5 shows it on a handheld device.

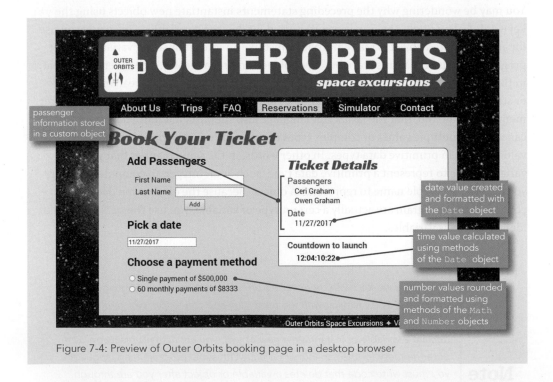

Figure 7-4: Preview of Outer Orbits booking page in a desktop browser

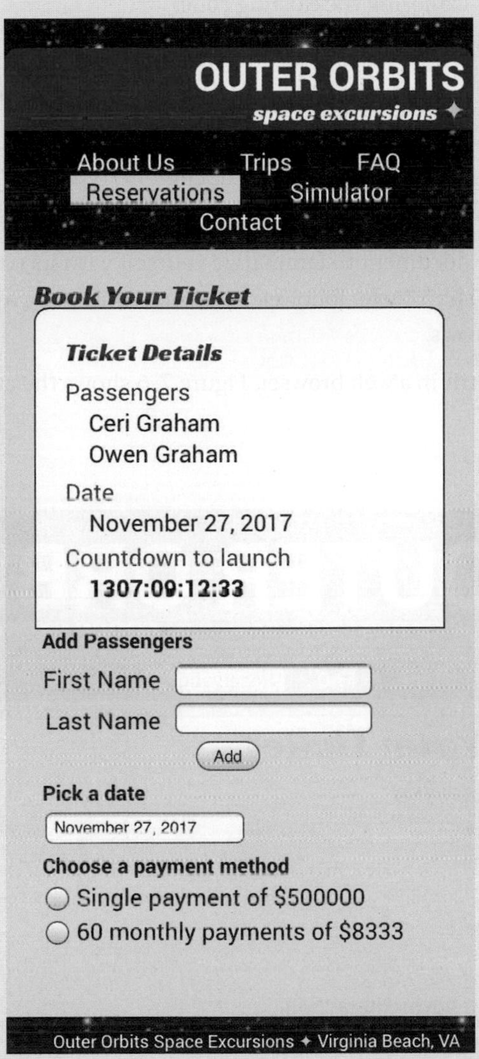

Figure 7-5: Preview of Outer Orbits booking page on a handheld device

You'll start your work by exploring the existing code.

To explore the code for the reservations page:

1. In your text editor, open the **booktrip.htm** file, located in your Chapter folder for Chapter 7.

2. In the comment section at the top of the document, type your name and today's date where indicated, and then save your work.

3. Scroll through the document to familiarize yourself with its content. The article section contains a short form, followed by a table containing a header row and six additional empty rows.

4. Open **booktrip.htm** in a web browser. Figure 7-6 shows the current content of the document.

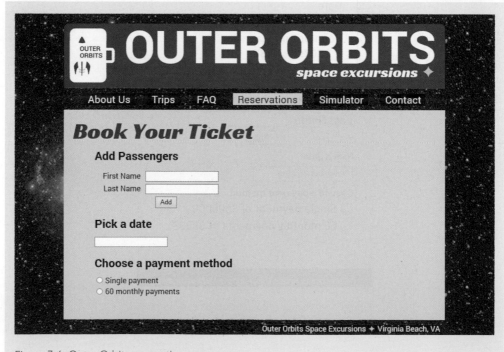

Figure 7-6: Outer Orbits reservation page

5. Return to your text editor, create a new JavaScript document, and then enter the following comment section, typing your name and today's date where indicated:

```
1    /*      JavaScript 6th Edition
2     *      Chapter 7
3     *      Chapter case
4
5     *      Outer Orbits
6     *      Author:
7     *      Date:
8
9     *      Filename: orbits.js
10   */
```

6. Below the comment section, enter the following statement:

```
"use strict"; // interpret contents in JavaScript strict mode
```

7. Save the document as **orbits.js**.

In the next section, you'll use the JavaScript Date, Number, and Math objects to enhance the reservations form.

Short Quiz 1

1. What is object-oriented programming? What is an object?

2. Name at least two built-in JavaScript classes.

Using the Date, Number, and Math Classes

In this section, you will learn how to work with three of the most commonly used JavaScript classes: Date, Number, and Math. First, you will explore the Date class.

Working with the Date and Time with the Date Class

The ability to work with dates in JavaScript programs unleashes a lot of possibilities. For instance, you can use dates in your programs to create calendars or to calculate how long it will take to do something. The **Date class** contains methods and properties for manipulating the date and time. It allows you to use the current date and time (or a specific date or time element, such as the current month) in your JavaScript programs. You create a Date object with one of the constructors listed in Table 7-2.

CONSTRUCTOR	DESCRIPTION
Date()	Creates a Date object that contains the current date and time provided by the device
Date(milliseconds)	Creates a Date object based on the number of milliseconds that have elapsed since midnight, January 1, 1970
Date(date_string)	Creates a Date object based on a string containing a date value
Date(year, month[, day, hours, minutes, seconds, milliseconds])	Creates a Date object with the date and time set according to the passed arguments; the year and month arguments are required

Table 7-2: Date class constructors

The following statement demonstrates how to create a Date object that contains the current date and time provided by the device running the program:

```
var today = new Date();
```

The day of the month and the year in a Date object are stored using numbers that match the actual date and year. However, the days of the week and months of the year are stored in a Date object using numeric representations, starting with zero, similar to an array. The numbers 0 through 6 represent the days Sunday through Saturday, and the numbers 0 through 11 represent the months January through December. The following statement demonstrates how to specify a specific date with a Date constructor function. In this example, the date assigned to the independenceDay variable is July 4, 1776.

```
var independenceDay = new Date(1776, 6, 4);
```

After you create a new Date object, you can then manipulate the date and time in the variable, using the methods of the Date class. Note that the date and time in a Date object are not updated over time like a clock. Instead, a Date object contains the static (unchanging) date and time as of the moment the JavaScript code instantiates the object.

Table 7-3 lists commonly used methods of the Date class. Note that the Date class does not contain any properties.

METHOD	DESCRIPTION
getDate()	Returns the date of a Date object
getDay()	Returns the day of a Date object
getFullYear()	Returns the year of a Date object in four-digit format
getHours()	Returns the hour of a Date object
getMilliseconds()	Returns the milliseconds of a Date object
getMinutes()	Returns the minutes of a Date object
getMonth()	Returns the month of a Date object
getSeconds()	Returns the seconds of a Date object
getTime()	Returns the time of a Date object
now()	Returns the current time as the number of milliseconds that have elapsed since midnight, January 1, 1970 (ECMAScript 5 and later only)
setDate(date)	Sets the date (1–31) of a Date object
setFullYear(year[, month, day])	Sets the four-digit year of a Date object; optionally allows you to set the month and the day
setHours(hours[, minutes, seconds, milliseconds])	Sets the hours (0–23) of a Date object; optionally allows you to set the minutes (0–59), seconds (0–59), and milliseconds (0–999)
setMilliseconds(milliseconds)	Sets the milliseconds (0–999) of a Date object
setMinutes(minutes[, seconds, milliseconds])	Sets the minutes (0–59) of a Date object; optionally allows you to set seconds (0–59) and milliseconds (0–999)
setMonth(month[, date])	Sets the month (0–11) of a Date object; optionally allows you to set the date (1–31)
setSeconds(seconds[, milliseconds])	Sets the seconds (0–59) of a Date object; optionally allows you to set milliseconds (0–999)
setTime()	Sets the time as the number of milliseconds that have elapsed since midnight, January 1, 1970
toLocaleString()	Converts a Date object to a string, set to the current time zone
toString()	Converts a Date object to a string
valueOf()	Converts a Date object to a millisecond format

Table 7-3: Commonly used methods of the Date class

Each portion of a Date object, such as the day, month, year, and so on, can be retrieved and modified using the Date object methods. For example, if you create a new Date object using the statement var curDate = new Date();, you can retrieve just the date portion stored in the curDate object by using the statement curDate.getDate();.

If you want to display the full text for days and months (for example, "Wednesday" or "January"), then you can use a conditional statement to check the value returned by the getDay() or getMonth() method. For example, the following code uses an if/else construct to store the full name of the day of the week returned by the getDay() method.

```
1   var today = new Date();
2   var curDay = today.getDay();
3   var weekday;
4   if (curDay === 0) {
5       weekday = "Sunday";
6   } else if (curDay === 1) {
7       weekday = "Monday";
8   } else if (curDay === 2) {
9       weekday = "Tuesday";
10  } else if (curDay === 3) {
11      weekday = "Wednesday";
12  } else if (curDay === 4) {
13      weekday = "Thursday";
14  } else if (curDay === 5) {
15      weekday = "Friday";
16  } else if (curDay === 6) {
17      weekday = "Saturday";
18  }
```

If you need to return the full text of the day of the week or the full text of the month, you should assign the days of the week or the months of the year to an array. You can then combine the getDay() or getMonth() method with the array name to return the full text of the day or month. For example, the following code includes an array named `months` with 12 elements that are assigned the full text names of the months of the year:

```
1    var today = new Date();
2    var months = ["January","February","March", ↵
3                  "April","May","June", ↵
4                  "July","August","September", ↵
5                  "October","November","December"];
6    var curMonth = months[today.getMonth()];
```

In the preceding code, the full text name of the month is assigned to the `curMonth` variable using the statement `var curMonth = months[today.getMonth()];`. The value of the array element is retrieved by placing the `today` object with the `getMonth()` method appended to it between the brackets of the months array name.

Next, you'll begin to add features to the Outer Orbits reservation page. You'll start by using the Date object to create a calendar widget, which is a program that displays a calendar that a user can click to select a date. Because there are many valid formats for dates, a calendar widget enables users to select a date using an interface, which then translates the selected date into a common format, while also displaying the result to users in a format they recognize.

> **Note**
>
> HTML5 supports a `date` value for the `type` attribute of the `input` element. However, at the time this book was written, major browsers had important differences in the date pickers they displayed for this input type. The Outer Orbits reservations page will use an input type of `text` along with the calendar widget you'll create to ensure that users have a consistent interface on all browsers and devices.

To create the calendar widget:

1. Return to **orbits.js** in your text editor, and then, below the code you entered in the previous section, enter the following code to declare a global variable to track the date a user is viewing or has selected:

```
var dateObject = new Date();
```

2. Below the global variable definition, add the following code to declare the `displayCalendar()` function:

```
function displayCalendar(whichMonth) {

}
```

3. Within the `displayCalendar()` function, add the following variable declarations:

```
1    var date;
2    var dateToday = new Date();
3    var dayOfWeek;
4    var daysInMonth;
5    var dateCells;
6    var captionValue;
7    var month;
8    var year;
9    var monthArray = ["January","February","March","April","May",↵
10       "June","July","August","September","October","November",↵
11       "December"];
```

4. Below the variables, add the following `if/else` statement to the function:

```
1    if (whichMonth === -1) {
2        dateObject.setMonth(dateObject.getMonth() - 1);
3    } else if (whichMonth === 1) {
4        dateObject.setMonth(dateObject.getMonth() + 1);
5    }
```

This statement enables users to navigate to the previous or next month using buttons in the calendar widget.

5. Below the `if/else` statement, add the following code to set variable values:

```
1    month = dateObject.getMonth();
2    year = dateObject.getFullYear();
3    dateObject.setDate(1);
4    dayOfWeek = dateObject.getDay();
5    captionValue = monthArray[month] + " " + year;
6    document.querySelector("#cal table caption").innerHTML =↵
7        captionValue;
```

6. Below the code setting the variable values, add the following `if/else` structure to determine the number of days in the selected month:

```
1    if (month === 0 || month === 2 || month === 4 ||↵
2        month === 6 || month === 7 || month === 9 ||↵
3        month === 11) { // Jan, Mar, May, Jul, Aug, Oct, Dec
```

```
 4        daysInMonth = 31;
 5    } else if (month === 1) { // Feb
 6        if (year % 4 === 0) { // leap year test
 7            if (year % 100 === 0) {
 8                // year ending in 00 not a leap year unless
 9                // divisible by 400
10                if (year % 400 === 0) {
11                    daysInMonth = 29;
12                } else {
13                    daysInMonth = 28;
14                }
15            } else {
16                daysInMonth = 29;
17            }
18        } else {
19            daysInMonth = 28;
20        }
21    } else { // Apr, Jun, Sep, Nov
22        daysInMonth = 30;
23    }
```

The first if statement and the final else statement set the number of days in a month for the 11 months that have the same number of days every year. If the selected month is February, the else if section in the middle determines whether the current year should be a leap year, incorporating two special rules for years that end in 00.

7. Below the if/else section, add the following code to clear the existing table contents:

```
1    dateCells = document.getElementsByTagName("td");
2    for (var i = 0; i < dateCells.length; i++) {
3        // clear existing table dates
4        dateCells[i].innerHTML = "";
5        dateCells[i].className = "";
6    }
```

8. Below the code from the preceding step, add the following code to add new dates to the appropriate calendar table cells:

```
1   for (var i = dayOfWeek; i < daysInMonth + dayOfWeek; i++) {
2       // add dates to days cells
3       dateCells[i].innerHTML = dateObject.getDate();
4       dateCells[i].className = "date";
5       if (dateToday < dateObject) {
6           dateCells[i].className = "futuredate";
7       }
8       date = dateObject.getDate() + 1;
9       dateObject.setDate(date);
10  }
```

9. After the code you entered in the previous step, add the following two statements:

```
1   dateObject.setMonth(dateObject.getMonth() - 1);
2   // reset month to month shown
3   document.getElementById("cal").style.display = "block";
4   // display calendar if it's not already visible
```

Your `displayCalendar()` function should match the following:

```
1   function displayCalendar(whichMonth) {
2       var date;
3       var dateToday = new Date();
4       var dayOfWeek;
5       var daysInMonth;
6       var dateCells;
7       var captionValue;
8       var month;
9       var year;
10      var monthArray = ["January","February",↵
11          "March","April","May","June","July","August",↵
12          "September","October","November","December"];
13      if (whichMonth === -1) {
14          dateObject.setMonth(dateObject.getMonth() - 1);
15      } else if (whichMonth === 1) {
```

```
16          dateObject.setMonth(dateObject.getMonth() + 1);
17      }
18      month = dateObject.getMonth();
19      year = dateObject.getFullYear();
20      dateObject.setDate(1);
21      dayOfWeek = dateObject.getDay();
22      captionValue = monthArray[month] + " " + year;
23      document.querySelector("#cal table caption").innerHTML =↵
24          captionValue;
25      if (month === 0 || month === 2 || month === 4 ||↵
26          month === 6 || month === 7 || month === 9 ||↵
27          month === 11) { // Jan, Mar, May, Jul, Aug, Oct, Dec
28          daysInMonth = 31;
29      } else if (month === 1) { // Feb
30          if (year % 4 === 0) { // leap year test
31              if (year % 100 === 0) {
32              // year ending in 00 not a leap year unless
33              // divisible by 400
34                  if (year % 400 === 0) {
35                      daysInMonth = 29;
36                  } else {
37                      daysInMonth = 28;
38                  }
39              } else {
40                  daysInMonth = 29;
41              }
42          } else {
43              daysInMonth = 28;
44          }
45      } else { // Apr, Jun, Sep, Nov
46          daysInMonth = 30;
47      }
48      dateCells = document.getElementsByTagName("td");
49      for (var i = 0; i < dateCells.length; i++) {
```

```
50          // clear existing table dates
51          dateCells[i].innerHTML = "";
52          dateCells[i].className = "";
53      }
54      for (var i = dayOfWeek; i < daysInMonth + dayOfWeek; i++) {
55          // add dates to days cells
56          dateCells[i].innerHTML = dateObject.getDate();
57          dateCells[i].className = "date";
58          if (dateToday < dateObject) {
59              dateCells[i].className = "futuredate";
60          }
61          date = dateObject.getDate() + 1;
62          dateObject.setDate(date);
63      }
64      dateObject.setMonth(dateObject.getMonth() - 1);
65      // reset month to month shown
66      document.getElementById("cal").style.display = "block";
67      // display calendar if it's not already visible
68  }
```

10. Below the `displayCalendar()` function, enter the following code to declare a `createEventListeners()` function:

```
function createEventListeners() {

}
```

11. Within the `createEventListeners()` function, add the following code:

```
1   var dateField = document.getElementById("tripDate");
2       if (dateField.addEventListener) {
3           dateField.addEventListener("click", displayCalendar, ↵
4               false);
5       } else if (dateField.attachEvent) {
6           dateField.attachEvent("onclick", displayCalendar);
7       }
```

12. Below the `createEventListeners()` function, add the following statements:

```
1    if (window.addEventListener) {
2       window.addEventListener("load", createEventListeners, false);
3    } else if (window.attachEvent) {
4       window.attachEvent("onload", createEventListeners);
5    }
```

13. Save your changes to **orbit.js**, open **booktrip.htm** in your browser, and then click the **Pick a date** field. The calendar widget is displayed showing the current month. Figure 7-7 shows the calendar for November 2017.

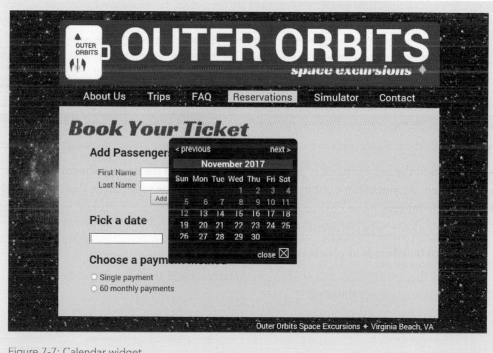

Figure 7-7: Calendar widget

14. Click one of the dates displayed in white, click the **previous** button, click the **next** button, and then click the **close** button. At this point, nothing happens when you click the calendar.

Ensuring that the logic of your JavaScript programs works is, of course, essential. However, you also need to make sure users intuitively understand how to use your programs. A judicious use of visual formatting can go a long way toward showing users how to interact with a program. For example, the `displayCalendar()` function you created includes the statement `dateCells[i].className = "futuredate";`, which uses CSS to change the appearance of valid future calendar dates from gray to white. This change adds a visual cue that helps users distinguish between future dates that are valid selections and past dates that are shown only for reference. Because clicking one of the past dates has no effect, this variation in appearance subtly reminds users of the difference between past and future dates. If all the dates in the calendar were the same color, users might erroneously conclude that the program was broken if they clicked a date in the past and nothing happened. Although you don't need to be an expert in design to be a successful JavaScript programmer, it can be useful to pay attention to the visual aspects of interfaces that you encounter on other web sites and apps, and draw lessons from them to strengthen your own programs.

Next you'll add the `selectDate()` function, which examines the date on the calendar that a user clicked, verifies that it's not in the past, and then sets the value of the Pick a date field to the selected date.

To add the `selectDate()` function:

1. Return to **orbits.js** in your text editor.

2. Above the `createEventListeners()` function, enter the following code to declare the `selectDate()` function:

```
1   function selectDate(event) {
2       if (event === undefined) { // get caller element in IE8
3           event = window.event;
4       }
5       var callerElement = event.target || event.srcElement;
6   }
```

This function takes a single parameter, `event`, which stores the event that triggered it. In modern browsers, this parameter lets you identify the element that called the function, which you can use to identify the date the user selected in the calendar widget. However,

IE8 doesn't do this, so the function includes an `if` statement that assigns the value of `window.event` to the `event` parameter if `event` is undefined. The function then creates the `callerElement` variable and assigns it the value of either the `target` attribute or the `srcElement` attribute of the `event` parameter. In most browsers, the `target` attribute of an event represents the element that received the event—in this case, the table cell that was clicked. IE8 instead has a `srcElement` attribute that fills the same role, so your code checks for whichever of these is supported by the current browser.

3. Below the `callerElement` declaration, enter the following code:

```
1    if (callerElement.innerHTML === "") {
2        // cell contains no date, so don't close the calendar
3        document.getElementById("cal").style.display = "block";
4        return false;
5    }
6    dateObject.setDate(callerElement.innerHTML);
```

This `if` statement checks if the cell the user clicked is empty. If so, the calendar remains displayed and the function ends. In all other cases, the next statement sets the date portion of the `dateObject` variable to the contents of the cell the user clicked.

4. Below the code from the previous step, add the following statements to the function:

```
1    var fullDateToday = new Date();
2    var dateToday = Date.UTC(fullDateToday.getFullYear(),↵
3        fullDateToday.getMonth(), fullDateToday.getDate());
4    var selectedDate = Date.UTC(dateObject.getFullYear(),↵
5        dateObject.getMonth(), dateObject.getDate());
6    if (selectedDate <= dateToday) {
7        document.getElementById("cal").style.display = "block";
8        return false;
9    }
10   document.getElementById("tripDate").value =↵
11       dateObject.toLocaleDateString();
```

This code creates a `fullDateToday` variable whose value is a `Date` object with the current date and time, and then it creates a `dateToday` variable with the value set to the year, month, and day from the `fullDateToday` variable. It then creates a `selectedDate` variable set to the year, month, and day of the date selected by the user. The `if` statement checks if the selected date is before today's date—and thus in the past. If so, the calendar remains displayed and the function ends, because the user must select a valid future date when making a reservation. In all other cases, the value of the Pick a date text box is set to the date in the Date object, using the toLocaleDateString() method to format the date according to the user's local conventions. Your selectDate function should match the following:

```
1   function selectDate(event) {
2       if (event === undefined) { // get caller element in IE8
3           event = window.event;
4       }
5       var callerElement = event.target || event.srcElement;
6       if (callerElement.innerHTML === "") {
7           // cell contains no date, so don't close the calendar
8           document.getElementById("cal").style.display = "block";
9           return false;
10      }
11      dateObject.setDate(callerElement.innerHTML);
12      var fullDateToday = new Date();
13      var dateToday = Date.UTC(fullDateToday.getFullYear(),↵
14          fullDateToday.getMonth(), fullDateToday.getDate());
15      var selectedDate = Date.UTC(dateObject.getFullYear(),↵
16          dateObject.getMonth(), dateObject.getDate());
17      if (selectedDate <= dateToday) {
18          document.getElementById("cal").style.display = "block";
19          return false;
20      }
21      document.getElementById("tripDate").value =↵
22          dateObject.toLocaleDateString();
23  }
```

5. Scroll down to the createEventListeners() function, and then before the closing }, add the following code:

```
1   var dateCells = document.getElementsByTagName("td");
2   if (dateCells[0].addEventListener) {
3       for (var i = 0; i < dateCells.length; i++) {
4           dateCells[i].addEventListener("click", selectDate,↵
5               false);
6       }
```

```
 7    } else if (dateCells[0].attachEvent) {
 8        for (var i = 0; i < dateCells.length; i++) {
 9            dateCells[i].attachEvent("onclick", selectDate);
10        }
11    }
```

This code creates a variable containing references to all the `td` elements in the document, which consists of all the calendar cells. The code to create an event listener or attach an event then loops through all the cells, setting the `click` event to trigger the `selectDate()` function you just created.

6. Save your changes to **orbits.js**, refresh or reload **booktrip.htm** in your browser, click the **Pick a date** box, and then click a date in the past. Notice that no date is displayed in the Pick a date box.

7. Click a date in the future. As Figure 7-8 shows, the selected date value is displayed in the Pick a date box.

Figure 7-8: Selected date displayed in Pick a date box

After a user selects a date, the calendar widget remains visible, even though it's no longer needed. Next you'll create a helper function called `hideCalendar()`, create an event listener that runs the function when a user clicks the close button, and add a statement that calls the `hideCalendar()` function after a user clicks a date in the calendar widget.

To create the `hideCalendar()` function:

1. Return to the **orbits.js** document in your text editor, and then above the `createEventListeners()` function, add the following:

```
function hideCalendar() {
    document.getElementById("cal").style.display = "none";
}
```

This function contains a single statement, which changes the display property for the calendar to `none`.

2. Within the `selectDate()` function, just before the closing }, add the following statement:

```
hideCalendar();
```

This statement closes the calendar after a valid date is selected.

3. Scroll down to the `createEventListeners()` function, and then before the closing }, add the following code:

```
1    var closeButton = document.getElementById("close");
2    if (closeButton.addEventListener) {
3        closeButton.addEventListener("click", hideCalendar, false);
4    } else if (closeButton.attachEvent) {
5        closeButton.attachEvent("onclick", hideCalendar);
6    }
```

This code calls the `hideCalendar()` function when a user clicks the close button on the calendar.

4. Save your changes to **orbits.js**, shift-refresh or shift-reload **booktrip.htm** in your browser to clear the form, click the **Pick a date** box, and then click the **Close** button. The calendar widget closes.

5. Click the **Pick a date** box, and then click a date in the future. As Figure 7-9 shows, the selected date value is displayed in the Pick a date box, and the widget closes.

Figure 7-9: Date selected and calendar widget closed

Next you'll add additional helper functions and event listeners to your code to enable users to navigate to different months using the previous and next buttons.

To add helper functions and event listeners for navigating between months:

1. Return to the **orbits.js** document in your text editor, and then above the `createEventListeners()` function, add the following:

```
1    function prevMo() {
2        displayCalendar(-1);
3    }
4    function nextMo() {
5        displayCalendar(1);
6    }
```

These function calls include arguments for the `displayCalendar()` function. The value -1 triggers code in the function to display the previous month, while the value 1 displays the next month.

2. Scroll down to the `createEventListeners()` function, and then before the closing }, add the following code:

```
1    var prevLink = document.getElementById("prev");
2    var nextLink = document.getElementById("next");
3    if (prevLink.addEventListener) {
4        prevLink.addEventListener("click", prevMo, false);
5        nextLink.addEventListener("click", nextMo, false);
6    } else if (prevLink.attachEvent) {
7        prevLink.attachEvent("onclick", prevMo);
8        nextLink.attachEvent("onclick", nextMo);
9    }
```

This code calls the `prevMo()` function when a user clicks the previous button, and the `nextMo()` function when a user clicks the next button.

3. Save your changes to **orbits.js**, shift-refresh or shift-reload **booktrip.htm** in your browser to clear the form, click the **Pick a date** box, and then click the **previous** button. The calendar widget displays the previous month.

4. Click the **next** button, and then click the **next** button again. The calendar widget displays the current month and then the month that follows.

Manipulating Numbers with the Number Class

The Number class contains methods for manipulating numbers and properties that contain static values representing some of the numeric limitations in the JavaScript language (such as the largest positive number that can be used in JavaScript). As with the Math object, you don't need to create a `Number` object to access the `Number` class methods or properties. Instead, you can simply append the name of any `Number` class method or property to the name of an existing variable that contains a numeric value.

Using **Number** Class Methods

Table 7-4 lists the methods of the `Number` class.

METHOD	DESCRIPTION
toExponential(*decimals*)	Converts a number to a string in exponential notation using the number of decimal places specified by *decimals*
toFixed(*decimals*)	Converts a number to a string using the number of decimal places specified by *decimals*
toLocaleString()	Converts a number to a string that is formatted with local numeric formatting style
toPrecision(*decimals*)	Converts a number to a string with the number of decimal places specified by *decimals*, in either exponential notation or in fixed notation
toString(*base*)	Converts a number to a string using the number system specified by *base*
valueOf()	Returns the numeric value of a `Number` object

Table 7-4: Number class methods

The primary reason for using any of the "to" methods listed in Table 7-4 is to convert a number to a string value with a specific number of decimal places that will be displayed to a user. If you don't need to display a number for a user, there is no need to use any of these methods. The most useful `Number` class method is the `toFixed()` method, which you can use to display a numeric value with a specified number of decimal places. For example, you may have a number in your program that represents a dollar value. However, depending on the result of a calculation or a value entered by a user, the number may contain more than the two decimal places that are acceptable in a currency value. The following code shows a simple example of a numeric variable named `salesTotal` that is assigned a value of 49.95. If you apply a discount of 10 percent to the variable, the new number is equal to 44.955. Before displaying the value, the final statement uses the `toFixed()` method to convert the value of the `salesTotal` variable to a string containing two decimal places.

```
1   var salesTotal = 49.95;
2   var discount = salesTotal * 0.1;
```

```
3    salesTotal -= discount; // new value is 44.955
4    document.getElementById("totalField").innerHTML = "$" +↵
5       salesTotal.toFixed(2); // displays $44.96
```

Another useful Number class method is the toLocaleString() method, which you can use to convert a number to a string that is formatted with local numeric formatting style. For example, in American numeric formatting style, you separate thousands with a comma. The following statements demonstrate how to convert the number 1210349 to the string $1,210,349:

```
1    var salesTotal = 1210349;
2    salesTotal = salesTotal.toLocaleString();
3    document.getElementById("totalField").innerHTML = "$" +↵
4       salesTotal; // displays $1,210,349
```

> **Note** Modern browsers have different rules about where to place number separators using the toLocaleString() method. In Chapter 8, you'll learn how to use regular expressions to enforce a common format across browsers.

Accessing Number Class Properties

Table 7-5 lists the properties of the Number class. Note that there is little reason for you to use these properties. However, they are listed here for the sake of completeness.

PROPERTY	DESCRIPTION
MAX_VALUE	The largest positive number that can be used in JavaScript
MIN_VALUE	The smallest positive number that can be used in JavaScript
NaN	The value NaN, which stands for "not a number"
NEGATIVE_INFINITY	The value of negative infinity
POSITIVE_INFINITY	The value of positive infinity

Table 7-5: Number class properties

> **Note** Just as the names of classes are capitalized in JavaScript, another convention is to write the names of fixed values, or constants, in all capital letters. The four properties in all caps in Table 7-5 represent constants.

The Outer Orbits reservation page gives each user the option of paying for the trip up front, or dividing the price into monthly payments over 5 years. Rather than hard-coding these values into the page, you'll work with the values as variables, enabling the company to easily incorporate future price changes. You'll use the `toFixed()` and `toLocaleString()` methods of the `Number` object to specify how the values should be displayed.

To calculate the monthly payment amount and format both prices:

1. Return to the **orbits.js** document in your text editor, and then above the `createEventListeners()` function, add the following code to declare the `updateTotalCost()` function:

```
function updateTotalCost() {

}
```

2. Within the `updateTotalCost()` function, add the following code:

```
var totalCost = 250000;
var monthlyCost = totalCost / 60;
var shortMonthlyCost = monthlyCost.toFixed(0);
```

   This statement declares three variables; `totalCost`, which has a fixed value, `monthlyCost` which is `totalCost` divided by 60 (the number of months in the payment plan), and `shortMonthlyCost`, which uses the `toFixed()` method of the `Number` object to store the `monthlyCost` value with no decimal places.

3. Below the variable declarations, add the following code:

```
1    document.getElementById("singleLabel").innerHTML =↵
2       "Single payment of $" + totalCost.toLocaleString();
3    document.getElementById("multipleLabel").innerHTML =↵
4       "60 monthly payments of $" +↵
5       shortMonthlyCost.toLocaleString();
```

   The first statement changes the label for the first option button to include the `totalCost` value, using the `toLocaleString()` method of the `Number` object to display the value according to the user's local conventions. The second statement does the same for the second option button, using the `shortMonthlyCost` value.

4. Within the `selectDate()` function, just before the closing }, enter the following statement:

```
updateTotalCost();
```

   This statement calls the `updateTotalCost()` function when a user selects a date.

5. Save your changes to **orbits.js**, shift-refresh or shift-reload **booktrip.htm** in your browser to clear the form, click the **Pick a date** box, and then click a future date. As Figure 7-10 shows, the option button labels are updated to show the prices, formatted according to local number formatting conventions, and with no decimal places. The figure shows the numbers in two different modern browsers; note that one includes a comma separator (250,000) in the first value, while the second (250000) doesn't. This behavior is entirely browser-specific.

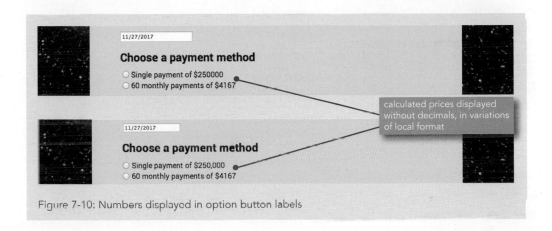

Figure 7-10: Numbers displayed in option button labels

Performing Math Functions with the Math Class

The Math class contains methods and properties for performing mathematical calculations in your programs.

Using Math Class Methods

Table 7-6 lists the methods of the Math class.

METHOD	RETURNS
abs(x)	The absolute value of x
acos(x)	The arc cosine of x
asin(x)	The arc sine of x
atan(x)	The arc tangent of x
atan2(x, y)	The angle from the x-axis of the point represented by x, y

Continued on next page...

METHOD	RETURNS
ceil(x)	The value of x rounded to the next highest integer
cos(x)	The cosine of x
exp(x)	The exponent of x
floor(x)	The value of x rounded to the next lowest integer
log(x)	The natural logarithm of x
max(x, y)	The larger of x or y
min(x, y)	The smaller of x or y
pow(x, y)	The value of x raised to the y power
random()	A random number
round(x)	The value of x rounded to the nearest integer
sin(x)	The sine of x
sqrt(x)	The square root of x
tan(x)	The tangent of x

Table 7-6: Math class methods

Unlike the Array, Date, and Number classes, the Math class does not contain a constructor. This means that you cannot instantiate a Math object using a statement such as the one below.

Not valid code:

```
var mathCalc = new Math();
```

Instead, you use the Math object and one of its methods or properties directly in your code. For example, the sqrt() method returns the square root of a number. The following code uses the sqrt() method to determine the square root of 144:

```
var curNumber = 144;
var squareRoot = Math.sqrt(curNumber); // returns 12
```

Accessing **Math** Class Properties

Table 7-7 lists the properties of the Math class.

PROPERTY	DESCRIPTION
E	Euler's constant e, which is the base of a natural logarithm; this value is approximately 2.7182818284590452354
LN10	The natural logarithm of 10, which is approximately 2.302585092994046
LN2	The natural logarithm of 2, which is approximately 0.6931471805599453
LOG10E	The base-10 logarithm of e, the base of the natural logarithms; this value is approximately 0.4342944819032518
LOG2E	The base-2 logarithm of e, the base of the natural logarithms; this value is approximately 1.4426950408889634
PI	A constant representing the ratio of the circumference of a circle to its diameter, which is approximately 3.1415926535897932
SQRT1_2	The square root of 1/2, which is approximately 0.7071067811865476
SQRT2	The square root of 2, which is approximately 1.4142135623730951

Table 7-7: Math class properties

As an example of how to use the properties of the Math object, the following code shows how to use the PI property to calculate the area of a circle based on its radius. The code also uses the pow() method to calculate the radius raised to the second power, and the round() method to round the value returned to the nearest whole number.

```
var radius = 25;
var area = Math.PI * Math.pow(radius, 2);
var roundedArea = Math.round(area); // returns 1963
```

The design of the Outer Orbits reservation page includes a countdown timer like those traditionally used for space launches, which calculates the days, hours, minutes, and seconds until the selected flight takes off. You'll assign the current date and time to a variable, and the date and time of the selected launch to another variable. You'll then use the Math.floor() method to determine the whole number of days, hours, minutes, and seconds between the two.

To calculate the days, hours, minutes, and seconds until launch:

1. Return to the **orbits.js** document in your text editor, and then above the createEventListeners() function, add the following code to create the updateCountdown() function and declare its variables:

```
1    function updateCountdown() {
2        var dateToday = new Date();
3        var dateFrom = Date.UTC(dateToday.getFullYear(),↵
```

```
4                dateToday.getMonth(), dateToday.getDate(),↵
5                dateToday.getHours(), dateToday.getMinutes(),↵
6                dateToday.getSeconds());
7       var dateTo = Date.UTC(dateObject.getFullYear(),↵
8                dateObject.getMonth(), dateObject.getDate(),↵
9                19, 0, 0); // all launches at 8:00pm UTC
10      }
```

The first statement sets the value of dateToday to the current date and time. The second creates a dateFrom variable containing the current year, month, date, hours, minutes, and seconds. The third statement creates a dateTo variable with a value containing the year, month, and date selected by the user, along with an hour of 19, a minute of 0, and a second of 0 to reflect that all launches take place at exactly 8:00 pm UTC.

2. Within the updateCountdown() function, add the following code:

```
1   // days
2   var daysUntil = Math.floor((dateTo - dateFrom) / 86400000);
3   document.getElementById("countdown").innerHTML = daysUntil;
```

Both the dateTo and dateFrom values are expressed in a value in milliseconds. The first statement calculates the difference in milliseconds between these two time values, and then divides it by 86400000 (the number of milliseconds in a day) to calculate the number of days between the two dates. The statement uses the Math.floor() method to convert the value to only the whole number portion of the difference. The second statement places the daysUntil value in the countdown element on the page.

3. Below the statements you entered in the previous step, add the following code:

```
1   // hours
2   var fractionalDay = (dateTo - dateFrom) % 86400000;
3   var hoursUntil = Math.floor(fractionalDay / 3600000);
4   if (hoursUntil < 10) {
5       hoursUntil = "0" + hoursUntil;
6   }
7   document.getElementById("countdown").innerHTML +=↵
8       ":" + hoursUntil;
```

The fractionalDay variable uses the modulus (%) operator to find the remainder from calculating the number of days. To calculate the hoursUntil variable, the fractionalDay variable is divided by 3600000 (the number of microseconds in an hour), and the Math.floor() method again provides just the whole number portion of the result. The final `if` statement checks if the number of minutes is a single digit and if so, appends a 0 to the start of the number; this is to represent the format generally seen in digital clocks. The final statement appends the `hoursUntil` value to the existing days value in the countdown element, with a colon between the two.

4. Below the statements you entered in the previous step, add the following code:

```
1   // minutes
2   var fractionalHour = fractionalDay % 3600000;
3   var minutesUntil = Math.floor(fractionalHour / 60000);
4   if (minutesUntil < 10) {
5       minutesUntil = "0" + minutesUntil;
6   }
7   document.getElementById("countdown").innerHTML +=↵
8       ":" + minutesUntil;
9   // seconds
10  var fractionalMinute = fractionalHour % 60000;
11  var secondsUntil = Math.floor(fractionalMinute / 1000);
12  if (secondsUntil < 10) {
13      secondsUntil = "0" + secondsUntil;
14  }
15  document.getElementById("countdown").innerHTML +=↵
16      ":" + secondsUntil;
```

This code uses the same sets of statements used to calculate the hours, dividing by 60000 (the number of microseconds in a minute) to calculate the remaining difference in minutes, and 1000 (the number of microseconds in a second) to calculate the remaining difference in seconds. Your `updateCountdown()` function should match the following:

```
1   function updateCountdown() {
2       var dateToday = new Date();
3       var dateFrom = Date.UTC(dateToday.getFullYear(),↵
4           dateToday.getMonth(), dateToday.getDate(),↵
5           dateToday.getHours(), dateToday.getMinutes(),↵
6           dateToday.getSeconds());
7       var dateTo = Date.UTC(dateObject.getFullYear(),↵
8           dateObject.getMonth(), dateObject.getDate(),↵
9           19, 0, 0); // all launches at 8:00pm UTC
10      // days
```

```
11      var daysUntil = Math.floor((dateTo - dateFrom) / 86400000);
12      document.getElementById("countdown").innerHTML = daysUntil;
13      // hours
14      var fractionalDay = (dateTo - dateFrom) % 86400000,
15          hoursUntil = Math.floor(fractionalDay / 3600000);
16      if (hoursUntil < 10) {
17          hoursUntil = "0" + hoursUntil;
18      }
19      document.getElementById("countdown").innerHTML +=↵
20          ":" + hoursUntil;
21      // minutes
22      var fractionalHour = fractionalDay % 3600000,
23          minutesUntil = Math.floor(fractionalHour / 60000);
24      if (minutesUntil < 10) {
25          minutesUntil = "0" + minutesUntil;
26      }
27      document.getElementById("countdown").innerHTML +=↵
28          ":" + minutesUntil;
29      // seconds
30      var fractionalMinute = fractionalHour % 60000,
31          secondsUntil = Math.floor(fractionalMinute / 1000);
32      if (secondsUntil < 10) {
33          secondsUntil = "0" + secondsUntil;
34      }
35      document.getElementById("countdown").innerHTML +=↵
36          ":" + secondsUntil;
37   }
```

5. At the top of the document, in the global variables section, add the following statement:

```
var countdown;
```

6. Within the `selectDate()` function, just before the closing }, enter the following statements:

```
countdown = setInterval(updateCountdown, 1000);
document.getElementById("countdownSection").style.display =↵
    "block";
```

The first statement uses the `setInterval()` method of the `Window` object to call the `updateCountdown()` function when a user selects a valid date, and to repeatedly call the function every second (every 1000 milliseconds). This simulates the behavior of a digital timer. The `setInterval()` method is set as the value of the global countdown variable so it can be cancelled later. The second statement makes the web page element containing the counter visible.

7. Within the `updateCountdown()` function, just before the `// days` comment, enter the following code:

```
1    if ((dateTo - dateFrom) < 1000) { // time will be less than 0↵
2       when setInterval runs next
3       clearInterval(countdown);
4       document.getElementById("countdownSection").style.↵
5          display = "none";
6    }
```

This `if` statement checks if the time left will be less than 0 on the next update. If so, it uses the `clearInterval()` method to clear the interval referenced by the `countdown` variable.

8. Save your changes to **orbits.js**, shift-refresh or shift-reload **booktrip.htm** in your browser to clear the form, click the **Pick a date** box, and then click a future date. As Figure 7-11 shows, the countdown timer is displayed on the right side of the page, and the time value changes once per second.

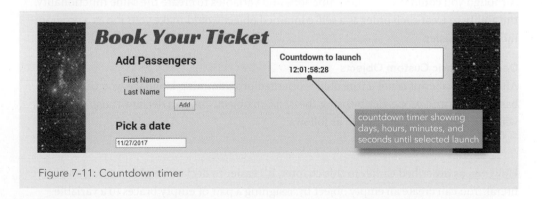

Figure 7-11: Countdown timer

Short Quiz 2

1. What code creates a `dateToday` variable and assigns the current date and time as its value?

2. Which method of the `Number` class do you use to convert a number to a string that is formatted with local numeric formatting style?

3. What is the result of applying the `floor()` method of the `Math` class to a numeric value?

Defining Custom JavaScript Objects

JavaScript is not a true object-oriented programming language. You can base objects in your programs on built-in JavaScript classes such as the `Array` and `Date` objects. However, you cannot create your own classes in JavaScript. For this reason, JavaScript is said to be an object-based programming language instead of an object-oriented programming language.

Nevertheless JavaScript does allow you to define your own custom objects. Unlike objects that are based on classes, custom objects in JavaScript are not encapsulated, which means that other programmers who use your custom object can see inside of the black box. Even though custom JavaScript objects cannot be encapsulated, you may find them useful, especially if you need to replicate the same functionality an unknown number of times in a script. For example, you may have a web site that allows customers to place online orders for items you sell. For each order, you may want to create a new object that uses properties to store information such as the customer's name, order date, payment method, shipping date, and so on. The object may also contain methods that calculate sales tax and sales total. Although you could use standard functions and variables to create the same functionality, the ability to treat each order as a self-contained object would make your job as a programmer a little easier.

Declaring Basic Custom Objects

Although JavaScript is not a true object-oriented programming language, you can create basic objects and properties by using the `Object` object. You can declare a custom object with the `Object()` constructor, as follows:

```
var objectName = new Object();
```

However, as described earlier in this chapter, it's easier to declare an object using an object literal. You can create an empty object by assigning a pair of empty braces to a variable name, as follows:

```
var objectName = {};
```

You can add a property to an object using dot syntax by specifying the object name followed by a dot and the property name, and then an equal sign and the value. For instance, you could use the following object literal to create an empty object named `InventoryList`:

```
var InventoryList = {};
```

You could then create an `inventoryDate` property within the `InventoryList` object and assign it a value using the following statement:

```
InventoryList.inventoryDate = new Date(2017, 11, 31);
```

One reason that creating objects using literals is generally preferred, however, is that you can declare an object and its properties all in a single statement with a literal. To declare a property within an object literal, you specify the property name within the braces followed by a colon and its value. You separate multiple property-value pairs with commas. The following code creates the `InventoryList` object and adds the `inventoryDate` property in a single statement:

```
var InventoryList = {
    inventoryDate: new Date(2017, 11, 31)
};
```

Note that even though this statement occupies multiple lines, it's still a single statement, and therefore must end with a semicolon. Also note that the final property name—in this case, the only property name—has no comma after it, and because a property declaration isn't a statement, it also doesn't end with a semicolon.

The following code creates a new object named `PerformanceTickets` and assigns four properties to it: `customerName`, `performanceName`, `ticketQuantity`, and `performanceDate`. You can access the values assigned to each property the same as you would for other types of objects, as demonstrated with the statements that assign innerHTML values. Notice that the `performanceDate` property is created as a `Date` object that stores the date and time of the performance. Figure 7-12 shows the output.

```
1   var PerformanceTickets = {
2       customerName: "Claudia Salomon",
3       performanceName: "Swan Lake",
4       ticketQuantity: 2,
5       performanceDate: new Date(2017, 6, 18, 20)
6   };
7   document.getElementById("custName").innerHTML =↵
8       PerformanceTickets.customerName;
9   document.getElementById("showName").innerHTML =↵
10      PerformanceTickets.performanceName;
11  document.getElementById("tixNum").innerHTML =↵
12      PerformanceTickets.ticketQuantity;
13  document.getElementById("showDate").innerHTML =↵
14      PerformanceTickets.performanceDate.toLocaleString();
```

Claudia Salomon

Swan Lake

2

Tue Jul 18 20:00:00 2017

Figure 7-12: Output using `PerformanceTickets` object values

The final feature you need to add to the Outer Orbits reservation page is a section summarizing the user's selections. This includes listing the name of each passenger, the selected launch date, and the payment plan. You'll create an object with the name `ticket` that will contain all of this information as a set of properties.

To create a custom ticket object containing passenger and launch data:

1. Return to the **orbits.js** document in your text editor, and then at the top of the document, add the following global variable declaration:

```
1   var ticket = {
2       date: "",
3       fName: "",
```

```
4        lName: ""
5    };
```

This code creates a new variable with the name `ticket`. The braces (`{ }`) around the value of this variable indicate that it's an object. The ticket object definition contains three properties: `date`, `fName`, and `lName`. Each property is assigned an empty string (`""`) as its value.

Caution

The first two property values should be followed by commas, not semicolons. The final property value should not be followed by any punctuation. The object value must end with a closing }, and the entire `var` statement must end with a semicolon.

2. Above the `createEventListeners()` function, add the following code to create the `registerName()` function and declare variables:

```
1    function registerName() {
2        var passengerList = document.getElementById("passengers");
3        var passengerName = document.createElement("li");
4    }
```

The `var` statement first creates a reference to the `passengers` element with the `passengerList` variable, and then it creates a new `li` element as an unattached document node and assigns it to the name `passengerName`.

3. Below the code from the previous step, add the following statements to the function:

```
ticket.fName = document.getElementById("fname").value;
ticket.lName = document.getElementById("lname").value;
```

The first statement assigns the value of the `fname` field in the form to the `fName` property of the `ticket` object. The second statement does the same for the `lname` field in the form and the `lName` property of the `ticket` object.

4. Below the code from the previous step, add the following statements to the function:

```
1    // add entered name to passenger list in ticket section
2    passengerName.innerHTML = ticket.fName + " " +↵
3        ticket.lName;
4    passengerList.appendChild(passengerName);
```

The first statement assigns the values of the `fName` and `lName` properties of the `ticket` object as the content of the `passengerName` element, with a space between the two values. The second statement appends the `passengerName` element to the `passengerList` element.

5. Below the code from the previous step, add the following statements to the function:

```
1   // clear first and last names from form
2   document.getElementById("fname").value = "";
3   document.getElementById("lname").value = "";
4   // display ticket and passengers section
5   document.getElementById("ticket").style.display = "block";
6   document.getElementById("passengersSection").style.display =↵
7      "block";
8   // return focus to First Name field to facilitate entry of
9   // another passenger name
10  document.getElementById("fname").focus();
```

6. In the `createEventListeners()` function, before the closing `}`, add the following code:

```
1   var nameButton = document.getElementById("addName");
2   if (nameButton.addEventListener) {
3     nameButton.addEventListener("click", registerName, false);
4   } else if (nameButton.attachEvent) {
5     nameButton.attachEvent("onclick", registerName);
6   }
```

This code registers an event listener to call the `registerName()` function whenever the Add button is clicked.

7. Within the `selectDate()` function, before the closing `}`, add the following code:

```
1   ticket.date = dateObject.toLocaleDateString();
2   document.getElementById("selectedDate").innerHTML =↵
3      ticket.date;
4   document.getElementById("dateSection").style.display =↵
5      "block";
```

The first statement sets the value of the `date` property of the `ticket` object to the date value of `dateObject` with local formatting conventions. The second statement then assigns the value of the `date` property of the ticket object as the text content of the `selectedDate` element. The third statement makes the element with the `id` value `dateSection` visible on the page.

8. Save your changes to **orbits.js**, shift-refresh or shift-reload **booktrip.htm** in your browser to clear the form, type your first name in the First Name box, type your last name in the Last Name box, click the **Add** button, click the **Pick a date** box, and then select a date. As Figure 7-13 shows, your name and the selected date are displayed on the right side of the page under the heading "Ticket Details."

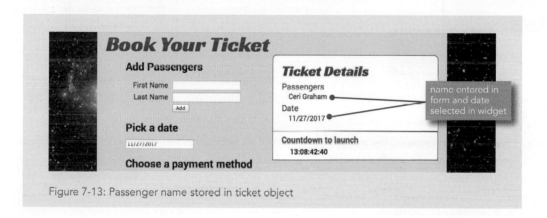

Figure 7-13: Passenger name stored in ticket object

9. Open your browser console and, if necessary, navigate to the command line.

10. Type **ticket**, and then press **Enter**. The console returns "Object" (or "object Object"), signifying that the value of the variable name you entered is an object.

11. If necessary, click **Object** to view the object's property names and values. Figure 7-14 shows the results in the major browsers.

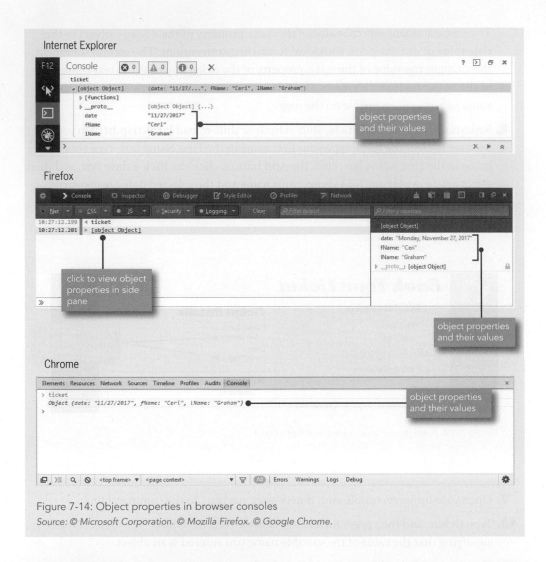

Figure 7-14: Object properties in browser consoles

Source: © Microsoft Corporation. © Mozilla Firefox. © Google Chrome.

Declaring Sub-Objects

In addition to strings or numeric values, object properties also support other types of values. The value of a property can be another object, which is known as a **sub-object**. For instance, the following code creates an object named `order` with a sub-object named `address`:

```
1   var order = {
2       orderNumber: "F5987",
3       address: {
4           street: "1 Main St",
```

```
5        city: "Farmington",
6        state: "NY",
7        zip: "14425"
8      }
9   };
```

The main object, with the name order, has two properties: orderNumber and address. The address property is itself a sub-object, and has four properties of its own: street, city, state, and zip.

Next you'll edit the definition of the ticket object to create a sub-object with the name passengers, containing the fname and lname properties.

To create the passengers sub-object:

1. Return to the **orbits.js** document in your text editor.

2. At the top of the document, within the global variable declaration, add a new line after the date property, and then type passengers: {

3. Increase the indent level for the fName and lName property definitions.

4. Add a new line after the lName property, and then type }. Your updated global variable declaration should match the following:

```
1   var dateObject = new Date(),
2       ticket = {
3          date: "",
4          passengers: {
5             fName: "",
6             lName: ""
7          }
8       };
```

The ticket object now has two properties, date and passengers. The passengers property is a sub-object of the ticket object, and the passengers property has two properties of its own: fName and lName.

5. Scroll down to the registerName() function. In the statement just below the first comment change ticket.fName to **ticket.passengers.fName**, and then in the statement that follows, change ticket.lName to **ticket.passengers.lName**.

6. In the statement just below the second comment, change `ticket.fName` to **ticket. passengers.fName**, and then change `ticket.lName` to **ticket.passengers. lName**. The start of your updated `registerName()` function should match the following:

```
1    function registerName() {
2        var passengerList = document.getElementById("passengers");
3        var passengerName = document.createElement("li");
4        // add first+last names to ticket object as new properties
5        ticket.passengers.fName =↵
6            document.getElementById("fname").value;
7        ticket.passengers.lName =↵
8            document.getElementById("lname").value;
9        // add entered name to passenger list in ticket section
10       passengerName.innerHTML = ticket.passengers.fName +↵
11           " " + ticket.passengers.lName;
12       passengerList.appendChild(passengerName);
```

7. Save your changes to **orbits.js**, shift-refresh or shift-reload **booktrip.htm** in your browser to clear the form, type your first name in the First Name box, type your last name in the Last Name box, click the **Add** button, click the **Pick a date** box, and then select a date. Your name and the selected date are again displayed on the right side of the page under the heading "Ticket Details."

8. At the command line, type **ticket**, and then press **Enter**.

9. Click the word **Object** or click the **triangle** next to the word "Object" to see the object properties, and then click the **triangle** next to the word "passengers" to see the properties of the sub-object. Figure 7-15 shows the results in the major browsers.

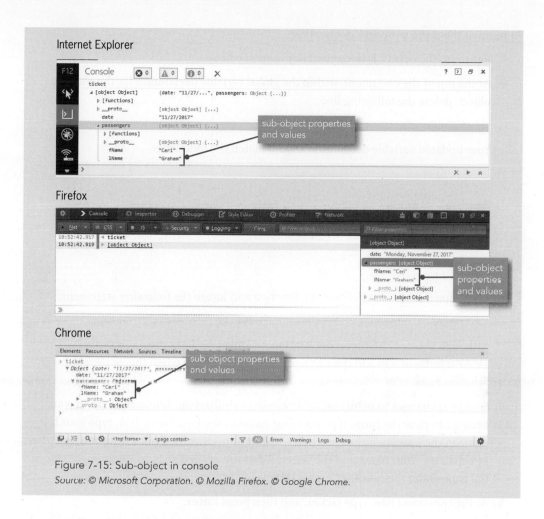

Internet Explorer

Firefox

Chrome

Figure 7-15: Sub-object in console

Source: © Microsoft Corporation. © Mozilla Firefox. © Google Chrome.

Adding Properties to an Existing Object

Although you can declare properties within an object definition, it's not required. As an alternative, you can add a new property simply by declaring its value. This is similar to the process of creating a new variable; however, unlike in a variable declaration, you don't use `var` or any other keyword to create a new object property.

For instance, to add a `shippingSpeed` property to the `order` object, you could use the following statement:

```
order.shippingSpeed = "overnight";
```

You'll remove the `date` property declaration from the `ticket` object in the orbits.js document, and then you'll verify that the property is still created by the existing code.

To remove the `date` property declaration:

1. Return to the **orbits.js** document in your text editor.

2. At the top of the document, within the global variable declaration for the `ticket` object, delete the following line:

```
date: "",
```

Your updated variable declaration should match the following:

```
1    var ticket = {
2            passengers: {
3                fName: "",
4                lName: ""
5            }
6        };
```

3. Scroll down to the `selectDate()` function and locate the following statement:

```
ticket.date = dateObject.toLocaleDateString();
```

Although the `ticket` object declaration no longer declares the `date` property, the above statement will add the `date` property to the object when the `selectDate()` function runs.

4. Save your changes to **orbits.js**, shift-refresh or shift-reload **booktrip.htm** in your browser to clear the form, type your first name in the First Name box, type your last name in the Last Name box, click the **Add** button, click the **Pick a date** box, and then select a date. Your name and the selected date are again displayed on the right side of the page under the heading "Ticket Details."

5. At the command line, type **ticket**, and then press **Enter**.

6. Click the word **Object** or click the **triangle** next to the word "Object" to see the object properties, and then click the **triangle** next to the word "passengers" to see the properties of the sub-object. The ticket object includes the `date` property added by the `selectDate()` function, and the object properties still match those shown earlier in Figure 7-15.

Referring to Object Properties as Associative Arrays

In a standard array, you can reference any value by its index number, which starts at 0 for the first array element and increments by 1 for each additional element. For instance, for the array

```
var stopLightColors = ["red","yellow","green"];
```

you could reference the second element, "yellow", with the code

```
stopLightColors[1];
```

JavaScript allows you to refer to object properties using associative array syntax. An **associative array** is an array whose elements are referred to with an alphanumeric key instead of an index number. For an object, the property name takes the place of an index number when using this syntax. For instance, if you instead stored the stoplight colors in an object, it might look as follows:

```
1    var stopLightColors = {
2        stop: "red",
3        caution: "yellow",
4        go: "green"
5    };
```

You've already seen how to refer to object property values with dot syntax using property names. You could reference the value for the caution property value using its property name, as follows:

```
stopLightColors.caution
```

Using associative array syntax, you instead put the property name in square brackets and enclose it in quotes, as follows:

```
stopLightColors["caution"]
```

Both dot syntax and associative array syntax return the value of the referenced property. To simply reference a property value, it's almost always easier to use dot syntax. However, associative array syntax can be powerful when an object contains multiple properties with similar names that also incorporate numbers. For instance, an object containing items in a customer's order might be structured as follows:

```
1    var order = {
2        item1: "KJ2435J",
3        price1: 23.95,
4        item2: "AW23454",
5        price2: 44.99,
6        item3: "2346J3B",
7        price3: 9.95
8    };
```

When creating an order summary, instead of referencing each property value with a separate statement, you could use a `for` loop like the following:

```
1    for (var i = 1; i < 4; i++) {
2        document.getElementById("itemList").innerHTML +=↵
3            "<p class='item'>" + order["item" + i] + "</p>";
4        document.getElementById("itemList").innerHTML +=↵
5            "<p class='price'>" + order["price" + i] + "</p>";
6    }
```

Associative array syntax also enables you to write generic code to add new object properties that incorporate numbers. For instance, if the customer with the order shown above decided to add an additional item to her shopping cart, your code could easily extend the order object with additional properties using the following code:

```
1    totalItems += 1; // increment counter of items in order
2    currentItem = document.getElementById("itemName").innerHTML;
3    currentPrice = document.getElementById("itemPrice").innerHTML;
4    newItemPropertyName = "item" + totalItems; // "item4"
5    newPricePropertyName = "price" + totalItems; // "price4"
6    order.newItemPropertyName = currentItem;
7    // order.item4 = (name)
8    order.newPricePropertyName = currentPrice;
9    // order.price4 = (price)
```

Because there should be no limit to the number of items a customer can order, this code enables your object to grow to incorporate details on as many items as a customer wants to purchase.

Outer Orbits wants users to be able to add as many people as they want to a single ticket. To make this possible, you'll remove the declarations for the `fName` and `lName` properties from the `ticket` object declaration, and you'll add code that uses associative array syntax to create numbered versions of these properties as necessary each time a user adds a passenger to the ticket.

To use associative array syntax to add numbered properties to the `ticket` object:

1. Return to the **orbits.js** document in your text editor.

2. At the top of the document, within the global variable declaration, remove the declarations for the `fName` and `lName` properties.

3. Before the declaration for the `passengers` property, add a declaration for the `passengersOnTicket` property with a value of 0, as follows:

```
1    var dateObject = new Date();
2    var ticket = {
3          passengersOnTicket: 0,
4          passengers: {}
5       };
```

The `ticket` object now has just two declared properties: `passengersOnTicket`, which will serve as a counter variable, and `passengers`, which is an empty sub-object.

4. Scroll down to the `registerName()` function, and then add declarations for the `newFnameProp` and `newLnameProp` variables without declaring values, as follows:

```
1    var passengerList = document.getElementById("passengers");
2    var passengerName = document.createElement("li");
3    var newFnameProp;
4    var newLnameProp;
```

5. Below the final `var` statement, add the following three statements:

```
ticket.passengersOnTicket += 1;
newFnameProp = "fname" + ticket.passengersOnTicket;
newLnameProp = "lname" + ticket.passengersOnTicket;
```

Because the `registerName()` function runs each time a user adds a passenger, the first statement increments the `passengersOnTicket` counter property by 1. The `newFnameProp` constructs a name for a new property that will store the new passenger's first name, concatenating the string "fname" with the current value of the `passengersOnTicket` property. For the first passenger, this will create a property value of `fname1`. The third statement does the same for the passenger's last name, creating a property value of `lname1` for the first passenger.

6. In the statement after the first comment, change `ticket.passengers.fName` to **`ticket.passengers[newFnameProp]`**. In the statement that follows, change `ticket.passengers.lName` to **`ticket.passengers[newLnameProp]`**, and then in the statement after the second comment, repeat both changes. The start of your updated `registerName()` function should match the following:

```
1    function registerName() {
2        var passengerList = document.getElementById("passengers");
3        var passengerName = document.createElement("li");
4        var newFnameProp;
5        var newLnameProp;
6        ticket.passengersOnTicket += 1;
7        newFnameProp = "fname" + ticket.passengersOnTicket;
8        newLnameProp = "lname" + ticket.passengersOnTicket;
9        // add first+last names to ticket object as new properties
10       ticket.passengers[newFnameProp] =↵
11           document.getElementById("fname").value;
12       ticket.passengers[newLnameProp] =↵
13           document.getElementById("lname").value;
14       // add entered name to passenger list in ticket section
15       passengerName.innerHTML =↵
16           ticket.passengers[newFnameProp] + " " +↵
17           ticket.passengers[newLnameProp];
18       passengerList.appendChild(passengerName);
```

7. Save your changes to **orbits.js**, shift-refresh or shift-reload **booktrip.htm** in your browser to clear the form, type your first name in the First Name box, type your last name in the Last Name box, click the **Add** button, click the **Pick a date** box, and then select a date. Your name and the selected date are again displayed on the right side of the page under the heading "Ticket Details."

8. At the command line, type **ticket**, and then press **Enter**.

9. Click the word **Object** or click the **triangle** next to the word "Object" to see the object properties, and then click the **triangle** next to the word "passengers" to see the properties of the sub-object. The `passengers` sub-object now includes the properties `fname1` and `lname1` added by the `selectDate()` function. Figure 7-16 shows the object structure in Internet Explorer.

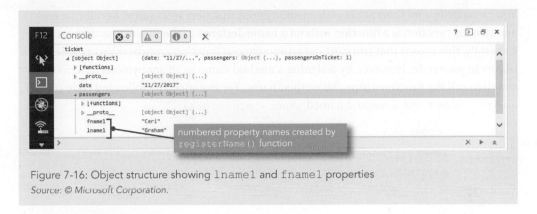

Figure 7-16: Object structure showing `lname1` and `fname1` properties
Source: © Microsoft Corporation.

10. Type another first name in the First Name box, type another last name in the Last Name box, and then click the **Add** button. The second name is added to the right side of the page below the first name.

11. At the command line, type **ticket**, press **Enter**, and then expand the `ticket` object and the `passengers` sub-object. As Figure 7-17 shows, the `passengers` sub-object now contains both names you added, stored in the properties `fname1`, `fname2`, `lname1`, and `lname2`.

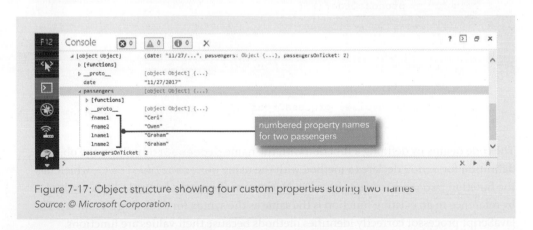

Figure 7-17: Object structure showing four custom properties storing two names
Source: © Microsoft Corporation.

Creating Methods

In addition to properties, objects in JavaScript can also have methods. A method of a custom object is simply a function that is assigned a name within the object.

There are two ways to add a method to an object: by providing code for the method in the object, or by referencing an external function.

You can specify a method name with an anonymous function as its value. Recall that an anonymous function is a function without a name declared in the function statement. Generally, this means that you can't use an anonymous function anywhere except where it occurs in your code. However, by assigning a method name to an anonymous function, you can then call the function using the method name. For instance, the following code creates an `order` object with a method named `generateInvoice()`:

```
1   var order = {
2       items: {},
3       generateInvoice: function() {
4           // function statements
5       }
6   };
```

Even though the `generateInvoice()` method is created using an anonymous function, you can call the `generateInvoice()` method using the statement

```
order.generateInvoice;
```

Another way to declare a method is to specify a method name and use the name of an existing function as its value, as in the following code:

```
1   function processOrder() {
2       // function statements
3   }
4   var order = {
5       items: {},
6       generateInvoice: processOrder
7   };
```

The code begins by defining a function with the name `processOrder`. Then the object definition for `order` declares a method with the name `generateInvoice()`, which has the function `processOrder` as its value. Notice that the syntax for declaring a method by reference to an existing function is the same as the syntax for declaring a property. The JavaScript processor correctly identifies methods because their values are functions.

Also notice that the `processOrder()` function is referenced without parentheses at the end. Using the code shown below to declare a method would not be valid because it includes parentheses.

Not valid code:

```
generateInvoice: processOrder()
```

Because the `updateTotalCost()` function operates on the `passengersOnTicket` property of the `ticket` object, you'll add a method to the `ticket` object that references the `updateTotalCost()` function. You'll then change the function call to use the object method.

To add the `updateTotalCost()` function as a method of the `ticket` object:

1. Return to the **orbits.js** document in your text editor.

2. At the top of the document, within the global variable declaration, add a **comma** at the end of the line that declares the `passengers` property, and then below it, add the code **calcCost: updateTotalCost** as shown below:

```
1    var dateObject = new Date();
2    var ticket = {
3         passengersOnTicket: 0,
4         passengers: {},
5         calcCost: updateTotalCost
6    };
```

3. Scroll down to the `updateTotalCost()` function, and then change the value for the `totalCost` variable to **this.passengersOnTicket * 250000**, as shown below:

```
1    function updateTotalCost() {
2         var totalCost = this.passengersOnTicket * 250000;
3         var monthlyCost = totalCost / 60;
4         var shortMonthlyCost = monthlyCost.toFixed(0);
```

The **this keyword** references the object that called the function where this statement is located. Because your code will use the `calcCost()` method of the `ticket` object to call this function, the `this` keyword in the statement you changed will refer to the `ticket` object, making the value equivalent to `ticket.passengersOnTicket * 250000`.

4. Scroll up to the `registerName()` function, and then on a new line before the closing `}`, enter the statement **ticket.calcCost();**. This statement calls the `calcCost()` method of the `ticket` object.

5. Scroll up to the `selectDate()` function, and then in the last line of the function, remove the statement `updateTotalCost()`. You've incorporated code to update the cost each time a name is added to the ticket, so you no longer need to call the function when a date is selected.

6. Save your changes to **orbits.js**, shift-refresh or shift-reload **booktrip.htm** in your browser to clear the form, type your first and last names in the name boxes, and then click **Add**. The labels under "Choose a payment method" are updated with rates for one passenger.

7. Type another first and last name in the name boxes, and then click **Add**. As Figure 7-18 shows, the labels under "Choose a payment method" are again updated, now displaying the rates for two passengers.

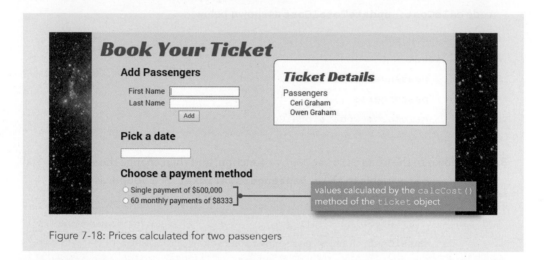

Figure 7-18: Prices calculated for two passengers

Programming Concepts | *Using the* `this` *Keyword*

Using the `this` keyword to calculate the total cost in your program has no great advantage over referencing the object name directly. However, it can be used to great effect in a program that includes multiple objects. For instance, if Outer Orbits added features to the reservations page that enabled users to view details on multiple tickets that they had purchased, the `this` keyword would enable the `updateTotalCost()` function to calculate the correct price for whichever object had called it, rather than referring only to a single hard-coded object. The following code illustrates this scenario, with two objects named `ticket1` and `ticket2`, each with a different value for `passengersOnTicket` and both with a `calcCost()` method that calls the

Continued on next page...

`updateTotalCost()` function. The two statements at the bottom show the results of calling the `calcCost()` method of each object.

```
1    var ticket1 = {
2        passengersOnTicket: 1,
3        calcCost: updateTotalCost
4    };
5    var ticket2 = {
6        passengersOnTicket: 3,
7        calcCost: updateTotalCost
8    };
9    ticket1.calcCost(); // 250000
10   ticket2.calcCost(); // 750000
```

The method for each object would calculate a different cost, even though both reference the same generic function: `updateTotalCost()`.

Enumerating Custom Object Properties

Some custom objects can contain dozens of properties. For example, a script may create new custom object properties that store sales prices for each item a customer wants to purchase. Suppose that you want to discount the individual sales prices by 10 percent of any items that cost more than $100. Because there is no way to determine in advance which items a customer will purchase, you have no way of knowing which properties have been added to the object for each individual customer. To execute the same statement or command block for all the properties within a custom object, you can use the **for/in statement**, which is a looping statement similar to the `for` statement. The syntax of the `for/in` statement is as follows:

```
for (variable in object) {
    statement(s);
}
```

The variable name in the `for/in` statement holds an individual object property. The object name in the constructor represents the name of an object that has been instantiated in a program. Unlike the other loop statements, the `for/in` statement does not require a counter or any other type of code to control how the loop functions. Instead, the `for/in` statement automatically assigns each property in an object to the variable name, performs the necessary statements on the property, then moves to the next property and starts over. The `for/in` statement ends automatically once it reaches the last property in an object.

One of the benefits of the `for/in` statement is that it **enumerates**, or assigns an index to, each property in an object. This is similar to the way elements in an array are indexed. You can use an enumerated object property to access the values contained within object properties. A typical use of the `for/in` statement is to validate the properties within an object. For instance, the following code checks if any of the properties has an empty string as a value, and if so, it calls the `generateErrorMessage()` method. The `if` statement refers to the `prop` variable as an index of the `order` object:

```
1   var item = {
2       itemNumber: "KJ2435J",
3       itemPrice: 23.95,
4       itemInstock: true,
5       itemShipDate: new Date(2017, 6, 18),
6   };
7   for (prop in order) {
8       if (order[prop] === "") {
9           order.generateErrorMessage();
10      }
11  }
```

In the preceding code, the variable name `prop` holds the names of each property in the `order` object. Each iteration of the `for/in` statement in the preceding code checks the value of a property. The code passes the `order` object to the `if` statement, along with the `prop` variable enclosed in brackets (`order[prop]`).

Sometimes program errors are caused by using the wrong object properties or by assigning the wrong value to an object property. You can use a `for/in` loop with `console.log()` statements to determine if values are being assigned to the correct properties in an object. This technique is useful when you have an object with many properties and you cannot trace the cause of incorrect values being assigned to properties.

Deleting Properties

You saw earlier how to add a property to a custom object by using a statement to declare it and assign it a value, as in the following statement:

```
ticket.date = dateObject.toLocaleDateString();
```

You can likewise use a statement to delete a property of a custom object. To do so, you use the delete operator with the syntax `delete object.property`. For example, the following statement deletes the itemInStock property of the order object:

```
delete order.itemInStock;
```

Defining Constructor Functions

Another way to define your own custom objects is by using a **constructor function**, which is a function that is used as the basis for a custom object. (Another term for constructor function is **object definition**.) As with traditional class-based objects, JavaScript objects inherit all the variables and statements of the constructor function on which they are based. Any JavaScript function can serve as a constructor.

> ## Best Practices
> *Deciding Whether to Use a Constructor Function or an Object Literal*
>
> The main difference between creating an object with an object literal and using a constructor function is that the constructor function serves as a template, enabling you to create any number of objects with the same set of properties and methods defined in the constructor function.
>
> The following code defines a function named `Order()` with four parameters that can serve as a constructor function:
>
> ```
> function Order(number, order, payment, ship) {
>     // statement(s);
> }
> ```
>
> You then use a `var` statement to instantiate an instance of the function, just as you do when using the constructor function for a built-in JavaScript object such as `Date`. For instance, to create an instance of the `Order` object named `shoppingBasket`, you would use the following statement:
>
> ```
> var shoppingBasket = new Order();
> ```
>
> If you need to create a unique object in a program, an object literal is the easiest solution. However, if your program will require multiple instances of an object with the same properties and methods, then creating a constructor function is more efficient.

Adding Properties to a Constructor Function

To add a property to a constructor function, you must add a statement to the function body that uses the `this` keyword with the following syntax: `this.property_name = value;`. In the case of a custom JavaScript object, the `this` keyword refers to the object that calls the constructor function. For example, the following constructor function includes four properties: `customerNumber`, `orderDate`, `paymentMethod`, and `shippingDate`.

```
1    function Order(number, order, payment, ship) {
2        this.customerNumber = number;
3        this.orderDate = order;
4        this.paymentMethod = payment;
5        this.shippingDate = ship;
6    }
```

The statements in the preceding constructor function use the `this` keyword to assign the values of the four arguments (`number`, `order`, `payment`, and `ship`) to the `customerNumber`, `orderDate`, `paymentMethod`, and `shippingDate` properties of whichever object called the function.

Adding Methods to a Constructor Function

You can create a function that will be used as an object method by referring to any object properties it contains with the `this` reference. For example, the following code defines a method that prints the `customerNumber`, `orderDate`, `paymentMethod`, and `shippingDate` properties of the `Order` constructor:

```
1    function displayOrderInfo() {
2        var summaryDiv = document.getElementById("summarySection");
3        summaryDiv.innerHTML += ("<p>Customer: " +↵
4            this.customerNumber + "</p>");
5        summaryDiv.innerHTML += ("<p>Order Date: " +↵
6            this.orderDate.toLocaleString()+ "</p>");
7        summaryDiv.innerHTML += ("<p>Payment: " +↵
8            this.paymentMethod + "</p>");
9        summaryDiv.innerHTML += ("<p>Ship Date: " +↵
10           this.shippingDate.toLocaleString() + "</p>");
11   }
```

After a method is created, it must be added to the constructor function, using the syntax `this.methodname = functionname;`. The `methodname` following the `this` reference is the name that is being assigned to the function within the object. Remember not to include the parentheses following the function name, as you would when calling a function in JavaScript. The statement `this.methodname = functionname();` is incorrect, because it includes parentheses. To add the `displayOrderInfo()` function to the `Order` object constructor definition as a method named `showOrder()`, you include the statement `this.showOrder = displayOrderInfo;` within the function definition braces.

The following code shows the `Order()` constructor function, the `displayOrderInfo()` function that creates the `showOrder()` method, and a statement that instantiates an `Order` object and prints the values of its properties.

```
1   function Order(number, order, payment, ship) {
2       this.customerNumber = number;
3       this.orderDate = order;
4       this.paymentMethod = payment;
5       this.shippingDate = ship;
6       this.showOrder = displayOrderInfo;
7   }
8   function displayOrderInfo() {
9       var summaryDiv = document.getElementById("summarySection");
10      summaryDiv.innerHTML += ("<p>Customer: " +↵
11          this.customerNumber + "</p>");
12      summaryDiv.innerHTML += ("<p>Order Date: " +↵
13          this.orderDate.toLocaleString()+ "</p>");
14      summaryDiv.innerHTML += ("<p>Payment: " +↵
15          this.paymentMethod + "</p>");
16      summaryDiv.innerHTML += ("<p>Ship Date: " +↵
17          this.shippingDate.toLocaleString() + "</p>");
18  }
19  var shoppingBasket = new Order("KJ2435J",↵
20      new Date(2017, 6, 17), "visa", new Date(2017, 6, 18));
21  shoppingBasket.showOrder();
```

Using the `prototype` Property

As explained earlier, an object inherits the properties and methods of the constructor function from which it is instantiated. When you instantiate a new object named `shoppingBasket`, based on the `Order` constructor function, the new object includes the `customerNumber`, `orderDate`, `paymentMethod`, and `shippingDate` properties along with the `showOrder()` method. After instantiating a new object, you can assign additional properties to the object, using dot syntax. The following code creates a new object based on the `Order` constructor function, then assigns to the object a new property named `trackingNumber`.

```
var shoppingBasket = new Order("KJ2435J",↵
    new Date(2017, 6, 17), "visa", new Date(2017, 6, 18));
shoppingBasket.trackingNumber = "Z205684738929";
```

When you add a new property to an object that has been instantiated from a constructor function, the new property is available only to that specific object; the property is not available to the constructor function or to any other objects that were instantiated from the same constructor function. However, if you use the `prototype` property with the name of the constructor function, any new properties you create will also be available to the constructor function and any objects instantiated from it. The **prototype property** is a built-in property that specifies the constructor from which an object was instantiated. The following code uses the `prototype` property to add the `trackingNumber` property to the `Order` constructor function. By using the `prototype` property, you ensure that all objects that extend the `Order` constructor function also have access to the `trackingNumber` property.

```
var shoppingBasket = new Order("KJ2435J",↵
    new Date(2017, 6, 17), "visa", new Date(2017, 6, 18));
shoppingBasket.prototype.trackingNumber = "Z205684738929";
```

Object definitions can use the `prototype` property to extend other object definitions. That is to say, you can create a new object based on an existing object. The new object inherits the properties and methods of the original object. You can then add additional properties and methods to the new object that will not be available to the existing object. Consider an object definition named `Event` that contains generic properties and methods that might be used for planning an event. You may need to create additional object definitions that extend `Event` and that contain properties and methods specific to certain types of events. To extend one object definition (the derived object definition) from another object definition (the base object definition), you append the `prototype` property to the derived object definition, followed by the new keyword and the name of the base object definition using the following syntax:

```
derived_object.prototype = new base_object();
```

The following code shows an example of a GraduationEvent object definition that extends the Event object definition. The Event class definition contains some generic properties—eventLocation, eventDate, and eventCost—that apply to all types of events, along with a calcEventCost() method that calculates the cost of an event. The GraduationEvent class includes guestOfHonor and schoolName properties along with a showEventDetails() method.

```
1    function Event(location, date) {
2        this.eventLocation = location;
3        this.eventDate = date;
4        this.eventCost - 0;
5        this.calcEventCost = calcCost;
6    }
7    function calcCost(guests) {
8        this.eventCost = quests * 25; // $25 per head
9    }
10   function GraduationEvent(graduate, school) {
11       this.guestOfHonor - graduate;
12       this.schoolName = school;
13       this.showEventDetails = eventDetails;
14   }
15   function eventDetails() {
16       var summaryDiv = document.getElementById("summarySection");
17       summaryDiv.innerHTML += ("<p>Guest of honor: " |↵
18           this.guestOfHonor + "</p>");
19       summaryDiv.innerHTML += ("<p>School: " +↵
20           this.schoolName + "</p>");
21       summaryDiv.innerHTML += ("<p>Event date: " +↵
22           this.eventDate + "</p>");
23       summaryDiv.innerHTML += ("<p>Event location: " +↵
24           this.eventLocation + "</p>");
25       summaryDiv.innerHTML += ("<p>Event cost: $"+↵
```

```
26              this.eventCost.toLocaleString() + "</p>");
27  }
28  GraduationEvent.prototype = new Event();
29  var wertherGraduation = new GraduationEvent("Jacob Werther", ↵
30      "UCSB");
31  wertherGraduation.eventLocation = "Santa Barbara, CA";
32  wertherGraduation.eventDate = "May 27, 2017";
33  wertherGraduation.calcEventCost(175);
34  wertherGraduation.showEventDetails();
```

> **Note** Some object-oriented programming languages allow objects to inherit from more than one object definition. JavaScript, however, allows objects to inherit from only a single object definition.

Short Quiz 3

1. What statement would you use to create a new empty object with the name `manifest` using an object literal?

2. What statement would you use to add a property named `itemNum` to the manifest object, and assign the property a numeric value of 1501?

3. What single statement would you use to create a new empty object with the name `manifest` that includes a property named `itemNum` with a value of 1501?

Summary

> The term object-oriented programming (or OOP) refers to the creation of reusable software objects that can be easily incorporated into another program.

> Reusable software objects are often referred to as components.

> In object-oriented programming, an object is programming code and data that can be treated as an individual unit or component. Data refers to information contained within variables or other types of storage structures.

> Objects are encapsulated, which means that all code and required data are contained within the object itself.

> An interface refers to the programmatic elements required for a source program to communicate with an object.

> The principle of information hiding states that any class members that other programmers do not need to access or know about should be hidden.

> In object-oriented programming, the code, methods, attributes, and other information that make up an object are organized using classes.

> An instance is an object that has been created from an existing class. When you create an object from an existing class, you are said to be instantiating the object.

> An object inherits, or takes on, the characteristics of the class on which it is based.

> The Date class contains methods and properties for manipulating the date and time.

> The Number class contains methods for manipulating numbers and properties that contain static values representing some of the numeric limitations in the JavaScript language (such as the largest positive number that can be used in JavaScript).

> The Math class contains methods and properties for performing mathematical calculations in your programs.

> You can easily define a custom object using an object literal.

> You can create a template for custom objects by creating a constructor function (also known as an object definition).

> In a function, the this keyword refers to the object that called the function.

> The prototype property is a built-in property that specifies the constructor from which an object was extended.

Key Terms

associative array—An array whose elements are referred to with alphanumeric keys instead of index numbers.

class—A template, or blueprint, that serves as the basis for new objects.

component—*See* object.

constructor function—A function that is used as the basis for a custom object.

data—Information contained within variables or other types of storage structures.

Date class—The built-in JavaScript class that contains methods and properties for manipulating the date and time.

encapsulated—Term used to refer to the self-contained quality of an object's code and data; all code and required data in an encapsulated object are contained within the object itself.

enumerate—To assign an index to; the `for/in` statement enumerates each property in an object.

for/in statement—A looping statement similar to the `for` statement that loops through the properties of an object.

garbage collection—Cleaning up, or reclaiming, memory that is reserved by a program.

information hiding—A principle that states that any methods and properties that other programmers do not need to access or know about should be hidden.

inherit—To take on the characteristics of a class; an object is said to inherit the properties and methods of the class on which it is based.

instance—An object that has been created from an existing class.

instantiate—To create an object from an existing class.

interface—The programmatic elements required for a source program to communicate with an object.

Math class—The built-in JavaScript class that contains methods and properties for performing mathematical calculations.

Number class—The built-in JavaScript class that contains methods for manipulating numbers and properties that contain static values representing some of the numeric limitations in the JavaScript language (such as the largest positive number that can be used in JavaScript).

object—Programming code and data that can be treated as an individual unit.

object definition—*See* constructor function.

object-oriented programming (OOP)—A programming practice that involves creating reusable software objects that can be easily incorporated into multiple programs.

OOP—*See* object-oriented programming.

prototype property—A built-in property that specifies the constructor from which an object was instantiated.

sub-object—A property value that is itself an object.

this keyword—References the object that called the function where this statement is located.

Review Questions

1. In object-oriented programming, a(n) _____ is a template, or blueprint, that serves as the basis for new objects.
   a. instance
   b. object
   c. method
   d. class

2. In object-oriented programming, a(n) _____ is an object that has been created from an existing template.
   a. instance
   b. property
   c. method
   d. class

3. Which of the following `Date` class constructors creates a `Date` object that contains the current date and time from the local computer?
   a. `Date()`
   b. `Date(milliseconds)`
   c. `Date(date_string)`
   d. `Date(year, month[, date, hours, minutes, seconds, milliseconds])`

4. Which of the following parts of a date value are stored in a `Date` object using numeric representations, starting with zero, similar to an array?
   a. Day of the month
   b. Month
   c. Year
   d. AM/PM

5. Which `Number` method converts a number to a string using a specified number of decimal places?
   a. `toFixed()`
   b. `toLocaleString()`
   c. `toString()`
   d. `valueOf()`

6. Which `Number` method converts a number to a string that is formatted with local numeric formatting style?
   a. `toFixed()`
   b. `toLocaleString()`
   c. `toString()`
   d. `valueOf()`

7. Which is the primary reason for using any of the "to" methods of the `Number` class?
   a. To convert a number for use in calculations
   b. To format a date
   c. To perform calculations
   d. To convert a number that will be displayed to a user

8. Which method of the `Math` class rounds a value to the next lowest integer?
   a. `floor()`
   b. `max()`
   c. `min()`
   d. `round()`

9. What is the correct syntax for rounding the number 39.75 to the nearest integer?
   a. `new Math = round(39.75);`
   b. `var mathCalc = new Math(round(39.75));`
   c. `Math.round(39.75);`
   d. `round(39.75);`

10. Which of the following statements creates an empty object with the name `registry`?
   a. `var registry;`
   b. `var registry = {};`
   c. `var registry = "";`
   d. `var registry = [];`

11. Which of the following statements adds a new property named `squareFeet` to an object named `RealEstate`?
   a. `var RealEstate.squareFeet;`
   b. `RealEstate.squareFeet = "";`
   c. `var squareFeed.RealEstate;`
   d. `squareFeet.RealEstate = "";`

12. A property whose value is itself an object is known as a(n) _____.
   a. sub-property
   b. instance
   c. constructor
   d. sub-object

13. Given the object definition

```
var members = {
    founder: "Luis"
};
```

which statement references the value of the `founder` property using an associative array?

   a. `founder`

   b. `members.founder`

   c. `members["founder"]`

   d. `members[0]`

14. Which statement declares a method named `calcTotal` and sets its value to the existing `calculateTotal()` function?

   a. `calcTotal: calculateTotal`

   b. `calcTotal: calculateTotal()`

   c. `calcTotal: function(calculateTotal)`

   d. `calcTotal: function(calculateTotal())`

15. The built-in property that specifies the constructor from which an object was extended is called the _____ property.

   a. default

   b. origination

   c. prototype

   d. source

16. Explain the principle of information hiding. What does the term "black box" refer to?

17. Explain why programmers use the terms "variable" and "object" interchangeably.

18. Explain why JavaScript is not a true object-oriented programming language.

19. Explain how to assign a new property to a custom object.

20. Explain when you would use an object literal and when you would create a constructor function.

Hands-On Projects

Hands-On Project 7-1

In this project, you'll create an app that calculates the square root of any number that a user enters.

1. In your text editor, open the **index.htm** file from the HandsOnProject7-1 folder in the Chapter07 folder, add your name and today's date where indicated in the comment section, and then save the file.

2. Before the closing `</body>` tag, add a `script` element containing the following global variable declarations:

```
var valueElement = document.getElementById("value");
var resultElement = document.getElementById("sqRoot");
```

3. Below the global variable declaration, add the following function to calculate the square root of the number entered and convert it to a string with two decimal places:

```
1   function convert() {
2       var root = Math.sqrt(valueElement.value);
3       resultElement.innerHTML = root.toFixed(2);
4   }
```

4. Below the `convert()` function, add the following function to create event listeners:

```
1   // add event listeners to Calculate square root
2   button and clear form
3   function createEventListener() {
4       var submitButton =↵
5           document.getElementById("convertButton");
6       if (submitButton.addEventListener) {
7         submitButton.addEventListener("click", convert, false);
8       } else if (submitButton.attachEvent) {
9         submitButton.attachEvent("onclick", convert);
10      }
11      document.getElementById('value').value = "";
12      // clear last starting value
13      document.getElementById('sqRoot').innerHTML = "";
14      // clear previous results
15  }
```

5. Below the `createEventListener()` function, add the following statements:

```
1   if (window.addEventListener) {
2       window.addEventListener("load", createEventListener, false);
3   } else if (window.attachEvent) {
4       window.attachEvent("onload", createEventListener);
5   }
```

6. Save your changes to **index.htm**, open **index.htm** in a browser, enter **25** in the Enter a number box, and then click the **Calculate square root** button. The Square root box should display the value 5.00, as shown in Figure 7-19.

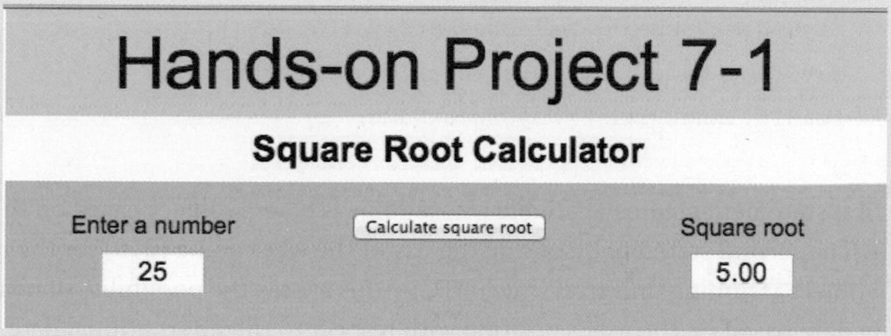

Hands-on Project 7-1

Square Root Calculator

Enter a number   [Calculate square root]   Square root

25   5.00

Figure 7-19: Square root calculator

7. Debug your code as necessary until it functions correctly.

Hands-On Project 7-2

In this project, you'll create an app that provides the day of the week for any date a user enters. You'll also explore the different interfaces available for selecting dates in modern browsers.

1. In your text editor, open the **index.htm** file from the HandsOnProject7-2 folder in the Chapter07 folder, add your name and today's date where indicated in the comment section, and then save the file.

2. Before the closing `</body>` tag, add a `script` element containing the following global variable declarations:

```
1   var selection = document.getElementById("dateSelected");
2   var result = document.getElementById("day");
3   var allDaysOfWeek = ["Sunday","Monday","Tuesday",↵
4        "Wednesday","Thursday","Friday","Saturday"];
5   var selectedDate;
6   var dayOfWeekNumber;
7   var dayOfWeekName;
```

3. Below the global variable declaration, add the following function to determine and display the day of the week for the date entered:

```
1  function lookUpDay() {
2      selectedDate = new Date(selection.value);
3      selectedDate.setUTCHours(12);
4      dayOfWeekNumber = selectedDate.getUTCDay();
5      dayOfWeekName = allDaysOfWeek[dayOfWeekNumber];
6      result.innerHTML = dayOfWeekName;
7  }
```

The first statement creates a variable whose value is a `Date` object based on the user's input. The second statement looks up the day of the week value (0–6) for the new `Date` object assuming universal time (UTC)—this avoids the possibility of using the wrong date based on the user's position with respect to the international date line. The third statement uses the day value from the previous statement to look up the corresponding day name from the `allDaysOfWeek` array. The final statement displays the resulting day name in the Day of the Week box on the page.

4. Below the `lookUpDay()` function, add the following function to create an event listener:

```
1  // add event listener to Find day button and clear form
2  function createEventListener() {
3      var submitButton = document.getElementById("determineDay");
4      if (submitButton.addEventListener) {
5        submitButton.addEventListener("click", lookUpDay, false);
6      } else if (submitButton.attachEvent) {
7        submitButton.attachEvent("onclick", lookUpDay);
8      }
9      document.getElementById("dateSelected").value = "";
10     // clear last starting value on reload
11     document.getElementById("day").innerHTML = "";
12     // clear previous results on reload
13 }
```

5. Below the `createEventListener()` function, add the following statements:

```
1  if (window.addEventListener) {
2      window.addEventListener("load", createEventListener, false);
3  } else if (window.attachEvent) {
```

```
4        window.attachEvent("onload", createEventListener);
5    }
```

6. Save your changes to **index.htm**, open **index.htm** in a browser, and then click the **Select a date** box. Notice if the browser displays a date picker or placeholder text to guide your entry.

7. Type **5/31/2017**, and then click the **Find day** button. The Day of the Week box should display "Wednesday," as shown in Figure 7-20. (*Note*: If no day is displayed or the day is incorrect, and your country uses a different standard date format, repeat this step with the date entered in your local date format.)

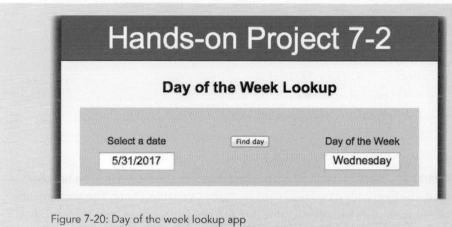

Figure 7-20: Day of the week lookup app

8. **Shift-reload** the page, enter today's date in the Select a date box in the format MM/DD/YYYY (or the format you used in Step 7, if different), and then click the **Find a day** button. Verify that the correct day of the week is displayed.

9. Repeat Steps 7 and 8 with at least one additional modern browser.

10. Debug your code as necessary until it functions correctly.

Hands-On Project 7-3

In this project, you'll create an app that totals the cost for selected items, calculates 5 percent tax on the selection, calculates the total, and displays all figures rounded to two decimal places.

1. In your text editor, open the **index.htm** file from the HandsOnProject7-3 folder in the Chapter07 folder, add your name and today's date where indicated in the comment section, and then save the file.

2. Before the closing `</body>` tag, add an empty `script` element.

3. Within the `script` element, add the following code to declare the `calcTotal()` function and its variables:

```
1    // function to add values of selected check boxes ↵
2       and display total
3    function calcTotal() {
4        var itemTotal = 0;
5        var tax = 0;
6        var totalWithTax = 0;
7        var items = document.getElementsByTagName("input");
8        var cells = document.getElementsByTagName("td");
9    }
```

4. Before the closing }, enter the following `for` statement:

```
1    for (var i = 0; i < 5; i++) {
2        if (items[i].checked) {
3            itemTotal += (items[i].value * 1);
4        }
5    }
```

This statement loops through all of the check boxes in the form. For each box that's checked, the loop adds its value to the `itemTotal` variable. (*Note*: The assignment statement multiplies each item's value by 1 to force JavaScript to treat the value as a number rather than a string.)

5. Before the closing }, enter the following statements:

```
1    tax = itemTotal * 0.05;
2    totalWithTax = itemTotal + tax;
3    cells[1].innerHTML = (itemTotal / 100).toFixed(2);
4    cells[3].innerHTML = (tax / 100).toFixed(2);
5    cells[5].innerHTML = "$" + (totalWithTax / 100).toFixed(2);
```

The first statement calculates 5 percent tax on the total order amount. The second statement adds the tax to the item total. Because the value for each check box is expressed in cents rather than in dollars (to avoid binary calculation errors), the remaining statements divide the calculated values by 100 to convert them to dollars. The third statement displays the total of selected items on the page with two decimal places. The fourth statement displays the calculated tax with two decimal places. The final statement displays that grand total with two decimal places.

6. Below the `calcTotal()` function, add the following code to create an event listener:

```
1   // add event listener to Submit button
2   var submitButton = document.getElementById("sButton");
3   if (submitButton.addEventListener) {
4     submitButton.addEventListener("click", calcTotal, false);
5   } else if (submitButton.attachEvent) {
6     submitButton.attachEvent("onclick", calcTotal);
7   }
```

7. Save your changes to **index.htm**, open **index.htm** in a browser, check the **Fried halibut** and **Side salad** boxes, click **Calculate**, and then verify that your page displays an Item total of 15.98, Tax of 0.80, and Total with tax of $16.78, as shown in Figure 7-21.

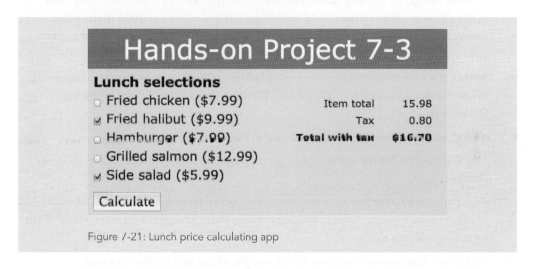

Figure 7-21: Lunch price calculating app

8. Retest the page using other combinations of items, and verify that the results shown for the calculated amounts are accurate.

9. Debug your code as necessary until it functions correctly.

Hands-On Project 7-4

In this project, you'll create a custom object containing delivery information entered by a user on a pizza delivery order form, and then you'll display the object property values in a confirmation section on the same page.

1. In your text editor, open the **index.htm** file from the HandsOnProject7-4 folder in the Chapter07 folder, add your name and today's date where indicated in the comment section, and then save the file.

2. Create a new document in your editor, add JavaScript comments containing the text **Hands-on Project 7-4**, your name, and today's date, and then save the file to the HandsOnProject7-4 folder with the name **script.js**.

3. Return to the **index.htm** file in your browser. Within the body section, just before the closing `</body>` tag, add a `script` element, and then specify the file **script.js** as the source.

4. In the **script.js** file, add code instructing processors to interpret the contents in strict mode. Declare two global variables: `delivInfo`, an empty object, and `delivSummary`, which points to the element with the `id` value `deliverTo`.

5. Create a function named `processDeliveryInfo()`. This function will add the value of each input field to the `delivInfo` object as a property value. Declare a local variable named `prop`. Add statements that store the value of the `name` input field in the `name` property of the `delivInfo` object, the `addr` input field in the `addr` property, the `city` input field in the `city` property, the `email` input field in the `email` property, and the `phone` input field in the `phone` property.

6. Within the `processDeliveryInfo()` function, add a `for/in` statement using the condition `(prop in delivInfo)`. The loop should contain the following statement:

    ```
    delivSummary.innerHTML += "<p>" + delivInfo[prop] + "</p>";
    ```

    This statement adds the value of the current property to the content of the `deliverTo` element.

7. Add a function named `previewOrder()` that contains two statements: a function call to `processDeliveryInfo()`, and a statement that changes the `display` style of the `section` element to `block`.

8. Add a function to create an event listener on the element with the `id` value `previewBtn`. The `click` event should call the `previewOrder()` function.

9. Add statements to run the function that creates the event listener when the page finishes loading.

10. Save your changes to **script.js**, open **index.htm** in a browser, enter fictitious information in all the boxes in the Delivery Information section, and then click **Preview Order**. A summary of the information you entered should be displayed on the right side of the page, as shown in Figure 7-22.

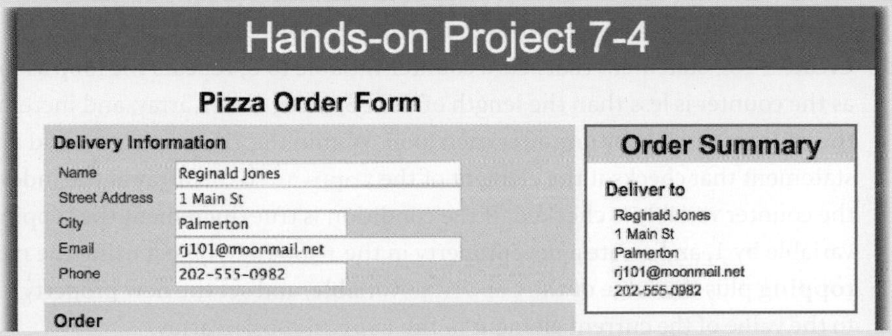

Figure 7-22: Pizza order form

11. Debug your code as necessary until it functions correctly.

Hands-On Project 7-5

In this project, you'll expand on the work you did in Hands-on Project 7-4 to create a custom object containing the order information entered on the pizza delivery order form, and then display those object property values in the confirmation section.

1. In the file manager for your operating system, copy the completed contents of the HandsOnProject7-4 folder to the HandsOnProject7-5 folder.

2. In your text editor, open the **index.htm** file from the HandsOnProject7-5 folder, change "Hands-on Project 7-4" to **Hands-on Project 7-5** in the comment section, in the `title` element, and in the `h1` element, and then save your changes.

3. Open **script.js**, and then in the comment section, change "Hands-on Project 7-4" to **Hands-on Project 7-5**.

4. In the **script.js** file, declare two additional global variables: `foodInfo`, an empty object, and `foodSummary`, which points to the element with the `id` value `order`.

5. Create a function with the name `processFood()`. Within the function, do the following:

   a. Declare five local variables: `prop`; `crustOpt`, which references the elements with the name `crust`; `toppings`, which has a value of 0; `toppingBoxes`, which references the elements with the name `toppings`; and `instr`, which references the element with the `id` value `instructions`.

   b. Add an `if/else` statement that checks if the first item in the `crustOpt` array is checked. If so, the crust property of the `foodInfo` object should be assigned the value of the first item in the `crustOpt` array; otherwise, the `crust` property of the `foodInfo` object should be assigned the value of the second item in the `crustOpt` array.

c. Add a statement that assigns the value of the element with the `id` value `size` as the value of the `size` property of the `foodInfo` object.

d. Create a `for` statement that sets a counter variable to 0, repeats the loop as long as the counter is less than the length of the `toppingBoxes` array, and increments the counter variable by one after each loop. Within the `for` statement, add an `if` statement that checks if the element of the `toppingBoxes` array at the index of the counter variable is checked. If the condition is true, increment the toppings variable by 1, and create a new property in the `foodInfo` object using the name **topping** plus the value of the `toppings` variable, and set the new property's value to the value of the current element in the `toppingBoxes` array.

e. Add an `if` statement that checks if the element referenced by the `instr` variable has any content, and if so, creates an `instructions` property for the `foodInfo` object and sets its value to the value of the element referenced by the `instr` variable.

f. Add the following statements to add the object properties to the Order Summary sidebar:

```
1   foodSummary.innerHTML += "<p><span>Crust</span>: " +↵
2       foodInfo.crust + "</p>";
3   foodSummary.innerHTML += "<p><span>Size</span>: " +↵
4       foodInfo.size + "</p>";
5   foodSummary.innerHTML += "<p><span>Topping(s)</span>: " +↵
6       "</p>";
7   foodSummary.innerHTML += "<ul>";
8   for (var i = 1; i < 6; i++) {
9       if (foodInfo["topping" + i]) {
10          foodSummary.innerHTML += "<li>" + foodInfo["topping" +↵
11              i] + "</li>";
12      }
13  }
14  foodSummary.innerHTML += "</ul>";
15  foodSummary.innerHTML += "<p><span>Instructions</span>: " +↵
16      foodInfo.instructions;
17  document.getElementById("order").style.display = "block";
```

6. In the `previewOrder()` function, add a call to the `processFood()` function after the existing call to the `processDeliveryInfo()` function.

7. Save your changes to **script.js**, open **index.htm** in a browser, enter fictitious information in all the boxes in the Delivery Information section, complete all the boxes in the Order section, and then click **Preview Order**. A summary of the information you entered should be displayed on the right side of the page, as shown in Figure 7-23.

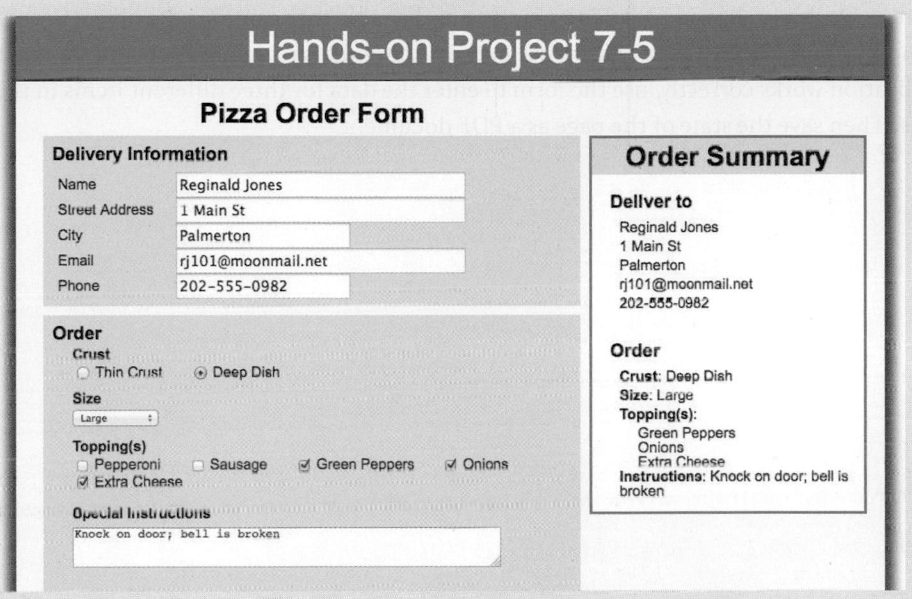

Figure 7-23: Enhanced pizza order form

8. Debug your code as necessary until it functions correctly.

Case Projects

Individual Case Project

Expand your individual website to include a page that calculates the time elapsed since a date entered by a user. The page should include a form that allows users to enter a day, month, and year. The page should then calculate and display the elapsed time in years, months, and days. Note that your program must include code to convert day values in excess of 31 into months, and months in excess of 12 into years.

Team Case Project

In your team website, add a page that enables users to add data to a table by entering data in a form for the contents of one row at a time. Start by deciding what kind of information you want to enable users to enter. Possiblities include players for a fantasy sports team or a summer reading list. Next create a page that contains a form with fields for each item of data you want to collect. The page should also include a table with heading rows corresponding to each of the form fields. As a team, design and code a constructor function to serve as a template for objects containing information about the subject of your page (such as football players or books). Also create code that (1) generates a new object each time the form content is submitted, and (2) adds a new row to the table that contains the object properties in the appropriate cells. If necessary, use `for/in` statements to debug your code. When the application works correctly, use the form to enter the data for three different items in the table. Then save the state of the page as a PDF document.

CHAPTER 8

MANIPULATING DATA IN STRINGS AND ARRAYS

When you complete this chapter, you will be able to:

> Manipulate strings with properties and methods of the `String` object
> Create regular expressions and use them to validate user input
> Manipulate arrays with properties and methods of the `Array` object
> Convert between strings and arrays, and between strings and JSON

One of the most common uses of JavaScript is for processing form data submitted by users. Because form data is submitted as strings, a good JavaScript programmer must be adept at dealing with strings. Another critical skill for a JavaScript programmer is the ability to manipulate arrays. Earlier in this book, you learned basic skills for working with both strings and arrays, including creating them and accessing and changing their values. In this chapter, you'll learn how to use advanced techniques for both strings and arrays to perform more complex operations on string values and array values. You'll also learn how to employ regular expressions, which are used for matching and manipulating strings according to specified rules. Finally, you'll learn how to convert string values to JSON, a data format commonly used to transmit object contents.

Manipulating Strings

As you learned in Chapter 1, a string is text contained within double or single quotation marks. You can use a text string as a literal value or assign it to a variable. For example, the first statement in the following code specifies a literal text string as element content, whereas the second statement assigns a text string to a variable.

```
1   document.getElementById("mainHeading").innerHTML = "24-Hour↵
2       Forecast";
3   var highSurfAdvisory = "Watch out for high waves and strong↵
4       rip currents.";
```

Whether you use single or double quotation marks, a string must begin and end with the same type of quotation mark. For example, the statement

```
subhead.innerHTML = "including hourly temperatures";
```

is valid because the string starts and ends with double quotation marks. Likewise,

```
subhead.innerHTML = 'including hourly temperatures';
```

is valid because the string begins and ends with single quotation marks. By contrast, the code below is invalid because the string starts with a double quotation mark and ends with a single quotation mark.

Not valid code:

```
subhead.innerHTML = "including hourly temperatures';
```

In this case, you would receive an error message because a JavaScript interpreter would not be able to tell where the literal string begins and ends.

The preceding example demonstrates the fundamentals of creating strings. You will often find it necessary to parse the text strings in your scripts. When applied to text strings, the term **parsing** refers to the act of extracting characters or substrings from a larger string. This is essentially the same concept as the parsing (rendering) that occurs in a web browser when the browser extracts the necessary formatting information from a web page before displaying it on the screen. In the case of a web page, the document itself is one large text string from which formatting and other information needs to be extracted. However, when working on a programming level, parsing usually refers to the extraction of information from string literals and variables.

To parse the text strings in your scripts, you use the methods and the property of the `String` class. All literal strings and string variables in JavaScript are represented by a `String class`, which contains methods for manipulating text strings.

In this chapter, you'll work on a website for Golden Rocks National Park in Golden Rocks, Alaska. The park wants to enable website users to create a profile, which they can use to reserve cabins or camping spots. To create a profile, a user needs to provide a username and a password that conform to a set of rules, along with an email address. In addition, each user will have the option of specifying one or more cabins or camping areas as favorites, which will be associated with their profile. Figure 8-1 shows a preview of the functionality you'll add to the existing page in a desktop browser, and Figure 8-2 shows the page on a handheld device.

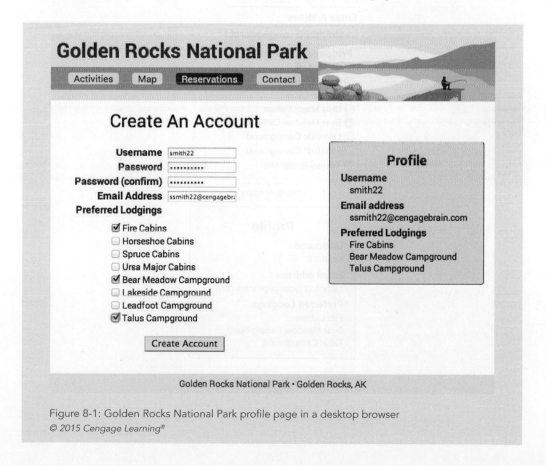

Figure 8-1: Golden Rocks National Park profile page in a desktop browser
© 2015 Cengage Learning®

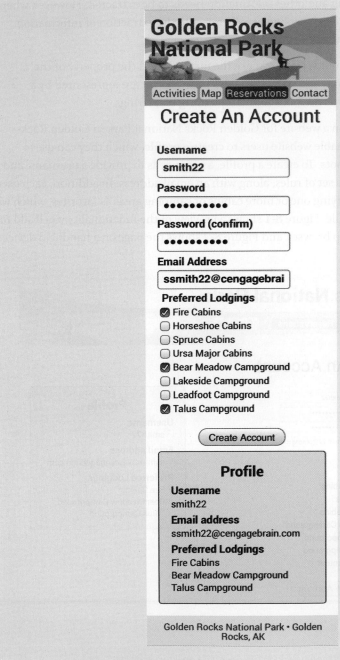

Figure 8-2: Golden Rocks National Park profile page in a handheld browser

Much of the code for the profile page has already been created. Your task will be to use properties and methods of the `String`, `Regex`, `Array`, and `JSON` objects to check and manipulate values entered by users. You'll start by reviewing the existing code.

To view the existing code for the profile page:

1. In your text editor, open the **account.htm** document, located in your Chapter folder for Chapter 8.

2. In the comment section, add your name and today's date where indicated, save your changes, and then scroll through the document and familiarize yourself with its content. The document contains a form in which users can enter information, and a `section` element that summarizes user selections.

3. Open the **goldrock.js** file in your text editor. In, in the comment section, add your name and today's date where indicated, save your changes, and then scroll through the file and familiarize yourself with its content. The file contains five functions. You'll finalize the `validateUsername()`, `validatePassword()`, and `validateEmail()` functions to check the relevant user input. You'll also finish the `registerLodging()` function so it adds the values of selected check boxes to an array. The `createEventListeners()` function creates event listeners for all the other functions.

4. Open **account.htm** in a browser, complete the text fields with fictitious information, and check at least one check box. As Figure 8-1 shows, all the information you enter, aside from the password, is displayed in the profile section on the right side of the page. Notice that clicking the Create Account button has no effect; you'll add code to process the form data later in this chapter.

> **Note** Modern browsers may add formatting indicating an invalid entry if your Email Address entry is not an email address. You'll enhance this validation later in this chapter.

Formatting Strings

This section describes how to use special characters and how to change a string from upper- to lowercase, or vice versa.

Using Special Characters

You learned in Chapter 2 that when you want to include basic types of special characters, such as quotation marks, within a literal string, you must use an escape sequence.

The escape sequence for double quotation marks is \" and the escape sequence for single quotation marks is \'. For example, in the statement

```
var mainHead = 'Today\'s Forecast';
```

the text string assigned to the mainHead variable includes an escape sequence for a single quotation mark. The value would be rendered in a browser as follows:

Today's Forecast

For other types of special characters, you need to use Unicode, which is a standardized set of characters from many of the world's languages. A number represents each character in the Unicode character set. For instance, the Unicode numbers for the uppercase letters *A*, *B*, and *C*, are 65, 66, and 67, respectively. In most cases, you can use HTML numeric character references or character entities to represent Unicode characters in text strings. For example, the copyright symbol (©) can be represented in HTML by the numeric character reference © or by the character entity ©. To assign the text "© 2006-2017" to a variable named copyrightInfo in JavaScript, you could use either of the following statements:

```
1  copyrightInfo = "<p>&#169; 2006-2017</p>";
2     // numeric character ref.
3  copyrightInfo = "<p>&copy; 2006-2017</p>";
4     // character entity
```

Instead of using numeric character references or character entities within text strings, as shown in the preceding example, you could instead use the **fromCharCode() method**, which constructs a text string from Unicode character codes that are passed as arguments. The fromCharCode() method is called a **static method** because it is not used as a method of any string objects (which can be literal strings or variables) in your scripts. Instead, you must call fromCharCode() as a method of the String class with the following syntax:

```
String.fromCharCode(char1, char2, ...)
```

The following code uses the fromCharCode() method to create the text "JavaScript" with Unicode characters:

```
String.fromCharCode(74,97,118,97,83,99,114,105,112,116)
```

The numeric characters in the preceding statement would be rendered in a web browser as "JavaScript". The following statement uses the fromCharCode() method to create the string value "© 2017":

```
copyrightInfo = String.fromCharCode(169) + " 2017";
```

Changing Case

To change the case of letters in a string, you use the `toLowerCase()` and `toUpperCase()` methods of the `String` class. The `toLowerCase()` method converts a text string to lowercase, whereas the `toUpperCase()` method converts a text string to uppercase. You append either method to a string or variable containing the text whose case you want to change. For example, the following code uses the `toUpperCase()` method to print the contents of the `agency` variable ("noaa") in uppercase letters ("NOAA"):

```
1   var agency = "noaa";
2   agencyName.innerHTML = agency.toUpperCase();
3   // browser displays "NOAA"
4   // but value of agency is still "noaa"
```

Note that the `toUpperCase()` method in the preceding statement does not convert the contents of the `agency` variable to uppercase letters; it only prints the text in uppercase letters. If you want to change the contents of a variable to upper- or lowercase letters, you must assign the value returned from the `toLowerCase()` or `toUpperCase()` method to that variable or to a different variable. The following statements demonstrate how to change the contents of the `agency` variable to uppercase letters:

```
1   var agency = "noaa";
2   agency = agency.toUpperCase();
3   // value of agency is "NOAA"
4   agencyName.innerHTML = agency;
5   // browser displays "NOAA"
```

Although email addresses are case insensitive, they are generally written in all lowercase letters. Next, you'll enhance the `validateEmail()` function so it converts the value entered in the Email Address field to lowercase letters.

To add code to convert the email address to lowercase:

1. Return to the **goldrock.js** document in your text editor.

2. Scroll down to the `validateEmail()` function, and locate the comment
   `// replace with code to convert email address to lowercase.`

3. Replace the comment with the following statement:

```
emailInput.value = emailInput.value.toLowerCase();
```

This statement looks up the value of the `emailInput` element—the input element for the email address—and then converts it to lowercase and assigns the result as the value of the same field.

4. Save your changes to **goldrock.js**, Shift-refresh or Shift-reload **account.htm** in your browser, click in the **Email Address** box, type **SSMITH22@CENGAGEBRAIN.COM**, and then press **Tab**. As Figure 8-3 shows, the email address is converted to all lowercase letters.

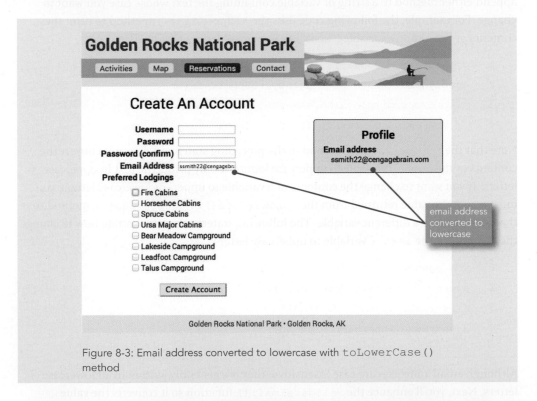

Figure 8-3: Email address converted to lowercase with `toLowerCase()` method

The event listeners for the text input boxes, including the Email Address box, listen for the `change` event, which fires when the focus leaves the box and the value has changed.

Counting Characters in a String

You will often find it necessary to count characters and words in strings, particularly with strings from form submissions. For example, you might need to count the number of characters in a password to ensure that a user selects a password with a minimum number of characters. Or, you might have a web page that allows users to submit classified ads that cannot exceed a maximum number of characters. The String class contains a single property, the **length property**, which returns the number of characters in a string. To return the total number of characters in a string, you append the length property of the String class to a literal string, variable, or object containing text. For example, the following code uses the length property to count the number of characters in a variable named country.

```
var country = "Kingdom of Morocco";
var stringLength = country.length;
// value of stringLength is 18
```

> **Note** The length property counts an escape sequence such as \n as a single character.

When creating a profile, the username must be at least 4 characters long, and the password must be at least 8 characters. You'll add conditional expressions to the validateUsername() and validatePassword() functions to check the length of user entries in the Username and Password (confirm) fields and display error messages if the entries are too short.

To add conditional statements to check for minimum username and password lengths:

1. Return to the **goldrock.js** document in your text editor.

2. In the validateUsername() function, locate the comment // replace with conditional expression.

3. Replace the comment with the following if statement:

```
if (unInput.value.length < 4) {
    throw "Username must be at least 4 characters long";
}
```

This statement checks the length property for the value in the unInput element (the Username box). If the length is less than 4—meaning a user has entered a username of 1–3 characters—the if statement throws an error.

4. In the validatePassword() function, locate the comment // replace with conditional expression.

5. Replace the comment with the following `if` statement:

```
if (pw1Input.value.length < 8) {
    throw "Password must be at least 8 characters";
}
```

This statement checks the `length` property for the value in the `pw1Input` element (the first Password box). If the length is less than 8—meaning a user has entered a password of 1–7 characters—the `if` statement throws an error. Note that this code checks only the first of the two password boxes. You'll add code later in this chapter that ensures that the entries in both password boxes match. This feature will make it unnecessary to check the length of both password boxes.

6. Save your changes to **goldrock.js**, Shift-refresh or Shift-reload **account.htm** in your browser, and then click in the **Username** box.

7. Type **abc**, press **Tab**; in the Password box type **abc**, press **Tab**; in the Password (confirm) box type **abc**, and then press **Tab**. As Figure 8-4 shows, error messages are displayed, indicating that a valid username must be at least 4 characters and a valid password must be at least 8 characters.

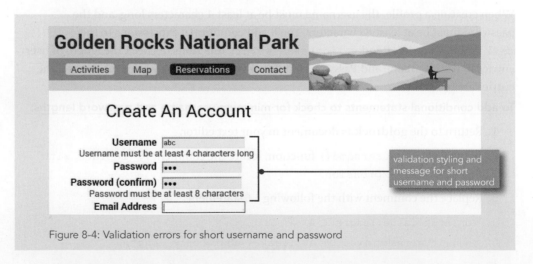

Figure 8-4: Validation errors for short username and password

8. Double-click the **Username** box, type **1234** to replace the existing contents, press **Tab**, type **12345678**, press **Tab**, type **12345678**, and then press **Tab**. The error messages and invalid styles are removed because the username you entered is 4 characters long, and the password you entered is 8 characters long.

Finding and Extracting Characters and Substrings

In some situations, you will need to find and extract characters and substrings from a string. For example, if your script receives an email address, you may need to extract the name portion of the email address or domain name. To search for and extract characters and substrings in JavaScript, you use the methods listed in Table 8-1.

METHOD	DESCRIPTION
charAt(index)	Returns the character at the specified position in a text string; returns an empty string if the specified position is greater than the length of the string
charCodeAt(index)	Returns the Unicode character code at the specified position in a text string; returns NaN if the specified position is greater than the length of the string
indexOf(text[, index])	Performs a case-sensitive search and returns the position number in a string of the first character in the text argument; if the index argument is included, then the indexOf() method starts searching at that position within the string; returns −1 if the character or string is not found
lastIndexOf(text[, index])	Performs a case-sensitive search and returns the position number in a string of the last instance of the first character in the text argument; if the index argument is included, then the lastIndexOf() method starts searching at that position within the string; returns −1 if the character or string is not found
match(pattern)	Performs a case-sensitive search and returns an array containing the results that match the pattern argument; returns null if the text is not found
search(pattern)	Performs a case-sensitive search and returns the position number in a string of the first instance of the first character in the pattern argument; returns −1 if the character or string is not found
slice(starting index [, ending index])	Extracts text from a string, starting with the position number in the string of the starting index argument and ending with the character immediately before the position number of the ending index argument; allows negative argument values
substring(starting index [, ending index])	Extracts text from a string, starting with the position number in the string of the starting index argument and ending with the character immediately before the position number of the ending index argument; does not allow negative argument values

Table 8-1: Search and extraction methods of the String class

Figure 8-5 illustrates some of these methods.

string	"	s	m	i	t	h	@	e	x	a	m	p	l	e	.	c	o	m	"
index values		0	1	2	3	4	5	6	7	8	9	10	11	12	13	14	15	16	
reverse index values		-17	-16	-15	-14	-13	-12	-11	-10	-9	-8	-7	-6	-5	-4	-3	-2	-1	

method	result
charAt(5)	"@"
charCodeAt(5)	40
indexOf("com")	14
lastIndexOf("e")	12
search("@")	5
slice(-11,-4)	"example"
substring(6,13)	"example"

Figure 8-5: Example uses of String class methods

There are two types of string search methods: methods that return a numeric position in a text string and methods that return a character or substring. To use methods that return the numeric position in a text string, it's important to remember that the position of characters in a text string begins with a value of 0, just like indexed array elements. For example, the **search() method** returns the position of the first instance of the first character of a text string that is passed as an argument. If the search string is not found, the search() method returns a value of –1. The following code uses the search() method to determine whether the email variable contains an @ character. The @ character is the 10th character in the string; however, because the position of text strings begins with 0, the second statement assigns a value of 9.

```
var email = "president@whitehouse.gov";
var atPosition = email.search("@"); // returns 9
```

As another example, the **indexOf() method** returns the position of the first occurrence of one string in another string. The primary difference between the search() method and the indexOf() method is that you can pass to the indexOf() method a second optional argument that specifies the position in the string where you want to start searching. If the search string is not found, the indexOf() method returns a value of –1. The following code uses the indexOf() method to determine whether the email variable contains an @ character. Because the indexOf() method includes a value of 10 as the second optional argument, the second statement assigns a value of –1 (indicating that the search string was not found) because the method began searching in the string after the position of the @ character.

```
var email = "president@whitehouse.gov";
var atIndex = email.indexOf("@", 10); // returns -1
```

To extract characters from a string, you use the **substring() method** or the **slice() method**. In both cases, you pass to the method the starting index and ending index of the characters you want to extract. Both methods return a substring containing the specified characters or an empty string if the specified starting index does not exist. For example, the second statement in the following code uses the search() method to identify the position of the @ character in the email variable. The substring() method then returns the name portion of the email address ("president") by using a starting index position of 0 (the first character in the string) and the value assigned to the nameEnd variable as the ending index position.

```
1   var email = "president@whitehouse.gov";
2   var nameEnd = email.search("@");
3   // value of nameEnd is 9
4   var nameText = email.substring(0, nameEnd);
5   // value of nameText is "president"
```

To extract characters from the middle or end of a string, you need to identify the position of the character in the string where you want to start the extraction. One way to do this is by using the search(), indexOf(), or lastIndexOf() methods. The **lastIndexOf() method** works the same way as the indexOf() method except that it returns the position of the last occurrence of one string in another string instead of the first. The following code uses the lastIndexOf() method to return the position of the period within the email address in the email variable. The substring() method then uses the index returned from the lastIndexOf() method to return the domain identifier ("gov") of the email address.

```
1   var email = "president@whitehouse.gov";
2   var startDomainID = email.lastIndexOf(".");
3   // startDomainID value is 20
4   var domainID = email.substring(startDomainID + 1);
5   // domainID value is "gov"
```

Note that the preceding example would produce the same results if you used indexOf() instead of lastIndexOf() because the starting string contains only one instance of the . character.

The only difference between the `slice()` and `substring()` methods is that the `slice()` method allows you to specify negative argument values for the index arguments. If you specify a negative value for the starting index, the `slice()` method starts at the end of the text string; –1 represents the last character in the string, –2 represents the second to last character, and so on. If you specify a negative value for the ending index, the number of characters that the `slice()` method extracts also starts at the end of the text string. Note that the `slice()` method does not return the character represented by the ending index; it returns the character immediately before the ending index. For example, the following statement uses the `slice()` method in two different ways:

```
1  var email = "president@whitehouse.gov";
2  var nameText = email.slice(0,9);
3  // nameText value is "president"
4  var domain = email.slice(-14,-4);
5  // domain value is "whitehouse"
```

The first `slice()` method uses a starting index of 0, which represents the letter *p* in the email text string, and an ending index of 9, which represents the @ symbol. Because the index values are positive, they are counted from the beginning of the text string. In comparison, the second `slice()` method uses a starting index of –14, which represents the letter *w*, and an ending index of –4, which represents the . character. Remember that both positions are counted from the end of the text string.

The following code uses the `slice()` method to return the domain identifier of the email address in the `email` variable:

```
var email = "president@whitehouse.gov";
var domainID = email.slice(-3);
// domainID value is "gov"
```

The following code contains another example of the `slice()` method. In this version, the code uses the `search()` and `lastIndexOf()` methods to return the domain name of the email address. Notice that the second statement increments the position returned from the `search()` method by 1. This prevents the @ character from being included in the substring returned from the `slice()` method.

```
1  var email = "president@whitehouse.gov";
2  var domainBegin = email.search("@") + 1;
3  var domainEnd = email.lastIndexOf(".");
4  var domain = email.slice(domainBegin, domainEnd);
5  // value of domain is "whitehouse"
```

Later in this chapter, you'll learn how to use regular expressions to validate strings, including email addresses. For now, you'll use the `search()` and `lastIndexOf()` methods simply to check whether an email address entered into the form contains an @ sign to separate the name and domain and a period to separate the domain and identifier.

To use the `search()` and `lastIndexOf()` methods to check whether an email address contains an @ sign and a period:

1. Return to **goldrock.js** in your text editor, and then in the `validateEmail()` function, locate the comment `// replace with conditional expression`.

2. Replace the comment with the following code:

```
if (emailInput.value.search("@") === -1 ||
    emailInput.value.lastIndexOf(".") === -1) {
    throw "Please provide a valid email address";
}
```

This code uses the `search()` and `lastIndexOf()` methods to determine whether the string passed to it contains an @ sign and a period. If the string is missing one or both of these characters, the `if` statement throws an error.

3. Save your changes to **goldrock.js**, and then Shift-refresh or Shift-reload **account.htm** in your browser.

4. Click in the **Email Address** box, type **ssmith22@cengagebrain**, and then press **Tab**. As Figure 8-6 shows, the box is highlighted in red and an error message is displayed, indicating that your entry is not a valid email address.

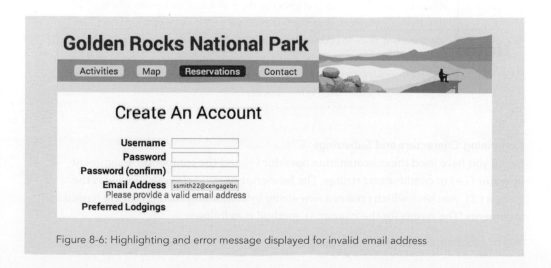

Figure 8-6: Highlighting and error message displayed for invalid email address

5. Click at the end of the **Email Address** box, if necessary use the right arrow key to move to the end of the text you entered, type **.com**, and then press **Tab**. The Email Address box now contains a complete email address, including an @ sign and a period, and the highlighting and error message are removed.

Replacing Characters and Substrings

In addition to finding and extracting characters in a string, you might also need to replace them. The `replace()` method of the `String` class creates a new string with the first instance of a specified pattern replaced with the value of the *text* argument. The syntax for the `replace()` method is *string.*`replace`*(pattern, text).* Essentially, the `replace()` method replaces the first matching pattern it finds in the string with the text.

> **Note** | *The* `replace()` *method is case sensitive.*

The following example demonstrates how to use the `replace()` method to replace "president" in the email variable with "vice.president":

```
var email = "president@whitehouse.gov";
var newEmail = email.replace("president", "vice.president");
// value of newEmail is "vice.president@whitehouse.gov"
```

> **Note** | *When you pass a simple text string as the* `pattern` *argument of the* `replace()` *method, only the first instance of the pattern is replaced with the specified text. To replace all instances of a pattern, you must use a regular expression as the* `pattern` *argument and set the property of the* `RegExp` *object's* `global` *property. Regular expressions and the* `RegExp` *object are discussed later in this chapter.*

Combining Characters and Substrings

So far, you have used the concatenation operator (+) and the compound assignment operator (+=) to combine text strings. The JavaScript `String` class also includes the `concat()` **method**, which creates a new string by combining strings that are passed as arguments. The syntax for the `concat()` method is as follows:

```
string.concat(value1, value2, ...)
```

Note that the `concat()` method does not change the original string but returns a new string. The *value* arguments are appended to the string in the order in which they are passed to the `concat()` method. For example, the following statements demonstrate how to use the `concat()` method to build a string that is stored in a new variable.

```
1    var name = "Theodor Seuss Geisel";
2    var penName = "Dr. Seuss";
3    var bio = penName.concat(" was the pen name of ", name);
4    // value of bio is
5    // "Dr. Seuss was the pen name of Theodor Seuss Geisel"
```

In most cases, you do not need to use the `concat()` method. Instead, it is usually easier to use the concatenation operator and the compound assignment operator to combine text strings. The following code shows the same statements from the preceding example, but this time using concatenation operators:

```
1    var name = "Theodor Seuss Geisel";
2    var penName = "Dr. Seuss";
3    var bio = penName + " was the pen name of " + name;
4    // value of bio is
5    // "Dr. Seuss was the pen name of Theodor Seuss Geisel"
```

Comparing Strings

In Chapter 2, you studied various operators that you can use with JavaScript, including comparison operators. Although comparison operators are most often used with numbers, they can also be used with strings. The following statements use the comparison operator (===) to compare two variables containing text strings:

```
1    var location1 = "Springfield, MO";
2    var location2 = "Springfield, MA";
3    var result;
4    if (location1 === location2) {
5        result = true;
6    } else {
7        result = false;
8    }
9    // value of result variable is false
```

Because the text strings are not the same, the `else` clause returns the value `false`. You can also use comparison operators to determine whether one letter is higher (that is, earlier) in the alphabet than another letter, as in the following code:

```
1   var firstLetter = "A";
2   var secondLetter = "B";
3   if (firstLetter < secondLetter) {
4       var letterOrder = firstLetter + ", " + secondLetter;
5   } else {
6       var letterOrder = secondLetter + ", " + firstLetter;
7   }
8   // letterOrder value is "A, B"
```

In this code, the `else` statement executes because the letter *B* is higher in the alphabet than the letter *A*.

The comparison operators compare individual characters according to their Unicode position. Lowercase letters are represented by the values 97 (*a*) to 122 (*z*). Uppercase letters are represented by the values 65 (*A*) to 90 (*Z*). Because lowercase letters have higher values than uppercase letters, the lowercase letters are evaluated as being "greater" than the uppercase letters. For example, an uppercase letter *A* is represented by Unicode value 65, whereas a lowercase letter *a* is represented by Unicode value 97. For this reason, the statement

```
"a" > "A"
```

returns a value of `true` because the uppercase letter *A* has a lower Unicode value than the lowercase letter *a*.

In addition to using standard comparison operators, the `String` class includes a **`localeCompare()` method**, which compares strings according to the particular sort order of a language or country. The syntax for the `localeCompare()` method is

```
sourceString.localeCompare(compareString)
```

If *compareString* is equivalent to *sourceString*, the method returns a value of 0; if *compareString* sorts before *sourceString*, the method returns a value greater than 0, usually 1; if *compareString* sorts after *sourceString*, the method returns a value less than 0, usually −1. For example, consider the following `localeCompare()` method:

```
1   var sourceString = "Don";
2   var compareString = "Dan";
3   var comparison = sourceString.localeCompare(compareString);
4   // returns 1
```

Because "Dan" sorts before "Don", the method returns a value of 1. In comparison, the following statement, which switches the "Dan" and "Don" arguments, returns a value of −1:

```
1    var sourceString = "Dan";
2    var compareString = "Don";
3    var comparison = sourceString.localeCompare(compareString);
4    // returns -1
```

If both string values are equal, the `localeCompare()` method returns a value of 0, as in the following example:

```
1    var sourceString = "Don";
2    var compareString = "Don";
3    var comparison = sourceString.localeCompare(compareString);
4    // returns 0
```

In modern browsers, the `localeCompare()` method can perform a case-sensitive comparison of two strings that differ only in capitalization. However, the syntax is not supported in older browsers such as IE8, and by default, browsers differ in whether they sort upper case letters before or after lower case letters for a given locale.

To perform a case-insensitive comparison of two strings, you must first use the `toLowerCase()` or `toUpperCase()` methods to convert the strings to the same case. The `localeCompare()` statement in the following code returns a value of 0 because both the source string and comparison string are converted to lowercase before the comparison is performed:

```
1    var sourceString = "Don";
2    var compareString = "don";
3    sourceString = sourceString.toLowerCase();
4    // value of sourceString is "don"
5    compareString = compareString.toLowerCase();
6    // value of compareString is "don"
7    var result = sourceString.localeCompare(compareString);
8    // returns 0
```

Next, you'll add code to the `validatePassword()` function that uses the `localeCompare()` method to verify that the user entries in the Password and Password (confirm) boxes are the same.

To use the `localeCompare()` method to verify that the password entries match:

1. Return to **goldrock.js** in your text editor.

2. Within the `validatePassword()` function, within the `try` statement, at the end of the `if` statement, add the following code:

```
else if (pw1Input.value.localeCompare(pw2Input.value) !== 0) {
    throw "Passwords must match";
}
```

This code uses the `localeCompare()` method of the `String` object to compare the values of `pw1Input` (the Password box) and `pw2Input` (the Password (confirm) box). A result of zero signifies that the two values are the same. If the result of this comparison is not zero, the `if` statement throws an error. Your `if/else` statement should match the following:

```
if (pw1Input.value.length < 8) {
    throw "Password must be at least 8 characters";
} else if (pw1Input.value.localeCompare(pw2Input.value) !== 0) {
    throw "Passwords must match";
}
```

3. Save your changes to **goldrock.js**, and then Shift-refresh or Shift-reload **account.htm** in your browser.

4. Click in the **Password** box, type **123456789**, press **Tab**, type **12345678**, and then press **Tab**. As Figure 8-7 shows, the boxes are highlighted in red and an error message is displayed, indicating that the passwords must match.

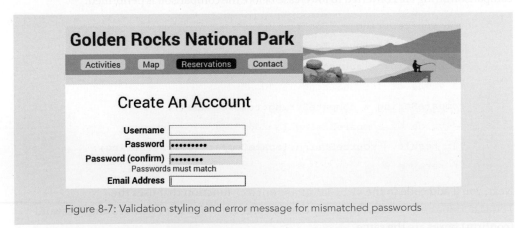

Figure 8-7: Validation styling and error message for mismatched passwords

5. Click at the end of the **Password (confirm) box**, type **9**, and then press **Tab**. Because the two passwords now match, the red highlighting and the error message are removed from the form.

Short Quiz 1

1. What string property returns the number of characters in a string?

2. Explain which values you provide for the two arguments of the `substring()` and `slice()` methods.

3. In the expression `var result = sourceString.localeCompare(compareString)`, what are the possible return values and what does each mean?

Working with Regular Expressions

One of the more complex methods of working with strings involves the use of **regular expressions**, which are patterns that are used for matching and manipulating strings according to specified rules. With scripting languages such as JavaScript, regular expressions are most commonly used for validating submitted form data. For example, you can use a regular expression to ensure that the value a user enters in a field matches a specific format, such as *mm/dd/yyyy* for a date, or (###) ###-#### for a phone number. Most scripting languages support some form of regular expressions.

> **Note** | ECMAScript regular expressions are based on the regular expression functionality of the Perl programming language.

Defining Regular Expressions in JavaScript

Regular expression patterns in JavaScript must begin and end with forward slashes. For example, the following statement defines a regular expression pattern for determining whether a text string contains "https" and assigns it to a variable named `urlProtocol`:

```
var urlProtocol = /https/;
```

Notice that the regular expression pattern is not enclosed in quotation marks.

You can use regular expressions with several of the `String` class methods, including the `search()` and `replace()` methods. The value you pass to either of these methods can be either a text string or a regular expression. For example, the following statements pass the `urlProtocol` regular expression to the `search()` method, which then searches the text contained within the `url` variable for "https":

```
var urlProtocol = /https/;
var url = "http://www.cengagebrain.com";
var searchResult = url.search(urlProtocol); // returns -1
```

Because the `url` variable contains a protocol of "http" instead of "https", the `search()` method returns a value of 1, indicating that the regular expression pattern was not found.

In addition to assigning a regular expression to a variable, you can also pass the pattern directly to a method that accepts regular expressions. The following example demonstrates how to pass the /https/ regular expression directly to the search() method:

```
var url = "http://www.cengagebrain.com";
var searchResult = url.search(/https/); // returns -1
```

Again, notice that the regular expression is not enclosed within quotation marks.

A final approach to creating a regular expression is to use the RegExp() constructor. The RegExp() constructor is part of the **RegExp object**, which contains methods and properties for working with regular expressions in JavaScript. To create a regular expression with the RegExp() constructor, you use the following syntax:

```
var regExpName = new RegExp("pattern"[, attributes]);
```

Notice that the pattern in the preceding syntax is surrounded by quotation marks instead of forward slashes. The following example demonstrates how to use the RegExp() constructor with the "https" pattern:

```
var urlProtocol = new RegExp("https");
var url = "http://www.cengagebrain.com";
var searchResult = url.search(urlProtocol); // returns -1
```

All three ways of defining regular expressions result in the same functionality, so which one you use makes little difference. Because the value passed to the RegExp() constructor is a text string, the JavaScript interpreter must convert it to a regular expression before it can be used as a regular expression. This added step can make RegExp() constructors slightly slower than assigning a regular expression to a text string or passing one as an argument. For this reason, some programmers prefer not to use RegExp() constructors to define regular expressions.

Next, you'll modify the search() method in the validateEmail() function so that it searches for the @ sign in the email address using a regular expression instead of the "@" text string.

Note You cannot use regular expressions with the indexOf() and lastIndexOf() methods.

To modify the search() method to use a regular expression:

1. Return to the **goldrock.js** document in your text editor.

2. In the validateEmail() function, within the try statement, locate the if statement you created earlier.

3. In the first line of the `if` statement, replace "@" with `/@/`, as shown below:

```
1    function validateEmail() {
2        var emailInput = document.getElementById("emailbox");
3        var errorDiv = document.getElementById("emailError");
4        try {
5            if (emailInput.value.search(/@/) === -1 ||
6                emailInput.value.lastIndexOf(".") === -1) {
7                throw "Please provide a valid email address";
8            }
9    ...
```

The value passed to the `search()` method is now passed as a regular expression instead of a string.

4. Save your changes to **goldrock.js**, and then Shift-refresh or Shift-reload **account.htm** in your browser.

5. Click in the **Password** box, type **123456789**, press **Tab**, type **12345678**, and then press **Tab**. As in Figure 8-7, the boxes are highlighted in red and an error message is displayed, indicating that the passwords must match.

6. Click at the end of the **Password (confirm) box**, type **9**, and then press **Tab**. As in the previous steps, the two passwords now match, so the red highlighting and the error message are removed from the form. The regular expression you substituted in the conditional statement performs the same function as the string it replaced.

Using Regular Expression Methods

Although you can use regular expressions with several of the `String` class methods, the `RegExp` object itself also includes two methods, `test()` and `exec()`, that are specifically designed for working with regular expressions. The `exec()` method is somewhat complex, so you will study only the `test()` method in this book. The **test() method** returns a value of `true` if a string contains text that matches a regular expression or `false` if it doesn't. The syntax for the `test()` method is

```
var pattern = test(string);
```

The following code demonstrates how to use the `test()` method to determine whether the `url` variable contains the text "cengagebrain".

```
var urlDomain = /cengagebrain/;
var url = "http://www.cengagebrain.com";
var testResult = urlDomain.test(url); // true
```

Because the variable does contain the text, the value of the `testResult` variable is `true`.

The preceding examples simply demonstrate how to use the `test()` method. In fact, there is no point in using regular expression methods with such examples because you can more easily determine whether the two strings match by using the `search()` method or one of the other `String` class methods. The real power of regular expressions comes from the patterns you write, which you'll learn more about in the next section.

Writing Regular Expression Patterns

The hardest part of working with regular expressions is writing the patterns and rules that are used for matching and manipulating strings. As an example of a common, albeit complicated, regular expression, consider the following code:

```
1   var emailPattern = /^[_a-zA-Z0-9\\-]+(\.[_a-zA-Z0-9\\-]+)*↵
2           @[a-zA-Z0-9\\-]+(\.[a-zA-Z0-9\\-]+)*(\.[a-z]{2,6})$/;
3   var email = "president@whitehouse.gov";
4   var result;
5   if (emailPattern.test(email)) {
6       result = true;
7   } else {
8       result = false;
9   }
10  // value of result is true
```

> **Note** You can find many types of prewritten regular expressions by searching the web for "regular expression library".

The preceding code uses the `test()` method to determine whether the `email` variable contains a valid email address. If the `test()` method returns a value of `true`, then the `if` statement returns `true`. As you can see, the logic is straightforward: If the email address doesn't match the regular expression, then the `else` statement returns `false`. The complex part of the code is the pattern that is defined in the first statement.

> **Note** You'll study the `emailPattern` regular expression shown above later in this chapter to understand its component parts and how it works.

Regular expression patterns consist of literal characters and metacharacters, which are special characters that define the pattern matching rules in a regular expression. Table 8-2 lists the metacharacters that you can use with JavaScript regular expressions.

METACHARACTER	DESCRIPTION
.	Matches any single character
\	Identifies the next character as a literal value
^	Matches characters at the beginning of a string
$	Matches characters at the end of a string
( )	Specifies required characters to include in a pattern match
[ ]	Specifies alternate characters allowed in a pattern match
[^]	Specifies characters to exclude in a pattern match
–	Identifies a possible range of characters to match
|	Specifies alternate sets of characters to include in a pattern match

Table 8-2: JavaScript regular expression metacharacters

Matching any Character

You use a period (.) to match any single character in a pattern. A period in a regular expression pattern really specifies that the pattern must contain a value where the period is located. For example, the following code specifies that the `zip` variable must contain five characters.

```
var zipPattern = /...../;
var zip = "015";
var testResult = zipPattern.test(zip); // false
```

Because the variable contains only three characters, the `test()` method returns a value of `false`. By comparison, the following `test()` method returns a value of `true` because the `zip` variable contains five characters:

```
var zipPattern = /...../;
var zip = "01562";
var testResult = zipPattern.test(zip); // true
```

Because the period specifies only that a character must be included in the designated location within the pattern, you can also include additional characters within the pattern. The following `test()` method returns a value of `true` because the `zip` variable contains the required five characters along with additional ZIP+4 characters:

```
var zipPattern = /...../;
var zip = "01562-2607";
var testResult = zipPattern.test(zip); // true
```

Matching Characters at the Beginning or End of a String

The ^ metacharacter matches characters at the beginning of a string, and the $ metacharacter matches characters at the end of a string. A pattern that matches the beginning or end of a line is called an **anchor**. To specify an anchor at the beginning of a line, the pattern must begin with the ^ metacharacter. The pattern in the following example matches a string that begins with "http":

```
var urlProtocol = /^http/;
var url = "http://www.cengagebrain.com";
var testResult = urlProtocol.test(url); // true
```

Because the url variable does begin with "http", the test() method returns true.

All literal characters following the ^ metacharacter in a pattern make up the anchor. This means that the following example returns false because the url variable does not begin with "https" (only "http" without the s), as is specified by the anchor in the pattern:

```
var urlProtocol = /^https/;
var url = "http://www.cengagebrain.com";
var testResult = urlProtocol.test(url); // false
```

To specify an anchor at the end of a line, the pattern must end with the $ metacharacter. The following code specifies a pattern that looks for "com" at the end of a string, and then checks a URL against the pattern:

```
var urlIdentifier = /com$/;
var url = "http://www.cengagebrain.com";
var testResult = urlIdentifier.test(url); // true
```

The preceding code returns true because the URL assigned to the urlIdentifier variable ends with "com". The following code uses a similar pattern, but checks for "gov" at the end of the string:

```
var urlIdentifier = /gov$/;
var url = "http://www.cengagebrain.com";
var testResult = urlIdentifier.test(url); // false
```

The preceding code returns false because the URL assigned to the url variable does not end with "gov".

Matching Special Characters

To match any metacharacter as a literal value in a regular expression, you must precede the character with a backslash. For example, a period (.) metacharacter matches any single character in a string. If you want to ensure that a string contains an actual period and not any character, you need to escape the period character with a backslash. In the following code, the domain identifier—com—is appended to the domain name with a comma instead of a period. However, the regular expression returns true because the period in the expression is not escaped.

Incorrect regular expression:

```
var urlIdentifier = /.com$/;
var url = "http://www.cengagebrain,com";
var testResult = urlIdentifier.test(url); // true
```

To correct the problem, you must escape the period as follows:

```
var urlIdentifier = /\.com$/;
var url = "http://www.cengagebrain,com";
var testResult = urlIdentifier.test(url); // false
```

Next, you modify the conditional expression in the validateEmail() function so it uses test() methods and determines whether a domain identifier is appended to the domain name with a period.

To add test() methods to the validateEmail() function:

1. Return to **goldrock.js** in your text editor.

2. Within the validateEmail() function, in the try statement, comment out the first two lines of the if statement, containing the conditions.

3. Below the commented out lines, but before the throw statement, add the following conditional statements:

```
1    if (
2        (/@/.test(emailInput.value) === false) || (
3            (/\...$/.test(emailInput.value) === false) &&
4            (/\....$/.test(emailInput.value) === false) &&
5            (/\.....$/.test(emailInput.value) === false) &&
6            (/\.......$/.test(emailInput.value) === false)
7        )
8    ) {
```

The first condition uses the `test()` method to check if the value of the `emailInput` element contains an @ symbol. The next four lines check if the value ends with a domain identifier of the correct length. At the time this book was written, domain identifiers in use contained 2, 3, 4, or 6 characters. The start of your revised `validateEmail()` function should match the following:

```
1   function validateEmail() {
2       var emailInput = document.getElementById("emailbox");
3       var errorDiv = document.getElementById("emailError");
4       try {
5   //      if (emailInput.value.search(/@/) === -1 ||
6   //          emailInput.value.lastIndexOf(".") === -1) {
7       if (
8           (/@/.test(emailInput.value) === false) || (
9               (/\...$/.test(emailInput.value) === false) &&
10              (/\....$/.test(emailInput.value) === false) &&
11              (/\.....$/.test(emailInput.value) === false) &&
12              (/\.......$/.test(emailInput.value) === false)
13          )
14      ) {
15          throw "Please provide a valid email address";
16      }
17  ...
```

> **Note** The nested parentheses are indented for clarity, using the same structure you might use when nesting braces. The indenting does not change their meaning.

4. Save your changes to **goldrock.js**, and then Shift-refresh or Shift-reload **account.htm** in your browser.

5. Click in the **Email Address** box, type **ssmith22@cengagebrain**, and then press **Tab**. As Figure 8-8 shows, the Email Address box is highlighted in red and an error message is displayed, indicating that the email address entered isn't valid.

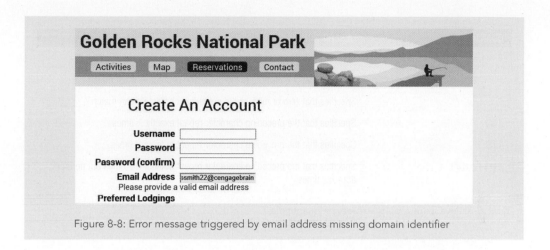

Figure 8-8: Error message triggered by email address missing domain identifier

6. Click at the end of the **Email Address box**. If necessary, use the arrow keys to move the insertion point to the end of the existing entry, type . and then press **Tab**. Even though you added a period to the email address, which would have satisfied the previous validation check, the highlight and error message remain, because the address is still missing the 2, 3, 4, or 6 characters of its domain identifier.

7. Click at the end of the **Email Address box**. If necessary, use the arrow keys to move the insertion point to the end of the existing entry, type **c**, and then press **Tab**. The highlight and error message still remain, because a one-character domain identifier does not meet the criteria you specified.

8. Click at the end of the **Email Address box**. If necessary, use the arrow keys to move the insertion point to the end of the existing entry, type **co**, and then press **Tab**. The highlight and error message are removed, because a two-character domain identifier satisfies the criteria for the email field.

Specifying Quantity

Metacharacters that specify the quantity of a match are called quantifiers. Table 8-3 lists the quantifiers that you can use with JavaScript regular expressions.

QUANTIFIER	DESCRIPTION
?	Specifies that the preceding character is optional
+	Specifies that one or more of the preceding characters must match
*	Specifies that zero or more of the preceding characters can match
{n}	Specifies that the preceding character repeat exactly n times
{n,}	Specifies that the preceding character repeat at least n times
{n1, n2}	Specifies that the preceding character repeat at least $n1$ times but no more than $n2$ times

Table 8-3: JavaScript regular expression quantifiers

The question mark quantifier specifies that the preceding character in the pattern is optional. The following code demonstrates how to use the question mark quantifier to specify that the protocol assigned to the beginning of the url variable can be either http or https:

```
var urlProtocol = /^https?/;
var url = "http://www.cengagebrain.com";
var testResult = urlProtocol.test(url); // true
```

The addition quantifier (+) specifies that one or more of the preceding characters must match, while the asterisk quantifier (*) specifies that zero or more of the preceding characters must match. As a simple example, URLs that contain information being passed from one page to another encode that information using the format *name=value*, where *name* is the name of a property and *value* is its value. The following code demonstrates how to ensure that a variable containing a string that should follow the format *name=value* contains at least one equal sign:

```
var stringPattern = /=+/;
var queryString = "color=green";
var testResult = stringPattern.test(queryString); // true
```

When a URL contains multiple *name=value* pairs, they are separated by ampersands (&). The following code demonstrates how to check whether the queryString variable contains zero or more ampersands:

```
var stringPattern = /=+&*/;
var queryString = "color=green&size=12";
var testResult = stringPattern.test(queryString); // true
```

The { } quantifiers allow you to specify more precisely the number of times that a character must repeat. The following code shows a simple example of how to use the { } quantifiers to ensure that a Zip code consists of at least 5 characters:

```
var zipPattern = /.{5}/;
var zip = "01562";
var testResult = zipPattern.test(zip); // true
```

> **Note** You can validate a Zip code much more efficiently with character classes, which are covered later in this chapter.

Next you'll use a single regular expression with quantifiers to replace the tests for the length of the domain identifier in the email address. You'll also replace the conditions that use the length property of the String object to verify the lengths of usernames and passwords with regular expressions using quantifiers.

To use quantifiers to specify minimum lengths for domain identifiers, usernames, and passwords:

1. Return to **goldrock.js** in your text editor.

2. Within the validateEmail() function, in the try statement, comment out the first eight lines of the if statement, containing the conditions you entered in the previous set of steps.

3. Below the commented out lines, but before the throw statement, add the following conditional statements:

```
if ((/@/.test(emailInput.value) === false) ||
    (/\..{2,6}$/.test(emailInput.value) === false)) {
```

The first condition is the same as the first condition from the previous steps. The second condition combines the tests for the domain identifier length into a single statement, which checks if the statement ends with a period (\.) followed by 2–6 characters. (Although no 5-character domain identifiers were in use at the time this was written, this test is sufficient for the validation purposes of this exercise.)

The start of your revised validateEmail() function should match the following:

```
1    function validateEmail() {
2        var emailInput = document.getElementById("emailbox");
3        var errorDiv = document.getElementById("emailError");
4        try {
```

```
5   //         if (emailInput.value.search(/@/) === -1 ||
6   //             emailInput.value.lastIndexOf(".") === -1) {
7   //     if (
8   //         (/@/.test(emailInput.value) === false) || (
9   //             (/\...$/.test(emailInput.value) === false) &&
10  //             (/\....$/.test(emailInput.value) === false) &&
11  //             (/\.....$/.test(emailInput.value) === false) &&
12  //             (/\.......$/.test(emailInput.value) === false)
13  //         )
14  //     ) {
15         if ((/@/.test(emailInput.value) === false) ||
16             (/\..{2,6}$/.test(emailInput.value) === false)) {
17             throw "Please provide a valid email address";
18         }
19  ...
```

4. In the `validateUsername()` function, in the `try` statement, comment out the first line of the `if` statement, containing the condition.

5. Below the commented out line, but before the `throw` statement, add the following conditional statement:

```
if (/.{4,}/.test(unInput.value) === false) {
```

This condition uses the quantifier `{4,}` to check if the `unInput` value is at least 4 characters long. Note that this quantifier does not specify an upper limit.

The start of your revised `validateUsername()` function should match the following:

```
1   function validateUsername() {
2       var unInput = document.getElementById("uname");
3       var errorDiv = document.getElementById("usernameError");
4       try {
5   //         if (unInput.value.length < 4) {
6           if (/.{4,}/.test(unInput.value) === false) {
7               throw "Username must be at least 4 characters long";
8           }
9   ...
```

6. In the `validatePassword()` function, in the `try` statement, comment out the first line of the `if` statement, containing the condition.

7. Below the commented out line, but before the first `throw` statement, add the following conditional statement:

```
if (/.{8,}/.test(pw1Input.value) === false) {
```

This condition uses the quantifier `{8,}` to check if the `pw1Input` value is at least 8 characters long. Note that this quantifier does not specify an upper limit.

The start of your revised `validatePassword()` function should match the following:

```
1    function validatePassword() {
2        var pw1Input = document.getElementById("pw1");
3        var pw2Input = document.getElementById("pw2");
4        var errorDiv = document.getElementById("passwordError");
5        try {
6    //       if (pw1Input.value.length < 8) {
7            if (/.{8,}/.test(pw1Input.value) === false) {
8                throw "Password must be at least 8 characters";
9            } else if (pw1Input.value.localeCompare(pw2Input.value)
10               !== 0) {
11               throw "Passwords must match";
12           }
13   ...
```

8. Save your changes to **goldrock.js**, and then Shift-refresh or Shift-reload **account.htm** in your browser.

9. Click in the **Username** box, type **123**, press **Tab**, in the **Password** box type **1234567**, press **Tab**, in the **Password (confirm)** box type **1234567**, press **Tab**, and then in the Email Address box type **ssmith22@cengagebrain.c**. As Figure 8-9 shows, all the boxes you typed in are highlighted in red and error messages are displayed, indicating that the username and password are too short, and the email address entered isn't valid.

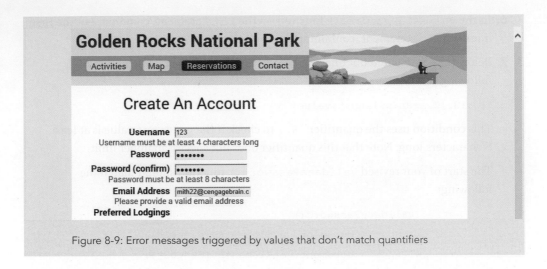

Figure 8-9: Error messages triggered by values that don't match quantifiers

10. Click at the end of the **Username box**, type **4**, click at the end of the **Password** box, type **8**, click at the end of the **Password (confirm)** box, type **8**, click at the end of the **Email Address** box, if necessary, use the arrow keys to move to the end of the existing entry, type **om**, and then press **Tab**. The highlights and error messages are removed because all of the entries now satisfy the length requirements specified using the regular expression quantifiers you added.

Specifying Subexpressions

As you learned earlier, regular expression patterns can include literal values; any strings you validate against a regular expression must contain exact matches for the literal values contained in the pattern. You can also use parentheses metacharacters ( ) to specify the required characters to include in a pattern match. Characters contained in a set of parentheses within a regular expression are referred to as a subexpression or subpattern. Subexpressions allow you to specify the format and quantities of the enclosed characters as a group.

For instance, a U.S. phone number has four distinct parts, which generally take the form 1-###-###-####. If you were creating a regular expression for a U.S. phone number, you could start by creating a subexpression for the first part—the number 1 followed by a hyphen:

```
/^(1-)/
```

You could add a question mark to indicate that the 1- may not be included in some valid phone numbers:

```
/^(1-)?/
```

You could then add a subexpression for the next three digits and the hyphen that follows them. This is the area code, and it is also optional:

```
/^(1-)?(.{3}\-)?/
```

You would add another subexpression for the next group of three characters followed by a hyphen, which is mandatory:

```
/^(1-)?(.{3}\-)?(.{3}\-)/
```

You could then finish the regular expression with one more subexpression for the final group of four characters, which is also mandatory:

```
/^(1-)?(.{3}\-)?(.{3}\-)(.{4})$/
```

> **Note**
> Notice that the preceding pattern includes the ^ and $ metacharacters to anchor both the beginning and end of the pattern. This ensures that a string exactly matches the pattern in a regular expression.

The first and second groups in the preceding pattern include the ? quantifier. This allows a string to optionally include a 1 and the area code. If the string does include these groups, they must be in the exact format of 1-*nnn*- (where *nnn* represents the area code), including the space following the area code. Similarly, the telephone number itself must include two groups that require the number to be in the format of "555-1212". Because the 1 and area code are optional, each of the test() methods in the following code returns a value of true:

```
1   var phonePattern = /^(1-)?(.{3}\-)?(.{3}\-)(.{4})$/;
2   var testResult = phonePattern.test("555-1234"); // true
3   testResult = phonePattern.test("707-555-1234"); // true
4   testResult = phonePattern.test("1-707-555-1234"); // true
```

Defining Character Classes

You use a **character class** in a regular expression to treat multiple characters as a single item. You create a character class by enclosing the characters that make up the class within bracket [] metacharacters. Any characters included in a character class represent alternate characters that are allowed in a pattern match. As an example of a simple character class, consider a word with alternative spellings, such as "analyze" (U.S.) or "analyse" (British).

The following code uses a character class to check for either spelling of this word by specifying that either *s* or *z* could be the sixth character in the string:

```
var wordPattern = /analy[sz]e/;
var testResult = wordPattern.test("analyse"); // true
testResult = wordPattern.test("analyze"); // true
```

Both statements return `true` because the character class allows either spelling of the word.

In comparison, the following test returns `false` because "analyce" is not an accepted spelling of the word:

```
testResult = wordPattern.test("analyce"); // false
```

You use a hyphen metacharacter (–) to specify a range of values in a character class. You can include alphabetical or numerical ranges. You specify all lowercase letters as "`[a-z]`" and all uppercase letters as "`[A-Z]`". The following code creates a pattern that matches only the values *A*, *B*, *C*, *D*, or *F*, and then tests the value of the `letterGrade` variable against the pattern. The character class in the regular expression specifies a range of *A–D* or the character *F* as valid values in the variable.

```
var gradeRange = /[A-DF]/;
var letterGrade = "B";
var testResult = gradeRange.test(letterGrade); // true
```

Because the variable is assigned a value of *B*, the `test()` method returns `true`.

In comparison, the following `test()` method returns `false` because *E* is not a valid value in the character class:

```
letterGrade = "E";
testResult = gradeRange.test(letterGrade); // false
```

To specify optional characters to exclude in a pattern match, include the ˆ metacharacter immediately before the characters in a character class. The following code specifies the same pattern as in the previous example, but by specifying unacceptable characters rather than acceptable characters:

```
1  var gradeRange = /[^EG-Z]/;
2  var letterGrade = "A";
3  var testResult = gradeRange.test(letterGrade); // true
4  letterGrade = "E";
5  testResult = gradeRange.test(letterGrade); // false
```

The `gradeRange` pattern excludes the letters *E* and *G–Z* from an acceptable pattern. The first `test()` method returns a value of `true` because the letter *A* is not excluded from the pattern match, while the second `test()` method returns a value of `false` because the letter *E* is excluded from the pattern match.

The following statements demonstrate how to include numeric characters in or exclude them from a pattern match:

```
var testResult = /[0-9]/.test("5"); // true
testResult = /[^0-9]/.test("5"); // false
```

The first statement returns `true` because it allows any numeric character, while the second statement returns `false` because it excludes any numeric character.

Note that you can combine ranges in a character class, as in the following statements:

```
var testResult = /[0-9a-zA-Z]/.test("7"); // true
testResult = /[^a-zA-Z]/.test("Q"); // false
```

The first statement demonstrates how to include all alphanumeric characters, and the second demonstrates how to exclude all lowercase and uppercase letters.

The following statements demonstrate how to use character classes to create a regular expression pattern for U.S. phone numbers:

```
1    var phonePattern = /^(1 )?(\([0-9]{3}\) )?([1-9]{3}) ↵
2         (\-[1-9]{4})$/;
3    var testResult = phonePattern.test("1 (707) 555-1234");
4        // value of testResult variable is true
```

As a more complex example of a character class, examine the following email validation regular expression, which you saw earlier in the chapter:

```
var emailPattern = /^[_a-zA-Z0-9\-]+(\.[_a-zA-Z0-9\-]+)*↵
    @[a-zA-Z0-9\-]+(\.[a-zA-Z0-9\-]+)*(\.[a-z]{2,6})$/;
```

At this point, you should recognize how the regular expression pattern is constructed. The anchor at the beginning of the pattern specifies that the first part of the email address must include one or more of the characters *A–Z* (upper- or lowercase), *0–9*, or an underscore (_) or hyphen (–). The second portion of the pattern specifies that the email address can optionally include a dot separator, as in "vice.president". The pattern also requires the @ character. Following the literal @ character, the regular expression uses patterns that are similar to the patterns in the name portion of the email address to specify the required structure of the domain name. The last portion of the pattern specifies that the domain identifier must consist of at least two, but not more than six, alphabetic characters.

Using subexpressions and character classes enables you to create powerful and flexible regular expressions. However, it's important to consider the trade-offs—especially the decreased readability of complex regular expressions by other programmers. In some cases, such as a phone number or email address, single, compact expressions are standardized and widely used. However, especially for custom regular expressions, it's important to stop and consider which is a higher priority for your organization and/or your team of developers: readability or compactness. In many cases, you can break a regular expression into smaller units and run a separate test on each. This has the side benefit of enabling you to identify specific issues with a string being tested, rather than simply learning that it does not meet all the requirements coded into a single complex regular expression. On the other hand, breaking a test into multiple statements results in more code, which can take longer for users to download and can negatively impact user experience. For these reasons, it's important to understand whether compact code or self-documenting code is a higher priority when creating regular expressions for a project.

JavaScript regular expressions include special escape characters that you can use in character classes to represent different types of data. For example, the `w` expression can be used instead of the `0-9a-zA-Z` pattern to allow any alphanumeric characters in a character class. Table 8-4 lists the JavaScript character class expressions.

EXPRESSION	DESCRIPTION
\w	Alphanumeric characters
\W	Any character that is not an alphanumeric character
\d	Numeric characters
\D	Nonnumeric characters
\s	White space characters
\S	All printable characters
\b	Backspace character

Table 8-4 JavaScript character class expressions

The following statements demonstrate how to use the \d class expression to test for numeric characters:

```
var testResult = /[\d]/.test("5"); // true
testResult = /[\d]/.test("A"); // false
```

As a more complex example, the following statement demonstrates another way to write an email validation regular expression, using class expressions:

```
var emailPattern = /^[_\w\-]+(\.[_\w\-]+)*@[\w\-]+↵
        (\.[\w\-]+)*(\.[\D]{2,6})$/;
```

Next, you'll use character classes to check the content of usernames, passwords, and email addresses in the account form. You'll add a conditional statement to verify that a username contains only letters and numbers. You'll add three additional statements to check the content of a password: one to verify that it contains at least one letter, another to verify that it contains at least one number, and a third to check that it contains one of the following four symbols: ! @ # _. Finally, you'll add a standard regular expression for email addresses to validate user input in the Email Address field.

To use regular expressions containing character classes to validate username, password, and email address values:

1. Return to **goldrock.js** in your text editor.

2. Within the `validateUsername()` function, in the `try` statement, add the following `else if` statement after the existing `if` statement:

```
else if (/\W/.test(unInput.value) === true) {
    throw "Username must contain only letters and numbers";
}
```

Your revised `if/else` statement should match the following:

```
1    if (/.{4,}/.test(unInput.value) === false) {
2        throw "Username must be at least 4 characters long";
3    } else if (/\W/.test(unInput.value) === true) {
4        throw "Username must contain only letters and numbers";
5    }
```

3. In the `validatePassword()` function, in the `try` statement, add the following `else if` statements after the existing `if/else if` statements:

```
1    else if (/[a-zA-Z]/.test(pw1Input.value) === false) {
2        throw "Password must contain at least one letter";
3    } else if (/\d/.test(pw1Input.value) === false) {
4        throw "Password must contain at least one number";
5    } else if (/[!@#_]/.test(pw1Input.value) === false) {
6        throw "Password must contain at least one of the following↵
7    symbols: ! @ # _";
8    }
```

The first statement checks if the password contains at least one uppercase or lowercase letter. The second statement checks if the password contains at least one digit from 0–9. The third statement checks if the password contains at least one of the following four characters: ! @ # _. Your revised `if/else if` statements should match the following:

```
1    if (/.{8,}/.test(pw1Input.value) === false) {
2        throw "Password must be at least 8 characters";
3    } else if (pw1Input.value.localeCompare(pw2Input.value) !== 0) {
4        throw "Passwords must match";
5    } else if (/[a-zA-Z]/.test(pw1Input.value) === false) {
6        throw "Password must contain at least one letter";
7    } else if (/\d/.test(pw1Input.value) === false) {
8        throw "Password must contain at least one number";
9    } else if (/[!@#_]/.test(pw1Input.value) === false) {
10       throw "Password must contain at least one of the following↵
11   symbols: ! @ # _";
12   }
```

4. In the `validateEmail()` function, insert a new line below the second `var` statement, and then add the following variable definition:

```
var emailCheck = /^[_\w\-]+(\.[_\w\-]+)*@[\w\-]+(\.[\w\-]+)*↵
(\.[\D]{2,6})$/;
```

5. In the `try` statement, comment out the first two lines of the `if` statement, containing the conditions.

6. Below the commented out lines, but before the first `throw` statement, add the following conditional statement:

```
if (emailCheck.test(emailInput.value) === false) {
```

This condition checks the value of the Email Address field against the email regular expression stored in the `emailCheck` variable. The start of your revised `validateEmail()` function should match the following:

```
1    function validateEmail() {
2       var emailInput = document.getElementById("emailbox");
3       var errorDiv = document.getElementById("emailError");
4       var emailCheck = /^[_\w\-]+(\.[_\w\-]+)*@[\w\-]+↵
5    (\.[\w\-]+)*(\.[\D]{2,6})$/;
6       try {
7    //       if (emailInput.value.search(/@/) === -1 ||
8    //           emailInput.value.lastIndexOf(".") === -1) {
9    //       if (
10   //           (/@/.test(emailInput.value) === false) || (
11   //               (/\...$/.test(emailInput.value) --- false) &&
12   //               (/\....$/.test(emailInput.value) === false) &&
13   //               (/\.....$/.test(emailInput.value) === false) &&
14   //               (/\.......$/.test(emailInput.value) === false)
15   //           )
16   //       ) {
17   //       if ((/@/.test(emailInput.value) === false) ||
18   //           (/\..{2,6}$/.test(emailInput.value) === false)) {
19            if (emailCheck.test(emailInput.value) === false) {
20               throw "Please provide a valid email address";
21            }
22   ...
```

7. Save your changes to **goldrock.js**, and then Shift-refresh or Shift-reload **account.htm** in your browser.

8. Click in the **Username** box, type **123!**, press **Tab**, in the **Password** box type **aaaaaaaa** (*a* eight times), press **Tab**, in the **Password (confirm)** box type **aaaaaaaa**, press **Tab**, and then in the **Email Address** box type **ssmith22@cengagebrain**. As Figure 8-10 shows, all the boxes you typed in are highlighted in red, with error messages displayed below, indicating that the username may contain only letters and numbers, the password must contain at least one number, and the email address entered isn't valid.

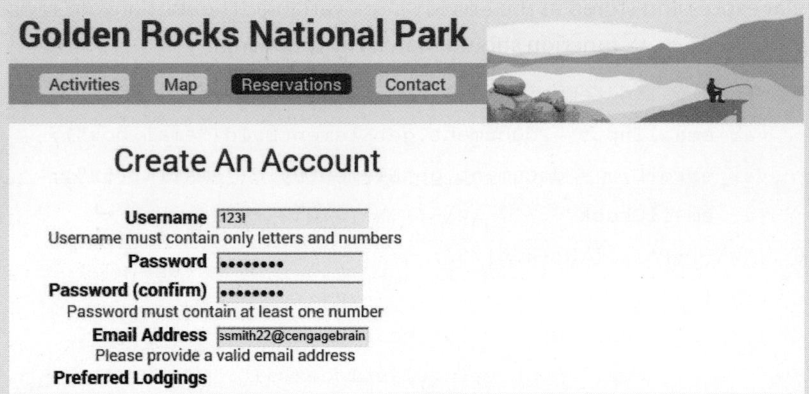

Figure 8-10: Error messages triggered by values that don't match character classes

9. Replace your entry in the **Username box** with **ssmith22**, replace your entries in the **Password** and **Password (confirm)** boxes with **aaaa1111**, click at the end of the **Email Address** box, if necessary, use the arrow keys to move to the end of the existing entry, type **.com**, and then press **Tab**. The highlights and error messages are removed from the Username and Email Address fields because the username consists of only letters and numbers, and the email address is complete. The Password and Password (confirm) boxes now generate a new error message because they do not contain one of the specified symbols.

10. Click at the end of the entry in the **Password** box, type **!**, click at the end of the entry in the **Password (confirm)** box, type **!**, and then press **Tab**. The highlights and error message are removed because the password (aaaa1111!) now contains letters, numbers, and one of the specified symbols.

Matching Multiple Pattern Choices

To allow a string to contain an alternate set of substrings, you separate the strings in a regular expression pattern with the | metacharacter. This is essentially the same as using the Or operator (||) to perform multiple evaluations in a conditional expression. For example, to allow a string to contain either "red" or "green", you include the pattern red|green.

The following code demonstrates how to check whether a domain identifier at the end of a string contains a required value of ".com", ".org", or ".net".

```
1   var domainPattern = /\.(com|org|net)$/;
2   var testResult = domainPattern.test↵
3         ("http://www.whitehouse.gov"); // false
4   testResult = domainPattern.test↵
5         ("http://www.cengagebrain.com"); // true
```

The first `test()` method returns a value of `false` because the URL contains a domain identifier of ".gov", while the second `test()` method returns a value of `true` because the domain name contains a valid identifier value of ".com".

Setting Regular Expression Properties

The `RegExp` object includes several properties that you can use to configure how JavaScript executes regular expressions. Table 8-5 lists the properties of the `RegExp` object. Note that several of the properties can be set with flags, which represent specific values that can be assigned to the property.

PROPERTY	FLAG	DESCRIPTION
global	g	Determines whether to search for all possible matches within a string
ignoreCase	i	Determines whether to ignore letter case when executing a regular expression
lastIndex		Stores the index of the first character from the last match (no flag)
multiline	m	Determines whether to search across multiple lines of text
source		Contains the regular expression pattern (no flag)

Table 8-5 Properties of the `RegExp` object

The values of the `lastIndex` and `source` properties are automatically set by the JavaScript interpreter, although you can set the values of the `global`, `ignoreCase`, and `multiline` properties from within your scripts. You have two options for setting the values of these properties. First, you can assign a value of `true` or `false` to a property by creating a regular expression with the `RegExp()` constructor. For example, the first statement in the following code declares a `RegExp` object named `opecCountry` that searches for the pattern "saudi arabia". The second statement then assigns a value of `true` to the `ignoreCase` property of the `opecCountry` variable so that the case of the regular expression is ignored when it executes.

```
var opecCountry = new RegExp("saudi arabia");
opecCountry.ignoreCase = true;
```

A second option for setting the values of the `global`, `ignoreCase`, and `multiline` properties is to use the flags that are listed in Table 8-5. You can pass the flags as text strings as the second argument of the `RegExp()` constructor. For example, the following statement creates a regular expression that ignores case:

```
var opecCountry = new RegExp("saudi arabia", "i");
```

A third option for setting the values of the `global`, `ignoreCase`, and `multiline` properties is to use the flags that are listed in Table 8-5 when you assign a regular expression to a variable without using the `RegExp()` constructor. To use one of the property flags, you place it after the closing slash at the end of the regular expression. For example, the first statement in the following code declares a regular expression that searches for the pattern "`saudi arabia`", and sets the `ignoreCase` attribute to `true` by appending the `i` flag after the closing forward slash:

```
1   var opecCountry = /saudi arabia/i;
2   var OPEC = "Algeria, Angola, Ecuador, Iran, Iraq, Kuwait, ↵
3           Libya, Nigeria, Qatar, Saudi Arabia, ↵
4           United Arab Emirates, Venezuela";
5   var testResult = opecCountry.test(OPEC); // true
```

The `test()` method in the second statement above returns a value of `true`, even though the letter case of "`Saudi Arabia`" in the `OPEC` variable does not match the letter case of "`saudi arabia`" in the `opecCountry` regular expression variable.

Recall that you can use regular expressions with several methods of the `String` class, including the `search()` and `replace()` methods. By default, the `replace()` method replaces only the first occurrence of a specified pattern in the target string. To replace all instances of a specified pattern with the `replace()` method, you set the value of the `RegExp` object's `global` property to `true`, either with the `RegExp()` constructor or by including the `g` flag in the regular expression pattern that is assigned to a variable. The following example demonstrates how to use the `g` flag to replace all instances of colon symbols in the `infoString` variable with equal signs:

```
1   var infoString = "color:green,size:12,shipping:ground";
2   infoString = infoString.replace(/:/g, "=");
3   // value of infoString is
4   // "color=green,size=12,shipping=ground"
```

Short Quiz 2

1. How do you use the `test()` method of the `RegExp` object to check a string against a regular expression?

2. What is an anchor in a regular expression? What two characters are used as anchors?

3. What characters surround a subexpression?

4. What characters surround a character class?

Manipulating Arrays

To manipulate arrays in your scripts, you use the methods and the `length` property of the **Array class**. When you create an array in your programs, you are really instantiating an object from the `Array` class. Table 8-6 lists the methods of the `Array` class.

METHOD	DESCRIPTION
`array1.concat(array2 [, array3, ...])`	Combines arrays
`pop()`	Removes the last element from the end of an array
`push(value1[, value2, ...])`	Adds one or more elements to the end of an array, where `value1`, `value2`, etc., are the values to add
`reverse()`	Reverses the order of the elements in an array
`shift()`	Removes and returns the first element from the beginning of an array

Continued on next page...

METHOD	DESCRIPTION
slice(*start*, *end*)	Copies a portion of an array to another array, where *start* is the array index number at which to begin extracting elements, and *end* is an integer value that indicates the number of elements to return from the array
sort()	Sorts an array alphabetically
splice(*start*, *elements_to_delete*[, *value1*, *value2*, ...])	Adds or removes elements within an array, where *start* indicates the index number within the array where elements should be added or removed; *elements_to_delete* is an integer value that indicates the number of elements to remove from the array, starting with the element indicated by the start argument; and *value1*, *value2*, etc., represent the values to add
unshift(*value1*[, *value2*, ...])	Adds one or more elements to the beginning of an array, where *value1*, *value2*, etc., are the values to add

Table 8-6: Methods of the Array class

Note that all Array methods are appended using dot syntax to the array name on which they are to run. For instance, to use the sort() method with the list array, you would use the statement

```
list.sort();
```

The Array methods are discussed throughout this section.

Finding and Extracting Elements and Values

This section discusses methods for finding and extracting elements and values in an array. The primary method for finding a value in an array is to use a looping statement to iterate through the array until you find a particular value. For example, the for statement in the following code loops through the hospitalDepts[] array to see if it contains "Neurology." If it does, the loop returns true.

```
1   var hospitalDepts = ["Anesthesia", "Molecular Biology", ↵
2         "Neurology", "Pediatrics"];
3   for (var i = 0; i < hospitalDepts.length; i++) {
4       if (hospitalDepts[i] === "Neurology") {
5           return true;
6       }
7   }
```

To extract elements and values from an array, you use the **slice() method** to copy a portion of an array and assign it to another array. The syntax for the slice() method is

```
array_name.slice(start, end);
```

The *array_name* argument indicates the name of the array from which you want to extract elements. The *start* argument indicates the start position within the array to begin extracting elements. The *end* argument is an integer value that indicates the number of elements to return from the array, starting with the element indicated by the *start* argument.

The following example demonstrates how to use the slice() method to return the first five elements in the largestStates[] array. The elements are assigned to a new array named fiveLargestStates[]. Figure 8-11 shows the output.

```
1    var largestStates = ["Alaska", "Texas", "California",↵
2        "Montana", "New Mexico", "Arizona", "Nevada",↵
3        "Colorado", "Oregon", "Wyoming"];
4    var fiveLargestStates = largestStates.slice(0, 5);
5    for (var i = 0; i < fiveLargestStates.length; i++) {
6        var newItem = document.createElement("p");
7        newItem.innerHTML = fiveLargestStates[i];
8        document.body.appendChild(newItem);
9    }
```

Alaska
Texas
California
Montana
New Mexico

Figure 8-11: List of states extracted using the slice() method

Manipulating Elements

As you use arrays in your scripts, you will undoubtedly need to add and remove elements. For example, suppose that you have a shopping cart program that uses an array to store the names of products that a customer plans to purchase. As the customer selects additional products to purchase, or changes her mind about an item, you will need to manipulate the elements in the array of products.

Adding Elements to and Removing Elements from the Beginning of an Array

To add elements to or remove elements from the beginning of an array, you need to use the shift() and unshift() methods. The **shift() method** removes and returns the first element from the beginning of an array, whereas the **unshift() method** adds one or more elements to the beginning of an array. You append the shift() method to the name of the array whose first element you want to remove. You append the unshift() method to the name of an array and pass to the method a comma-separated list of values for the elements you want to add. For example, the following code declares and initializes an array containing the names of five colors, and then uses the shift() and unshift() methods to change the array contents:

```
1   var colors = ["mauve", "periwinkle", "silver", "cherry",↵
2         "lemon"];
3   colors.shift(); // colors value now
4   // ["periwinkle", "silver", "cherry", "lemon"]
5   colors.unshift("yellow-orange", "violet");
6   // colors value now ["yellow-orange", "violet",
7   // "mauve", "periwinkle", "silver", "cherry", "lemon"]
```

The shift() method removes the first color, mauve, from the top of the array and the unshift() method adds two new colors, yellow-orange and violet, to the top of the array.

Adding Elements to and Removing Elements from the End of an Array

The easiest way to add additional elements to the end of an array is to use the array's length property to determine the next available index. For example, the first statement in the following code creates an array of color names. The second statement then adds a new value, "lemon," as the fourth element of the array by using the array's length property as the element index.

```
1   var colors = ["mauve", "periwinkle", "silver", "cherry"];
2   colors[colors.length] = "lemon";
3   // colors value now ["mauve", "periwinkle", "silver",
4   // "cherry", "lemon"]
```

You can also add elements to and remove elements from the end of an array by using the pop() and push() methods. The **pop() method** removes the last element from the end of an array, whereas the **push() method** adds one or more elements to the end of an array. You append the pop() method to the name of the array whose last element you want to remove. You append the `push()` method to the name of an array and pass to the method a comma-separated list of values for the elements you want to add. In the following example, the `pop()` method removes the last color, "cherry," from the end of the array and the `push()` method adds two additional colors, "yellow-orange" and "violet," to the end of the array.

```
1   var colors = ["mauve", "periwinkle", "silver", "cherry"];
2   colors.pop();
3   // colors value now ["mauve", "periwinkle", "silver"]
4   colors.push("yellow-orange", "violet");
5   // colors value now ["mauve", "periwinkle", "silver",
6   // "yellow-orange", "violet"]
```

Adding and Removing Elements within an Array

So far, you have learned to add and remove elements from the beginning and end of an array. To add or remove elements anywhere else in an array, you need to use the **splice()** **method**. After adding or removing array elements, the `splice()` method also renumbers the indexes in the array. The syntax for the `splice()` method is

```
array.splice(start, elements_to_delete, value1, value2, ...);
```

The *array* argument indicates the name of the array you want to modify. The *start* argument indicates the index number within the array where elements should be added or removed. The *elements_to_delete* argument is an integer value that indicates the number of elements to remove from the array, starting with the element indicated by the *start* argument. The *value1*, *value2*, ... arguments represent the values you want to add as new elements to an array.

To add an element within an array, include a value of 0 as the second argument to the `splice()` method. The `splice()` method in the following code adds a new element with a value of "Ophthalmology" between the "Neurology" and "Pediatrics" elements, and renumbers the elements:

```
1   var hospitalDepts = ["Anesthesia", "Molecular Biology",↵
2           "Neurology", "Pediatrics"];
3   hospitalDepts.splice(3, 0, "Ophthalmology");
4   // value now ["Anesthesia", "Molecular Biology",
5   // "Neurology", "Ophthalmology", "Pediatrics"]
```

To add more than one element within an array, you must pass them as additional values to the `splice()` method. The following example shows how to add two new elements, "Ophthalmology" and "Otolaryngology", between the "Neurology" and "Pediatrics" elements:

```
1   var hospitalDepts = ["Anesthesia", "Molecular Biology", ↵
2         "Neurology", "Pediatrics"];
3   hospitalDepts.splice(3, 0, "Ophthalmology", ↵
4         "Otolaryngology");
5   // value now ["Anesthesia", "Molecular Biology",
6   // "Neurology", "Ophthalmology", "Otolaryngology",
7   // "Pediatrics"]
```

You can also delete array elements by omitting the third argument from the `splice()` method. After you delete array elements with the `splice()` method, the remaining indexes are renumbered, just as when you add new elements. For example, to delete the second and third elements in the `hospitalDepts[]` array, you use the following statement:

```
1   var hospitalDepts = ["Anesthesia", "Molecular Biology", ↵
2         "Neurology", "Pediatrics"];
3   hospitalDepts.splice(1, 2);
4   // value now ["Anesthesia", "Pediatrics"]
```

> **Note**
>
> If you do not include the second argument (`elements_to_delete`), the `splice()` method deletes all the elements from the first argument (`start`) to the end of the array.

This `splice()` statement removes the elements "Molecular Biology" and "Neurology" from the array.

The plan for the Golden Rocks State Park account page is to add the value of each item selected in the Preferred Lodgings section to an array, which will be submitted along with the other user information when a user completes the form. The goldrock.js document contains the `registerLodging()` function, which adds a value to the Profile section on the page when the associated check box is checked, and removes it from the list when the check box is unchecked. You'll add statements to the `registerLodging()` function to add values to and remove values from the `lodging` array as well.

To use methods of the `Array` class to add values to and remove values from the `lodging` array:

1. Return to **goldrock.js** in your text editor.

2. Scroll down to the `registerLodging()` function, and examine it until you understand how it works.

3. Within the first `if` statement, locate the comment `// replace with statement to add checkbox value to lodging array`, delete the comment, and then enter the following two statements in its place:

```
// add checkbox value to lodging array
lodging.push(lodgingName);
```

The `lodgingName` variable stores the value of the check box that called the function. The `if` statement checks if the check box is checked, and if so, the second statement you entered uses the `push()` method of the `Array` object to add the value of the `lodgingName` variable to the end of the `lodging` array.

4. Near the end of the function, within the second `if` statement, locate the comment `// replace with statement to remove element at index i from array`.

5. Delete the comment and then enter the following two statements in its place:

```
// remove element at index i from array
lodging.splice(i, 1);
```

This section of the code executes if the check box that called the function is unchecked. If so, the code uses a `for` statement to loop through the lodging array until it finds the element with a value equal to the `lodgingName` variable. The second statement you entered then uses the `splice()` method of the `Array` object to delete a single element of the `lodging` array at the current index. Your revised `registerLodging()` function should match the following:

```
1    function registerLodging(event) {
2        if (event === undefined) { // get caller element in IE8
3            event = window.event;
4        }
5        var callerElement = event.target || event.srcElement;
6        var lodgingName = callerElement.value;
7        if (callerElement.checked) { // if box has just been checked
8            // add checkbox value to lodging array
9            lodging.push(lodgingName);
```

```
10        // add checkbox value to list in profile section
11        var newLodging = document.createElement("li");
12        newLodging.innerHTML = lodgingName;
13        document.getElementById("profileLodgings").↵
14           appendChild(newLodging);
15        // make profile section and lodging section visible
16        document.getElementById("profile").style.display =↵
17           "block";
18        document.getElementById("lodgingsSection").style.↵
19           display = "block";
20     } else { // if box has just been unchecked
21        var listItems = document.querySelectorAll↵
22           ("#profileLodgings li");
23        for (var i = 0; i < listItems.length; i++) {
24           if (listItems[i].innerHTML === lodgingName) {
25              // remove element at index i from array
26              lodging.splice(i, 1);
27              // remove lodging from profile list
28              listItems[i].parentNode.removeChild(listItems[i]);
29              break;
30           }
31        }
32     }
33  }
```

6. Save your changes to **goldrock.js**, and then Shift-refresh or Shift-reload **account.htm** in your browser.

7. Click the check boxes for **Fire Cabins**, **Spruce Cabins**, and **Talus Campground**. The three selections are displayed in the profile section on the page.

8. Open your browser console, type **lodging**, press **Enter**, if necessary, press **Enter** again, and then if necessary, click the text **object Array** to view the contents of the array. The contents of the lodging array are displayed. Each of the elements was added by the first statement you entered, using the push() method. Figure 8-12 shows the console in Internet Explorer.

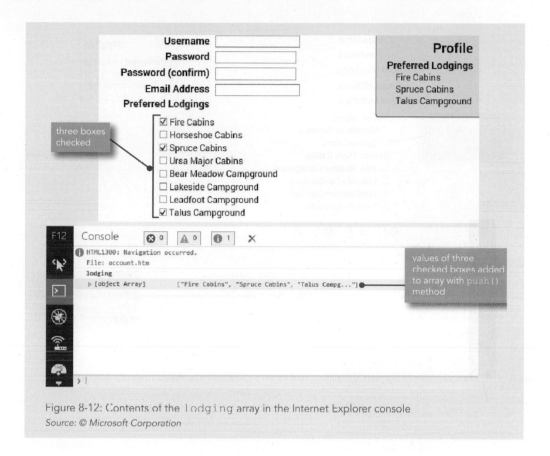

Figure 8-12: Contents of the lodging array in the Internet Explorer console

Source: © Microsoft Corporation

9. Click the **Spruce Cabins** check box to uncheck it. The profile section now lists only Fire Cabins and Talus Campground, which are the values of the remaining checked check boxes.

10. In the console, type **lodging**, press **Enter**, if necessary, press **Enter** again, and then if necessary, click the newly displayed text **object Array** to view the contents of the array. The updated contents of the lodging array are displayed. Notice that the value "Spruce Cabins" was removed by the second statement you entered, using the splice() method. Figure 8-13 shows the updated console in Internet Explorer.

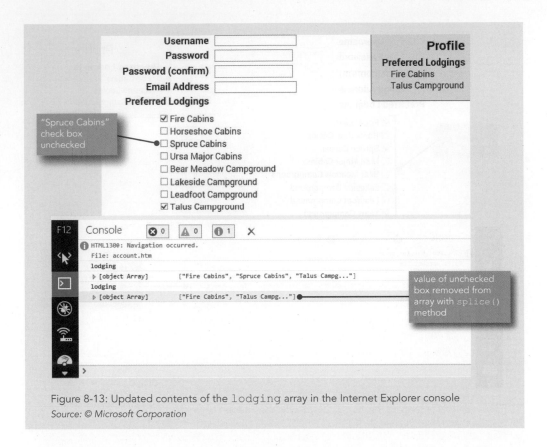

Figure 8-13: Updated contents of the `lodging` array in the Internet Explorer console

Source: © Microsoft Corporation

Sorting and Combining Arrays

In the preceding section, you studied techniques for working with the individual elements in an array. In this section, you'll study techniques for manipulating entire arrays. More specifically, this section discusses how to sort and compare arrays. First, you learn how to sort arrays.

Sorting Arrays

To sort elements of an array alphabetically, you use the **sort() method**. You append the `sort()` method to the name of the array you want to sort using the following syntax:

```
array_name.sort()
```

For example, the following code shows how to use the `sort()` method to sort the elements of an array named `scientificFishNames[]`. Notice the order in which

the values are specified when the array is created, and their order after executing the
sort() method.

```
1    var scientificFishNames = ["Quadratus taiwanae",↵
2        "Macquaria australasica", "Jordania zonope",↵
3        "Abudefduf sparoides", "Dactylopterus volitans",↵
4        "Wattsia mossambica", "Bagrus urostigma"];
5    scientificFishNames.sort();
6    // scientificFishNames value now
7    // ["Abudefduf sparoides", "Bagrus urostigma",
8    // "Dactylopterus volitans", "Jordania zonope",
9    // "Macquaria australasica", "Quadratus taiwanae",
10   // "Wattsia mossambica"]
```

The **reverse() method** simply transposes, or reverses, the order of the elements in an
array; it does not perform a reverse sort (Z to A instead of A to Z). If you want to perform
a reverse sort on an array, then you first need to execute the sort() method to sort the
array alphabetically and then call the reverse() method to transpose the array elements. The following code shows the results of executing the reverse() method on the
scientificFishNames[] array:

```
1    scientificFishNames.reverse();
2    // scientificFishNames value now
3    // ["Wattsia mossambica", "Quadratus taiwanae",
4    // "Macquaria australasica", "Jordania zonope",
5    // "Dactylopterus volitans", "Bagrus urostigma",
6    // "Abudefduf sparoides"]
```

Combining Arrays

If you want to combine arrays, you use the **concat() method**. The syntax for the
concat() method is

```
array1.concat(array2, array3, ...);
```

The *array2* array is appended to the *array1* array, the *array3* array is appended to the
array2 array, and so on. For example, consider the following code, which declares and
initializes the Provinces[] and Territories[] arrays. The Territories[] array is

appended to the `Provinces[]` array with the `concat()` method, and the result is then assigned to a new array named `Canada[]`.

```
1    var Provinces = ["Newfoundland and Labrador", ↵
2            "Prince Edward Island", "Nova Scotia", ↵
3            "New Brunswick", "Quebec", "Ontario", ↵
4            "Manitoba", "Saskatchewan", "Alberta", ↵
5            "British Columbia"];
6    var Territories = ["Nunavut", "Northwest Territories", ↵
7            "Yukon"];
8    var Canada = [];
9    Canada = Provinces.concat(Territories);
10   // value of Canada now ["Newfoundland and Labrador",
11   // "Prince Edward Island", "Nova Scotia",
12   // "New Brunswick", "Quebec", "Ontario",
13   // "Manitoba", "Saskatchewan", "Alberta",
14   // "British Columbia", "Nunavut",
15   // "Northwest Territories", "Yukon"];
```

Short Quiz 3

1. When you use the `slice()` method, you provide two values as arguments. Explain what these two values signify.

2. What is the difference between the `shift()` and `unshift()` methods?

3. How do the `pop()` and `push()` methods work?

Converting Between Data Types

Another common task when working with strings and arrays is to convert them to different data types. In addition to converting strings to arrays and arrays to strings, it's also important to be able to convert objects to strings using a standard format, and to be able to convert those strings back to objects. In this section, you'll learn about methods for performing all of these conversions.

Converting Between Strings and Arrays

Depending on the type of data stored in a string, you may sometimes find it easier to manipulate the data by converting it into an array. You use the **`split()` method** of the `String` class to split a string into an indexed array. The `split()` method uses the syntax

```
array = string.split(separator[, limit]);
```

The *separator* argument specifies the character or characters where the string will be separated into array elements, and the *limit* argument determines the maximum length of the array. If the string does not contain the specified separators, the entire string is assigned to the first element of the array. To split the individual characters in a string into an array, pass an empty string ("") as the *separator* argument.

The following code demonstrates how to convert a variable named OPEC into an array named opecArray.

```
1   var OPEC = "Algeria, Angola, Ecuador, Iran, Iraq, Kuwait,↵
2          Libya, Nigeria, Qatar, Saudi Arabia,↵
3          United Arab Emirates, Venezuela";
4   // The value of OPEC is a string
5   var opecArray = OPEC.split(", ");
6   // The value of opecArray is the following array:
7   // ["Algeria", "Angola", "Ecuador", "Iran", "Iraq",
8   // "Kuwait", "Libya", "Nigeria", "Qatar", "Saudi Arabia",
9   // "United Arab Emirates", "Venezuela"]
```

Because a comma and a space separate the country names in the OPEC variable, these characters are specified as the *separator* argument.

The opposite of the split() method is the Array class's join() method, which combines array elements into a string, separated by a comma or specified characters. The syntax for the join() method is

```
array.join(["separator"]);
```

The *separator* argument specifies the character or characters that will separate the contents of each array element in the returned string. If you do not include the *separator* argument, the join() method automatically separates elements with a comma. To prevent the elements from being separated by any characters in the new string, pass an empty string ("") as the *separator* argument. The following code demonstrates how to use the join() method to create a string from an array containing the names of the OPEC nations.

```
1   var OPEC = ["Algeria", "Angola", "Ecuador", "Iran",↵
2      "Iraq", "Kuwait", "Libya", "Nigeria", "Qatar",↵
3      "Saudi Arabia", "United Arab Emirates", "Venezuela"];
4   // value of OPEC is an array
5   var opecString = OPEC.join();
6   // value of opecString is the following string:
```

```
7   // "Algeria, Angola, Ecuador, Iran, Iraq, Kuwait, Libya,
8   // Nigeria, Qatar, Saudi Arabia, United Arab Emirates,
9   // Venezuela"
```

Because the `join()` method does not include a *separator* argument, the OPEC nations are automatically separated by commas in the new string value.

In comparison, the following code specifies "`;`" for the *separator* argument:

```
1   var OPEC = ["Algeria", "Angola", "Ecuador", "Iran",↵
2       "Iraq", "Kuwait", "Libya", "Nigeria", "Qatar",↵
3       "Saudi Arabia", "United Arab Emirates", "Venezuela"];
4   // value of OPEC is an array
5   var opecString = OPEC.join(";");
6   // value of opecString is the following string:
7   // "Algeria;Angola;Ecuador;Iran;Iraq;Kuwait;Libya;
8   // Nigeria;Qatar;Saudi Arabia;United Arab Emirates;
9   // Venezuela"
```

Because the `join()` method in the preceding code includes a *separator* argument of "`;`", the OPEC nations are separated by semicolons in the new string value.

In addition to the `join()` method, you can also use the `toString()` and `toLocaleString()` methods to convert an array to a string. The **`toString()` method** automatically separates converted array elements with commas. The **`toLocaleString()` method** formats the returned string according to the conventions of the user's language or country and also automatically separates each converted array element with that locale's separator character. The syntax for the `toString()` method is

```
array.toString();
```

The syntax for the `toLocaleString()` method is

```
array.toLocaleString();
```

Golden Rocks National Park needs the contents of the `lodging` array converted to a string for submission to the server program that processes new accounts. Next, you'll create a function called `convertToString()` and add code to it that converts the value of the `lodging` array to a string.

To convert the value of the `lodging` array to a string:

1. Return to **goldrock.js** in your text editor.

2. Before the `createEventListeners()` function, insert the following code to create the `convertToString()` function:

```
1   // convert form input to strings for submission
2   function convertToString() {
3      // convert lodging array to string
4      arrayString = lodging.toString();
5   }
```

The `arrayString` variable is a global variable that's declared at the start of the goldrock.js file. The function uses the `toString()` method to convert the contents of the `lodging` array to a string, and then assigns this value to the `arrayString` variable.

3. Scroll down to the `createEventListeners()` function and then, before the closing `}`, enter the following code to create an event listener for the `convertToString()` function you just created:

```
1   var button = document.getElementById("createBtn");
2   if (button.addEventListener) {
3      button.addEventListener("click", convertToString, false);
4   } else if (button.attachEvent) {
5      button.attachEvent("onclick", convertToString);
6   }
```

This code calls the `convertToString()` function when the `click` event fires on the Create Profile button.

4. Save your changes to **goldrock.js**, and then Shift-refresh or Shift-reload **account.htm** in your browser.

5. Click the check boxes for **Fire Cabins**, **Spruce Cabins**, and **Talus Campground**, and then click the **Create Account** button. The three selections are displayed in the profile section on the page.

> **Caution** | Be sure to click the Create Account button to convert the array contents to a string.

6. In your browser console, type **lodging**, press **Enter**, if necessary, press **Enter** again, and then if necessary, click the text **object Array** to view the contents of the array. The contents of the `lodging` array match those shown previously in Figure 8-12.

7. In the console, type **arrayString** and then press **Enter**. The value of the arrayString variable is displayed. The string consists of the three array values concatenated by commas. Figure 8-14 shows the console output in Internet Explorer.

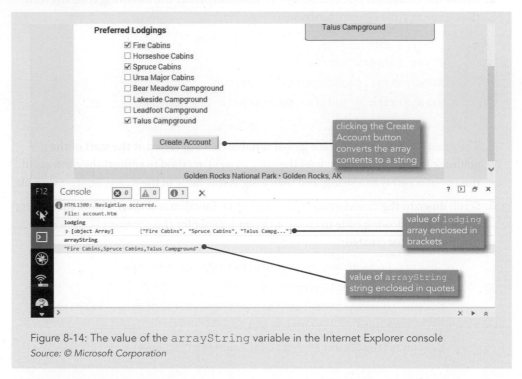

Figure 8-14: The value of the `arrayString` variable in the Internet Explorer console
Source: © Microsoft Corporation

Converting Between Strings and JSON

Besides converting between strings and arrays, another common task in working with application data is converting between strings and JSON. **JavaScript Object Notation (JSON)** is a data format that represents a JavaScript object as a string. JSON is commonly used to send data from an application to a server, or from a server to an application.

Programming Concepts | *Exchanging Information*

Websites generally need to pass information collected from users to other systems, including programs running on web servers and systems run by other organizations. Because so many different systems and programs exist, developers have created standards for exchanging information,

Continued on next page...

so that the information sent by one program is formatted in a way that another program can interpret. Information exchange on the Internet today makes use of two primary formats: XML and JSON. XML (Extensible Markup Language) is both powerful and complex. JSON grew out of the recognition that for many tasks involving information exchange from and to web documents, much of the complexity of XML wasn't needed, and the structure used for JavaScript objects already supported almost all of the most commonly needed features.

ECMAScript 5 was the first version of the specification to include a JSON object. However, browsers started supporting the JSON object before it became part of the specification, so in addition to being supported in modern browsers, the JSON object is supported in Internet Explorer version 8 and later.

The JSON object has two methods, which are described in Table 8-7. The JSON object has no properties.

METHOD	DESCRIPTION
parse()	Converts a string value to an object
stringify()	Converts an object to a string value

Table 8-7 Methods of the JSON object

Converting an Object to a String

To convert a JavaScript object to a JSON string, you use the **stringify() method** of the JSON object. The stringify() method has the syntax

```
string = JSON.stringify(value [, replacer [, space]]);
```

The string value is the name of the variable that will contain the JSON string. The value argument represents the JavaScript object to be converted to a string. You can use the replacer argument to specify a function that affects the conversion process or a list of object properties to be included in the string. If you use the space argument, you specify either a value between 0 and 10 indicating the number of spaces that should separate values in the string, or one or more characters to serve as separators.

For instance, the following code declares an object containing information about a user, and then converts it to a string:

```
1   var newUser = {
2           fName: "Tony",
3           lName: "Chu"
4       },
5       newUserString = JSON.stringify(newUser);
6   // value of newUserString is
7   // '{"fName":"Tony","lName":"Chu"}'
```

In the string produced by the `stringify()` method, each property name is enclosed in double quotes, each string value is enclosed in double quotes, each property is concatenated with its value with a colon, and property-value pairs are separated with commas. In addition, the entire set of object properties and values is enclosed in braces.

To instead separate each property-value pair with a semicolon and a space, you could use the following statement:

```
newUserString = JSON.stringify(newUser, "; ");
// value of newUserString is
// '{"fName":"Tony"; "lName":"Chu"}'
```

This string is the same as the previous one, except that the first property-value pair is followed by a semicolon and a space instead of by a comma.

Converting a String to an Object

The **parse() method** of the JSON object performs the opposite action of the `stringify()` method: it converts a JSON string to a JavaScript object. The `parse()` method has the syntax

```
object = JSON.parse(string [, function]);
```

The `object` value is the name of the variable that will contain the JavaScript object. The `string` argument represents the JSON string to be converted to an object. You can use the `function` argument to specify a function that affects the conversion process.

For instance, the following statement defines a JSON string:

```
var newUser = '{"fName":"Tony","lName":"Chu"}';
```

Note that this value is a string because it is enclosed in quotes. Without the quotes, the braces would instead make it an object. The value is enclosed in single quotes to distinguish from the double quotes surrounding the property names and values.

To convert the `newUser` string value to a JavaScript object, you use the following `parse()` statement:

```
1    var newUserObject = JSON.parse(newUser);
2    // value of newUserObject is
3    // {
4    //     fName: "Tony",
5    //     lName: "Chu"
6    // };
```

In addition to the array, Golden Rocks National Park needs the contents of the `profile` object converted to a JSON string for submission to the server. Next, you'll add a statement to the `convertToString()` function to convert the value of the `profile` object to a JSON string.

To convert the value of the `profile` object to a JSON string:

1. Return to **goldrock.js** in your text editor.

2. Within the `convertToString()` function, before the closing }, insert the following statements:

```
// convert profile object to string
objectString = JSON.stringify(profile);
```

The `profile` variable is a global variable that's declared at the start of the goldrock.js file. The second statement uses the `stringify()` method of the JSON object to convert the contents of the `profile` array to a JSON string, and then assigns this value to the `objectString` variable.

3. Save your changes to **goldrock.js**, and then Shift-refresh or Shift-reload **account.htm** in your browser.

4. Enter the following data in the Create An Account form:

Username:	**smith22**
Password:	**kR@yF15h**
Password (confirm):	**kR@yF15h**
Email address:	**ssmith22@cengagebrain.com**

5. Click the **Create Account** button.

> **Caution** | *Be sure to click the Create Account button to convert the object contents to a* JSON *string.*

6. In your browser console, type **profile**, press **Enter**, if necessary, press **Enter** again, and then if necessary, click the text **object Object** to view the contents of the object. The contents of the `profile` object are displayed.

7. In the console, type **objectString**, and then press **Enter**. The value of the `objectString` variable is displayed. The string consists of the three object properties and their values separated by colons, with the property-value pairs concatenated by commas. Figure 8-15 shows the console output in Internet Explorer.

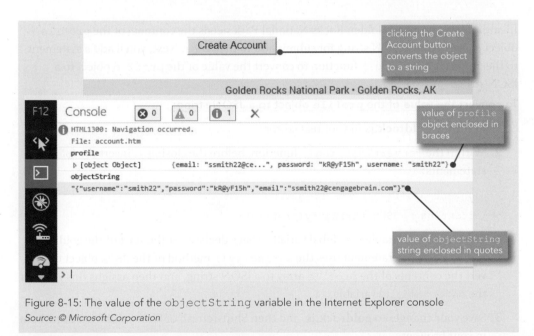

Figure 8-15: The value of the `objectString` variable in the Internet Explorer console
Source: © Microsoft Corporation

Short Quiz 4

1. Which method do you use to convert a string to an array? Which object is this a method of?

2. What is the difference between the `toString()` and `toLocaleString()` methods of the `String` object?

3. What is JSON? What is it used for?

Summary

> You can parse and manipulate strings using methods of the `String` class. These methods enable you to count characters, find and extract characters and substrings, replace characters and substrings, combine characters and substrings, and compare strings.

> The `fromCharCode()` method of the `String` class constructs a text string from Unicode character codes that are passed as arguments.

> To change the case of letters in a string, you use the `toLowerCase()` and `toUpperCase()` methods of the `String` class.

> The `String` class contains a single property, the `length` property, which returns the number of characters in a string.

> There are two types of string search methods: methods that return a numeric position in a text string and methods that return a character or substring.

> The `replace()` method of the `String` class creates a new string with all instances of a specified pattern replaced with the value of the text argument.

> The `concat()` method of the JavaScript `String` class creates a new string by combining strings that are passed as arguments.

> The `localeCompare()` method of the `String` class compares strings according to the particular sort order of a language or country.

> Regular expressions are patterns that are used for matching and manipulating strings according to specified rules.

> The `RegExp` class enables you to compare and manipulate strings using patterns you specify.

> Regular expression patterns consist of literal characters and metacharacters, which are special characters that define the pattern matching rules in a regular expression.

> A pattern that matches the beginning or end of a line is called an anchor.

> Metacharacters that specify the quantity of a match are called quantifiers.

> Characters contained in a set of parentheses within a regular expression are referred to as a subexpression or subpattern.

> You use character classes in regular expressions to treat multiple characters as a single item.

> To allow a string to contain an alternate set of substrings, you separate the strings in a regular expression pattern with the | metacharacter.

> The `Array` class includes methods for manipulating array contents.

> To extract elements and values from an array, you use the `slice()` method of the `Array` class to return (copy) a portion of an array and assign it to another array.

> You use the `shift()` and `unshift()` methods of the `Array` class to add elements to or remove elements from the beginning of an array.

> You use the `pop()` and `push()` methods of the `Array` class to add elements to or remove elements from the end of an array.

> The `splice()` method of the `Array` class adds or removes elements within an array.

> The `sort()` method of the `Array` class alphabetically sorts the elements of an array.

> The `reverse()` method of the `Array` class transposes, or reverses, the order of the elements in an array.

> The `concat()` method of the `Array` class combines arrays.

> The `String` and `Array` classes include methods for converting between string values and array values.

> The `split()` method of the `String` class splits a string into an indexed array.

> The `join()` method of the `Array` class combines array elements into a string, separated by a comma or specified characters.

> The `JSON` class includes methods for converting between string values and object values.

> To convert a JavaScript object to a JSON string, you use the `stringify()` method of the `JSON` object.

> The `parse()` method of the `JSON` object performs the opposite action of the `stringify()` method: it converts a JSON string to a JavaScript object.

Key Terms

anchor—A regular expression pattern that matches the beginning or end of a line.

Array class—The JavaScript class that includes methods and a property for manipulating arrays in your scripts.

character class—Characters in a regular expression grouped within bracket metacharacters and treated as a single item; any characters included in a character class represent alternate characters that are allowed in a pattern match.

concat() method—A method of the `String` class that creates a new string by combining strings that are passed as arguments.

fromCharCode() method—A method of the `String` class that constructs a text string from Unicode character codes that are passed as arguments.

indexOf() method—A method of the `String` class that returns the position of the first occurrence of one string in another string.

JavaScript Object Notation (JSON) —A data format that represents a JavaScript object as a string.

join() method—The method of the `Array` class that combines array elements into a string, separated by a comma or specified characters.

JSON—*See* JavaScript Object Notation.

lastIndexOf() method—A method of the `String` class that returns the position of the last occurrence of one string in another string.

length property—The only property of the `String` class, which returns the number of characters in a string.

localeCompare() method—A method of the `String` class that compares strings according to the particular sort order of a language or country.

metacharacters—Special characters that define the pattern matching rules in a regular expression.

parse() method—The method of the `JSON` object that converts a JSON string to a JavaScript object.

parsing—The act of extracting characters or substrings from a larger string.

pop() method—The method of the `Array` class that removes the last element from the end of an array.

push() method—The method of the `Array` class that adds one or more elements to the end of an array.

quantifiers—Metacharacters that specify the quantity of a match.

regular expression—A pattern used for matching and manipulating strings according to specified rules.

RegExp object—A JavaScript object that contains methods and properties for working with regular expressions.

replace() method—A method of the `String` class that creates a new string with the first instance of a specified pattern replaced with a text value supplied as an argument.

reverse() method—The method of the `Array` class that you use to simply transpose, or reverse, the order of the elements in an array.

search() method—A method of the `String` class that returns the position of the first instance of the first character of a text string that is passed as an argument.

shift() method—The method of the `Array` class that removes and returns the first element from the beginning of an array.

slice() method (arrays)—A method of the Array class that you use to copy a portion of an array and assign it to another array.

slice() method (strings)—A method of the String class that you use to extract characters from a string; slice() allows you to specify negative index values as arguments.

sort() method—The method of the Array class that you use to sort elements of an array alphabetically.

splice() method—The method of the Array class that you use to add or remove elements anywhere in an array, and then renumber the indexes in the array.

split() method—The method of the String class that you use to split a string into an indexed array.

static method—A method that you call using its class name rather than the name of an object of that class.

String class—A JavaScript class that represents all literal strings and string variables and contains methods for manipulating text strings.

stringify() method—The method of the JSON object that you use to convert a JavaScript object to a JSON string.

subexpression—Characters contained in a set of parentheses within a regular expression, which allow you to specify the format and quantities of the enclosed characters as a group.

subpattern—*See* subexpression.

substring() method—A method of the String class that you use to extract characters from a string; substring() does not allow you to specify negative index values as arguments.

test() method—A method of the RegExp class that returns a value of true if a string contains text that matches a regular expression or false if it doesn't.

toLocaleString() method—The method of the Array class that combines array elements into a string, formats the returned string according to the conventions of the user's language or country, and also automatically separates each converted array element with that locale's separator character.

toLowerCase() method—A method of the String class that converts a text string to lowercase.

toString() method—The method of the Array class that combines array elements into a string, automatically separated by commas.

toUpperCase() method—A method of the String class that converts a text string to uppercase.

Unicode—A standardized set of characters from many of the world's languages, with a number representing each character.

unshift() method—The method of the Array class that adds one or more elements to the beginning of an array.

Review Questions

1. Extracting characters or substrings from a larger text string is known as _____.
   a. parsing
   b. compiling
   c. rendering
   d. stripping

2. What is the property of the `String` class that returns the number of characters in a string?
   a. `chars`
   b. `size`
   c. `width`
   d. `length`

3. Regular expression patterns in JavaScript must begin and end with which characters?
   a. `{ }`
   b. `/ /`
   c. `( )`
   d. `[ ]`

4. Which of the following is a method of the `RegExp` class for working with regular expressions?
   a. `search()`
   b. `subexpression()`
   c. `test()`
   d. `class()`

5. Which metacharacter in a regular expression represents any single character?
   a. `$`
   b. `^`
   c. `\`
   d. `.`

6. Which metacharacter(s) in a regular expression represent characters to exclude?
   a. `()`
   b. `[]`
   c. `[^]`
   d. `-`

7. A pattern that matches the beginning or end of a line is called a(n) _____.

    a. anchor

    b. root

    c. metacharacter

    d. class

8. To match any metacharacter as a literal value in a regular expression, you must _____.

    a. enclose the character in brackets ([ ])

    b. enclose the character in parentheses (( ))

    c. precede the character with a slash (/)

    d. precede the character with a backslash (\ )

9. Which of the following expressions would return `false`?

    a. `/^1./.test("1.10")`

    b. `/^1\./.test("1.10")`

    c. `/1.$/.test("1.10")`

    d. `/1\.$/.test("1.10")`

10. Which of the following quantifiers specifies that the preceding character repeat at least 2 times?

    a. `{2}`

    b. `{2,}`

    c. `+`

    d. `?`

11. Which of the following characters do you use to create a subexpression?

    a. `[ ]`

    b. `/ /`

    c. `( )`

    d. `{ }`

12. Which of the following expressions represents numeric characters?

    a. `\s`

    b. `\b`

    c. `\d`

    d. `\D`

13. Which method of the `Array` class removes the last element from the end of an array?

    a. `pop()`

    b. `push()`

    c. `shift()`

    d. `unshift()`

14. What array would result from the following statement?

```
[white, silver, blue].splice(1, 0, "gray");
```
   a. [gray, silver, blue]
   b. [white, gray, blue]
   c. [white, gray, silver, blue]
   d. [gray, white, silver, blue]

15. The JSON.parse() method converts a value to which data type?
   a. Object
   b. String
   c. Array
   d. Number

16. After running the statements

```
var media = "dvd", label = media.toUpperCase();
```

   what is the value of the media variable, and why?

17. What is the difference between the indexOf() and lastIndexOf() methods?

18. Explain why you would specify negative argument values for the slice() method.

19. Does the expression "a" < "A" evaluate to true or false? Why?

20. What is the difference between the shift() and unshift() methods of the Array class?

Hands-On Projects

Hands-On Project 8-1

In this project, you'll enhance a form to create an account ID value based on the user's first and last initials, and then you'll add all the account information to an array.

1. In your text editor, open the **index.htm** file from the HandsOnProject8-1 folder in the Chapter08 folder, add your name and today's date where indicated in the comment section, and then save the file.

2. Before the closing </body> tag, add the following script element, save your changes, and then close **index.htm**:

```
<script src="script.js"></script>
```

3. Create a new file in your text editor, create a JavaScript comment section containing the text **Hands-on Project 8-1**, your name, today's date, and the filename **script.js**, and then save the file with the name **script.js** to the HandsOnProject8-1 folder.

4. Add a statement instructing processors to interpret the document contents in strict mode. Add another statement declaring a global variable named `newAccountArray` with an empty array as its value.

5. Declare a new function named `createID()`. Declare the local variables listed in Table 8-8, with values referencing the elements with the id values shown.

VARIABLE	ELEMENT ID VALUE
fname	fnameinput
lname	lnameinput
zip	zipinput
account	accountidbox

Table 8-8: Variable names and corresponding element ids

Also declare a local variable named `fields` with a value that references all elements with the tag name `input`. Finally, declare the local variables `acctid`, `firstInit`, and `lastInit` with no values.

6. Within the `createID()` function, create an `if` statement that checks if the values of the elements referenced by the `fname`, `lname`, and `zip` variables are all non-null. (*Hint*: Check if each value is not equal to an empty string (`""`).) Add the following statements to run if the condition is true:

```
1   firstInit = fname.value.charAt(0).toUpperCase();
2   lastInit = lname.value.charAt(0).toUpperCase();
3   acctid = firstInit + lastInit + zip.value;
4   account.value = acctid;
5   newAccountArray = [];
6   for (var i = 0; i < fields.length - 1; i++) {
7       newAccountArray.push(fields[i].value);
8   }
```

This code uses the `charAt()` method of the `String` object to assign the first letter of the user's first and last names to the `firstInit` and `lastInit` variables. Next it creates the `acctid` value by concatenating the first initial, last initial, and zip code, then assigns that value to the Account ID field in the form. Finally, it ensures that the newAccountArray variable is empty, and then uses a `for` loop to add the value of each form field to the array with the `push()` method.

7. Add the following function to create event listeners:

```
1   function createEventListeners() {
2       var fname = document.getElementById("fnameinput");
3       var lname = document.getElementById("lnameinput");
4       var zip = document.getElementById("zipinput");
5       if (fname.addEventListener) {
6           fname.addEventListener("change", createID, false);
7           lname.addEventListener("change", createID, false);
8           zip.addEventListener("change", createID, false);
9       } else if (fname.attachEvent) {
10          fname.attachEvent("onchange", createID);
11          lname.attachEvent("onchange", createID);
12          zip.attachEvent("onchange", createID);
13      }
14  }
15  if (window.addEventListener) {
16      window.addEventListener("load", createEventListeners,↵
17          false);
18  } else if (window.attachEvent) {
19      window.attachEvent("onload", createEventListeners);
20  }
```

8. Save your changes to **script.js**, then open **index.htm** in your browser. Enter your name and address (or a fictitious name and address) in the form. After entering a Zip value, press **Tab**. The Account ID value is created automatically.

9. Open your browser console, type **newAccountArray**, press **Enter**, and then, if necessary, click **object Array** to view the array contents. As Figure 8-16 shows, the array contents, including the Account ID, are all elements in the newAccountArray variable.

Hands-on Project 8-1

New Account Information

First Name	Tony
Last Name	Chu
Street Address	1 Main St
City	Romeo
State	MI
Zip	48065
Account ID	TC48065

Create Account

```
F12    Console      ⊗ 0    ⚠ 0    ⓘ 1    ✕
ⓘ JavaScript Console is attached and accepting commands.
   newAccountArray
   ▷ [object Array]        ["Tony", "Chu", "1 Main St", "Oakland", "MI", "48065", "TC48065"]



   > |
```

Figure 8-16: Completed form with array contents in console
Source: © Microsoft Corporation

Hands-On Project 8-2

In this project, you'll modify the document you worked with in Hands-on Project 8-1 to store input in an object rather than an array. You'll also convert the object contents to a JSON string.

1. In the file manager for your operating system, copy the completed contents of the HandsOnProject8-1 folder to the HandsOnProject8-2 folder.

2. In your text editor, open the **index.htm** file from the HandsOnProject8-2 folder, change "Hands-on Project 8-1" to **Hands-on Project 8-2** in the comment section, in the `title` element, and in the `h1` element, and then save your changes.

3. Open **script.js**, and then in the comment section, change "Hands-on Project 8-1" to **Hands-on Project 8-2**.

4. In the **script.js** file, comment out the global variable `newAccountArray`, and then declare two global variables: `newAccountObject`, with an empty object as its value, and `newAccountSubmission`, with no value.

5. In the `createID()` function, in the `if` statement, just before the `for` loop, comment out the statement that resets the value of the `newAccountArray` variable, and then add the following statement to reset the value of the `newAccountObject` variable:

    ```
    newAccountObject = {};
    ```

6. Within the `for` loop, comment out the statement that uses the `push()` method of the `Array` object. Within the `for` loop, add the following new statement to create an object property based on the value of each object value:

    ```
    newAccountObject[fields[i].name] = fields[i].value;
    ```

7. Below the `createID()` function, declare a new function with the name `createString()`. Add the following statement to the `createString()` function:

    ```
    newAccountSubmission = JSON.stringify(newAccountObject);
    ```

8. Within the `createEventListeners()` function, just before the closing }, add the following code to call the `createString()` function when the form button is clicked:

    ```
    1   var button = document.getElementById("submitBtn");
    2   if (button.addEventListener) {
    3      button.addEventListener("click", createString, false);
    4   } else if (button.attachEvent) {
    5      button.attachEvent("onclick", createString);
    6   }
    ```

9. Save your changes to **script.js**, and then open **index.htm** in a browser. Enter your name and address (or a fictitious name and address) in the form. After entering a Zip value, press **Tab**. The Account ID value is created automatically, as in the previous case.

10. Open your browser console, type **newAccountObject**, press **Enter**, and then, if necessary, click **object Object** to view the object contents. The object properties include all the form fields and their values, including the Account ID.

11. Click the **Create Account** button on the web page. This calls the `createString()` function, which creates a JSON string from the `newAccountObject` object.

12. In your console, type **newAccountSubmission**, and then press **Enter**. As Figure 8-17 shows, the value of `newAccountSubmission` is a JSON string containing all the `newAccountObject` properties and their values.

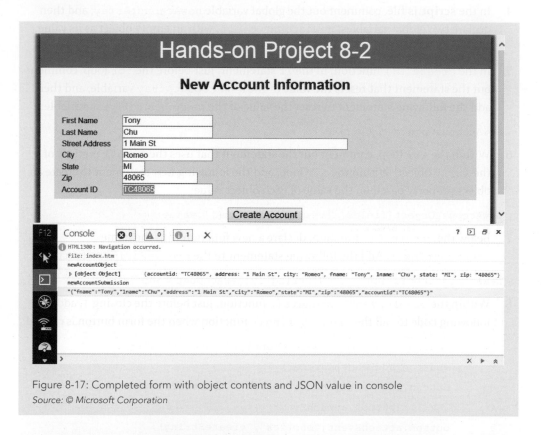

Figure 8-17: Completed form with object contents and JSON value in console
Source: © Microsoft Corporation

Hands-On Project 8-3

When you make an online purchase using a credit card, many sites require you to identify which type of card you're using (Visa, MasterCard, etc.) before entering the card number. However, numbers for each card company follow different rules, and the type of card can be deduced from the card number itself. In this project, you'll enhance a section of an order form using regular expressions. After a credit card number is entered, you'll use a series of `if/else` statements to check the number against regular expressions for four major card companies, and then to select the option button for the matching card type automatically. Major credit card numbers must be in the following formats:

> **American Express**—Numbers start with 34 or 37 and consist of 15 digits.
> **Discover**—Numbers begin with 6011 or 65 and consist of 16 digits.
> **MasterCard**—Numbers start with the numbers 51 through 55 and consist of 16 digits.
> **Visa**—Numbers start with a 4; new cards consist of 16 digits and old cards consist of 13 digits.

Note | *More information on credit card numbers and regular expressions is available at http://www.regular-expressions.info/creditcard.html.*

1. In your text editor, open the **index.htm** file from the HandsOnProject8-3 folder in the Chapter08 folder, add your name and today's date where indicated in the comment section, and then save the file.

2. Before the closing `</body>` tag, add the following `script` element, save your changes, and then close **index.htm**:

   ```
   <script src="script.js"></script>
   ```

3. Create a new file in your text editor, create a JavaScript comment section containing the text **Hands-on Project 8-3**, your name, today's date, and the filename **script.js**, and then save the file with the name **script.js** to the HandsOnProject8-3 folder.

4. Add a statement instructing processors to interpret the document contents in strict mode.

5. Declare a new function named `selectCardType()`. Declare the local variables listed in Table 8-9 with the values shown:

VARIABLE NAME	VALUE
cardNumValue	document.getElementById("ccNum").value
visa	/^4[0-9]{12}(?:[0-9]{3})?$/
mc	/^5[1-5][0-9]{14}$/
discover	/^6(?:011|5[0-9]{2})[0-9]{12}$/
amex	/^3[47][0-9]{13}$/

Table 8-9: Variable names and values

6. Within the `selectCardType()` function, add the following series of `if`/`else` statements to test the card number entered by a user against the regular expressions and check the option button for the matching card type:

```
1   if (visa.test(cardNumValue)) {
2      document.getElementById("visa").checked = "checked";
3   } else if (mc.test(cardNumValue)) {
4      document.getElementById("mc").checked = "checked";
5   } else if (discover.test(cardNumValue)) {
6      document.getElementById("discover").checked = "checked";
7   } else if (amex.test(cardNumValue)) {
8      document.getElementById("amex").checked = "checked";
9   }
```

7. Below the `selectCardType()` function, add the following code to create an event listener:

```
1   function createEventListeners() {
2      var cardNum = document.getElementById("ccNum");
3      if (cardNum.addEventListener) {
4        cardNum.addEventListener("change", selectCardType, false);
5      } else if (cardNum.attachEvent) {
6        cardNum.attachEvent("onchange", selectCardType);
7      }
8   }
9   if (window.addEventListener) {
10     window.addEventListener("load", createEventListeners, false);
11  } else if (window.attachEvent) {
12     window.attachEvent("onload", createEventListeners);
13  }
```

8. Save your changes to **script.js**, and then open index.htm in a browser.

9. Click in the **Card #** box, type **378282246310005**, and then press **Tab**. As Figure 8-18 shows, the American Express option is selected because this card number matches the regular expression for American Express cards.

Hands-on Project 8-3

Payment Information

Card # 378282246310005

☐ Visa ○ Master Card ○ Discover ⦿ American Express

Figure 8-18: Completed form with correctly identified card number

10. Create a document in a text editor, and then repeat Step 9 to test the following card numbers, recording the credit card type for each number in your document. Each card number should be identified as a different card type.
    a. 4012888888881881
    b. 371449635398431
    c. 5105105105105100
    d. 6011000990139424

Hands-On Project 8-4

In this project, you'll add functionality to a web page that displays a to-do list. You'll add code to store the text of each item in an array, as well as code that creates an ordered list containing the array items. You'll also incorporate a "first" button before the text of each list item that a user can click to move that list item to the top of the list.

1. In your text editor, open the **index.htm** file from the HandsOnProject8-4 folder in the Chapter08 folder, add your name and today's date where indicated in the comment section, and then save the file.

2. Before the closing `</body>` tag, add the following `script` element, save your changes, and then close **index.htm**:

```
<script src="script.js"></script>
```

3. Create a new file in your text editor, create a JavaScript comment section containing the text **Hands-on Project 8-4**, your name, today's date, and the filename **script.js**, and then save the file with the name **script.js** to the HandsOnProject8-4 folder.

4. Add a statement instructing processors to interpret the document contents in strict mode. Also declare a global variable named `list` with an empty array as its value.

5. Declare a new function named `generateList()` containing the following statements:

```
1   var listItems = document.getElementsByTagName("li");
2   for (var i = listItems.length - 1; i >= 0; i--) {
```

```
3       document.getElementsByTagName("ol")[0].↵
4           removeChild(listItems[i]);
5    }
6    for (var i = 0; i < list.length; i++) {
7        var newItem = "<span class='first'>first</span>" + list[i];
8        var newListItem = document.createElement("li");
9        newListItem.innerHTML = newItem;
10       document.getElementsByTagName("ol")[0].↵
11           appendChild(newListItem);
12       var firstButtons = document.querySelectorAll(".first");
13       var lastFirstButton = firstButtons[firstButtons.length - 1];
14       if (lastFirstButton.addEventListener) {
15         lastFirstButton.addEventListener("click",↵
16             moveToTop, false);
17       } else if (lastFirstButton.attachEvent) {
18         lastFirstButton.attachEvent("onclick", moveToTop);
19       }
20   }
```

This function loops through the existing `li` elements in the HTML document and removes them all. It then loops through the `list` array, and for each array element, it creates a new `li` element. It then generates the content of that element using the current array element along with a `span` element to create the "first" button. Finally, the function adds an event listener to the "first" button to call the `moveToTop()` function, which you'll create in a later step.

6. Below the `generateList()` function, declare a new function named `addItem()` containing the following statements:

```
1    var newItem = document.getElementById("newItem");
2    list.push(newItem.value);
3    newItem.focus();
4    newItem.value = "";
5    generateList();
```

This code adds the value in the text box to the end of the `list` array using the `push()` method. After returning the focus to the text box and clearing its value, the function calls the `generateList()` function.

7. Below the `addItem()` function, declare a new function named `moveToTop()` that takes a single parameter, `evt`. Add the following statements to the function:

```
1   if (evt === undefined) { // get caller element in IE8
2       evt = window.event;
3   }
4   var callerElement = evt.target || evt.srcElement;
5   var listItems = document.getElementsByTagName("li");
6   var parentItem = callerElement.parentNode;
7   for (var i = 0; i < list.length; i++) {
8       if (parentItem.innerHTML.search(list[i]) !== -1) {
9           var itemToMove = list.splice(i, 1);
10          list.unshift(itemToMove);
11      }
12  }
13  generateList();
```

This code creates variables that reference the collection of `li` elements in the document and the parent `li` element of the "first" button that was clicked to call the function. It then uses a `for` loop and the string `search()` method to check each value in the `list` array against the content of the parent `li` element. When it identifies the matching text in the array, it uses the `splice()` array method to remove that array element from the array and assign it to a variable. It then uses the array `unshift()` method to add the variable value as a new element at the start of the array. Finally, it calls the `generateList()` function to recreate the ordered list based on the new order of the array.

8. Below the `moveToTop()` function, add the following code to create an event listener for the button:

```
1   function createEventListener() {
2       var addButton = document.getElementById("button");
3       if (addButton.addEventListener) {
4           addButton.addEventListener("click", addItem, false);
5       } else if (addButton.attachEvent) {
6           addButton.attachEvent("onclick", addItem);
7       }
8   }
9   if (window.addEventListener) {
```

```
10        window.addEventListener("load", createEventListener, false);
11    } else if (window.attachEvent) {
12        window.attachEvent("onload", createEventListener);
13    }
```

9. Save your changes to **script.js**, and then open **index.htm** in a browser. Click in the text box, type **Finish JavaScript projects**, click **Add Item**, type **Make dinner**, click **Add Item**, type **Renew license**, and then click **Add Item**. Your list should now contain three items, each with its own "first" button, as shown in Figure 8-19.

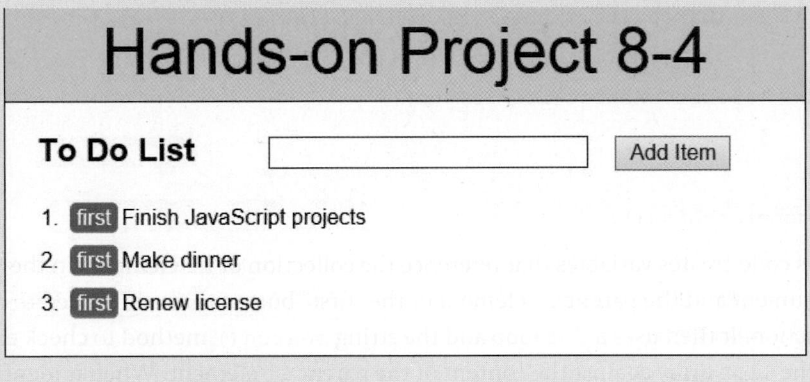

Hands-on Project 8-4

To Do List [   ] [Add Item]

1. [first] Finish JavaScript projects
2. [first] Make dinner
3. [first] Renew license

Figure 8-19: To-do list with "first" buttons

10. Click the **first button** for item 3. The "Renew license" list item moves to the top of the list, as shown in Figure 8-20.

Hands-on Project 8-4

To Do List [   ] [Add Item]

1. [first] Renew license
2. [first] Finish JavaScript projects
3. [first] Make dinner

Figure 8-20: To-do list with rearranged items

Hands-On Project 8-5

In this exercise, you'll enhance Hands-on Project 8-4 to include a "last" button for each item. You'll add a function to your code so a user can click the "last" button for an item to move that item to the last position on the list.

1. In the file manager for your operating system, copy the completed contents of the HandsOnProject8-4 folder to the HandsOnProject8-5 folder.

2. In your text editor, open the **index.htm** file from the HandsOnProject8-5 folder, change "Hands-on Project 8-4" to **Hands-on Project 8-5** in the comment section, in the `title` element, and in the `h1` element, and then save your changes.

3. Open **script.js**, and then in the comment section, change "Hands-on Project 8-4" to **Hands-on Project 8-5**.

4. In the **script.js** file, within the `generateList()` function, in the second `for` statement, add the code `"<span class='last'>last</span>"` + within the declaration of the `newItem` variable, as follows:

```
var newItem = "<span class='first'>first</span>" +↵
   "<span class='last'>last</span>" + list[i];
```

This code adds the text "last" before each list item, to serve as a button for moving a list item to the end of the list.

5. Just before the first `if` statement, add declarations for the `lastButtons` and `lastLastButton` variables, as follows:

```
1   var firstButtons = document.querySelectorAll(".first");
2   var lastFirstButton = firstButtons[firstButtons.length - 1];
3   var lastButtons = document.querySelectorAll(".last");
4   var lastLastButton = lastButtons[lastButtons.length - 1];
```

6. Within the code that adds event listeners in the `generateList()` function, add statements to add an event listener or attach an event to the element referenced by the `lastLastButton` variable, calling the `moveToBottom()` function, as follows:

```
1   if (lastFirstButton.addEventListener) {
2     lastFirstButton.addEventListener("click", moveToTop, false);
3     lastLastButton.addEventListener("click", moveToBottom,↵
4       false);
5   } else if (lastFirstButton.attachEvent) {
6     lastFirstButton.attachEvent("onclick", moveToTop);
7     lastLastButton.attachEvent("onclick", moveToBottom);
8   }
```

7. Below the `moveToTop()` function, declare a new function called `moveToBottom()`. This function should accept a single parameter with the name `evt`. Add the following statements to the function:

```
1    if (evt === undefined) { // get caller element in IE8
2        evt = window.event;
3    }
4    var callerElement = evt.target || evt.srcElement;
5    var listItems = document.getElementsByTagName("li");
6    var parentItem = callerElement.parentNode;
7    for (var i = 0; i < list.length; i++) {
8        if (parentItem.innerHTML.search(list[i]) !== -1) {
9            var itemToMove = list.splice(i, 1);
10           list.push(itemToMove);
11       }
12   }
13   generateList();
```

This function contains the same statements as the `moveToTop()` function, with one exception: instead of using the `unshift()` method to add the selected item to the beginning of the array, this function uses the `push()` method to add it to the end of the array.

8. Save your changes to **script.js**, and then open **index.htm** in a browser. Click in the text box, type **Finish JavaScript projects**, click **Add Item**, type **Make dinner**, click **Add Item**, type **Renew license**, and then click **Add Item**. Your list should now contain three items, each with its own "first" and "last" buttons, as shown in Figure 8-21.

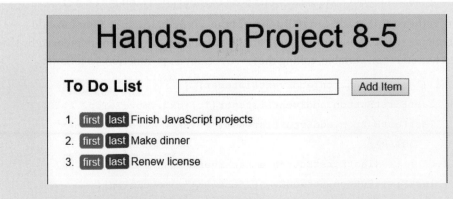

Figure 8-21: To-do list with "first" and "last" buttons

9. Click the **last button** for item 1. The "Finish JavaScript projects" list item moves to the bottom of the list, as shown in Figure 8-22.

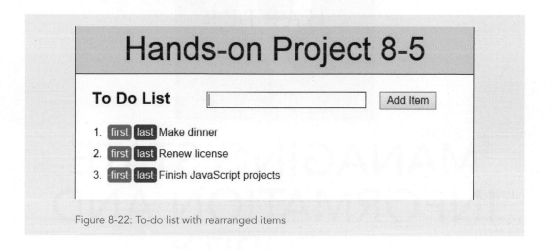

Figure 8-22: To-do list with rearranged items

Case Projects

Individual Case Project

Enhance the feedback form in your project to enable users to choose one or more options from a list of at least five options. Include code that adds user selections to either an array or an object, and ensure that if a user deselects one of the options, it is removed from the array or object. Add code to convert the array or object to a string.

Group Case Project

Have each group member demonstrate the enhancements they created for the Individual Case Project to the group, including reviewing the code. From the different group members' implementations, decide on what information would be most useful to collect on the group feedback form, and whether to store it in an array or an object. Then write the code together to add these features to the group site, ensuring that the code removes an option from the array or object if a user deselects it. Add code to convert the array or object to a string.

CHAPTER 9

MANAGING STATE INFORMATION AND SECURITY

When you complete this chapter, you will be able to:

> Save state information with query strings, hidden form fields, and cookies

> Describe JavaScript security issues and employ coding practices designed to address them

The web was not originally designed to store information about a user's visit to a web site. However, the ability to store user information, including preferences, passwords, and other data, is important on the web today because it significantly improves a site's usability. The three most common tools for maintaining this type of information are query strings, hidden form fields, and cookies, which you will study in this chapter. Given the sensitive nature of user information, it's also essential that you have a good understanding of the JavaScript security issues described in this chapter.

Note | *To complete the steps in this chapter, you should have access to a local web server. For instructions on installing one, see Appendix A.*

Understanding State Information

Hypertext Transfer Protocol (HTTP) is a set of rules used by browsers and servers to exchange information about web documents. These rules also ensure that web browsers correctly process and display the various types of information contained in web pages. Information about individual visits to a web site is called state information. HTTP was originally designed to be stateless, which means that web browsers stored no persistent data about a visit to a web site. The original stateless design of the web allowed early web servers to quickly process requests for web pages, since they did not need to remember any unique requirements for different clients. Similarly, web browsers did not need to know any special information to load a particular web page from a server. Although this stateless design was efficient, it was also limiting; because a web server could not remember individual user information, the web browser was forced to treat every visit to a web page as an entirely new session. This was true regardless of whether the browser had just opened a different web page on the same server. This design hampered interactivity and limited the amount of personalization a web site could provide. Today, there are many reasons for maintaining state information. Among other things, maintaining state information allows a server to:

> Customize individual web pages based on user preferences.

> Temporarily store information as a user navigates within a multipart form.

> Provide shopping carts that store items selected until checkout.

In this chapter, you'll work with a two-part order form for Eating Well in Season (EWS), a business in Glover, Vermont, that delivers produce from local farms to its customers. EWS wants to enable new customers to sign up online. However, the company is concerned that making a web form to collect all the necessary information would be challenging to fill out on a handheld device like a mobile phone. To address this concern, they hired a designer to create a form that's split into two parts: one document that collects basic customer information, and a second document that allows users to specify their service preferences. EWS has asked you to write the JavaScript code necessary for all of the form information to be submitted at once. Figures 9-1 and 9-2 show the first and second form pages in a desktop browser, and Figures 9-3 and 9-4 show the pages on a handheld device.

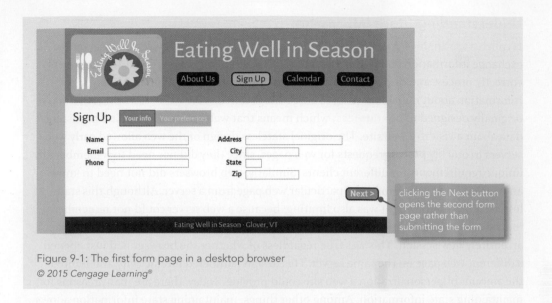

Figure 9-1: The first form page in a desktop browser
© 2015 Cengage Learning®

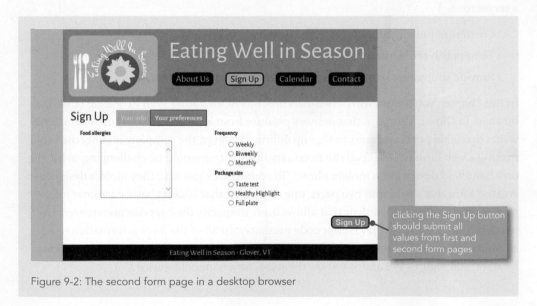

Figure 9-2: The second form page in a desktop browser

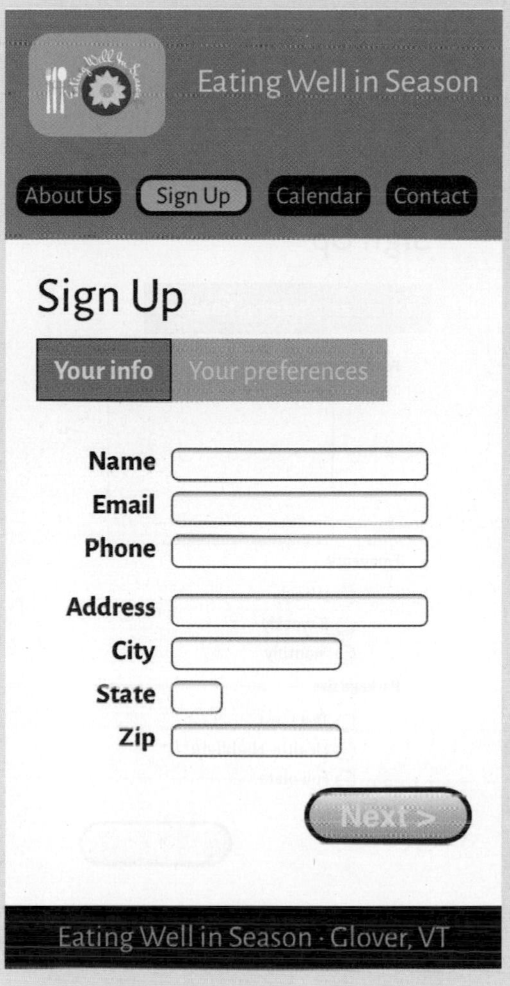

Figure 9-3: The first form page on a handheld device

Figure 9-4: The second form page on a handheld device

The forms are designed so that data entered by the user on both forms can be submitted to a web server simultaneously. This makes sense because the data collected by both forms are really part of the same data set; the forms are broken into two web pages only to make it easier for users to enter the necessary information. The problem with these web pages is that, if a user moves from the Your info page to the Your preferences page, the data entered on the Your info page is lost. In this chapter, you will learn how to make the data entered into the first web pages available to the second by using query strings, hidden form fields, and cookies.

Saving State Information with Query Strings

One way to preserve information following a user's visit to a web page is to append a query string to the end of a URL. A **query string** is a set of name-value pairs appended to a target URL. It consists of a single text string containing one or more pieces of information. You can use a query string to pass information, such as search criteria, from one web page to another.

Passing Data with a Query String

To pass data from one web page to another using a query string, you add a question mark (?) immediately after a URL, followed by the query string (in name-value pairs) for the information you want to preserve. In this manner, you are passing information to another web page, similarly to the way you can pass arguments to a function or method. You separate individual name-value pairs within the query string by using ampersands (&). For instance, the following link code incorporates a query string consisting of a single name-value pair:

```
<a href="http://www.example.com/↵
    addItem.html?isbn=9780394800165&quantity=2">Order Book</a>
```

The passed query string is then assigned to the `search` property of the `Location` object of the target web page. The `search` property of the `Location` object contains a URL's query or search parameters. For the preceding example, after the addItem.html document opens, the query string `?isbn=9780394800165&quantity=2` is available as the value of the `search` property of the `Location` object.

> **Note**
>
> The `search` property of the `Location` object gets its name from the fact that many Internet search engines use the query string it contains to store search criteria.

You can use methods of the `String` class to concatenate names and values into a query string. For instance, the following code creates a URL including a query string that contains the values from the `fname`, `lname`, and `city` fields:

```
1   var savedData = "?fname=" +↵
2       document.getElementById("fName").value;
3   savedData += "&lname=" +↵
4       document.getElementById("lName").value;
5   savedData += "&city=" +↵
6       document.getElementById("city").value;
7   location.href = "contact.html" + savedData;
```

This code adds the literal text `?fname=` to the value in the `fname` field, `&lname=` to the value in the `lname` field, and `&city=` to the value in the `city` field. The last line adds the document name `contact.html` to the start of the query string, and assigns the result to the `href` property of the `Location` object, opening the page in the browser while passing the query string data to the new page.

The `submit` method of a form automatically creates a query string from its field values and passes that to the location specified by the `action` attribute. Because the Next button on the first order page for the EWS website is configured as a submit button, the form will create a query string containing user entries when the Next button is clicked. You'll test this now by entering sample data in the order.htm page, clicking the Next button, and then examining the query string in your browser's address bar for the page that opens.

To examine the query string generated when a user submits the form on the first order page:

1. If you are using a local web server, copy the Chapter09 folder from your data files to the root folder of the web server. If you installed XAMPP using the instructions in Appendix A, the root folder is C:/xampp/htdocs (Windows) or /Applications/XAMPP/xampfiles/htdocs (Mac).

2. In your text editor, open the **order.htm**, **order2.htm**, and **results.htm** documents, located in your Chapter folder for Chapter 9.

3. In the comment section of each file, add your name and today's date where indicated, save your changes, and then scroll through the document and familiarize yourself with its content. The order.htm and order2.htm documents contain forms in which users can enter information. You'll use the results.htm document to simulate submitting form data to a server by displaying data received from the forms.

4. Open **order.htm** in a browser, complete the text fields with fictitious information, and then click the **Next** button. The second order page opens and the address displayed in the browser's address bar includes a query string that incorporates the names and values from the fields on the previous page. Figure 9-5 shows the page in Firefox.

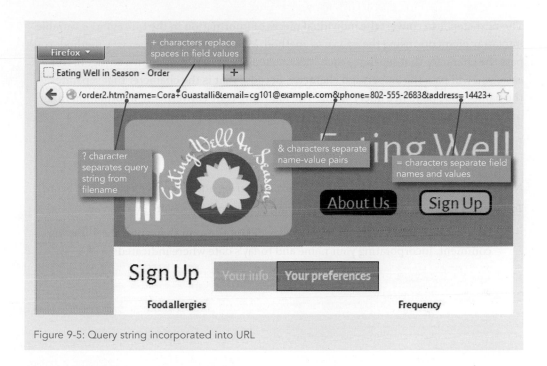

Figure 9-5: Query string incorporated into URL

Parsing Data from a Query String

For a web page to use the information in a query string, your JavaScript program must first parse the string, using a combination of several methods and the length property of the String object. The first parsing task is to extract all the string contents except for the question mark at the start of the query string. To do this, you use the substring() method combined with the length property. As you learned in Chapter 8, the substring() method takes two arguments: a starting index number and an ending index number. The first character in a string has an index number of 0, similar to the first element in an array. Because you want to exclude the first character of the string (the question mark), which has an index of 0, you use a starting index of 1 for the substring() method. For the ending index number you use the length property, which tells the substring() method to include the rest, or length, of the string. The following code assigns the search property of the Location object to a variable named queryData and uses the substring() method and length property to extract all of the string except the starting question mark:

```
1    // Assign the query string to the queryData variable
2    var queryData = location.search;
3    // Remove the opening question mark from the string
4    queryData = queryData.substring(1, queryData.length);
```

The next step is to convert the individual pieces of information in the `queryData` variable into array elements, using the `split()` method. When you call the `split()` method, you pass the character that separates each individual piece of information in a string. In this case, you will pass the ampersand character, because that is the character that separates the name-value pairs in a query string. The following code converts the information in the `queryData` variable into an array named `queryArray[]`:

```
// split queryData into an array
var queryArray = queryData.split("&");
```

Next, you'll create a function that parses the query string and stores the result in an array.

To create a function to parse the query string and store the results in an array:

1. In your text editor, create a new, blank JavaScript file, and then enter the following comment, incorporating your name and today's date where indicated:

```
1    /*      JavaScript 6th Edition
2      *      Chapter 9
3      *      Chapter case
4      *      Eating Well in Season
5      *      Author:
6      *      Date:
7      *      Filename: script2.js
8      */
```

2. Add a statement instructing processors to interpret the document contents in strict mode, and then save the file with the name **script2.js** to the Chapter folder for Chapter 9. If you are using a local web server, be sure to save the file to the location of your files on the server.

3. Declare a global variable named **queryArray** with an empty array as its value.

4. Declare a function named **populateInfo()** containing the following statements:

```
1    if (location.search) {
2            var queryData = location.search;
3            queryData = queryData.substring(1, queryData.length);
4            queryArray = queryData.split("&");
5    }
```

The `if` statement checks if the `search` property of the `Location` object has a value; if not, the page has no query string to parse. If so, the `var` statement creates the `queryData` variable, which stores the value of `location.search`. The next statement uses the `substring()` method of the `String` class to copy all but the first character (the ?) from the `queryData` variable and assign the new value to the `queryData`. The final statement uses the `split()` method of the `String` class to extract each name-value pair from the `queryData` variable and assign it as an element in the `queryArray` variable.

5. Below the `populateInfo()` function, add the following code to run the function when the page finishes loading:

```
1   if (window.addEventListener) {
2       window.addEventListener("load", populateInfo, false);
3   } else if (window.attachEvent) {
4       window.attachEvent("onload", populateInfo);
5   }
```

Your completed code should match the following:

```
1    "use strict";
2    var queryArray = [];
3    function populateInfo() {
4        if (location.search) {
5            var queryData = location.search;
6            queryData = queryData.substring(1, queryData.length);
7            queryArray = queryData.split("&");
8        }
9    }
10   if (window.addEventListener) {
11       window.addEventListener("load", populateInfo, false);
12   } else if (window.attachEvent) {
13       window.attachEvent("onload", populateInfo);
14   }
```

6. Save your changes to **script2.js**, and then in your text editor return to **order2.htm**.

7. Before the closing `</body>` tag, add a `script` element that specifies **script2.js** as the source.

8. Save your changes to **order2.htm**, reload **order.htm** in your browser, complete the form with fictitious information, and then click the **Next** button. As in the previous steps, the second form page is displayed with the query string in the URL.

9. Open your browser's console, type **queryArray**, press **Enter**, and then, if necessary, click **object Array** to view the array contents. As Figure 9-6 shows, each name-value pair from the query string is an element in the array.

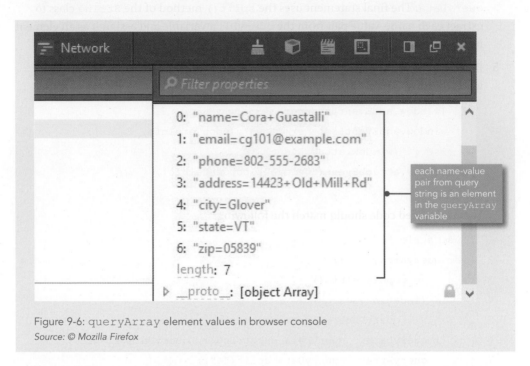

Figure 9-6: `queryArray` element values in browser console
Source: © Mozilla Firefox

By storing the query string contents in the `queryArray` array, you now have access to this data from within the second form page. However, when a user enters data in the second form page and then clicks the Order button, only the field values from the second form are submitted. To incorporate the values from the first form into the second without confusing users, you can use hidden form fields.

Saving State Information with Hidden Form Fields

A special type of `input` element, called a **hidden form field**, is not displayed by web browsers and, therefore, allows developers to hide information from users. Hidden form fields temporarily store data that needs to be sent to a server along with the rest of a form, but that a user does not need to see. Examples of data stored in hidden fields include the result of a calculation or some other type of information that a program on a web server might need. You create hidden form fields by using the same syntax used for other fields created with the `input` element: `<input type="hidden">`.

The form on the second EWS order page includes hidden form fields that correspond to the fields from the first page. However, they are empty, and users can't interact with them. Next, you'll enhance the `populateInfo()` function to assign the value portion of each element in the `queryArray` as the value of its corresponding hidden field in the second form. This will enable users to submit all input from the first and second form pages when they click the Order button on the second form. Figure 9-7 illustrates this process.

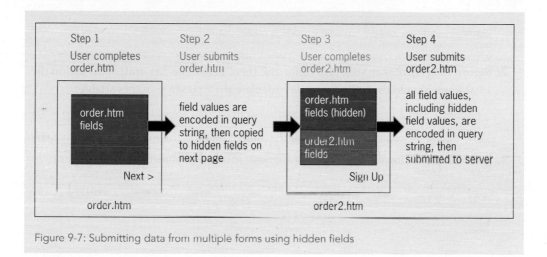

Figure 9-7: Submitting data from multiple forms using hidden fields

To enhance the `populateInfo()` function to assign values from the `queryArray` array to the hidden fields:

1. In your text editor, return to **order2.htm** and examine the `input` elements within the `article` element. As Figure 9-8 shows, the first seven `input` elements have type values of `hidden`, indicating that they are hidden fields. Each field has `name` and `id` values that correspond to one of the fields from the form on the order.htm page.

```
                                                    ┌─────────────────────────┐
                                                    │ input elements with type │
                                                    │ values of "hidden" are   │
                                                    │ not visible to users     │
                                                    └─────────────────────────┘
<form action="results.htm">

    <input type="hidden" id="name" name="name" />

    <input type="hidden" id="email" name="email" />

    <input type="hidden" id="phone" name="phone" />

    <input type="hidden" id="address" name="address" />

    <input type="hidden" id="city" name="city" />

    <input type="hidden" id="state" name="state" />

    <input type="hidden" id="zip" name="zip" />

    ...
```

Figure 9-8: Code for hidden form fields in order2.htm

2. Return to **script2.js** in your text editor and then, below the `var` statement within the `if` statement, add the following code to declare the `hiddenInputs` variable:

```
var hiddenInputs = document.querySelectorAll("input[type=hidden]");
```

This statement stores references to all the hidden fields in the `hiddenInputs` variable.

3. Just before the closing `}` for the `if` statement, insert the following `for` statement:

```
1   for (var i = 0; i < queryArray.length; i++) {
2       hiddenInputs[i].value = queryArray[i].↵
3           substring(queryArray[i].lastIndexOf("=") + 1);
4   }
```

Each time through the `for` loop, the `hiddenInputs[]` element for the current counter value is assigned the value of the corresponding `queryArray` element. Because each `queryArray` element contains a name-value pair (such as `state=VT`), the statement uses the `substring()` method of the `String` class to extract the element content starting with the character following the equal sign (=). Your updated `populateInfo()` function should match the following:

```
1   function populateInfo() {
2       if (location.search) {
3           var queryData = location.search;
4           var hiddenInputs = document.querySelectorAll↵
5               ("input[type=hidden]");
6           queryData = queryData.substring(1, queryData.length);
```

```
7        queryArray = queryData.split("&");
8        for (var i = 0; i < queryArray.length; i++) {
9            hiddenInputs[i].value = queryArray[i].↵
10               substring(queryArray[i].lastIndexOf("=") + 1);
11       }
12   }
13 }
```

4. Save your changes to **script2.js**, shift-refresh or shift-reload **order.htm** in your browser, complete all the fields with fictitious information, and then click the **Next** button. The order2.htm page opens. Even though your code added values to the hidden fields, the page is unchanged because the fields aren't displayed in the browser window.

5. In your browser's console, type **document.getElementById("name").value**, and then press **Enter**. As Figure 9-9 shows, the value you entered in the Name field on the previous page is displayed, because the populateInfo() function copied its value into the name field on the current page.

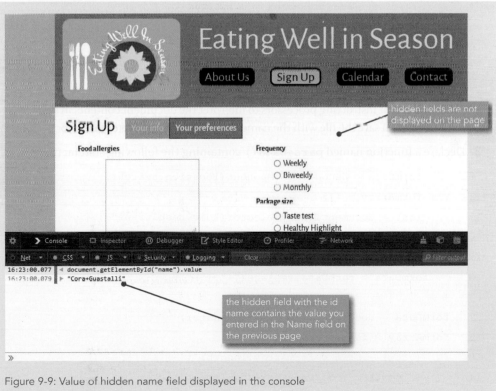

Figure 9-9: Value of hidden name field displayed in the console
Source: © Mozilla Firefox

6. Repeat Step 5 to verify that the hidden fields with the following ids all contain values that correspond to the information you entered on the first page: `email`, `phone`, `address`, `city`, `state`, `zip`.

Because the form on order2.htm now contains fields with values from the order.htm page, when the form is submitted it should include all the entries from both forms. To test this, you'll first create a function for the results.htm page that will parse and display all the name-value pairs in the query string. Then you'll enter data in both of the forms and verify that all the data you entered is displayed in the results.htm page.

To create a function to parse and display data from the query string on the results.htm page:

1. In your text editor, create a new, blank JavaScript file, and then enter the following comment, incorporating your name and today's date where indicated:

```
1   /*      JavaScript 6th Edition
2    *      Chapter 9
3    *      Chapter case
4    *      Eating Well in Season
5    *      Author:
6    *      Date:
7    *      Filename: script3.js
8    */
```

2. Add a statement instructing processors to interpret the document contents in strict mode, and then save the file with the name **script3.js** to the Chapter folder for Chapter 9.

3. Declare a function named **parseData()** containing the following statements:

```
1    var formData = decodeURIComponent(location.search);
2    var formArray = [];
3    var list = document.querySelector("div.results ul");
4    formData = formData.substring(1, formData.length);
5    while (formData.indexOf("+") !== -1) {
6        formData = formData.replace("+", " ");
7    }
8    formData = decodeURIComponent(formData);
9    formArray = formData.split("&");
10   for (var i = 0; i < formArray.length; i++) {
11       var newItem = document.createElement("li");
```

```
12      newItem.innerHTML = formArray[i];
13      list.appendChild(newItem);
14   }
```

The `var` statement first replaces any encoded characters in the query string with their character equivalents and then assigns the value to the `formData` variable. It then creates an empty array named `formArray`, and finally creates a variable named `list` that stores a reference to the unordered list within the `div` in the `results` class. The next statement removes the leading `?` from the query string and assigns the new value to the `formData` variable. The `while` statement then replaces each occurrence of `+` in the `formData` variable value with a space, which converts the entries from a machine-readable form to a more human-readable form. The next statement converts any remaining encoded characters in the `formData` variable to their character equivalents. The statement that follows uses the `split()` method of the `String` class to divide the `formData` value at each `&` and store the results as elements in the `formArray` array. Finally, each time through the `for` loop, a new `li` element is created, then the array element whose index number corresponds to the current counter value is assigned as the `innerHTML` of the `li` element, and then the `li` element is added as a child of the `ul` element referenced by the `list` variable.

4. Below the `parseData()` function, add the following code to call the function when the page finishes loading:

```
1    if (window.addEventListener) {
2        window.addEventListener("load", parseData, false);
3    } else if (window.attachEvent) {
4        window.attachEvent("onload", parseData);
5    }
```

5. Save your changes to **script3.js**.

6. Return to **results.htm** in your text editor. Just above the closing `</body>` tag add a `script` element that specifies **script3.js** as its source, and then save your changes to **results.htm**.

7. In your browser, shift-refresh or shift-reload **order.htm**, complete the form with fictitious information, click the **Next** button, complete the **order2.htm** form with fictitious information, and then click **Sign Up**. As Figure 9-10 shows, all the name-value pairs that are part of the query string submitted by order2.htm are displayed in the results.htm page. Note that the results include the values you entered on the first form page as well as on the second.

Figure 9-10: Results page showing name-value data from order.htm and order2.htm

Short Quiz 1

1. How do you reference a passed query string in your code?

2. How is data in a query string separated from a URL? How are individual name-value pairs distinguished within a query string?

3. How is a hidden form field different from other form fields?

Storing State Information

Query strings do not permanently maintain state information. The information contained in a query string is available only during the current session of a web page. Once a web page that reads a query string closes, the query string is lost. Hidden form fields maintain state information between web pages, but the data they contain are also lost once the web page that reads the hidden fields closes. You can save the contents of a query string or hidden form fields by submitting the form data by using a server-side scripting language, but that method requires a separate, server-based application. In this section, you'll study two different means of storing state information on a user's computer. The most widespread way of doing this on the web today is using cookies, which are small pieces of information that are stored in text files on a user's computer. As you will learn later in this chapter, a newer specification, known as Web Storage, sets out standards for storing more information than cookies allow, using a syntax and methods that are more intuitive than cookies. Although Web Storage is not yet as widely supported as cookies, you'll study how to use it in this chapter as well.

Storing State Information with Cookies

Each time a web client makes a request to a web server, the client also sends saved cookies for the requested web page to the server. The server can then use the cookies to customize the web page for the client. Alternatively, scripts that are part of the web page can access information in cookies and use it to customize the page without involving the server. Cookies are most often used to store information that helps the server identify you.

> **Note**
>
> Cookies are stored on a user's computer as plain text files. If a user's computer is infected with malware, any data, including the contents of cookies, is vulnerable to being stolen and used fraudulently by a third party. For this reason, your programs should never place sensitive information, such as a password or credit card information, in a cookie. All modern browsers offer secure storage of logins and other personal information, which users can choose to enable; note that this information is not stored in cookies, but instead it is stored using a separate browser-specific mechanism. For more information on the hazards of storing sensitive information in cookies, use a search engine to search on "storing passwords in cookies."

Cookies can be temporary or persistent. Temporary cookies remain available only for the current browser session. Persistent cookies remain available beyond the current browser session and are stored in a text file on a client computer.

The cookie specification limits the number and size of cookies stored for a particular page or domain. According to the specification, each individual server or domain should be able to store only a maximum of 20 cookies on a user's computer. In addition, the total cookies per browser should not be able to exceed 300, and the largest cookie size is 4 KB. Modern browsers don't necessarily enforce these rules because storage space on a client computer is not the issue it was in the early days of the web. However, some browsers may still enforce these rules, so it's important to be mindful of them when creating cookies.

Creating and Modifying Cookies

You use the `cookie` property of the `Document` object to create cookies in name-value pairs, the same way you use name-value pairs with a query string. The syntax for the `cookie` property is

```
document.cookie = name + "=" + value;
```

The `cookie` property is created with a required `name` attribute and four optional attributes: `expires`, `path`, `domain`, and `secure`. Table 9-1 describes the five attributes.

ATTRIBUTE	DESCRIPTION
domain=*domain*	For a web server with multiple subdomains, specifies whether the cookie is available only to the subdomain from which it originated (default)
expires=*date*	When a cookie will be deleted from the system, where *date* is a date in UTC format; setting `expires` to a date value in the past and deletes a cookie immediately
name=*name*	The name of the cookie (required)
path=*path*	A path on the web server in which documents must be located to have access to the cookie; by default, a cookie is available to all web pages in the same directory
secure=*boolean*	Whether the cookie can be transmitted only over a secure protocol, such as HTTPS (`true`), or may be transmitted over a nonsecure protocol (`false`, the default)

Table 9-1: Cookie attributes

 Note | *To modify an existing cookie, you simply assign a new name-value pair to the* `document.cookie` *property. If the name-value pair already exists it will be overwritten.*

The **name** Attribute

The only required parameter of the `cookie` property is the `name` attribute, which specifies the cookie's name-value pair. Cookies created with only the `name` attribute are temporary cookies, because they are available for only the current browser session. The following code creates a cookie with a name-value pair of `username=mw101`:

```
document.cookie = "username=mw101";
```

The `cookie` property of the `Document` object can be confusing. For other JavaScript properties, assigning a new value to a property *replaces* the old value. In contrast, assigning a new value to the `cookie` property adds another entry to a list of cookies, rather than simply replacing the last value. The following example builds a list of cookies:

```
document.cookie = "username=mw101";
document.cookie = "member=true";
document.cookie = "audio=false";
```

A web browser automatically separates each name-value pair in the `cookie` property with a semicolon and a space. Therefore, the value assigned to the `cookie` property for the preceding cookies contains the following value:

```
username=mw101; member=true; audio=false
```

By default, cookies themselves cannot include semicolons or other special characters, such as commas or spaces. Cookies cannot include special characters because they are transmitted between web browsers and web servers using HTTP, which does not allow certain nonalphanumeric characters to be transmitted in their native format. However, you can use special characters in your cookies if you use encoding, which involves converting each special character in a text string to its corresponding hexadecimal ASCII value, preceded by a percent sign. For example, 20 is the hexadecimal ASCII equivalent of a space character, and 25 is the hexadecimal ASCII equivalent of a percent sign (%). In URL encoded format, each space character is represented by %20. After encoding, the contents of the string `fullname=Mitchell Ward` would read as follows:

```
fullname=Mitchell%20Ward
```

The built-in `encodeURIComponent()` function is used in JavaScript for encoding the individual parts of a URI. More specifically, the `encodeURIComponent()` function converts each special character in a URI to its corresponding hexadecimal ASCII value, preceded by a percent sign. The syntax for the `encodeURIComponent()` function is `encodeURIComponent(text)`. The `encodeURIComponent()` function does not encode standard alphanumeric characters such as *A*, *B*, *C*, or 1, 2, 3, or any of the following special characters: - _ . ! ~ * ' ( ). It also does not encode the following characters, which have a special meaning in a URI: ; / ? : % @ & = + $,. For example, the / character is not encoded because it is used for designating a path on a file system. To use a cookie or other text string encoded with the `encodeURIComponent()` function, you must first decode it with the `decodeURIComponent()` function. The syntax for the `decodeURIComponent()` function is

```
decodeURIComponent(text)
```

The following encodes several cookies with the `encodeURIComponent()` function and assigns them to the `cookie` property of the `Document` object:

```
1   var username = document.getElementById("username").value;
2   var member = document.getElementById("member").value;
3   var audio = document.getElementById("audio").value;
4   document.cookie = "username=" +↵
5       encodeURIComponent(username);
```

```
6    document.cookie = "member=" +↵
7        encodeURIComponent(member);
8    document.cookie = "audio=" +↵
9        encodeURIComponent(audio);
```

> **Note**
>
> JavaScript also includes the `encodeURI()` and `decodeURI()` functions, which can be used to encode and decode entire URIs, leaving colon and slash characters as literals. Be sure to distinguish these functions from the `encodeURIComponent()` and `decodeURIComponent()` functions, which encode and decode characters including colon and slash for URI parameters.

If you transmit a URI containing spaces using a modern web browser, the browser automatically encodes the spaces for you before transmitting the cookie. However, special characters, such as the percent sign, are not automatically encoded. This can cause problems with older browsers and web servers that do not recognize certain special characters unless they are encoded. Additionally, older browsers do not automatically encode spaces in URIs. For these reasons, you should manually encode and decode cookies using the `encodeURIComponent()` and `decodeURIComponent()` functions if you anticipate that your scripts will run in older web browsers.

Testing Applications That Use Cookies

Cookies are part of the specification for HTTP, which is the protocol used to request files from a web server. However, when you're developing and testing web documents on your local machine, browsers open them without using HTTP, by accessing the local file system directly. You can verify this by inspecting a file's URL in a browser's address bar; for a local file opened without HTTP, the URL starts with the `file:///` prefix. Although some browsers support setting cookies on local files requested without HTTP, some browsers do not. As a result, you may get inconsistent results when testing code that creates or modifies cookies on local files.

There are a few methods you can use to work around this issue when writing and testing code. First, you can research which browsers allow cookies to be set on local files and focus your testing on those browsers. At the time this book was written, only Chrome refused to set cookies for local files. However, other browsers were inconsistent in some of the details of implementation. Although this method can be useful for initial testing, note that you cannot complete full cross-browser testing of an application that uses cookies with this method.

A more robust option is to run a web server on your local computer, and to open files for testing using the server rather than by accessing the local file system. When a browser opens files from a server, even one running on your local machine, it uses the HTTP protocol, and therefore sets cookies just as it would for any other server. Some code editors include built-in testing servers that you can use for this purpose; one free option is Aptana Studio 3, which is available for both Windows and Mac. Another option is to install a full web server on your computer, or to enable a server that may be included with your operating system. For instructions on installing a web server, see Appendix A, "Installing and Configuring a Testing Server."

As you complete the steps in this chapter, you should test your work using a browser that you've confirmed allows you to set and modify cookies on local files, or you should open files from a local web server using the HTTP protocol.

Next, you'll add code to the script2.js file so that, before a user submits the contents of the form, the page creates cookies containing the form field names and their values.

To enhance the script2.js file to create cookies containing the form field names and their values:

1. In your text editor, return to the **script2.js** file.

2. Below the `populateInfo()` function, declare a new function named `createCookies()` containing the following code:

```
1    var formFields =↵
2            document.querySelectorAll("input[type=hidden],↵
3            input[type=radio], textarea");
4    for (var i = 0; i < formFields.length; i++) {
5        var currentValue =↵
6            decodeURIComponent(formFields[i].value);
7        currentValue = currentValue.replace(/\+/g, " ");
8        document.cookie = formFields[i].name + "=" + currentValue;
9    }
```

The `formFields` variable stores references to all hidden and radio `input` elements, as well as to all `textarea` elements; this results in references to all the fields in the form, but not to the submit button. The `for` statement iterates through the fields. For each field, it decodes any encoded characters in the fields value, and then replaces each occurrence of the + symbol with a space. Finally, it creates a cookie consisting of the current field name followed by an equal sign and the current field value.

3. Below the `createCookies()` function, add the following `handleSubmit()` function:

```
1    function handleSubmit(evt) {
2        if (evt.preventDefault) {
3            evt.preventDefault(); // prevent form from submitting
4        } else {
```

```
5      evt.returnValue = false; // prevent form from submitting⏎
6           in IE8
7      }
8      createCookies();
9      document.getElementsByTagName("form")[0].submit();
10   }
```

You'll create an event handler to call this function when the form is submitted. This function prevents the form from being submitted immediately, then calls the `createCookies()` function to create cookies based on the completed form, and then fires the `submit` event on the form.

4. Below the `handleSubmit()` function, add the following two functions:

```
1    function createEventListeners() {
2        var form = document.getElementsByTagName("form")[0];
3        if (form.addEventListener) {
4            form.addEventListener("submit", handleSubmit, false);
5        } else if (form.attachEvent) {
6            form.attachEvent("onsubmit", handleSubmit);
7        }
8    }
9    function setUpPage() {
10       createEventListeners();
11       populateInfo();
12   }
```

The `createEventListeners()` function creates an event listener for the form that calls the `handleSubmit()` function you created in the previous step when the `submit` event fires on the form. The `setUpPage()` function calls the `createEventListeners()` and `populateInfo()` functions; you'll edit the `window .onload` statement in the next step to call this function when the page finishes loading.

5. Modify the event listener code at the bottom of the document to call the `setUpPage()` function as follows:

```
1    if (window.addEventListener) {
2        window.addEventListener("load", setUpPage, false);
3    } else if (window.attachEvent) {
4        window.attachEvent("onload", setUpPage);
5    }
```

Your completed code should match the following:

```
1    function createCookies() {
2        var formFields =↵
3                document.querySelectorAll("input[type=hidden],↵
4                input[type=radio], textarea");
5        for (var i = 0; i < formFields.length; i++) {
6            var currentValue =↵
7                decodeURIComponent(formFields[i].value);
8            currentValue = currentValue.replace(/\+/g, " ");
9            document.cookie = formFields[i].name + "=" +↵
10               currentValue;
11       }
12   }
13   function handleSubmit(evt) {
14       if (evt.preventDefault) {
15           evt.preventDefault(); // prevent form from submitting
16       } else {
17           evt.returnValue = false; // prevent form from submitting↵
18               in IE8
19       }
20       createCookies();
21       document.getElementsByTagName("form")[0].submit();
22   }
23   function createEventListeners() {
24       var form = document.getElementsByTagName("form")[0];
25       if (form.addEventListener) {
26           form.addEventListener("submit", handleSubmit, false);
27       } else if (form.attachEvent) {
28           form.attachEvent("onsubmit", handleSubmit);
29       }
30   }
31   function setUpPage() {
32       createEventListeners();
33       populateInfo();
34   }
```

```
35   if (window.addEventListener) {
36      window.addEventListener("load", setUpPage, false);
37   } else if (window.attachEvent) {
38      window.attachEvent("onload", setUpPage);
39   }
```

6. Save your changes to **script2.js**.

> **Caution** | From this point forward, you must open files for testing either in a browser that supports setting cookies on the local filesystem, or from a local web server. Otherwise, your browser may not set or modify cookies as you expect.

7. In your browser, shift-refresh or shift-reload **order.htm**, complete the form with fictitious information, click **Next**, complete the second form with fictitious information, and then click **Sign Up**.

8. In your browser's console, type **document.cookie**. As Figure 9-11 shows, the value of the `cookie` property is a single string, with each name-value pair separated by a semicolon and a space, and each parameter and value from the query string is part of the `cookie` property.

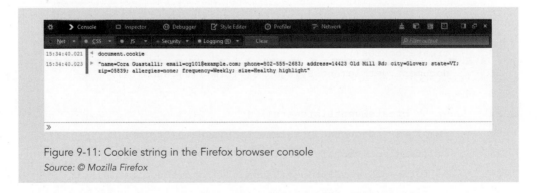

Figure 9-11: Cookie string in the Firefox browser console
Source: © Mozilla Firefox

Setting Cookie Expiration Dates

For a cookie to persist beyond the current browser session, you must use the `expires` attribute of the `cookie` property. The **expires attribute** of the `cookie` property determines how long a cookie can remain on a client system before it is deleted. Cookies created without an `expires` attribute are available for the current browser session only. The syntax for assigning the `expires` attribute to the `cookie` property, along with an associated name-value pair, is `expires=date`. The name-value pair and the `expires=date` pair are separated by a semicolon. The *date* portion of the `expires` attribute must be a text string in Coordinated Universal Time (usually abbreviated as UTC) format, which looks like this:

```
Weekday Month DD HH:MM:SS Time_Zone YYYY
```

> **Note** Coordinated Universal Time is also known as Greenwich Mean Time (GMT), Zulu time, and world time.

The following is an example of Coordinated Universal Time:

```
Mon Mar 27 14:15:18 PST 2017
```

> **Note** Take care not to encode the `expires` attribute using the `encodeURIComponent()` method. JavaScript does not recognize a UTC date when it is in URI-encoded format. If you use the `encodeURIComponent()` method with the `expires` attribute, JavaScript is not able to set the cookie expiration date.

You can manually type a string in UTC format, or you can create the string with the `Date` object, which automatically creates the string in UTC format. To use a `Date` object with the `expires` attribute, you specify the amount of time you want the cookie to be valid by using a combination of the set and get methods of the `Date` object. The following statement declares a `Date` object named `cookieDate`, and then changes the date portion of the new object by using the `setDate()` and `getDate()` methods.

```
cookieDate.setDate(myDate.getDate() + 7);
```

In the example, the `setDate()` method sets the date portion of `cookieDate` by using the `getDate()` method to retrieve the date, and adding 7 to increase the date by 1 week. You might use a cookie that expires after 1 week (or less) to store data that needs to be maintained for a limited amount of time. For example, a travel agency might store data in a cookie that temporarily holds a travel reservation that expires after a week.

After you create a `Date` object and specify the date you want the cookie to expire, you must use the `toUTCString()` method to convert the `Date` object to a string, formatting it in Coordinated Universal Time. The following code creates a new cookie and assigns an expiration date one year from now:

```
1   var expiresDate = new Date();
2   var username = document.getElementById("username").value;
```

```
3    expiresDate.setFullYear(expiresDate.getFullYear() + 1);
4    document.cookie = "username=" +↵
5        encodeURIComponent(username) + "; expires=" +↵
6        expiresDate.toUTCString();
```

Before the `expires` attribute is assigned to the cookie property, the `Date` object uses the `toUTCString()` method to convert the date to a string in Coordinated Universal Time.

Because you didn't specify the `expires` parameter for the cookies you set, they should expire when your browser session ends. Next, you'll verify this, and then you'll revise the `createCookies()` function to make the cookies persistent.

To verify that the EWS cookies are session cookies and then convert them to persistent cookies:

1. In your browser, shift-refresh or shift-reload **order.htm**.

2. In the browser console, type **document.cookie** and then press **Enter**. If you haven't closed your browser since completing the last set of steps, the session cookies created by the results.htm page are still set and the cookie string is displayed in the console.

3. Close your browser, reopen it, and then reopen **order.htm**.

4. In the browser console, type **document.cookie** and then press **Enter**. As Figure 9-12 shows, the cookie value is an empty string (`""`) because the cookies you set earlier were deleted when you closed the browser, ending your browser session.

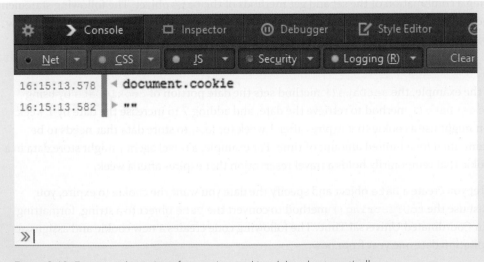

Figure 9-12: Empty cookie string after session cookies deleted automatically
Source: © Mozilla Firefox

5. In your text editor, return to **script2.js**, and then within the `createCookies()` function, below the `var` statement, add a statement to declare a variable named **expiresDate** with the current date as its value.

6. Before the `for` statement, add the following statement:

```
expiresDate.setDate(expiresDate.getDate() + 7);
```

This statement sets the value of the `expiresDate` variable to 1 week in the future.

7. In the last statement within the `for` loop, add code to specify an expires date, as follows:

```
document.cookie = formFields[i].name + "=" + currentValue↵
    + "; expires=" + expiresDate.toUTCString();
```

This code adds a semicolon, a space, and the text `expires=` to the cookie being set, followed by the date stored in the `expiresDate` variable, formatted as a string. Your updated `createCookies()` function should match the following:

```
1    function createCookies() {
2        var formFields =
3                document.querySelectorAll("input[type=hidden],
4                input[type=radio], textarea");
5        var expiresDate = new Date();
6        expiresDate.setDate(expiresDate.getDate() + 7);
7        for (var i = 0; i < formFields.length; i++) {
8            var currentValue =↵
9                decodeURIComponent(formFields[i].value);
10           currentValue = currentValue.replace(/\+/g, " ");
11           document.cookie = formFields[i].name + "=" +↵
12               currentValue + "; expires=" +↵
13               expiresDate.toUTCString();
14       }
15   }
```

8. Save your changes to **script2.js**, shift-refresh or shift-reload **order.htm** in your browser, complete the form with fictitious information, click **Next**, complete the second form with fictitious information, click **Sign Up**, and then in the browser console, type **document.cookie** and press **Enter**. The cookie string displayed should include all the same name-value pairs as in earlier steps.

9. Close your browser, reopen it, and then open **order.htm**.

10. In your browser console, type **document.cookie**, and then press **Enter**. The cookie string displays all the name-value pairs displayed in Step 8, verifying that the cookies are persistent, and that closing the browser doesn't delete them.

Configuring Availability of Cookies to Other Web Pages on the Server

The `path attribute` determines the availability of a cookie to other web pages on a server. The `path` attribute is assigned to the `cookie` property, along with an associated name-value pair, using the syntax `path=path`. By default, a cookie is available to all web pages in the same directory. However, if you specify a path, then a cookie is available to all web pages in the specified path as well as to all web pages in all subdirectories in the specified path. For example, the following statement makes the cookie named `username` available to all web pages located in the */advertising* directory or any of its subdirectories:

```
1    var username = document.getElementById("username").value;
2    document.cookie = "username=" +↵
3      encodeURIComponent(username + "; path=/advertising");
```

To make a cookie available to all directories on a server, you use a slash to indicate the root directory, as in the following example:

```
document.cookie = "username=" +↵
    encodeURIComponent(username + "; path=/");
```

When you are developing JavaScript programs that create cookies, your programs may not function correctly if the directory containing your web page contains other programs that create cookies. Cookies from other programs that are stored in the same directory along with unused cookies you created during development can cause your JavaScript program to run erratically. Therefore, you should always place a JavaScript program that creates cookies in its own directory and use the `path` attribute to specify any subdirectories your program requires.

Sharing Cookies Across a Domain

Using the `path` attribute allows cookies to be shared across a server. Some web sites, however, are very large and use a number of servers. The `domain attribute` is used for sharing cookies across multiple servers in the same domain. The domain attribute is assigned to the cookie property, along with an associated name-value pair, using the syntax domain=*domain*. For example, if the web server *advertising.example.com* needs to share cookies with the web server *content.example.com*, the domain attribute for cookies set by *advertising.example.com* should be set to *.example.com*. That way, cookies created by *advertising.example.com* are available to *content.example.com* and to all other servers in the domain *example.com*.

The following code shows how to make a cookie at *advertising.example.com* available to all servers in the *example.com* domain:

```
1    var username = document.getElementById("username").value;
2    document.cookie = "username=" +↵
3        encodeURIComponent(username +↵
4        "; domain=.example.com");
```

Note that you cannot share cookies outside of a domain. This is a result of the same-origin policy, which you'll learn about later in this chapter.

Securing Cookie Transmissions

Internet connections are not always safe for transmitting sensitive information. It is possible for unscrupulous people to steal personal information, such as credit card numbers, passwords, Social Security numbers, and other types of private information online. To protect private data transferred across the Internet, web servers and browsers can encrypt data and transfer it across a secure connection. The URLs for web sites that implement encryption usually start with the HTTPS protocol instead of HTTP.

> ## Programming Concepts | *Encryption*
>
> The main protocol used to encrypt data on web sites is Secure Sockets Layer, or SSL. The use of SSL encryption is widespread on the web. However, the SSL standard is being replaced by Transport Layer Security (TLS), which will eventually replace SSL. Both SSL and TLS encryption can be used to prevent a man-in-the-middle attack, in which data being exchanged between two parties is read and potentially changed in transit. SSL and TLS encrypt data between the client and the server, making it essentially impossible for anyone who might intercept that data in transit to read or change it.

The **secure attribute** indicates that a cookie can be transmitted only across a secure Internet connection using HTTPS or another security protocol. You assign this attribute to the `cookie` property with a Boolean value of `true` or `false`, along with an associated name-value pair, using the syntax `secure=value`. For example, to activate the `secure` attribute for a cookie, you use a statement similar to the following:

```
var username = document.getElementById("username").value;
document.cookie = "username=" +↵
    encodeURIComponent(username + "; secure=true");
```

The `secure` attribute is most useful for sites that use the HTTPS protocol for all connections. At the time this book was written, a number of large sites had implemented this practice, but a large portion of Internet traffic was still HTTP.

Because cookies are stored unencrypted on a user's hard drive, where they can be read by malicious programs, sensitive information should never be stored in cookies to begin with. However, adding the `secure` attribute to all cookies can be one part of an overall plan for site security.

Reading Cookies with JavaScript

So far, you have stored both temporary and persistent cookies. To make use of the cookies you've created, you need to retrieve stored cookie values—in other words, you need to read the cookies. The cookies for a particular web page are available in the `cookie` property of the `Document` object. Each cookie consists of one continuous string that must be parsed before the data it contains can be used. Parsing a cookie is a two-step process:

1. Decode the cookie using the `decodeURIComponent()` function.
2. Use methods of the `String` object to extract individual name-value pairs.

Parsing cookie data is very similar to parsing query strings, except that there is no question mark at the beginning of the string to work around; also, individual cookies are separated by a semicolon and a space instead of an ampersand. To give you an idea of what is involved in extracting data from cookies, the following code creates three encoded cookies, then reads them from the `cookie` property and decodes them. The `split()` method is then used to copy each name-value pair into an array named `cookieArray[]`.

```
1    document.cookie = "username=" +↵
2        encodeURIComponent(username);
3    document.cookie = "member=" +↵
4        encodeURIComponent(member);
5    document.cookie = "audio=" +↵
```

```
6        encodeURIComponent(audio);
7    var cookieString = decodeURIComponent(document.cookie);
8    var cookieArray = cookieString.split("; ");
```

Notice that the split() method in the preceding code splits the cookies by using two characters: a semicolon and a space. If you do not include the space in the split() method, then the name portion of each name-value pair in the new array has an extra space before it. Once you split the cookies into separate array elements, you still need to determine which cookie holds the value you need. The following for loop cycles through each element in the array, using an if statement and several string methods to check if the name portion of each name-value pair is equal to "team":

```
1    var currentUsername;
2    var unBox = document.getElementById("username");
3    for (var i = 0; i < 3; i++) {
4       currentUsername = cookieArray[i];
5       if ↵
6       (currentUsername.substring(0,currentUsername.indexOf("=")) ↵
7       === "username") {
8          unBox.value =↵
9             currentUsername.substring(currentUsername. ↵
10            indexOf("=") + 1,currentUsername.length);
11         break;
12      }
13   }
```

The conditional expression in the if statement uses the substring() method to return the name portion of the name-value pair in the variable named currentUsername. The first argument in the substring() method specifies the starting point of the substring as the first character (0). The second argument in the substring() method is the indexOf() method appended to the currentUsername variable, which returns the index number of the equal sign. If the substring is equal to username, then the for loop ends using a break statement, and the value of the username cookie is copied as the value of the unBox element. The statements that return the value portion of the name-value pair also use the substring() method along with the indexOf() method. However, this time the first argument starts the substring at the index number of the equal sign plus one, which is the character following the equal sign. The second argument in the substring() method specifies that the ending point of the substring is the length of the data variable.

Next, you will modify the parseData() function in script3.js so it reads the stored cookies instead of query strings. The code for the function is almost identical to the query string version, except that the cookie string is split with a semicolon and a space instead of an ampersand.

To modify the parseData() function so it reads the stored cookies instead of query strings:

1. In your text editor, return to the **script3.js** file.

2. Comment out the existing parseData() function.

3. Add the following new parseData() function:

```
1    function parseData() {
2        var formData = document.cookie;
3        var formArray = [];
4        var list = document.querySelector("div.results ul");
5        formArray = formData.split("; ");
6        for (var i = 0; i < formArray.length; i++) {
7            var newItem = document.createElement("li");
8            newItem.innerHTML = formArray[i];
9            list.appendChild(newItem);
10       }
11   }
```

The new function declares the same variables as the previous version, but assigns the value of document.cookie to the formData variable. The new function excludes the statement using the substring() method because the cookie string does not include a leading & to remove. The new function also excludes the statements to replace and decode characters because you already performed these steps on the cookie data before you created the cookies. Finally, the split() method splits the contents of the string at each occurrence of a semicolon followed by a space, which is the divider between cookies.

4. Save your changes to **script3.js**, shift-refresh or shift-reload **order.htm** in your browser, complete the form with fictitious information, click **Next**, complete the second form with fictitious information, and then click **Sign Up**. As Figure 9-13 shows, the submitted content is displayed on the results page just as it was previously. However, this content is now based on the cookies rather than on the query string.

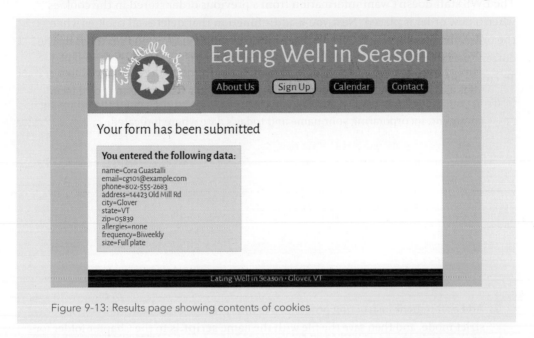

Figure 9-13: Results page showing contents of cookies

Deleting Cookies

When a user closes a browser tab or window, any temporary cookies associated with the session are deleted, while persistent cookies remain on the user's computer until they expire. In some cases, however, persistent cookies need to be deleted. You can use JavaScript to delete persistent cookies in your programs. In addition, as a developer, sometimes you need to manually delete cookies in your own browser that are set while you are testing your programs. This section describes how to delete cookies using JavaScript, as well as how to delete them manually from your browser.

Deleting Cookies with JavaScript

You can delete cookies in your code, although the way in which you delete them is not intuitive. To delete a cookie, you must set its expiration to a date in the past. The following code deletes the `username` cookie by setting its `expires` attribute to one week ago:

```
var expiresDate = new Date();
var username = document.getElementById("username").value;
```

```
expiresDate.setDate(expiresDate.getDate() - 7);
document.cookie = "username=" +↵
   encodeURIComponent(username) + "; expires=" +↵
   expiresDate.toUTCString();
```

The EWS staff doesn't want information from a previous order stored in the cookies when a new order is placed. Next you'll add a function that deletes all cookies when the order.htm page opens, to ensure that any information submitted is entered by the current user.

To create a function to delete cookies when order.htm opens:

1. In your text editor, create a new, blank JavaScript file, and then enter the following comment, incorporating your name and today's date where indicated:

```
1    /*      JavaScript 6th Edition
2     *      Chapter 9
3     *      Chapter case
4     *      Eating Well in Season
5     *      Author:
6     *      Date:
7     *      Filename: script.js
8     */
```

2. Add a statement instructing processors to interpret the document contents in strict mode, and then save the file with the name **script.js** to the Chapter folder for Chapter 9.

3. Declare a function named **clearCookies()** containing the following statements:

```
1    var cookieString = document.cookie;
2    var cookieArray = cookieString.split("; ");
3    var expiresDate = new Date();
4    expiresDate.setDate(expiresDate.getDate() - 7);
5    for (var i = 0; i < cookieArray.length; i++) {
6       document.cookie = cookieArray[i] + "; expires=" +
7    expiresDate.toUTCString();
8    }
```

The `var` statement creates a variable containing the cookie string, an array containing each cookie as a separate element, and a date object set to the current date. The next statement uses the `setDate()` and `getDate()` methods to set the value of the `expiresDate` variable to 7 days in the past. The `for` statement then recreates each cookie in the array, appending an expires attribute that uses the `expiresDate` value. This sets each cookie to expire on a date in the past, meaning that browsers delete the cookie immediately.

4. Below the `clearCookies()` function, add the following code to call the function after the page finishes loading:

```
1    if (window.addEventListener) {
2        window.addEventListener("load", clearCookies, false);
3    } else if (window.attachEvent) {
4        window.attachEvent("onload", clearCookies);
5    }
```

5. Save your changes to **script.js**, and then in your text editor return to **order.htm**.

6. Before the closing `</body>` tag, add a `script` element that specifies **script.js** as the source.

7. Save your changes to **order.htm**, and then reload **order.htm** in your browser.

8. In the browser console, type **document.cookie** and then press **Enter**. As Figure 9-14 shows, the value of the `cookie` property is an empty string, confirming that the script you created deleted all the cookies when the page loaded.

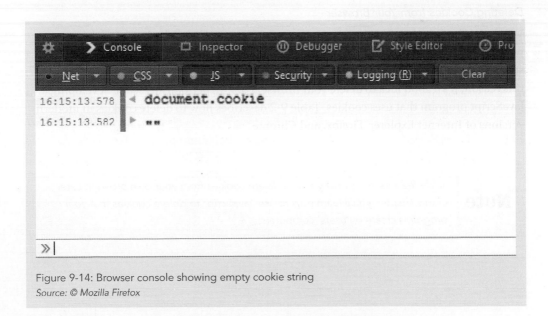

Figure 9-14: Browser console showing empty cookie string
Source: © Mozilla Firefox

Web sites and applications that require users to log into a server commonly have the ability to keep a user logged in for weeks or months at a time without compromising the security of the user's login information. Such sites often display a checkbox with the label "Remember me" or "Keep me logged in" as part of the login form, and enable you to continue to access customized content in the future, without repeatedly providing your login information. Because cookies store data in plain text, they can be read from a user's drive by malicious applications; for this reason, sensitive information such as passwords should never be stored in cookies.

In a system that supports persistent logins, when a user logs into the system, the web server provides the browser a string of random characters known as a **token**. The token is stored in a cookie, which the web server uses to verify the user's identity the next time the user requests access. Because the token is a random string, malicious programs can't anticipate its value to log into a user's account from another location. A web server stores the token value and compares it to the username to verify the user's identity. At that time, the server generates a new token, which is stored in a cookie on the user's machine.

Deleting Cookies from Your Browser

When developing a JavaScript program, you may accidentally create, but not delete, persistent cookies that your program does not need. Unused persistent cookies can sometimes interfere with the execution of a JavaScript program that uses cookies. For this reason, it's a good idea to delete your browser cookies periodically while developing a JavaScript program that uses cookies. Table 9-2 describes how to delete cookies in modern versions of Internet Explorer, Firefox, and Chrome.

Note | *Table 9-2 describes how you can delete cookies from your own browser. Later in this chapter, you'll learn how to use JavaScript to delete cookies that your programs create on users' computers.*

BROWSER	KEYBOARD SHORTCUT	MENU STEPS
Internet Explorer 9+	Press **Ctrl** + **Shift** + **Del**, then in the window that opens, make sure the **Cookies and website data** box is checked, and then click **Delete**.	Click the **Tools** icon, if necessary point to **Safety** on the menu, click **Delete browsing history** in the submenu, then in the window that opens, make sure the **Cookies and website data** box is checked, and then click **Delete**.
Firefox	Press **Ctrl** + **Shift** + **Del** (Windows) or **command** + **shift** + **delete** (Mac), then in the window that opens, select the desired time range in the "Time range to clear" list, if necessary click the Details arrow, make sure the **Cookies** box is checked, and then click **Clear Now** (Windows) or **OK** (Mac).	Click the **Open menu** button, click **History**, click **Clear Recent History**, then in the window that opens, select the desired time range in the "Time range to clear" list, if necessary click the Details arrow, make sure the **Cookies** box is checked, and then click **Clear Now** (Windows) or **OK** (Mac).
Chrome	Press **Ctrl** + **H** (Windows) or **command** + **Y** (Mac), click **Clear browsing data**, then in the window that opens, select the desired time range in the "Obliterate the following items from" list, make sure the **Cookies and other site and plug-in data** box is checked, and then click **Clear browsing data**.	Click the **Customize and control Google Chrome** button, click **History**, click **Clear browsing data**, then in the window that opens, select the desired time range in the "Obliterate the following items from" list, make sure the **Cookies and other site and plug-in data** box is checked, and then click **Clear browsing data**.

Table 9-2: Steps to delete cookies in IE, Firefox, and Chrome

Storing State Information with the Web Storage API

Many common uses of cookies today were never envisioned in the original implementations of the `cookie` object. Creating, reading, and removing cookies requires complex code that's not always straightforward. In addition, all cookies are sent to the server with each HTTP request. In recent years, an effort has been underway to deal with these shortcomings and add new functionality to browsers by creating a standard to replace cookies. The result is a draft specification of the W3C known as Web Storage. Because Web Storage is not supported by a number of older browser versions, cookies are still the standard for storing information on the client about a user's interactions with a web server. However, Web Storage offers additional features that cookies don't support, so developers creating web applications for users of specific browsers can take advantage of these features now.

Web Storage includes two different properties of the `Window` object: `localStorage` and `sessionStorage`. You use the `localStorage` property for storage that remains until you run code to delete it, similar to persistent cookies. Data stored using the `sessionStorage` property, on the other hand, is removed automatically when a user closes the browser tab or window that generated it, much like temporary cookies. Data stored using either property is placed in a `Storage` object, which is similar to a standard JavaScript object: it contains named properties that are paired with values.

Storing and reading data with Web Storage is much more straightforward than using cookies. For instance, the following code stores the value entered by a user in a field with the `id` value of `fname`, and then stores that value using the `localStorage` property with the name `fName`:

```
var firstName = document.getElementById("fname").value;
localStorage.fName = firstName;
```

The Web Storage specification includes several methods for creating, reading, and deleting stored data. Table 9-3 describes several of these methods.

METHOD	DESCRIPTION
clear()	Removes all data
getItem(*name*)	Retrieves the value of the item with the name *name*
removeItem(*name*)	Removes the item with the name *name* from storage
setItem(*name*, *value*)	Stores an item with the name *name* and the value *value*

Table 9-3: Methods of the Web Storage API

To use a method, you preface it with either the `localStorage` or `sessionStorage` property. For instance, you could use the `setItem()` method with the `localStorage` property to declare the `fname` property and sets its value in a single statement using the following code:

```
localStorage.setItem(fname, firstName);
```

This statement declares a property with the name `fname` and sets its value to the value of the `firstName` variable. Because the statement starts with the `localStorage` property, the data is available until it is deleted. You can delete a property using the `removeItem()` method, as follows:

```
localStorage.removeItem(fname);
```

This statement removes the `fname` property and its value from storage. Note that the process of removing data stored using Web Storage is much more straightforward than when using cookies, which require you to specify an expiration date in the past in order to remove data.

Web storage is available only to documents from the domain that created it, similar to cookies.

Short Quiz 2

1. What are the two main types of cookies? What is the difference between them?

2. How do you delete a cookie in your code?

3. What are some advantages of using Web Storage rather than cookies? Why might a developer choose to continue using cookies?

Understanding Security Issues

Viruses, worms, data theft by hackers, and other types of security threats are now a fact of life when it comes to web-based applications. If you put an application into a production environment without considering security issues, you are asking for trouble. To combat security violations, you need to consider both web server security issues and secure coding issues. Web server security involves technologies such as firewalls, which combine software and hardware to prevent access to private networks connected to the Internet. One very important technology is the Secure Sockets Layer (SSL) protocol, which encrypts data and transfers it across a secure connection. This type of security technology works well in the realm of the Internet. However, JavaScript programs are downloaded and executed locally within the web browser of a client computer, and are not governed by security technologies such as firewalls and SSL.

This section discusses security issues that relate to web browsers and JavaScript.

> **Note** Although web server security issues are critical, they are properly covered in books on Apache, Nginx, Internet Information Services, and other types of web servers. Be sure to research security issues for your web server and operating system before activating a production web site.

Secure Coding with JavaScript

The terms secure coding and defensive coding refer to writing code in a way that minimizes any intentional or accidental security issues. Secure coding has become a major goal for many information technology companies, primarily because of the exorbitant cost of fixing security flaws in commercial software. According to one study, it is 100 times more expensive to fix security flaws in released software than it is to apply secure coding techniques during the development phase. The National Institute of Standards & Technology estimates that $60 billion a year is spent identifying and correcting software errors.

Basically, all code is insecure unless proven otherwise. Unfortunately, there is no magic formula for writing secure code, although there are various techniques that you can use to minimize security threats in your scripts. Your first line of defense in securing your JavaScript programs is to validate all user input. You have studied various techniques in this book for validating user input, including how to validate data with regular expressions and how to use exceptions to handle errors as they occur in your scripts. Be sure to use these techniques in your scripts, especially scripts that run on commercial web sites. The remainder of this section discusses security issues that relate to web browsers and JavaScript.

JavaScript Security Concerns

The web was originally designed to be read-only, which is to say its primary purpose was to locate and display documents that existed on other areas of the web. With the development of programming languages such as JavaScript, web pages can now contain programs in addition to static content. This ability to execute programs within a web page raises several security concerns. The security areas of most concern to JavaScript programmers are:

> Protection of a web page and JavaScript program against malicious tampering

> Privacy of individual client information

> Protection of the local file system of the client or web site from theft or tampering

JavaScript code on a web page that is not written securely is vulnerable to a **code injection attack**, in which a program or user enters JavaScript code that changes the function of the web page. For instance, a malicious program could open a web page containing a form and enter JavaScript code in one of the form fields designed to retrieve sensitive information from the server. Such a program could then relay this information to a person other than the owner.

Validating forms before submission is an important part of preventing injection attacks. In addition, it's important to **escape** characters in form field values that could be part of malicious code, which involves converting the characters to their character code equivalents, as you do when URL encoding cookie data. For form input, escaping is generally performed by the web server before processing user input.

Another security concern is the privacy of individual client information in the web browser window. Your contact information and browsing history are valuable pieces of information that many advertisers would like to access in order to tailor their advertising based on your personal tastes. Without security restrictions, a JavaScript program could read this information from your web browser. One of the most important JavaScript security features is its *lack* of certain types of functionality. For example, many programming languages include objects and methods that make it possible for a program to read, write, and delete files. To prevent mischievous scripts from stealing information or causing damage by changing or deleting files, JavaScript does not allow any file manipulation aside from cookies, Web Storage, and a few other emerging standards, which are site specific. Similarly, JavaScript does not include any sort of mechanism for creating a network connection. This limitation prevents JavaScript programs from infiltrating a private network or intranet from which information may be stolen or damaged. Another helpful limitation is the fact that JavaScript cannot run system commands or execute programs on a client. The ability to read and write cookies is the only type of access to a client that JavaScript has. Web browsers, however, strictly govern cookies and do not allow access to cookies from outside the domain that created them.

The Same Origin Policy

Another JavaScript security feature restricts how JavaScript code in one window, tab, or frame accesses a web page in another window, tab, or frame on a client computer. Under the same origin policy, windows, tabs, and frames can view and modify the elements and properties of documents displayed in other windows, tabs, and frames only if they share the same protocol (such as HTTP) and exist on the same web server.

> **Note** In modern web design, web page objects created with the `iframe` element are known as frames. The `iframe` element enables you to display the content of one HTML document within another HTML document.

For example, documents from the following two domains cannot access each other's elements and properties because they use different protocols.

> *http://www.example.com*
> *https://www.example.com*

The first domain's protocol is HTTP and the second domain's protocol is HTTPS (indicating that the connection to the server uses SSL encryption). The same origin policy applies not only to the domain name but also to the server on which a document is located. Therefore, documents from the following two domains cannot access each other's elements and properties, because they are located on different servers, even though they exist in the same domain of example.com:

> *http://marketing.example.com*
> *http://content.example.com*

The same origin policy prevents malicious scripts from modifying the content of other windows and tabs and prevents the theft of private browser information and information displayed on secure web pages. How crucial is the same origin policy? Consider the `src` attribute of the `Document` object, which determines the URL displayed in a window, tab, or frame. If the same origin policy did not exist, then a web page in one window, tab, or frame could change the web pages displayed in other windows, tabs, or frames, inserting advertising or simply redirecting to a new URL. The security of private networks and intranets would also be at risk without the same origin policy. Consider a user who has one web browser open to a page on the Internet and another web browser open to a secure page from his or her private network or intranet. Without the same origin policy, the Internet web page would have access to the information displayed on the private web page.

The same origin policy also protects the integrity of your web page's design. For example, without the same origin policy, a page in one window, tab, or frame could modify the elements and properties of JavaScript objects and HTML code in other windows, tabs, and frames.

In some circumstances, you might want two documents from related web sites on different servers to be able to access each other's elements and properties. Consider a situation in which a document in the *marketing.example.com* domain needs to access content, such as form data, from a document in the *content.example.com* domain. To allow documents from different origins in the same domain to access each other's elements and properties, you use the `domain` property of the `Document` object. The **domain property** of the `Document` object changes the origin of a document to its root domain name by using the statement

```
document.domain = "domain"
```

Adding the statement `document.domain = "example.com";` to documents from both *marketing.example.com* and *content.example.com* allows the documents to access each other's elements and properties, even though they are located on different servers.

Using Third-Party Scripts

Although the same-origin policy is an important part of web browser security, in some cases you want scripts from other domains, known as **third-party scripts**, to be able to run on your web pages. For instance, some companies provide widgets, which are programs that you can add to your web pages but that run from the provider's web server, rather than from your own. Another common situation requiring third-party scripts is the use of a **content delivery network (CDN)**, which is a company that maintains web servers optimized for fast delivery of content. CDNs are commonly used by large organizations, and generally provide content from their own domain rather than from the client's domain.

To enable a third-party script in a web document, you simply include a `script` element with a `src` value pointing to the third-party content. The same origin policy limits scripts to those referenced by HTML documents from the original web server; this enables web pages to use third-party scripts.

Short Quiz 3

1. What is a code injection attack?

2. What is the same origin policy?

3. What is a third-party script? How do you include one in a web document?

Summary

> Your programs can temporarily save information by passing it from one page to another with a query string, and by storing it in hidden form fields.

> Your programs can store information for longer periods by creating cookies, which are small pieces of information about a user that are stored in text files on the user's computer.

> JavaScript includes safeguards such as the same origin policy to prevent some security issues. However, it's still important to write code with an eye toward security to avoid other potential problems, including code injection attacks.

Key Terms

CDN—*See* content delivery network.

code injection attack—A security threat in which a program or user enters JavaScript code that changes the function of the web page.

content delivery network (CDN)—A company that maintains web servers optimized for fast delivery of content.

cookies—Small pieces of information that are stored in text files on a user's computer.

decodeURIComponent() function—A built-in function used in JavaScript for decoding the individual parts of a URI.

defensive coding—*See* secure coding.

domain attribute—The attribute of the `cookie` property that specifies how widely a cookie can be shared across multiple servers in the same domain.

domain property—The property of the `Document` object that you use to change the origin of a document to its root domain name.

encodeURIComponent() function—A built-in function used in JavaScript for encoding the individual parts of a URI.

encoding—The process of converting each special character in a text string to its corresponding hexadecimal ASCII value, preceded by a percent sign.

escape—To convert characters to their character code equivalents, similar to encoding.

expires attribute—The attribute of the `cookie` property that determines how long a cookie can remain on a client system before it is deleted.

hidden form field—A special type of `input` element that is not displayed by web browsers and, therefore, allows developers to hide information from users.

HTTP—*See* Hypertext Transfer Protocol (HTTP).

Hypertext Transfer Protocol (HTTP)—A set of rules used by browsers and servers to exchange information about web documents.

localStorage property—The Web Storage property that you use for storage that remains until you run code to delete it, similar to persistent cookies.

man-in-the-middle attack—An attack in which data being exchanged between two parties is read and potentially changed in transit.

path attribute—The attribute of the `cookie` property that determines the availability of a cookie to other web pages on a server.

persistent cookies—Cookies that remain available beyond the current browser session and are stored in a text file on a client computer.

query string—A set of name-value pairs appended to a target URL.

same origin policy—A JavaScript security feature that restricts how JavaScript code in one window, tab, or frame accesses a web page in another window, tab, or frame on a client computer.

secure attribute—The attribute of the `cookie` property that indicates whether a cookie can be transmitted only across a secure Internet connection using HTTPS or another security protocol.

secure coding—Writing code in a way that minimizes any intentional or accidental security issues.

Secure Sockets Layer (SSL)—The main protocol used to encrypt data on web sites.

sessionStorage property—The Web Storage property that you use for storage that is removed automatically when a user closes the browser tab or window that generated it, much like temporary cookies.

SSL—*See* Secure Sockets Layer.

state information—Information about individual visits to a web site.

stateless—Describes a protocol that doesn't accommodate storing persistent data.

temporary cookies—Cookies that remain available only for the current browser session.

third-party scripts—Scripts from other domains.

TLS—*See* Transport Layer Security.

token—A string of random characters used to verify a user's identity in a system that supports persistent logins.

Transport Layer Security (TLS)—The encryption standard planned to eventually replace SSL.

Web Storage—A newer specification for storing data about a web session, which sets out standards for storing more information than cookies allow and uses a syntax and methods that are more intuitive than cookies.

Review Questions

1. HTTP was originally designed to be _____, which means that web browsers stored no persistent data about a visit to a web site.
   a. hidden
   b. encrypted
   c. stateless
   d. stateful

2. What character is used to separate individual name-value pairs within a query string?
   a. &
   b. $
   c. ?
   d. %

3. To concatenate names and values into a query string, you can use methods of the _____ class.
   a. `Array`
   b. `String`
   c. `Number`
   d. `Date`

4. The _____ method of a form automatically creates a query string from its field values.
   a. `reset`
   b. `change`
   c. `click`
   d. `submit`

5. Which `type` value for the `input` element creates a field that is not displayed by web browsers?
   a. `hidden`
   b. `invisible`
   c. `none`
   d. `text`

6. Which is the only required attribute of the `cookie` property?
   a. `path`
   b. `domain`
   c. `expires`
   d. `name`

7. You can use special characters in your cookies if you use _____.
   a. secure coding
   b. encoding
   c. a CDN
   d. the `secure` attribute

8. Cookies created without a(n) _____ attribute are available for the current browser session only.
   a. `path`
   b. `domain`
   c. `expires`
   d. `name`

9. Which function do you use as part of the process of parsing a cookie?
   a. `encodeURI()`
   b. `decodeURI()`
   c. `encodeURIComponent()`
   d. `decodeURIComponent()`

10. To delete cookies in your code, you change the value of which `cookie` attribute?
    a. `path`
    b. `domain`
    c. `expires`
    d. `name`

11. Which property of the Web Storage API do you use to store data that remains until you run code to delete it, similar to persistent cookies?
    a. `localStorage`
    b. `sessionStorage`
    c. `persistentStorage`
    d. `webStorage`

12. Which method do you use to delete a specific item from Web Storage?
    a. `clear()`
    b. `getItem()`
    c. `removeItem()`
    d. `setItem()`

13. Your first line of defense in securing your JavaScript programs is to _____.
    a. require a login for every user
    b. validate all user input
    c. encode all data
    d. restrict access to a single subdomain

14. An attack in which a program or user enters JavaScript code that changes the function of a web page is known as a(n) _____ attack.
    a. code injection
    b. secure coding
    c. cross-site
    d. SSL

15. It's important to _____ characters in form field values that could be part of malicious code, which involves converting the characters to their character code equivalents.

    a. encrypt
    b. decrypt
    c. encode
    d. escape

16. Why should a password never be stored in a cookie?

17. What is the difference between temporary and persistent cookies?

18. Explain how to modify an existing cookie.

19. Describe one advantage and one disadvantage of using Web Storage rather than cookies.

20. Explain what a code injection attack is, and one step you can take to prevent such attacks.

Hands-On Projects

Hands-On Project 9-1

In this project, you'll start work on a web app that enables users to create a greeting card. As a first step, you'll add functionality that allows users to submit the text of a greeting on one page and then view the text formatted as it would appear on a card. To accomplish this, you'll create code to parse the value of the variable passed from the first web page to the second web page in a query string. You'll then add code to display the value in the second web page.

1. In your text editor, open the **index.htm** file from the HandsOnProject9-1 folder in the Chapter09 folder, add your name and today's date where indicated in the comment section, and then save the file.

2. Before the closing `</body>` tag, add a `script` element that references **script.js** as the source, save your changes, and then close **index.htm**.

3. Repeat Steps 1 and 2 for the file **preview.htm**.

4. Create a new file in your text editor, create a JavaScript comment section containing the text **Hands-on Project 9-1**, your name, today's date, and the filename **script.js**, and then save the file with the name **script.js** to the HandsOnProject9-1 folder.

5. Add a statement instructing processors to interpret the document contents in strict mode.

6. Declare a new function named `populateInfo()`. Within the function, add the following `if` statement:

```
1   if (location.search) {
2       var greeting = location.search;
3       greeting = greeting.replace("+", " ");
```

```
4       greeting = greeting.substring(greeting.lastIndexOf("=")↵
5           + 1);
6       document.getElementById("greetingtext").innerHTML =↵
7           decodeURIComponent(greeting);
8   }
```

7. Below the `populateInfo()` function, add the following code to run the function when the page finishes loading:

```
1   if (window.addEventListener) {
2       window.addEventListener("load", populateInfo, false);
3   } else if (window.attachEvent) {
4       window.attachEvent("onload", populateInfo);
5   }
```

8. Save your changes to **script.js**, and then return to **index.htm** in your browser.

9. In the Greeting Text box, type **Happy Birthday!** and then click the **Preview** button. The preview.htm page is displayed with the text "Happy Birthday!" formatted as shown in Figure 9-15.

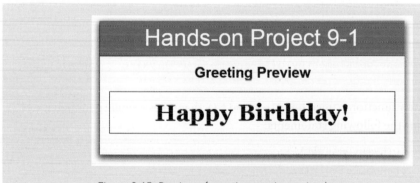

Figure 9-15: Preview of greeting text in preview.htm page

Hands-On Project 9-2

One common use of cookies on a site that requires logging in is to save a user's login name. In this project, you'll add code that automatically creates a cookie containing a user's login name (but not password) when the user submits the login form. You'll also add code to populate the Username field with the cookie value if the cookie exists.

Remember that to protect your users' identities, passwords should never be stored in cookies. The web pages that you'll be working with simulate the login process without requiring a password. On a real-life website, the entered username and password would be submitted to a web server for verification.

1. In your text editor, open the **index.htm** file from the HandsOnProject9-2 folder in the Chapter09 folder, add your name and today's date where indicated in the comment section, and then save the file.

2. Before the closing `</body>` tag, add a `script` element that references **script.js** as the source, save your changes, and then close **index.htm**.

3. Repeat Step 1 for **results.htm**.

4. Create a new file in your text editor, create a JavaScript comment section containing the text **Hands-on Project 9-2**, your name, today's date, and the filename **script.js**, and then save the file with the name **script.js** to the HandsOnProject9-2 folder.

5. Add a statement instructing processors to interpret the document contents in strict mode.

6. Declare a new function named **processCookie()** containing the following statement:

```
document.cookie = "username=" +
    document.getElementById("usernameinput").value;
```

7. Declare a new function named **populateInfo()** containing the following if statement:

```
1  if (document.cookie) {
2      var uname = document.cookie;
3      uname = uname.substring(uname.lastIndexOf("=") + 1);
4      document.getElementById("usernameinput").value = uname;
5  }
```

8. Declare a new function named **handleSubmit()** that takes a single parameter, evt, and contains the following statements:

```
1  if (evt.preventDefault) {
2      evt.preventDefault();
3  } else {
4      evt.returnValue = false;
5  }
6  processCookie();
7  document.getElementsByTagName("form")[0].submit();
```

9. Add the following code to create an event listener, and to call the populateInfo() and createEventListener() functions when the page finishes loading:

```
1  function createEventListener() {
2      var loginForm = document.getElementsByTagName("form")[0];
```

```
3        if (loginForm.addEventListener) {
4            loginForm.addEventListener("submit", handleSubmit, ↵
5                false);
6        } else if (loginForm.attachEvent) {
7            loginForm.attachEvent("onsubmit", handleSubmit);
8        }
9    }
10   function setUpPage() {
11       populateInfo();
12       createEventListener();
13   }
14   if (window.addEventListener) {
15       window.addEventListener("load", setUpPage, false);
16   } else if (window.attachEvent) {
17       window.attachEvent("onload", setUpPage);
18   }
```

10. Save your changes to **script.js**, and then open **index.htm** in a browser.

11. In the **Username** box, type your email address, and then click the **Login** button. The results.htm page, containing the text "Login successful," is displayed because this page is specified in the form's `action` attribute.

12. Return to **index.htm** in your browser, and then shift-refresh or shift-reload the page. Even though you reloaded or refreshed the page using Shift to clear the form, when the page finished loading, the code you created populated the Username field with the username stored in a cookie, as shown in Figure 9-16.

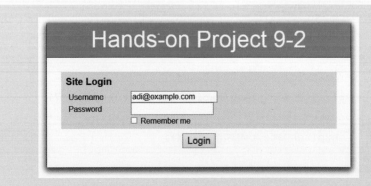

Figure 9-16: Username field populated with cookie value

Hands-On Project 9-3

In this project, you'll enhance the login script you created in Hands-on Project 9-2. You'll add code that checks whether the "Remember me" box is checked, and sets a cookie only if the box is checked. In addition, you'll add code to delete any existing cookie if the "Remember me" box is unchecked when the form is submitted.

1. In the file manager for your operating system, copy the completed contents of the HandsOnProject9-2 folder to the HandsOnProject9-3 folder.

2. In your text editor, open the **index.htm** file from the HandsOnProject9-3 folder, change "Hands-on Project 9-2" to **Hands-on Project 9-3** in the comment section, in the `title` element, and in the `h1` element, and then save your changes. Repeat for **results.htm**.

3. Open **script.js**, and then in the comment section, change "Hands-on Project 9-2" to **Hands-on Project 9-3**.

4. In the **script.js** file, in the `processCookie()` function, enclose the existing statement to set a cookie within an `if` clause, using the following condition:

```
document.getElementById("rememberinput").checked
```

5. After the `if` clause, add an `else` clause containing the following statements:

```
1    var expiresDate = new Date();
2    expiresDate.setDate(expiresDate.getDate() - 7);
3    document.cookie = "username=null; expires=" +↵
4        expiresDate.toUTCString();
```

Your completed `processCookie()` function should match the following:

```
1    function processCookie() {
2        if (document.getElementById("rememberinput").checked) {
3            document.cookie = "username=" +↵
4                document.getElementById("usernameinput").value;
5        } else {
6            var expiresDate = new Date();
7            expiresDate.setDate(expiresDate.getDate() - 7);
8            document.cookie = "username=null; expires=" +↵
9                expiresDate.toUTCString();
10       }
11   }
```

6. Save your changes to **script.js**, and then open **index.htm** in a browser.

7. If necessary, enter your email address in the **Username** box, click the **Remember me** box to check it, and then click **Login**. The results.htm page is displayed, with the text "Login successful." Because you checked the Remember me box, the browser also stored a cookie containing your username.

8. Return to **index.htm** and then shift-refresh or shift-reload the page. The code you created populated the Username field with the username stored in a cookie.

9. Ensure that the Remember me box is not checked, click **Login** to open the **results.htm** page, return to the **index.htm** page, and then shift-refresh or shift-reload the page. Because you last submitted the form with the "Remember me" box unchecked, the code you created deleted the cookie, and the Username field is blank as shown in Figure 9-17.

Figure 9-17: Blank Username field after cookie is deleted

Hands-On Project 9-4

Some websites save login information only for a limited time, and require users to reenter it periodically. In this project, you'll modify the login page you've worked with in Hands-on Projects 9-2 and 9-3 to create a cookie that expires after a set period. Although real-life websites typically expire such cookies after a number of weeks, you'll create one that expires 2 minutes after its creation in order to facilitate testing.

1. In the file manager for your operating system, copy the completed contents of the HandsOnProject9-3 folder to the HandsOnProject9-4 folder.

2. In your text editor, open the **index.htm** file from the HandsOnProject9-4 folder, change "Hands-on Project 9-3" to **Hands-on Project 9-4** in the comment section, in the `title` element, and in the `h1` element, and then save your changes. Repeat for **results.htm**.

3. Open **script.js**, and then in the comment section, change "Hands-on Project 9-3" to **Hands-on Project 9-4**.

4. In the **script.js** file, in the `processCookie()` function, move the statement `var expiresDate = new Date();` from the `else` clause to above the `if` clause, making it the first statement in the function.

5. Within the `if` clause, add the following line of code before the existing statement:

```
expiresDate.setMinutes(expiresDate.getMinutes() + 2);
```

6. Edit the second line of code in the `if` clause so it matches the following:

```
document.cookie = "username="↵
    + document.getElementById("usernameinput").value↵
    + "; expires=" + expiresDate.toUTCString();
```

Your completed `processCookie()` function should match the following:

```
1    function processCookie() {
2        var expiresDate = new Date();
3        if (document.getElementById("rememberinput").checked) {
4            expiresDate.setMinutes(expiresDate.getMinutes() + 2);
5            document.cookie = "username="↵
6                + document.getElementById("usernameinput").value↵
7                + "; expires=" + expiresDate.toUTCString();
8        } else {
9            expiresDate.setDate(expiresDate.getDate() - 7);
10           document.cookie = "username=null; expires="↵
11               + expiresDate.toUTCString();
12       }
13   }
```

7. Save your changes to **script.js**, and then open **index.htm** in a browser.

8. In the Username box, enter your email address, click the **Remember me** box to check it, and then click the **Login** button. The results.htm page is displayed as a confirmation that the form has been submitted.

9. Return to **index.htm** in your browser, and then shift-refresh or shift-reload the page. If it's been less than 2 minutes since you submitted the page, the Username box should be prepopulated with your email address, which was stored in a cookie in the previous step.

10. In the browser console, type **document.cookie** and then press **Enter**. As Figure 9-18 shows, the cookie contains the email address you entered in Step 8.

Figure 9-18: Cookie value displayed in console
Source: © Microsoft Corporation

11. Wait 2 minutes, and then shift-refresh or shift-reload the page. The Username box remains empty because the cookie has expired.

12. In the browser console, type **document.cookie** and then press **Enter**. As Figure 9-19 shows, the cookie is an empty string.

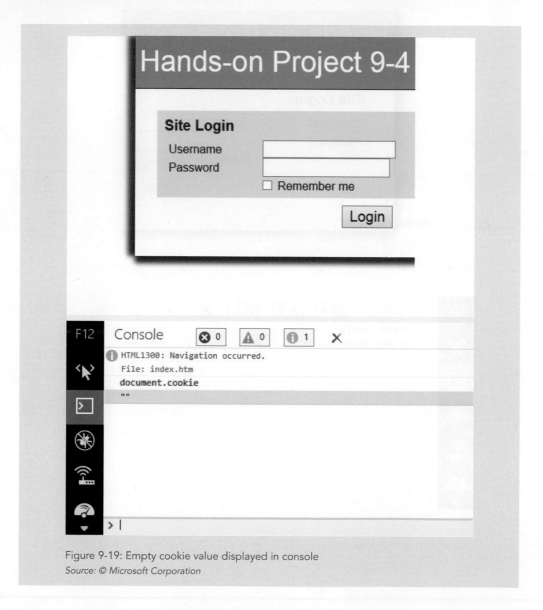

Figure 9-19: Empty cookie value displayed in console
Source: © Microsoft Corporation

Hands-On Project 9-5

In this project, you'll continue to work with the login page you've coded in Hands-on Projects 9-2 through 9-4. You'll replace the cookie storage functionality you created for the login page with code that instead uses the Web Storage `sessionStorage` property. Note that the final result in this project will work only in browsers that support Web Storage, which includes all modern browsers and IE8. For a detailed list of browser support for this API, see *caniuse.com* and search for "Web Storage".

1. In the file manager for your operating system, copy the completed contents of the HandsOnProject9-4 folder to the HandsOnProject9-5 folder.

2. In your text editor, open the **index.htm** file from the HandsOnProject9-4 folder, change "Hands-on Project 9-4" to **Hands-on Project 9-5** in the comment section, in the `title` element, and in the `h1` element, and then save your changes. Repeat for **results.htm**.

3. Open **script.js**, and then in the comment section, change "Hands-on Project 9-4" to **Hands-on Project 9-5**.

4. In the **script.js** file, comment out the `processCookie()` and `populateInfo()` functions.

5. Below the commented out functions, create a new `processStorage()` function. Add an `if` statement that checks if the element with the `id` value of `rememberinput` is checked, and if so, runs the following statement:

```
sessionStorage.username =
    document.getElementById("usernameinput").value;
```

   This statement adds a name-value pair to the `sessionStorage` property, assigning the name "username" and the value in the Username box.

6. Below the `processStorage()` function, add a new `populateInfo()` function. Add an `if` statement that uses the condition `sessionStorage.username` and runs the following statement:

```
document.getElementById("usernameinput").value =
    sessionStorage.username;
```

This function checks if the `sessionStorage` property contains data with the name `username`, and if so, it sets the value assigned to this name as the value of the Username box. Your new functions should match the following:

```
1   function processStorage() {
2       if (document.getElementById("rememberinput").checked) {
3           sessionStorage.username =↵
4               document.getElementById("usernameinput").value;
5       }
6   }
7   function populateInfo() {
8       if (sessionStorage.username) {
9           document.getElementById("usernameinput").value =↵
10              sessionStorage.username;
11      }
12  }
```

7. Save your changes to **script.js**, and then open **index.htm** in a browser.

8. In the Username box, enter your email address, click the **Remember me** box to check it, and then click the **Login** button. The results.htm page is displayed as a confirmation that the form has been submitted.

9. Return to **index.htm** in your browser, and then shift-refresh or shift-reload the page. The Username box is prepopulated with your email address, which was added to the `sessionStorage` property in the previous step.

10. In the browser console, type **sessionStorage**, press **Enter**, and then if necessary, click **object Storage**. As Figure 9-20 shows, the storage contents are displayed, including the name-value pair created by your code.

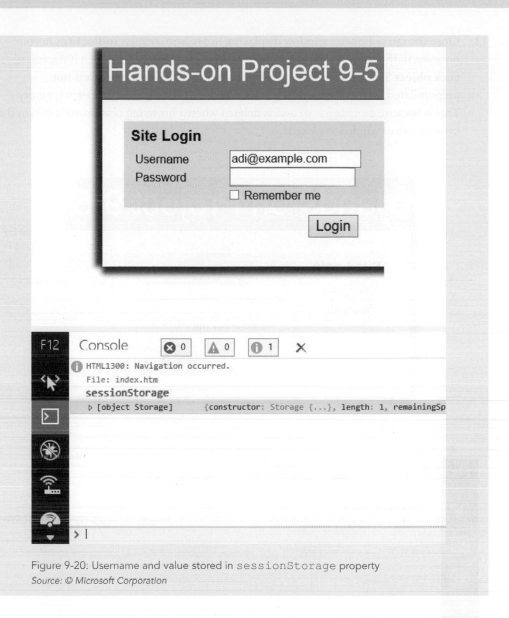

Figure 9-20: Username and value stored in `sessionStorage` property
Source: © Microsoft Corporation

11. Close the tab or browser window displaying index.htm, reopen **index.htm** in your browser, in the console type **sessionStorage**, press **Enter**, and then if necessary click **object Storage** to view the storage contents. The Username box is not prepopulated, and as Figure 9-21 shows, the sessionStorage property is empty. This is because sessionStorage is deleted when a browsing session ends (when the browser tab or window is closed).

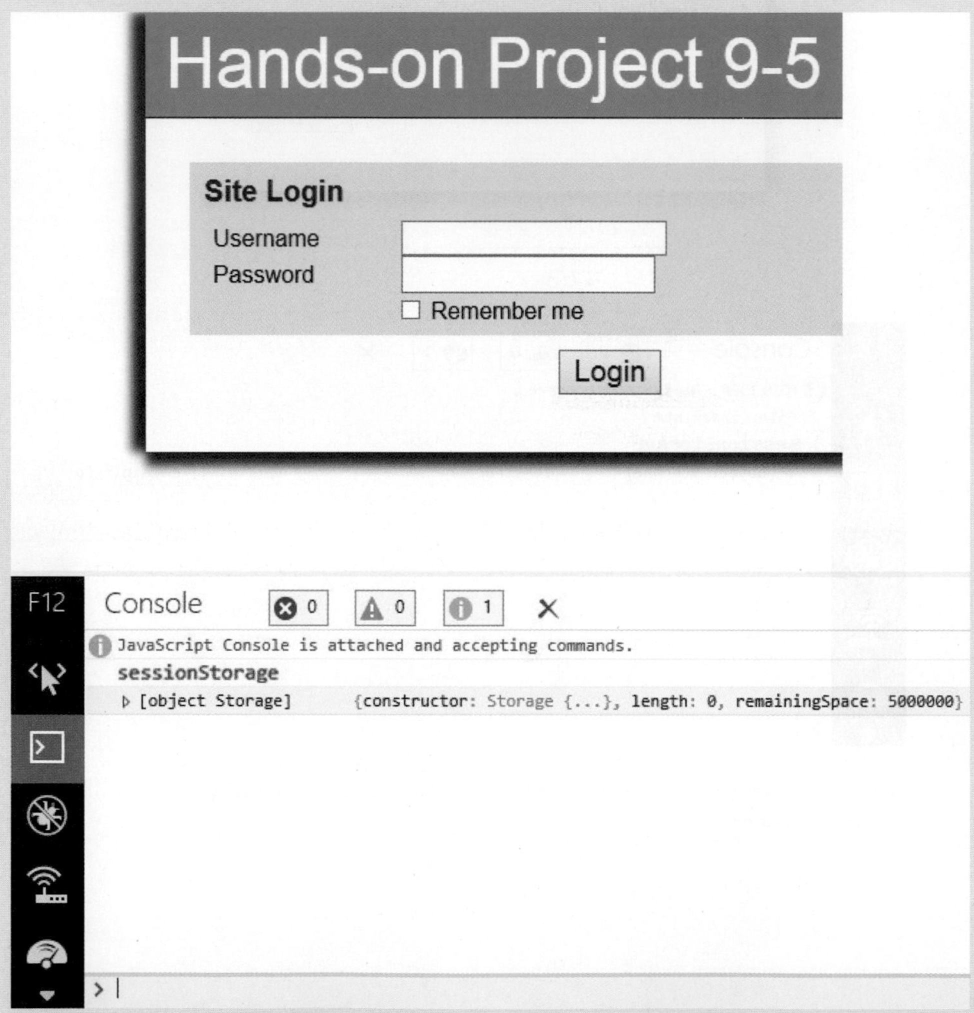

Figure 9-21: Empty sessionStorage property
Source: © Microsoft Corporation

Case Projects

Individual Case Project

Enhance the personal website you've created in the preceding chapters of this book to prevent security issues. To do this, review each form field in your site and identify any additional validation that you could reasonably add. In particular, look for situations where you could use a regular expression to limit the allowable characters in order to exclude characters used in creating JavaScript code. Use word-processing software to create a table like Table 9-4, which includes an example. Add a row for each form field in your website.

FILENAME	FIELD LABEL	VALIDATION PERFORMED BEFORE SUBMISSION	VALIDATION LEFT TO WEB SERVER
index.htm	Zip	Numbers and hyphen only no more than 10 digits	Verifying that Zip value is appropriate for provided State value

Table 9-4. Table for planning additional validation

When you've reviewed each field in your website, add the validation described in your table. Test each field until you're satisfied with your new validation code.

Group Case Project

Have each group member present the table and website from their Individual Case Project to the group. When presenting your website, solicit feedback from other group members regarding additional validation that you could add to your site, and discuss as a group the pros and any cons of the suggested enhancement. After all group members have presented their sites and received feedback, implement any suggestions for your site that your group generally felt would be good additions.

CHAPTER

10

PROGRAMMING FOR TOUCHSCREENS AND MOBILE DEVICES

When you complete this chapter, you will be able to:

> Integrate mouse, touch, and pointer events into a web app

> Obtain and work with a user's geolocation information

> Optimize a mobile web app to accommodate the common constraints experienced by mobile users

Developing a web page that's usable across different devices requires HTML that accurately describes the content and CSS that accounts for different screen sizes and resolutions. In addition, it's important to write JavaScript that accurately captures user actions no matter the type of device on which a user accesses your site.

While touchscreen devices generally support mouse-based events for basic user actions, programming some behaviors for touchscreen users in a web app requires supporting touch-specific events in your code. In this chapter, you'll learn about some of the most commonly supported touch events and you'll integrate them into a web app. You'll also explore some of the HTML5 APIs that can enhance the experience of mobile device users, and you'll integrate one of them—the Geolocation API—into a web app.

Using Touch Events and Pointer Events

On a touchscreen device without a mouse, most browsers fire the `click` event when a user touches the screen. As a result, JavaScript code that responds to this basic user action works predictably across devices. All the web apps you've worked with so far in this book incorporate events that work on both desktop and mobile browsers. However, other mouse-based events don't translate neatly to touchscreen devices.

In this chapter, you'll enhance a website for Oak Top House, an event venue in Columbus, Ohio. Oak Top House is available for daily or multiday rentals, and is commonly used for weddings, graduation parties, quinceañeras, and other special events. The owners of Oak Top House want a web app that will enable users to learn about the facility, book rentals, and make arrangements for events. As a first step, they would like the web app to have two parts: a diagram of the banquet hall where users can specify the arrangement of furniture for their events, and a map that shows the venue's location. They've already contracted a developer to create the initial HTML and CSS, and they'd like you to program the app. Figures 10-1, 10-2, and 10-3 show previews of the functionality you'll add to the app's two sections.

Figure 10-1: Default arrangement of Setup tab
© 2015 Cengage Learning®

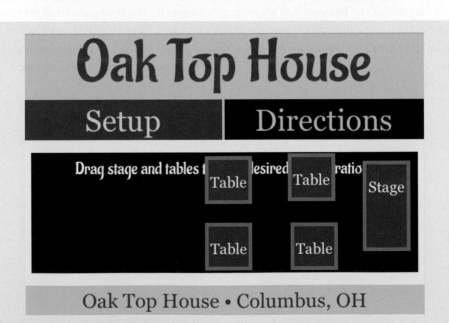

Figure 10-2: Setup tab with furniture rearranged

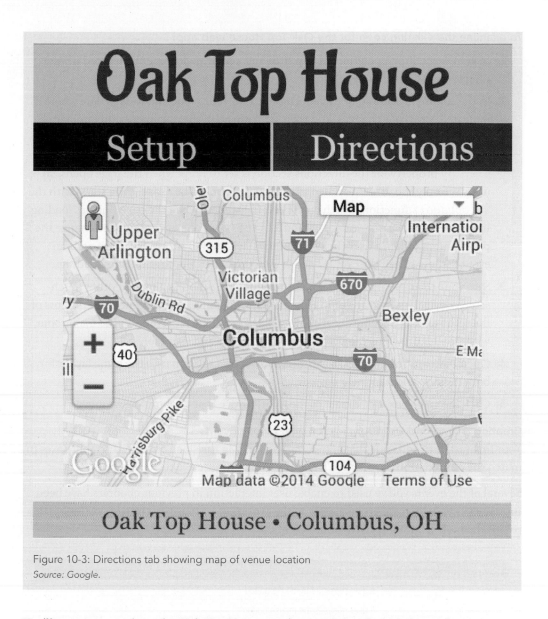

Figure 10-3: Directions tab showing map of venue location
Source: Google.

You'll start your work on the Oak Top House app by examining the existing code.

Note | To keep the amount of code in this chapter manageable, the app you create will not be compatible with IE8.

To examine the existing code for the Oak Top House web app:

1. In your text editor, open the **oaktop.htm** and **script.js** documents, located in your Chapter folder for Chapter 10.

2. In the comment section for each document, add your name and today's date where indicated, save your changes, and then scroll through the document and familiarize yourself with its content. The oaktop.htm document contains two `article` elements—one for the room layout and one for directions to the venue. The CSS `display` property for the directions section is set to `none` when the page opens, so users see only the content related to the setup section. The script.js file starts with the `setUpPage()` function, which creates event listeners when the page finishes loading. It also contains the `loadSetup()` and `loadDirections()` functions to change the page contents when a user clicks one of the navigation buttons. Finally, it adds an event listener to call the `setUpPage()` function when the page finishes loading.

3. Save your changes, and then open **oaktop.htm** on a mobile phone or other touch-screen device. As you can see in Figure 10-1, by default the app shows the contents of the setup article. Specifically, it shows a black rectangle representing the main room, with smaller brown rectangles representing a stage and four tables.

4. Open **oaktop.htm** in a desktop browser. Note that the app uses the same layout for both desktop and handheld devices.

5. Click the stage box, and drag it to the right. Notice that the box doesn't move.

Creating a Drag-and-Drop Application with Mouse Events

Your first task is to add code that allows the user to drag the stage box and the table boxes to match the desired room layout. You'll start by adding mouse events for desktop users.

Several of the events you've used to enable user interaction in previous chapters have been **mouse events**, which are events based on the actions of a mouse or a touchpad. Table 10-1 recaps the most commonly used mouse events.

EVENT	DESCRIPTION
`mousedown`	A user presses the mouse button
`mouseup`	A user releases the mouse button
`click`	A user clicks an element; equivalent to `mousedown` followed by `mouseup`
`mousemove`	A user moves the mouse pointer
`mouseover`	A user moves the mouse pointer within an element
`mouseout`	A user moves the mouse pointer off of an element

Table 10-1: Mouse events

Your app will let users drag an element after a `mousedown` event. The `mousedown` event will add an event listener to the current element that calls a function that will change the position of the current element in response to the `mousemove` event. It will also add an event listener to the element that responds to the `mouseup` event by removing the `mousemove` and `mouseup` event listeners. This ensures that a mouse movement only affects the element the mouse pointer is pointing to when the user presses the mouse button.

You'll create two additional functions to manage moving the current element on the screen. The `getCoords()` function will check the `clientX` and `clientY` properties of the `mousemove` event to identify the coordinates where the move started. The `moveDrag()` function will then use the `getCoords()` function again to check the new location of the mouse pointer. Next, it will calculate the changes in the *x* and *y* coordinates, and finally change the `left` and `top` properties of the element to the calculated positions. Figure 10-4 illustrates the `evt.clientX` and `evt.clientY` coordinates, as well as the calculated `deltaX` and `deltaY` values.

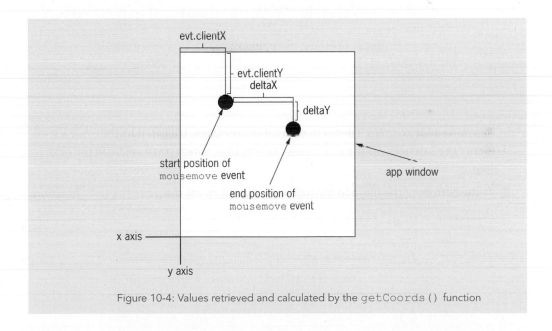

Figure 10-4: Values retrieved and calculated by the `getCoords()` function

Next you'll revise the app by adding event listeners for mouse events to enable users to drag the furniture in the diagram on a desktop computer.

To add mouse events to the Oak Top House web app:

1. Return to **script.js** in your text editor, and then below the `use strict` declaration, add the following comment and global variables:

```
1    // declare global variables for setup page
2    var zIndexCounter;
3    var pos = [];
4    var origin;
```

2. In the `setUpPage()` function, just before the closing }, add the following code to set the value of the `zIndexCounter` variable and add event listeners to each of the furniture objects:

```
1    var movableItems = document.querySelectorAll("#room div");
2    zIndexCounter = movableItems.length + 1;
3    for (var i = 0; i < movableItems.length; i++) {
4        if (movableItems[i].addEventListener) {
5            movableItems[i].addEventListener("mousedown", startDrag, ↵
6                false);
7        } else if (movableItems[i].attachEvent) {
8            movableItems[i].attachEvent("onmousedown", startDrag);
9        }
10   }
```

This code adds an event listener to each furniture object, triggered by the `mousedown` event. The listener calls the `startDrag()` function, which you'll create in the next step.

3. At the bottom of the file, add the following code to create the `startDrag()` function:

```
1    // add event listeners and move object
2    // when user starts dragging
3    function startDrag(evt) {
4        // set z-index to move selected element on top of others
5        this.style.zIndex = zIndexCounter;
6        // increment z-index counter so next selected element is
7        // on top of others
8        zIndexCounter++;
```

```
9        this.addEventListener("mousemove", moveDrag, false);
10       this.addEventListener("mouseup", removeDragListener, ↵
11          false);
12       pos = [this.offsetLeft,this.offsetTop];
13       origin = getCoords(evt);
14    }
```

The z-index property sets the stacking order in which overlapping elements are displayed. In lines 4–8, the function sets the current element's z-index property to a value higher than all other draggable elements, ensuring it will be displayed on top of the other elements. The code then increments the zIndexCounter variable so the next dragged item, if any, will be displayed on top of the current one. Line 9 adds an event listener to call both the moveDrag() function when the mousemove event fires, and the removeDragListener() function when the mouseup event fires. The moveDrag() function will reposition the element as the mouse pointer changes position, and the removeDragListener() function will end the dragging process when a user releases the mouse button. Line 12 places the distances of the left and top edges of the current object from the relevant edges of the containing element in the pos variable, and line 13 uses the getCoords() function to get the coordinates of the mouse click and store them in the origin variable.

4. Below the startDrag() function, enter the following moveDrag() function:

```
1    // calculate new location of dragged object
2    function moveDrag(evt) {
3        var currentPos = getCoords(evt);
4        var deltaX = currentPos[0] - origin[0];
5        var deltaY = currentPos[1] - origin[1];
6        this.style.left = (pos[0] + deltaX) + "px";
7        this.style.top = (pos[1] + deltaY) + "px";
8    }
```

Line 3 uses the getCoords() function, which you'll create next, to get the current mouse coordinates and assign them to the currentPos variable. Line 4 creates a deltaX variable that calculates the difference between the *x* coordinates of the currentPos and origin variables, and line 5 does the same for the *y* coordinates. Line 6 then adds the *x* value of the pos array to the deltaX variable, concatenates the characters "px", and assigns the result as the value of the element's left CSS property. Line 7 does the same for the *y* values and the top property.

5. Below the `moveDrag()` function, enter the following `getCoords()` function:

```
1    // identify location of object
2    function getCoords(evt) {
3        var coords = [];
4        coords[0] = evt.clientX;
5        coords[1] = evt.clientY;
6        return coords;
7    }
```

This function, which you've already called in the previous two functions, simply fetches the current mouse coordinates, assigns them to the `coords[]` variable, and then returns the variable.

6. Below the `getCoords()` function, enter the following `removeDragListener()` function:

```
1    // remove mouse event listeners when dragging ends
2    function removeDragListener() {
3        this.removeEventListener("mousemove", moveDrag, false);
4        this.removeEventListener("mouseup", removeDragListener, ↵
5            false);
6    }
```

This is the function called in response to the `mouseup` event, based on the event listener in the `startDrag()` function. It removes the event listeners from the `mousemove` and `mouseup` events, ensuring that subsequent mouse movements don't change the position of the current element.

7. Save your changes to **script.js**, refresh or reload **oaktop.htm** in your desktop browser, and then drag the stage box. The box moves when you drag it and stops moving when you release the mouse button.

8. Refresh or reload **oaktop.htm** in your mobile browser, and then drag the stage box. The box doesn't move.

Understanding Mouse Events on a Touchscreen Device

On a touchscreen device, some web page elements respond to mouse events, while others don't. The `div` element, which is used to create the stage and table boxes in the Oak Top House app, is not considered a clickable element, and for this reason it does not fire mouse events on a touchscreen. However, mobile operating systems consider other elements, such as links and form elements, to be clickable. On these elements, mobile browsers respond to a touch by initiating a touch cascade. In a touch cascade, a browser checks a touched element for an event handler for multiple events, including some mouse events. Figure 10-5 shows the order of the touch cascade.

Note that the touch cascade starts with the `touchstart` and `touchend` events, which you'll learn about next.

```
touchstart

touchend

mouseover

mousemove

mousedown

mouseup

click
```

Figure 10-5: Touch cascade order

The furniture objects don't move on a touchscreen device because they are not clickable elements, and therefore mobile browsers do not fire mouse events on them. To make your code work with touchscreen devices as well, you'll need to add event listeners for touchscreen-specific events.

When rendered on touchscreen devices, most elements don't respond to mouse-specific events, such as `mousedown`, `mousemove`, and `mouseup`. Instead, touchscreen devices fire a set of touchscreen-specific events on these elements. Apple created a set of events for iOS known as touch events, which are implemented in the native browsers on both the Apple iOS and Google Android platforms. More recently, Microsoft created a different specification, known as pointer events, which it has implemented in the native browsers on its Windows Phone platform and Windows operating system (starting with Windows 8). Both touch events and pointer events are now maintained by the W3C. Touch events and pointer events take different approaches to working with events on a touchscreen device.

Implementing Touch Events

Touch events, as the name implies, focus on responding to a user's finger touches on a touchscreen. Table 10-2 describes the events in the touch events model.

EVENT	DESCRIPTION
touchstart	A user places a finger on the screen
touchmove	A user moves a finger on the screen
touchend	A user removes a finger from the screen
touchcancel	A user moves a finger out of the browser window, or the interface or app cancels the touch

Table 10-2: Touch events

The `touchstart` event is roughly analogous to the `mousedown` mouse event. Likewise, `touchmove` corresponds to `mousemove`, and `touchend` performs a similar function to `mouseup`. The fourth mouse event, `touchcancel`, addresses a situation that doesn't occur with a mouse: when a touch moves off the screen or outside of an object's containing element, or when the operating system or application cancels the touch.

Next, you'll add touch events to your code for the Oak Top House setup app. Figure 10-6 shows the existing mouse event for which a touch event will play a corresponding role for a touchscreen device.

Mouse event	Touch event
mousedown	touchstart
mousemove	touchmove
mouseup	touchend

Figure 10-6: Touch events in the setup app

You can integrate touch events into your existing code simply by adding event listeners for them in the `setUpPage()` and `startDrag()` functions. You'll add a `touchstart` event listener corresponding to each `mousedown` event listener, and likewise you'll add a `touchmove` event listener for each `mousemove` event listener and a `touchend` event listener for each `mouseup` event listener. You'll also create a `removeTouchListener()` function that serves the same role as the existing `removeDragListener()` function, but for touch events rather than for mouse events.

To integrate touch events into the setup app:

1. Return to **script.js** in your text editor, and then in the `setUpPage()` function, within the `for` loop, add the statement highlighted in the following code:

```
1    for (var i = 0; i < movableItems.length; i++) {
2        if (movableItems[i].addEventListener) {
3            movableItems[i].addEventListener("mousedown", ↵
4                startDrag, false);
5            movableItems[i].addEventListener("touchstart", ↵
6                startDrag, false);
7    } else if (movableItems[i].attachEvent) {
8            movableItems[i].attachEvent("onmousedown", startDrag);
9        }
10   }
```

This code originally looped through all of the `div` elements within the `div` with the `id` value of `room`, and added an event listener for the `mousedown` event to each one. The statement you entered replicates the same behavior for the `touchstart` event, using the same function, `startDrag()`, as the event handler. Notice that you do not attach a touch event in the `else if` section of the code. This is because the `attachEvent()` method works only in IE8, which supports only mouse events.

2. Scroll down to the `startDrag()` function and then, below the statement `zIndexCounter++`, enter the following statements:

```
1    if (evt.type !== "mousedown") {
2        this.addEventListener("touchmove", moveDrag, false);
3        this.addEventListener("touchend", removeTouchListener, ↵
4            false);
5    } else {
```

3. Near the bottom of the function, before the statement that sets the value of the `pos` variable, add a closing `}` to mark the end of the `else` statement. The statements you added create event listeners corresponding to those for the `mousemove` and `mouseup` events. The `touchend` event listener calls `removeTouchListener()` as its event handler. You'll create this function in the next step. Your updated code for the `startDrag()` function should match the following code:

```
1    function startDrag(evt) {
2        // set z-index to move selected element on top of others
3        this.style.zIndex = zIndexCounter;
```

```
4        // increment z-index counter so next selected element is
5        // on top of others
6        zIndexCounter++;
7        if (evt.type !== "mousedown") {
8            this.addEventListener("touchmove", moveDrag, false);
9            this.addEventListener("touchend", removeTouchListener, ↵
10               false);
11       } else {
12           this.addEventListener("mousemove", moveDrag, false);
13           this.addEventListener("mouseup", removeDragListener, ↵
14               false);
15       }
16       pos = [this.offsetLeft, this.offsetTop];
17       origin = getCoords(evt);
18   }
```

4. Scroll down to the `removeDragListener()` function and then, below this function, add the following `removeTouchListener()` function:

```
1    // remove touch event listeners when dragging ends
2    function removeTouchListener() {
3        this.removeEventListener("touchmove", moveDrag, false);
4        this.removeEventListener("touchend", removeTouchListener, ↵
5            false);
6    }
```

This function performs the same task for touches as the `removeDragListener()` function, which you created in the previous steps, performs for mouse events. The `removeTouchListener()` function removes the `touchmove` and `touchend` event listeners for the current element. This ensures that when a user stops touching the current element, it does not respond to future touches on another part of the screen.

5. Save your changes, refresh or reload **oaktop.htm** on a touchscreen device, and then drag one of the table boxes up or down. The box itself does not move and, depending on your device, the entire page may move up or down on the screen.

Working with Touch Coordinates

In addition to the touch events you've added to your existing code, you need to add code to account for an additional difference between mouse and touch events. The `getCoords()`

function you created references `evt.clientX` and `evt.clientY`—the *x* and *y* coordinates of the event that fired, such as `mousedown`. However, touch events are built to support **multitouch** devices, which allow for multiple touches on the screen at the same time. Therefore, touch events don't include `clientX` or `clientY` properties as direct children. Instead, each touch event has the properties `touches`, `targetTouches`, and `changedTouches`, each of which contains an array of coordinates. Table 10-3 describes the information that each array contains.

ARRAY	CONTENTS
touches	Coordinates of all touches currently on the screen
targetTouches	Coordinates of all touches on the current element
changedTouches	Coordinates of all touches involved in the event

Table 10-3: Array properties of touch events

To identify the starting location of the moving element, you'll use the `targetTouches` array. The Oak Top House setup app interface needs just one touch (a single finger) to move a piece of furniture, so you need to reference just the first item in the `targetTouches` array—`targetTouches[0]`. This means that you can use the references `evt.targetTouches[0].clientX` and `evt.targetTouches[0].clientY` to identify the starting *x* and *y* coordinates, respectively, of the initial touch on an element. You'll add this to the `getCoords()` function using an `if/else` statement that checks if the `targetTouches` property exists for the current event and if the `targetTouches` property has a value for its `length` property. If both of these conditions are true, then `targetTouches` is associated with at least one set of coordinates, which your code will use. Otherwise, the code will use the existing `clientX` and `clientY` events associated with `mousedown` events.

To add support for `targetTouches` coordinates to the `getCoords()` function:

1. Return to **script.js** in your text editor, and then locate the `getCoords()` function.

2. Below the declaration of the `coords` variable, enter the following code:

```
1    if (evt.targetTouches && evt.targetTouches.length) {
2       var thisTouch = evt.targetTouches[0];
3       coords[0] = thisTouch.clientX;
4       coords[1] = thisTouch.clientY;
5    } else {
```

The conditions for the `if` statement check that the `evt` parameter has a `targetTouches` property, and that this `targetTouches` property has a `length` value. If so, lines 2–4 of this code are executed. Line 2 declares a `thisTouch` variable equal to the first element in the `targetTouches` array for the event. Then lines 3 and 4 add two values to the `coords` array, equal to the values of the `clientX` and `clientY` properties for `thisTouch`.

3. Near the end of the function, just before the `return coords` statement, add a closing } to end the else statement. Your updated code for the `getCoords()` function should match the following:

```
1    function getCoords(evt) {
2        var coords = [];
3        if (evt.targetTouches && evt.targetTouches.length) {
4            var thisTouch = evt.targetTouches[0];
5            coords[0] = thisTouch.clientX;
6            coords[1] = thisTouch.clientY;
7        } else {
8            coords[0] = evt.clientX;
9            coords[1] = evt.clientY;
10       }
11       return coords;
12   }
```

4. Save your changes, refresh or reload **oaktop.htm** on a touchscreen device, and then drag one of the table boxes up or down. This time, the box moves. However, the touch experience is still not as user-friendly as dragging with a mouse. On some devices, dragging a table box also drags the page within the device window, making it hard to predict how far a finger motion will move the box. On other devices, each drag moves the box only a short distance and then stops, no matter where your finger moves.

Distinguishing Between App and Device Interaction

In addition to the handlers you've added to your app for touch events, you need to add additional code to ensure that the touch events fire on the target element. This can be complicated because touchscreen devices use touch events for more than one purpose, as illustrated in Figure 10-7.

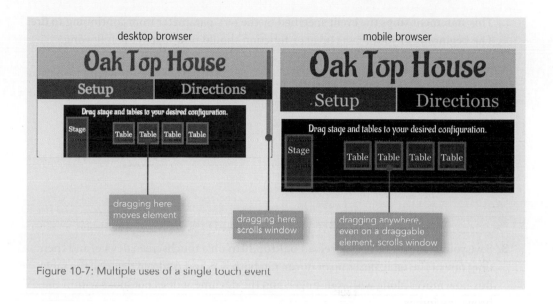

Figure 10-7: Multiple uses of a single touch event

While users can interact via touch with an app like yours, they also use touch to perform browser and device interactions, known as **gestures**, for activities such as scrolling the page and viewing device notifications. In addition to executing your code in response to the touchmove event, the device's operating system may also interpret the touchmove event as the user interacting with the interface to scroll the page, for instance. As you can imagine, users would find such unpredictable results frustrating.

To ensure that the operating system interface does not respond to events generated when users interact with your app, you can use the preventDefault() method. By adding the preventDefault() method within event handler code, you prevent touch actions on specific elements from also triggering interface gestures. You'll add the prevent.Default() method to the startDrag() function to ensure that when a user drags the stage and table boxes, the operating system doesn't also attempt to run its own code in response to the event.

To add the `preventDefault()` method to the `startDrag()` function:

1. Return to **script.js** in your text editor, and then locate the startDrag() function.

2. Just below the first line of the if statement, enter the following code:

```
evt.preventDefault();
```

This statement stops the event specified by the `evt` parameter from continuing to fire. The beginning of your `startDrag()` function should now match the following:

```
1   function startDrag(evt) {
2       // set z-index to move selected element on top of others
3       this.style.zIndex = zIndexCounter;
4       // increment z-index counter so next selected element is
5       // on top of others
6       zIndexCounter++;
7       if (evt.type !== "mousedown") {
8           evt.preventDefault();
9           this.addEventListener("touchmove", moveDrag, false);
```

3. Save your changes, refresh or reload **oaktop.htm** on a touchscreen device, and then drag one of the table boxes up or down. On both iOS and Android devices, the table box now moves along with your finger, and the document does not move within the browser window.

4. Place one finger on a table box, place another finger on another table box, and then drag both fingers. Because the code you wrote supports multitouch devices, both elements move simultaneously in response to the two separate touches.

5. If you have access to a Windows touchscreen device, use it to repeat Steps 3 and 4. Depending on your device, the touches may have no effect on the table elements.

You have successfully created an app that works with a mouse as well as on touchscreen devices running iOS and Android. To make your app work with Windows touchscreen devices as well, you'll need to incorporate pointer events.

Implementing Pointer Events

As touchscreens moved to different devices, including tablets and notebook computers, creating code that responded to both touch and mouse events became more complicated. For instance, consider the code you've created so far in this chapter. What would happen if a user interacted with your app using a **stylus**, which is a pointing device that looks like a pencil and allows for precise touch input on a touchscreen? Likewise, imagine if a user opened your app on a device such as a Google Chromebook or Microsoft Surface, which have both touchscreens and trackpads. While you could use a combination of mouse and touch events for both of these situations, you would need to add additional logic to your app to decide on a user's intent in some cases.

In response to this issue, Microsoft created pointer events, which take a different approach to user input than the method you've used so far. Pointer events aim to handle input from a mouse, finger, or stylus with each event. Table 10-4 describes some events in the pointer events model.

EVENT	FINGER/STYLUS DESCRIPTION	MOUSE DESCRIPTION
pointerdown	A touch is initiated over the element	The mouse button is pressed while the pointer is over the element
pointerup	A touch is ended over the element	The mouse button is released while the pointer is over the element
pointercancel	An active touch or click is cancelled by the app or the interface	
pointermove	An active touch or active mouse pointer moves	
pointerover	An active touch or click moves within the boundaries of an element	
pointerout	An active touch or active mouse pointer leaves the boundaries of an element	
pointerenter	An active touch or active mouse pointer moves within the boundaries of an element or one of its descendant elements	
pointerleave	An active touch or active mouse pointer leaves the boundaries of an element and all of its descendant elements	

Table 10-4: Pointer events

> **Note** Internet Explorer 10 and Internet Explorer Mobile 10 respond only to pointer events with the `ms` prefix, such as `mspointerdown`. If your code needs to support users of either IE10 browser, you should duplicate each pointer event reference with a matching reference to the `ms` prefixed pointer event. You'll practice this in the next section.

In addition to combining events for multiple input devices into a single set of events, the pointer events specification was also created to incorporate event properties that mouse and touch events didn't support. Pointer events can respond to the amount of pressure a user is placing on the screen or the angle at which a user is holding a stylus.

If all devices supported a pointer events specification that covered all possible scenarios, then programmers would be able to code apps using just one set of events, rather than alternate cases for mouse or touch. However, at the time this book was written, only Internet

Explorer Mobile and Internet Explorer 10 and later supported pointer events. This means that you cannot yet create code using only pointer events that works on a significant proportion of devices. However, because some versions of Internet Explorer do not recognize touch events, for maximum compatibility you should incorporate pointer events into your code along with mouse and touch events.

Pointer events include the same `clientX` and `clientY` properties as mouse events, so your existing code for working with screen coordinates is compatible with pointer events. However, stopping operating system interface gestures from firing in response to a pointer event works differently in current implementations of pointer events than it does for touch events. Rather than the `preventDefault()` method, pointer events in Microsoft browsers rely on a CSS property, `msTouchAction`. To disable interface gestures, you set the value of `msTouchAction` for the current element to `none`.

You'll complete the setup portion of the Oak Top House web app by adding support for pointer events as well as code that sets the `msTouchAction` property for the current element to `none`.

To add support for pointer events to the app:

1. Return to **script.js** in your text editor, and then locate the `setUpPage()` function.

2. Below the `for` statement, enter the following code:

```
// disable IE10+ interface gestures
movableItems[i].style.msTouchAction = "none";
movableItems[i].style.touchAction = "none";
```

3. Within the `for` loop, just before the `if else` statement, add the following code:

```
1    movableItems[i].addEventListener("mspointerdown", startDrag, ↵
2        false);
3    movableItems[i].addEventListener("pointerdown", startDrag, ↵
4        false);
```

   Recall that Internet Explorer 10 and Internet Explorer Mobile 10 support pointer events only with the `ms` prefix. To support all versions of Internet Explorer that support pointer events, you add both the prefixed and unprefixed versions of the event name.

4. Scroll down to the `startDrag()` function, and then within the `if` clause, add the code highlighted below:

```
1    if (evt.type !== "mousedown") {
2        evt.preventDefault();
```

```
3        this.addEventListener("touchmove", moveDrag, false);
4        this.addEventListener("mspointermove", moveDrag, false);
5        this.addEventListener("pointermove", moveDrag, false);
6        this.addEventListener("touchend", removeTouchListener,↵
7           false);
8        this.addEventListener("mspointerup", removeTouchListener,↵
9           false);
10       this.addEventListener("pointerup", removeTouchListener,↵
11          false);
12   } else {
```

The `mspointermove` and `pointermove` events use the same event handler as the existing `touchmove` event, and the `mspointerup` and `pointerup` events use the same event handler as the existing `touchend` event.

5. Scroll down to the `removeTouchListener()` function, and then add the statements highlighted below:

```
1    function removeTouchListener() {
2        this.removeEventListener("touchmove", moveDrag, false);
3        this.removeEventListener("mspointermove", moveDrag,↵
4           false);
5        this.removeEventListener("pointermove", moveDrag, false);
6        this.removeEventListener("touchend",↵
7           removeTouchListener, false);
8        this.removeEventListener("mspointerup",↵
9           removeTouchListener, false);
10       this.removeEventListener("pointerup",↵
11          removeTouchListener, false);
12   }
```

6. Save your changes, and then if you have access to a touchscreen device with Internet Explorer 10 or higher, or Internet Explorer Mobile 10 or higher, open **oaktop.htm**, and drag one of the table boxes. The dragging behavior matches that on iOS and Android devices.

You have completed the code that makes the boxes on the Setup tab of the Oak Top House app draggable on different devices that support various mechanisms for user input. To complete the app, the owners of Oak Top House would like you to show directions from the user's current location to Oak Top House along with a map when users click the Directions tab. To accomplish this, you need to learn more about programming interfaces for mobile devices.

Short Quiz 1

1. What is a touch cascade?

2. What is the difference between touch events and pointer events?

3. Why do touch events not support `clientX` and `clientY` properties? What do they use instead of these properties?

Using Programming Interfaces for Mobile Devices

Ever since mobile devices began to make up a significant proportion of devices accessing the web, mobile browser makers have continually created new APIs to allow developers of web apps to access information provided by mobile device hardware. Recall that API stands for "application programming interface," which is a specification that standardizes how certain software interacts with other software. While native apps—the kind that you download and install, with icons that are displayed in a menu or on the home screen—have long had access to the data generated by this hardware, mobile browsers have only recently begun to support access for web apps. The W3C has taken over coordinating future development of many of these APIs, and browser makers are creating new APIs on a regular basis. Table 10-5 lists some hardware APIs for mobile devices. The following sections describe these APIs in more detail.

API	PURPOSE
Geolocation	Provides user's latitude and longitude coordinates (user opt-in required)
Battery Status	Reports charge level of device battery
Device Orientation	Provides access to device orientation and changes in orientation
WebRTC	Provides access to device camera, microphone, and/or screen (user opt-in required for all)

Table 10-5: Selected hardware APIs for mobile devices

Using the Geolocation API

The **Geolocation API** provides access to a user's latitude and longitude coordinates. You access methods of the Geolocation API using the `geolocation` property of the `Navigator` object. Table 10-6 describes the methods of the Geolocation API.

METHOD	DESCRIPTION
getCurrentPosition(*success* [, *fail, options*])	Provides current position of device, subject to user authorization, where *success* is code to run if the request is successful, *fail* is code to run if the request fails, and *options* represents one or more optional parameters
watchPosition(*success* [, *fail, options*])	Provides current position of device, and continues to monitor position, providing updated position when position changes
clearWatch(*number*)	Stops monitoring position, where *number* is the number returned by the original watchPosition() statement

Table 10-6: Methods of the Geolocation API

The *success* and *fail* arguments of the first two methods are executable code. Arguments that contain or reference executable code are known as **callbacks**.

Using the **getCurrentPosition()** Method

To request a user's position a single time, you use the getCurrentPosition() method. This method takes up to three arguments. The first is code that is executed if the request is successful. This is the only argument that is required. The getCurrentPosition() method automatically passes an object containing the device's location information to the function specified in the first argument. The object contains a single property, coords, which contains the subproperties described in Table 10-7.

PROPERTY	DESCRIPTION
latitude	Geographic latitude, in degrees
longitude	Geographic longitude, in degrees
altitude	Elevation, in meters
accuracy	Accuracy of latitude and longitude values, in meters
altitudeAccuracy	Accuracy of altitude value, in meters
heading	Direction of travel, in degrees
speed	Current speed, in meters per second

Table 10-7: Properties passed on a successful geolocation request

The function that handles a successful geolocation request must include a parameter name for the object passed to it. Statements within the function can then reference the coords properties with the syntax

```
parameter.coords.property
```

For instance, the following code calls the `showLocation()` function on a successful geolocation call. The `showLocation()` function assigns the name `position` to the object containing position information. The function includes statements that reference nested properties, such as `position.coords.longitude`.

```
1   navigator.geolocation.getCurrentPosition(showLocation);
2   function showLocation(position) {
3       console.log("Longitude: " + position.coords.longitude);
4       console.log("Latitude: " + position.coords.latitude);
5   }
```

The `getCurrentPosition()` method allows two optional arguments. The function to handle a successful request can be followed by a function to handle an unsuccessful request. This option is generally used to display a message to users letting them know that their position information could not be determined. The optional third argument is an object containing optional properties for the geolocation request. Table 10-8 describes these properties.

PROPERTY	DESCRIPTION
enableHighAccuracy	Request for high-accuracy results (Boolean)
timeout	Maximum time to wait before cancelling request, in milliseconds
maximumAge	Maximum age of cached request to use; if set to 0, new request is always triggered, and if set to `infinity`, any existing cached data is always used

Table 10-8: Available properties for geolocation request

Skills at Work | *Making Your Apps Transparent to Users*

The geolocation specification mandates that apps secure a user's permission before acquiring geolocation data. This part of the specification is implemented by browsers, so no additional steps are required by app developers to carry it out. However, it serves as a useful model of **data transparency**, which is the process of making it clear to users what information your app wants to collect from them and how you intend to use it. The more transparent you are with your data requests and use, the more trust you build with the users of your apps.

You could enhance the previous example to include a function to handle a failed request and to set a 10-second timeout as follows:

```
1   navigator.geolocation.getCurrentPosition(showLocation, fail,↵
2       {timeout: 10000});
3   function showLocation(position) {
4       console.log("Longitude: " + position.coords.longitude);
5       console.log("Latitude: " + position.coords.latitude);
6   }
7   function fail() {
8       var content = document.getElementById("mainParagraph");
9       content.innerHTML = "<p>Geolocation information not↵
10          available or not authorized.</p>";
11  }
```

This code now includes two additional arguments to the `getCurrentPosition()` method. The second argument is a call to the `fail()` function, which adds a message to the document if the request is unsuccessful. The third argument is a JavaScript object containing a single property and value, which specifies that the method should wait only 10,000 milliseconds (10 seconds) for a response from the browser.

Although this code now specifies what to do if the geolocation request is unsuccessful, the code still generates an error in older browsers that don't recognize the `geolocation` property of the `Navigator` object. To ensure that this error is handled gracefully, you can wrap the call to the `getCurrentPosition()` method in an `if/else` statement that checks if the `navigator.geolocation` property exists, and if not, calls the `fail()` function.

```
1   if (navigator.geolocation) {
2       navigator.geolocation.getCurrentPosition(createDirections, ↵
3           fail, {timeout: 10000});
4   } else {
5       fail();
6   }
```

Oak Top House would like the app to give users an option to view a map showing the location of Oak Top House. You'll start your work on this feature by adding basic code to query a user's position and log the latitude and longitude results in the console.

To add a request for geolocation information to the app:

1. Return to **script.js** in your text editor, and then below the `loadDirections()` function, enter the following code to create the `geoTest()` function:

```
function geoTest() {

}
```

2. Within the `geoTest()` function, enter the following `if/else` statement:

```
1    if (navigator.geolocation) {
2        navigator.geolocation.getCurrentPosition(createDirections,↵
3            fail, {timeout: 10000});
4    } else {
5        fail();
6    }
```

3. Within the `loadDirections()` function, just before the closing `}`, add the following statement to call the `geoTest()` function:

```
geoTest();
```

4. Below the `geoTest()` function, add the following two functions:

```
1    function createDirections(position) {
2        console.log("Longitude: " + position.coords.longitude);
3        console.log("Latitude: " + position.coords.latitude);
4    }
5    function fail() {
6        console.log("Geolocation information not available or not↵
7            authorized.");
8    }
```

The `createDirections()` function is called when a geolocation request succeeds. It assigns the name position to the object containing the geolocation data and then writes the `position.coords.longitude` and `position.coords.latitude` values to the console. The `fail()` function is called when a geolocation request fails, and simply writes an error message to the console.

5. Save your changes, refresh or reload **oaktop.htm** in your browser, and then make sure the browser console is open.

6. Click the **Directions** tab. In response to the geolocation request in your code, the browser displays a dialog box asking your permission to provide your geolocation information to the requester. Figure 10-8 shows the dialog box in IE.

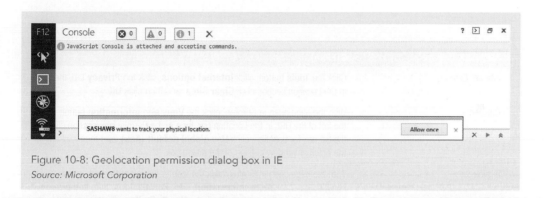

Figure 10-8: Geolocation permission dialog box in IE
Source: Microsoft Corporation

7. Click the **Allow once**, **Share Location**, or similar button to authorize your browser to share your geolocation information with your app. After a few moments, your latitude and longitude values are logged to the console, as shown in Figure 10-9.

Figure 10-9: Latitude and longitude logged to console
Source: Microsoft Corporation

BROWSER	STEPS
Internet Explorer	Click the **Tools** button, click **Internet options**, click the **Privacy** tab, then in the Location section click **Clear Sites**, and then click **OK**
Chrome	With the page open in Chrome, click the **View site information** button to the left of the URL in the Location bar, then in the Permissions section click the list box for Location, click **Use global default (Ask)**, and then click in the browser window outside of the dialog box
Firefox	With the page open in Firefox, click the icon to the left of the URL in the Location bar, click **More Information**, click **Permissions**, then in the Access Your Location section check the **Use Default** box, and then close the dialog box.

Table 10-9: Steps to clear saved geolocation history

Your app now successfully obtains location information, and displays alternate content if a user denies the app's request. However, sometimes users don't notice or ignore the browser's request to share their location information. In this case, your `getCurrentPosition()` method neither fails or succeeds, leaving the page empty, as illustrated in Figure 10-10.

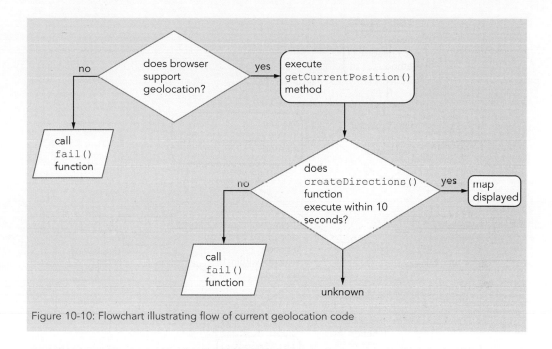

Figure 10-10: Flowchart illustrating flow of current geolocation code

Your code currently includes a 10 second (10,000 millisecond) timeout as part of the getCurrentPosition() method. However, in most browsers this timeout takes effect only after a user has granted permission for your app to access location data. If a user ignores or doesn't notice the request, this timeout never starts counting. In addition, some browsers offer users the option of saying "Not now" to the permission request, instead of "Never," and these browsers treat a "Not now" answer the same as they would treat a lack of response to the request. Therefore, your code must include one additional layer to deal with this scenario.

One simple way to handle the lack of a yes or no response from the user is to use the setTimeout() method of the Window object to start a countdown immediately before the if/else statement. If the if/else statement waits without a response for the amount of time specified by the setTimeout() method, the timeout triggers the fail() function. But if the if/else statement receives a response before the timeout finishes, it calls the createDirections() function, which cancels the timeout. Figure 10-11 shows a revised flowchart that incorporates this extra layer.

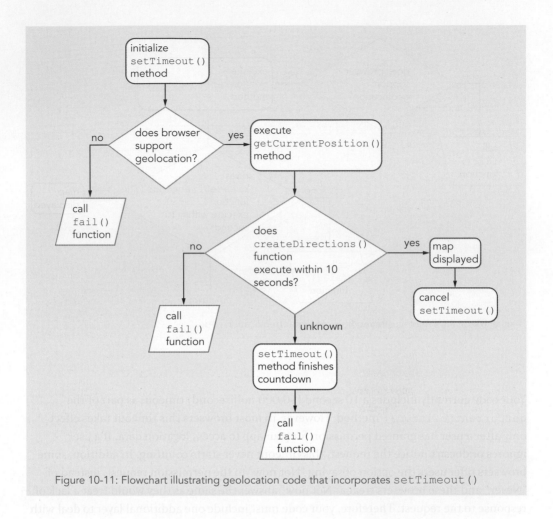

Figure 10-11: Flowchart illustrating geolocation code that incorporates setTimeout()

Next you'll examine what happens when you don't respond to a location request in your browser, and then you'll add setTimeout() code to handle this situation.

To use the setTimeout() method to handle a lack of response to a location query:

1. Return to **oaktop.htm** in your browser, and then follow the instructions in Table 10-9 to clear the location settings for your data files.

2. Refresh or reload **oaktop.htm**, and then click **Directions**, but *do not* respond to the browser prompt asking for permission to share your location information. Notice that the console remains blank, displaying neither coordinates nor an error message.

3. Click the **close** button in the box requesting your location. In Chrome, your error message is displayed in the console. However, in Firefox and Internet Explorer, the console remains blank.

4. Return to **script.js** in your editor, scroll to the top of the file, and then in the global variables section, add the following declaration:

```
var waitForUser;
```

You'll use a global variable to create a named timeout that you can cancel.

5. Scroll down to the geoTest() function, and then before the if statement, add the following statement:

```
waitForUser = setTimeout(fail, 10000);
```

This statement sets a 10-second (10000 millisecond) timeout that calls the fail() function at the end of the countdown. The timeout is assigned to the waitForUser variable name.

6. Scroll down to the createDirections() function, and then add the following statement as the first line of the function:

```
clearTimeout(waitForUser);
```

If the createDirections() function is called, this statement ends the waitForUser timeout. Your geoTest() and createDirections() functions should match the following:

```
1    function geoTest() {
2        waitForUser = setTimeout(fail, 10000);
3        if (navigator.geolocation) {
4            navigator.geolocation.getCurrentPosition(↵
5                createDirections, fail, {timeout: 10000});
6        } else {
7            fail();
8        }
9    }
10   function createDirections(position) {
11       clearTimeout(waitForUser);
12       console.log("Longitude: " + position.coords.longitude);
13       console.log("Latitude: " + position.coords.latitude);
14   }
```

7. Refresh or reload **oaktop.htm** in your browser, and then click **Directions**, but do not respond to the browser prompt asking for permission to share your location information. After 10 seconds, the error message "Geolocation information not available or not authorized." is logged to the console as a result of the expiration of the timeout set with the `setTimeout()` method.

Now that your code can successfully acquire geolocation information and deal with other possible user responses, you can use any information received from users to add features to your app. To do so, you have to integrate the information with databases and JavaScript functionality that can identify the location specified by your geographic coordinates and illustrate that location on a map.

A few companies maintain publicly accessible databases mapping geographic coordinates to maps and determining driving routes between points. In addition to providing you much of the information you need, these companies have also written much of the code needed to use this information. They provide APIs that enable you to customize and display the information you want with a minimum of JavaScript. To complete the Directions section of the Oak Top House web app, you'll use the Google Maps API, which enables you to display maps and directions provided by Google.

> **Note** Integrating Google Maps into an app is free for low-volume use. However, if Google receives a large volume of requests from a site each day, the requesting site must pay a usage fee. Google then provides an *API key*, which is a string of characters that you incorporate into any request your code makes to Google to verify that your use is licensed. Because you're using the service on your computer rather than on a website with many users, you do not need to obtain an API key.

Using the Google Maps API

The Google Maps API enables you to add content provided by the Google Maps service to your own apps. You can use the Google Maps API to display a map centered on the user's current location or on a location you specify, a map showing a route between two locations, or written directions between two locations.

> **Note** This chapter describes how to use the Google Maps JavaScript API v3. Because the code references the version number, it will continue to work even after new versions of the API are released.

To see how the Google Maps API works, you'll start by adding a map to the Oak Top House page that's centered on the user's current location. To create a map, you need to use two constructors that are part of the Google Maps API—Map() and LatLng(). Recall that a constructor is a function that creates a new instance of an object. The Map() constructor creates a map object and uses the following syntax:

```
var name = new google.maps.Map(element, options);
```

The word *name* represents a variable name assigned to the object that the Map() constructor creates. The term *element* is a reference to a web page element where the map is displayed, and *options* is a JavaScript object containing parameters for the map. The API supports many properties, but only two are required—zoom and center. The zoom property is a whole number that specifies the level of zoom where 0 shows the entire Earth, and larger numbers show more detailed views. The center property specifies the latitude and longitude on which the map is centered. You specify the coordinates using an object created with the LatLng() constructor, as follows:

```
center: new google.maps.LatLng(latitude, longitude)
```

In this expression, *latitude* and *longitude* represent latitude and longitude coordinates, respectively.

The following code creates a new map centered on the user's current position with a zoom level of 11:

```
1    var currPosLat = position.coords.latitude;
2    var currPosLng = position.coords.longitude;
3    var mapOptions = {
4        center: new google.maps.LatLng(currPosLat, currPosLng),
5        zoom: 11
6    };
7    var map = new google.maps.Map(document.getElementById("map"),↵
8        mapOptions);
```

Lines 1 and 2 assign the user's latitude and longitude to variables. Lines 3–6 create an object with the name mapOptions that specifies the required parameters for the map. Line 4 sets the center of the map to a LatLng object that references the user's current latitude and longitude, and line 5 sets the zoom level to 11. Lines 7 and 8 create a Map object assigned to the variable name map, displayed in the element with the id value map, and using the options stored in the mapOptions variable.